1 MONTH OF
FREE
READING

at

www.ForgottenBooks.com

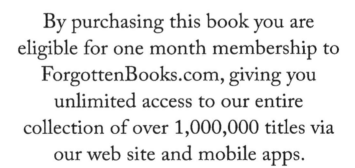

By purchasing this book you are
eligible for one month membership to
ForgottenBooks.com, giving you
unlimited access to our entire
collection of over 1,000,000 titles via
our web site and mobile apps.

To claim your free month visit:

www.forgottenbooks.com/free1116391

ISBN 978-0-331-38791-9
PIBN 11116391

Historic, Archive Document

Do not assume content reflects current scientific knowledge, policies, or practices.

R23

United States
Department of
Agriculture

Forest Service

Tongass
National
Forest
10-MB-90

January 1990

Analysis of the Management Situation

Appendix, Volume I

Tongass National Forest Land and Resource Management Plan Revision

949595

Analysis of the Management Situation

Appendix, Volume I

Tongass National Forest Land and Resource Management Plan Revision

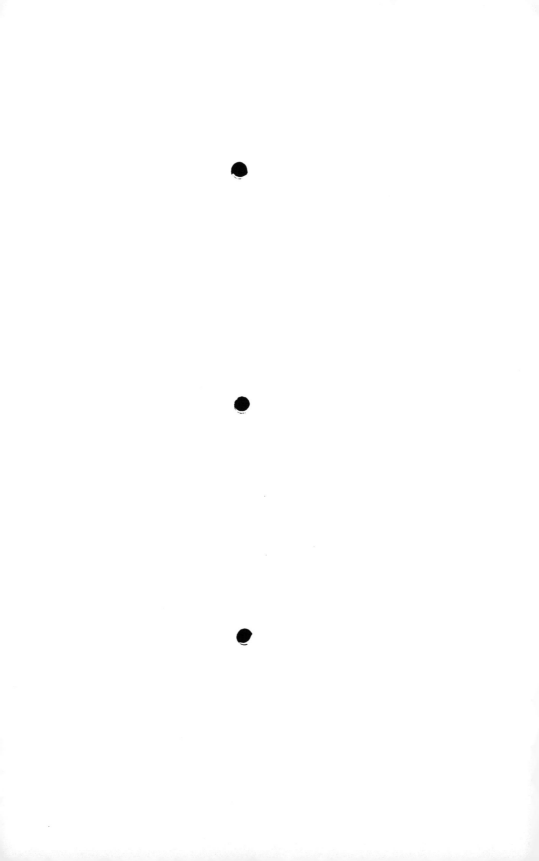

APPENDIXES

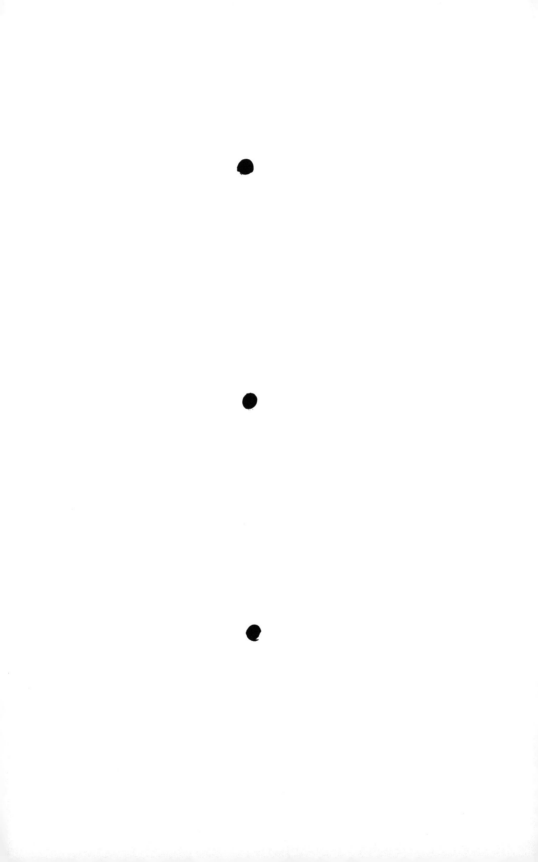

APPENDIX A

Background on Pending Legislation

Moratorium Areas

House of Representatives Bill H R. 987 proposes 23 Areas on the Tongass
National Forest for Wilderness designation   Sec 201 of H.R 987 describes
these 23 Areas often referred to as the "23 Moratorium Areas " See George
Leonard's statement to the Subcommittee on Water, Power and Offshore Energy
Resources for a description of each of the 23 Areas (attached)

The Southeast Conference Board of Directors has adopted a policy statement on
management and access to the Tongass National Forest which is endorsed by
Governor Cowper of the State of Alaska (attached)   The Southeast Conference
calls for the following 12 Moratorium Areas to remain in a roadless condition

    Yakutat Forelands
    Kadashan
    Chuck River
    Lisianski/Upper Hoonah Sound
    Nutkwa
    Karta River
    Calder/Holbrook
    Young Lake
    Outside Islands
    Trap Bay
    Goose Flats
    Berners Bay

A summary of the Southeast Conference position is outlined in a memo dated
March 17, 1989 from William B Privett, President of Southeast Conference to
Regional Forester Mike Barton (attached)

The Alaska Loggers Association (ALA) policy statement on the Tongass lists 6
Moratorium Areas "for removal from multiple use management   The 6 Areas are:

    Yakutat Forelands
    Kadashan
    Lisianski
    Karta River
    Nutkwa
    Chuck River

ALA's position is documented in a column of the Ketchikan Daily News dated
march 22, 1989 (attached)

Other aspects of Congressional legislation that has been introduced and their
affects on ANILCA are summarized in a Table titled Proposed Tongass Legislation
dated May 31, 1989 (attached)

STEVEN A. BRINK
Tongass Plan Revision Team Leader

PROPOSED TONGASS LEGISLATION

Comparison of Proposed Tongass Timber Legislation				
* CURRENT LAW (Alaska National Interest Lands Conservation Act)	H.R. 987 (Mrazek) (Miller Substitute)	H.R. 1368 (Volkmer) Mark-up Before House Ag. Subcommittee	* S.237 (Murkowski)	* S 346 (Wirth)
Tongass Timber Supply Fund (TTSF): ANILCA Sec. 705(a) makes available at least $40 million annually in order to make timber available to dependent industry. Provides for a timber supply of 4.5 billion board feet per decade.	TTSF: Repeals ANILCA Section 705(a). Makes timber supply subject to review and appropriation by Congress.	TTSF: Repeals ANILCA Section 705(a). Makes timber supply subject to review and appropriation by Congress.	TTSF: Repeals ANILCA Section 705(a). Makes timber supply subject to review and appropriation by Congress.	TTSF: Repeals ANILCA Section 705(a). Makes timber supply subject to review and appropriation by Congress.
Timber Supply Provides for a timber supply of 4.5 billion board feet per decade.	Timber Supply. Secretary of Agriculture is authorized to make available sufficient volume to meet actual market demand as determined by the planning process.	Timber Supply Repealed. Requires secretary, subject to applicable planning and management statistics to prepare sufficient timber for sale to meet market demands up to 4.5 billion BF/Decade.	Timber Supply Repealed.	Timber Supply Repealed.
NFMA Planning: ANILCA Sec. 705(d) exempts Tongass from the planning process requirement of Sec. 6(k) of NFMA.	NFMA Planning: Repeals ANILCA Section 705(d) exemption from planning process requirement of NFMA.	NFMA Planning: Repeals ANILCA Section 705(d) exemption from the planning process requirement of Sec. 6(k) of NFMA.	NFMA Planning: Does not address ANILCA Section 705(d).	NFMA Planning: Repeals ANILCA Section 705(d) exemption from the planning process requirement of Sec 6(k) of NFMA.

* CURRENT LAW (Continued)	H.R. 987 (Mrazek) (Miller Substitute)	H.R. 1368 (Volkmer)	* S.237 (Murkowski)	* S.346 (Wirth)
50-year Contracts: Does not specifically address long term contracts.	50-year Contracts: Requires that the long term timber contracts with APC & KPC be terminated within 90 days of passage of this legislation.	50-year Contracts: Requires Forest Service to enter into negotiations with both APC & KPC to make changes that would make the long term timber contracts more similar to the Forest Service short term timber contracts. Forest Service to report back to Congress in 1 year as to the success of the negotiations and also what effect cancellation of the long term contracts would have if negotiations are not successful.	50-year Contracts: Does not specifically address long term contracts.	50-year Contracts: Requires that the long term timber contracts with APC & KPC be terminated within 90 days of passage of this legislation.
Tongass Land Management Plan Revision: Not addressed by ANILCA.	TLMP Revision: Require that new revision plans would increase the base of protection of both fish habitat and wildlife. Increase public participation in the plan, insuring the volume of timber harvest doesn't negatively impact other industries. Mandates a non logging buffer strip of at least 100 ft. on each side of all salmon streams and their tributaries. Bars construction of road between Hoonah and Tenakee Springs.	TLMP Revision: Requires the Forest Service to change planning and management priorities so as to assure a greater emphasis be given to the "long-term best interest of the commercial fishing, recreation, and tourism industries. subsistence communities in Southeast Alaska and the national interest in the fish and wildlife and other natural resources of the Tongass National Forest."	TLMP Revision: Not addressed.	TLMP Revision: Current revision superseded by new TLMP revision which must significantly increase protection of fish, wildlife, watershed, recreation, cultural, biological diversity, and old growth ecosystem resources and subsistence values" from the protection contained in existing plan.

Comparison of Proposed Tongass Timber Legislation				
* CURRENT LAW (Continued)	H.R. 987 (Mrazek) (Miller Substitute)	H.R. 1368 (Volkmer)	* S.237 (Murkowski)	* S.346 (Wirth)
Wilderness: ANILCA Sec. 704 designated 5.4 million acres of wilderness.	Wilderness: Creates an additional 23 wilderness area totaling 1.8 million acres. Proposes Young Lake wilderness shall be managed as part of the Admiralty Island National Monument.	Wilderness: Does not address the issue of Wilderness/Moratorium area.	Wilderness: Does not address the issue of Wilderness/Moratorium area.	Wilderness: Creates 23 "moratorium areas" where timber harvesting and road building would be prohibited until completion of new revised plan. The moratorium will remain in effect until 90 days after publication of the Record of Decision.

State Position

TESTIMONY OF ERIC S. LASCHEVER
BEFORE THE HOUSE SUBCOMMITTEE ON
WATER AND POWER AND OFFSHORE ENERGY RESOURCES
March 14, 1989

Mr. Chairman and Members of the Subcommittee:

My name is Eric S. Laschever. I am the Special Assistant to
Governor Steve Cowper for the Tongass National Forest. I
want to thank you for the opportunity to present the views
of the State of Alaska on H.R. 987.

As you know, the State is a long-standing opponent of the
cancellation of the long-term contracts, the creation of
substantial additional wilderness areas, and outright repeal
of Section 705 of ANILCA. We oppose these measures because
of the uncertainty which they would create for the timber
industry that relies upon timber from the Tongass National
Forest. In addition, we are concerned that the enactment of
these measures could disrupt the stability of communities
which rely upon this industry. These concerns are
documented in prior testimony which I ask be submitted for
the record.

Since last fall, when the House of Representatives passed a
similar version of this bill, a number of Alaskans, under
the auspices of the Southeast Conference have been engaged
in an effort to work out a compromise. The Southeast Conference is an organization comprising elected officials and
business leaders from the region.

The Conference appointed a committee to try to reach a
compromise. The committee consisted of the mayors from
Ketchikan, Sitka, Pelican, and Wrangell and a member of the
Juneau Assembly. The committee began its deliberations by
identifying the interests of the various communities,
recognizing that community interests were not always identi-
cal to those of any specific industry or other discreet
interest group within the community.

The efforts of this group have garnered support from many
fishermen, elected officials from large and small
communities, and Native leaders. Last week, Governor Cowper
announced his support for key components of this compromise
and believes that a broad spectrum of the residents of the
region are prepared to advocate a balanced and
forward-looking approach to management of the National
Forest. The State of Alaska believes that an approach of
conciliation here in Washington would produce a better
outcome than continued confrontation.

I would like to focus the rest of my testimony on some of
the key provisions of this compromise.

CONTRACT RENEGOTIATION

The State of Alaska supports renegotiation but not cancellation of the long-term contracts to address concerns which have been raised regarding the effect of the contracts on overall management of the forest. This approach is the approach taken in the measure which this committee and the House passed last year, and is the approach recommended by the Southeast Conference and the Sealaska Corporation, the regional Native corporation established under federal law. We oppose contract cancellation because of the risk that one or both of the pulp mills would close with attendant impacts on the communities which rely upon them. In a survey, commissioned by Sealaska Corporation, only 9 percent of Southeastern Alaska residents favored cancelling the contracts.

PROTECTION OF IMPORTANT FISH AND WILDLIFE HABITAT

The State of Alaska concurs with the Southeast Conference goal of maintaining fisheries-related employment and associated protection of anadromous fish streams. The State also supports permanent legislative protection of a limited number of specific areas which possess important fish and wildlife habitat. This special status would not be wilderness, but would prohibit commercial timber harvesting and associated road building. Other activities such as mining, primitive recreation facilities, water and power developments, and fisheries improvements could be permitted. Access would be less restricted than under wilderness status.

The Southeast Conference has proposed twelve areas for special attention, based on the input of affected communities. The State recognizes the high value of these areas as fish and wildlife habitat, and the importance of many of them to the fishing and tourism industries, subsistence users, and a number of communities in Southeast Alaska.

We have not made a final decision about each area and the boundaries of each area; however, the concept and overall impact on the timber base is workable. Permanent non-wilderness protection of a limited number of areas appears to be favored by the majority of residents of Southeast Alaska. In the Sealaska survey, seventy-six percent favored such protection while sixty percent did not favor additional wilderness.

SECTION 705 OF ANILCA

Perhaps the most difficult issue to resolve has been the matter of the requirement in ANILCA that the Secretary provide 4.5 billion board feet of timber per decade to the dependent industry.

The Southeast Conference has proposed language which authorizes the Secretary to provide "up to 4.5 billion board feet per decade" subject to market factors and multiple use concerns.

The above approaches increase the flexibility of the Secretary to adjust the timber made available to the industry for the decade to take into account market conditions and other natural resource values. The State supports Secretarial discretion on this matter.

With regard to funding, the State believes that funds will continue to be required to conduct intensive management activities such as pre-commercial thinning of second-growth stands. The State supports sufficient funding to accomplish this task.

ECONOMIC DIVERSIFICATION

The State of Alaska is also reviewing a regional economic development proposal offered by the Sealaska Corporation. With regard to this proposal, the State agrees with Sealaska's central message that we should use the pending legislation as an opportunity to strengthen the diversity of the regional economy. The State endorses the following concepts outlined in the corporation's proposal: the need for regional transportation coordination, fisheries enhancement, community stabilization, and promotion of recreation and tourism including adequate funding by the Forest Service for recreational facilities and trails.

In addition, the Southeast Conference has proposed an economic diversification fund which would be used to strengthen the Southeast economy. This proposal could be adapted to finance a number of the elements of the Sealaska proposal such as fisheries enhancement. We strongly support this concept and look forward to working with interested members of the committee to develop the idea further.

The State recognizes that in the legislative process it is often necessary to stake out a bargaining position to retain room for negotiations with the other house. The State's position is not such a postion. We offer this compromise, not as a new starting point for negotiations, but as our concept of where the legislation will settle when the negotiations have come to an end.

To conclude, the State of Alaska is strongly opposed to the legislation before you today. However, we believe that a bill which contained the key elements outlined in our testimony would address the concerns which have been raised during the last three years of deliberations.

STATEMENT OF
GEORGE M. LEONARD, ASSOCIATE CHIEF
FOREST SERVICE
UNITED STATES DEPARTMENT OF AGRICULTURE

Before the
Subcommittee on Water, Power and Offshore Energy Resources
Committee on Interior and Insular Affairs
House of Representatives

H.R. 987, a bill "To amend the Alaska National Interest Lands Conservation Act,
to designate certain lands in the Tongass National Forest as wilderness,
and for other purposes"

March 14, 1989

MR. CHAIRMAN AND MEMBERS OF THE SUBCOMMITTEE:

Thank you for the opportunity to present the Administration's views on

H.R. 987, a bill, "To amend the Alaska National Interest Lands Conservation

Act, to designate certain lands in the Tongass National Forest as wilderness,

and for other purposes." With me today is Mike Barton, Regional Forester for

Alaska.

The Administration strongly opposes enactment of H.R. 987.

H.R. 987 would repeal sections 705(a) and 705(d) of the Alaska National

Interest Lands Conservation Act (ANILCA), terminate the existing long-term

timber sale contracts in Alaska, and create wildernesses on 23 areas of the

Tongass National Forest.

Tongass Land and Resource Management Plan

Using National Forest Management Act (NFMA) planning procedures, we are well
into the process of revising the 1979 Tongass Land and Resource Management
Plan.

We recognize that Section 705(a) of ANILCA presently requires us to maintain
the timber supply from the Tongass National Forest at a rate of 4.5 billion
board feet per decade. However, this requirement does not restrict us from
examining other alternative timber supply levels during the revision process
for the Tongass plan. We, in fact, are considering a full range of alternative
management strategies. If, as a result of our resource analysis and review of
public comment, we determine that an alternative not consistent with the goal
of 4.5 billion board feet per decade is appropriate, we will recommend that the
current statutory direction be modified.

The Tongass plan revision team is also working on an analysis of the Forest's
capability to supply goods and services in response to public demands and the
physical capabilities of the Forest. This analysis is referred to as the
Analysis of the Management Situation (AMS). It is targeted for completion in
June.

New resource inventories for timber, soils, streams, wildlife, and fisheries
have been or are being completed. Studies relating to projected demands for
timber, fish, and wildlife are also underway. New research results will also
be incorporated. Based on this new information, the draft plan will describe

the allowable sale quantity as defined in the Tongass Land and Resource
Management Plan.

In conclusion, we are doing our best to carry out congressional direction in
fulfilling our land stewardship responsibilities on the Tongass National
Forest. We believe that a major statutory change would be premature at this
time. We are only 10 months from completion of the draft revision of the
Tongass Land and Resource Management Plan. The revision will provide the
public and Congress with updated, comprehensive information and analyses of
resources, markets, and the perspective of different publics. We urge the
Congress to wait for information developed through the Forest Plan revision
process before considering major statutory changes such as those in H.R. 987.

Mr. Barton and I would be happy to answer your questions or provide any
additional information you may desire.

USDA SUPPLEMENT
TO STATEMENT OF GEORGE M. LEONARD, ASSOCIATE CHIEF

WILDERNESS AREA ANALYSIS
DIRECT AND INDIRECT EFFECTS ON TIMBER

NAME	TOTAL ACREAGE	ACRES CFL	ACRES SUITABLE	ASQ (MMBF)	LUD1 ASQ	LUD2 ASQ	INDIRECT CFL	INDIRECT SUITABLE	ASQ
Yakutat Forelands	220,278	70,363	32,465	8.97	0	.9	17,478	14,623	4.14
Berners Bay	46,147	7,178	208	.04	0	.29	0	0	0
Young Lake	18,728	8,987	5,864	1.35	0	0	0	0	0
Chichagof	347,771	97,200	37,139	8.11	0	2.86	14,723	8,413	1.17
Kadashan	34,304	17,787	10,570	2.5	0	0	10,947	7,423	1.46
Trap Bay	8,667	4,471	2,704	.66	0	0	5,312	2,813	0.61
Chuck River	125,233	47,941	18,915	3.51	0	1.35	0	0	0
South Kuiu	191,566	105,563	36,720	7.56	0	2.03	10,665	8,075	1.20
Rocky Pass	78,366	23,954	0	0	0	2.86	14,059	8,779	1.88
West Duncan Canal	134,680	41,556	23,648	4.64	0	0	12,462	9,529	1.51
South Etolin Is.	83,642	36,640	0	0	4.0	0	5,770	4,478	.82
Nana	31,621	16,329	0	0	0	2.60	0	0	0
Calder/Holbrook	66,693	34,266	16,621	4.53	0	0	36,460	22,601	5.13
Sarkar Lake	25,650	11,269	0	0	0	1.46	0	0	0
Outside Islands	96,606	52,186	16,569	3.61	0	0	0	0	0
Karta River	36,566	24,159	0	0	3.96	0	0	0	0
Nutkwa	52,674	24,758	12,526	2.63	0	0	1,836	306	.07
Kegan Lake	24,960	11,305	0	0	0	1.53	0	0	0
Anan Creek *	36,415	8,923	0	0	0	.39	0	0	0
Pt. Adolphus / Mud Bay *	73,324	26,777	16,491	4.09	0	0	3,836	2,149	.47
Pleasant/Lemesurier Islands *	18,571	6,620	0	0	0	.79	0	0	0
Sullivan Island *	4,032	3,100	2,666	.36	0	0	0	0	0
Port Houghton/Sanborn Canal *	56,916	10,377	7,956	1.27	0	6	0	0	0
TOTAL	1,821,480	698,750	250,086	53.90	7.96	16.63	133,795	98,366	18.25

* New areas not included in HR 1516.

WILDERNESS AREA ANALYSIS
LAND STATUS ACREAGE

NAME	TOTAL ACREAGE	NON-FED	HR1516	NOTES
Yakutat Forelands *	220,278	10	229,963	Both CFL and ASQ boundaries change.
Berners Bay *	46,147	2	66,522	Both CFL and ASQ - LUD II boundaries.
Young Lake	18,726	24	18,702	CFL - Correction.
Chichagof *	347,771	42	332,645	Both CFL and ASQ boundary.
Kadashan *	34,204	160	34,044	Difference in CFL correction.
Trap Bay	6,667	0	6,667	
Chuck River	125,233	694	124,539	
South Kuiu *	191,565	33	191,532	Both CFL and ASQ - LUD II.
Rocky Pass *	76,368	634	75,734	Both CFL and ASQ - LUD II.
West Duncan Canal *	134,680	53	134,627	Both CFL and ASQ.
South Etolin Is. *	83,642	0	83,642	Both CFL and ASQ LUD I released.
Naha *	31,821	27	47,319	Both CFL and ASQ. LUD II and boundary.
Calder/Holbrook*	66,693	0	168,539	Both CFL and ASQ boundary change.
Sarkar Lake *	25,850	0	50,625	Both CFL and ASQ boundary change LUD II.
Outside Islands	96,606	36	96,572	
Karta River *	39,586	5	39,586	Both CFL and ASQ - LUD I release boundary.
Nutkwa *	52,674	20	52,654	Both CFL and ASQ boundary change.
Kegan Lake *	24,990	335	24,655	Both CFL and ASQ LUD II.
Anan Creek	38,415	0	0	
Pt. Adolphus/Mud Bay	73,524	178	0	
Pleasant/Lemesurier Islands	18,931	46	0	
Sullivan Island	4,032	0	0	
Port Houghton/Sanborn Canal	58,915	0	0	
TOTAL	1,821,460	2,299	1,755,565	

* - CFL and ASQ different in HR 967 than in HR1516.

WILDERNESS AREAS IN HR 987

Wilderness Study Area 1: Yakutat Forelands
(RESOURCE ASSESSMENTS ASSUME AREAS ARE MANAGED AS WILDERNESS)

Federal Acreage - 220,268
Non-Federal Acreage - 10
Total Acreage - 220,278

VCU's - 377(East side of Dangerous River), 379, 381, 382, 383, 384, 385, 387, 388, 389, 390, 391, 392, 393, 394, 395

Land Status - Open to State selection.

Fisheries - All VCU's are rated as having high value fisheries habitat which supports significant commercial fisheries for sockeye and coho salmon. Recreational fisheries for steelhead and coho salmon are world class. Salmon are an important subsistence resource in the area.

Wildlife - All VCU's have high wildlife value particularly for moose, brown bear, and migratory waterfowl. The area is known internationally for trophy big game. Moose and furbearers are important local subsistence resources.

Fish and Wildlife Impacts - Wilderness designation would foreclose future wildlife habitat management/ habitat enhancement opportunities in these areas. Wilderness designation could preclude some future fisheries development opportunities, or at a minimum, significantly increase the analysis required before any such opportunities would be approved for development.

Minerals Impacts - Moderate to low oil and gas potential and historic mining district on east end. May contain extensive beach deposits of chromite.

Timber Harvest Impacts -

Suitable CFL - 32,465 acres

Annual Volume (mmbf) - 8.97 mmbf

Transportation Impacts - The proposed Wilderness would not eliminate, but would complicate any future plans for road access along the Alsek River to Canada, and through the Yakutat Forelands. Congressional approval as outlined under ANILCA Section XI would be required prior to any construction of roads or utilities across Wilderness areas. The latter road would provide land transportation to a number of fishing camps. Glacial plugging of Russell Fiord would isolate this proposed Wilderness.

Recreation - The Yakutat Forelands Area has a history of a variety of commercial, subsistence, and recreational uses. Activities are associated with subsistence, commercial and sport fishing especially at the mouths of rivers such as the Dangerous, Akwe, Italio, Alsek, etc. Both sport and subsistence hunting activities occur throughout the Foreland Area. There are numerous private fish camps especially on the Forelands near the mouths of the Akwe and Italio Rivers. Three airplane landing strips, receiving annual maintenance by the FS, are located within the proposed area, as well as, six FS public recreation cabins. Motorized access by all-terrain vehicles, helicopters, and wheeled or floatplane occur in conjunction with the sportfishing, hunting and the private or public cabin use. The proximity to the community of Yakutat contributes to the frequent and consistent recreational uses of the area, as does it's international reputation for sportfishing and hunting. Public recreation cabins in the area are so popular, reservations are allotted by lottery for specific dates.

VCU 377- FS public recreation cabin and airstrip.
VCU 379- Private tent frames and two FS public recreation cabins.
VCU 381- Several private cabins, four miscellaneous buildings and a tractor road.
VCU 382- Privately-owned cabin.
VCU 387- FS public recreation cabin, guide camp with three tent platforms.
VCU 389- Two FS public recreation cabins, two air strips, and a guide camp with tent platform.

Recreation Impacts: Wilderness designation could place limitations on existing use and facilities. Existing uses and developed facilities, and their maintenance, do not provide the opportunities for solitude and primitive recreation envisioned by the 1964 Wilderness Act. Management guidelines of Wilderness designated through ANILCA, provides for semi-primitive roadless recreation opportunities. Traditional activities and some facilities that would be precluded from use under the 1964 Act, are authorized under ANILCA. Limitations on use of mechanical equipment and some forms of motorized use not authorized by ANILCA would have to be administered and managed. Management options and flexibility are narrowed by Wilderness designation.

Subsistence: Heavy subsistence use occurs throughout the Forelands for fish, wildlife, shellfish and plants.

Subsistence Impacts - Subsistence rights authorized by ANILCA is defined as the customary and traditional use by rural Alaska residents of wild, renewable resources for direct personal or family consumption. Reasonable access to subsistence resources are ensured by ANILCA. Snowmobiles, motorboats, and other means of surface transportation traditionally employed for subsistence, subject to reasonable regulation, is likewise ensured by ANILCA regardless of Wilderness designation. Wilderness designation of this area would have little impact on subsistence over the short-term. However, subsistence use does affect the Wilderness resource by removing the opportunity for solitude and a primitive recreation experience when snowmobiles, motorboats, and other means of surface transportation are employed.

Miscellaneous Impacts - Designation would isolate VCU 375. Timber impacts are shown above.

Wilderness Study Area 2: Berners Bay
(RESOURCE ASSESSMENTS ASSUME AREAS ARE MANAGED AS WILDERNESS)

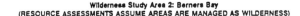

VCU's - 12(South 1/2), 13(Southern portion), 16(East 1/2), 17, and 25(extreme NE portion, only).

Federal Acreage - 46,145
Non-Federal Acreage - 2
Total Acreage - 46,147

Land Status - Open to State selection. None are currently proposed.

Fisheries - All VCU's have high value fisheries habitat that produce coho and sockeye salmon for important local commercial, subsistence, and recreational fisheries.

Wildlife - All VCU's are rated as having medium wildlife values. Moose, brown bear and mountain goat are important recreational use species. The area is important for migratory waterfowl. Commercial trapping is a important source of income for some area residents.

Fish and Wildlife Impacts - Wilderness designation would foreclose future wildlife habitat management/ habitat enhancement opportunities in these areas. Wilderness designation could preclude some future fisheries development opportunities, or at a minimum, significantly increase the analysis required before any such opportunities would be approved for development.

Minerals Impacts - Western edge includes a small portion of known mineralization and Historic Mining District which is undergoing further exploration and development. Adjacent active operations include the Jualin complex (some 383 acres of patented claims) which has an approved operating plan for an access road which was constructed in 1988 as well as an extensive drilling program and the Kensington complex (769 acres of patented claims as well as 118 unpatented claims) with an approved operating plan including an access road, 5,500 foot exploration adit, waste rock disposal and other facilities. Environmental studies are under way for further activities.

Timber Harvest Impacts -

        Suitable CFL - 208 acres

        Annual Volume (mmbf) - .04 mmbf

Transportation Impacts - Pending Congressional approval per ANILCA Section XI, the proposed wilderness would isolate existing rights of way from the end of the existing highway north to Berners Bay. The proposal affects an identified terminus of a cross Lynn Canal ferry or the right of way for a road connecting Haines to Juneau.

Recreation - The Berners Bay proposed Wilderness contains several private recreation cabins under special use permit. Recreation use is primarily associated with air boats, jet boats, kayaking, fishing and hunting. Associated upland camping also occurs in the Area. The proximity to Juneau makes this area especially attractive to recreationists and use of the area is significant. There are no public use facilities in the area.

Recreation Impacts - Public service facilities are needed in this area. Wilderness designation would preclude building those needed either by the Forest Service or private commercial services. Public use would need to be managed and perhaps in the long-term limited to maintain the Wilderness resource if so designated. Limitations would be costly to administer.

Subsistence: A moderate amount of subsistence use occurs in this Area.

Subsistence Impacts - Subsistence use could affect the Wilderness use of the area. Wilderness designation would not affect subsistence use over the short-term.

Wilderness Study Area 3: Young Lake
(RESOURCE ASSESSMENTS ASSUME AREAS ARE MANAGED AS WILDERNESS)

VCU's - 133

Federal Acreage - 18,702
Non-Federal Acreage -24
Total Acreage - 18,726

Land Status - 11/87 State selection nomination dropped due to provisions in the Green's Creek Mine Development EIS restricting residential development.

Fisheries - The area has medium value fish habitat. Young Lake supports a popular recreational fishery for cutthroat trout.

Wildlife - The area has high value wildlife habitat. Brown bear and Sitka black-tailed deer are important recreational resources.

Fish and Wildlife Impacts - Wilderness designation would foreclose future wildlife habitat management/ habitat enhancement opportunities in these areas. Wilderness designation could preclude some future fisheries development opportunities, or at a minimum, significantly increase the analysis required before any such opportunities would be approved for development.

Minerals Impacts - Known mineralization including a probable zinc prospect. Access for exploration for minerals adjacent to Green's Creek could also be affected.

Timber Harvest Impacts -

       Suitable CFL - 5,664 acres

       Annual Volume (mmbf) - 1.35 mmbf

Transportation Impacts - The proposed wilderness does not affect any identified road access, either within or related to adjacent lands.

Recreation - VCU 133C is located in land use designation (LUD) III. It includes three Forest Service recreation cabins, including one of the top three cabins in use on Juneau Ranger District (Admiralty Cove cabin). There is a trail from the cove to Young's Lake. The area is very popular for deer hunting and brown bear are abundant in the area.

Recreation Impacts - Increasing public use of this area would need to be closely managed to maintain the Wilderness resource including some use limitations over the long-term, in particular in the vicinity of the cabins. The cabins and their concentrated use have an effect on solitude and primitive recreation opportunities.

Miscellaneous Impacts - There is a research natural area that may be affected.

Wilderness Study Area 4: Chichagof
(RESOURCE ASSESSMENTS ASSUME AREAS ARE MANAGED AS WILDERNESS)

VCU's - 189, 190, 224, 225, 226, 228, 229, 246, 247, 248, 249, 262, 279, 280, 281, 282, 283, 285, 286.

Federal Acreage - 347,729
Non-Federal Acreage -42
Total Acreage - 347,771

Land Status - Federal acreage includes the approved Idaho Inlet State selection (370 acres). Includes all of the 1/89 State selection nomination at Goose Flats (1192 acres) which is currently under public review. Also includes a small portion of the 1/89 Tenakee/Frederick Portage nomination which is under public review.

Fisheries - All VCU's have very high fisheries habitat values and contribute significantly to northern Southeast Alaska commercial and subsistence fisheries. The area supports an important recreational and commercial charter boat fishery.

Wildlife - All VCU's have high wildlife habitat value. Brown bear trophy hunting in the area is world class. Sitka black-tailed deer is an important local subsistence and recreational users resource.

Fish and Wildlife Impacts - Wilderness designation would foreclose future wildlife habitat management/ habitat enhancement opportunities in these areas. Wilderness designation could preclude some future fisheries development opportunities, or at a minimum, significantly increase the analysis required before any such opportunities would be approved for development.

Minerals Impacts - Known mineralization and Historic District. There are 19 known mineral occurances in the unit mostly for lode and placer gold, copper-nickel and molybdenum. Three separate mineralized zones occur within the unit and have potential for further discovery.

Timber Harvest Impacts -

   Suitable CFL - 37,139 acres

   Annual Volume (mmbf) - 8.11 mmbf

Transportation Impacts - The transportation system included in the final decision for the 86-90 Alaska Pulp Company Operating Plan for the Patterson Bay to Deep Bay Area would be precluded at least until a decision on Wilderness designation was made for the area. A corridor for possible connection between Chichagof and Baranof Islands would be affected requiring Congressional approval as per ANILCA Section XI.

On the North side of Hoonah Sound, the road paralleling the beach at the upper end of the Sound would be eliminated, as would a possible connection between Crab Bay of Tenakee Inlet and Hoonah Sound unless State receives approval from Congress as per ANILCA Section XI.

Recreation - The Chichagof area contains a variety of activities including outfitter/guiding permits on both sides of Hoonah Sound, old mining and logging sites, all-terrain motor vehicle use, and hunting and fishing both for recreation and subsistence. Visually, logging activities are evident in some of the VCU's. A new recreation cabin is proposed in upper Hoonah Sound in response to public demand.

Recreation Impacts - All-terrain motor vehicle use, except for subsistence purposes, would be eliminated if this area is designated Wilderness. Cabins, except for health and safety or administrative purposes, would not be constructed.

Subsistence - A considerable amount of hunting and fishing subsistence use occurs in this area.

Subsistence Impacts - Wilderness solitude and primitive recreation experiences would be affected by ATV use of the area. Over the short-term, Wilderness designation would not seriously affect subsistence.

Wilderness Study Area 5: Kadashan
(RESOURCE ASSESSMENTS ASSUME AREAS ARE MANAGED AS WILDERNESS)

VCU's - 235

Federal Acreage - 34,044
Non-Federal Acreage - 160
Total Acreage - 34,204

Land Status - Open to State land selection. There are private land parcels with cabins at the head of Corner Bay.

Fisheries - This VCU has very high fisheries habitat values and contribute significantly to northern Southeast Alaska commercial and subsistence fisheries. The area is an important local recreational fishery.

Wildlife - The area has high wildlife habitat value. Brown bear trophy hunting in the area is world class. Sitka black-tailed deer is an important local subsistence and recreational resource.

Fish and Wildlife Impacts - Wilderness designation would foreclose future wildlife habitat management/ habitat enhancement opportunities in these areas. Wilderness designation could preclude some future fisheries development opportunities, or at a minimum, significantly increase the analysis required before any such opportunities would be approved for development.

Minerals Impacts - Mineralization occurs in the northeast third of the unit. One known mineral deposit occurs in the unit.

Timber Harvest Impacts -

    Suitable CFL - 10,570 acres

    Annual Volume (mmbf) - 2.5 mmbf

No activity at present. 651 mbf of decked road right-of-way log removal scheduled in 1989. Logs currently under contract as part of independent sale program.

Transportation Impacts - The completion of the road from Corner Bay to the False Island-Sitkoh Bay portion would be foreclosed. The lack of road access not only eliminates timber harvest, it also increases general management costs by forcing employees to fly or take boats around the island. The current high level of air transportation would continue rather than allow for use of land transportation.

Recreation - The VCU 235C is currently in a LUD III designation. Motorized access occurs on the partially constructed road from Corner Bay up into the Kadashan drainage and is used for hunting waterfowl, brown bear, and deer. Commercial trapping also occurs in this area. This proposed Wilderness is near the community of Tenakee Springs, which frequently uses the area for recreational purposes.

Recreation Impacts - Wilderness designation could limit the level of recreation use to maintain the wilderness resource for solitude and a primitive recreation experience. Motorized use, except for subsistence purposes, would be eliminated. Any restrictions would be costly to administer.

Subsistence - Heavy subsistence use occurs over most of the area.

Subsistence Impacts - Opportunities for solitude or a primitive recreation experience would be affected during heavy subsistence use periods. Wilderness designation would not affect subsistence use over the short-term.

Miscellaneous Impacts - Eliminates administrative access between False Island and Corner Bay already partially roaded (7 miles).

Wilderness Study Area 6: Trap Bay
(RESOURCE ASSESSMENTS ASSUME AREAS ARE MANAGED AS WILDERNESS)

VCU's - 237

Federal Acreage - 6,667
Non-Federal Acreage - 0
Total Acreage - 6,667

Land Status - State selection proposed in public review process as a State recreation area recommended to be dropped by the Planning Team.

Fisheries - The short stream in this VCU has high fisheries habitat values and contributes somewhat to northern Southeast Alaska commercial and subsistence fisheries. The area is used occasionally as a local recreational fishery.

Wildlife - This VCU has high wildlife habitat value. Brown bear trophy hunting in the area is world class. Sitka black-tailed deer is an important local subsistence and recreational users resource.

Fish and Wildlife Impacts - Wilderness designation would foreclose future wildlife habitat management/ habitat enhancement opportunities in these areas. Wilderness designation could preclude some future fisheries development opportunities, or at a minimum, significantly increase the analysis required before any such opportunities would be approved for development.

Minerals Impacts - A stone quarry occurs on the western boundary of the unit. Mineralization occurs in the southern and southwestern side of the unit.

Timber Harvest Impacts -

　　　Suitable CFL - 2,704 acres

　　　Annual Volume (mmbf) - .65 mmbf

Transportation Impacts - The proposed Wilderness would prohibit the Trap Bay facility for transfer of logs with associated roads. The preferred alternative in the FEIS for the 86-90 Alaska Pulp Company Operating Plan was to construct a road connection rather than construct the facilities for log transfer. A Wilderness designation would block this alternative.

Recreation - Trap Bay is a popular anchorage for subsistence, commercial and recreational fishing boats. Upland recreational use is usually in connection with big game hunting. No public recreation facilities have been developed. This area receives a moderate amount of recreational use from the community of Tenakee Springs, located across Tenakee Inlet.

Recreation Impacts - Wilderness designation would have no heavy effect on recreation opportunities, in the short term. It is possible that future recreation use restrictions may be necessary to maintain Wilderness characteristics.

Subsistence - A moderate amount of subsistence use occurs over most of the area.

Subsistence Impacts - Opportunities for solitude or a primitive recreation experience could be affected during heavy subsistence use periods. Wilderness designation would not affect subsistence use over the short-term.

Miscellaneous Impacts -

Subsistence - A moderate amount of subsistence use occurs over most of the area.

Subsistence Impacts - National Forest administered lands surrounding private lands could receive increased subsistence use if Hobart becomes a long-term stable community. Subsistence use could increase which might reduce the opportunity for solitude in certain areas. Presently there are no conflicts.

Miscellaneous Impacts - Eliminates proposed Williams Cove Terminal Transfer Facility site for proposed Gilbert Bay Sale. Isolates a portion of VCU 74 including Goldbelt land. An active cost-share road construction agreement with Goldbelt would have to be terminated.

Wilderness Study Area 8: South Kuiu
(RESOURCE ASSESSMENTS ASSUME AREAS ARE MANAGED AS WILDERNESS)

VCU's - 403, 408, 409, 410, 411, 412, 413, 414, 415, 416, 417, 418

Federal Acreage - 191,532
Non-Federal Acreage - 33
Total Acreage - 191,565

Land Status - Federal acreage includes two 11/87 State selection nominations. One dropped by Planning Team and the No Name Bay (approximately 3500 acres) proposed for selection.

Fisheries - The area is rated as having high value fish habitat that contribute significantly to commercial fisheries of southern Southeast.

Wildlife - The area is rated as having medium value wildlife habitat. Black bear and furbearers in the area are important recreation and subsistence resources. The area is currently closed to deer hunting.

Fish and Wildlife Impacts - Wilderness designation would foreclose future wildlife habitat management/habitat enhancement opportunities in these areas. Wilderness designation could preclude some future fisheries development opportunities, or at a minimum, significantly increase the analysis required before any such opportunities would be approved for development.

Minerals Impacts - Known mineralization includes two zinc prospects in the southwestern sector of the unit.

Timber Harvest Impacts -

Suitable CFL - 38,720 acres
Annual Volume (mmbf) - 7.55 mmbf
Com-   Additional 18,000 acres of Operable CFL in VCU 403 if the allocation were to change in
ment: the TLMP Revision.

Transportation Impacts - Transportation connections from VCU 419 to the proposed log transfer facility in No Name Bay would be precluded by this proposal. VCUs 415, 416 and 417 are included in the study area for the
APC 81-90 Supplemental Environmental Impact Statement. Alternatives for meeting the harvest committments of the Alaska Pulp Corporation's long term contract could be limited in scope should these three VCUs become wilderness.

There is a mainhaul road through the Bay of Pillars (VCU 403) bordering the proposed wilderness. The current Tongass Land Management Plan allocated this VCU LUD 2, maintaining its wildland character. No other roads are proposed under the current management plan.

Recreation - Area is adjacent to the Tebenkof Wilderness. Associated bays and coves provide anchorages for subsistence users, commercial fisherman and some pleasure boaters. Planned construction of a trail from Kell Bay to Table Bay.

Recreation Impacts - Wilderness designation could reduce the opportunity to provide private recreation developments through special use permits. In the long-term, recreation use might be limited in order to maintain the Wilderness environment and primitive recreation opportunities. VCU 403, although adjacent to existing Tebenkof Wilderness does not connect to the remaining VCU's of this proposal. Wilderness designation may restrict future recreational developments or activities.

Subsistence - A moderate amount of subsistence use occurs over most of the area, primarily from the communities of Kake, Point Baker, Port Protection, and others.

Subsistence Impacts - Wilderness designation would not affect subsistence use over the short-term.

Wilderness Study Area 9: Rocky Pass
(RESOURCE ASSESSMENTS ASSUME AREAS ARE MANAGED AS WILDERNESS)

VCU's - 427, 428 (Both LUD II)

Federal Acreage - 75,734
Non-Federal Acreage - 634
Total Acreage - 76,368

Land Status - Non-federal acreage includes High Island State selection.

Fisheries - The area is rated as having moderate value fish habitat which contributes to commercial fisheries in Frederick Sound and Sumner Strait.

Wildlife - The area is rated as having high value wildlife habitat. Sitka black-tailed deer, black bear, furbearers and waterfowl in the area are important recreation and subsistence resources. The area is currently closed to deer hunting.

Fish and Wildlife Impacts - Wilderness designation would foreclose future wildlife habitat management/ habitat enhancement opportunities in these areas. Wilderness designation could preclude some future fisheries development opportunities, or at a minimum, significantly increase the analysis required before any such opportunities would be approved for development.

Minerals Impacts - The northern end of the unit is underlain by mineral terranes. There is a good possibility for deposits in this area.

Timber Harvest Impacts -

Suitable CFL - 0 acres
Annual Volume (mmbf) - 0 mmbf
Comment: 24,000 acres Operable CFL in the area if the allocation were to change in the TLMP Revision.

Transportation Impacts - No transportation facilities or corridors are to be constructed in this area which is to be managed to maintain its wildland characteristics as prescribed in the Tongass Land Management Plan.

Recreation - Significant hunting and fishing use in and around Big John Bay. Forest Service public recreation cabin located at Big John Bay (VCU 427), with trail to established interior road system (FDR 6314) which provides access to other road systems linking to the community of Kake.

Recreation Impacts - Wilderness designation could restrict current use, facility improvements, and operation and maintenance of existing public use facilities. Administration of public use would need to be increased to maintain Wilderness environment.

Subsistence - Heavily used subsistence area by the community of Kake, appx. 15 miles to the north.

Subsistence Impacts - Opportunities for solitude or a primitive recreation experience could be affected during heavy subsistence use periods. Wilderness designation would not affect subsistence use.

Miscellaneous Impacts - Eliminates access to VCU 427.15 and result in an access problem for the North Irish Creek sale under contract to Alaska Timber Corp.

Wilderness Study Area 10: West Duncan Canal
(RESOURCE ASSESSMENTS ASSUME AREAS ARE MANAGED AS WILDERNESS)

VCU's - 434, 435, 436, 438, 440, 448 (West Duncan Canal and Woewodski Island)

Federal Acreage - 134,627
Non-Federal Acreage - 53
Total Acreage - 134,680

Land Status - One parcel of private land within proposed wilderness boundary (Woewodski Island). Homesite development has occured on the southern tip of Lindenburg Peninsula (Beecher Pass) and the east side of the Wrangell Narrows through the State of Alaska land lottery program. The waterfront now appears developed.

Fisheries - These VCU's have high value fish habitat. Recreational fisheries for coho salmon, steelhead trout, and cutthroat trout are world class. The crab and shrimp fisheries are excellent in the Duncan Canal area.

Wildlife - The area has high value wildlife habitat. Black bear, Sitka black-tailed deer, and furbearers are important subsistence and recreational resources. The area is closed to deer hunting. The area is important migratory waterfowl habitat. The Alaska Department of Fish and Game classifies the area as Class 1 having high wildlife and fisheries value.

Fish and Wildlife Impacts - Wilderness designation would foreclose future wildlife habitat management/ habitat enhancement opportunities in these areas. Wilderness designation could preclude some future fisheries development opportunities, or at a minimum, significantly increase the analysis required before any such opportunities would be approved for development.

Minerals Impacts - Known mineralization occurs. There are 10 known deposits including 3 past producers including the Castle Island barite deposit. Nearly 400 claims were active in 1986 and the area has potential for further discovery/production.

Timber Harvest Impacts -

       Suitable CFL - 23,548 acres
       Annual Volume (mmbf) - 4.64 mmbf
       Comment: Proposed wilderness designation would affect the Totem Timber Sale.

Transportation Impacts - The planned roads from Douglas Bay North would be included in this proposed Wilderness. On the East side of Wrangell Narrows, existing roads and non-federal lands appear to be included in the proposed wilderness.

Recreation - Area adjacent to Petersburg Creek - Duncan Salt Chuck Wilderness. Area heavily used by residents of Petersburg. Excellent fishing and hunting opportunities. Motor boat use common. Three historic mines in the area, that receive visitor use. Forest Service recreation cabins in these VCUs are: Kah Sheets Bay, Kah Sheets Lake, Beecher Pass, Breilland Slough, Castle Flats, Castle River, Harvey Lake, Towers Arm and Towers Lake. Maintained trails in these VCUs are: Castle River (.5 mile), Harvey Lake (1 mile) and Kah Sheets Lake (2.5 mile).

Recreation Impacts - Wilderness designation could limit current use and operation/maintenance of existing public use facilities in order to maintain a Wilderness environment. Management intensity of the public use of the area would be increased to maintain the opportunity fo solitude and a primitive recreation experience. Present use reduces opportunities for solitude and privitive recreation experiences.

Subsistence - The area is popular for subsistence gathering in part due to the convenience of the nine public cabins in the general vicinity. Cabins are used in conjunction with subsistence gathering activities.

Subsistence Impacts - Opportunities for solitude or a primitive recreation experience could be affected during heavy subsistence use periods. Wilderness designation would not affect subsistence use.

Wilderness Study Area 11: South Etolin Island
(RESOURCE ASSESSMENTS ASSUME AREAS ARE MANAGED AS WILDERNESS)

VCU's - 471, 472, 473, 474 (all LUD I Release)

Federal Acreage - 83,642
Non-Federal Acreage - 0
Total Acreage - 83,642

Land Status - 11/87 State selection nomination dropped. Federal acreage includes the approved McHenry Anchorage State selection.

Fisheries - This area is rated as having moderate value fish habitat that produces significant harvests of coho, pink, and chum salmon in the southern Southeast commercial fisheries.

Wildlife - The area is rated as having medium value wildlife habitat. Sitka black-tailed deer, black bear, and furbearers in the area are important recreation and subsistence resources. Elk were transplanted to Etolin Island in cooperation with Alaska Department of Fish and Game and may establish on South Etolin Island.

Fish and Wildlife Impacts - Wilderness designation would foreclose future wildlife habitat management/habitat enhancement opportunities in these areas. Wilderness designation could preclude some future fisheries development opportunities, or at a minimum, significantly increase the analysis required before any such opportunities would be approved for development.

Minerals Impacts - Known mineralization underlies the unit and one uranium prospect is known to occur.

Timber Harvest Impacts -

> Suitable CFL - 0 acres
> Annual Volume (mmbf) - 0 MMbf
> Com-   35,000 acres of operable CFL in the area could be available if the allocation were to
> ment: change in the TLMP Revision.

Transportation Impacts - This portion of Etolin Island was proposed as wilderness in the Tongass Land Management Plan, but was not included in the Alaska National Interest Lands Conservation Act. No road corridors are involved.

Recreation - Islands at southern tip of Etolin Island provide many recreational anchorages. Excellent deer hunting and beachcombing opportunities. Canoe passage provides scenic route for small boat travel.

Recreation Impacts - Wilderness designation would have little effect on existing recreation opportunities, in the short term. It is possible that future recreation use restrictions may be necessary to maintain Wilderness characteristics.

Subsistence - This area is a popular subsistence use area for the community of Wrangell, and others.

Subsistence Impacts - Opportunities for solitude or a primitive recreation experience could be affected during heavy subsistence use periods. Wilderness designation would not affect subsistence use.

Miscellaneous Impacts - This area has been extensively studied for mariculture sites, which might be precluded, but no apparent impact on adjacent VCU's.

Wilderness Study Area 12: Naha River
(RESOURCE ASSESSMENTS ASSUME AREAS ARE MANAGED AS WILDERNESS)

VCU's - 742.

Federal Acreage - 31,794
Non-Federal Acreage - 27
Total Acreage - 31,821

Land Status - Open to State land selection.

Fisheries - This area has high value fish habitat. Recreational fisheries for coho salmon, steelhead trout, and cutthroat trout are world class.

Wildlife - The area has high value wildlife habitat. Black bear, Sitka black-tailed deer, and furbearers are important subsistence and recreational resources. The Alaska Department of Fish and Game classifies the area as Class 1 having high wildlife and fisheries value.

Fish and Wildlife Impacts - Wilderness designation would foreclose future wildlife habitat management/habitat enhancement opportunities in these areas. Wilderness designation could preclude some future fisheries development opportunities, or at a minimum, significantly increase the analysis required before any such opportunities would be approved for development.

Minerals Impacts - No known mineralization.

Timber Harvest Impacts -

Suitable CFL - 0 acres

Annual Volume (mmbf) - 0 mmbf

Wilderness Study Area 13: Calder/Holbrook
(RESOURCE ASSESSMENTS ASSUME AREAS ARE MANAGED AS WILDERNESS)

VCU's - 527 (The portion only around the basin forming Hole-in-the-Wall), 528 (Western 2/3rd), 531 (Southerly 1/2), 536 (Southerly 1/2), 537 (West side of El Capitan Passage), 541 (Easterly 2/3rd), 542, 548 and 549 (West side of El Capitan Passage).

Federal Acreage - 68,693
Non-Federal Acreage - 0
Total Acreage - 68,693

Land Status - State selection nomination at Hole In The Wall (500 acres) recommended in State Prince of Wales Area Plan Public Review Draft.

Fisheries - This area is rated as having high value fish habitat that contribute significantly to Sumner Strait commercial fisheries.

Wildlife - The area is rated as having medium value wildlife habitat. Sitka black-tailed deer, black bear, and furbearers in the area are important recreation and subsistence resources.

Fish and Wildlife Impacts - Wilderness designation would foreclose future wildlife habitat management/ habitat enhancement opportunities in these areas. Wilderness designation could preclude some future fisheries development opportunities, or at a minimum, significantly increase the analysis required before any such opportunities would be approved for development.

Minerals Impacts - Seven mineral deposits are known in the unit which include past producers of marble and zinc. There are 39 patented claims and numerous unpatented claims. The area has potential for further discovery/production. Limestone is found throughout the area.

Timber Harvest Impacts -

> **Suitable CFL** - 18,821 acres

> **Annual Volume (mmbf)** - 4.53 mmbf

Transportation Impacts - The proposed wilderness includes lands with some existing roads.

Recreation - VCU's 527, 528, 531, 536, 537, 542, 548 and 549 contain no developed recreation facilities. VCU 541, has a very popular upland FS public recreation cabin accessible from saltwater. El Capitan Passage is a dredged inside passage for log rafts and commercial fishing. There are known major limestone caves within the Area that have potential for significant recreational attractions and management challenges.

Recreation Impacts - Existing public recreation cabins are authorized in ANILCA Wilderness' as are a number of other recreation activities and facilities. Little impact would occur on the recreation activities, however, these activities and developments may diminish the opportunity for Wilderness solitude and primitive recreation experiences envisioned in the 1964 Wilderness Act.

Subsistence - A significant amount of subsistence use occurs over most of the area.

Subsistence Impacts - Opportunities for solitude or a primitive recreation experience could be affected during heavy subsistence use periods. Wilderness designation would not affect subsistence use.

Wilderness Study Area 14: Sarkar Lakes
(RESOURCE ASSESSMENTS ASSUME AREAS ARE MANAGED AS WILDERNESS)

VCU's - 554(8,938 acs. deleted), 571, 572, 574, and 577.

Federal Acreage - 25,650
Non-Federal Acreage - 0
Total Acreage - 25,650

Land Status - Open to State selection.

Fisheries - All VCU's have high value fisheries habitat. Sockeye salmon and coho salmon production is important to commercial, subsistence, and recreational fisheries in the area. The Alaska Department of Fish and Game has classified the area as a Class 1 area having high fish and wildlife value.

Wildlife - The area has high value wildlife habitat. Sitka black-tailed deer, black bear, and furbearers are important subsistence and recreational resources.

Fish and Wildlife Impacts - Wilderness designation would foreclose future wildlife habitat management/ habitat enhancement opportunities in these areas. Wilderness designation could preclude some future fisheries development opportunities, or at a minimum, significantly increase the analysis required before any such opportunities would be approved for development.

Minerals Impacts - One copper sulfide prospect occurs in the unit and there are active unpatented mining claims in the area.

Timber Harvest Impacts -

    Suitable CFL - 0 acres

    Annual Volume (mmbf) - 0 mmbf

Transportation Impacts - This proposed wilderness includes VCU 554, designated to be managed to maintain its wildland character in the Tongass Land Management Plan.

Recreation - This Area is very popular for both recreational and subsistence hunting and fishing. Canoeing the Sarkar Area watercourses and lakes is a rapidly increasing public use. Two FS public recreation cabins which are only accessible by floatplane are within this Area. Outboard motors are used on the lakes. The Area is bordered by an extensive road system which receives increasingly heavy motorized recreation use. The sights and sounds of this use are evident. Hiking on improved and unimproved trails from the road system is increasing in popularity.

Recreation Impacts - All of the recreation activities and facilities would be authorized under ANILCA Wilderness designation. It is possible that future recreation use restrictions may be necessary to maintain Wilderness characteristics. Opportunities to provide some services to recreation users might be forgone if the area is designated Wilderness.

Subsistence - The area is popular for subsistence by residents of Thorne Bay, Coffman Cove, and other rural communities on Prince of Wales Island. Road along the border of this area provides easy access to subsistence users.

Subsistence Impacts - Opportunities for solitude or a primitive recreation experience could be affected during heavy subsistence use periods. Wilderness designation would not affect subsistence use.

Miscellaneous Impacts -

Wilderness Study Area 15: Outside Islands
(RESOURCE ASSESSMENTS ASSUME AREAS ARE MANAGED AS WILDERNESS)

VCU's - 626, 627, 628, 567, 568, 569

Federal Acreage - 98,572
Non-Federal Acreage - 36
Total Acreage - 98,608

Land Status - The State Prince of Wales Area Plan included three nominations on Baker and Noyes Islands. These were not recommended due to public opposition.

Fisheries - This area is rated as having moderate value fish habitat that produces coho, pink, and chum salmon in the southern Southeast commercial fisheries.

Wildlife - The area is rated as having medium value wildlife habitat. Sitka black-tailed deer, black bear, and furbearers in the area are important recreation and subsistence resources.

Fish and Wildlife Impacts - Wilderness designation would foreclose future wildlife habitat management/ habitat enhancement opportunities in these areas. Wilderness designation could preclude some future fisheries development opportunities, or at a minimum, significantly increase the analysis required before any such opportunities would be approved for development.

Minerals Impacts - Known mineralization consists of 5 or 6 metals deposits. There are also several unpatented claims present.

Timber Harvest Impacts -

> Suitable CFL - 18,569 acres

> Annual Volume (mmbf) - 3.51 mmbf

Transportation Impacts - Little planning for transportation has occurred on these lands except as was done with the State of Alaska South West Prince of Wales Tideland Plan. With the exception of Noyes Island, access was provided to these lands.

Recreation - Little recreation activity. Steamboat Bay used by fisherman as anchorage. A public use facility is planned.

Recreation Impacts - Wilderness designation would have little effect on existing recreation activities. ANILCA authorizes cabins and shelters for public health and safety within Wilderness.

Subsistence - Some upland subsistence use occurs.

Subsistence Impacts - Wilderness designation would not affect subsistence use over the short-term.

Miscellaneous Impacts - No apparent impact on adjacent VCU's.

Wilderness Study Area 16: Karta River
(RESOURCE ASSESSMENTS ASSUME AREAS ARE MANAGED AS WILDERNESS)

VCU's - 605, 606, 607, 608

Federal Acreage - 39,881
Non-Federal Acreage - 5
Total Acreage - 39,886

Land Status - Open to State land selection. Proposal includes a small parcel of Native Corporation land.

Fisheries - All VCU's have high value fisheries habitat. Sockeye salmon and coho salmon production is important to commercial, subsistence, and recreational fisheries in the area. The Alaska Department of Fish and Game has classified VCU 607 as a Class 1 area having high fish and wildlife value.

Wildlife - VCU 607 has high value wildlife habitat. VCU 608 has medium value wildlife habitat. Sitka black-tailed deer, black bear, and furbearers are important subsistence and recreational resources.

Fish and Wildlife Impacts - Wilderness designation would foreclose future wildlife habitat management/habitat enhancement opportunities in these areas. Wilderness designation could preclude some future fisheries development opportunities, or at a minimum, significantly increase the analysis required before any such opportunities would be approved for development.

Minerals Impacts - Known mineralization and Historic District with 5 mineral deposits including a past gold producer.

Timber Harvest Impacts -

    Suitable CFL - 0 acres

    Annual Volume (mmbf) - 0 mmbf

Transportation Impacts - This area was recommended in the Tongass Land Management Plan for wilderness but was not included in ANILCA. The State of Alaska has identified a potential road corridor through the Karta area to connect at Tolstoi Bay.

Recreation - Very popular recreation area used by residents and visitors. Four Forest Service recreation cabins are so heavily used in the Karta system, reservations are selected by a lottery system. Heavy subsistence use.

Recreation Impacts - This area already receives heavy public use. Wilderness designation would increase use pressure, diminishing the quality of Wilderness experience. Public use would need to be restricted. Operation and maintenance of public facilities could be constrained.

Subsistence - Very popular and heavily used for subsistence activities.

Subsistence Impacts - Subsistence use takes priority over public hunting and fishing. Wilderness designation could result in conflicts between the general user and subsistence activities. Regulation of both activities might be necessary at some point.

Wilderness Study Area 17: Nutkwa
(RESOURCE ASSESSMENTS ASSUME AREAS ARE MANAGED AS WILDERNESS)

VCU's - 685, 686, 688, 689

Federal Acreage - 52,654
Non-Federal Acreage - 20
Total Acreage - 52,674

Land Status - State South Prince of Wales Area Plan included two nominations. The Mabel Bay selection (1150 acres) is recommended and the other was dropped.

Fisheries - All VCU's are rated as having very high value fish habitat. Sockeye and coho salmon production is significant. VCU 685 is classified by the Alaska Department of Fish and Game as a Class 1 area having high fish and wildlife value. Subsistence use of sockeye salmon is significant.

Wildlife - VCU 685 is rated as having high value wildlife habitat. VCU 686 is rated as medium value wildlife habitat. Sitka black-tailed deer and furbearers are important recreation and subsistence resources in the area.

Fish and Wildlife Impacts - Wilderness designation would foreclose future wildlife habitat management/ habitat enhancement opportunities in these areas. Wilderness designation could preclude some future fisheries development opportunities, or at a minimum, significantly increase the analysis required before any such opportunities would be approved for development.

Minerals Impacts - Five mineral properties occur including one past producer. Most are copper sulfide and lode gold occurances. One claim is patented.

Timber Harvest Impacts -

    Suitable CFL - 12,526 acres

    Annual Volume (mmbf) - 2.83 mmbf

Transportation Impacts - Planning for access of these lands has occurred with the State of Alaska Southwest Prince of Wales Island Tidelands Plan. Cooperative development between National Forest lands and private lands was foreseen at that time, and planned accordingly.

Recreation - Area receives light recreation use a present. Area borders South Prince of Wales to the east.

Recreation Impacts - Area is adjacent to private land. Wilderness designation could increase recreation use of area.

Subsistence - A moderate amount of subsistence use occurs primarily from the community of Hydaburg and others.

Subsistence Impacts - Opportunities for solitude or a primitive recreation experience would not be affected by subsistence activities. Wilderness designation would not affect subsistence use over the short-term.

Miscellaneous Impacts -

Wilderness Study Area 18: Kegan Lake
(RESOURCE ASSESSMENTS ASSUME AREAS ARE MANAGED AS WILDERNESS)

VCU's - 684

Federal Acreage - 24,655
Non-Federal Acreage - 335
Total Acreage - 24,990

Land Status - Open to State land selection.

Fisheries - This VCU has high value fish habitat. Recreational fisheries for coho salmon, steelhead trout, and rainbow trout are world class.

Wildlife - The area has high value wildlife habitat. Black bear, Sitka black-tailed deer, and furbearers are important subsistence and recreational resources. The area is important migratory waterfowl habitat. The Alaska Department of Fish and Game classifies the area as Class 1 having high wildlife and fisheries value.

Fish and Wildlife Impacts - Wilderness designation would foreclose future wildlife habitat management/ habitat enhancement opportunities in these areas. Wilderness designation could preclude some future fisheries development opportunities, or at a minimum, significantly increase the analysis required before any such opportunities would be approved for development.

Minerals Impacts - Known mineralization and Historic District includes past producing copper and marble mines of some importance. There are 30 patented claims in the unit as well as numerous unpatented claims. There is a high potential for further discovery/production.

Timber Harvest Impacts -

    Suitable CFL - 0 acres

    Annual Volume (mmbf) - 0 mmbf

Transportation Impacts - No roads have been planned in this VCU identified to be managed to maintain its wildland characteristics in the Tongass Land Management Plan.

Recreation - Heavily used by recreationists for sportfishing and hunting. Recreation facilities consist of two public recreation cabins, trails and mooring buoy. Area is adjacent to South Prince of Wales Wilderness.

Recreation Impacts - Wilderness designation would attract more users to this area, diminishing the quality of wilderness experience. Some use restrictions may be necessary to maintain Wilderness experience.

Subsistence - A very popular subsistence use area from nearby rural communities.

Subsistence Impacts - Opportunities for solitude or a primitive recreation experience could be affected during heavy subsistence use periods. Wilderness designation would not affect subsistence use over the short-term.

Wilderness Study Area 19: Anan Creek
(RESOURCE ASSESSMENTS ASSUME AREAS ARE MANAGED AS WILDERNESS)

VCU - 522 (LUD II)

Federal Acreage - 38,415
Non-Federal Acreage - 0
Total Acreage - 38,415

Land Status - Open to State land selection, but none proposed. Native selection proposed at mouth of Anan Creek, where there's an historical use site. A power transmission line for the Tyee Hydroelectric Project crosses the Area.

Fisheries - The Anan Creek system is one of the premier salmon producing streams in Southeast Alaska. There are two large lakes on the west fork of this system supporting sockeye, cutthroat and rainbow trout and Dolly Varden. This system supports one of the largest runs of pink salmon in Southeast Alaska with annual escapements averaging more than 100,000 fish. The area supports a large commercial fishery, as well as growing recreational fishing. A fish ladder, constructed late 1970's in cooperation with the State of Alaska, allows migrating salmon to access spawning grounds above the lower falls.

Wildlife - The area is considered to have medium value wildlife habitat. Deer, black bear, and grouse are important recreation and subsistence resources. Anan Creek is also an important wildlife viewing area for local residents and tourists.

Fish and Wildlife Impacts - Wilderness designation would foreclose future wildlife habitat management/ habitat enhancement opportunities in this area. Wilderness designation could preclude some future fisheries development opportunities, or at a minimum, significantly increase the analysis required before any such opportunities would be approved for development.

Minerals Impacts - Open to mineral entry but no potential identified.

Timber Harvest Impacts -

    Suitable CFL: 0
    Annual Volume (MMBF): 0
    Comment: 1700 acres of Operable CFL in the area.

Transportation Impacts - Unroaded, trail present. No impacts.

Recreation - VCU 522 has a LUD II designation and includes Anan Bay, Anan Creek and Anan Lake. The recreational attributes of this area are heavily utilized by local and non-resident visitors. Public use facilities in the area include a FS recreation cabin, a popular bear viewing observatory and maintained trails. Other facilities include an unmaintained cabin and trails. There are eight outfitter/guides operating in the area authorized by FS special use permit. A mooring buoy located in Anan Bay is heavily used by boats travelling the Inside Passage.

Recreation Impacts - Wilderness designation could increase use of this area to a point that restrictions would need to be implemented and administered. Heavy use reduces the quality of Wilderness experience which is presently occuring.

Subsistence - This a very popular subsistence area.

Subsistence Impacts - Wilderness designation could increase use of the area, resulting in conflicts that could arise between subsistence users and recreation users. Wilderness designation would not affect subsistence.

Miscellaneous Impacts - None

Wilderness Study Area 20: Pt Adolphus/Mud Bay
(RESOURCE ASSESSMENTS ASSUME AREAS ARE MANAGED AS WILDERNESS)

VCU'S - 191,192,193(2/3),194,195,196

Federal Acreage - 73,346
Non-Federal Acreage - 178
Total Acreage - 73,524

Land Status - Open to State land selection, but none proposed.

Fisheries - Pt Adolphus/Mud Bay have many inland lakes and other water areas important to both anadromous and resident fish. This area supports important subsistence, recreational, and commercial fisheries. Coho, sockeye, pink and chum salmon, cutthroat trout, and Dolly Varden utilize the spawning and rearing area within this system. Pink and chum salmon are periodically abundant with high pink salmon escapements on odd years and Otter Lake reportedly receives runs of Sockeye salmon and cutthroat trout. Dolly Varden are abundant throughout the system with two to three pounders being common.

Wildlife - The many inland and coastal wetland areas provide important waterfowl habitats. The estuarine areas of Mud Bay are particularly important to brown bears. The upland areas are important to pine martin and alpine areas provide important deer summer range. Beaver populations are found throughout the area.

Fish and Wildlife Impacts - Wilderness designation would foreclose future wildlife habitat management/habitat enhancement opportunities in this area. Wilderness designation could preclude some future fisheries development opportunities, or at a minimum, significantly increase the analysis required before any such opportunities would be approved for development.

Minerals Impacts - Open to mineral entry with occurrences of epigentic and polymetalic vein as well as disseminated deposits.

Timber Harvest Impacts -

Suitable CFL - 18,491

Annual Volume (mmbf) - 4.09

Transportation Impacts - No impact other than access for timber harvest.

Recreation - Recreation use of this Area is by sport and subsistence hunting with upland use by commercial and sportfishing visitors who anchor-up in Mud Bay, Idaho Inlet and the various smaller unnamed bays and bites along the seacoast.

Recreation Impacts - Wilderness designation would increase interest and use of this area.

Subsistence - The area is popular with subsistence users from Elfin Cove and other communities.

Subsistence Impacts - Conflicts between subsistence users and recreation users may arise. Wilderness designation would not affect subsistence use.

Miscellaneous Impacts -

Wilderness Study Area 21: Pleasant/Lemesurier Islands
(RESOURCE ASSESSMENTS ASSUME AREAS ARE MANAGED AS WILDERNESS)

VCU'S - 185,186

Federal Acreage - 18,925
Non-Federal Acreage - 46
Total Acreage - 18,971

Land Status - Open to State land selection, but none proposed. There are two private holdings totaling 46 acres on the south side of Lemesurier Island.

Fisheries - There are no major fish streams on these islands.

Wildlife - These islands are considered to have medium value wildlife habitat. The islands do provide good deer and grouse habitat and deer and grouse are important recreation and subsistence resources.

Fish and Wildlife Impacts - Wilderness designation would foreclose future wildlife habitat management/ habitat enhancement opportunities in this area.

Minerals Impacts - Open to mineral entry with occurrences of epigentic and polymetalic vein as well as disseminated deposits on Lemesuner Island.

Timber Harvest Impacts -

    Suitable CFL - 0

    Annual Volume (mmbf) - 0

Transportation Impacts - No impact.

Recreation - VCU 185 has been proposed as a Research Natural Area. Upland use by recreation visitors is casual and in connection with commercial and sport fishing. The area is composed of two small islands in Icy Strait near the communities of Gustavus, Elfin Cove, and Hoonah. Presently the area is being managed for semi-primitive roadless recreation opportunities.

Recreation Impacts - The two islands are small and rugged. They would be increasingly visited if designated as Wilderness, which may cause some conflicts with subsistence users.

Subsistence - Some subsistence use occurs.

Subsistence Impacts - Wilderness designation would not affect subsistence use.

Miscellaneous Impacts -

Wilderness Study Area 22: Sullivan Island
(RESOURCE ASSESSMENTS ASSUME AREAS ARE MANAGED AS WILDERNESS)

VCU - 94

Federal Acreage - 4,032
Non-Federal Acreage - 0
Total Acreage - 4,032

Land Status - Includes all the island except the approved State selection (600 acres).

Fisheries - There are no major fish streams on this island. There are no known anadromous and few resident fish populations inhabiting Sullivan Island. Sculpin, Stickleback, and Dolly Varden may be found in the limited fresh waters areas on the island.

Wildlife - The island has good wildlife habitat for several species. Sitka black-tailed deer inhabit the island and use beach areas during periods of high snow fall. Sixteen bald eagle nests have been active recently near the island coast. The island also supports populations of mink and pine martin.

Fish and Wildlife Impacts - Wilderness designation would foreclose future wildlife habitat management/ habitat enhancement opportunities in this area. Wilderness designation could preclude some future fisheries development opportunities, or at a minimum, significantly increase the analysis required before any such opportunities would be approved for development.

Minerals Impacts - Open to mineral entry, but no potential identified.

Timber Harvest Impacts -

    Suitable CFL - 2,568

    Annual Volume (mmbf) - 0.35

Transportation Impacts - No impact.

Recreation - Light recreation use by kayakers and residents of Haines occurs.

Recreation Impacts - Wilderness designation would forego the opportunity to provide public / private recreation facilities and services on the island as use increases. The approved State selection are within VCU 94 could eventually become a community inside or adjacent to Wilderness.

Subsistence - Some subsistence use occurs by residents of the rural community of Haines and others.

Subsistence Impacts - Wilderness designation would not affect subsistence use over the short-term. Eventually there may be a rural community developed on the approved State selected land. In this event there could be conflicts between subsistence users of this community and Wilderness use.

Miscellaneous Impacts -

Wilderness Study Area 23: Port Houghton/Sanborn Canal
(RESOURCE ASSESSMENTS ASSUME AREAS ARE MANAGED AS WILDERNESS)

VCU'S - 79,84

Federal Acreage - 58,915
Non-Federal Acreage - 0
Total Acreage - 58,915

Land Status - Open to State land selection, but none proposed. Federal acreage includes approximately 3,000 acres on which subsurface estate was patented to the Sealaska Corporation.

Fisheries - Rusty, Roberts Island and Negro Creeks constitute the major fish producing systems. The principle commercial species include pink, chum and coho salmon with steelhead, rainbow trout and Dolly Varden providing opportunities for sport fishing which however, is presently very limited. This Area support commercial salmon, crab and halibut fisheries.

Wildlife - These areas are considered to have high value wildlife habitat and have high populations of black bears, mountain goats, and eagle nests. High waterfowl populations use the inland and coastal wetland areas. Deer populations in both areas are currently low.

Fish and Wildlife Impacts - Wilderness designation would foreclose future wildlife habitat management/ habitat enhancement opportunities in this area. Wilderness designation could preclude some future fisheries development opportunities, or at a minimum, significantly increase the analysis required before any such opportunities would be approved for development.

Minerals Impacts - Open to mineral entry with occurrences of epigentic and polymetalic vein, massive sulfides as well as disseminated deposits.

Timber Harvest Impacts -

   Suitable CFL - 7,958

   Annual Volume (mmbf) - 1.27

Transportation Impacts - No impact.

Recreation - Recreation and subsistence use of this Area is increasing due to the extensive development and logging community in the Hobart Bay area, ten miles to the north. Upland use of the Tongass National Forest is generally in connection with commercial and sport fishing. Some sport and subsistence hunting occurs. VCU 79 is adjacent to the Tracy Arm-Fords Terror Wilderness. This proposed area is contiguous with Area 7-Chuck River.

Recreation Impacts - Little immediate impact on recreation activities as a result of Wilderness designation. With residential development in Hobart Bay and private land at Port Houghton, use would increase.

Subsistence - Light subsistence use presently occurs. This use will increase with the further development of private lands at Hobart Bay - Port Houghton. Residents will need to qualify for subsistence status.

Subsistence Impacts - Wilderness designation would not affect subsistence use.

Miscellaneous Impacts -

Tongass compromise endorsed

Governor Steve Cowper has announced his endorsement of key provisions of a compromise on the Tongass National Forest supported by elected Southeast government officials, fishermen, and Native leaders.

Cowper said the compromise proposed by the Southeast Conference's Tongass Committee is "fair and reasonable and realistically takes into account the political situation in Washington, D.C."

"Alaska cannot sit by and let a radical bill get pushed through Congress or perhaps be attached to ANWR legislation," said the Governor, who spent a week in Washington meeting with key officials on Tongass. "We've got to make sure such legislation doesn't decimate the economy and the people of Southeast Alaska. I believe this compromise meets that test."

At issue are proposed changes to the Alaska National Interest Lands Conservation Act that directly affect people who live in the Tongass Forest. A committee of the Southeast Conference has proposed a compromise, subsequently endorsed by the Conference Board on February 20th, between strict conservationist legislation and that supported by the timber industry.

The Conference is composed of local elected government officials and Chamber of Commerce members of Southeast communities.

The Governor said he especially endorses the compromise provisions that guarantee balanced multiple use management and appropriate enough money to supply the market demand up to 4.5 billion board feet of timber per decade. He said the compromise also protects in non-wilderness status important fish and wildlife areas identified by local communities and provides for an economic diversification program to stimulate local economies.

Cowper said his chief concern is protecting the jobs of Southeast residents who rely on the national forest, and that key elements of the compromise attempt to do that.

The Governor criticized radical bills introduced in Congress that would cancel long-term timber contracts, create 1.7 million additional acres of wilderness, and repeal the 4.5 billion board feet timber supply.

Cowper said his visit to Washington made it clear "that the train is leaving the station on the Tongass. We cannot afford to stand around and pretend things will get better because we'll be left at the station."

He said that he continues to review a progressive regional economic development proposal made by the Sealaska Corporation, which seeks to strengthen Southeast's economy. He also said he will continue to work with the state's congressional delegation to fine-tune Alaska's strategy on Tongass.

The Governor's views were delivered to the House Interior and Agriculture committees in Washington last week.

ALA announces Tongass position

130 567 0385 0460 0620

By KERRY WATSON
Daily News Staff Writer

Alaska Loggers Association on Friday released its own policy statement on Tongass legislation.

The board of directors spent two days reviewing Tongass legislation policy in developing the statement, according to a press release from ALA.

The policy statement was drafted after ALA members came back from the U.S. House Interior and Agriculture Committee hearings last week on the Tongass. After "reviewing the concerns of communities expressed through the Southeast Conference and others, we decided to take a fresh look at our position concerning Tongass legislation," said board president Virgil Soderberg.

It is time that ALA, the Southeast Alaska Conservation Council, the Southeast, Conference, and the State of Alaska work with the Alaska Congressional Delegation "to forge an 'All Alaska' position to present to Congress," said Soderberg.

The loggers' association seeks a Tongass bill that "meets the concerns of the majority of people in Southeast Alaska, namely protects the economic well-being of the people and Southeast Alaska communities associated with the forest products industry; the resources of the forest used by other Southeast Alaskans for their livelihood-namely commercial fishing and tourism; and maintains the subsistence, hunting and recreational resources of the Tongass National Forest," according to the ALA release.

Firm on 4.5

ALA recommends that the U.S. Forest Service be allowed to make available 4.5 billion board feet of timber per decade "subject to ongoing and annual review to meet timber industry needs based on market demand, industry capacity and economics." However, the policy states that the loggers' association doesn't support the concept of 'mandated' cut. "The ALA believes harvest levels should be driven by economics, markets and sound principles of forestry," reads the policy statement.

The Tongass policy statement addresses individual contracts. "Perceived problems" with contracts "should not drive legislation which can have far-reaching impacts on the people and the communities of Southeast Alaska," it reads. Those matters should be handled by the federal government and the private party, according to the statement.

The Tongass policy statement calls for "intensive management monies of up to $18 million per year needed to access marginal timber stands," The money would be subject to the annual appropriations process, according to the statement.

ALA is critical of the time a timber sale takes from conception to its award - four to seven years. Steps to hasten the process by streamlining the appeals process are listed in policy.

Six grudging areas

ALA is opposed to new land allocations prior to the completion of the Tongass Land Management. However, if Congress decides to allocate land in advance of TLMP, ALA lists six areas that are the "only" ones that should be considered for removal from multiple use management. They are: Yakutat Forelands, Kadashan, Lisianski, Karta, Nutkwa and Chuck River.

The areas boundaries should be clear so that access to multiple use areas is not blocked. Protected status areas could provide substitutes for portions of the areas listed above, suggest ALA.

Southeast Conference released a

See ALA, page 12

ALA · · · · · · page 1—

· · · · · · · · OCLO policy statement in late February. It called for the designation of 12 areas as non-commercial timber areas. In addition to those listed by ALA, the Conference asked for Berners Bay, Couse Flats, Tray Bay watershed, Salt Lake and Baker Islands, Young Lake and Mt. Calder/Mt. Holbrook area.

Other provisions of Southeast's Conference statement were an allowable harvest of up to 4.5 billion board feet per decade and an intensive management fund of up to $15 million yearly.

Regional Forester
U.S. Forest Service
P.O. Box 21628
Juneau, AK 99802-1628

Dear Mr. Barton,

The Southeast Conference Board of Directors has adopted the
enclosed policy statement as the official position of the
Conference on management and access to the Tongass National
Forest. The document was prepared by a five member committee of
the Conference with input from the timber industry, the
environmental community, and fishing groups. As you know, the
communities of the Tongass were consulted and played a major role
in forming the key provisions of the document. We hereby request
that the Forest Service carefully analyze this management scenario
and incorporate it into the alternatives for the revision of the
Tongass Land Management Plan (TLMP).

The document represents a true compromise between those residents
and communities interested in continuation of a viable and healthy
logging industry and those concerned about preservation of other
values of the forest, including fishing, subsistence and habitat.
As a compromise it must be viewed as representing a delicate
balance between those interested parties. Any significant change
to the document will result in loss of support from some major
constituent group.

The statement has been endorsed by Governor Cowper and a growing
number of communities and local organizations. The letters and
resolutions of support generally recognize that the statement does
not completely satisfy anyone. However, it does represent a true
middle ground where all residents of Southeast Alaska can rally to
maintain those economic, social and cultural interests which are
of critical importance to our region. It serves to provide a
meaningful backdrop to the TLMP process and offers valuable tools
to the Forest Service in addressing the underlying interests of
communities in Southeast Alaska.

As always your assistance is appreciated.

Sincerely,

William B. Privett
President, Southeast Conference

"Working For All Alaska"

SOUTHEAST CONFERENCE

A Policy Statement on the Tongass National Forest Legislation and Management

AN ALASKAN PERSPECTIVE

FINAL ADOPTION 3/10/89

"Working For All Alaska"

P O Box 22286   Juneau, Alaska 99802

                                           March 10, 1989

To Whom It May Concern:

The Southeast Conference has worked long and hard to develop the
enclosed policy position regarding legislation and management of the
Tongass National Forest. This policy position is intended to close the
argument and stop further erosion of the economy of Southeast Alaska.
It is not intended to diminish the role of the timber industry or any
other industry in our effort to build a stable diversified economy.

This position has been developed with input from communities of
Southeast Alaska and provides a balanced resolution that is intended
to ensure continued employment and opportunities in timber, fisheries,
tourism, recreation, mining, and subsistence. The policy was
developed with a focus on the families in Southeast Alaska by a
special committee representing large and small communities with varied
interests. The policy position recommended to the Board was supported
unanimously by the special committee. Although concerns of special
interests were taken into consideration, and frequently paralleled
that of communities, they were not (and cannot be) the primary focus.
It is important to note that this is a unique approach that provides a
fragile package that is balanced by five key elements of equal
importance. These key elements are:

- Clarifying the mission of the National Forest Service in the
  Tongass to include an allowable harvest of up to 4.5 billion
  board feet per decade adjusted at Secretary discretion depending
  on market conditions and subject to multiple use values of the
  Tongass Forest. (This serves to maintain existing jobs in the
  forest while protecting fish and wildlife and their habitat.)

- Establishing a specific intensive management fund to ensure that
  the Forest Service is able to make marginal timber stands viable
  sales for the industry and sustain other values.

- Setting aside 12 areas for protection due to the high values of
  fish and wildlife production and community use of those areas.

- Providing for land trades, exchanges, or purchases of non-
  wilderness lands to increase the timber base for the allowable
  harvest level (to include potential use of harvested land).

- Establishing an economic diversification fund of grants and
  loans to provide opportunities to strengthen the Southeast
  economy.

A reaffirmation of this policy was duly supported by the Southeast
Conference Board of Directors on March 10th. Two minor amendments to
the document were made at that time. The amendments are not intended
to substantively change the intent of the original Conference position
that provides the Secretary with authority to adjust the decade
harvest level _and_ the annual harvest level based on market conditions,
concerns of local communities, and a multiple use mission as we have
outlined.

                        "Working For All Alaska"

We believe that the intensive management fund and land trades/purchase provision of our position serve to ensure a land base for a timber supply to maintain a viable industry.

The set aside of 12 areas is of great import to many communities and while it somewhat reduces the timber base, is essential to our position. Further, the economic diversification fund provides the opportunity for the economy of Southeast Alaska to stabilize. This fund allows the people of Southeast Alaska to continue to live and work in Southeast while the Tongass is managed to meet the needs and ideals of people throughout America. Again, no element of our position can stand alone. If there is any concern for the people of Southeast Alaska, then the key elements of our position must be incorporated into any final legislation or management plan of the Tongass National Forest.

We are not professional drafters of federal legislation and therefore ask indulgence for our presentation. We respectfully offer our position paper to Alaskans, the U.S. Congress, and the American people as a fair and reasonable resolution to the conflict in the Tongass.

Respectfully Submitted,

William B. Privett
President, Southeast Conference

SOUTHEAST CONFERENCE

P O Box 22286   Juneau, Alaska 99802

TONGASS NATIONAL FOREST
Policy Position

Table of Contents:

3/10/89

I. INTRODUCTION

The Southeast Conference is a Non-Profit Corporation comprised of
local elected officials, business leaders and community members
representing Southeast Alaska dedicated to improving the well being
of Alaskans through the prudent expansion of the Alaskan economy.
The Conference was formed in 1963 to spearhead efforts to establish a
transportation infrastructure in the land locked panhandle of
Southeast upon which to build viable local and regional economies.
The Conference was successful in that endeavor; working with the
State and Federal governments the Southeast Conference built a
"sailing bridge" from Seattle throughout Southeast, the Alaska Marine
Highway System. It is a billion dollar example of what the people
of Southeast can do when they work together to overcome an obstacle
or challenge. That system is only one of many varied accomplishments
of the Southeast Conference efforts ranging from the Ketchikan
shipyard to the continued development and expansion of the University
of Alaska Southeast. The successes can all be attributed to the
people of Southeast striving together for a common purpose, while
maintaining mutual respect for community differences, quality of
life, and the importance of cultural heritage. The Southeast
Conference knows that the well being of the region is dependent on
the well being of the individual communities.

The mission of the Southeast Conference is to build and maintain a
stable, diversified economy that provides for an improved standard of
living, quality employment and business development opportunities for
the people of Southeast Alaska through prudent use of our resources.
Use of these resources should reflect respect of the culture and the
individual community perspective of quality of life by taking strong
deliberate actions to affect business and government decisions and
markets; while encouraging a family centered society, a clean
environment and maximum realization of our mental, physical,
emotional and spiritual well being.

It was with this history and spirit that the Board of Directors met
in September and launched an all out effort to resolve the conflicts
and economic peril surrounding the Tongass National Forest management
and legislation. During the Annual Meeting last Fall in Ketchikan
the Southeast Conference engaged in conversations and work sessions
with timber industry personnel, conservationists, as well as the
Governor and the Regional Forester about the problems in the
Tongass. One thing became abundantly clear, if there was going to be
an acceptable resolution to the Tongass conflict, there needed to be
an effort toward developing a consensus, at least in Southeast.

The Conference established a five member Tongass Committee comprised
of representatives from large and small southeast Alaskan communities
reflecting the interests of timber, subsistence, fisheries, tourism

Working For All Alaska"

and mining. In order to understand the complexity of the problem, the Tongass Committee decided to look at the southeast economy and community interests in depth. The committee used a process of principled negotiation while working on the project and constantly notified communities of progress and sought input. The work of the committee was divided into three phases: analysis, option development, and the decision stage. The majority of the 18 weeks of work was spent in the analysis stage. Following is a brief discussion of the committee's findings.

The State's economy will, increasingly in the future, be affected and directed by the regional economies rather than a single industry (oil). The regional economy of Southeast is necessarily the future of the Tongass. The well being of the people of Southeast Alaska is inextricably linked to the management of the Tongass National Forest. The economic stability of Southeast is subject to the decisions that the Forest Service makes regarding permits, sales, practices and day to day management of the Tongass. The 65,000 residents of Southeast Alaska rely on four primary industries, timber, tourism, fisheries, and mining, and in many cases a subsistence way of life, for employment and the economic infrastructure. Our economy is beginning to show more strength in traditional industries, i.e. fishing, mining, and forest products. It appears that if our trading markets do not falter, we will see continued growth and diversification.

The Southeast Alaska region, over the past fifty years, has given its residents one of the State's most economically diverse and stable geographic areas. However, the future of this economic unit is tied to continued vitality in the timber, fishing, tourism and mining industries, as well as subsistence. These industries are inter-related and dependent on one another for their viability. Our Southeast industrial base is fragile, inter-related, and dependent on the price and frequency of goods and services established by the combined demand of fishing, tourism, mining and timber.

At the present time total employment, earnings to workers and value of finished product from fishing, tourism, and timber are achieving a rough balance. The latest estimates by the Alaska Department of Labor indicates that for the month of July, 1988 there were at least 3,205 workers in the timber industry in Southeast. Actual employment in fishing and tourism is extremely difficult to compare across the board. Using baseline data from the USFS and the State, both fishing and tourism may have total employment at similar levels. It is currently estimated by the State of Alaska that 20 to 25 percent of earnings in Southeast are timber industry dependent. By extrapolation, similar levels are assumed in fishing and tourism. Mining has made a startling comeback in the past three years and will soon be an equal partner. Further, subsistence is a significant part of the economies of most small communities throughout Southeast.

Although certainly employment is not equal across the board, one thing is clear; taken on the average and over time, there is beginning a real "leveling" between these basic industries, their

-2-

employment and total impact. This mutual support effect results in a broader economic base and will allow a community to experience a setback in one industry or segment of an industry without area wide recession. It also allows costs of community development and infrastructure to be born by that broader base.

The goal of the U.S. Congress, when the long term timber sale was approved, was the formation of a stable and enduring economy for Southeast Alaska. With diversification, including fishing, tourism, timber, mining, and subsistence, there is a growing realization that each has an important contribution to the overall competitive position of Southeast Alaska in the world market. The regional economic well-being is directly tied to continued health of the other partners in that industrial base. Every unit of the economy benefits from the transportation infrastructure, localized roads, and community development, so long as that does not infringe or threaten the quality of life or the other industries. The committee found it essential in these discussions to develop an option that reinforced economic "value added" diversification.

The underlying interests raise complicated questions and challenges. Debate is serious, sometimes hateful, but always reflective of a need to clarify the mission of the U.S. Forest Service in the Tongass. Southeast opponents of continuation of the large scale logging and specific subsidized harvest levels are using congressional debates for airing their concerns about the Forest Service management practices. They argue that the supposition of a multiple use mission is skewed, or even impossible given the mandates of Section 705 of ANILCA to provide 4.5 billion board feet per decade from the Tongass. These proponents for change say that this harvest mandate skews the mission of the Forest Service. Their concerns include a lack of protection of important fish and wildlife habitat , let alone enhancement. The argument comes to economic point on details that suggest a threat to the fisheries, subsistence as well as the recreation and tourism industries.

Opponents of the status quo suggest that the communities' areas of special interests, quality anadramous streams and wildlife habitat all fall second consideration to the skewed mission. They add that there is no opportunity for competition.

Proponents of the pulp timber industry counter by claiming that the pulp mills are only economically viable with reasonable long term commitments of access to productive timber stands. Ketchikan Pulp Company has for example recently invested some 35 million dollars to "retool their mill" for more cost effective value added use of the timber coming to them. The mills maintain they must have contracts and commitments of large volumes of timber to sustain their financial stability. Further, proponents point out that roads constructed provide long term use by tourists, fishermen, and hunters; and that they provide valuable recreation, and subsistence opportunities. Further, there are four smaller log mills that operate efficiently by selling the pulp which some estimate is up to 50% of the timber, to the pulp mills and lumber milling the other for market.

The major concern of many of the people of Southeast is of course that a threat to the financial stability of the mills corresponds to a potential loss of jobs and ultimately places families in crisis!

Further, irrespective of changes to the status quo, it is obvious that the limitations of Tongass National Forest designations will cause some drop in employment due to the decline in production on private land and the unavailable timber for open sale. The total employment currently cannot be absorbed in the Tongass. Perhaps diversification is the only long term opportunity for those that will ultimately be displaced.

The current level of harvest of 400 mbf and the resultant jobs within the Tongass (i.e. existing employment that is a function of the harvest within the Tongass National Forest) may be sustainable. However, the Forest Service as well as others have shown us in gruesome detail that the current total Southeast harvest is definitely not sustainable under any circumstances. This poignant reality is due to harvest levels on private land that are not on a sustained yield basis. This harvest level which is not bound by primary manufacturing restrictions, allowing round log exports, brings the total harvest in Southeast to almost 800 mbf this year. There is a contraction coming irrespective of changes to 705. The focus of the Southeast Conference has been to balance this reality with other community interests.

Another critical point raised within the Committee debate is the question of the twelve special areas that communities have requested be removed from commercial harvest designation. The Southeast Conference Tongass Committee spent hours reviewing and discussing these areas. There is no question that they have high quality unique intrinsic values. The Southeast Conference worked with the Forest Service, the Department of Fish and Game, and others in narrowing the scope of these requests. But they are real and the consequences of the withdrawals mean a loss of a little more than 23 million board feet.

Further, the Forest Service indicates that this will increase the pressure for intensive management and questions of sustaining a 4.5 billion board foot harvest level. The opponents of status quo also mention this may further skew the mission.

This issue received further investigation and consideration because the timber industry and the Forest Service maintain that the proposals for withdrawal would cause a commensurate loss of jobs. (The GAO estimates that the loss would be 4.2 jobs per million board feet.) This is further complicated by an argument that these are potential jobs, since the approximately 23 million board feet is far short of impacting the 400 million board feet currently harvested from the Tongass, not existing jobs. But again the industry counters that these are potential jobs for those who may ultimately lose employment from the private harvest that will be shut down (within the next 5 to 10 years) since it is not a sustainable harvest.

The Southeast Conference has determined that no industry as
aforementioned is safe or potentially stable until the Tongass issues
are resolved. Therefore, the committee has ferreted out the major
underlying interests of the communities and through principled
negotiation, developed a proposed resolution to the major conflicts.

The vast expanse of land and natural resources in the Tongass are
both a blessing and a curse. On the one hand, wilderness, personal
freedom and unlimited opportunity are available to anyone. On the
other, the outstanding natural beauty, the relatively small
population and the widely held mistrust of development invites
congressional intervention. In the Tongass we have an inter-
dependent, fragile economy. Legislation being considered by Congress
could weaken this fabric. It could start a chain reaction resulting
in serious regional recession and economic de-stabilization. It
could cause multiple-use areas to become one-industry towns.

The Southeast Conference has a vested interest in assuring that when
the dust clears in Washington D.C., there will be no winners or
losers in the Tongass. The Southeast Conference has developed this
position through a principled negotiation process involving
representatives of communities and interests from throughout
Southeast. It is fair, reasonable, and critical to all Alaskans.

II. UNDERLYING INTERESTS/OBJECTIVES OF SOUTHEAST ALASKAN COMMUNITIES

Following is the Southeast Conference policy position on Tongass
National Forest Legislation and Management. We propose that this
position be used for the development of reasonable legislation and
Tongass land management practices that are sensitive to the people
whose lives are physically, mentally, emotionally and spiritually
interwoven with the Tongass.

A. Objectives reflecting the underlying interests of the Southeast
   Communities:

   1) To maintain the employment within the Southeast Timber
      industry including providing for diversification (perhaps
      Federal-State assistance for retooling and small mills, etc.).
   2) To maintain employment within the fisheries industry including
      State and Federal efforts to provide for research, protection,
      and mitigation for anadromous streams.
   3) To maintain employment within the mining industry and to
      recognize the unique mining opportunities that benefit
      communities.
   4) To maintain employment within the tourism industry including
      sensitivity to respective communities' unique tourism
      opportunities (e.g. RVs, parks, docks, and highly visible
      areas), and dispersal of Pacific Rim and other Independent
      travelers.
   5) To have Congress recognize and provide for respective
      communities' social, personal, and cultural uses.
   6) To have Congress recognize that all of these uses are important
      to the people of Southeast and that these uses, the people, and
      the management of the Tongass are interrelated and mutually
      supportive.
   7) To have Congress recognize the respective communities' interest
      in protecting specific areas from commercial harvest.
   8) To have Congress recognize that the timber industry needs
      access to "appropriate and productive" stands to maintain
      a viable industry and timber employment.
   9) To insure that Southeast Alaskans have a voice "at the table"
      in any and all discussions and decisions regarding the Tongass
      legislation. (This includes congressional hearings; and if a
      hearing is held in Alaska, it should be held in Sitka.)
   10) To maintain a stable and diversified economy throughout
      Southeast.
   11) To maintain at least the current level of federal commitment to
      the economy of Southeast Alaska and to provide opportunities
      for diversification, particularly for those that may be
      disenfranchised by legislation.
   12) To separate Tongass legislation from other political issues or
      legislation.

III. ANILCA CONSIDERATIONS

Section 705(a) of the Alaska National Interest Lands Conservation Act (16 U.S.C. 539(a) is hereby repealed and reenacted to read as follows:

(a) Congress finds that the Tongass National Forest possesses rich and diverse natural resources of inestimable value to the citizens of Alaska and the Nation. Many of these resources are vital to the regional economy of Southeast Alaska and, in differing mixes, to its varied communities. To foster and clarify a balanced multiple use mission for management of the Tongass Forest and the importance to the people of Southeast Alaska of clean air and water, timber harvesting and processing, commercial fishing, mining, subsistence, tourism (including sport fishing, hunting and other outdoor recreation), and associated support services, and to provide for broader distribution of the economic benefits of the Tongass Forest to the residents of Southeast Alaska, it is hereby enacted —

(1) The Congress authorizes and directs the Secretary of Agriculture to utilize federal funds of up to 15 million dollars, adjusted annually for inflation and appropriated on an annual basis, to ensure a multiple use mission and carry out an intensive management program. The fund is to be utilized so as to make available up to 4 billion five hundred million board feet per decade to maintain a timber supply to a dynamic and dependent industry necessary to meet annual market demand and subject to protecting and enhancing other resource industries and uses. The Secretary is authorized to adjust the allowable annual harvest, through the Land Management Planning Process, based on market conditions for timber, sustained yield principles of management of maintaining fish and wildlife, and recognition of other considerations of the multiple use mission.

(2) On the first day of each fiscal year, the Secretary of the Treasury shall transfer funds into the intensive management account equal to the amount expended from the account during the prior fiscal year. The Secretary of Agriculture is authorized and directed to use funds from the account exclusively for:
(A) Construction of the facilities needed to access new and existing timber sale areas which have been awarded or released and which meet the criteria for added investments contained in the 1986 Forest Service Region X's Timber Sale Preparation Handbook; and
(B) Timber stand improvement; and
(C) The Secretary is authorized and directed to use up to 20% of the intensive management funds to promote, protect and enhance subsistence, sport and commercial fisheries, the wildlife, and recreation resources. The Secretary shall provide a report to Congress annually regarding the use and effectiveness of the fund.

(3) The Secretary is authorized to adjust the maximum clear cut size to optimize economic harvesting of timber sale areas, and make other adjustments deemed appropriate so long as such clear cut size

and other adjustments are not inconsistent with the multiple use
mission and objectives of the Tongass Land Management Plan (TLMP).

Sections 705(b)(1) and (2) are repealed and reenacted to read as
follows:

(1) The Secretary is authorized and directed to establish a
special fund and program of economic diversification loans and grants
to stimulate enhancement and diversification of the economy of
Southeast Alaska. The Secretary is authorized to promulgate
regulations deemed necessary to define eligibility requirements
providing for at least fifty percent of the fund to be utilized for
grants to small businesses, community, and regional efforts that
stimulate the economy of Southeast Alaska. The Secretary is
authorized to establish a loan program to provide loans to industries
within Southeast Alaska for "value added" initiatives or more
efficient utilization of natural resources of the Tongass.

(2) To carry out the special economic diversification program
established by this Section, there is hereby authorized beginning
after Fiscal Year 1989 to be appropriated $20,000,000. from the
National Forest Fund receipts, to be deposited in a special fund in
the Treasury of the United States to remain available until expended.
    (A) On the first day of each fiscal year, the Secretary of the
Treasury shall transfer funds into the economic diversification fund
equal to the amount expended for grants during the prior fiscal
year. Repayments of principle and interest of loans and other
recoveries of funds authorized by this Section shall be credited to
the fund. The Secretary shall provide Congress with a report
annually regarding the use and effectiveness of the fund. The report
shall be prepared in consultation with the Southeast Conference, a
corporation representing municipalities and individuals of Southeast
Alaska.

(3) Sections 705(b)(1)and (2) are repealed effective September 30,
1999.

Section 705(c) is repealed and reenacted to read:

(c) The Secretary of Agriculture shall review and if necessary
renegotiate the long term sale contracts to ensure:
    1) employment stabilization to the maximum extent possible for
those working in the Tongass National Forest;
    2) fair and reasonable accommodation to the contract holders
considering their investment in requiring fair market value rated for
timber;
    3) fair and reasonable competition within the timber industry in
the Tongass National Forest;
    4) that the contracts are consistent with the the Tongass Land
Management Plan and any revisions thereto;
    5) that Southeast Alaskan communities are given consideration in
their respective interests;

-8-

6) that the contractors are given a clear definition and commitment
of location and amounts of timber available through the contract
period as part of the forest plan revision;
7) clear statements of the responsibility and authority of the
Forest Service to protect fish and wildlife resources and habitats.

Title VII is amended by adding a new section to read:

Section 709(a)(1) The following public lands within the Tongass
National Forest are hereby designated as protected non-commercial
timber areas:

			Impact Potential
Yakutat Forelands	134,822 acres		3.75 million bd.ft./year*
Kadashan River Watershed	33,641	"	2.52 "
Chuck River/Windham Bay	74,942	"	2.00 "
Lisianski and			
Upper Hoonah Sound	134,657	"	3.62
Nutkwa River Watershed	22,507	"	1.87
Karta River Watershed	38,701	"	0.00
Mt. Calder/Mt. Holbrook	48,000	"	3.79
Young Lake	18,173	"	1.35
Outside Islands —			
Noyes	24,651	"	1.64
Lulu	18,517	"	.24
Baker	31,946	"	1.24
Trap Bay Watershed	6,446	"	.65
Goose Flats	23,798	"	.60
Berners Bay	35,379	"	.04

- -

TOTAL: 646,180 acres   23.31 million bd.ft./year

(* These volume/year figures are to be compared to the '450' million
board ft/yr timber supply goal managed on a 100 year rotation.)

The Secretary shall manage the protected areas designated in this
section in accordance with Land Use Designation II as defined in the
Tongass Land Management Plan (amended 85-86). The Secretary shall
establish a management direction specific to the above areas
including allowed uses other than timber harvest, through the Land
Management Planning Process in consultation with the communities of
Southeast Alaska.

(2) The Secretary is authorized and directed to pursue reasonable
opportunities for non-wilderness land exchanges, trades, and/or
purchases with the State of Alaska and/or any appropriate private
land owners of property that may add to the timber base to mitigate
or eliminate the potential economic impacts of 709(a)(1) in Southeast
Alaska. The Secretary shall provide Congress with a written report
and recommendations including a complete description of any proposed
exchanges or trades. The report shall be prepared in consultation
with the Southeast Conference.

-9-

IV. DESCRIPTIONS OF SPECIAL AREAS

Yakutat Forelands

The Tongass Land Management Plan recognized the area as the most diverse and productive fish and wildlife area in the Tongass, with the highest rankings for wilderness values and ecological diversity. The Alaska Department of Fish and Game (ADF&G) has rated the entire area as having the highest value habitat for both fish and wildlife as well as being a very important commercial, sport, and subsistence harvest area.

The Italio, Akwe, and Ustay-Tanis river systems together produce all five species of salmon and are especially productive of coho and sockeye. Peak escapements (the number of fish reported on their spawning grounds after surviving the commercial and subsistence fisheries) reported are 37,000 sockeye and 54,000 coho salmon. These systems are also good habitat for rainbow, steelhead, and cutthroat trout and for Dolly Varden. Brown bear, moose, mountain goat, wolves, marten, mink, land otter, beaver, bald eagles, trumpeter swans, sandhill cranes, and a myriad of other birds and small mammals are abundant in this diverse and productive ecosystem. The rare glacier phase of black bear occurs in the Ustay-Tanis area.

The local subsistence and commercial gillnetters benefit from the abundant salmon. The high quality of sport fishing on the Ustay, Italio, and Akwe rivers attracts approximately 1600 anglers from Yakutat, other areas of Alaska, the USA, and foreign countries providing significant income to the local economy (the average non-local angler spends about $550 per fishing trip). Hunting information is only available for the entire Yakutat Forelands, of which the proposed area comprises roughly 50 percent. The proposed area is an important area for moose hunting, an activity for which public demand far exceeds the level of opportunity, as well as brown and black bears and mountain goats. Trappers harvest marten, wolves, wolverine, beaver, and land otters. It is an important waterfowl hunting area for local residents.

Berners Bay

The Tongass Land Management Plan rated the area as high for fish and moderate for estuarine resources. The ADF&G rated the area as high for fish and wildlife. The area is intensively used by residents of Juneau due to its close proximity, road access, and resource values.

The Berners, Lace, and Antler/Gilkey rivers are the major anadromous streams flowing into Berners Bay and produce four species of salmon as well as rainbow, steelhead, and cutthroat trout and Dolly Varden. The peak recorded escapements in these three systems combined are 13,300 coho, 4000 sockeye, 9100 chum, and up to 10,000 pink salmon. Brown bear, black bear, moose, wolves, mink, marten, land otter, beaver, and land and water birds are abundant in the area. Mountain goats and bald eagles are moderately abundant. Seals, sea lions, and whales are common in the bay.

The Berners Bay area is intensively used by sport fishers, moose, bear, and deer hunters, kayakers, hikers, and campers. The Berners River is used by the ADF&G as an indicator of the coho salmon production for the management of the northern southeast coho fishery.

Young Lake

The Tongass Land Management Plan rated the Young's Lake watershed and estuary as being of the highest productivity class for fish. The ADF&G rates the area as being of the highest value for fisheries, wildlife, and sport fishing. The proximity of the area to Juneau makes it an extremely popular recreation spot for fishing, hunting, beach combing, camping, and hiking.

Admiralty Creek and adjacent streams produce three species of salmon, with peak reported escapements of 90,000 pink, 10,000 chum, and several hundred coho. These drainages also produce substantial populations of steelhead and cutthroat trout, kokanee, and Dolly Varden. Admiralty Creek is important in the management of the commercial salmon fishery for the ADF&G has historically sampled the density of pre-emergent fry in the stream gravels to estimate the over-winter survival rate of salmon streams in the general area. Sitka black-tailed deer, brown bear, marten, mink, red squirrels, raptors, and waterfowl are abundant. Land otters and beaver are moderately abundant. Whales and seals are commonly observed in the nearshore waters.

The Young Lake area is near Juneau/Douglas and accessible by boat, skiff, floatplane, and wheel plane. The three Forest Service cabins in the drainage receive the highest use of any watershed on Admiralty Island. The area is intensively used in the spring for steelhead fishing and brown bear and grouse hunting. Summer use of the area includes fishing, picnicking, camping, hiking, and bird-watching. Autumn brings deer and duck hunters to the area. The area is one of the most popular deer hunting areas for Juneau/Douglas residents, with 1654 hunters harvesting 468 deer in the Young's Bay-Hawk Inlet area in 1987 (see attached map). The system is classified by the ADF&G as a quality watershed for sport fishing because of the quantity, quality, and diversity of resident and anadromous fish and the high level of recreational use.

Lisianski River

The Tongass Land Management Plan rated the area as having the highest value for the production of salmon. The ADF&G ranked the area as the highest value for the quality of sport fishing and the production of salmon and trout and of moderate value for the production of wildlife. The fish produced in the Lisianski drainage supports a commercial fishery worth over a million dollars every year to fishermen. The area is used heavily by residents of Pelican for fishing, hunting, and general recreation.

The Lisianski River is one of the top five salmon producers in the region, with reported peak escapements of 220,000 pink, 5000 chum, 1500 coho, and 100 sockeye salmon. It also produces significant populations of rainbow, steelhead, and cutthroat trout and Dolly Varden. Brown bear, Sitka-black-tailed deer, marten, mink, land otter, bald eagles, waterfowl, and other old-growth forest species are moderately abundant.

Detailed information on hunting and fishing is not available for this small area, although it is important to the residents of Pelican for at least deer hunting (see attached map).

Upper Hoonah Sound

The Tongass Land Management Plan rated the area as having moderate values for fisheries, with the exception of Paterson Creek watershed which was rated high value. The ADF&G considers the area a moderate producer of fish and wildlife and an important harvest area for the residents of Sitka.

Several drainages each produce over 50,000 pink, over 6000 chum, and up to 500 coho salmon in an average year. Most drainages also produce moderate populations of rainbow, steelhead, and cutthroat trout and Dolly Varden. The estuarine sedge-grass flats and salmon streams are brown bear concentration areas. Waterfowl concentrate on the sedge-grass flats during spring and fall migrations. The area supports moderate populations of Sitka black-tailed deer, marten, land otter, mink, wolves, bald eagles, nesting waterfowl, and other old-growth forest species.

Residents of Sitka use the area to harvest salmon, halibut, crabs, deer, and furbearers. In 1987, around 590 deer were harvested in the area by Sitka hunters in 1100 hunter-days.

Goose Flats

The Tongass Land Management Plan rated the Goose Flats watershed as having moderately high fishery value and high estuarine resource values. The ADF&G rates the area as a moderate producer of fish and wildlife and as an important harvest area for the residents of Tenakee Springs.

All three drainages in the area each produce 10,000-50,000 pink salmon and over 6000 chum salmon in an average year and also support cutthroat trout and Dolly Varden. The extensive intertidal sedge-grass flats support spring concentrations of brown bear and spring and fall concentrations of migratory waterfowl. There are moderate populations of deer. Information on the population status of other species is lacking.

Tenakee Springs residents rely heavily on the area for the harvest of deer, waterfowl, furbearers, and shellfish.

Kadashan River

The Tongass Land Management Plan rated the drainage the highest value for fisheries and estuarine resources. The ADF&G rated the area as the highest class for fish and wildlife production. It is an important harvest area for residents of Tenakee Springs as well as the basis for a large commercial fishery and non-local hunting and sport fishing. The ADF&G/U.S. Forest Service have monitored pink and chum salmon escapements into the Kadashan River since 1969 and the out-migration of the juveniles since 1977 to predict the run strength and manage the commercial salmon fishery in the general area. Since no other stream in northern southeast Alaska has this quality of data, maintenance of this drainage in its natural condition is very important to the management of the salmon fishery. Research has also been conducted in this drainage on coho salmon, deer, and brown bear.

Kadashan is one of the top five producers of pink salmon in southeast Alaska, with a peak recorded escapement of 282,000 and average escapement of over 130,000 fish. It is among the top ten chum salmon streams in southeast Alaska, with a peak recorded escapement of 66,000 and average escapement of 25,000 fish. Coho salmon escapement is estimated at 2000-4000 fish. The drainage also supports rainbow, steelhead, and cutthroat trout and very high numbers of Dolly Varden.

Kadashan has one of the largest estuarine sedge-grass flats and intertidal mud flats in northern southeast Alaska. This extremely productive habitat is a major nursery for Dungeness crabs, important herring spawning area, major spring and fall feeding and resting stop-over for migratory waterfowl, and brown bear concentration area during spring.

The Kadashan drainage supports one of the highest concentrations of brown bears in southeast Alaska. Deer, marten, mink, land otter, red squirrels, and bald eagles are also abundant. Large numbers of seals are attracted to the abundant salmon as they mill around the mouth of the river.

The commercial fishery based on Kadashan salmon is typically worth over a million dollars annually to fishermen. Residents of Tenakee Springs depend on the area for the harvest of deer, salmon, shellfish, and furbearers. The ADF&G classifies the Kadashan River as the highest quality for sport fishing.

Trap Bay

The Tongass Land Management Plan rated the area as high value for estuarine resources and moderate value for fish production. The ADF&G rated the area as the highest value for wildlife and moderate value for fish. Hydrologic and fisheries research has been conducted in the area over the last decade.

The river which runs into Trap Bay supports moderate populations of coho, pink and chum salmon and Dolly Varden. Brown bear are abundant with spring concentrations on the estuarine sedge-grass flats and subalpine meadows and summer concentrations along the salmon streams. Although specific studies are lacking, the area is undoubtedly good habitat for other old-growth forest species.

Residents of Tenakee Springs depend on Trap Bay area for the harvest of deer (see attached map), waterfowl, and furbearers.

Chuck River

The Tongass Land Management Plan rated the Chuck River watershed as the highest value for fish and moderately high for estuarine resources. The ADF&G rated The Chuck River drainage as the highest value for fish and the areas around Windham Bay, the lower Chuck River, and Endicott Arm as the highest value for wildlife. The area is popular both with tour boat operators and Juneau residents.

Chuck River is among one of the highest producers of pink salmon in southeast Alaska, with a recorded peak escapement of 220,000. It also supports good populations of the other four salmon species and rainbow, steelhead, and cutthroat trout and Dolly Varden. The area is good habitat for black bears and mountain goats.

The Chuck River supports a significant commercial salmon fishery worth around a million per year to fishermen. The area is hunted frequently by Juneau residents in pursuit of black bear and mountain goats. The coastal areas in Endicott Arm and Windham Bay are used by recreational boaters, fishermen, and charter boats.

Calder-Holbrook

The Tongass Land Management Plan rated subareas within the boundary of the proposed area as moderately high to high value for fish and for estuarine values. The ADF&G rated the subareas as moderate for fish, with the exception of a high value for the Shipley drainage, and moderate to high

-14-

for wildlife, with the highest values for the watersheds draining into Shakan Bay, Dry Pass, Tokeen Bay, and Shipley Bay. The area is important to the residents of Port Protection, Point Baker, Cape Pole, Edna Bay, Craig, and Klawock for the harvest of fish and wildlife.

There are many productive streams in the area supporting pink, chum, and coho salmon and rainbow, steelhead and cutthroat trout and Dolly Varden. Shipley and Sutter drainages also support sockeye salmon. The combined peak escapements for the more important streams in the area is 680,000 pink and 14,000 chum salmon. Herring spawn in Labouchere Bay. Dungeness crab rear in the area. Harbor seals are abundant and haulout in the Barrier Islands. Sitka black-tailed deer and black bear occur throughout the area in moderately high density. Black bears and migratory waterfowl concentrate on the estuarine sedge-grass flats at the head of Calder Bay. Bluff Island is a seabird colony and a harbor seal haulout. Protection Head is a seabird colony. Waterfowl concentrate in Dry Pass, Shakan Strait, and Tokeen Bay.

Residents of Point Baker, Port Protection, Cape Pole, Edna Bay, Klawock, and Craig use the area for the harvest of deer, salmon, furbearers, geoducks, crab, waterfowl, and other resources. Shipley Creek is intensively fished by Port Protection residents for sockeye salmon. Point Baker residents gillnet salmon in Shakan Strait. Residents of Klawock trap throughout Tokeen Bay. Commercial salmon fishing and crabbing occurs throughout the area.

Karta River

The Tongass Land Management Plan rated the Karta watershed as the highest value for fish. The ADF&G considers the Karta drainage to be one of the most productive anadromous fish systems on Prince of Wales Island, as well as having the highest values for wildlife. The area is very important for fishing and hunting to local residents as well as non-resident sport fishers.

The peak recorded escapements to the Karta River are 136,000 pink, 42,000 sockeye, and 41,000 chum salmon. The drainage also supports rainbow trout, spring and fall runs of steelhead, cutthroat trout, and Dolly Varden. The Karta River watershed is an extremely productive and diverse area. Black bear, furbearers, waterfowl, and other birds are abundant. There are moderate populations of deer, wolves, bald eagles, and marine mammals. The area is important for Trumpeter swans in the winter. The estuary is a rearing area for shrimp and dungeness crab and a herring spawning area.

There is an excellent trail system linking the series of lakes from salt water up to the highest lake. The area is a very popular area for bear hunting, trapping, sport fishing, and subsistence sockeye fishing by residents of Kasaan. The Forest Service considers the Karta drainage to be one of the top two recreation areas on the south Tongass.

Noyes-Lulu-Baker Islands

The Tongass Land Management Plan rated the islands as moderate to moderately high value for fish and estuarine resources. The ADF&G rated the area as moderate for wildlife and low for fisheries production. The islands are in the midst of a major commercial fishing ground that provides fishermen with over $16 million a year and are important for the harvests of fish and wildlife for residents of Craig and Klawock. These dramatic outer-coast islands are also becoming increasingly popular with tourists.

The islands' anadromous fish streams support pink and chum salmon. The two largest systems each produce 10,000-50,000 pinks, with one system also producing more than 6000 chum salmon a year and the other system producing up to 6000 chum salmon. Marine mammals are abundant along the coast, including sea otters, sea lions, and humpback whales. The islands also support deer and wolves.

Residents of Craig and Klawock use the islands to harvest salmon, other finfish, shellfish, seals, and deer. The commercial purse seining fleet, along with the associated fish buyers, packers and processors, depend on the safe anchorages provided by these islands which could be jeopardized by log storage in the limited areas of safe anchorage.

Nutkwa River

The Tongass Land Management Plan rated the drainage as high value for fish and estuarine resources. The ADF&G rated the area as high value for fish and wildlife. The fishery production makes the area extremely important to the commercial salmon industry and the residents of Hydaburg.

The Nutkwa system, with its large, shallow salt chuck, is an exceptional producer of pink salmon, with a peak recorded escapement of 215,000, and a major producer of sockeye, with a peak escapement of 1400. It also produces chum and coho salmon as well as rainbow, steelhead, and cutthroat trout and Dolly Varden. The salt chuck is important habitat for marine mammals and waterfowl, including trumpeter swans.

APPENDIX B

The Modelling and Analysis Processes

(not available at this time)

APPENDIX C

Roadless Areas

(data not complete for some areas)

APPENDIX C - ROADLESS AREA

This Appendix describes the 106 Roadless Areas to be evaluated in the Tongass
Land Management Plan revision process. Areas are included in the following
order

Unit	No.	Area Name	National Forest Acres
TSA	201	FANSHAW	48,869
TSA	202	SPIRES	536,653
TSA	203	THOMAS	4,517
TSA	204	MADAN	68,998
TSA	205	AARON	78,884
TSA	206	CONE	128,574
TSA	207	HARDING	177,598
TSA	208	BRADFIELD	212,872
TSA	209	ANAN	37,933
TSA	210	FROSTY	41,395
TSA	211	NORTH KUPREANOF	116,666
TSA	212	MISSIONARY	14,005
TSA	213	FIVE MILE	19,438
TSA	214	SOUTH KUPREANOF	209,957
TSA	215	CASTLE	49,360
TSA	216	LINDENBERG	22,797
TSA	217	GREEN ROCKS	10,380
TSA	218	WOEWODSKI	10,376
TSA	219	NORTH MITKOF	5,876
TSA	220	EAST MITKOF	10,250
TSA	223	MANZANITA	7,850
TSA	224	CRYSTAL	19,293
TSA	225	KADIN	1,623
TSA	226	GREYS	361
TSA	227	NORTH WRANGELL	11,624
TSA	229	SOUTH WRANGELL	71,173
TSA	231	WORONKOFSKI	9,773
TSA	232	NORTH ETOLIN	46,887
TSA	233	MOSMAN	57,974
TSA	234	SOUTH ETOLIN	113,031
TSA	235	WEST ZAREMBO	6,945
TSA	236	EAST ZAREMBO	8,990
TSA	237	SOUTH ZAREMBO	32,288
TSA	238	KASHEVAROF ISLANDS	16,487
TSA	239	KEKU	12,126
TSA	240	SECURITY	41,105
TSA	241	NORTH KUIU	9,741
TSA	242	CAMDEN	54,730
TSA	243	ROCKY PASS	78,976
TSA	244	PILLARS	28,570
TSA	245	EAST KUIU	46,271
TSA	246	SOUTH KUIU	124,065
TCA	301	JUNEAU-SKAGWAY ICE	1,209,199
TCA	302	TAKU-SNETTISHAM	736,112
TCA	303	SULLIVAN	66,657
TCA	304	CHILKAT-W LYNN	207,277
TCA	305	JUNEAU URBAN	104,970

Unit	No.	Area Name	National Forest Acres
TCA	306	MANSFIELD PENINSULA	52,994
TCA	307	GREENS CR -YOUNG BAY	48,078
TCA	308	WINDHAM-PORT HOUGHT	240,296
TCA	309	JUNEAU ISLANDS	7,051
TCA	310	DOUGLAS ISLAND	27,390
TCA	311	CHICHAGOF	637,238
TCA	312	TRAP BAY	22,008
TCA	314	POINT CRAVEN	11,837
TCA	317	POINT AUGUSTA	19,479
TCA	318	WHITESTONE	6,100
TCA	319	PAVLOF-EAST POINT	10,900
TCA	321	TENAKEE RIDGE	24,262
TCA	323	GAME CREEK	67,046
TCA	324	PLEASANT ISLAND	12,239
TCA	325	FRESHWATER BAY	63,206
TCA	326	NORTH KRUZOF	31,170
TCA	327	MIDDLE KRUZOF	15,540
TCA	328	HOONAH SOUND	97,257
TCA	329	SOUTH KRUZOF	56,701
TCA	330	NORTH BARANOF	341,417
TCA	331	SITKA URBAN	120,536
TCA	332	SITKA SOUND	19,475
TCA	333	REDOUBT	75,732
TCA	334	POINT ALEXANDER	126,120
TCA	338	BRABAZON ADDITION	500,374
TCA	339	YAKUTAT FORELANDS	305,871
TCA	341	UPPER SITUK	61,722
TKA	501	DALL ISLAND	108,260
TKA	502	SUMEZ ISLAND	36,327
TKA	503	OUTER ISLANDS	102,881
TKA	504	SUKKWAN	46,145
TKA	505	SODA BAY	76,596
TKA	507	EUDORA	233,933
TKA	508	CHRISTOVAL	7,750
TKA	509	KOGISH	76,175
TKA	510	KARTA	121,440
TKA	511	THORNE RIVER	112,460
TKA	512	RATZ	8,349
TKA	513	SWEETWATER	11,104
TKA	514	SARKAR	73,565
TKA	515	KOSCIUSKO	70,216
TKA	516	CALDER	12,687
TKA	517	EL CAPITAN	43,604
TKA	518	SALMON BAY	36,366
TKA	519	POLK	149,205
TKA	520	KASAAN	8,536
TKA	521	DUKE	46,785
TKA	522	GRAVINA	38,952
TKA	523	SOUTH REVILLA	71,358
TKA	524	REVILLA	138,393
TKA	525	BEHM ISLANDS	2,042
TKA	526	NORTH REVILLA	163,771

Unit No		Area Name	National Forest Acres
TKA	527	NEETS	6,315
TKA	528	CLEVELAND	193,473
TKA	529	NORTH CLEVELAND	114,158
TKA	530	HYDER	128,585
TKA	531	NUTKWA	59,318
TKA	532	FAKE PASS	798
TKA	577	QUARTZ	149,107
	Total For All Areas		10,442,893

INDIVIDUAL ROADLESS AREA DESCRIPTION

NAME: Fanshaw (201)   ACRES (GROSS): 48,889   ACRES (NFS): 48,869

GEOZONE: S08
GEOGRAPHIC PROVINCE: Coast Range

1989 WILDERNESS ATTRIBUTE RATING: 25

a. Description

(1) **Relationship to RARE II areas:** The table below displays the VCU 1/ names, VCU numbers, original WARS 2/ rating, and comments. This enables the reader to compare the roadless areas evaluated in Appendix C with previous analyses.

VCU Name	VCU No.	1979 WARS Rating	Comments
Fanshaw Bay	85	17	
Fanshaw	86	22	
Cat	87	23	
Tangent	88	22	
Bay Point	89	23	

(2) **History:** The Fanshaw area was probably inhabited by the Tlingit in prehistoric times. In modern times, a fox farm was located in Fanshaw Bay during the 1930-40's. Evidence of the farm remains to this day Cape Fanshaw is the site of an abandoned village and cannery which became active in 1901 with the establishment of a post office.

(3) **Location and Access:** The area is located on the mainland at Cape Fanshaw and extends south to the North Arm of Farragut Bay It abuts Frederick Sound and is accessible by water and floatplane Anchorage is available in Steamboat Bay and Cleveland Passage at Fanshaw Bay, and in the North Arm of Farragut Bay. Accessible shorelines suitable for landing small craft and floatplanes are found in both bays The shoreline along Frederick Sound is exposed and often difficult to access There are no sites suitable for landing wheeled aircraft. There is no ferry service or road access to the area.

1/ A VCU (Value Comparison Unit) is one of 867 watersheds which make up the forest and were differentiated for planning purposes in the Tongass Land Management Plan.
2/ Wilderness Attribute Rating System (WARS) was the nationwide system used to rate the wilderness attributes of roadless areas in the Roadless Area Review and Evaluation (RARE II).

(4) Geography and Topography: The Fanshaw area is characterized by four
separate peaks and ridges with an average elevation of about 3,000 feet
One peak reaches over 3,500 feet   Between the isolated mountains are
low-lying valleys   About 180 acres are alpine, and another 241 acres are
rock   Freshwater lakes account for 20 acres   The area contains 33 miles
of shoreline on saltwater

(5) Ecosystem:

    (a) Classification: The area is classified as being in the Coast
    Range Geographic Province   The area is characterized by broad,
    low-lying valleys and several steeply-rising peaks   Productive forest
    lands exist in river bottoms and on mountain slopes. Vegetation
    ranges from sub-alpine to saltwater marshes.

    (b) Vegetation: Much of the low-lying land is covered with muskeg and
    scrub lodgepole pine (1,581 acres). Hills and side slopes of the
    mountains where drainage is better are covered with dense stands of
    Sitka spruce, western hemlock and Alaska-cedar. Spruce trees are
    typically found as stringers along the streams.

    There are approximately 46,068 acres of forested land of which 29,358
    acres are commercial forest land. Of the commercial forest land,
    25,620 acres are non-riparian old growth and 3,678 acres are riparian
    old growth.

    (c) Soils: Soils in this area are formed in a wide variety of parent
    material, including bedrock and glacial drift   In general, well- or
    moderately-well-drained soils occur on moderate to steep mountain
    slopes with permeable parent materials   These soils are very acidic,
    have cold soil temperatures, and are very high in organic matter
    Rooting is largely limited to the surface organic layers and the top
    few inches of mineral soil. These soils are usually moist, sometimes
    wet, but are never dry.

    More-poorly-drained soils developed on less-sloping areas and/or areas
    with impermeable soil materials   These soils have deep accumulations
    of organic matter and range from scrubby forested wetlands to open
    muskeg.

    Alpine soils, generally above an elevation of 2,000 feet, are mostly
    shallow, very wet organic soils or are extremely shallow and rocky

    (d) Fish Resource: Fish resources have been rated as part of the
    Tongass Land Management Plan (1979) and by the Alaska Department of
    Fish and Game in its Forest Habitat Integrity Program (1983)   These
    ratings describe the value of VCU's for sport fish, commercial fish
    and estuaries

    VCU 89 was rated as highly valued for estuaries

There are seven Alaska Department of Fish and Game numbered salmon
producing streams within the area   Cat Creek is the largest producer
with an average annual peak escapement of 10,600 pink salmon   Coho.
steelhead and a few chum salmon are also present

(e) Wildlife Resource: A small population of mountain goats lives on
the isolated mountains within the area. Black bears and Sitka
black-tailed deer are found in the area, as are an occasional brown
bear and a few moose   Waterfowl use the limited grass flats at the
head of the North Arm   There are no known concentrations of marine
wildlife or sea lion haul out sites

(f) **Threatened and Endangered Species:** The area contains no known
threatened or endangered species.

(6) **Current Use and Management:** The entire area was allocated to LUD 4 in
the Tongass Land Management Plan. A timber sale was planned at one time,
in conjunction with the a proposed sale in Port Houghton, but was
subsequently dropped from the schedule and no resource development
activities have yet occurred in the area. There is a 540 acre Research
Natural Area near Fanshaw Bay. There is also a lighthouse reserve on the
tip of Cape Fanshaw. Fanshaw Bay is frequently used by small boats   Lack
of cabins or commercial overnight facilities limits use by recreationists
The area is not identified as a significant subsistence area in the Tongass
Resource Use Cooperative Survey (TRUCS)

(7) **Appearance (Apparent Naturalness):** The area appears unmodified except
for the remains of an abandoned fox farm in Fanshaw Bay   Much of the area
is visible from the Alaska Marine Highway and cruise ship routes   Almost
the entire roadless area, 99 percent, is in Existing Visual Condition (EVC)
Type I, where only ecological change has occurred   The remaining one
percent of the area appears to be untouched by human activity (EVC
Type II).

About 39 percent of this roadless area is inventoried Variety Class B
(possessing landscape diversity that is common for the character type)
The remaining 61 percent is inventoried Variety Class C (possessing a low
degree of landscape diversity).

(8) **Surroundings (External Influences):** Moderately-heavy boat traffic
passes through Frederick Sound and evidence of timber harvest on Kupreanof
Island may be visible in the background when viewed from some portions of
the Fanshaw Roadless Area.

(9) **Attractions and Features of Special Interest:** The area contains seven
inventoried recreation places totaling 14,526 acres. These recreation
places include the old fox farm. While the streams in the area offer some
sport fishing opportunity, the area does not receive much use. The
available anchorages provide safety for boaters waiting for the weather to
improve in Frederick Sound and Stephens Passage. Cape Fanshaw is not known
to be a good anchorage.

b   Capability of Management as Wilderness or in an Unroaded Condition

(1) Manageability and management area boundaries: The area is
well-defined on the west, southwest and south by saltwater   The
topographic divides on the north and east are low and in some cases poorly
defined   Feasibility of management in a roadless condition is high

(2) Natural Integrity: The area is essentially unmodified   Some evidence
of old structures is present at the abandoned fox farm in Fanshaw Bay but
is of limited magnitude and effect.

(3) Opportunity for Solitude: There is a high opportunity for solitude
within the area. At times, low-flying airplanes may disrupt visitors for
brief periods. Boats bypassing the area are generally far enough offshore
so as not to cause any distraction. Present recreation use levels are low,
and generally a person camped inland is unlikely to see others   The troll
fishery brings boat use to this area.

(4) Opportunity for Primitive Recreation: The area provides primarily
semi-primitive motorized and non-motorized recreation opportunities

ROS Class	Acres
Primitive (P)	23,496
Semi-Primitive Non-Motorized (SPNM)	15,719
Semi-Primitive Motorized (SPM)	9,654

The area contains seven inventoried recreation places

ROS CLASS	# OF REC. PLACES	TOTAL ACRES	CAPACITY BY RVD
P	1	5,730	320
SPNM	2	3,866	470
SPM	4	4,930	2,689

There are no developed recreation facilities within the area   The
character of the landforms in the area generally allows the visitor to feel
remote from the sights and sounds of human activity   The area is
accessible by boat from the community of Petersburg in two to four hours on
somewhat exposed waters. The presence of bears also presents a degree of
challenge and a need for woods skills and experience.

(5) Special Features (Ecologic, Geologic, Scientific, Cultural): The
abandoned fox farm site attracts some visitors. The Research Natural Area
was established for protection and study of a stand of Alaska-cedar,
however that stand is not particularly unique. Cape Fanshaw is also known
to be a good site for collecting the wild Sitka rose.

c. Availability for Management as Wilderness or in an Unroaded Condition

(1) Resource Potentials

(a) Recreation Potential: There is potential for additional
outfitter and guide permits, trails, and cabins or shelters

(b) Fish Resource: The Tongass Land Management Plan, amended Winter 1985-86, identifies fish habitat enhancement projects   Fish enhancement projects continue to surface and there is potential for additional projects in this area   Construction of a fish pass at Cat Creek is being considered by the Forest Service to enhance pink salmon production.

(c) Wildlife Resource: As identified in the Tongass Land Management Plan, amended 1985-86, several moose habitat improvement projects are planned in the area   These projects typically consist of browse enhancement.

(d) Timber Resource: There are 20,831 acres inventoried as tentatively suitable for harvest. This includes 2,539 acres of riparian old growth and 18,252 acres of non-riparian old growth   None of the area is second growth except as a result of older stands being blown down by the wind.

(e) Land Use Authorizations: None.

(f) Minerals: There are no inventoried areas with high mineral development potential in the area and no known mining claims

(g) Areas of Scientific Interest: The area contains no inventoried potential Research Natural Areas. Cape Fanshaw is an existing Research Natural Area. The area has not been identified for any other scientific value.

(2) Management Considerations

(a) Timber: The potential for managing timber in this roadless area is dependent on the development of a road system in the adjoining roadless area to the north. There are no suitable sites for a log transfer facility (LTF) in this area. Any significant amounts of timber harvested from this area would have to be hauled to a LTF in Port Houghton to be placed in the water and towed to a mill   Overall timber values are not high, and development is not likely in the near future.

(b) Wilderness: Maintenance of the area in a roadless condition enhances opportunities to manage the adjacent roadless areas as Wilderness and to provide enhanced opportunities for solitude and primitive recreation.

(c) Fire: The area has no significant fire history

(d) Insects and Disease: Endemic tree diseases common to Southeast Alaska are present; there are no know epidemic disease occurrences

(e) Land Status: The State has selected 700 acres within this area

d. Relationship to Communities and Other Roadless and Wilderness Areas

   (1) Nearby Roadless and Wilderness Areas and Uses: Admiralty Island
   Wilderness lies across Stephens Passage about 15 miles to the west   The
   Fanshaw area is part of a larger mainland land mass that is unroaded and is
   located between the Tracy Arm-Fords Terror Wilderness to the north and the
   Stikine-LeConte Wilderness to the south   The mainland areas receive light
   use inland with slightly higher use along saltwater shorelines   Admiralty
   gets slightly higher use because of its hunting opportunities

   (2) Distance From Population Centers (Accessibility): Approximate
   distances from population centers are as follows.

Community		Air Miles	Water Miles
Juneau	(Pop. 23,729)	85	90
Petersburg	(Pop. 4,040)	25	30
Wrangell	(Pop. 2,836)	55	70
Ketchikan	(Pop. 12,705)	135	150

   Petersburg is the nearest stop on the Alaska Marine Highway

   (3) Interest by Proponents:

      (a) Moratorium areas: The area has not been identified as a
      "moratorium" area or proposed as Wilderness in legislative initiatives
      to date.

      (b) Local users/residents: There has been little interest on the
      part of any interest groups to retain the roadless character of this
      area.

e. Environmental Consequences

   ALTERNATIVE ANALYSIS TO BE DONE LATER

INDIVIDUAL ROADLESS AREA DESCRIPTION

NAME: Spires (202)   ACRES (GROSS): 537,376   ACRES (NFS): 536,653

GEOZONE: S08
GEOGRAPHIC PROVINCE: Coast Range

1989 WILDERNESS ATTRIBUTE RATING: 27

a. Description

    (1) Relationship to RARE II areas: The table below displays the VCU 1/
    names, VCU numbers, original WARS 2/ rating, and comments. This enables
    the reader to compare the roadless areas evaluated in Appendix C with
    previous analyses.

| | | 1979 | |
VCU Name	VCU No.	WARS Rating	Comments
Farragut	90	26	Farragut Bay & lower Farragut River, contains State land
Glory	91	26	Farragut & Glory Lakes
Gray	92	25	
Baird	481	23	
Dana	482	23	Borders Thomas Bay
Jefferson	483	22	
Spurt	484	21	Borders Thomas Bay
Scenery	485	21	
Swan	486	21	
Thomas	487	22	Borders Thomas Bay and contains State land
Paterson	488*	22	
Muddy	489*	22	Contains State land

*--The roadless area includes only part of this VCU

    (2) History: The Farragut and Thomas Bay areas were inhabited by the
    Tlingit in prehistoric times. In 1958, logging began in the Muddy and
    Patterson River drainages and continued until recently Minor amounts of
    A-frame beach logging occurred in Farragut Bay and on Point Vandeput
    Gravel was excavated near the mouth of Muddy River on a commercial basis
    for several years. Several homesteads were located near the mouth of
    Farragut River and on Point Agassiz Peninsula near Thomas Bay From 1930
    to 1942 there was a fishing and agriculture village on the mainland south
    of Point Agassiz.

1/ A VCU (Value Comparison Unit) is one of 867 watersheds which make up the
    forest and were differentiated for planning purposes in the Tongass Land
    Management Plan.
2/ Wilderness Attribute Rating System (WARS) was the nationwide system used to
    rate the wilderness attributes of roadless areas in the Roadless Area
    Review and Evaluation (RARE II).

(3) Location and Access: The area is located on the mainland from the Port Houghton drainage and Tracy Arm-Fords Terror Wilderness on the north to the Stikine-LeConte Wilderness on the south It abuts Frederick Sound on the southwest and the Canadian boarder on the east The area is accessed by boat on saltwater and by floatplane on saltwater and several freshwater lakes. Anchorage is available in Farragut and Thomas Bays   Accessible shorelines suitable for landing small craft and floatplanes are found in both bays The shoreline along Frederick Sound is exposed and often difficult to access There are no sites suitable for landing wheeled aircraft There is no ferry service or road access to the area from outside, but there is road access from the south end of Thomas Bay up Muddy and Patterson Rivers. Vehicles are typically transported via landing craft from Petersburg.

(4) Geography and Topography: The area is generally characterized as highly complex terrain dominated by rugged mountains, many of which reach elevations of over 5,000 feet The tallest is over 9,000 feet Between the mountains are deep valleys and numerous glaciers About 237,543 acres are ice and snow, 132,296 acres are classified as rock, and another 2,862 acres are alpine. Near the shore, the landforms become more gentle and. include large outwash plains from Farragut, Muddy, and Patterson Rivers These rivers are rather short (four to 12 miles) and of glacial origin Dominant waterforms include two major saltwater bays and several high-elevation lakes totaling 4,999 acres. Swan, Spurt, DeBoer, Scenery, Ruth, Farragut and Glory Lakes are in this roadless area. The area contains 52 miles of saltwater shoreline.

(5) Ecosystem:

    (a) Classification: The Spires Roadless Area is classified as being in the Coast Range Geographic Province, which is characterized as having broad, low-lying valleys and several steeply-rising peaks Productive forest lands exist in river bottoms and on mountain slopes. There are no known areas of unique or uncommon plant/soils associations or geologic formations in the area.

    (b) Vegetation: Alpine vegetation dominates above an elevation of 2,500 feet. Below that elevation, the mountains, hills, and well-drained outwash plains are dominated by heavy stands of western hemlock, Sitka spruce, and Alaska-cedar Some of the low-lying, poorly-drained land is covered with muskeg (901 acres) and scrub lodgepole pine. Spruce trees are also typically found as stringers along the streams.

    There are approximately 132,977 acres of forested land of which 64,209 acres are commercial forest land. Of the commercial forest land, 54,824 acres are non-riparian old growth and 9,165 acres are riparian old growth.

    (c) Soils: Soils in this area are formed in a wide variety of parent material, including bedrock and glacial drift In general, well- or moderately-well-drained soils are on moderate to steep mountain slopes with permeable parent materials These soils are very acidic, have cold soil temperatures, and are very high in organic matter Rooting

is largely limited to the surface organic layers and the top few
inches of mineral soil   These soils are usually moist, sometimes wet,
but are never dry

More-poorly-drained soils developed on less sloping areas and/or areas
with impermeable soil materials   These soils have deep accumulations
of organic matter and range from scrubby forested wetlands to open
muskeg

Alpine soils, generally above an elevation of 2,000 feet, are mostly
shallow, very wet organic soils or are extremely shallow and rocky

(d) Fish: Fish resources have been rated as part of the Tongass Land
Management Plan (1979) and by the Alaska Department of Fish and Game
in its Forest Habitat Integrity Program (1983). These ratings
describe the value of VCU's for sport fish, commercial fish and
estuaries.

VCU's 90 and 489 are rated as high value for sport fish.   VCU's rated
as highly valued for commercial fish are 90, 91, 92, 483, 489   VCU's
90, 482, 484, 485, 486, 489 rated as having highly valued estuaries

Thirteen Alaska Department of Fish and Game numbered salmon producing
streams are present within the area. The Farragut River and Dry Bay
Creek are the best salmon producers. There are runs of pink, chum,
coho, king and steelhead in the Farragut, however increased sediment
in glacial water has prevented spawning-ground counts in the river
Dry Bay Creek has an average annual peak escapement of 8,200 pink and
2,000 chum salmon. Coho and steelhead are also present   Good rainbow
trout are available in Swan Lake.

(e) Wildlife: A small population of mountain goats lives in the
area. Black bears and Sitka black-tailed deer are found in the area,
as are an occasional brown bear and a moderate population of moose
Waterfowl use the extensive grassflats at the head of Farragut Bay and
smaller areas around Thomas Bay   There are no known concentrations of
marine wildlife or sea lion haul-out sites

(f) Threatened and Endangered Species: The area contains no known
threatened or endangered species

(6) Current Use and Management: The lower portion of Farragut River (VCU
90) was allocated in the Tongass Land Management Plan to Land Use
Designation (LUD) 2 (27,342 acres), to be managed for roadless recreation
opportunities. The Muddy River drainage (VCU 489), the Patterson River
drainage (VCU 487), and the Dry Bay drainage (VCU 483) were allocated to
LUD 4 (51,520 acres) which allows for timber harvest and roads   VCU 484
around Spurt Lake, and VCU 486 around Swan Lake were allocated to LUD 3
(28,035 acres) which also allows development, but at a reduced scale   The
rest of the area, which includes the higher elevations, was allocated to
LUD 1 (428,698 acres) and recommended for Wilderness designation   However,
Congress did not designate the area as Wilderness, so it reverted to a
"LUD 1 Release" status to be managed to protect its wilderness character to
allow for reconsideration at the time the Forest Plan is revised

Thomas and Farragut Bays are frequently used by small pleasure and
commercial fishing boats   There are two public recreation cabins on the
shore of Thomas Bay, one at Swan Lake, and one at DeBoer Lake   All of
these cabins get high use   Trails in the area include the Cascade Creek
Trail (4 5 miles), Spurt Lake Trail (1 1 miles), and a trail from the
Thomas Bay cabin to the Cascade Creek Trail   There are no commercial
overnight facilities in the area   Moose hunting is popular during the
fall   Current information indicates that some subsistence activities
occur, primarily from residents of Petersburg

(7) Appearance (Apparent Naturalness): Most of the area appears
unmodified. However, the logging around the south side of Thomas Bay and
in the Muddy and Patterson River valleys gives the adjacent roadless areas
a modified appearance. The area exists in an unmodified visual condition
Some of the foreground along Frederick Sound and the higher elevation area
are visible from present ferry and small cruiseship routes   At higher
elevations, the landscape offers spectacular scenery

The majority of this roadless area (99 percent) is in Existing Visual
Condition (EVC) Type I, where only ecological change has occurred   The
remaining one percent of the area is in EVC Type V where changes in the
landscape are obvious to the average person, and appear to be major
disturbances.

About 83 percent of this roadless area is inventoried Variety Class A
(possessing landscape diversity that is unique for the character type), 15
percent is inventoried Variety Class B (possessing landscape diversity that
is common for the character type), and the remaining two percent is Variety
Class C (possessing a low degree of landscape diversity)

(8) Surroundings (External Influences): The area abuts the Fanshaw
Roadless Area and the Tracy Arm-Fords Terror Wilderness on the north, and
the Stikine-LeConte Wilderness on the south. Land across the Canadian
boarder to the east is mostly rugged mountains and glaciers
Moderately-heavy boat traffic passes offshore along this area in Frederick
Sound and in Thomas and Farragut Bays   Evidence of timber harvest in the
Muddy and Patterson River valleys and along one slope of Farragut Bay are
seen from some locations within the roadless area   Inhabited and abandoned
buildings on the private land adjoining the area may be visible from some
places in the roadless area. Jet aircraft approaching Petersburg may
occasionally pass over portions of the area at elevations of less than ten
thousand feet. Small aircraft may land in parts of this roadless area

(9) Attractions and Features of Special Interest: Thomas Bay and, to a
slightly lesser degree, Farragut Bay are destination attractions for
residents of Petersburg. The public recreation cabins, the saltwater
fishing, the outstanding scenery, opportunities to hunt waterfowl and
moose, opportunities to run small boats on Farragut River, and the
opportunity to walk the trails and logging roads are special features
This area also offers opportunities for mountain climbing and backcountry
skiing. The public cabins at DeBoer and Swan Lakes offer a unique fly-in
trip and freshwater fishing opportunities   The area contains 20
inventoried recreation places totaling 121,642 acres   There are a total of
6 0 miles of improved trails in the area   Opportunities to see and hunt

mountain goats and moose are also attractions   The presence of good
anchorage sites allows boaters to stay in the area overnight

b   Capability of Management as Wilderness or in an Unroaded Condition

(1) Manageability and Management Area Boundaries: The area is well
defined on the southwest by saltwater. The topographic divides are, for
the most part, well defined   Feasibility of management in a roadless
condition is high except around the Muddy and Patterson Rivers

(2) Natural Integrity: Except for the Muddy and lower Patterson River
valleys, the area is essentially unmodified.

(3) Opportunity for Solitude: There is a high opportunity for solitude
within the area. At times, moderately-low-flying airplanes may disrupt
visitors for brief periods. Passing boats are generally far enough
offshore so as not to cause any distraction. Present recreation use levels
are low except in the immediate vicinity of the recreation cabins or along
the saltwater shore where use is relatively high. Generally, a person
camped inland is unlikely to see others.

(4) Opportunity for Primitive Recreation: The area provides primarily
primitive, and semi-primitive motorized and non-motorized opportunity

ROS class	Acres
Primitive (P)	448,850
Semi-Primitive Non-Motorized (SPNM)	59,913
Semi-Primitive Motorized (SPM)	17,692
Roaded Modified (RM)	10,197

The area contains 20 recreation places.

ROS CLASS	# OF REC. PLACES	TOTAL ACRES	CAPACITY BY RVD
P	4	89,720	4,236
SPNM	5	8,676	1,673
SPM	8	11,048	8,845
RM	3	10,197	2,111

There are four public recreation cabins, three maintained trails and two
abandoned trails in the area. The character of the landforms generally
allows the visitor to feel remote from the sights and sounds of human
activity. The area is accessible by boat from the community of Petersburg
in one to four hours on somewhat exposed waters. The presence of bears
also presents a degree of challenge and a need for woods skills and
experience.

(5) Special Features (Ecologic, Geologic, Scientific, Cultural): Besides
outstanding scenery, there are opportunities to observe a wide spectrum of
ecological progressions, from bare rock at the face of receding glaciers to
climax stands of old-growth forest, all within a short geographic
distance. Near Patterson Glacier are the remains of a once-buried forest
This area is also the setting for some local accounts of strange phenomenon
featured in the book "The Strangest Story Ever Told".

c. Availability for Management as Wilderness of in an Unroaded Condition

   (1) Resource Potentials

       (a) Recreation Potential: There is high potential for additional
       outfitter and guide permits and for additional trails, cabins, or
       shelters The existing Cascade Creek Trail is scheduled for
       reconstruction to the lower falls in fiscal year 91, with portions of
       it designed to be barrier free. A trail from Spurt Cove to the Spurt
       Lake Trail is also being considered. The Thomas Bay area is a likely
       area for an additional cabin, though no specific site has been
       selected. The beauty, diversity and accessibility of Thomas Bay makes
       it a likely area for increased sightseeing and excursion trip
       opportunities.

       (b) Fish Resource: The Tongass Land Management Plan, amended Winter
       1985-86, identifies fish habitat enhancement projects Fish
       enhancement projects continue to surface and there is potential for
       additional projects in this area. Fish habitat enhancement at Dry Bay
       may be considered to provide access for pink salmon to the upper
       watershed. The possibility exists for an egg incubation box project
       on the Muddy River

       (c) Wildlife Resource: As identified in the Tongass Land Management
       Plan, amended 1985-86, several moose and big game browse habitat
       improvement projects are planned in the area. These projects
       typically consist of thinning, planting, and releasing of browse
       species.

       (d) Timber Resource: There are 33,551 acres inventoried as
       tentatively suitable for harvest. This includes 6,381 acres of
       riparian old growth and 26,990 acres of non-riparian old growth A
       small amount of second growth exists in the area, either as a result
       of older stands being blown down by the wind or as a result of A-frame
       harvest.

       (e) Land Use Authorizations: The Scenery Lake and Swan Lake
       drainages have been identified by the Federal Power Commission as
       potential hydropower generation sites and are withdrawn from other
       management considerations. Several proposals have been made over the
       years to develop the hydropower potential at Swan Lake, but to date no
       development has taken place and is not likely in the immediate
       future. There are two special use permits in the area One is for a
       recreation residence in the North Arm of Farragut Bay, and the other
       is a for a waterline in Thomas Bay, which provides water for a fish
       camp.

       (f) Minerals: There are no inventoried areas with high mineral
       development potential in the area and no known mining claims There
       has been some mineral exploration in the past

       (g) Areas of Scientific Interest: The area contains no inventoried
       potential Research Natural Areas The area has not been identified
       for any other scientific value

(2) **Management Considerations**

(a) **Timber:** The potential for managing timber in this roadless area is closely linked to the existing road system near Thomas Bay, or development of additional log transfer facilities (LTF's) in Thomas and Farragut Bays. Any significant amounts of timber harvested from this area would have to be hauled to either of those bays to be placed in the water and towed to a mill.

(b) **Wilderness:** Maintenance of the area in a roadless condition enhances opportunities to manage the adjacent roadless areas as Wilderness and to provide enhanced opportunities for solitude and primitive recreation.

(c) **Fire:** The area has no significant fire history.

(d) **Insects and Disease:** Endemic tree diseases common to Southeast Alaska are present; there are no know epidemic disease occurrences

(e) **Land Status:** The entire area is National Forest land.

d. **Relationship to Communities and Other Roadless and Wilderness Areas**

(1) **Nearby Roadless and Wilderness Areas and Uses:** Petersburg Creek-Duncan Salt Chuck Wilderness is across Frederick Sound about 10 miles to the west. The Spires area is part of a larger mainland land mass that is unroaded and is located between the Tracy Arm-Fords Terror Wilderness tn the north and the Stikine-LeConte Wilderness to the south The mainland areas receive light use inland, except at two or three lakes, with higher use around saltwater bays

(2) **Distance From Population Centers (Accessibility):** Approximate distances from population centers are as follows

Community		Air Miles	Water Miles
Juneau	(Pop. 23,729)	105	115
Petersburg	(Pop. 4,040)	10	15
Wrangell	(Pop. 2,836)	40	50
Ketchikan	(Pop. 12,705)	125	140

Petersburg is the nearest stop on the Alaska Marine Highway

(3) **Interest by Proponents:**

(a) **Moratorium areas:** The area has not been identified as a "moratorium" area or proposed as Wilderness in legislative initiatives to date.

(b) **Local users/residents:** Local Petersburg residents have a high degree of interest in how this area is managed There was a strong protest when the State considered subdividing and selling land in Thomas Bay

e. Environmental Consequences

   ALTERNATIVE ANALYSIS TO BE DONE LATER

INDIVIDUAL ROADLESS AREA DESCRIPTION

NAME: Thomas (203)   ACRES (GROSS): 4,697   ACRES (NFS)· 4,517

GEOZONE: S08
GEOGRAPHIC PROVINCE: Coast Range

1989 WILDERNESS ATTRIBUTE RATING: 18

a. **Description**

(1) **Relationship to RARE II areas:** The following table displays the VCU 1/ names, VCU numbers, original WARS 2/ rating, and comments. This enables the reader to compare the roadless areas evaluated in Appendix C with previous analyses.

VCU Name	VCU No.	1979 WARS Rating	Comments
Thomas	487*	22	
Muddy	489*	22	

*--The roadless area includes only part of this VCU

(2) **History:** Thomas Bay was within the territory of the Talquedi clan of the Stikine Tlingit. Evidence of their use of the bay includes a village site, hunting and fishing camps, petroglyphs and bark-stripped trees Unconfirmed reports suggest a large Tlingit village with 500 residents was buried under an avalanche of rocks A three-masted Russian gunboat was reported sunk within the bay Evidence of historic use of the bay includes an abandoned shrimp cannery, mining camps, fox farms, and log cabins

(3) **Location and Access:** The area is located between Thomas Bay and Frederick Sound on the Point Agassiz Penninsula. The area is part of the coastal mainland. The area is accessed by boat and floatplane on saltwater within Thomas Bay. Anchorage is available in Thomas Bay The shoreline along·Frederick Sound is exposed and often difficult to access There are no sites suitable for landing wheeled aircraft There is no ferry service or road access to the area from outside. There is road access from the southern end of Thomas Bay to the southern end of the roadless area

1/ A VCU (Value Comparison Unit) is one of 867 watersheds which make up the forest and were differentiated for planning purposes in the Tongass Land Management Plan.

2/ Wilderness Attribute Rating System (WARS) was the nationwide system used to rate the wilderness attributes of roadless areas in the Roadless Area Review and Evaluation (RARE II).

(4) Geography and Topography: The area is generally characterized by gently-rolling terrain with little relief This area is peninsular and separates Frederick Sound from Thomas Bay Though the roadless area is part of the mainland, its size, location and shape display few characteristics typical of the mainland. The terrain rises gradually from shoreline, to a height of about 400 feet near the center Several small streams drain the area, and several small lakes lie near the center of the area The area contains seven miles of shoreline on saltwater with about 420 acres of beach Muskeg covers about 100 acres, and the lakes total about 40 acres

(5) Ecosystem:

(a) Classification: The area is classified as being in the Coast Range Geographic Province. This province is generally characterized by large, massive, bulky landforms. Mountains are typically 5,000 to 7,000 feet in elevation, with summits and ridges rising even higher Glacial streams and valleys are typical

(b) Vegetation: Vegetation consists of typical spruce-hemlock forests. Muskegs are interspersed among low elevation timber stands where drainage is restricted. Trees are sparse and consist mainly of stunted lodgepole pine, western hemlock and Alaska-cedar.

There are approximately 4,217 acres of forested land of which 1,599 acres are commercial forest land. Of the commercial forest land, 1,459 acres are non-riparian old growth and 120 acres are riparian old growth.

(c) Soils: Soils in this area are formed in a wide variety of parent material, including bedrock and glacial drift In general, well- or moderately-well-drained soils are on moderate to steep mountain slopes with permeable parent materials. These soils are very acidic, have cold soil temperatures, and are very high in organic matter Rooting is largely limited to the surface organic layers and the top few inches of mineral soil. These soils are usually moist, sometimes wet, but are never dry .

More-poorly-drained soils developed on less sloping areas and/or areas with impermeable soil materials. These soils have deep accumulations of organic matter and range from scrubby, forested wetlands to open muskeg.

Alpine soils, generally above 2,000 feet elevation, are mostly shallow, very wet organic soils or are extremely shallow and rocky

(d) Fish Resource: Fish resources have been rated as part of the Tongass Land Management Plan (1979) and by the Alaska Department of Fish and Game in its Forest Habitat Integrity Program (1983) These ratings describe the value of VCU's for sport fish, commercial fish, and estuaries

VCU 489 is rated as high value for sport fish, commercial fish, and
estuaries   However, most of the values that contributed to the high
rating are found outside the roadless area

(e) Wildlife Resource: The area contains moose, brown bear and Sitka
black-tailed deer

(f) Threatened and Endangered Species: The area contains no known
threatened or endangered species.

(6) Current Use and Management: The entire roadless area was allocated to
Land Use Designation (LUD) 4 under the Tongass Land Management Plan   LUD
4 lands are to be managed for intensive resource use and development   The
area is popular for moose hunting in the fall. Other hunting activities
occur as well. There are no developed recreation facilities in the area
Some subsistence activities occur in the area, primarily from residents of
Petersburg.

(7) Appearance (Apparent Naturalness): Most of the area appears
unmodified. Exceptions are areas adjacent to logging, which give the
adjacent roadless areas a modified appearance. The visual character type
for this area, Coast Range, is not typical of this roadless area. The area
displays a low profile compared to the backdrop across Thomas Bay where the
large mountains of the Coast Range stand. About 21 percent of the area is
inventoried in Variety Class B (possessing landscape diversity that is
common for the character type), and the remaining 79 percent is inventoried
as Class C (possessing a low degree of landscape diversity)

The majority of the roadless area (62 percent) is in Existing Visual
Condition (EVC) I, where the natural landscape appears to be untouched by
human activity. EVC II makes up about eight percent of the area. These
are areas in which changes to the landscape are not noticed by the average
person unless pointed out. Another eight percent of the area is in EVC IV.
in which changes to the landscape are easily noticed by the average person
and may attract some attention. These areas appear to be disturbances but
resemble natural patterns. EVC V accounts for the remaining 22 percent, in
which changes in the landscape are in glaring contrast to the natural
landscape and appear to be drastic disturbances. The area is highly
sensitive as viewed from Frederick Sound, the primary travel route of the
Alaska Marine Highway   This Sensitivity Level I area affects about 42
percent of the roadless area

(8) Surroundings (External Influences): The area is a peninsula forming
the southern entrance to Thomas Bay. Thomas Bay is a popular recreation
destination for residents of Petersburg. Relatively heavy boat traffic can
occur at times. Frederick Sound is a major passage for commercial boat
traffic, including Alaska State ferries. Evidence of beach logging, and
adjacent and distant clearcuts are visible from parts of this roadless
area. Inhabited and abandoned buildings on the private land nearby may be
visible from some places in the roadless area. Jet aircraft approaching
and leaving Petersburg may occasionally pass over portions of the area at
elevations of less than ten thousand feet   Small aircraft frequently pass
by the area

(9) **Attractions and Features of Special Interest:** Thomas Bay is a destination attraction for residents of Petersburg This roadless area makes up a substantial portion of the southern entrance to the bay The area contains three inventoried recreation places totaling 4,517 acres. There are no developed recreation facilities in the area

b   Capability of Management as Wilderness or in an Unroaded Condition

(1) **Manageability and Management Area Boundaries:** The west boundary of the area is defined by saltwater and beach logged cutting units Cutting units generally define the eastern and southern boundaries Feasability of management in a Wilderness condition is low, due to the size and shape of the area. Feasability of management in a roadless condition is low to moderate.

(2) **Natural Integrity:** The area is unmodified. However, adjacent management and recreational activities make it likely that the natural integrity has been impacted to some degree.

(3) **Opportunity for Solitude:** There is a moderate opportunity for solitude within the area. At times low-flying airplanes may disrupt visitors for brief periods. Boats bypassing the area are generally offshore far enough so as not to cause any distraction Present recreation use levels are low, except in the immediate vicinity of shorelines Generally, a person camped inland is unlikely to see others

(4) **Opportunity for Primitive Recreation:** The area provides primarily semi-primitive motorized and non-motorized recreation opportunities.

ROS Class	Acres
Primitive (P)	0
Semi-Primitive Non-Motorized (SPNM)	3,258
Semi-Primitive Motorized (SPM)	839
Roaded Modified (RM)	420

The area contains three inventoried recreation places.

ROS CLASS	# OF REC. PLACES	TOTAL ACRES	CAPACITY BY RVD
SPNM	1	3,258	150
SPM	1	839	351
RM	1	420	69

The character of the landforms generally allows the visitor to feel remote from the sights and sounds of human activity. The area is accessible by boat from the community of Petersburg in one to three hours on somewhat exposed waters. The presence of bears presents a degree of challenge and a need for woods skills and experience.

(5) Special Features (Ecologic, Geologic, Scientific, Cultural): The character of the roadless area, which makes up most of the Point Agassiz peninsula, is the result of glacial moraines The retreat of these glaciers shaped the Thomas Bay area This peninsula defines the southern entrance to the bay from Frederick Sound

c Availability for Management as Wilderness or in an Unroaded Condition

   (1) Resource Potentials

       (a) Recreation Potential: There is potential for outfitter and guide permits, and for trails, cabins, or shelters

       (b) Fish Resources: The Tongass Land Management Plan, amended Winter 1985-86 does not identify any fish enhancement projects in this area.

       (c) Wildlife Resources: As identified in the Tongass Land Management Plan, amended 1985-86 moose habitat improvement projects are planned in this area. These typically involve enhancement of browse species

       (c) Timber Resource: There are 1,099 acres inventoried as tentatively suitable for harvest. This includes 40 acres of riparian old growth, and 1,039 acres of non-riparian old growth

       (d) Land Use Authorizations: There are currently no special uses or other land authorizations.

       (e) Minerals: There are no inventoried areas with high mineral development potential, and no known mining claims

       (f) Areas of Scientific Interest: The area has not been identified as a potential Research Natural Area, or for any other scientific purpose.

   (2) Management Considerations

       (a) There is potential for managing timber in this roadless area Log transfer facilities are connected to an existing road system adjacent to the southern end of this roadless area.

       (b) Maintenance of the area in a roadless condition enhances opportunities for semi-primitive recreation, visual management, and for low levels of wildlife disturbance

       (c) Fire: The area has no significant fire history

       (d) Insects and Disease: Endemic tree diseases common to Southeast Alaska are present; there are no know epidemic disease occurrences

       (e) Land Status: The entire area is National Forest land

d. Relationship to Communities and Other Roadless and Wilderness Areas

(1) Nearby Roadless and Wilderness Areas and Uses: The Spires Roadless Area, lies just to the east across Thomas Bay. It is a large area on the mainland and extends to the Stikine-Leconte Wilderness Overall use in these areas is light to moderate depending upon accessibility and attractions.

(2) Distance From Population Centers (Accessibility): Approximate distances from population centers are as follows·

Community		Air Miles	Water Miles
Juneau	(Pop. 23,729)	100	110
Petersburg	(Pop. 4,040)	10	15
Wrangell	(Pop. 2,836)	38	59
Ketchikan	(Pop. 12,705)	115	120

Petersburg is the nearest stop on the Alaska Marine Highway

(3) Interest by Proponents:

(a) Moratorium areas: The area has not been identified as a "moratorium" area or proposed as Wilderness in legislative initiatives to date.

(b) Local users/residents: Local Petersburg residents have a high degree of interest in how this area is managed There was a strong protest when the State considered subdividing and selling land in Thomas Bay

e. Environmental Consequences

ALTERNATIVE ANALYSIS TO BE DONE LATER

INDIVIDUAL ROADLESS AREA DESCRIPTION

NAME: Madan (204)   ACRES (GROSS): 72,958   ACRES (NFS): 68,998

GEOZONE: S09
GEOGRAPHIC PROVINCE: Coast Range

1989 WILDERNESS ATTRIBUTE RATING: 24

a. Description

     (1) Relationship to RARE II areas: The table below displays the VCU 1/
     names, VCU numbers, original WARS 2/ rating, and comments. This enables
     the reader to compare the roadless areas evaluated in Appendix C with
     previous analyses.

| | | 1979 | |
VCU Name	VCU No.	WARS Rating	Comments
Cottonwood	497*	22	This part of VCU 497 was not included in the Wilderness
Garnet	501	22	
Virginia	502	18	Virginia Lake drainage
Madan	504*	21	

     *--The roadless area includes only part of this VCU

     (2) History: The area was inhabited by the Tlingit in prehistoric times
     A sawmill and a stampmill operated at the mouth of Mill Creek during the
     early 1900's. Extensive prospecting has occurred in the area over the
     years, resulting in numerous claims and the patent of one group of claims
     At least two of the potential road routes to Canada which have been
     discussed in the past pass through this area. The State has selected land
     in the area which has been tentatively approved for conveyance

     (3) Location and Access: The area is located on the mainland and is
     bounded on the north by the Stikine-LeConte Wilderness; on the west by the
     Eastern Passage, on the south by Blake Channel, and on the east by the
     Aaron Creek divide. The area is accessed by boat on saltwater and is
     floatplane on saltwater and to Virginia Lake. The Mill Creek Trail
     provides access to the outlet of Virginia Lake. Accessible shorelines
     suitable for landing small craft and floatplanes are abundant when weather
     conditions are favorable. The shoreline along Eastern Passage is
     relatively protected. There are no sites suitable for landing wheeled
     aircraft in the area, however, the Wrangell airport, located on Wrangell
     Island, is within one mile of the area. There is no ferry service or road
     access to the area from outside.

1/ A VCU (Value Comparison Unit) is one of 867 watersheds which make up the
    forest and were differentiated for planning purposes in the Tongass Land
    Management Plan.
2/ Wilderness Attribute Rating System (WARS) was the nationwide system used to
    rate the wilderness attributes of roadless areas in the Roadless Area
    Review and Evaluation (RARE II).

(4) Geography and Topography: The area is generally characterized as highly-complex terrain dominated by rugged mountains, many of which reach elevations of over 3,000 feet. The tallest is over 5,000 feet Between the mountains are deep, broad valleys containing several sizable streams Near the shore, the landforms become more gentle Dominant waterforms include a relatively small glacier which occupies the highest mountains, Virginia Lake, and the waterfall on Mill Creek. Freshwater Lakes account for a total of 540 acres, with another 420 acres in ice and snow, and 6,281 acres in rock Alpine accounts for about 4,221 acres The area contains 16 miles of shoreline on saltwater

(5) Ecosystem:

(a) Classification: The area is classified as being in the Coast Range Geographic Province This region is generally characterized as a core of massive, angular mountains capped with ice fields at high elevations along the Canadian border, with somewhat lower mountains, deeply-incised valleys and glacier-fed streams closer to the coast This roadless area is more characteristic of the lower coastal portion of the region. There are no known areas of unique or uncommon plant/soils associations or geologic formations in the area

(b) Vegetation: Alpine vegetation dominates above an elevation of 2,500 feet. Below that elevation the mountains, hills, and well-drained outwash plains are dominated by heavy stands of western hemlock, Sitka spruce, Alaska-cedar, and scattered stands of redcedar Much of the low-lying, poorly-drained land is covered with muskeg and scrub lodgepole pine (20 acres) Spruce is also typically found as stringers along the streams.

There are approximately 49,774 acres of forested land of which 32,370 acres are commercial forest land. Of the commercial forest land 28,309 acres are non-riparian old growth and 3,621 acres are riparian old growth.

(c) Soils: Soils in this area are formed in a wide variety of parent material, including bedrock and glacial drift In general, well- or moderately-well-drained soils are on moderate to steep mountain slopes with permeable parent materials These soils are very acidic, have cold soil temperatures, and are very high in organic matter Rooting is largely limited to the surface organic layers and the top few inches of mineral soil. These soils are usually moist, sometimes wet, but are never dry.

More-poorly-drained soils developed on less-sloping areas and/or areas with impermeable soil materials. These soils have deep accumulations of organic matter and range from scrubby, forested wetlands to open muskeg

Alpine soils, generally above 2,000 feet elevation, are mostly shallow, very wet organic soils or are extremely shallow and rocky

(d) Fish: Fish resources have been rated as part of the Tongass Land
Management Plan (1979) and by the Alaska Department of Fish and Game
in its Forest Habitat Integrity Program (1983)   These ratings
describe the value of VCU's for sport fish, commercial fish and
estuaries.

VCU 497 is rated high for sport fishing, and VCU 497 is rated high in
estuary values

Seven Alaska Department of Fish and Game numbered fish streams are
present in the area. Generally, salmon production from the area is
low   Good cutthroat trout fishing occurs in Virginia Lake   A fish
ladder has been constructed at a barrier to Virginia Lake, and sockeye
fry have been stocked into the lake. First returns will be in 1992.

(e) Wildlife: A small population of mountain goats lives in the
area. Black bear and Sitka black-tailed deer are found in the area,
as are an occasional brown bear and a small population of moose
There are no known concentrations of marine wildlife or sea lion
haul-out sites.

(f) Threatened and Endangered Species: The area contains no known
threatened or endangered species.

(6) Current Use and Management: The portion of VCU 497 (1,302 acres)
included in this area was originally recommended for Wilderness allocation
in the Tongass Land Management Plan, but was not included when the final
· Wilderness boundary was drawn. It has subsequently been managed as a "LUD
1 Release" area under which its wilderness attributes are maintained for
reconsideration in the Tongass Land Management Plan revision. The
remainder of the roadless area (67,696 acres) was allocated to LUD 3, which
allows resource development such as roads and timber harvest with
consideration for other resources.

The waters offshore are frequently used by small pleasure and commercial
fishing boats   There are two public recreation cabins in the area, one on
the shore of Virginia Lake, and one at saltwater near Garnet Mountain
Both receive moderate use. The Mill Creek Trail (0 9 miles) provides some
access within the area. There are no commercial overnight facilities in
the area. Current information indicates that some subsistence activities
occur in the area, primarily from residents of Wrangell using Mill Creek
sockeye salmon for subsistence/personal use.

(7) Appearance (Apparent Naturalness): The majority of this roadless area
(99 percent) is natural appearing, where only ecological change has
occurred (Existing Visual Condition (EVC) Type I). However, the recreation
cabin and the remnants of past mining activities are evident from the Mill
Creek Trail (one percent scattered through EVC Types II, III, and IV)
Most of the foreground along Eastern Passage and higher elevation areas in
the background are visible from boats using those waters   Some of the area
is visible from the community of Wrangell. Jet aircraft fly over the area
in their approach to the Wrangell Airport.

Eight percent of this roadless area is inventoried Variety Class A
(possessing landscape diversity that is unique for the character type), 59
percent is inventoried Variety Class B (possessing landscape diversity that
is common for the character type) and the remaining 33 percent is
inventoried Variety Class C (possessing a low degree of landscape
diversity)

(8) **Surroundings (External Influences):** The area is part of a much larger
roadless land mass It abuts the Stikine-LeConte Wilderness on the north
and the Aaron Creek Roadless Area on the east Moderately-heavy boat
traffic passes offshore along this area in Eastern Passage Jet and other
aircraft approaching Wrangell may pass over portions of the area at
elevations of less than ten thousand feet, and may be heard from the area
as they land and take off. Other sights and sounds from Wrangell may also
be detectable. Evidence of timber harvest on Wrangell Island may be
visible from some parts of the roadless area. The State has not yet
indicated what it intends to do with its selected lands in the area If a
road to Canada materializes, the State lands will likely be used for a
deep-water port and community development.

(9) **Attractions and Features of Special Interest:** Virginia Lake is the
major recreation feature of the area, attracting people by floatplane and
on the Virginia Lake Trail from saltwater. The public recreation cabin,
the offshore saltwater fishing, the scenery provided by the mainland
setting, the opportunity to hunt moose and brown bear, and the Mill Creek
Trail are special features found in this area. The area contains 10
inventoried recreation places totaling 5,845 acres There is a total of
0 9 miles of improved trail in the area.

b. **Capability of Management as Wilderness or in an Unroaded Condition**

(1) **Manageability and management area boundaries:** The area is well
defined on the southwest by saltwater. The topographic divides are, for
the most part, well defined. Feasibility of management in a roadless
condition is high unless the mining claims are developed or the State
establishes a community on the State land.

(2) **Natural Integrity:** The area is essentially unmodified Exceptions
are recreation cabin sites, Mill Creek Trail, and the fish pass at the
mouth of Mill Creek.

(3) **Opportunity for Solitude:** There is a moderate to high opportunity for
solitude within the area. Low-flying aircraft (floatplanes and jet
aircraft) may disrupt visitors for brief periods. Boats bypassing the area
are generally far enough offshore so as not to cause any distraction
Present recreation use levels are low except in the immediate vicinity of
the recreation cabins, on the Virginia Lake Trail or along the saltwater
shore. Generally, a person camped inland is unlikely to see others

(4) Opportunity for Primitive Recreation: The area provides primarily
semi-primitive motorized and non-motorized recreation opportunities

ROS class	Acres
Primitive (P)	49,391
Semi-Primitive Non-Motorized (SPNM)	6,641
Semi-Primitive Motorized (SPM)	10,606
Roaded Natural (RN)	2,360

The area contains 10 recreation places

ROS CLASS	# RECREATION PLACES	TOTAL ACRES	CAPACITY BY RVD
P	2	100	14
SPNM	1	280	. 80
SPM	5	4,324	2,930
RN	2	1,140	721

There are two public recreation cabins and one short maintained trail in
the area. The character of the landforms generally allows the visitor to
feel remote from the sights and sounds of human activity. The area is
accessible by boat from the community of Wrangell in less than one hour on
somewhat protected waters. The presence of both black and brown bears also
presents a degree of challenge and a need for woods skills and experience

(5) Special Features (Ecologic, Geologic, Scientific, Cultural): There
are opportunities to observe and study petroglyphs on the beach near Mill
Creek and to watch returning salmon work their way upstream though the
fishpass at Mill Creek Falls.

c. Availability for management as Wilderness or in an Unroaded Condition

(1) Resource Potentials

(a) Recreation Potential: There is potential for additional
outfitter and guide permits and for additional trails, cabins, or
shelters. Virginia Lake recreation cabin is being considered for
conversion to barrier-free accessibility

(b) Fish Resource: The Tongass Land Management Plan, amended Winter
1985-86 identifies fish habitat enhancement projects Fish
enhancement projects continue to surface, and there is potential for
additional projects in this area. Fish habitat enhancement at
Crittenden Creek may be considered by the Forest Service to enhance
salmon production.

(c) Wildlife Resource: As identified in the Tongass Land Management
Plan, amended 1985-86 several habitat improvement projects are planned
in the area. Moose habitat enhancement is planned along the main
tributary streams

(d) **Timber Resource:** There are 22,366 acres inventoried as tentatively suitable for harvest. This includes 2,361 acres of riparian old growth and 19,725 acres of non-riparian old growth None of the area is second growth except a small stand at the mouth of Mill Creek or as result of older stands being blown down by the wind

(e) **Land Use Authorizations:** The Virginia Lake drainage has been identified by the Federal Energy Regulatory Commission (FERC) as a potential hydropower generation site and is withdrawn from competing management No serious proposals have been received to develop the hydropower potential of this site There is one special use permit in Madan Bay and two private parcels at Green Point

(f) **Minerals:** There are numerous mining claims in the area and one group of claims has been patented. The potential for development of those claims is unknown

(g) **Areas of Scientific Interest:** The area contains no inventoried potential Research Natural Areas. The area has not been identified for any other scientific value.

(2) **Management Considerations**

(a) **Timber:** The area was analyzed for timber sale opportunities. After a preliminary analysis with extensive reconnaissance, timber values, overall, were not sufficient to warrant further investment at this time. In the near future, if timber values change as predicted, or other resource values encourage development, a timber sale could be possible.

(b) **Wildlife:** Maintenance of the area in a roadless condition enhances opportunities to manage the adjacent roadless areas as Wilderness and to provide enhanced opportunities for solitude and primitive recreation. It also maintains opportunities for wildlife such as wolves, bears, and moose, to move between the Wilderness and other areas to the southeast

(c) **Fire:** The area has no significant fire history

(d) **Insects and Disease:** Endemic tree diseases common to Southeast Alaska are present; there are no know epidemic disease occurrences

(e) **Land Status:** Native Land Selections include a four acre Sealaska Historical site at Green Point.   Part of the 9910 acre Zimovia Strait/Eastern Passage State selection is in this area   There are 60 acres of private land holdings.

d. **Relationship to Communities and Other Roadless and Wilderness Areas**

(1) **Nearby Roadless and Wilderness Areas and Uses:** The Madan area is part of a larger mainland unroaded land mass that is located between the Stikine-LeConte Wilderness on the north and the Aaron Roadless Area to the south. The mainland areas receive light use inland, except around Virginia Lake, which receives moderately-high use.

(2) **Distance From Population Centers (Accessibility):** Approximate distances from population centers are as follows:

Community			Air Miles	Water Miles
Juneau	(Pop	23,729)	145	170
Petersburg	(Pop.	4,040)	30	50
Wrangell	(Pop	2,836)	5	8
Ketchikan	(Pop	12,705)	80	104

Wrangell is the nearest stop on the Alaska Marine Highway

(3) **Interest by Proponents:**

(a) **Moratorium areas:** The area has not been identified as a "moratorium" area or proposed as Wilderness in legislative initiatives to date.

(b) **Local users/residents:** Local Wrangell residents have a high degree of interest in maintaining the integrity of the area around Virginia Lake, but many would like to see mining, logging, or other development in other parts of the area, including a road link between Wrangell and the Canadian highway system.

e. **Environmental Consequences**

ALTERNATIVE ANALYSIS TO BE DONE LATER

INDIVIDUAL ROADLESS AREA DESCRIPTION

NAME: Aaron (205)   ACRES (GROSS): 78,884   ACRES (NFS): 78,884

GEOZONE: S09
GEOGRAPHIC PROVINCE: Coast Range

1989 WILDERNESS ATTRIBUTE RATING: 27

a   Description

(1) **Relationship to RARE II areas:** The table below displays the VCU 1/ names, VCU numbers, original WARS 2/ rating, and comments. This enables the reader to compare the roadless areas evaluated in Appendix C with previous analyses

VCU Name	VCU No.	1979 WARS Rating	Comments
Berg	503	26	
Aaron	506	21	
Derns	508	21	

(2) **History:** The area was used by the Tlingit in prehistoric times Extensive prospecting has occurred in the area over the years, resulting in the filing of numerous mining claims. Some development once occurred in Berg Basin. Aaron Creek is an alternative route for a road from the saltwater to the Canadian border, and has received considerable attention in the past few years A connection to Wrangell is also possible The flats at Aaron Creek provide storage for log rafts

(3) **Location and Access:** The area is located on the mainland and is bounded on the north by the Stikine-LeConte Wilderness, on the west by the Madan Roadless Area; on the south by Blake Channel and the Canal Roadless Area; and on the east by the Cone Roadless Area. The area is accessed by boat or floatplane from Berg Bay. Good anchorage is available in Berg Bay for small boats. There are no sites suitable for landing wheeled aircraft. There is no ferry service or road access to the area from outside There is an old trail from saltwater up Berg Creek to one of the mining prospects

1/ A VCU (Value Comparison Unit) is one of 867 watersheds which make up the forest and were differentiated for planning purposes in the Tongass Land Management Plan.
2/ Wilderness Attribute Rating System (WARS) was the nationwide system used to rate the wilderness attributes of roadless areas in the Roadless Area Review and Evaluation (RARE II).

(4) Geography and Topography: The area is generally characterized as highly-complex terrain dominated by rugged mountains, many of which reach elevations of over 3,000 feet; the tallest is over 5,000 feet Between the mountains are deep, broad valleys containing several sizable streams which ultimately feed into the main channel of Aaron Creek Near its mouth, Aaron Creek forms a wide floodplain and ends in a large grassflat at tidewater. Dominant waterforms include relatively small glaciers which occupy the highest mountains, Aaron Creek, and numerous small cirque lakes at high elevations The freshwater lakes account for 120 acres, snow and ice for another 10,903 acres, and rock covers 19,520 acres Alpine accounts for 3,480 acres The area contains 10 miles of saltwater shoreline

(5) Ecosystem:

(a) Classification: The area is classified as being in the Coast Range Geographic Province. The region is generally characterized as a core of massive, angular mountains capped with ice fields at high elevations along the Canadian border, with somewhat lower mountains, deeply-incised valleys, and glacier-fed streams near the coast This roadless area is more characteristic of the lower coastal portion of the region. There are no known areas of unique or uncommon plant/soils associations or geologic formations in the area

(b) Vegetation: Alpine vegetation dominates above an elevation of 2,500 feet Below that elevation, the mountains, hills, and well-drained outwash plains are dominated by heavy stands of western hemlock, Sitka spruce, Alaska-cedar, and scattered stands of western redcedar There are pockets of poorly-drained land along the valley bottoms which are covered with muskeg (480 acres) and scrub lodgepole pine The many snowslide and landslide paths on the steep slopes are typically covered with grass, alders and willows

There are approximately 31,638 acres of forested land of which 17,359 acres are commercial forest land. Of the commercial forest land, 14,519 acres are non-riparian old growth and 2,440 acres are riparian old growth.

(c) Soils: Soils in this area are formed in a wide variety of parent materials, including bedrock and glacial drift In general, well- or moderately-well-drained soils are on moderate to steep mountain slopes with permeable parent materials. These soils are very acidic, have cold soil temperatures, and are very high in organic matter Rooting is largely limited to the surface organic layers and the top few inches of mineral soil. These soils are usually moist, sometimes wet, but are never dry.

More-poorly-drained soils developed on less sloping areas and/or areas with impermeable soil materials. These soils have deep accumulations of organic matter and range from scrubby forested wetlands to open muskeg.

Alpine soils, generally above 2,000 feet elevation, are mostly shallow, very wet organic soils or are extremely shallow and rocky

(d) **Fish Resource:** Fish resources have been rated as part of the Tongass Land Management Plan (1979) and by the Alaska Department of Fish and Game in its Forest Habitat Integrity Program (1983) These ratings describe the value of VCU's for sport fish, commercial fish and estuaries

VCU's 503 and 506 are rated as high value for sport fish and for commercial fish

Two Alaska Department of Fish and Game numbered salmon producing streams are present within the area. Aaron Creek, the largest producer, has an average annual escapement of 1,500 pink, and 2,600 chum, coho, and king salmon

(e) **Wildlife Resource:** A small population of mountain goats lives in the area. Black bears and Sitka black-tailed deer are found in the area, as are an occasional brown bear and a small population of moose. Wolves are often seen on the grassflats This area is a major north-south travel corridor connecting the Stikine and Bradfield rivers. There are no known concentrations of marine wildlife or sea lion haul-out sites.

(f) **Threatened and Endangered Species:** The area contains no known threatened or endangered species

(6) **Current Use and Management:** The main Aaron Creek drainage (44,947 acres) was allocated to Land Use Designation (LUD) 4 in the Tongass Land Management Plan, which would allow road construction and timber harvest Two of the side drainages were allocated to LUD 2 (33,937 acres), which prohibits timber harvest They are managed for roadless recreation The narrow channel and small bay at the mouth of Aaron Creek are used by small pleasure and commercial fishing boats There is a public recreation cabin in Berg Bay near the mouth of the creek. The cabin receives moderate to high use and is seasonal in nature. Aaron Creek Trail provides access from the cabin to the grassflats beyond, and continues in a more primitive condition up Berg Creek into Berg Creek basin, a total of five miles There are no commercial overnight facilities in the area Current information indicates that some subsistence activities occur in the area primarily from residents of Wrangell.

(7) **Appearance (Apparent Naturalness):** Most of the area appears unmodified. However, minor intrusions such as the recreation cabin and the results of activities on mining claims, are evident when one is close to them. In addition, there is a stand of trees on the steep hillside on the north side of the larger bay that was harvested in 1960, and the difference in vegetation is noticeable. The area exists in a predominantly natural condition, except near the Berg Bay cabin, where some of the foreground around Berg Bay and the larger bay is visible from boats using Blake Channel A striking view of high peaks framed by the narrow entrance to Aaron Creek is also seen from the channel Overall, the area provides spectacular scenery

The majority of this roadless area, 99 percent, is natural appearing, where only ecological change has occurred (Existing Visual Condition (EVC) Type I) Less than one percent of the area appears to be untouched by human activity (EVC Type II) EVC Type III, where changes in the landscape are noticed by the average forest visitor, and EVC Type IV, where changes in the landscape are easily noticed by the average person and may attract some attention, also account for minor portions of less than one percent

Seventy-nine percent of this roadless area is inventoried Variety Class A (possessing landscape diversity that is unique for the character type), 17 percent is inventoried Variety Class B (possessing landscape diversity that is common for the character type) and the remaining four percent is inventoried Variety Class C (possessing a low degree of landscape diversity).

(8) **Surroundings (External Influences):** The area is part of a much larger roadless land mass. It abuts the Stikine-LeConte Wilderness on the north and other roadless areas on the south and east. The narrow entrance to this area and the high mountains on the boundaries effectively cut off outside influences. It is possible that public desire for a road to Canada may lead to developing the route along Aaron Creek which would change the roadless character. Moderately-heavy boat traffic frequents the Berg Bay area, and the potential for activity exists in the log storage area in the bay

(9) **Attractions and Features of Special Interest:** The public recreation cabin; the secure anchorage; the spectacular scenery; the trail, and the opportunity to view or hunt birds, bears, and moose on the grassflat and river valley, and goats on the hillsides are all special features The area contains five inventoried recreation places totaling 22,059 acres.

b. **Capability of Management as Wilderness or in an Unroaded Condition**

(1) **Manageability and management area boundaries:** The area is very well defined by topographic features with entrance at the mouth of Aaron Creek or at Berg Bay Feasibility of management in a roadless condition is high unless the mining claims are developed or the State decides to construct a highway through it to Canada.

(2) **Natural Integrity:** The area is essentially unmodified, except for minor impacts from mining and at the cabin site.

(3) **Opportunity for Solitude:** There is a high opportunity for solitude within the area. Low-flying aircraft follow Blake Channel and boats bypass the area. Present recreation use levels are low except in the immediate vicinity of the recreation cabin or around the grassflats during the fall waterfowl hunting season. Generally, a person camped inland is unlikely to see others.

(4) **Opportunity for Primitive Recreation:** The area provides primarily semi-primitive motorized and non-motorized recreation opportunities

ROS class	Acres
Primitive (P)	71,464
Semi-Primitive Non-Motorized (SPNM)	4,520
Semi-Primitive Motorized (SPM)	2,700
Roaded Natural (RN)	200

The area contains five recreation places

ROS CLASS	# OF REC. PLACES	TOTAL ACRES	CAPACITY BY RVD
P	2	16,120	1,909
SPNM	1	3,100	928
SPM	1	2,700	2,134
RN	1	140	75

There is one public recreation cabin and one maintained short trail in the area. The character of the landforms generally allows the visitor to feel remote from the sights and sounds of human activity. The area is accessible by boat from the community of Wrangell in less than two hours on somewhat protected waters. The presence of both black and brown bears also presents a degree of challenge and a need for woods skills and experience

(5) **Special Features (Ecologic, Geologic, Scientific, Cultural):** There are opportunities to observe and study wildlife, geologic formations, ecology, and the forces and processes which formed these mountains   The area has high scenic quality

c. Availability for Management as Wilderness or in an Unroaded Condition

(1) Resource Potentials

(a) **Recreation Potential:** There is potential for additional trails and shelters located at high elevations.

(b) **Fish Resource:** The Tongass Land Management Plan, amended Winter 1985-86 identifies fish habitat enhancement projects. No projects have been identified for this area.

(c) **Wildlife Resource:** As identified in the Tongass Land Management Plan, amended 1985-86 habitat improvement projects are planned in the area. The grassflats have been burned several times to improve waterfowl habitat. Enhancement opportunities include slashing portions of the older, decadent willow to promote new growth for moose, and improvement of habitat for waterfowl.

(d) **Timber Resource:** There are 7,219 acres inventoried as tentatively suitable for timber harvest. This includes 1,500 acres of riparian old growth and 5,520 acres of non-riparian old growth Some acres of second-growth spruce and alder have resulted from timber harvest in 1960

(e) **Land Use Authorizations:** The log storage area at the mouth of Aaron Creek is under special use permit with the State

(f) **Minerals:** There are numerous mining claims in the area The potential for development of those claims is unknown

(g) **Areas of Scientific Interest:** The area contains no inventoried potential Research Natural Areas. The area has not been identified for any other scientific value.

(2) Management Considerations

(a) **Timber:** The potential for managing timber in this roadless area is closely linked to the development of an access road up the main river valley and the development of a log transfer facility (LTF).

(b) **Transportation:** This valley has been studied in the past, and continues to be considered as a possible road route to link the community of Wrangell to the Canadian highway system

(c) **Wilderness/Wildlife:** Maintenance of the area in a roadless condition enhances opportunities to manage the adjacent roadless areas as Wilderness and to provide enhanced opportunities for solitude and primitive recreation. It also maintains opportunities for wildlife, such as wolves, bears, and moose, to move between the Stikine-LeConte Wilderness and other areas to the southeast.

(d) **Fire:** The area has no significant fire history

(e) **Insects and Disease:** Endemic tree diseases common to Southeast Alaska are present; there are no know epidemic disease occurrences

(f) **Land Status:** The entire area is National Forest Systems Land

d. Relationship to Communities and Other Roadless and Wilderness Areas

(1) **Nearby Roadless and Wilderness Areas and Uses:** The Aaron Creek area is part of a larger mainland unroaded land mass that is located between the Madan Roadless Area to the west, the Cone Roadless Area to the east, and the Harding Roadless Area to the south. The mainland areas receive light use inland, except around Berg Bay and at the mouth of Aaron Creek

(2) **Distance From Population Centers (Accessibility):** Approximate distances from population centers are as follows·

Community		Air Miles	Water Miles
Juneau	(Pop. 23,729)	150	180
Petersburg	(Pop. 4,040)	35	60
Wrangell	(Pop. 2,836)	8	18
Ketchikan	(Pop. 12,705)	78	98

Wrangell is the nearest stop on the Alaska Marine Highway.

(3) Interest by Proponents:

(a) Moratorium areas: The area has not been identified as a "moratorium" area or proposed as Wilderness in legislative initiatives to date

(b) Local users/residents: Local Wrangell residents have a moderate degree of interest in maintaining the integrity of the area   Some would like to see mining development take place and construction of a road connecting Wrangell to the Canadian road network   Others support maintaining the roadless character of the area for wildlife and scenic values.

e. Environmental Consequences

ALTERNATIVE ANALYSIS TO BE DONE LATER

INDIVIDUAL ROADLESS AREA DESCRIPTION

NAME: Cone (206)   ACRES (GROSS): 128,574   ACRES (NFS)· 128,574

GEOZONE: S09
GEOGRAPHIC PROVINCE: Coast Range

1989 WILDERNESS ATTRIBUTE RATING: 27

a. Description

(1) Relationship to RARE II areas: The table below displays the VCU 1/
names, VCU numbers, original WARS 2/ rating, and comments. This enables
the reader to compare the roadless areas evaluated in Appendix C with
previous analyses.

VCU Name	VCU No.	1979 WARS Rating	Comments
Cone	507	24	The area drains entirely into Canada

(2) History: Since the area drains entirely into Canada and is accessible
only with great difficulty from the Alaskan side, there has been little use
of the area in the past. The area has been prospected for minerals and
claims have been located

(3) Location and Access: The Cone Roadless Area is located on the
mainland. It is bounded on the north by the Canadian border, on the west
by the Stikine-LeConte Wilderness and the Aaron Roadless Area, and on the
south by the Harding and Bradfield Roadless Areas Access is only by foot
or by helicopter. No suitable sites exist for landing wheeled aircraft

(4) Geography and Topography: The area is generally characterized as
highly-complex terrain dominated by rugged mountains, many of which reach
elevations of over 5,000 feet; the tallest is over 6,800 feet Between the
mountains are deep, narrow valleys containing several sizable streams which
ultimately feed into the Stikine and Iskut Rivers. Dominant waterforms
include the high velocity streams and small glaciers which occupy the
highest mountains. Alpine covers 2,397 acres, ice and snow cover another
32,363 acres, and rock accounts for about 39,961 acres. The area does not
contain any shoreline on saltwater or freshwater lakes

1/ A VCU (Value Comparison Unit) is one of 867 watersheds which make up the
   forest and were differentiated for planning purposes in the Tongass Land
   Management Plan.
2/ Wilderness Attribute Rating System (WARS) was the nationwide system used to
   rate the wilderness attributes of roadless areas in the Roadless Area
   Review and Evaluation (RARE II).

(5) Ecosystem:

(a) Classification: The area is classified as being in the Coast
Range Geographic Province. That region is generally characterized as
a core of massive, angular mountains capped with ice fields at high
elevations along the Canadian border, with somewhat lower mountains,
deeply-incised valleys and glacier-fed streams closer to the coast
This roadless area is more characteristic of the higher, mountainous
portion but without the massive ice fields. There are no known areas
of unique or uncommon plant/soils associations or geologic formations
in the area

(b) Vegetation: Alpine vegetation dominates above an elevation of
2,500 feet. Below that elevation, the steep mountain sides are
heavily marked with snowslide and landslide paths which are typically
covered with grass, alders and willows. Occasionally, cottonwoods may
be found along the valley bottoms and floodplains About 100 acres
are classified as muskeg.

There are approximately 29,552 acres of forested land of which 11,591
acres are commercial forest land. Of the commercial forest land,
9,242 acres are non-riparian old growth and 2,214 acres are riparian
old growth

(c) Soils: Soils in this area are formed in a wide variety of parent
materials, including bedrock and glacial drift In general, well- or
moderately-well-drained soils are on moderate to steep mountain slopes
with permeable parent materials. These soils are very acidic, have
cold soil temperatures, and are very high in organic matter Rooting
is largely limited to the surface organic layers and the top few
inches of mineral soil These soils are usually moist, sometimes wet,
but are never dry.

More-poorly-drained soils developed on less sloping areas and/or areas
with impermeable soil materials These soils have deep accumulations
of organic matter and range from scrubby, forested wetlands to open
muskeg.

Alpine soils, generally above 2,000 feet elevation, are mostly
shallow, very wet organic soils or are extremely shallow and rocky

(d) Fish Resource: Fish resources have been rated as part of the
Tongass Land Management Plan (1979) and by the Alaska Department of
Fish and Game in its Forest Habitat Integrity Program (1983) These
ratings describe the value of VCU's for sport fish, commercial fish
and estuaries.

None of the VCU's in this area are rated high for any of the values

Several drainages in this area form the headwaters of the Katete and
other rivers which empty into the Stikine River The Katete River is
in Canada, and no escapement data is available

(e) **Wildlife Resource:** A small population of mountain goats ranges over the area, as do black and brown bears, and moose

(f) **Threatened and Endangered Species:** The area contains no known threatened or endangered species.

(6) **Current Use and Management:** The area was allocated to Land Use Designation 2 (128,394 acres) in the Tongass Land Management Plan, which prohibits timber harvest and is managed for roadless recreation Land or water access to the area is difficult, requiring entry into Canada on the Stikine River then up the Katete River, entering the area on foot There are no facilities of any kind. The area gets little use There is no known subsistence use.

(7) **Appearance (Apparent Naturalness):** The area appears unmodified Some of the area may be seen in the background from boaters on the Stikine River.

The majority of this roadless area (98 percent) is natural appearing, where only ecological change has occurred (Existing Visual Condition (EVC) Type I). Two percent of this roadless area is EVC Type III, where changes in the landscape are noticed by the average forest visitor. The natural appearance of the landscape remains dominant.

About 82 percent of this roadless area is inventoried Variety Class A (possessing landscape diversity that is unique for the character type), and 17 percent is inventoried Variety Class B (possessing landscape diversity that is common for the character type).

(8) **Surroundings (External Influences):** The area is part of a much larger roadless land mass. Activities on the Canadian side of the border are most likely to influence this area. While there are no known intrusions at the present time, the area around the Iskut River is heavily mineralized and mining discoveries could lead to mine development in the area The impact of a dam for hydroelectric power generation on the Iskut River in Canada may impact this area to some degree.

(9) **Attractions and Features of Special Interest:** The natural features of the area, remoteness, solitude, the scenery, and the opportunity to see wildlife and to study the processes which formed this country may all be attractions. The area contains no inventoried recreation places, and there are no improved trails.

b. Capability of Management as Roadless or in an Unroaded Condition

(1) **Manageability and Management Area Boundaries:** The area is very well defined by topographic features. Feasibility of management in a roadless condition is very high unless minerals are discovered and developed

(2) **Natural Integrity:** The area is unmodified.

(3) **Opportunity for Solitude:** There is a high opportunity for solitude within the area   Low-flying airplanes traveling between Wrangell and the Canadian mines near the Iskut River may at times pass over the area and be observed by people in this roadless area   Present recreation use levels are very low

(4) **Opportunity for Primitive Recreation:** The area provides primarily primitive opportunities

ROS Class	Acres
Primitive (P)	128,488

The area contains no recreation places.

There are no developed recreation facilities in the area. The character of the landforms allows the visitor to feel remote from the sights and sounds of human activity. The area is accessible with difficulty and requires entry into Canada by way of the Stikine River Valley and then on foot up the Katete River drainage, presenting a high degree of physical challenge The presence of both black and brown bears also presents a degree of challenge and a need for woods skills and experience.

(5) **Special Features (Ecologic, Geologic, Scientific, Cultural)·** There are opportunities to observe and study wildlife and the various forces which formed these mountains

c. Availability for Management as Wilderness or in an Unroaded Condition

(1) Resource Potentials

(a) **Recreation Potential:** Potential for increased use or facility development is low until access is improved If a road to Canada is constructed through the area, then use and demand will likely increase somewhat. However, lack of specific destination features will limit use.

(b) **Fish Resource:** The Tongass Land Management Plan, amended Winter 1985-86, identifies fish habitat enhancement projects. No known enhancement projects are planned for this area.

(c) **Wildlife Resource:** As identified in the Tongass Land Management Plan, amended 1985-86, no habitat improvement projects are planned in the area. There is potential for moose and goat habitat enhancement however.

(d) **Timber Resource:** There are 4,229 acres considered tentatively suitable for harvest at this time This includes 1,036 acres of riparian old growth, and 3,159 acres of non-riparian old growth Harvest is not likely unless a road is built into the area for other purposes No harvest has occurred in the area in the past

(e) Land Use Authorizations: A 69 KV powerline has been authorized to be constructed from the Tyee power plant at the head of Bradfield Canal, up the North Fork of the Bradfield River and entering Canada by way of the Craig River That portion in the headwaters of the Craig River would traverse this area

(f) Minerals: There are several invalid mining claims in the area The potential for development of new claims is unknown

(g) Areas of Scientific Interest: The area contains no inventoried potential Research Natural Areas The area has not been identified for any other scientific value

(2) **Management Considerations**

(a) **Timber:** There is no potential for managing timber in this roadless area without road access. The nature of the steep slopes and scattered timber make it doubtful that the timber harvest would be economical even if the road were financed by other sources

(b) **Transportation:** Two routes being considered for a possible road like between saltwater and the Canadian highway system include portions of this roadless area. One route would come from Wrangell, up Aaron Creek, and would enter this area in the West Fork of the Katete River, accessing the main Stikine River Valley Another proposal is to build a road from Bradfield Canal up the North Fork of the Bradfield River and entering Canada through this area by way of the Craig River drainage.

(c) **Wilderness/Wildlife:** Maintenance of the area in a roadless condition enhances opportunities to manage the adjacent roadless areas as wilderness and to provide enhanced opportunities for solitude and primitive recreation It also maintains opportunities for wildlife, such as wolves, bears, and moose, to move between the Stikine River Valley and other areas to the southeast.

(d) **Fire:** The area has no significant fire history

(e) **Insects and Disease:** Endemic tree diseases common to Southeast Alaska are present; there are no know epidemic disease occurrences

(f) **Land Status:** All National Forest lands.

d. **Relationship to Communities and Other Roadless and Wilderness Areas**

(1) **Nearby Roadless and Wilderness Areas and Uses:** The Cone area is part of a larger mainland unroaded land mass that is located between the Bradfield Roadless Area to the southeast, the Harding Roadless Area to the southwest, the Aaron Roadless Area to the west, and the Canadian mountains to the north. The mainland areas receive light use inland, away from saltwater access.

(2) **Distance From Population Centers (Accessibility):** Approximate distances from population centers are as follows

Community			Air Miles	Water/Overland Miles
Juneau	(Pop	23,729)	156	186
Petersburg	(Pop	4,040)	41	66
Wrangell	(Pop	2,836)	14	24
Ketchikan	(Pop.	12,705)	84	104

Wrangell is the nearest stop on the Alaska Marine Highway

(3)   Interest by Proponents:

(a) **Moratorium areas:** The area has not been identified as a "moratorium" area or proposed as Wilderness in legislative initiatives to date.

(b) **Local users/residents:** There is virtually no local use of the area. Local Wrangell residents have a high degree of interest in developing a road from Wrangell through this area to the Canadian highway system.

e. **Environmental Consequences**

ALTERNATIVE ANALYSIS TO BE DONE LATER

INDIVIDUAL ROADLESS AREA DESCRIPTION

NAME: Harding (207)   ACRES (GROSS): 177,598   ACRES (NFS): 177,598

GEOZONE: S09
GEOGRAPHIC PROVINCE: Coast Range

1989 WILDERNESS ATTRIBUTE RATING: 22

a. Description

    (1) Relationship to RARE II areas: The table below displays the VCU 1/ names, VCU numbers, acres, original WARS 2/ rating, and comments This enables the reader to compare the roadless areas evaluated in Appendix C with previous analyses.

VCU Name	VCU No.	1979 WARS Rating	Comments
Blake	505*	22	
Marten	509	23	
Campbell	510	22	
Harding	511	23	
Tyee	518	22	
Eagle	519	26	
Hoya	520	21	
Canal	521	22	

*--The roadless area includes only part of this VCU

    (2) History: The area was used by the Tlingit in prehistoric and historic times. While the area has probably been prospected for minerals, there are no known mining claims. In 1984, a 138 KV powerline was constructed through part of the area along the south side of Bradfield Canal

    (3) Location and Access: The area is located on the mainland and is bounded on the west by Blake Channel and on the southeast by Misty Fiords National Monument. It is bounded by other roadless areas on all other sides. The area is accessed by saltwater along Blake Channel and by Bradfield Canal which bisects the area. Several freshwater lakes are accessible by floatplane. There are no sites suitable for landing wheeled aircraft.

1/ A VCU (Value Comparison Unit) is one of 867 watersheds which make up the forest and were differentiated for planning purposes in the Tongass Land Management Plan.
2/ Wilderness Attribute Rating System (WARS) was the nationwide system used to rate the wilderness attributes of roadless areas in the Roadless Area Review and Evaluation (RARE II).

(4) Geography and Topography: The area is generally characterized as highly-complex terrain dominated by rugged mountains, many of which reach elevations of over 3,000 feet   The tallest is over 4,000 feet   Between the mountains are deep, narrow valleys containing several sizable streams which ultimately feed into Blake Channel or Bradfield Canal   Dominant waterforms include numerous streams, several lakes covering a total area of about 1,000 acres, and relatively small glaciers which occupy the highest mountains   Alpine accounts for 3,500 acres, ice and snow 4,280 acres, and rock covers 20,660 acres   The area contains 32 miles of shoreline on saltwater

(5) Ecosystem:

(a) Classification: The area is classified as being in the Coast Range Geographic Province   That region is generally characterized as a core of massive, angular mountains capped with ice fields at high elevation along the Canadian border, with somewhat lower mountains, deeply-incised valleys, and glacier-fed streams closer to the coast This roadless area is more characteristic of the lower coastal portion.   There are no known areas of unique or uncommon plant/soils associations or geologic formations in the area.

(b) Vegetation: Above 2,500 feet, alpine vegetation dominates Below that elevation the steep mountain sides are heavily marked with snowslide and landslide paths that are typically covered with grass, alders and willows. Occasionally, cottonwoods may be found along the valley bottoms and floodplains   Muskeg occupies about 580 acres

There are approximately 72,006 acres of forested land of which 37 125 acres are commercial forest land   Of the commercial forest land 31,564 acres are non-riparian old growth and 5,000 acres are riparian old growth.

(c) Soils: Soils in this area are formed in a wide variety of parent materials, including bedrock and glacial drift. In general, well- or moderately-well-drained soils are found on moderate to steep mountain slopes with permeable parent materials   These soils are very acidic, have cold soil temperatures, and are very high in organic matter Rooting is largely limited to the surface organic layers and the top few inches of mineral soil   These soils are usually moist, sometimes wet, but are never dry.

More-poorly-drained soils developed on less-sloping areas and/or areas with impermeable soil materials. These soils have deep accumulations of organic matter and range from scrubby, forested wetlands to open muskeg.

Alpine soils, generally above 2,000 feet elevation, are mostly shallow, very wet organic soils or are extremely shallow and rocky.

(d) **Fish Resource:** Fish resources have been rated as part of the Tongass Land Management Plan (1979) and by the Alaska Department of Fish and Game in its Forest Habitat Integrity Program (1983). These ratings describe the value of VCU's for sport fish, commercial fish and estuaries.

VCU's 509, 511, and 519 rated as high value for sport fish. VCU's rated as highly valued for commercial fish are 510, 511, and 519.

Eleven ADF&G numbered salmon producing streams are present in the area. The most productive are Harding River, Eagle River and Martin Creek. The Harding has an average annual peak escapement of 8,200 pink, 14,000 chum, numerous coho, several hundred kings, and some steelhead. Eagle River has escapements of 271,400 pink, and some kings, coho, and steelhead. Martin Creek has escapements of 11,300 pink, and a good run of steelhead. Eagle River and Martin Creek are presently attracting local and guided steelhead fishermen.

(e) **Wildlife Resource:** A small population of mountain goats ranges over the area, as do black and brown bears, and moose.

(f) **Threatened and Endangered Species:** The area contains no known threatened or endangered species.

(6) **Current Use and Management:** Four drainages in the area (VCU's 509, 511, 518, and 519) were allocated to Land Use Designation 2 (55,240 acres) in the Tongass Land Management Plan, which prohibits timber harvest and is managed for roadless recreation. The other four drainages (VCU's 505, 510, 520, and 521) were allocated to Land Use Designation 4 (56,786 acres) which allows road construction and timber harvest. Blake Channel and Bradfield Canal receive moderately-heavy use by commercial and pleasure boats. The shoreline is mostly rocky and receives little recreation use. There are two public recreation cabins on inland lakes and one at saltwater near the mouth of Harding River. There is no known subsistence use in the area.

Adjacent to and partially within this area is development for the Tyee power project. This includes an underground intake and helicopter pad at Tyee Lake, and support facilities below along saltwater. The support facilities include a powerhouse, powerlines, small dock and storage building, three houses for permanent residences, and a gravel landing strip. All of this area has been State selected. Also nearby are a small administrative cabin, log transfer facility, and a log storage area.

(7) **Appearance (Apparent Naturalness):** That part of the area north of Bradfield Canal appears unmodified. The area south of Bradfield Canal appears essentially unmodified except for occasional sightings of the Tyee powerline.

The majority of this roadless area (96 percent) is natural appearing, where only ecological change has occurred (Existing Visual Condition (EVC) Type I). Four percent of this roadless area is EVC Type III, where changes in the landscape are noticed by the average forest visitor, but the natural appearance of the landscape remains dominant.

Forty-three percent of this roadless area is inventoried Variety Class A
(possessing landscape diversity that is unique for the character type), 49
percent is inventoried Variety Class B (possessing landscape diversity that
is common for the character type) and the remaining eight percent is
inventoried Variety Class C (possessing a low degree of landscape
diversity)

(8) **Surroundings (External Influences):** The area is part of a much larger
roadless land mass Boats plying the waters of Blake Channel and Bradfield
Canal may be visible from within parts of the area but usually are not
intrusive Low-flying airplanes and helicopters accessing the Tyee power
site or the freshwater lakes may temporarily distract visitors in the
area The development at the Tyee Power site is also an external impact

(9) **Attractions and Features of Special Interest:** The natural features of
the area, the scenery, and the opportunity to see wildlife and to study the
processes which formed this country may all be attractions High quality
fishing opportunities in the streams and lakes are also an attraction The
area contains 13 inventoried recreation places totaling 21,762 acres
There are no improved trails in the area.

b. **Capability of Management as Wilderness or in an Unroaded Condition**

(1) **Manageability and Management Area Boundaries:** The area is generally
well defined by topographic features. Feasibility of management in a
roadless condition is high on the northern side of Bradfield Canal and
somewhat less on the southern side where there is an existing power
transmission line and associated developments There is the potential for
development of another powerline on the south side of the area

(2) **Natural Integrity:** The area is unmodified except for the existing
powerline and development, and minor timber harvest conducted in 1955 on
the north shore of Bradfield Canal.

(3) **Opportunity for Solitude:** There is a high opportunity for solitude
within the area. Low-flying airplanes traveling to the Tyee power plant or
to the inland lakes may at times pass over the area and be observed by
people in this roadless area. Present recreation use levels are low except
around the public recreation cabins and occasionally at the mouths of some
streams. Generally, a person camped or traveling inland is unlikely to see
others

(4) **Opportunity for Primitive Recreation:** The area provides primarily
primitive recreation opportunities:

ROS Class	Acres
Primitive (P)	90,701
Semi-Primitive Non-Motorized (SPNM)	10,722
Semi-Primitive Motorized (SPM)	10,603

The area contains 13 recreation places

ROS CLASS	# OF REC. PLACES	TOTAL ACRES	CAPACITY BY RVD
P	5	16,709	·3,674
SPNM	2	1,661	. 940
SPM	6	3,981	1,743

There are three public recreation cabins in the area. The character of the
landforms generally allows the visitor to feel remote from the sights and
sounds of human activity. The area is accessible by boat from the
community of Wrangell in less than four hours, and from Ketchikan in
approximately eight hours. Access on land is difficult, offering a high
degree of physical challenge The presence of both black and brown bears
also presents a degree of challenge and a need for woods skills and
experience.

(5) Special Features (Ecologic, Geologic, Scientific, Cultural): There
are opportunities to observe and study fish and wildlife and the various
forces which formed these mountains.

c. Availability for Management a Wilderness or in an Unroaded Condition

(1) Resource Potentials

(a) Recreation Potential: There is potential for additional
outfitter and guide permits and for developed trails and additional
cabins or shelters

(b) Fish Resource: The Tongass Land Management Plan, amended Winter
1985-86 identifies fish habitat enhancement projects Fish
enhancement projects continue to surface and there is potential for
additional projects in this area.

The Forest Service is presently studying both the Harding River and
the Eagle River for possible fish ladders All species could use the
upper Harding, and coho would be the target for the Eagle River

(c) Wildlife Resource: As identified in the Tongass Land Management
Plan, amended 1985-86 moose habitat improvement projects are planned
in the area These projects typically consist of thinning, slashing
pruning and planting for preferred browse species

(d) Timber Resource: There are 16,442 acres inventoried as
tentatively suitable for harvest. This includes 3,040 acres of
riparian old growth, and 13,142 acres of non-riparian old growth
Minor areas of second growth (thirty-five-year-old stand) are along
the shore of Bradfield Canal.

(e) Land Use Authorizations: A 138 KV powerline under special use
permit crosses part of the area south of Bradfield Canal Tyee Lake
drainage has been identified by the Federal Power Commission as a
hydropower generation site and is withdrawn from competing
management. In 1984, a tunnel was drilled from a powerhouse in the
Bradfield drainage through the mountain to the bottom of Tyee Lake to
provide water for electrical generation. This and the associated
developments previously described are under permit, but were selected
by the state and approved for conveyance.

(f) Minerals: The area generally has a low minerals rating and there
are no known current claims

(g) **Areas of Scientific Interest:** The area contains no inventoried potential Research Natural Areas The area has not been identified for any other scientific value

(2) Management Considerations

(a) The potential for managing timber in this roadless area is dependant upon market values and the development of harvest methods which will allow extraction without need for extensive roading It will also require numerous sites for transferring logs to saltwater

(b) Proposals to connect electricity generation sites and communities together in Southeast Alaska have identified the Eagle River drainage as a likely route for a transmission line to connect the Tyee station with Ketchikan. That would affect one currently unroaded drainage within this roadless area. One of the larger lakes in the area is in the Eagle River drainage and one of the existing public recreation cabins is on the shore of that lake

(c) Maintenance of the area in a roadless condition enhances opportunities to manage the adjacent roadless areas as Wilderness, and to provide enhanced opportunities for solitude and primitive recreation. It also maintains opportunities for wildlife, such as wolves, bears, and moose, to move freely through the area

(d) Fire: The area has no significant fire history

(e) **Insects and Disease:** Endemic tree diseases common to Southeast Alaska are present; there are no know epidemic disease occurrences

(f) **Land Status:** The State-selected lands for the Tyee power site include acres within this roadless area.

d. Relationship to Communities and Other Roadless and Wilderness Areas

(1) **Nearby Roadless and Wilderness Areas and Uses:** The Harding area is part of a larger mainland unroaded landmass. Adjacent roadless areas include the Aaron, Cone, Bradfield, and Anan Roadless Areas The Stikine-LeConte Wilderness is located about 10 miles to the north The mainland areas receive light use inland away from saltwater access

(2) **Distance From Population Centers (Accessibility):** Approximate distances from population centers are as follows:

Community		Air Miles	Water Miles
Juneau	(Pop. 23,729)	175	215
Petersburg	(Pop. 4,040)	65	90
Wrangell	(Pop. 2,836)	35	40
Ketchikan	(Pop. 12,705)	55	90

Wrangell is the nearest stop on the Alaska Marine Highway

(3) Interest by Proponents:

(a) **Moratorium areas:** The area has not been identified as a "moratorium" area or proposed as Wilderness in legislative initiatives to date

(b) **Local users/residents:** Most use of the area is associated with commercial fishing in Bradfield Canal and Blake Channel and with sport fishing in some of the major streams in the area There has been some interest by residents of Wrangell in limiting the number of outfitter guides in the area.

e. **Environmental Consequences**

ALTERNATIVE ANALYSIS TO BE DONE LATER

INDIVIDUAL ROADLESS AREA DESCRIPTION

NAME: Bradfield (208)   ACRES (GROSS): 212,872   ACRES (NFS): 212,872

GEOZONE: S09
GEOGRAPHIC PROVINCE: Coast Range

1989 WILDERNESS ATTRIBUTE RATING: 25

a   Description

(1) **Relationship to RARE II areas:** The following table displays the VCU 1/ names, VCU numbers, original WARS 2/ rating, and comments. This enables the reader to compare the roadless areas evaluated in Appendix C with previous analyses.

VCU Name	VCU No.	1979 WARS Rating	Comments
White	512	24	
North Fork	513	23	
Bradfield	514*	20	
Cloud	515*	23	
Glacier	516*	24	
East Fork	517*	20	

*--The roadless area includes only part of this VCU

(2) **History:** The area may have been used by the Tlingit in prehistoric and historic times. From 1966 to 1982, the Bradfield River, North Fork, and East Fork Timber Sales were logged in the Bradfield drainage In 1984, a 138 KV power generation plant was constructed near the mouth of the Bradfield River to the west of this roadless area.

(3) **Location and Access:** The area is located on the mainland and is bounded on the west by the Harding Roadless Area, and on the southeast and east by Misty Fiords National Monument. A minor portion is bounded on the northeast by the Canadian border. The area is accessible by saltwater along Bradfield Canal There is a gravel landing strip near the power generation site suitable for landing small wheeled aircraft

1/ A VCU (Value Comparison Unit) is one of 867 watersheds which make up the forest and were differentiated for planning purposes in the Tongass Land Management Plan.
2/ Wilderness Attribute Rating System (WARS) was the nationwide system used to rate the wilderness attributes of roadless areas in the Roadless Area Review and Evaluation (RARE II).

(4) **Geography and Topography:** The area is generally characterized as highly-complex terrain dominated by rugged mountains, many of which reach elevations of over 4,000 feet, the tallest is over 6,800 feet Between the mountains are deep, narrow valleys containing the high-energy Bradfield and White Rivers which feed the head of Bradfield Canal Dominant waterforms include relatively small glaciers which occupy the highest mountains, numerous streams, waterfalls and several small cirque lakes The lakes occupy 320 acres, with ice and snow covering 36,201 acres Rock covers 64,957 acres, and alpine accounts for 2,335 acres The area contains no saktwater shoreline

(5) **Ecosystem:**

(a) **Classification:** The area is classified as being in the Coast Range Geographic Province. That region is generally characterized as a core of massive, angular mountains capped with ice fields at high elevation along the Canadian border, with somewhat lower mountains, deeply-incised valleys and glacier-fed streams closer to the coast This roadless area is more characteristic of the higher portion of the region but without the massive ice fields. There are no known areas of unique or uncommon plant/soils associations There is a small hot spring in the area.

(b) **Vegetation:** Alpine vegetation dominates above 2,500 feet elevation Below that elevation the steep mountain sides and river floodplains are heavily forested with Sitka spruce and lesser amounts of western hemlock. The steep slopes are heavily marked with snowslide and landslide paths which are typically covered with grass, alders and willows. Stands of cottonwood are also found along the valley bottoms and floodplains There are about 40 acres of muskeg inventoried in this area

There are approximately 53,950 acres of forested land of which 18,298 acres are commercial forest land Of the commercial forest land, 15,860 acres are non-riparian old growth and 2,338 acres are riparian old growth.

(c) **Soils:** Soils in this area are formed in a wide variety of parent material, including bedrock and glacial drift In general, well- or moderately-well-drained soils are on moderate to steep mountain slopes with permeable parent materials These soils are very acidic, have cold soil temperatures, and are very high in organic matter Rooting is largely limited to the surface organic layers and the top few inches of mineral soil. These soils are usually moist, sometimes wet, but are never dry.

More-poorly-drained soils developed on less-sloping areas and/or areas with impermeable soil materials. These soils have deep accumulations of organic matter and range from scrubby forested wetlands to open muskeg.

Alpine soils, generally above 2,000 feet elevation, are mostly shallow, very wet organic soils or are extremely shallow and rocky

(d) **Fish Resource:** Fish resources have been rated as part of the Tongass Land Management Plan (1979) and by the Alaska Department of Fish and Game in its Forest Habitat Integrity Program (1983) These ratings describe the value of VCU's for sport fish, commercial fish and estuaries.

The VCU's which are rated as high value for sport fish are 513, 514, and 515 VCU's rated as highly valued for commercial fish are 513, 514, 515, 516, and 517

The two main channels of the Bradfield River are identified by the Alaska Department of Fish and Game as important for producing salmon. The river produces coho, pink, chum, sockeye and king salmon and steelhead.

(e) **Wildlife Resource:** Brown bear are prevalent in the area A small population of mountain goats ranges over the area, as do black bear, and moose. Bald eagles nest in the area.

(f) **Threatened and Endangered Species:** The area contains no known threatened or endangered species.

(6) **Current Use and Management:** Two drainages in the area (VCU's 512 and 513) were allocated to Land Use Designation 2 (65,583 acres) in the Tongass Land Management Plan, which prohibits timber harvest and is managed for roadless recreation. The other four drainages (VCU's 505, 510, 520, and 521) were allocated to Land Use Designation 4 (117,907 acres) which allows road construction and timber harvest.

The area at the head of Bradfield Canal around the power generation facility receives moderately-heavy use by people visiting and working at the site. Moderate amounts of brown bear and waterfowl hunting takes place in the lower Bradfield area. Goat hunting is popular in the higher elevations. There are no public recreation facilities in the area There is no known subsistence use in the area.

(7) **Appearance (Apparent Naturalness):** The White River drainage and the area at higher elevations appear natural and unmodified However, the area at the mouth of the Bradfield River, and areas extending up the valley bottoms of both forks of that river appear extensively modified by past roading and timber harvest. Although these modified areas are outside this roadless area boundary, the effects of the past timber harvest are evident as seen from the roadless area.

The majority of this roadless area (85 percent) is natural appearing, where only ecological change has occurred (Existing Visual Condition (EVC) Type I). One percent of this roadless area is EVC Type III, where changes in the landscape are noticed by the average forest visitor The natural appearance of the landscape remains dominant. Six percent of the area is in EVC Type IV, where changes in the landscape are easily noticed by the average person and may attract some attention. They appear to be disturbances but resemble natural patterns Eight percent is in EVC Type V where changes in the landscape are obvious to the average person, and appear to be major disturbances.

The entire roadless area is inventoried Variety Class A (possessing landscape diversity that is unique for the character type)

(8) **Surroundings (External Influences):** The area is part of a much larger roadless land mass Low-flying aircraft accessing the Tyee power site are common and may attract attention in the southwestern portion of the area Timber harvest in the valley bottoms which penetrate the roadless area is also an external influence. Generally, the remainder of the area is isolated.

(9) **Attractions and Features of Special Interest:** The natural features of the area, the scenery, and the opportunity to see wildlife and to study the processes which formed this country may all be attractions The area contains four inventoried recreation places totaling 6,473 acres There are no improved trails in the area.

b. **Capability of Management as Wilderness or in an Unroaded Condition**

(1) **Manageability and Management Area Boundaries:** The area is well defined by topographic features. Entry into the area is largely restricted to the single location at the head of Bradfield Canal.

(2) **Natural Integrity:** The White River drainage, the upper elevations , and the upper reaches of both branches of the Bradfield River have not been modified The valley bottoms and lower slopes along much of the Bradfield River have been extensively roaded, and timber stands have been harvested. The natural high energy movement of the river in its floodplain has reclaimed the roads in several places

(3) **Opportunity for Solitude:** There is a high opportunity for solitude within the area. Boats and low-flying airplanes traveling to the Tyee power plant are common and may be observed by people in this roadless area   Present recreation use levels are low except around the grassflats at the mouths of the rivers. Generally, a person camped or traveling inland is unlikely to see others.

(4) **Opportunity for Primitive Recreation:** The area provides primarily primitive non-motorized recreation opportunities

ROS Class	Acres
Primitive (P)	142,028
Semi-Primitive Non-Motorized (SPNM)	24,945
Semi-Primitive Motorized (SPM)	200
Roaded Modified (RM)	16,656

The area contains four recreation places.

ROS CLASS	# OF REC. PLACES	TOTAL ACRES	CAPACITY BY RVD
P .	2	920	355
SPM	1	100	9
RM	1	5,453	608

There are no public recreation facilities in the area. The character of
the landforms generally allows the visitor to feel remote from the sights
and sounds of human activity The area is accessible by boat from the
community of Wrangell in less than four hours, and from Ketchikan in
approximately eight hours Access on land is difficult, offering a high
degree of physical challenge The presence of both black and brown bears
also presents a degree of challenge and a need for woods skills and
experience.

(5) Special Features (Ecologic, Geologic, Scientific, Cultural): There
are opportunities to observe and study fish and wildlife and the various
forces which formed the landscape There is also a small undeveloped hot
spring in the area.

c. Availability for Management as Wilderness or in an Unroaded Condition

   (1) Resource Potentials

      (a) Recreation Potential: There is potential for outfitter and guide
      permits and for developed trails and cabins or shelters

      (b) Fish Resource: The Tongass Land Management Plan, amended Winter
      1985-86 identifies fish habitat enhancement projects No fish
      enhancement projects are planned in this area. There may be an
      opportunity for rehabilitation of stream channels damaged by roading
      and logging on the Bradfield River.

      (c) Wildlife Resource: As identified in the Tongass Land Management
      Plan, amended 1985-86 wildlife habitat improvement projects are
      planned in the area. There is potential for waterfowl enhancement and
      browse regeneration (willow slashing) for moose

      (d) Timber Resource: There are 5,735 acres inventoried as
      tentatively suitable for harvest. This includes 979 acres of riparian
      old growth and 4,696 acres of non-riparian old growth

      (e) Land Use Authorizations: A support camp and a power generating
      plant which uses water from Tyee Lake are under special use permit
      near the head of Bradfield Canal. Authorization has been given for
      the development of a 69 KV power transmission line up the North Fork
      of the Bradfield River to the Canadian border to serve mining
      developments in Canada. No construction has begun on this project to
      date. The State of Alaska has appropriated $150,000 to complete an
      Environmental Impact Statement addressing the impacts associated with
      a road up the North Fork of the Bradfield River

      (f) Minerals: The area generally has a low minerals rating although
      the White River drainage is rated fairly high. There are several
      claims near the mouth of the Bradfield River.

      (g) Areas of Scientific Interest: The area contains no inventoried
      potential Research Natural Areas The area has not been identified
      for any other scientific value

(2) Management Considerations

(a) **Timber:** The areas along the river bottoms have been extensively harvested and roaded . The roads which cross rivers in the flat valley bottoms were bridged, and were washed out by high water flows or were removed following harvest activities   Because harvesting has concluded, roaded access stops at the first bridge crossing which is approximately two miles from saltwater   The timber remaining for harvest is in areas where high development costs will preclude development for the immediate future   The areas which have been harvested are production sites and will be managed for second growth

(b) **Utilities:** There are current proposals to construct a 69 KV powerline and a road from the head of Bradfield Canal along the North Fork of the Bradfield River to the Canadian border. Those proposals would affect VCU's 513 and 514. In addition the State is in the process of selecting 5,500 acres of land at the head of Bradfield Canal which could become a deep water port and community if the powerline and road to Canada are built.

(c) **Wilderness/Wildlife:** Maintenance of the area in a roadless condition enhances opportunities to manage the adjacent roadless areas as Wilderness and to provide enhanced opportunities for solitude and primitive recreation   It also maintains opportunities for wildlife. such as wolves, bears, and moose, to move freely through the area

(d) **Fire:** The area has no significant fire history

(e) **Insects and Disease:** Endemic tree diseases common to Southeast Alaska are present; there are no know epidemic disease occurrences

(f) **Land Status:** Bradfield Canal (4,090 acres) and Tyee Lake (980 acres) which are State land selections are located west of the roadless area, and may overlap the roadless area in some places

d. **Relationship to Communities and Other Roadless and Wilderness Areas**

(1) **Nearby Roadless and Wilderness Areas and Uses:** The Bradfield area is part of a larger mainland unroaded land mass that is located between the Stikine-LeConte Wilderness on the northwest, the roadless Canadian mountains to the north, and Misty Fiords National Monument on the southeast. The mainland areas receive light use inland away from saltwater access.

(2) **Distance From Population Centers (Accessibility):** Approximate distances from population centers are as follows·

Community		Air Miles	Water Miles
Juneau	(Pop. 23,729)	185	225
Petersburg	(Pop 4,040)	75	100
Wrangell	(Pop. 2,836)	45	50
Ketchikan	(Pop 12,705)	65	100

Wrangell is the nearest stop on the Alaska Marine Highway

(3) Interest by Proponents:

(a) Moratorium areas: The area has not been identified as a "moratorium" area or proposed as Wilderness in legislative initiatives to date.

(b) Local users/residents: Most use of the area is associated with power generation site and with brown bear, moose, and waterfowl hunting.

(c) Other: Interest has developed from both the Canadian and Alaska State governments for a potential road access to Canada through this area.

e. Environmental Consequences

ALTERNATIVE ANALYSIS TO BE DONE LATER

INDIVIDUAL ROADLESS AREA DESCRIPTION

NAME: Anan (209)   ACRES (GROSS): 37,933   ACRES (NFS): 37,933

GEOZONE: S09
GEOGRAPHIC PROVINCE: Coast Range

1989 WILDERNESS ATTRIBUTE RATING: 23

a. Description

(1) **Relationship to RARE II areas:** The table below displays the VCU 1/ names, VCU numbers, original WARS 2/ rating, and comments. This enables the reader to compare the roadless areas evaluated in Appendix C with previous analyses.

VCU Name	VCU No.	1979 WARS Rating	Comments
Anan	522	26	

(2) **History:** The area was inhabited by the Tlingit in prehistoric times Several cultural sites are known. In 1984, a 138 KV power transmission line was constructed through a portion of the area. The strong salmon runs have been an important commercial resource. Fish enhancement and recreation facilities have been developed in the area.

(3) **Location and Access:** The area is located on the mainland and is bounded on the northeast by the Harding Roadless Area, on the southwest by the Frosty Roadless Area, and on the northwest by Ernest Sound The area is accessible by saltwater along Ernest Sound and Bradfield Canal Floatplanes can land on Anan and Boulder Lakes There are no sites suitable for landing small wheeled aircraft.

(4) **Geography and Topography:** The area is generally characterized as complex terrain, dominated by rounded mountains and hills, many of which reach elevations of over 2,000 feet. The tallest is approximately 3,000 feet Between the mountains are deep, narrow valleys containing two forks of Anan Creek and two long, narrow lakes. Several smaller lakes exist near the headwaters and numerous small cirque lakes occur in the alpine These lakes total 1,781 acres. About 340 acres are classified as alpine, and 2,081 acres as rock. The area contains six miles of shoreline on saltwater

---

1/ A VCU (Value Comparison Unit) is one of 867 watersheds which make up the forest and were differentiated for planning purposes in the Tongass Land Management Plan.
2/ Wilderness Attribute Rating System (WARS) was the nationwide system used to rate the wilderness attributes of roadless areas in the Roadless Area Review and Evaluation (RARE II).

(5) Ecosystem:

(a) Classification: The area is classified as being in the Coast
Range Geographic Province   That province is generally characterized
as a core of massive, angular mountains capped with ice fields at high
elevation along the Canadian border, with somewhat lower mountains,
deeply-incised valleys and glacier-fed streams closer to the coast
This roadless area is more characteristic of the lower portion of the
region with no glaciers and relatively low, rounded landforms   There
are no known areas of unique or uncommon plant/soils associations

(b) Vegetation: Alpine vegetation dominates above 2,500 feet
elevation. Below that elevation, there are extensive areas of muskeg
(40 acres) and scrub lodgepole pine. Hillsides and steeper slopes
with better drainage are heavily forested with Sitka spruce and lesser
amounts of western hemlock.

There are approximately 33,192 acres of forested land of which 16,126
acres are commercial forest land. Of the commercial forest land,
15,105 acres are non-riparian old growth and 1,020 acres are riparian
old growth.

(c) Soils: Soils in this area are formed in a wide variety of parent
material, including bedrock and glacial drift. In general, well- or
moderately-well-drained soils are on moderate to steep mountain slopes
with permeable parent materials. These soils are very acidic, have
cold soil temperatures, and are very high in organic matter   Rooting
is largely limited to the surface organic layers and the top few
inches of mineral soil. These soils are usually moist, sometimes wet,
but are never dry.

More-poorly-drained soils developed on less-sloping areas and/or areas
with impermeable soil materials. These soils have deep accumulations
of organic matter and range from scrubby, forested wetlands to open
muskeg.

Alpine soils, generally above 2,000 feet elevation, are mostly
shallow, very wet organic soils or are extremely shallow and rocky

(d) Fish Resource: Fish resources have been rated as part of the
Tongass Land Management Plan (1979) and by the Alaska Department of
Fish and Game in its Forest Habitat Integrity Program (1983) These
ratings describe the value of VCU's for sport fish, commercial fish
and estuaries.

The one VCU for this area, 522, is rated high for both sport and
commercial values.

Anan Creek produces the most pink salmon of any stream on the Stikine
Area. Average annual peak escapement is 166,000   Coho and steelhead
are also abundant. Anan Creek has increased in popularity with sport
fishermen. The State of Alaska with cooperation with the Forest
Service constructed a fish ladder to help pink salmon over a partial
barrier.

(e) Wildlife Resource: The area has the largest concentration of black bears in Southeast Alaska. Brown bears are also present   Bald eagles nest in the area, and gulls, ravens, and crows concentrate here due to the fish runs   Goats are hunted in the Anan and Boulder Lakes vicinity

(f) Threatened and Endangered Species: The area contains no known threatened or endangered species

(6) Current Use and Management: The entire roadless area was allocated to Land Use Designation 2 in the Tongass Land Management Plan, which prohibits timber harvest and is managed for roadless recreation   The area at the mouth of Anan Creek receives heavy use by people who come to camp, fish, and observe the wildlife. Good anchorage, frequently used by outfitter guides, is found off the mouth of the creek. Black bear hunting is prohibited in the immediate vicinity of the stream mouth. There is one public recreation cabin in the area, a bear observatory, and trails up both forks of the creek. The trail from the recreation cabin to the observatory, and the observatory were reconstructed in 1989   Salmon have been gathered from this area for subsistence use in the past   A fish ladder at the bear observatory is managed by the Alaska Department of Fish and Game.

(7) Appearance (Apparent Naturalness): Most of the area appears natural and unmodified. However, the area at the mouth of Anan Creek has a cabin, trail, bear observatory, and fishpass. All facilities are constructed of natural materials, blending well with the surroundings   The scale and concentration of the facilities reduces the natural character of the Anan Bay area. A float and anchor buoy exist in the bay also   A 138 KV power transmission line crosses the northernmost edge of the area and is not evident to the visitor   The marine terminus located at the water's edge is evident as one approaches the bay from the north

The majority of this roadless area (98 percent) is natural appearing, where only ecological change has occurred (Existing Visual Condition (EVC) Type I). Two percent of this roadless area is EVC Type III, where changes in the landscape are noticed by the average forest visitor   The natural appearance of the landscape remains dominant.

Twenty-three percent of this roadless area is inventoried Variety Class A (possessing landscape diversity that is unique for the character type), 29 percent is inventoried Variety Class B (possessing landscape diversity that is common for the character type) and the remaining 48 percent is inventoried Variety Class C (possessing a low degree of landscape diversity).

(8) Surroundings (External Influences): The area is part of a much larger roadless land mass   Low-flying aircraft accessing the Tyee power site, or landing on one of the lakes or in the outer bay, are not uncommon   Boats passing close by or anchored in Anan Bay may also distract users near the mouth of the creek

(9) **Attractions and Features of Special Interest:** Many attractions and features are present. They include the opportunity to fish for, and observe, pink salmon and steelhead moving over a waterfall and through a fishpass structure, observing black bear, eagles, and occasional brown bears feeding on the salmon; hiking the trails, enjoying the scenery, and overnighting in the cabin. The area contains four inventoried recreation places totaling 14,505 acres

The significance of the salmon runs attract the concentrations of black bear and other wildlife, which in turn contribute highly to its recreation values.

b. **Capability of Management as Wilderness or in an Unroaded Condition**

(1) **Manageability and Management Area Boundaries:** The area is well defined by topographic features. Entry into the area is largely restricted to the single location at the mouth of Anan Creek.

(2) **Natural Integrity:** Except for the minor facilities and the fishpass at the falls near saltwater, the area has not been modified. Continued public demand and increases in use will likely chip away at the areas natural integrity.

(3) **Opportunity for Solitude:** There is low opportunity for solitude in the bay. Opportunity increases as one moves away from the mouth of the creek, or in the off season. Boats or airplanes entering Anan Bay or airplanes landing on the lakes may commonly be observed by people in this roadless area, but such influences are not widespread Present recreation use levels are low except around the mouth of the creek and at the cabin which has high use   Generally, a person camped or traveling inland is unlikely to see others.

(4) **Opportunity for Primitive Recreation:** The area provides primarily primitive recreation opportunities:

ROS Class	Acres
Primitive (P)	33,572
Semi-Primitive Non-Motorized (SPNM)	2,901
Semi-Primitive Motorized (SPM)	1,461

The area contains four recreation places.

ROS CLASS	# OF REC. PLACES	TOTAL ACRES	CAPACITY BY RVD
P	2	13,145	2575
SPNM	1	780	1120
SPM	1	580	437

The recreation cabin, bear observatory, and trails have been improved and provide access within the area   The character of the landforms generally allows the visitor to feel remote from the sights and sounds of human activity   The area is accessible by boat from the community of Wrangell in less than two hours, and from Ketchikan in approximately six hours   Travel

on land is difficult, offering a high degree of physical challenge The
presence of brown bears also presents a degree of challenge and a need for
woods skills and experience

(5) **Special Features (Ecologic, Geologic, Scientific, Cultural):** There
are numerous opportunities to observe and study fish and wildlife, all
within a small, easily-accessible area. The pink salmon run is the highest
of any river on the Stikine Area.

c. **Availability for Management as Wilderness or in an Unroaded Condition**

(1) **Resource Potentials**

(a) **Recreation Potential:** There is potential for additional
outfitter and guide permits and for developed trails and additional
cabins or shelters, as well as for further improvements to existing
facilities for barrier-free access. This is dependent on the level of
development and recreation experience desired at the Anan Bay area
There is also potential to provide barrier-free access to the Bear
Observatory.

(b) **Fish Resource:** The Tongass Land Management Plan, amended Winter
1985-86 identifies fish habitat enhancement projects Fish
enhancement projects continue to surface, and there is potential to
improve fish access into the two large lakes in the upper watershed

(c) **Wildlife Resource:** As identified in the Tongass Land Management
Plan, amended 1985-86, no habitat improvement projects are planned in
the area

Public demand to observe the black bear concentrations has increased
dramatically in the past few years Levels of disturbance to bears
needs to be determined along with future recreation goals for the
area

(d) **Timber Resource:** There are 8,063 acres inventoried as
tentatively suitable for harvest. This includes 640 acres of riparian
old growth and 7,423 acres of non-riparian old growth

(e) **Land Use Authorizations:** The 138 KV Tyee power transmission line
crosses the north edge of the area A Native historic site has been
selected in the Anan Bay area. Several outfitter guides operate
frequently in the bay area

(f) **Minerals:** The area has a low minerals rating and there are no
known mining claims.

(g) **Areas of Scientific Interest:** The area contains one inventoried
potential Research Natural Area. This area is recommended as an
"other recommended Research Natural Area", and not as a priority area

(2) **Management Considerations**

(a) **Timber:** There are no plans to harvest timber in the area, since
it is currently managed for its roadless character

(b) Cultural: There is a Native claim of a historic village site at the mouth of Anan Creek.

(c) Wilderness/Wildlife: Maintenance of the area in a roadless condition enhances opportunities to manage the adjacent roadless areas as Wilderness and to provide enhanced opportunities for solitude and primitive recreation for those using it   It also maintains opportunities for wildlife, such as wolves and bears, to move freely through the area.

(d) Fire: The area has no significant fire history

(e) Insects and Disease: Endemic tree diseases common to Southeast Alaska are present; there are no know epidemic disease occurrences

(f) Land Status: Native land selections in this area total 7.5 acres.

d. Relationship to Communities and Other Roadless and Wilderness Areas

(1) Nearby Roadless and Wilderness Areas and Uses: The Anan area is part of a larger mainland unroaded land mass that is located between the Stikine-LeConte Wilderness on the northwest, the roadless Canadian mountains to the north, and Misty Fiords National Monument on the southeast. The mainland areas receive light use inland away from saltwater access.

(2) Distance From Population Centers (Accessibility): Approximate distances from population centers are as follows·

Community		Air Miles	Water Miles
Juneau	(Pop 23,729)	175	230
Petersburg	(Pop. 4,040)	60	80
Wrangell	(Pop. 2,836)	30	40
Ketchikan	(Pop. 12,705)	55	· 75

Wrangell is the nearest stop on the Alaska Marine Highway and the "gateway" to this area.

(3) Interest by Proponents:

(a) Moratorium areas: The area has been identified as a "moratorium" area for special congressional consideration in a recent legislative initiative.

(b) Local users/residents: Many local people from Wrangell, Petersburg, and Ketchikan visit the area during the salmon run and often take visitors there to observe the wildlife

(c) Other: There is a high interest in the area by outfitters and guides.

e. Environmental Consequences

ALTERNATIVE ANALYSIS TO BE DONE LATER

INDIVIDUAL ROADLESS AREA DESCRIPTION

NAME: Frosty (210)   ACRES (GROSS): 41,395   ACRES (NFS): 41,395

GEOZONE: S09
GEOGRAPHIC PROVINCE: Coast Range

1989 WILDERNESS ATTRIBUTE RATING: 25

a. Description

(1) Relationship to RARE II areas: The table below displays the VCU 1/
names, VCU numbers, original WARS 2/ rating, and comments. This enables
the reader to compare the roadless areas evaluated in Appendix C with
previous analyses.

VCU Name	VCU No.	1979 WARS Rating	Comments
Ward	523	20	
Frosty	524	23	
Sunny	526	23	

(2) History: The area was inhabited by the Tlingit in prehistoric times
In the 1930'S and 1940's there were salmon canneries located at Point Ward
and in Santa Anna Inlet   About 30 years ago, limited timber harvest
occurred on the north side of Frosty Bay approximately 30 years ago

(3) Location and Access: The area is located on the mainland and is
bounded on the west by Ernest Sound and Seward Passage, and on the east by
the Anan Roadless Area. The area is accessible by boat or floatplane from
Ernest Sound. There are no sites suitable for landing small, wheeled
aircraft.

(4) Geography and Topography: The area is generally characterized as
complex terrain dominated by rounded mountains and hills rising steeply
from saltwater. Many reach elevations of over 2,000 feet, and the tallest
is approximately 3,000 feet   Between the mountains and hills are low
valleys containing short streams.   There are numerous small lakes in the
area totaling about 1,020 acres. Twenty acres are classified as rock   the
area contains 18 miles of shoreline on saltwater

1/ A VCU (Value Comparison Unit) is one of 867 watersheds which make up the
    Forest and were differentiated for planning purposes in the Tongass Land
    Management Plan.
2/ Wilderness Attribute Rating System (WARS) was the nationwide system used to
    rate the wilderness attributes of roadless areas in the Roadless Area
    Review and Evaluation (RARE II).

(5) Ecosystem:

(a) **Classification:** The area is in the Coast Range Geographic
Province This province is generally characterized as a core of
massive, angular mountains capped with ice fields at high elevations
along the Canadian Border, with somewhat lower mountains,
deeply-incised valleys and glacier-fed streams closer to the coast
This roadless area is characteristic of the lower portion of the
region with no glaciers and relatively low, rounded landforms There
are no known areas of unique or uncommon plant/soils associations

(b) **Vegetation:** Alpine vegetation dominates the few areas above
2,500 feet in elevation. Below that elevation there are minor areas
of muskeg and scrub lodgepole pine. Hillsides and steeper slopes with
better drainage are generally heavily forested with Sitka spruce and
western hemlock.

There are approximately 39,533 acres of forested land of which 19,480
acres are commercial forest land. Of the commercial forest land,
16,513 acres are non-riparian old growth and 2,767 acres are riparian
old growth.

(c) **Soils:** Soils in this area are formed in a wide variety of parent
materials, including bedrock and glacial drift. In general, well- or
moderately-well-drained soils are on moderate to steep mountain slopes
with permeable parent materials These soils are very acidic, have
cold soil temperatures, and are very high in organic matter Rooting
is largely limited to the surface organic layers and the top few
inches of mineral soil These soils are usually moist, sometimes wet
but are never dry.

More-poorly-drained soils developed on less-sloping areas and/or areas
with impermeable soil materials. These soils have deep accumulations
of organic matter and range from scrubby, forested wetlands to open
muskeg.

Alpine soils, generally above 2,000 feet in elevation, are mostly
shallow, very wet organic soils or are extremely shallow and rocky

(d) **Fish Resource:** Fish resources have been rated as part of the
Tongass Land Management Plan (1979) and by the Alaska Department of
Fish and Game in its Forest Habitat Integrity Program (1983) These
ratings describe the value of VCU's for sport fish, commercial fish
and estuaries

VCU 526 is rated as high value for sport fish. The one VCU rated as
highly valued for commercial fish is 523.

Four Alaska Department of Fish and Game numbered fish streams are
present. The largest producer is June Creek, with average annual peak
escapements of 1,800 pink salmon. Generally, this area is not a large
producer of anadromous fish

Lake Helen in Santa Anna Inlet is a popular sport fishing site for resident trout. Large trout are also found in Standing Rock Lake, but the lake is rarely fished because access is poor

(e) Wildlife Resource: Black bears, brown bears, and wolves range over the area, as well as a small goat population Sitka black-tailed deer are also present. Geese nest in Frosty Creek, and swans winter at Helen Lake and a small lake in Frosty Creek drainage

(f) Threatened and Endangered Species: The area contains no known threatened or endangered species

(6) Current Use and Management: This roadless area was allocated to Land Use Designation 4 in the Tongass Land Management Plan, which allows road construction and timber harvest. A timber sale which is centered in VCU 524 (Frosty Bay area) is now being planned. If approved, the sale would be offered in 1990. Ernest Sound and Seward Passage receive moderately-heavy use by recreation and commercial fishing boats. Frosty and Sunny Bays provide good anchorages. Trapping occurs along the beach fringe There are no public recreation facilities and inland use is light There is no known subsistence use in the area.

(7) Appearance (Apparent Naturalness): Most of the area appears natural and unmodified. However, near the mouth of Frosty Bay, areas were harvested about 50 years ago, and second growth is apparent. There are also obvious remains of the cannery in Santa Anna Inlet.

The majority of this roadless area (99 percent) is in Existing Visual Condition (EVC) Type I where the landscape is natural appearing, and only ecological change has occurred. One percent of this roadless area is EVC Type III, where changes in the landscape are noticed by the average forest visitor. The natural appearance of the landscape remains dominant

Twenty-six percent is inventoried Variety Class A (possessing landscape diversity that is unique for the character type) Twenty-four percent is inventoried Variety Class B (possessing landscape diversity that is common for the character type) and the remaining 40 percent is inventoried Variety Class C (possessing a low degree of landscape diversity)

(8) Surroundings (External Influences): The area is part of a much larger roadless land mass. Boats passing close by or anchored in one of the bays may distract users near saltwater. Views of clearcut timber harvest (cut in 1989) on Deer Island may become apparent by users in some of this area

(9) Attractions and Features of Special Interest: Attractions include the opportunity for secure anchorage and the opportunity to observe remains of the old canneries. The area contains six inventoried recreation places totaling 3,973 acres.

b. Capability of Management as Wilderness or in an Unroaded Condition

(1) Manageability and Management Area Boundaries: The seaward boundary is well defined, but many of the drainage divides in this area are not distinct

(2) **Natural Integrity:** Except for the minor timber harvest in Frosty Bay and the cannery remains, the area has not been modified

(3) **Opportunity for Solitude:** There is a high opportunity for solitude within the area, especially once one moves away from the beach a short distance Boats or airplanes passing by or entering one of the bays may, at times, be observed by people in this roadless area, but such influences are not widespread. Present recreation use levels are low Generally, a person using the area is unlikely to see others.

(4) **Opportunity for Primitive Recreation:** The area provides primarily opportunities for primitive recreation.

ROS Class	Acres
Primitive	28,114
Semi-Primitive Non-Motorized	7,438
Semi-Primitive Motorized	5,200
Roaded Modified	60
Rural	582

The area contains six recreation places.

ROS CLASS	# OF REC. PLACES	TOTAL ACRES	CAPACITY BY RVD
P	4	3,132	2,048
SPM	2	560	771

The character of the landforms generally allows the visitor to feel remote from the sights and sounds of human activity The area is accessible by boat from the community of Wrangell in less than four hours, and from Ketchikan in approximately six hours Travel on land is difficult, offering a high degree of physical challenge. The presence of brown bears also presents a degree of challenge and a need for woods skills and experience.

(5) **Special Features (Ecologic, Geologic, Scientific, Cultural):** There are no known outstanding features in the area.

c. **Availability for Management as Wilderness or in an Unroaded Condition**

(1) **Resource Potentials**

(a) **Recreation Potential:** There is potential for outfitter and guide permits, and for developed trails to some of the lakes Additional cabins or shelters are also possible.

(b) **Fish Resource:** The Tongass Land Management Plan, amended Winter 1985-86, does not identify any fish habitat enhancement projects in this roadless area. However, potential exists to provide fish passage into upper Frosty Creek. Three falls would have to be modified

(c) **Wildlife Resource:** As identified in the Tongass Land Management Plan, amended 1985-86, no habitat improvement projects are planned in the area However, the potential exists for waterfowl enhancement along Frosty Creek

(d) **Timber Resource:** There are 11,411 acres inventoried as tentatively suitable for harvest. This includes 1,463 acres of riparian old growth and 9,848 acres of non-riparian old growth Areas of 45-year-old second growth are located near the mouth of Frosty Bay.

(e) **Land Use Authorizations:** There are no special uses authorized for this area. A grow-fish site has been proposed in Santa Anna Inlet.

(f) **Minerals:** The area has a low minerals rating and there are no known mining claims.

(g) **Areas of Scientific Interest:** The area contains no inventoried potential Research Natural Areas and has not been identified for any other scientific value.

(2) **Management Considerations**

(a) A timber sale is currently being planned for the Frosty drainage (VCU 524) with construction of a log transfer facility near the mouth of Frosty Bay.

(b) Maintenance of the area in a roadless condition enhances opportunities to manage the adjacent roadless areas as Wilderness, and to provide enhanced opportunities for solitude and primitive recreation. It also maintains opportunities for wildlife, such as wolves and bears to move freely through the area.

(c) **Fire:** The area has no significant fire history

(d) **Insects and Disease:** Endemic tree diseases common to Southeast Alaska are present; there are no know epidemic disease occurrences

(e) **Land Status:** All National Forest System land

d. **Relationship to Communities and Other Roadless and Wilderness Areas**

(1) **Nearby Roadless and Wilderness Areas and Uses:** The Frosty area is part of a larger mainland unroaded land mass that is located between the Stikine-LeConte Wilderness on the northwest, the roadless Canadian mountains to the north, and Misty Fiords National Monument and other roadless lands on the southeast. The mainland areas receive light use inland, away from saltwater access

(2) **Distance From Population Centers (Accessibility):** Approximate
distances from population centers are as follows

Community			Air Miles	Water Miles
Juneau	(Pop	23,729)	175	230
Petersburg	(Pop	4,040)	60	80
Wrangell	(Pop	2,836)	30	45
Ketchikan	(Pop	12,705)	50	70

Wrangell is the nearest stop on the Alaska Marine Highway.

(3) **Interest by Proponents:**

(a) **Moratorium areas:** The area has not been identified as a
"moratorium" area or other special consideration in legislative
initiative

(b) **Local users/residents:** Local fishermen and Ketchikan residents
traveling to Anan Creek use the waters and anchorages associated with
this area.

e. **Environmental Consequences**

ALTERNATIVE ANALYSIS TO BE DONE LATER

INDIVIDUAL ROADLESS AREA DESCRIPTION

NAME: North Kupreanof (211)   ACRES (GROSS): 138,623   ACRES (NFS): 116,666

GEOZONE: S03
GEOGRAPHIC PROVINCE: Central Interior Islands

1989 WILDERNESS ATTRIBUTE RATING: 23

a   Description

    (1) **Relationship to RARE II areas:** The table below displays the VCU 1/
names, VCU numbers, original WARS 2/ rating, and comments   This enables
the reader to compare the roadless areas evaluated in Appendix C with
previous analyses.

VCU Name	VCU No.	1979 WARS Rating	Comments
Turn	422*	22	
Kake	423*	-	Not Rated in 1979
Bohemia	424	22	
Cathedral	425*	14	
Hamilton	426*	23	
Salt Chuck	441*	24	LUD II leftover
Portage	442*	23	
Twelvemile	444*	24	

*--The roadless area includes only part of this VCU

(2) **History:** This area adjoins the community of Kake   Traditional and
subsistence uses have been concentrated around the lower reaches of
Cathedral Falls Creek and the Hamilton River. No known unique cultural or
historic resources exist in this area. In modern times, portions of this
area have been selected by Sealaska Native Corporation under the provisions
of Alaska Native Claims Settlement Act (ANCSA) and the Alaska National
Interest Lands Conservation Act (ANILCA)   This area receives low
recreation use.

1/ A VCU (Value Comparison Unit) is one of 867 watersheds which make up the
forest and were differentiated for planning purposes in the Tongass Land
Management Plan.
2/ Wilderness Attribute Rating System (WARS) was the nationwide system used to
rate the wilderness attributes of roadless areas in the Roadless Area
Review and Evaluation (RARE II).

(3) Location and Access: North Kupreanof Roadless Area lies along the southern shore of Frederick Sound, on Kupreanof Island It is accessed primarily by saltwater by boat or floatplane. This area is open to northeasterly winds No sheltered anchorages are available along the shore, except in Portage Bay The community of Kake lies 15 air miles to the southwest, and the community of Petersburg lies 30 miles to the southeast Logging roads provide access to the southwest side of the area from Kake There are no sites suitable for landing wheeled aircraft or floatplanes in the interior of this area.

(4) Geography and Topography: Landforms along this area are characterized by uniformly rolling lowlands Bohemia Ridge rises to an elevation of 2,200 feet, providing topographic relief to essentially flat terrain The ridge parallels other ridges on Kupreanof Island in a roughly northwest to southeast direction, with extensive areas of lowlands in between Two major drainage systems, the Hamilton River and Cathedral Falls Creek wind across much of this area. Small lakes cover a total of 379 acres. The area contains 27 miles of shoreline on saltwater

(5) Ecosystem:

(a) Classification: The area is classified in the Central Interior Islands Geographic Province. This province is characterized by generally subdued, rolling topography and extensive muskegs

(b) Vegetation: Muskeg/scrub timber complexes on wet areas are extensive, interspersed with mature mixed conifer plant communities on better-drained sites along creeks and on steeper slopes Muskeg covers about 16,732 acres. Timbered hill slopes are dominated by western hemlock, Sitka spruce and Alaska-cedar plant communities Minor amounts of redcedar are present, this is the northern limit of redcedar.

There are approximately 98,392 acres of forested land of which 26,606 acres are commercial forest land. Of the commercial forest land, 22,801 acres are non-riparian old growth and 3,587 acres are riparian old growth.

(c) Soils: Soils in this area are formed in a wide variety of parent materials, including bedrock and glacial drift. In general, well- or moderately-well-drained soils are on moderate to steep mountain slopes with permeable parent materials. These soils are very acidic, have cold soil temperatures, and are very high in organic matter Rooting is largely limited to the surface organic layers and the top few inches of mineral soil. These soils are usually moist, sometimes wet, but are never dry.

More-poorly-drained soils developed on less sloping areas and/or areas with impermeable soil materials. These soils have deep accumulations of organic matter and range from scrubby forested wetlands to open muskeg.

Alpine soils, generally above 2,000 feet elevation, are mostly shallow, very wet organic soils or are extremely shallow and rocky

(d) **Fish Resource:** Fish resources have been rated as part of the
Tongass Land Management Plan (1979) and by the Alaska Department of
Fish and Game in its Forest Habitat Integrity Program (1983) These
ratings describe the value of VCU's for sport fish, commercial fish
and estuaries.

VCU's 425 and 426 are rated as high value for sport fish   VCU's rated
as highly valued for commercial fish are 422, 424, 425, 426, and 441.
VCU's rated as highly valued estuaries are 425, 441, and 442

About 12 Alaska Department of Fish and Game numbered salmon streams
are present   The Hamilton River is by far the best producer with
average annual peak escapements of 7,900 pink and 400 chum salmon
Although no spawning data is available, the Hamilton produces very
good runs of steelhead and coho salmon. Sport anglers and Kake
residents fish in the Hamilton River.

(e) **Wildlife Resource:** The majority of this study area has low
habitat qualities, with only occasional deer and moose tracks
noticed. Recent surveys (Spring 1989) seem to indicate a growing
moose population here. Waterfowl and black bear hunting are popular
sports in this area.   .

(f) **Threatened and Endangered Species:** The area contains no known
threatened or endangered species.

(6) **Current Use and Management:** The majority of this area was allocated
to Land Use Designation (LUD) 4 (113,573 acres). In 1983, the Bohemia
Timber Sale Environmental Assessment and Decision Notice were approved
Due to poor timber markets, this timber sale has never been sold   A
portion of Forest Road 6030 was constructed using Tongass Timber Supply
Fund money in an effort to offset the lower value timber in this area
This road is adjacent to the southern side of this roadless area
Currently, this area is undergoing additional scoping and interdisciplinary
review for a proposed Bohemia Mountain Timber Sale which is scheduled to be
offered in 1991-92. A small portion of the area (2,895 acres) is allocated
to LUD 2. This is an area that was excluded from designation of the
Petersburg Creek-Duncan Salt Chuck Wilderness.

(7) **Appearance (Apparent Naturalness):**   The area is essentially
unmodified. The portion of Forest Road 6030 is far inland and not readily
visible by viewers from saltwater.

The majority of this roadless area (90 percent) is natural appearing, where
only ecological change has occurred (Existing Visual Condition (EVC) Type
I). Three percent of this roadless area is EVC Type III, where changes in
the landscape are noticed by the average forest visitor. The natural
appearance of the landscape remains dominant. Less than one percent of the
area is in EVC Type IV, where changes in the landscape are easily noticed
by the average person and may attract some attention   They appear to be
disturbances but resemble natural patterns. Six percent is in EVC Type V
where changes in the landscape are obvious to the average person, and
appear to be major disturbances

None of this roadless area is inventoried Variety Class A (possessing
landscape diversity that is unique for the character type), 15 percent is
inventoried Variety Class B (possessing landscape diversity that is common
for the character type) and the remaining 85 percent is inventoried Variety
Class C (possessing a low degree of landscape diversity)

(8) **Surroundings (External Influences):** North Kupreanof Roadless Area
adjoins the community of Kake to the west, and South Kupreanof Roadless
Area and the Petersburg Creek-Duncan Salt Chuck Wilderness to the south and
east To the north is saltwater Harvest activities on Native lands to
the west are evident from Frederick Sound and the adjacent areas Forest
Service harvest activities are evident in the area to the west around
Portage Bay

(9) **Attractions and Features of Special Interest:** The areas immediately
adjacent to saltwater or major creeks are valued for recreation uses such
as black bear and waterfowl hunting, camping, beach combing and sport
fishing, as well as subsistence activities The area contains 12
inventoried recreation places which contain 12,388 acres.

b. Capability of Management as Wilderness or in an Unroaded Condition

(1) **Manageability and Management Area Boundaries:** The adjacency of this
area to the community of Kake, and to planned timber sales originating from
the Portage Bay area will influence the future management of North
Kupreanof Roadless Area.

(2) **Natural Integrity:** The area is essentially unmodified.

(3) **Opportunity for Solitude:** There is a high opportunity for solitude in
the North Kupreanof Roadless Area. Use of floatplanes and powerboats may
be present for brief periods. Current recreation use levels are low to
moderate in specific locations adjacent to the major creeks and drainages

(4) **Opportunity for Primitive Recreation:** The area provides primarily
primitive and semi-primitive non-motorized opportunity

ROS Class	Acres
Primitive	51,611
Semi-Primitive Non-Motorized	50,071
Semi-Primitive Motorized	9,218
Roaded Natural	2,234
Roaded Modified	3,532

The area contains 12 recreation places.

ROS CLASS	# OF REC. PLACES	TOTAL ACRES	CAPACITY BY RVD
P	2	3,111	598
SPNM	4	4,951	2,426
SPM	4	2,053	1,772
RN	1	2,234	4,337
RM	1	20	54

(5) Special Features (Ecologic, Geologic, Scientific, Cultural): No known
special features exist in this area

c. Availability for Management as Wilderness or in an Unroaded Condition

(1) Resource Potentials

(a) **Recreation Potential:** Recreation potential in this area is
moderate, reflecting its proximity to the community of Kake   The area
could be accessed by foot from the adjacent road system, with
appropriate trail development.

(b) **Fish Resource:** The Tongass Land Management Plan, amended Winter
1985-86, identifies non-structual fish habitat enhancement projects
Fish enhancement projects continue to surface, and there is potential
for additional projects in this area.

Cathedral Falls Creek has abundant habitat above large falls.
Laddering is not presently feasible but fish may be trapped and
transported above the falls.

(c) **Wildlife Resource:** As identified in the Tongass Land Management
Plan, amended 1985-86, moose and deer habitat improvement projects are
planned in the area. These projects typically consist of browse
enhancement through thinning, seeding, and plantings

(d) **Timber Resource:** There are 19,928 acres inventoried as
tentatively suitable for timber harvest. This includes 2,152 acres of
riparian old growth, and 17,598 acres of non-riparian old growth
None of the area is second growth.

(e) **Land Use Authorizations:** None.

(f) **Minerals:** There are no inventoried areas with high mineral
development potential within this roadless area.

(g) **Areas of Scientific Interest:** The area contains no inventoried
potential Research Natural Areas and has not been identified for any
other scientific value.

(2) **Management Considerations**

(a) Maintenance of all or parts of this area in a roadless condition
could benefit the Petersburg Creek-Duncan Salt Chuck Wilderness area
Other roadless areas would benefit only marginally by having North
Kupreanof remain roadless.

(b) Timber values are generally low (with the exception of
Alaska-cedar). Development costs, though moderate, are still too high
for economical development. Future market values, if improved, should
make the timber resource profitable for management

The portion of VCU 441 located within this roadless area, was consciously left out when the adjacent Petersburg Creek-Duncan Salt Chuck Wilderness was created The intent was to allow for future road access options from Portage Bay to the Bohemia Mountain area, and a future tie-in with Forest Road 6030.

(c) Fire: The area has no significant fire history

(d) Insects and Disease: Endemic tree diseases common to Southeast Alaska are present; there are no know epidemic disease occurrences.

(e) Land Status: A proposed 240 acres have been selected by the State

d. Relationship to Communities and Other Roadless and Wilderness Areas

(1) **Nearby Roadless and Wilderness Areas and Uses:** North Kupreanof is one of four contiguous roadless areas on the western half of Kupreanof Island Rocky Pass, South Kupreanof, Castle Roadless Areas are located on the western half of Kupreanof Island, and Missionary Roadless Area on the northeast corner of the island. The Petersburg Creek-Duncan Salt Chuck Wilderness also adjoins these roadless units. This area receives low recreational use.

(2) **Distance From Population Centers (Accessibility):** Approximate distances from population centers are as follows

Community		Air Miles	Water Miles	
Juneau	(Pop 23,729)	110	98	
Petersburg	(Pop 4,040)	25	22	
Wrangell	(Pop. 3,000)	55	75	
Ketchikan	(Pop. 12,705)	130	155	

Petersburg and Kake are the nearest stops on the Alaska Marine Highway.

(3) Interest by Proponents:

(a) **Moratorium areas:** The area has not been identified as a "moratorium" area or other special consideration in legislative initiatives.

(b) **Local users/residents:** The area is of concern to local residents of Kake. Future timber sales may provide employment and other opportunities. A road connection from Kake to Petersburg has been proposed for some time. It would utilize Forest Road 6030 from Kake, and tie into the Portage Bay road system. This would involve crossing this roadless area.

e. Environmental Consequences

ALTERNATIVE ANALYSIS TO BE DONE LATER

INDIVIDUAL ROADLESS AREA DESCRIPTION

NAME: Missionary (212)   ACRES (GROSS): 14,005   ACRES (NFS): 14,005

- GEOZONE: S03
GEOGRAPHIC PROVINCE: Central Interior Islands

1989 WILDERNESS ATTRIBUTE RATING: 23

a. Description

    (1) Relationship to RARE II areas: The table below displays the VCU 1/
    names, VCU numbers, original WARS 2/ rating, and comments   This enables
    the reader to compare the roadless areas evaluated in Appendix C with
    previous analyses.

VCU Name	VCU No.	1979 WARS Rating	Comments
Portage	442*	23	
Kane	443*	21	
Twelvemile	444*	24	

    *--The roadless area includes only part of this VCU.

    (2) History: The area was once inhabited by the Stikine Tlingit
    Evidence indicates that the surrounding area was used for hunting and
    fishing, but no cultural resources have been found in the interior areas
    The remains of an historic cabin are located near the mouth of Twelvemile
    Creek.

    (3) Location and Access: This roadless area is located on the northern
    portion of the Lindenberg Peninsula, on Kupreanof Island   It is located
    about 12 miles northwest of the city of Petersburg. Petersburg is served
    by the Alaska Marine Highway and daily jet service   Access to the
    Missionary Roadless Area is by floatplane or boat. From Portage Bay to the
    west, a logging road system accesses three sides of this roadless area

    (4) Geography and Topography: This roadless area is dominated by the
    upper flanks of the Missionary Mountain Range. These mountains are
    characterized by steep slopes, glacial cirque lakes, and an alpine ridge
    line. Elevation ranges from sea level to 3,253 feet at Kane Peak. The
    area contains one mile of shoreline on saltwater. There are four lakes
    high on the flanks of the mountains. The majority of the area, 12,545
    acres, is covered by forest. Rock covers 100 acres. The lakes cover a
    combined area of 120 acres.

1/ A VCU (Value Comparison Unit) is one of 867 watersheds which make up the
    forest and were differentiated for planning purposes in the Tongass Land
    Management Plan.
2/ Wilderness Attribute Rating System (WARS) was the nationwide system used to
    rate the wilderness attributes of roadless areas in the Roadless Area
    Review and Evaluation (RARE II).

(5) Ecosystem:

(a) Classification: The area is classified as being in the Central
Interior Islands Geographic Province   This province is characterized
by generally subdued, rolling topography and extensive muskeg areas,
with localized, rugged topography. This roadless area has rugged
topography, and glacial cirques are present   Because of its small
size, it does not have the land and waterform variety characteristic
of the province.

The area contains the watersheds of three medium-sized streams and
several small streams which empty directly to saltwater   Streams
within the area are high gradient and generally short

(b) Vegetation: Spruce-hemlock forests dominate the mountain sides
of this area. Alpine vegetation dominates the mountainous ridge top
There are minor amounts of muskeg vegetation in small pockets

There are 12,545 acres of forested land, of which 7,144 acres are
commercial forest land   Of the commercial forest land, 6,404 acres
are non-riparian old growth and 740 acres are riparian old growth

(c) Soils: Soils in this area are formed in a wide variety of parent
materials, including bedrock and glacial drift. In general, well- or
moderately-well-drained soils are on moderate to steep mountain slopes
with permeable parent materials   These soils are very acidic, have
cold soil temperatures, and are very high in organic matter   Rooting
is largely limited to the surface organic layers and the top few
inches of mineral soil   These soils are usually moist, sometimes wet,
but are never dry.

More-poorly-drained soils developed on less sloping areas and/or areas
with impermeable soil materials. These soils have deep accumulations
of organic matter and range from scrubby forested wetlands to open
muskeg.

Alpine soils, generally above 2,000 feet in elevation, are mostly
shallow, very wet organic soils or are extremely shallow and rocky

(d) Fish Resource: Fish resources have been rated as part of the
Tongass Land Management Plan (1979) and by the Alaska Department of
Fish and Game in its Forest Habitat Integrity Program (1983)   These
ratings describe the value of VCU's for sport fish, commercial fish,
and estuaries

VCU's 442 and 444 were rated as moderately-high value for commercial
fish and VCU 442 rated as highly valued for estuary values   No VCU's
were rated high for sport fish, since none of the streams within the
roadless area have significant fish habitat

(e) Wildlife Resource: A population of Sitka black-tailed deer and
black bear range over the roadless area.

(f) Threatened and Endangered Species: The area contains no known
threatened or endangered species.

(6) Current Use and Management: That portion of VCU 443 which is part of
this roadless area is allocated to Land Use Designation (LUD) 3
(5,781 acres). LUD 3 allows the land to be managed for a variety of uses,
with the emphasis on managing for uses in a compatible and complementary
manner to provide the greatest combination of benefits The other two
partial VCU's in the roadless area are allocated to LUD 4 (7,822 acres),
which provides for intensive resource use and development

Fishing and hunting are the main recreational uses in the area One of the
lakes was stocked with grayling and receives occasional use Deer hunting
has been closed in the area for the last fifteen years Most use is
concentrated along the outside edges of the area which are accessible by
roads, but overall use levels are low. There is some subsistence use in
the area.

(7) Appearance (Apparent Naturalness): About one-third of the area
appears unmodified. The remainder of the area has been heavily influenced
by adjacent management activities, mainly timber harvest and roads.

Thirty-six percent of this roadless area was inventoried in Variety Class A
(possessing landscape diversity that is unique for the character type) and
64 percent of the acreage was inventoried Variety Class B (possessing
landscape diversity that is common for the character type) None was
inventoried in Variety Class C (possessing a low degree of landscape
diversity).

Most of the roadless area (36 percent) is in Existing Visual Condition
(EVC) I; these areas appear to be untouched by human activity. About 16
percent is in EVC IV, in which changes to the landscape are easily noticed
by the average person and may attract some attention. The disturbances are
apparent, but resemble natural patterns. EVC V accounts for the remaining
48 percent. These are areas in which changes to the landscape are obvious
to the average person, and appear to be major disturbances

(8) Surroundings (External Influences): Roads and timber management
activities occur on three sides of the roadless area. Noise and sights of
vehicles and active timber sales may occur periodically, being greatest in
magnitude near the roads and lessening as one moves away Portage Bay,
adjacent to the west of this roadless area, has a log transfer site and
logging camp. At times, it is busy with activity. Frederick Sound, which
receives heavy boat traffic, is adjacent to the east. Low-flying aircraft
may temporarily distract visitors in the area.

(9) Attractions and Features of Special Interest: Although the area is
relatively close to Petersburg and there is anchorage in Portage Bay, there
are few attractions which historically draw visitors into the roadless
area. The main attractions are opportunities for deer hunting when the
season is open, and grayling fishing in the one lake where they are found
The area contains two inventoried recreation places totalling 280 acres

b   Capability of Management as Wilderness or in an Unroaded Condition

(1) Manageability and Management Area Boundaries: The area is bounded on
three sides by roads and timber management activities Cutting units along
some of the drainages have impacted parts of the core of the roadless
setting There are few topographic breaks or other natural features to
define the area, as cutting units exist on the lower flanks of the
mountains Feasibility of management in a Wilderness condition is low to
moderate, due to the amount of cultural activities adjacent to this
roadless area. Feasibility of management in an unroaded condition is
moderate, as it maintains traditional opportunities

(2) Natural Integrity: The area is unmodified, however its overall
integrity is not considered pristine. Adjacent management activities have
likely impacted some of the natural integrity of this area, such as
wildlife. The irregular shape of the area, and penetration of roads and
timber harvest up the Todahl Creek Valley, also have likely impacted the
area's natural integrity

(3) Opportunity for Solitude: There is a moderate opportunity for
solitude within the area. Air and boat traffic, and occasional vehicle
traffic pass nearby, and may be heard and observed by people in this
roadless area. Overall recreation use levels are low, being higher along
the fringes near road and water access. Generally, a person camped or
traveling inland is unlikely to encounter others Timber harvest or other
activities in the adjacent areas, which occur periodically, would have a
significant impact on the opportunity for solitude when they are occurring

(4) Opportunity for Primitive Recreation: The area provides
Semi-Primitive Recreation opportunity as inventoried with the Recreation
Opportunity Spectrum (ROS) System.

ROS class	Acres
Semi Primitive Non-Motorized (SPNM)	6,061
Semi Primitive Motorized (SPM)	3,402
Roaded Modified (RM)	4,543

The area contains two inventoried recreation places

ROS CLASS	# OF REC. PLACES	TOTAL ACRES	CAPACITY BY RVD
SPM	2	140	280

There are no developed recreation opportunities in this area. The broken
nature of the landforms and the heavy vegetation at lower elevations
provides a visitor the opportunity to find locations remote from the sights
and sounds of human activity. The area is accessible from the community of
Petersburg by boat.

(5) Special Features (Ecologic, Geologic, Scientific, Cultural): The
grayling found in one small lake are uncommon in the region An unusual
mineral outcrop is located near the east side of the area . Saltwater
access is also likely to attract recreationists

c. Availability for Management as Wilderness or in an Unroaded Condition

    (1) Resource Potentials

        (a) Recreation Potential: There is some potential for outfitter and
guide permits, trails, and cabins and/or shelters There is some
potential for adjacent recreation activities to spill into the
roadless area, such as mountain biking or off-road vehicle use

        (b) Fish Resource: No fish habitat enhancement projects were
identified in the Tongass Land Management Plan, amended Winter
1985-86

        (c) Wildlife Resource: As identified in the Tongass Land Management
Plan, amended Winter 1985-86, no wildlife enhancement projects are
planned within the roadless area.

        (d) Timber Resource: There are 3,683 acres inventoried as
tentatively suitable for harvest This includes 240 acres of riparian
old growth, and 3,443 acres of non-riparian old growth.

        (e) Land Use Authorizations: Numerous special use permits exist
within parts of this roadless area. They include a Coast Guard
reservation, roads, logging camp, log dump, and public recreation
cabin.

        (f) Minerals: The area has low minerals potential Although claims
have been filed on locations within the area in the past, no
development has been conducted

        (g) Areas of Scientific Interest: The area has not been identified
as an Inventoried Potential Research Natural Area or for any other
scientific purpose.

    (2) Management Considerations

        (a) The potential for managing timber in this roadless area is
dependent on market values. A road system and/or logging systems
capable of harvesting the area would be necessary Nearby roads could
be extended to accomplish much of this

        (b) Maintenance of the area in a roadless condition enhances
opportunities for certain wildlife and traditional recreation
activities.

        (c) Fire: The area has no significant fire history.

        (d) Insects and Disease: Endemic tree diseases common to Southeast
Alaska are present; there are no know epidemic disease occurrences

        (e) Land Status: All National Forest System land.

d Relationship to communities and other roadless and Wilderness areas.

(1) **Nearby Roadless and Wilderness Areas and Uses:** The nearest roadless areas are Five Mile, and North Kupreanof. The Petersburg Creek-Duncan Salt Chuck Wilderness is located four miles to the south

(2) **Distance From Population Centers (Accessibility):** Approximate distances from population centers are as follows·

Community	Air Miles	Water Miles
Juneau (Pop. 23,729)	100	110
Petersburg (Pop. 4,040)	12	15
Wrangell (Pop. 2,836)	46	56
Ketchikan (Pop. 12,705)	115	120

Petersburg is the nearest stop on the Alaska Marine Highway.

(3) **Interest by Proponents:**

(a) **Moratorium areas:** The area has not been identified as a "moratorium" area or proposed as Wilderness in legislative initiatives to date.

(b) **Local users/residents:** Portions of the area are traditional and/or popular recreation areas

e. Environmental Consequences

ALTERNATIVE ANALYSIS TO BE DONE LATER

INDIVIDUAL ROADLESS AREA DESCRIPTION

NAME: Five Mile (213)   ACRES (GROSS): 20,297   ACRES (NFS): 19,438

GEOZONE: S03
GEOGRAPHIC PROVINCE: Central Interior Islands

1989 WILDERNESS ATTRIBUTE RATING: 25

a. Description

(1) **Relationship to RARE II areas:** The following table displays the VCU
1/ names, VCU numbers, original WARS 2/ rating, and comments. This enables
the reader to compare the roadless areas evaluated in Appendix C with
previous analyses.

VCU Name	VCU No.	1979 WARS Rating	Comments
Twelvemile	444*	24	LUD IV
Sukoi	446	22	LUD III
Narrows	447*	20	LUD III

*--The roadless area includes only part of this VCU.

(2) **History:** This area lies along the eastern shore of the Lindenberg
Peninsula on Kupreanof Island at Five Mile Creek, and includes the Sukoi
Islets. Several historic resources exist in this area. This area has
relatively moderate recreation use One developed trail leads from
saltwater to Colp Lake

(3) **Location and Access:** Five Mile Roadless Area lies along the eastern
shore of the Lindenberg Peninsula on Kupreanof Island This area is
accessed primarily by saltwater by boat. Good anchorages exist near the
Sukoi Islets, and about eight miles south of Cape Strait The Petersburg
Mountain Trail provides access into the southern part of this area
Logging roads from Portage Bay access portions on the west. The community
of Kake lies 33 air miles to the west, and the community of Petersburg lies
five miles to the south. There are no sites suitable for landing wheeled
aircraft or floatplanes in the interior of this area.

1/ A VCU (Value Comparison Unit) is one of 867 watersheds which make up the
   forest and were differentiated for planning purposes in the Tongass Land
   Management Plan.
2/ Wilderness Attribute Rating System (WARS) was the nationwide system used to
   rate the wilderness attributes of roadless areas in the Roadless Area
   Review and Evaluation (RARE II).

(4) **Geography and Topography:** Landforms along this area are characterized by a glacier-fed stream, Five Mile Creek, and steeply-rising mountain slopes   The highest peak, Del Monte, rises to 2,250 feet from saltwater   The area contains 13 miles of shoreline on saltwater   The Sukoi Islands account for 200 acres of this roadless area, freshwater lakes cover another 140 acres, and alpine terrain covers 1,300 acres

(5) **Ecosystem:**

(a) **Classification:** The area is classified as being in the Central Interior Islands Geographic Province   This province is generally characterized by rolling, subdued topography and extensive muskeg areas, but may have rugged terrain in localized areas

(b) **Vegetation:** Muskeg/scrub timber complexes on wet areas account for about 80 acres, interspersed with mature mixed conifer plant communities on better-drained sites along creeks and on steeper slopes. Timbered hill slopes are dominated by western hemlock, Sitka spruce, and Alaska-cedar plant communities. Minor amounts of redcedar are present.

There are approximately 16,998 acres of forested land of which 8,658 acres are commercial forest land. Of the commercial forest land, 7,978 acres are non-riparian old growth and 500 acres are riparian old growth.

(c) **Soils:** Soils in this area are formed in a wide variety of parent materials, including bedrock and glacial drift. In general, well- or moderately-well-drained soils are on moderate to steep mountain slopes with permeable parent materials. These soils are very acidic, have cold soil temperatures, and are very high in organic matter   Rooting is largely limited to the surface organic layers and the top few inches of mineral soil. These soils are usually moist, sometimes wet, but are never dry.

More-poorly-drained soils developed on less-sloping areas and/or areas with impermeable soil materials. These soils have deep accumulations of organic matter and range from scrubby forested wetlands to open muskeg.

Alpine soils, generally above 2,000 feet elevation, are mostly shallow, very wet organic soils or are extremely shallow and rocky.

(d) **Fish Resource:** Fish resources have been rated as part of the Tongass Land Management Plan (1979) and by the Alaska Department of Fish and Game in its Forest Habitat Integrity Program (1983)   These ratings describe the value of VCU's for sport fish, commercial fish and estuaries.

One VCU, 447, is rated as high value for sport fish.

Five Mile Creek, the only ADF&G numbered stream in this area, has an average annual peak escapement of 1,800 pink salmon   Petersburg anglers often fish in the stream

(e) Wildlife Resource: The majority of this study area has moderate habitat qualities, with only occasional deer and moose track sign noticed. Waterfowl and black bear hunting are popular sports associated with the estuary at the head of Five Mile Creek.

(f) Threatened and Endangered Species: The area contains no known threatened or endangered species.

(6) Current Use and Management: This area was designated as a combination of Land Use Designation (LUD) 3 (12,837 acres) and LUD 4 (6,401 acres) areas. A tentative road corridor has been identified along the shoreline to connect the Lindenberg Peninsula to Portage Bay, and possibly to Kake. There is high public concern of a possible connection of Kupreanof to Kake.

Two trails exist in this area, both beginning at saltwater. The Petersburg Mountain Trail receives relatively heavy use and climbs up to Petersburg Mountain. The Colp Lake Trail receives light use and accesses Colp Lake. Use is primarily by day users from nearby Petersburg.

The Sukoi Islands lie in a primary marine route for pleasure and commercial boat traffic. This includes the Alaska State ferries which cruise between the islands and view much of this roadless area.

Several small buildings exist on two private parcels of land at the mouth of Five Mile Creek. Navigation markers are maintained in the vicinity of the Sukoi Islands.

(7) Appearance (Apparent Naturalness): The area is essentially unmodified. It is visible from major marine travel routes and provides a backdrop for the city of Petersburg.

The majority of this roadless area (88 percent) is natural appearing, where only ecological change has occurred (Existing Visual Condition (EVC) Type I). Less than one percent of this roadless area is EVC Type III, where changes in the landscape are noticed by the average forest visitor. The natural appearance of the landscape remains dominant. Five percent is in EVC Type V where changes in the landscape are obvious to the average person, and appear to be major disturbances.

Forty-seven percent of this roadless area is inventoried Variety Class A (possessing landscape diversity that is unique for the character type), 52 percent is inventoried Variety Class B (possessing landscape diversity that is common for the character type) and the remaining one percent is inventoried Variety Class C (possessing a low degree of landscape diversity).

(8) Surroundings (External Influences): The northern end of the Lindenberg Peninsula is roaded and connected to Portage Bay. To the east is saltwater (Frederick Sound) which receives heavy boat traffic. To the southeast this roadless area adjoins the community of Kupreanof (West Petersburg). Across Wrangell Narrows from Kupreanof is the city of Petersburg. Immediately to the south is the Petersburg Creek-Duncan Salt Chuck Wilderness area.

(9) **Attractions and Features of Special Interest:** The areas immediately adjacent to saltwater or major creeks are valued for recreation uses such as black bear hunting, hiking, and beach combing. Sport fishing is popular around the Sukoi Islets Colp Lake Trail includes views of small glaciers and ice fields The Petersburg Mountain Trail is readily accessible from the state dock in Kupreanof, across Wrangell Narrows from the city of Petersburg It provides outstanding views from the top of Petersburg Mountain and provides access to alpine. The area contains six inventoried recreation places totaling 6,139 acres

b Capability of Management as Wilderness or in an Unroaded Condition

(1) **Manageability and Management Area Boundaries:** Areas to the north are defined by roads and harvest areas. The east is well defined by saltwater. The Petersburg Creek-Duncan Salt Chuck Wilderness lies to the south.

(2) **Natural Integrity:** The area is essentially unmodified

(3) **Opportunity for Solitude:** There is a high opportunity for solitude in the Five Mile Roadless Area. Use of floatplanes and motorboats may disrupt visitors for brief periods. Present recreation use levels are low to moderate in specific locations adjacent to the major creeks and drainages A visitor camped on the beach may see or be seen by fishing boats offshore

(4) **Opportunity for Primitive Recreation:** The area provides primarily primitive and semi-primitive motorized opportunity·

ROS Class	Acres
Primitive (P)	5,400
Semi-Primitive Non-Motorized (SPNM)	4,581
Semi-Primitive Motorized (SPM)	7,691
Roaded Modified (RM)	1,760

The area contains six recreation places.

ROS CLASS	# OF REC. PLACES	TOTAL ACRES	CAPACITY BY RVD
P	1	3,479	175
SPM	5	2,659	1,684

(5) **Special Features (Ecologic, Geologic, Scientific, Cultural):** Features in the southern portion of the area form a backdrop for Petersburg and the marine gateway from the north.

c. Availability for Management as Wilderness or in an Unroaded Condition

(1) Resource Potentials

(a) **Recreation Potential:** Recreation potential for Five Mile area is moderate to high. Use of the developed trails is primarily by residents of Petersburg or Kupreanof Additional trails, cabins and/or shelters all have potential. The area displays a wide variety of settings--from offshore islands to alpine--in a compact area that is easily accessible from Petersburg and Kupreanof.

(b) **Fish Resource:** The Tongass Land Management Plan, amended Winter 1985-86 identifies fish habitat enhancement projects. However none are planned at this time.

(c) **Wildlife Resource:** As identified in the Tongass Land Management Plan, amended 1985-86, habitat improvement projects are planned in the area. These projects typically consist of browse enhancement

(d) **Timber Resource:** There are 5,259 acres inventoried as tentatively suitable for timber harvest. This includes 360 acres of riparian old growth and 4,719 acres of non-riparian old growth   None of the area is second growth.

(e) **Land Use Authorizations:** A special use permit exists for an electronics site on top of Petersburg Mountain

(f) **Minerals:** There are no inventoried areas with high mineral development potential in the area.

(g) **Areas of Scientific Interest:** The area contains no inventoried potential Research Natural Areas and has not been identified for any other scientific value.

(2) **Management Considerations**

(a) Maintenance of this area in a roadless condition enhances the opportunity to manage the adjacent Petersburg Creek-Duncan Salt Chuck Wilderness area. It also maintains existing recreation opportunities and the visual backdrop for the towns of Petersburg and Kupreanof

(b) There are good timber values in this area, however high roading costs and high scenic values will need to be recognized. An additional log transfer facility is also desirable to lessen the haul cost to Portage Bay, the nearest log transfer facility

(c) There is continued interest in future road access from Kake to Kupreanof. Access through the Five Mile Roadless Area would be necessary to accomplish this, and would likely be along the eastern boundary, along or just above the saltwater shoreline

(d) **Fire:** The area has no significant fire history.

(e) **Insects and Disease:** Endemic tree diseases common to Southeast Alaska are present; there are no know epidemic disease occurrences

(f) **Land Status:** Fifty acres of this area is made up of private landholdings. Six hundred acres are proposed for State land selection.

d. Relationship to Communities and Other Roadless and Wilderness Areas .
(1) Nearby Roadless and Wilderness Areas and Uses: The western and
southern boundaries of the Five Mile Roadless Area adjoin the eastern and
northern boundaries of the Petersburg Creek-Duncan Salt Chuck Wilderness
area The remaining roadless units on Kupreanof Island are separated from
the Five Mile Roadless Area by saltwater or roaded areas Overall, this
area receives moderate recreational use

(2) Distance From Population Centers (Accessibility): Approximate
distances from population centers are as follows:

Community		Air Miles	Water Miles
Juneau	(Pop. 23,729)	115	115
Petersburg	(Pop. 4,040)	5	5
Wrangell	(Pop. 2,836)	35	40

Petersburg is the nearest stop on the Alaska Marine Highway

(3) Interest by Proponents:

(a) Moratorium areas: The area has not been identified as a
"moratorium" area or proposed as Wilderness in legislative initiatives
to date.

(b) Local users/residents: Interest has developed in this roadless
area concerning potential road access from Kake to Kupreanof

e. Environmental Consequences

ALTERNATIVE ANALYSIS TO BE DONE LATER

INDIVIDUAL ROADLESS AREA DESCRIPTION

NAME: South Kupreanof (214) ACRES (GROSS): 209,957   ACRES (NFS): 209,957

GEOZONE: S03 and S10
GEOGRAPHIC PROVINCE: Central Interior Islands

1989 WILDERNESS ATTRIBUTE RATING: 26

a. Description

(1) **Relationship to RARE II areas:** The table below displays the VCU 1/ names, VCU numbers, original WARS 2/ rating, and comments This enables the reader to compare the roadless areas evaluated in Appendix C with previous analyses.

VCU Name	VCU No.	1979 WARS Rating	Comments
Irish	429*	24	LUD 4
Lovelace	430*	22	LUD 4
Barrie	431*	21	LUD 4
Totem	432*	23	LUD 4
Douglas	433*	18	LUD 4
Castle River	436	21	LUD 4
Indian	438*	24	LUD 4
Towers	440	25	LUD 3

*--The roadless area includes only part of this VCU

(2) **History:** The shorelines along the southern boundary and along Duncan Canal were probably used extensively by the Tlingit. No extensive cultural evaluation has been completed for the South Kupreanof Roadless Area Incidental evidence, such as pitch trees, and remains of fox farms and villages, indicates that additional cultural sites may be discovered through intensive archeological investigation. In modern times, although this area was designated as a LUD 4, activities have been minimal to non-existent on South Kupreanof Roadless Area, except for A-frame logging along the beach areas

1/ A VCU (Value Comparison Unit) is one of 867 watersheds which make up the Forest and were differentiated for planning purposes in the Tongass Land Management Plan.
2/ Wilderness Attribute Rating System (WARS) was the nationwide system used to rate the wilderness attributes of roadless areas in the Roadless Area Review and Evaluation (RARE II).

(3) Location and Access: South Kupreanof Roadless Area is east of Rocky Pass Roadless Area and west of Castle Roadless Area, on Kupreanof Island On the northeast corner, it adjoins the Petersburg Creek-Duncan Salt Chuck Wilderness area Technically, this roadless area does not reach to the shoreline along Sumner Strait, due to the presence of clearcutting and road construction which occurred in the late 1960's through the mid-1970's It is accessible primarily by saltwater by boat or floatplane A few good anchorages are located along the southern shoreline, and within Duncan Canal Several of the inland lakes are large enough to land small floatplanes The community of Kake lies 65 air miles from the heart of this area. There are no sites suitable for landing wheeled aircraft.

(4) Geography and Topography: Landforms in this area are characterized by uniformly-rolling to moderately-steep hills, typically less than 1,500 feet in elevation. The ridges parallel each other in a roughly northwest to southeast direction. The area contains 38 miles of shoreline on saltwater. Freshwater lakes occupy 1,203 acres, alpine about 1,282 acres, and rock makes up another 40 acres.

(5) Ecosystem:

(a) Classification: The area is classified as being in the Central Interior Islands Geographic Province. The area typifies the low-lying, rolling terrain with little relief, and rounded gentle ridges characteristic of this province.

(b) Vegetation: Muskeg/scrub timber complexes on wet areas (10,339 acres) are interspersed with mature mixed conifer plant communities on better-drained sites Timbered hill slopes are dominated by western hemlock and Alaska-cedar plant communities Minor amounts of redcedar are present

There are approximately 195,353 acres of forested land of which 83,617 acres are commercial forest land. Of the commercial forest land, 70,394 acres are non-riparian old growth and 12,962 acres are riparian old growth.

(c) Soils: Soils in this area are formed in a wide variety of parent materials, including bedrock and glacial drift. In general, well- or moderately-well-drained soils are on moderate to steep mountain slopes with permeable parent materials. These soils are very acidic, have cold soil temperatures, and are very high in organic matter Rooting is largely limited to the surface organic layers and the top few inches of mineral soil. These soils are usually moist, sometimes wet but are never dry.

More-poorly-drained soils developed on less-sloping areas and/or areas with impermeable soil materials These soils have deep accumulations of organic matter and range from scrubby forested wetlands to open muskeg.

Alpine soils, generally above 2,000 feet elevation, are mostly shallow, very wet organic soils or are extremely shallow and rocky

(d) Fish Resource: Fish resources have been rated as part of the
Tongass Land Management Plan (1979) and by the Alaska Department of
Fish and Game in its Forest Habitat Integrity Program (1983)   These
ratings describe the value of VCU's for sport fish, commercial fish
and estuaries

There are four VCU's which are rated as high value for sport fish
These are VCU's 429, 431, 436, 440.   VCU's rated as highly valued
for commercial fish are 431, 432, 436, 440 VCU's rated as highly
valued estuaries include 430, 432, 433, 438, 440

The area contains either the entire stream or the headwaters of
approximately twenty ADF&G numbered salmon producing streams   The
most important include Castle River, Irish Creek, Tunehean Creek, and
Kushnahean Creek. All are very good producers of Coho salmon and
steelhead. Castle River is a very popular sport fishing area for
Coho. Additionally, these streams produce pink and chum salmon
Tunehean has an average peak escapement of 23,600 pink. Generally,
this area is a good producer of anadromous fish   Irish Creek Fish
Ladder was constructed in 1984 to open an extensive watershed to
salmon.

(e) Wildlife Resource: Historically, South Kupreanof was known for a
moderate to high Sitka black-tailed deer population. In the late
1960's and early 1970's, all of Southeast Alaska experienced a decline
in deer populations. Moose are also present and recent surveys
(Spring 1989) seem to indicate a growing moose population here

(f) Threatened and Endangered Species: The area contains no known
threatened or endangered species

(6) Current Use and Management: With the exception of VCU 440 (Towers)
which is allocated as Land Use Designation (LUD) 3 (26,346 acres), the
remaining area was designated as LUD 4 (183,551 acres)   There currently is
one operating timber sale within this roadless area. Harvesting and
roading will occur primarily in the northern half of VCU 429 (Irish Creek).

Some timber harvest has been planned to the south of this area   In 1984
the Totem Timber Sale was planned which provides for a log transfer
facility in Douglas Bay. This sale was laid out but never offered   The
Totem is within VCU's 429, 432, 433, 434 and 436. Implementation of this
sale has been delayed because of the lack of road funds

Overall, this roadless area receives light recreational use

(7) Appearance (Apparent Naturalness): Portions of the roadless area are
viewed from Sumner Strait, a major travel route used by cruiseships and
Alaska State ferries. The Tunehean Creek drainage is seen as background
from Rocky Pass, a secondary travel route used frequently by recreationists
in small boats. Most of the roadless area appears unmodified from
established travel routes, although the beach area adjacent to the roadless
area appears highly modified where logging has occurred in the past

The majority of this area (97 percent) is natural appearing, where only
ecological change has occurred (Existing Visual Condition (EVC) Type I)
Less than one percent of the area appears to be untouched by human activity
(EVC Type II)   Less than one percent is in EVC Type IV, where changes in
the landscape are easily noticed by the average person and may attract some
attention   They appear to be disturbances but resemble natural patterns
Two percent is in EVC Type V where changes in the landscape are obvious to
the average person, and appear to be major disturbances

Less than one percent of this roadless area is inventoried Variety Class A
(possessing landscape diversity that is unique for the character type)
About 16 percent is inventoried Variety Class B (possessing landscape
diversity that is common for the character type)   The remaining 84 percent
is inventoried Variety Class C (possessing a low degree of landscape
diversity).

(8) **Surroundings (External Influences):** South Kupreanof Roadless Area is
generally surrounded by other roadless areas. Road construction is
occurring in the northern portion and is planned for the southern arm
Much of the adjacent southern beach areas have been logged. In addition,
this area is relatively flat, lessening the external impacts from within

(9) **Attractions and Features of Special Interest:** The areas immediately
adjacent to saltwater or major creeks are highly valued for recreation uses
such as black bear and waterfowl hunting, camping, trapping, beach combing,
and sport fishing. Beaches between Point Barrie and Totem Point are made
up of small multi-colored and agate-like stones. Stone columns produced by
erosion formed the "totems" at the head of Totem Bay The Forest Service
once maintained recreation cabins in Towers Arm and at Towers Lake, but the
cabins were eliminated   There are 14 inventoried recreation places which
contain 26,056 acres   Bear hunting and sport fishing occur throughout.

b. Capability of Management as Wilderness or in an Unroaded Condition

(1) **Manageability and management area boundaries:** South Kupreanof
Roadless Area is surrounded by roadless areas on all sides, except for the
fringe of clearcut units on saltwater facing Sumner Strait

(2) **Natural Integrity:** The area is essentially unmodified

(3) **Opportunity for Solitude:** There is a high opportunity for solitude in
the South Kupreanof Roadless Area. Use of floatplanes and motorboats may
disrupt visitors for brief periods. Present recreation use levels are low.

(4) **Opportunity for Primitive Recreation:** The area provides primarily
primitive and semi-primitive non-motorized opportunity·

ROS Class	Acres
Primitive (P)	165,881
Semi-Primitive Non-Motorized (SPNM)	30,945
Semi-Primitive Motorized (SPM)	8,901
Roaded Natural (RN)	40
Roaded Modified (RM)	4,050

The area contains 14 recreation places.

ROS CLASS	# OF REC. PLACES	TOTAL ACRES	CAPACITY BY RVD
P	3	15,780	2,109
SPNM	1	20	13
SPM	4	8,178	5,696
RN	1	40	71
RM	5	2,038	678

There are two Forest Service recreation cabins in the area, both of which are out of service.

(5) **Special Features (Ecologic, Geologic, Scientific, Cultural):** Rock hounding, beach combing and hiking occur in the lower section of Rocky Pass, and around to the beaches in Totem Bay. Waterfowl hunting occurs in the major estuaries, and sport fishing is popular.

c. **Availability for Management as Wilderness or in an Unroaded Condition**

(1) **Resource Potentials**

(a) **Recreation Potential:** Overall recreation potential for South Kupreanof is low. A variety of recreation opportunities which are of interest to the average visitor are limited in the area.

(b) **Fish Resource:** The Tongass Land Management Plan, amended Winter 1985-86 identifies fish habitat enhancement projects. There is potential for additional projects in this area   West Douglas Bay Creek may have rock work to improve passage of anadromous fish   A proposed fishway has been identified in upper Keku Creek

(c) **Wildlife Resource:** As identified in the Tongass Land Management Plan, amended 1985-86 habitat improvement projects are planned in the area. These projects typically consist of waterfowl and deer winter range enhancement through seeding, thinning, and planting.

(d) **Timber Resource:** There are 45,602 acres inventoried as tentatively suitable for timber harvest. This includes 5,249 acres of riparian old growth, and 40,192 acres of non-riparian old growth None of the area is second growth.

(e) **Land Use Authorizations:** None

(f) **Minerals:** There are no inventoried areas with high mineral development potential in the area.

(g) **Areas of Scientific Interest:** The area contains no inventoried potential Research Natural Areas and has not been identified for any other scientific value.

(2) **Management Considerations**

(a) The North Irish Timber Sale activities will continue to occur in the northern half of VCU 429 (Irish) Significant investment was made in sale design and layout of the Totem Timber Sale in 1984 Totem Timber Sale was never offered, and an analysis will be done in the near future as to its viability.

(b) Maintenance of the area in a roadless condition might be , beneficial to the Rocky Pass and Castle Roadless Areas Based on known characteristics of South Kupreanof, it lacks the variety to provide significant interest to the recreation visitor

(c) **Fire:** The area has no significant fire history

(d) **Insects and Disease:** Endemic tree diseases common to Southeast Alaska are present; there are no know epidemic disease occurrences

(e) **Land Status:** All National Forest System land

d. **Relationship to Communities and Other Roadless and Wilderness Areas**

(1) **Nearby Roadless and Wilderness Areas and Uses:** South Kupreanof is one of four contiguous roadless areas on the western half of Kupreanof Island Roadless areas that make up the larger area are Rocky Pass, Castle, North Kupreanof and the Petersburg Creek-Duncan Salt Chuck Wilderness This area receives light recreational use.

(2) **Distance From Population Centers (Accessibility):** Approximate distances from population centers are as follows

Community		Air Miles	Water Miles
Juneau	(Pop. 23,729)	120	143
Petersburg	(Pop. 4,040)	20	65
Wrangell	(Pop. 2,836)	45	60

Wrangell, Kake, and Petersburg are the nearest stops on the Alaska Marine Highway

(3) **Interest by Proponents:**

(a) **Moratorium areas:** VCU's 440, 438, and 436 have been identified as part of the West Duncan Moratorium Area

(b) **Local users/residents:** The areas immediately adjacent to saltwater and majors streams receive light recreational use There is high interest in maintaining Duncan Canal in its natural state for recreational use. Remaining lowlands are lacking interest to the average user.

e. Environmental Consequences

ALTERNATIVE ANALYSIS TO BE DONE LATER

INDIVIDUAL ROADLESS AREA DESCRIPTION

NAME: Castle (215)   ACRES (GROSS): 49,360   ACRES (NFS): 49,360

GEOZONE: S10
GEOGRAPHIC PROVINCE: Central Interior Islands

1989 WILDERNESS ATTRIBUTE RATING: 25

a. Description

   (1) **Relationship to RARE II areas:** The following table displays the VCU
   1/ names, VCU numbers, original WARS 2/ rating, and comments This enables
   the reader to compare the roadless areas evaluated in Appendix C with
   previous analyses.

VCU Name	VCU No.	1979 WARS Rating	Comments
Kah Sheets	434	21	LUD 4
Castle Island	435	19	LUD 3

   (2) **History:** The shorelines along the southern boundary and along Duncan
   Canal were probably used by the Tlingit. No extensive cultural evaluation
   has been completed for the Castle Roadless Area. Remains of fox farms on
   some of the associated islands in Duncan Canal provide evidence that
   additional historical sites may be discovered through intensive
   archeological investigation. A barite mine operated in the area until the
   1970's. In modern times, this area has fairly intense recreation use

   (3) **Location and Access:** Castle Roadless Area lies along the southwest
   shore of Duncan Canal on the southeast corner of Kupreanof Island It is
   just north of Kah Sheets Bay, and includes Castle River Estuary and flats
   Technically, this roadless area does not reach to the shoreline along Kah
   Sheets Bay or Little Duncan Bay due to the presence of clearcutting and
   road construction which occurred in the mid 1970's. Much of the
   recreational interest is focused along saltwater. It is accessed primarily
   by saltwater by boat or floatplane. Only a few good anchorages can be
   found along Duncan Canal. Kah Sheets Lake is large enough to land small
   floatplanes. The community of Kake lies 35 air miles to the northwest, and
   the community of Petersburg lies 20 miles to the northeast. There are no
   sites suitable for landing wheeled aircraft.

1/ A VCU (Value Comparison Unit) is one of 867 watersheds which make up the
    forest and were differentiated for planning purposes in the Tongass Land
    Management Plan.
2/ Wilderness Attribute Rating System (WARS) was the nationwide system used to
    rate the wilderness attributes of roadless areas in the Roadless Area
    Review and Evaluation (RARE II).

(4) Geography and Topography: Landforms along this area are characterized by uniformly-rolling to moderately-steep hills, typically less than 1,500 feet in elevation The ridges parallel each other in a roughly northwest to southeast direction, with fairly extensive areas of lowlands in between. This area is classified as part of the Kupreanof Lowlands The area contains 26 miles of shoreline on saltwater Small offshore islands make up 100 acres of this area, while alpine covers about 100 acres Freshwater lakes, the main one being Kah Sheets Lake, cover another 639 acres

(5) Ecosystem:

(a) Classification: The area is classified as being in the Central Interior Islands Geographic Province. This province is generally characterized by subdued, rolling topography and extensive muskeg areas, but may have rugged terrain in localized areas.

(b) Vegetation: Muskeg/scrub timber complexes on wet areas (7,172 acres), are interspersed with mature mixed conifer plant communities on better-drained sites. Timbered hill slopes are dominated by western hemlock, Sitka spruce, and Alaska-cedar plant communities Minor amounts of redcedar are present.

There are approximately 41,268 acres of forested land of which 19,766 acres are commercial forest land. Of the commercial forest land, 17,388 acres are non-riparian old growth and 2,378 acres are riparian old growth.

(c) Soils: Soils in this area are formed in a wide variety of parent materials, including bedrock and glacial drift In general, well- or moderately-well-drained soils are on moderate to steep mountain slopes with permeable parent materials. These soils are very acidic, have cold soil temperatures, and are very high in organic matter Rooting is largely limited to the surface organic layers and the top few inches of mineral soil. These soils are usually moist, sometimes wet, but are never dry.

More-poorly-drained soils developed on less-sloping areas and/or areas with impermeable soil materials. These soils have deep accumulations of organic matter and range from scrubby forested wetlands to open muskeg.

Alpine soils, generally above 2,000 feet elevation, are mostly shallow, very wet organic soils or are extremely shallow and rocky

(d) Fish Resource: Fish resources have been rated as part of the Tongass Land Management Plan (1979) and by the Alaska Department of Fish and Game in its Forest Habitat Integrity Program (1983) These ratings describe the value of VCU's for sport fish, commercial fish and estuaries.

There are two VCU's which are rated as high value for sport fish and commercial fish These are VCU's 434 and 435. These two VCU's are also rated as highly valued estuaries

Castle River and Kah Sheets are noted for good spring steelhead
fishing, and coho fishing in the late summer. Fifteen ADF&G numbered
salmon producing streams are present. Kah Sheets and Castle River are
the most well known   Kah Sheets produces good steelhead fishing in
the spring, and sockeye in July. Castle River is a very popular coho
fishing stream in the late summer

(e) Wildlife Resource: Historically, South Kupreanof was known for a
moderate to high Sitka black-tailed deer population   In the late
1960's and early 1970's all of Southeast Alaska experienced a decline
in deer populations due to severe winters and wolf predation   This
combined with beach logging along the southern shore, has resulted in
poor recovery of deer populations on South Kupreanof   Recent surveys
(Spring 1989) seem to indicate a growing moose population here
Waterfowl and black bear hunting are popular sports in this area.

(f) **Threatened and Endangered Species:** The area contains no known
threatened or endangered species.

(6) Current Use and Management: This area has high recreation use   There
are two Forest Service recreation cabins in Castle River, one cabin at Kah
Sheets Lake, and one cabin at Breiland Slough. Planked trails connect the
Castle River cabins and provide good fishing opportunities along Castle
River. A planked trail connects the Kah Sheets Bay cabin, just outside of
the roadless area, with the cabin on Kah Sheets Lake. The cabin at Kah
Sheets Lake is being reconstructed to provide barrier-free access   The
Castle River drainage was designated as a LUD 3 (30,839 acres), while the
Kah Sheets drainage was designated LUD 4 (18,401 acres)   Other than beach
logging, no activity has taken place.

(7) Appearance (Apparent Naturalness): This area appears largely
unmodified and natural along Duncan Canal. Portions of the area along
little Duncan Bay and Kah Sheets Bay were harvested along the beach in the
mid-1970's and the cut is visible. Inland is mostly low lying and is not
visible, except for the basin around Kah Sheets Lake.

The majority of this roadless area (99 percent) is natural appearing, where
only ecological change has occurred (Existing Visual Condition (EVC) Type
I). Less than one percent exists in EVC Types III, IV, and V

None of this roadless area is inventoried Variety Class A (possessing
landscape diversity that is unique for the character type), 41 percent is
inventoried Variety Class B (possessing landscape diversity that is common
for the character type) and the remaining 59 percent is inventoried Variety
Class C (possessing a low degree of landscape diversity)

(8) Surroundings (External Influences): Castle Roadless Area is
surrounded by other roadless areas and saltwater. Beach logging and
roading along the saltwater fringe, which is just out of the roadless area,
has affected the character of this area. However, most of these areas have
recovered into lush plantations and do not dominate the setting   Views of
timber sale activity across Duncan Canal are visible from parts of this
roadless area.

(9) Attractions and Features of Special Interest: The areas immediately adjacent to saltwater or major creeks are highly valued for recreation uses such as black bear and waterfowl hunting, camping, beach combing, and sport fishing Recreation cabins are popular and often in use, as weather permits, from late April through October Kah Sheets Lake Cabin offers a unique fly in opportunity that will be accessible to all The area contains seven inventoried recreation places totaling 11,551 acres

b   Capability of Management as Wilderness or in an Unroaded Condition

(1) Manageability and Management Area Boundaries: Castle Roadless Area is surrounded by roadless areas or saltwater on all sides, except for the fringe of clearcut units on saltwater in Kah Sheets Bay and Little Duncan Canal. Management of this area as roadless would be influenced by road construction in the adjacent South Kupreanof area should the Totem Timber Sale be developed.

(2) Natural Integrity: The area is essentially unmodified

(3) Opportunity for Solitude: There is a high opportunity for solitude in the Castle Roadless Area. Use of floatplanes and motorboats may disrupt visitors for brief periods. Present recreation use levels are moderate to high in specific locations. Visitors would expect to see or to be seen by others in passing boats if camped directly on the beach.

(4) Opportunity for Primitive Recreation: The area provides primarily primitive and semi-primitive non-motorized recreation opportunities

ROS Class	Acres
Primitive (P)	22,304
Semi-Primitive Non-Motorized (SPNM)	17,683
Semi-Primitive Motorized (SPM)	8,793
Roaded Modified (RM)	459

The area contains seven recreation places.

ROS CLASS	# OF REC. PLACES	TOTAL ACRES	CAPACITY BY RVD
P	1	3,357	1,890
SPNM	2	2,918	1,537
SPM	3	5,116	6,920
RM	1	160	116

There are four Forest Service recreation cabins and three developed trails in the Castle Roadless Area.

(5) Special Features (Ecologic, Geologic, Scientific, Cultural): Exploring by skiff, beach combing and hiking are popular along saltwater access. There are a series of small islands off the mouth of Castle River which have limestone cliffs and caves There is an abandoned barite mine developed in the 1960's, which includes an old mill site located on private land Black bear and waterfowl hunting in the major estuaries are popular, as is sport fishing

c. Availability for Management as Wilderness or in an Unroaded Condition

(1) Resource Potentials

(a) **Recreation Potential:** Recreation potential for Castle Roadless Area is high due its proximity on relatively sheltered waters to Petersburg   There is potential for additional recreation cabins, trails and outfitter and guide permits

(b) **Fish Resource:** The Tongass Land Management Plan, amended Winter 1985-86 identifies fish habitat enhancement projects   Fish enhancement projects continue to surface and there is potential for additional projects in this area. Kah Sheets Lake has been identified as a candidate for fertilization to increase its productivity A ladder may be constructed at Kah Sheets Creek to provide passage for pink and chum salmon to the upper watershed.

(c) **Wildlife Resource:** As identified in the Tongass Land Management Plan, amended 1985-86 deer winter range and waterfowl habitat improvement projects are planned in the area. These projects typically consist of thinning, seeding and planting for preferred browse species.

(d) **Timber Resource:** There are 10,972 acres inventoried as tentatively suitable for timber harvest   This includes 1,059 acres of riparian old growth and 9,913 acres of non-riparian old growth None of the area is second growth.

(e) **Land Use Authorizations:** None.

(f) **Minerals:** There are no known active claims in the area   A barite mine operated from the 1960's into the 1970's

(g) **Areas of Scientific Interest:** The area contains no inventoried potential Research Natural Areas and has not been identified for any other scientific value.

(2) Management Considerations

(a) Maintenance in a roadless condition does not appear to directly affect the roadless areas adjoined the Castle Roadless Area

(b) The potential for managing timber in this roadless area is dependent upon the development of high market values and the development of less expensive access to make consideration of this area economically feasible.

(c) **Fire:** The area has no significant fire history

(d) **Insects and Disease:** Endemic tree diseases common to Southeast Alaska are present; there are no know epidemic disease occurrences

(e) **Land Status:** Private lands make up 5.3 acres of this roadless area.

d. Relationship to Communities and Other Roadless and Wilderness Areas

(1) **Nearby Roadless and Wilderness Areas and Uses:** Castle is one of four contiguous roadless areas on the western half of Kupreanof Island The roadless units on the western half of Kupreanof Island are Rocky Pass, South Kupreanof, Castle, and North Kupreanof The Petersburg Creek-Duncan Salt Chuck Wilderness also adjoins these roadless units This area receives heavy recreational use

(2) **Distance From Population Centers (Accessibility):** Approximate distances from population centers are as follows

Community		Air Miles	Water Miles
Juneau	(Pop. 23,729)	120	143
Petersburg	(Pop. 4,040)	18	24
Wrangell	(Pop 2,836)	45	32

Wrangell and Petersburg are the nearest stops on the Alaska Marine Highway.

(3) **Interest by Proponents:**

(a) **Moratorium areas:** Most of the area is identified in a moratorium area in at least one legislative proposal.

(b) **Local users/residents:** The areas immediately adjacent to recreation cabins and trails receive moderate to high recreational use. High interest exists by local users in maintaining Duncan Canal in a natural state for recreational use Remaining lowlands are lacking interest to the average user.

e. Environmental Consequences

ALTERNATIVE ANALYSIS TO BE DONE LATER

INDIVIDUAL ROADLESS AREA DESCRIPTION

NAME: Lindenberg (216)   ACRES (GROSS): 28,337   ACRES (NFS): 22,797

GEOZONE: S03
GEOGRAPHIC PROVINCE: Central Interior Islands

1989 WILDERNESS ATTRIBUTE RATING: 24

a. Description

(1) Relationship to RARE II areas: The table below displays the VCU 1/
names, VCU numbers, original WARS 2/ rating, and comments This enables
the reader to compare the roadless areas evaluated in Appendix C with
previous analyses.

VCU Name	VCU No.	1979 WARS Rating	Comments
Mitchell	437*	22	LUD 4
Duncan	439*	18	LUD 4
Narrows	447*	20	LUD 3

*--The roadless area includes only part of this VCU

(2) History: This area was within the former territory of the Stikine
Tlingit. Evidence of their use includes campsites, fort sites, garden
areas and fish weirs. Most, if not all, cultural activity occurred along
the shoreline No cultural resources are recorded for the interior areas

(3) Location and Access: This area lies inland on the Lindenberg
Peninsula, directly south of the Petersburg Creek-Duncan Salt Chuck
Wilderness. The community of Kake lies 30 air miles to the northwest, the
city of Petersburg lies one mile to the east across Wrangell Narrows, and
the city of Kupreanof is adjacent to the east side of the area There are
no sites suitable for landing wheeled aircraft or floatplanes in the
interior of this area. Saltwater access is by way of the Wrangell Narrows
(transportation link to Petersburg via the Alaska Marine Highway) The
Duncan Canal Portage Trail provides access through the interior of this
area.

1/ A VCU (Value Comparison Unit) is one of 867 watersheds which make up the
   Forest and were differentiated for planning purposes in the Tongass Land
   Management Plan.
2/ Wilderness Attribute Rating System (WARS) was the nationwide system used to
   rate the wilderness attributes of roadless areas in the Roadless Area
   Review and Evaluation (RARE II).

(4) Geography and Topography: Landforms along this area are characterized
by steep mountain slopes divided by two major drainages, Duncan Creek and
Coho Creek This area bisects the Lindenberg Peninsula from Ohmer Slough
to the mouth of Coho Creek and then runs south along Wrangell Narrows just
past Mountain Point. The highest peak rises to 3,250 feet from saltwater
This area is classified as part of the Kupreanof Lowlands which is typical
of Kuiu, Kupreanof and Zarembo Islands on the Stikine Area Freshwater
lakes cover 20 acres, alpine 60 acres and rock 40 acres There are five
miles of shoreline on saltwater

(5) Ecosystem:

    (a) Classification: The area is classified as being in the Central
    Interior Islands Geographic Province This province is generally
    characterized by rolling, subdued topography and extensive muskeg
    areas, but may have rugged terrain in localized areas.

    (b) Vegetation: Muskeg/scrub timber complexes vegetate the lowlands
    (100 acres) below Mountain Point to the Coho Creek drainage Timbered
    hill slopes are dominated by western hemlock and Alaska-cedar plant
    communities. Minor amounts of redcedar are present

    There are approximately 21,578 acres of forested land of which 10,420
    acres are commercial forest land. Of the commercial forest land,
    9,080 acres are non-riparian old growth and 1,340 acres are riparian
    old growth.

    (c) Soils: Soils in this area are formed in a wide variety of parent
    material, including bedrock and glacial drift In general, well- or
    moderately-well-drained soils are on moderate to steep mountain slopes
    with permeable parent materials These soils are very acidic, have
    cold soil temperatures, and are very high in organic matter Rooting
    is largely limited to the surface organic layers and the top few
    inches of mineral soil. These soils are usually moist, sometimes wet,
    but are never dry.

    More-poorly-drained soils developed on less-sloping areas and/or areas
    with impermeable soil materials These soils have deep accumulations
    of organic matter and range from scrubby forested wetlands to open
    muskeg.

    Alpine soils, generally above 2,000 feet elevation, are mostly
    shallow, very wet organic soils or are extremely shallow and rocky

    (d) Fish Resource: Fish resources have been rated as part of the
    Tongass Land Management Plan (1978) and by the Alaska Department of
    Fish and Game in its Forest Habitat Integrity Program (1983) These
    ratings describe the value of VCU's for sport fish, commercial fish
    and estuaries.

    VCU 447 is rated as high value for sport fish. VCU's 437 and 430
    rated as highly valued estuaries

(e) **Wildlife Resource:** The majority of this study area has low
habitat qualities, with only occasional deer and moose track sign
noticed. Waterfowl and black bear hunting are popular sports
associated with the estuaries along Wrangell Narrows

(f) **Threatened and Endangered Species:** The area contains no known
threatened or endangered species

(6) **Current Use and Management:** This area was designated as a combination
of Land Use Designation (LUD) 3 (10,679 acres) and LUD 4 (12,099 acres)
areas   There is moderate recreation use of Duncan Creek and Coho Creek
The Duncan Canal Portage Trail runs across the area in the Duncan Creek and
Coho Creek drainages   This primitive trail, which is not officially on the
trail system, is part of a planned larger loop system which runs through
the adjacent Petersburg Creek-Duncan Salt Chuck Wilderness

(7) **Appearance (Apparent Naturalness):** The area is unmodified   The
existing visual condition of the area is predominantly natural

The majority of this roadless area (81 percent) is natural appearing, where
only ecological change has occurred (Existing Visual Condition (EVC) Type
I)   Less than one percent of the area appears to be untouched by human
activity (EVC Type II). Five percent of the area is in EVC Type IV, where
changes in the landscape are easily noticed by the average person and may
attract some attention. They appear to be disturbances but resemble
natural patterns. Thirteen percent is in EVC Type V where changes in the
landscape are obvious to the average person, and appear to be major
disturbances.

Eight percent of this roadless area is inventoried Variety Class A
(possessing landscape diversity that is unique for the character type) 68
percent is inventoried Variety Class B (possessing landscape diversity that
is common for the character type) and the remaining 24 percent is
inventoried Variety Class C (possessing a low degree of landscape
diversity).

(8) **Surroundings (External Influences):** The area is within close range of
the Petersburg Community   The Petersburg Creek-Duncan Salt Chuck
Wilderness directly adjoins the Lindenberg Roadless Area to the north   The
community of Kupreanof and the State of Alaska own the majority of land
surrounding Coho Creek and adjacent to Wrangell Narrows   Development on
these lands of other ownership could influence the setting

(9) **Attractions and Features of Special Interest:** The areas immediately
adjacent to saltwater or major creeks are valued for recreation uses such
as black bear hunting, hiking, and beach combing. Sport fishing is popular
and sightseeing is popular on Duncan Creek. The Duncan Canal Portage Trail
provides one of the few extended hiking opportunities in the area   This
loop trail of about 30 miles includes the adjacent Wilderness, and ties in
numerous recreation amenities. There is one inventoried recreation place
totaling 880 acres

b   Capability of Management as Wilderness or in an Unroaded Condition

(1) **Manageability and Management Area Boundaries:** This roadless area is adjacent to the community of Kupreanof, and to land owned by State of Alaska and Petersburg This will most likely lead to continued development of homesites, which may not be compatible with maintenance of parts of the area as roadless in the long term. On the other hand, this roadless area directly adjoins the Petersburg Creek-Duncan Salt Chuck Wilderness, which enhances the opportunity to mutually support the roadless, undeveloped character of each area. The northern part of the area is easily defined, the rest of the area is not Feasibility of management in a roadless condition is fair to high.

(2) **Natural Integrity:** The area is essentially unmodified Areas adjacent to private land are likely to change in character as development occurs

(3) **Opportunity for Solitude:** There is a high opportunity for solitude in the Lindenberg Roadless Area Use of floatplanes and powerboats may disrupt visitors for brief periods. Present recreation use levels are low to moderate in specific locations adjacent to the major creeks and drainages. A visitor camped on the creeks has a low chance of seeing or being seen by other visitors in the area

(4) **Opportunity for Primitive Recreation:** The area provides primarily semi-primitive non-motorized recreation opportunities.

ROS Class	Acres
Semi-Primitive Non-Motorized (SPNM)	18,237
Semi-Primitive Motorized (SPM)	2,920
Roaded Modified (RM)	1,640

The area contains one recreation place.

ROS CLASS	# OF REC. PLACES	TOTAL ACRES	CAPACITY BY RVD
SPM		880	932

The Duncan Canal Portage Trail provides access to the interior of this roadless area Fishing, hunting, and sightseeing are the basic activities provided in this primitive and semi-primitive setting The area is accessible by boat from the town of Petersburg in less then one-half hour

(5) **Special Features (Ecologic, Geologic, Scientific, Cultural):** A visitor hiking the Duncan Canal Portage Trail, in conjunction with the loop opportunity afforded by the Petersburg Lake Trail, will encounter numerous ecotypes: muskeg, coniferous forest, hardwood riparian, freshwater and saltwater marshes, and saltwater and freshwater bodies

c. Availability for Management as Wilderness or in an Unroaded Condition

   (1) Resource Potentials

      (a) Recreation Potential: Recreation potential for Lindenberg
      Roadless Area is high, due to the proximity to Petersburg and the
      adjacent Wilderness area. There is potential for additional outfitter
      and guide permits, and development of cabins and/or shelters
      Additional opportunities for trails would create more loop options,
      and could increase the diversity of settings and ecotypes encountered

      (b) Fish Resource: The Tongass Land Management Plan, amended Winter
      1985-86 identifies no specific fish habitat enhancement projects

      (c) Wildlife Resource: As identified in the Tongass Land Management
      Plan, amended 1985-86 browse, winter range, and waterfowl habitat
      improvement projects are planned in the area. These projects
      typically consist of planting, thinning, and burning

      (d) Timber Resource: There are 7,920 acres inventoried as
      tentatively suitable for timber harvest. This includes 820 acres of
      riparian old growth, and 7,100 acres of non-riparian old growth   None
      of the area is second growth.

      (e) Land Use Authorizations: Three recreation cabin special use
      permits are present.

      (f) Minerals: There are no inventoried areas with high mineral
      development potential.

      (g) Areas of Scientific Interest: The area contains no inventoried
      potential Research Natural Areas and has not been identified for any
      other scientific value.

   (2) Management Considerations

      (a) Maintenance of this area in a roadless condition enhances the
      opportunity to manage the adjacent Petersburg Creek-Duncan Salt Chuck
      Wilderness, and current and potential recreation opportunities

      (b) The potential for managing timber in this roadless area is
      dependent upon the development of stable market values to make
      consideration of this area economically feasible, and the ability to
      develop cost effective transportation of logs to saltwater

      (c) Fire: The area has no significant fire history.

      (d) Insects and Disease: Endemic tree diseases common to Southeast
      Alaska are present; there are no know epidemic disease occurrences

      (e) Land Status: The State has selected 3,515 acres at Coho Creek

d   Relationship to Communities and Other Roadless and Wilderness Areas

(1) **Nearby Roadless and Wilderness Areas and Uses:** The northern boundary
of the Lindenberg Roadless Area adjoins the Petersburg Creek-Duncan Salt
Chuck Wilderness   The remaining roadless units on Kupreanof Island are
separated from Lindenberg area by saltwater or roaded areas   This area
receives moderate recreational use

(2) **Distance From Population Centers (Accessibility):** Approximate
distances from population centers are as follows.

Community		Air Miles	Water Miles
Juneau	(Pop 23,729)	110	130
Petersburg	(Pop. 4,040)	3	4
Wrangell	(Pop. 2,836)	30	40

Wrangell and Petersburg are the nearest stops on the Alaska Marine Highway.

(3) **Interest by Proponents:**

(a) **Moratorium areas:** The area has not been identified as a
"moratorium area" in legislative initiatives to date

(b) **Local users/residents:** Many local residents want this area
remain unroaded and undeveloped as long as possible.

e. Environmental Consequences

ALTERNATIVE ANALYSIS TO BE DONE LATER

INDIVIDUAL ROADLESS AREA DESCRIPTION

NAME: Green Rocks (217)   ACRES (GROSS): 12,439   ACRES (NFS): 10,380

GEOZONE: S03
GEOGRAPHIC PROVINCE: Central Interior Islands

1989 WILDERNESS ATTRIBUTE RATING: 22

a. Description

(1) **Relationship to RARE II areas:** The table below displays the VCU 1/
names, VCU numbers, original WARS 2/ rating, and comments. This enables
the reader to compare the roadless areas evaluated in Appendix C with
previous analyses.

VCU Name	VCU No.	1979 WARS Rating	Comments
Mitchell	437*	22	
Narrows	447*	20	
Woewodski	448*	24	

*--The roadless area includes only part of this VCU.

(2) **History:** The area was used by the Stikine Tlingit in prehistoric and
historic times. Their use is evidenced by the remains of a village site,
fort site, and several fish weirs. The Green Rocks area was a popular
recreation destination in the early 1900's for area residents Green Rocks
Lake was known by local people as Mary's Lake, for Mary Allen whose family
lived near Green Rocks. A saltery and floating cannery operated in Beecher
Pass at the turn of the century.

(3) **Location and Access:** The area is on the Lindenberg Peninsula of
Kupreanof Island, adjacent to Wrangell Narrows. The area is within 10
miles of Petersburg. Roadless areas exist to the south and southwest.
across Wrangell Narrows. Saltwater access is by way of Wrangell Narrows
(transportation link to Petersburg via the Alaska Marine Highway), Duncan
Canal, and Beecher Pass. There are no sites suitable for landing wheeled
aircraft.

1/ A VCU (Value Comparison Unit) is one of 867 watersheds which make up the
Forest and were differentiated for planning purposes in the Tongass Land
Management Plan.
2/ Wilderness Attribute Rating System (WARS) was the nationwide system used to
rate the wilderness attributes of roadless areas in the Roadless Area
Review and Evaluation (RARE II).

(4) Geography and Topography: The area is comprised of one major drainage and several smaller ones The east is gently rolling with muskegs   In the western portion, gently rolling landscapes rise to timbered hillsides up to 2,600 feet The landform drops steeply to Duncan Canal on the west side There is one sizable stream in the area Dominant waterforms include Green Rocks Lake in the eastern portion of the area. The area contains six miles of shoreline on saltwater The area exists in a predominantly natural condition

(5) Ecosystem:

    (a) Classification: The area is classified as being in the Central Interior Islands Geographic Province. The area is generally characterized by rolling, subdued topography and extensive muskeg areas. There are no known areas of unique or uncommon plant/soils associations or geologic formations in the area.

    (b) Vegetation: Low-lying, interior portions of the area are muskeg (480 acres) Typical Sitka spruce and western hemlock forest covers the area, and is concentrated on the steep landform on the northern end.

    There are approximately 9,799 acres of forested land of which 4,539 acres are commercial forest land. Of the commercial forest land, 4,239 acres are non-riparian old growth and 260 acres are riparian old growth.

    (c) Soils: Soils in this area are formed in a wide variety of parent material, including bedrock and glacial drift In general, well- or moderately-well-drained soils are on moderate to steep mountain slopes with permeable parent materials These soils are very acidic, have cold soil temperatures, and are very high in organic matter Rooting is largely limited to the surface organic layers and the top few inches of mineral soil. These soils are usually moist, sometimes wet, but are never dry.

    More-poorly-drained soils developed on less-sloping areas and/or areas with impermeable soil materials. These soils have deep accumulations of organic matter and range from scrubby forested wetlands to open muskeg.

    Alpine soils, generally above 2,000 feet elevation, are mostly shallow, very wet organic soils or are extremely shallow and rocky

    (d) Fish Resource: Fish resources have been rated as part of the Tongass Land Management Plan (1978) and by the Alaska Department of Fish and Game in its Forest Habitat Integrity Program (1983) These ratings describe the value of VCU's for sport fish, commercial fish and estuaries.

    VCU 447 is rated as high value for sport fish VCU's 437 and 448 rated as having highly valued estuaries.

(e) Wildlife Resource: A population of Sitka black-tailed deer and black bear range over the area   Moose are occasionally sighted

(f) Threatened and Endangered Species: The area contains no known threatened or endangered species.

(6) Current Use and Management: The eastern portion of the area, 7,861 acres, was allocated to Land Use Designation (LUD) 3 in the Tongass Land Management Plan, which allows for development with consideration for amenity resources. The western half of the area, 2,558 acres, is designated LUD 4, which allows a full range of resource use and development. There is a one-mile trail, which is currently in poor condition, from saltwater to Green Rocks Lake   There is no known subsistence use in the area.

Land adjacent to this area was selected by the State of Alaska and lots were awarded at a public drawing. Some lots have been developed.

(7) Appearance (Apparent Naturalness): The area generally appears unmodified, with exceptions being recreation cabins, and private residences. Several units along the west side of the area adjacent to Duncan Creek have been harvested.

The majority of this roadless area (57 percent) is natural appearing, where only ecological change has occurred (Existing Visual Condition (EVC) Type I)   Three percent of this roadless area is EVC Type III, where changes in the landscape are noticed by the average forest visitor. The natural appearance of the landscape remains dominant. Seventeen percent of the area is in EVC Type IV, where changes in the landscape are easily noticed by the average person and may attract some attention. They appear to be disturbances but resemble natural patterns   About 23 percent is in EVC Type V where changes in the landscape are obvious to the average person, and appear to be major disturbances

Six percent of this roadless area is inventoried Variety Class A (possessing landscape diversity that is unique for the character type), 62 percent is inventoried Variety Class B (possessing landscape diversity that is common for the character type) and the remaining 32 percent is inventoried Variety Class C (possessing a low degree of landscape diversity).

(8) Surroundings (External Influences): The area is within close range of the Petersburg community   In 1980, the State of Alaska sold numerous parcels of land, through the land lottery program, along the eastern boundary of the roadless area. Many of these land owners have built permanent, year-round residences on their property. The Alaska Marine Highway ferries, as they travel through Wrangell Narrows, pass within one-quarter mile of the east side of the area. Extensive logging and roading occurs on the north side of the area.

(9) Attractions and Features of Special Interest: Green Rocks Lake, Green Rocks Trail, and several popular waterfowl hunting areas provide the greatest attraction to the recreating public. The scenery of the area is typical of much of the lowlands of Southeast Alaska   The area contains two inventoried recreation places totaling 1,541 acres

b. Capability of Management as Wilderness or in an Unroaded Condition

(1) Manageability and Management Area Boundaries: The area is bounded by saltwater to the south, and logging areas to the north. The west side is bounded by a combination of logging areas and saltwater Feasibility of management in a roadless condition is high To the east is state and private land.

(2) Natural Integrity: The area is unmodified except for the existing recreation cabins, residences and trail

(3) Opportunity for Solitude: There is a moderate opportunity for solitude within the area. Low-flying airplanes traveling to and from Petersburg, Alaska State ferries, and recreational boaters may at times pass over the area and be observed by people in this roadless area Present recreation use levels are low except around the trail. Generally, a person camped or traveling inland is unlikely to see others

(4) Opportunity for Primitive Recreation: The area provides primarily semi-primitive motorized and non-motorized opportunities

ROS Class	Acres
Semi-Primitive Non-Motorized (SPNM)	4,021
Semi-Primitive Motorized (SPM)	4,719
Roaded Modified (RM)	1,559
Rural (R)	80

The area contains two recreation places.

ROS CLASS	# OF REC. PLACES	TOTAL ACRES	CAPACITY BY RVD
SPNM	1	1,141	390
SPM	1	400	60

There are no developed recreation facilities in the area, except the trail to Green Rocks Lake. The character of the landforms generally allows the visitor to feel remote from the sights and sounds of human activity, except for the frequent drone of airplanes flying over and nearby The area is accessible by boat from the community of Petersburg in less than an hour, and from Wrangell in approximately two hours.

(5) Special Features (Ecologic, Geologic, Scientific, Cultural): There are opportunities to observe wildlife, enjoy the Green Rocks Lake Trail, and hunt waterfowl.

c. Availability for Management as Wilderness or in an Unroaded Condition

(1) Resource Potentials

(a) Recreation Potential: There is potential for additional outfitter and guide permits, and for developed trails and additional cabins or shelters

(b) **Fish Resource:** The Tongass Land Management Plan, amended Winter 1985-86 identifies no specific fish habitat enhancement projects

(c) **Wildlife Resource:** As identified in the Tongass Land Management Plan, amended 1985-86, browse, winter range, and waterfowl habitat improvement projects are planned in the area These projects typically consist of thinning, planting, and burning

(d) **Timber Resource:** There are 3,360 acres inventoried as tentatively suitable for harvest This includes 220 acres of riparian old growth and 3,120 acres of non-riparian old growth

(e) **Land Use Authorizations:** There are no special uses

(f) **Minerals:** There are no inventoried areas with high mineral development potential in the area and no known mining claims.

(g) **Areas of Scientific Interest:** The area contains no inventoried potential Research Natural Areas. The area has not been identified for any other scientific value.

(2) **Management Considerations**

(a) The potential for managing timber in this roadless area is dependent on the development of a road system or harvest methods which will allow extraction without need for extensive roading although one log transfer facility may be necessary.

(b) Maintenance of the area in a roadless condition enhances opportunities to manage the adjacent roadless areas as Wilderness. and provides greater opportunities for solitude and semi-primitive recreation It also maintains opportunities for wildlife, such as deer and bear, to move freely through the area.

(c) **Fire:** The area has no significant fire history

(d) **Insects and Disease:** Endemic tree diseases common to Southeast Alaska are present, there are no know epidemic disease occurrences

(e) **Land Status:** The State has selected about 2,000 acres concentrated near the shoreline. Some of these State-selected lands are currently private landholdings.

d. **Relationship to Communities and Other Roadless and Wilderness Areas**

(1) **Nearby Roadless and Wilderness Areas and Uses:** Green Rocks Roadless Area is adjacent to the Woewodski Island, Crystal, and Castle Roadless Areas. It is about four miles from the Lindenburg Roadless Area

(2) **Distance From Population Centers (Accessibility):** Approximate distances from population centers are as follows.

Community		Air Miles	Water Miles
Juneau	(Pop. 23,729)	115	135
Petersburg	(Pop. 4,040)	10	10
Wrangell	(Pop 2,836)	25	45
Ketchikan	(Pop. 12,705)	95	90

Petersburg and Wrangell are the nearest stops on the Alaska Marine Highway.

(3) Interest by Proponents:

(a) **Moratorium areas:** The area has not been identified as a
"moratorium" area or proposed as Wilderness in legislative initiatives
to date.

(b) **Local users/residents:** The area is primarily used for recreation
by residents of Petersburg and Kupreanof

e. Environmental Consequences

ALTERNATIVE ANALYSIS TO BE DONE LATER

INDIVIDUAL ROADLESS AREA DESCRIPTION

NAME: Woewodski (218)   ACRES (GROSS): 10,396   ACRES (NFS): 10,376

GEOZONE: S10
GEOGRAPHIC PROVINCE: Coast Range

1989 WILDERNESS ATTRIBUTE RATING: 22

a. Description

    (1) Relationship to RARE II areas: The table below displays the VCU 1/
names, VCU numbers, original WARS 2/ rating, and comments This enables
the reader to compare the roadless areas evaluated in Appendix C with
previous analyses.

		1979	
VCU Name	VCU No.	WARS Rating	Comments
Woewodski	448*	24	

*--The roadless area includes only part of this VCU.

    (2) History: The area was used by the Tlingit in prehistoric and historic
times. The area is unique in its extent of mineral wealth, minerals
include gold and its associated minerals. Various companies have held
rights to the island's mineral wealth since the early 1900's.

    (3) Location and Access: The area is across Wrangell Narrows (one-quarter
mile) from Mitkof Island. Kupreanof Island lies to the west and north.
Woewodski Island is within 16 miles of Petersburg It is surrounded by
roadless areas in all directions. Saltwater access is by way of Wrangell
Narrows (transportation link to Petersburg via Alaska Marine Highway),
Duncan Canal, Beecher Pass, and Sumner Strait. Floatplanes can access
Harvey Lake, where there is a Forest Service recreation cabin. There are
no sites suitable for landing wheeled aircraft.

    (4) Geography and Topography: The area is an island comprised of four
major drainages To the northeast there are flat muskegs rising to
timbered hillsides of 1,100 feet. To the southwest, landforms rise
gradually to 500 feet. There are no sizable streams on the island
Dominant waterforms include Harvey Lake in the northwest portion of the
island. Freshwater lakes total about 220 acres. The area contains 23
miles of shoreline on saltwater. The island exists in a predominantly
natural condition.

1/ A VCU (Value Comparison Unit) is one of 867 watersheds which make up the
Forest and were differentiated for planning purposes in the Tongass Land
Management Plan.
2/ Wilderness Attribute Rating System (WARS) was the nationwide system used to
rate the wilderness attributes of roadless areas in the Roadless Area
Review and Evaluation (RARE II).

(5) Ecosystem:

(a) Classification: The area is classified as being in the Coast Range Geographic Province. This province is generally characterized as a core of massive angular mountains capped with ice fields at high elevations, with somewhat lower mountains, deeply incised valleys and glacier-fed streams closer to the coast. This roadless area is more characteristic of the lower coastal portion There are no known areas of unique or uncommon plant/soils associations or geologic formations in the area

(b) Vegetation: Muskeg covers about 160 acres of the low-lying, interior portions of the island. Sitka spruce/western hemlock old growth is concentrated on the steep landform on the northern end of the island. The island also is a local source for spruce trolling poles and redcedar cabin logs.

There are approximately 9,917 acres of forested land of which 5,978 acres are commercial forest land. Of the commercial forest land, 5,318 acres are non-riparian old growth and 500 acres are riparian old growth.

(c) Soils: Soils in this area are formed in a wide variety of parent materials, including bedrock and glacial drift. In general, well- or moderately-well-drained soils are on moderate to steep mountain slopes with permeable parent materials These soils are very acidic, have cold soil temperatures, and are very high in organic matter Rooting is largely limited to the surface organic layers and the top few inches of mineral soil. These soils are usually moist, sometimes wet, but are never dry

More-poorly-drained soils developed on less-sloping areas and/or areas with impermeable soil materials. These soils have deep accumulations of organic matter and range from scrubby forested wetlands to open muskeg.

Alpine soils, generally above 2,000 feet elevation, are mostly shallow, very wet organic soils or are extremely shallow and rocky

(d) Fish Resource: Fish resources have been rated as part of the Tongass Land Management Plan (1979) and by the Alaska Department of Fish and Game in its Forest Habitat Integrity Program (1983) These ratings describe the value of VCU's for sport fish, commercial fish and estuaries.

The one VCU in this area, 448, rated as having highly valued estuaries.

There are two Alaska Department of Fish and Game numbered salmon producing streams Harvey Creek is the more important of the two streams, producing medium sized runs of coho salmon Harvey Lake is a popular fishing area for cutthroat trout.

(e) Wildlife Resource: Black bear and a small population of Sitka black-tailed deer range over the island.

(f) **Threatened and Endangered Species:** The area contains no known threatened or endangered species.

(6) **Current Use and Management:** All of the area was allocated to Land Use Designation 3 in the Tongass Land Management Plan, which allows for development with consideration for amenity resources In the late 1970's and early 1980's, the Woewodski Timber Sale was being planned to harvest approximately 15 million board feet of timber from this area It was scheduled for sale in 1990, but will not be offered This decision was due to a combination of significant resource concerns and marginal economic returns.

There is one public recreation cabin on Harvey Lake, and one at saltwater near the west end of Beecher Pass. Forest Service Recreation Trail 488 connects Harvey Lake to Duncan Canal. There is no known subsistence use in the area.

Land on islands adjacent to this area was selected by the State of Alaska and lots were awarded at a public drawing. Many lots have been developed and have dwellings on them. In addition, several old and current mines exist in the area.

(7) **Appearance (Apparent Naturalness):** The island generally appears unmodified, with exceptions being the recreation cabins, trail and two private residences. On the southeast end of the island, areas of blown-down timber are visible from Wrangell Narrows.

The majority of this roadless area (95 percent) is natural appearing, where only ecological change has occurred (Existing Visual Condition (EVC) Type I) Two percent of the area appears to be untouched by human activity (EVC Type II) Three percent of this roadless area is EVC Type III, where changes in the landscape are noticed by the average forest visitor. The natural appearance of the landscape remains dominant

Two percent of this roadless area is inventoried Variety Class A (possessing landscape diversity that is unique for the character type), 92 percent is inventoried Variety Class B (possessing landscape diversity that is common for the character type) and the remaining six percent is inventoried Variety Class C (possessing as low degree of landscape diversity).

(8) **Surroundings (External Influences):** The area is within close range of the Petersburg community. Numerous recreation residences are in the Beecher Pass area. In 1980, the State of Alaska sold numerous parcels of land through the land lottery program. Many of the land owners have built permanent, year-round residences on their properties. The Alaska Marine Highway ferries pass within one-quarter mile of the island on its east side.

(9) **Attractions and Features of Special Interest:** The Harvey Lake Trail and cabin, and proximity to Petersburg, provide the greatest attraction to the recreating public. The scenery of the area is typical of much of the lowlands of Southeast Alaska. The area contains six inventoried recreation places totaling 3,618 acres

b. Capability of Management as Wilderness or in an Unroaded Condition

(1) Manageability and Management Area Boundaries: The area is surrounded by saltwater and is easily defined. Feasibility of management in a roadless condition is high.

(2) Natural Integrity: The area is unmodified except for the existing recreation cabins, residences and trail located at the northern end of the island.

(3) Opportunity for Solitude: There is moderate opportunity for solitude within the area. Low-flying airplanes traveling to and from Petersburg, the ferry, and recreational boaters may at times pass by the area and be observed by people in this roadless area. Present recreation use levels are low except around the public recreation cabins and trail. Generally, a person camped or traveling inland is unlikely to see others.

(4) Opportunity for Primitive Recreation: The area provides primarily primitive non-motorized opportunity:

ROS Class	Acres
Semi-Primitive Non-Motorized (SPNM)	6,138
Semi-Primitive Motorized (SPM)	2,158
Roaded Natural (RN)	1,880
Roaded Modified (RM)	200

The area contains six recreation places.

ROS CLASS	# OF REC. PLACES	TOTAL ACRES	CAPACITY BY RVD
SPNM	1	839	70
SPM	2	718	2,059
RN	3	1,060	6,360

There are two public recreation cabins in the area. At the Harvey Lake cabin, the character of the landforms generally allows the visitor to feel remote from the sights and sounds of human activity. The area is accessible by boat from the community of Petersburg in less than an hour, and from Wrangell in approximately two hours. In July and August, fishing for silver salmon takes place around the recreation cabin.

(5) Special Features (Ecologic, Geologic, Scientific, Cultural): There are opportunities to observe wildlife and enjoy the Harvey Lake Trail and recreation cabin. There are remnants of old mines which could be of interest. The area is close to Petersburg on relatively sheltered waters

c. Availability for Management as Wilderness or in an Unroaded Condition

   (1) Resource Potentials

      (a) Recreation Potential: There is potential for additional
      outfitter and guide permits and for developed trails and additional
      cabins or shelters   The area's proximity to Petersburg make its
      potential higher than many other roadless areas

      (b) Fish Resource: The Tongass Land Management Plan, amended Winter
      1985-86 identifies fish habitat enhancement projects   No fish
      enhancement projects are identified in the plan for this area

      (c) Wildlife Resource: As identified in the Tongass Land Management
      Plan, amended 1985-86, habitat improvement projects are planned in the
      area. These projects typically consist of browse enhancement for big
      game through seeding, thinning, and planting.

      (d) Timber Resource: There are 5,379 acres inventoried as
      tentatively suitable for harvest. This includes 480 acres of riparian
      old growth, and 4,679 acres of non-riparian old growth. There is no
      second growth on the island.

      (e) Land Use Authorizations: There is one special use recreation
      residence permit on the north shore of the island, one private
      residence and one private mining property near the Harvey Lake
      trailhead

      (f) Minerals: The area has an abundant supply of minerals, and
      mineral exploration activity has increased in the last few years
      Claims cover 90 percent of the island.

      (g) Areas of Scientific Interest: The area contains no inventoried
      potential Research Natural Areas, and has not been identified for any
      other scientific value.

   (2) Management Considerations

      (a) The potential for managing timber in this roadless area is
      dependent on high market values, and the resolution of resource
      conflicts. One site for transferring logs to saltwater would be
      necessary   At present, timber values are not sufficient to cover
      development costs. Timber development could occur in conjunction with
      mining activities.

      (b) Maintenance of the area in a roadless condition enhances
      opportunities to manage the adjacent roadless areas as Wilderness and
      to provide enhanced opportunities for solitude and primitive
      recreation. It also maintains opportunities for wildlife to move
      freely through the area.

      (c) Fire: The area has no significant fire history

      (d) Insects and Disease: Endemic tree diseases common to Southeast
      Alaska are present, there are no known epidemic disease occurrences

(e) Land Status: Private landholdings total 38 72 acres   There are
no State or Native land selections within this roadless area

d. Relationship to Communities and Other Roadless and Wilderness Areas

(1) Nearby Roadless and Wilderness Areas and Uses: Woewodski Island is
adjacent to the Castle, Crystal, and Green Rocks Roadless Areas   The
Petersburg Creek-Duncan Salt Chuck Wilderness lies 20 miles north of this
roadless area

(2) Distance From Population Centers (Accessibility): Approximate
distances from population centers are as follows

Community		Air Miles	Water Miles
Juneau	(Pop. 23,729)	128	140
Petersburg	(Pop. 4,040)	12	16
Wrangell	(Pop. 2,836)	23	26
Ketchikan	(Pop. 12,705)	94	102

Petersburg and Wrangell are the nearest stops on the Alaska Marine Highway.

(3) Interest by Proponents:

(a) Moratorium areas: The area has not been identified as a
"moratorium" area or proposed as Wilderness in legislative initiatives
to date.

(b) Local users/residents: The area is primarily used for
recreational purposes, with Petersburg residents and those from the
Beecher Pass homesites making use of the Harvey Lake Trail and
recreation cabins.

(c) Other: During the planning for the Woewodski Timber Sale,
intense local opposition developed from residents in the Beechers Pass
area.

e. Environmental Consequences

ALTERNATIVE ANALYSIS TO BE DONE LATER

INDIVIDUAL ROADLESS AREA DESCRIPTION

NAME: North Mitkof (219)   ACRES (GROSS): 9,713   ACRES (NFS): 5,876

GEOZONE: S04
GEOGRAPHIC PROVINCE: Coast Range

1989 WILDERNESS ATTRIBUTE RATING: 19

a Description

(1) Relationship to RARE II areas: The table below displays the VCU 1/ names, VCU numbers, original WARS 2/ rating, and comments This enables the reader to compare the roadless areas evaluated in Appendix C with previous analyses.

VCU Name	VCU No.	1979 WARS Rating	Comments
Narrows	447*	20	
Frederick	449*	20	

*--The roadless area includes only part of this VCU.

(2) History: The area was claimed by several Stikine Tlingit clans who used the area for hunting and trapping. There are, however, no recorded cultural resources within the area boundaries. This may be a reflection of the low number of cultural resource inventories conducted in the area During historic times, there was activity in the Petersburg and Scow Bay areas.

(3) Location and Access: This roadless area is located on the northern portion of Mitkof Island, adjacent to and just southeast of the city of Petersburg. The Mitkof Highway generally makes up the eastern boundary of this roadless area, and Forest Road 6209 (Twin Creeks Road) makes up the southern portion. Forest Road 6204 makes up a portion of the eastern boundary. The northeastern portion of this area is adjacent to Frederick Sound. All of these roads and the body of water provide access to portions of this roadless area. The Ravens Roost Trail provides access from the city of Petersburg into the northwest portion of the roadless area Several other roads also provide access from Petersburg. Petersburg is served by the Alaska Marine Highway and daily jet service Helicopters have also been used to access areas inside this roadless area.

1/ A VCU (Value Comparison Unit) is one of 867 watersheds which make up the Forest and were differentiated for planning purposes in the Tongass Land Management Plan.
2/ Wilderness Attribute Rating System (WARS) was the nationwide system used to rate the wilderness attributes of roadless areas in the Roadless Area Review and Evaluation (RARE II).

(4) Geography and Topography: The area rises fairly steeply and uniformly from the west side, with drainages running to the east and north   Ridges are rounded and separate the drainages. Several gently-rolling plateaus exist at higher elevations. The highest point is just over 2,500 feet in elevation and the lowest point is at sea level. The area contains no shoreline on saltwater   The majority of the area, 5,696 acres, is covered by forest   Muskeg and alpine cover about 40 acres each

(5) Ecosystem:

   (a) Classification: The area is classified as being in the Coast Range Geographic Province   The area is characterized by landforms consisting of blocky mountains, separated by flat-floored, U-shaped valleys. During the last ice age, the area was covered by glaciers and the mountains have rounded hummocky summits, knobs and ridges

   The streams are short (less than 5 miles long) with steep to moderate gradients to saltwater. The lower parts of most valleys contain numerous small muskeg ponds.

   (b) Vegetation: Vegetation of this roadless area primarily consists of typical spruce-hemlock forests. Low-lying, poorly-drained portions of the area support peatmoss "muskeg" and scrub lodgepole pine

   There are 5,696 acres of forested land, of which 3,298 acres are commercial forest land. Of the commercial forest land, 3,018 acres are non-riparian old growth and 200 acres are riparian old growth

   (c) Soils: Soils in this area are formed in a wide variety of parent materials, including bedrock and glacial drift   In general, well- or moderately-well-drained soils are on moderate to steep mountain slopes with permeable parent materials. These soils are very acidic, have cold soil temperatures, and are very high in organic matter   Rooting is largely limited to the surface organic layers and the top few inches of mineral soil. These soils are usually moist, sometimes wet, but are never dry.

   More-poorly-drained soils developed on less-sloping areas and/or areas with impermeable soil materials   These soils have deep accumulations of organic matter and range from scrubby forested wetlands to open muskeg.

   Alpine soils, generally above 2,000 feet in elevation, are mostly shallow, very wet organic soils or are extremely shallow and rocky

   (d) Fish Resource: VCU 447 was rated "high" for sport fish, and "moderately high" for commercial fish values as part of the Tongass Land Management Plan (1979) and by the Alaska Department of Fish and Game in its Forest Habitat Integrity Program (1983). However, the streams that contributed to those ratings are not located within the roadless area. There is no estuarine habitat in the roadless area   The portion of the roadless area in VCU 449 does not contain any significant fish streams

(e) **Wildlife Resource:** A small population of Sitka black-tailed deer and black bear range over the roadless area.

(f) **Threatened and Endangered Species:** The area contains no known threatened or endangered species

(6) **Current Use and Management:** VCU 447 is allocated to Land Use Designation (LUD) 3 (3,737 acres). LUD 3 allows the land to be managed for a variety of uses. Emphasis is on managing for uses in a compatible and complementary manner to provide the greatest combination of benefits VCU 449 is allocated to LUD 4, (2,139) which provides for intensive resource use and development. Much of the land in this roadless area has been selected or is being considered for selection by the State and by the city of Petersburg. Areas which may possibly be selected are concentrated on the western, northern and eastern sides. The city of Petersburg gets its drinking water from a watershed which is located primarily in this roadless area.

Due to its proximity and accessibility, the North Mitkof Roadless Area receives relatively heavy recreational use. The Ravens Roost Trail begins on the edge of the community of Petersburg and climbs to a scenic view along the ridgeline. It accesses the Ravens Roost Cabin, also located along this scenic ridge. In the winter, the Twin Ridge Ski Trail provides access from the Twin Creek Road, along this same ridgeline to the Ravens Roost Cabin. Helicopters are used to access this area both summer and winter. Wintertime use of the area is growing Other cross-country ski use of the area occurs in the vicinity off the Twin Creek Road, where the terrain is suitable. Portions of the area have been studied for downhill skiing opportunities.

The roads which bound three sides of the area bring in other uses as well Hunting, fishing, and woodcutting are all popular activities There is some subsistence use in the area. The Tyee Powerline corridor skirts the edge of the area in places along the west side.

(7) **Appearance (Apparent Naturalness):** The majority of the area appears unmodified. Exceptions are some of the residences which have developed on State-selected land along Frederick Sound, development of private land along the western and northern boundaries, and the Ravens Roost Trail and Cabin.

Seventy-nine percent of the acreage was inventoried Variety Class B (possessing landscape diversity that is common for the character type) The remaining 21 percent was inventoried in Variety Class C (possessing a low degree of landscape diversity). Most of the roadless area (96 percent), is in Existing Visual Condition (EVC) I; these areas appear to be untouched by human activity. The other four percent is in EVC IV, in which changes to the landscape are easily noticed by the average person and may attract some attention. They appear to be disturbances but resemble natural patterns.

(8) **Surroundings (External Influences):** Many external influences affect
this area, and generally lessen in magnitude as one leaves the influences
of roads, accessible saltwater, and the city of Petersburg. Roads, and
timber management activities occur on three sides of the roadless area
Noise and sights of vehicles and active timber sales may occur
periodically   Along Frederick Sound, fishing and pleasure craft may be
visible and heard. The town of Petersburg can be seen and heard from some
locations as well   The presence of the airport provides a concentrated
area for airplanes and helicopters   Low-flying aircraft may temporarily
distract visitors in the area at times.

(9) **Attractions and Features of Special Interest:** The proximity to
Petersburg makes portions of this roadless area attractive to a variety of
uses. These include a municipal watershed, community expansion,
recreation, and various forms and intensities of resource utilization such
as timber, rock sources, utility corridors, and special uses   The area
contains three inventoried recreation places, totaling 3,398 acres

b. **Capability of Management as Wilderness or in an Unroaded Condition**

(1) **Manageability and Management Area Boundaries:** The area is bounded on
three sides by non-National Forest lands. These landlines generally follow
legal subdivisions. As they are developed, many external influences will
develop affecting various portions of the roadless area. Feasibility of
management in a Wilderness condition is low due to the amount of
distractions and inconsistent settings which may evolve. Feasibility of
management as an unroaded area is moderate to high for most of the area.
Some of the area is domestic watershed.

(2) **Natural Integrity:** The area is unmodified, and has maintained its
overall integrity

(3) **Opportunity for Solitude:** There is a moderate to low opportunity for
solitude within the area. Air traffic and marine traffic pass nearby, and
may be heard and observed by people in this roadless area, especially in
the northern portions   The trail and cabin also concentrate users,
lessening the probability of solitude. Overall recreation use levels are
moderate, except along the trail corridor and some easily-accessible
locales where use is high. Generally, a person camped or traveling inland
is unlikely to see others. Timber harvest or periodic activities in
adjacent areas would have a significant impact on the opportunity for
solitude when they are occurring.

(4) **Opportunity for Primitive Recreation:** The area provides primarily
Semi-Primitive Recreation opportunity as inventoried with the Recreation
Opportunity Spectrum (ROS) System.

ROS Class	Acres
Semi-Primitive Non-Motorized (SPNM)	4,157
Semi-Primitive Motorized (SPM)	160
Roaded Modified (RM)	1,159

The area contains three inventoried recreation places, two of which are in
the Semi-Primitive ROS class

ROS CLASS	# OF REC. PLACES	TOTAL ACRES	CAPACITY BY RVD
SPNM	2	3,078	4,950
RM	1	320	152

The Ravens Roost Trail and Twin Ridge Ski Trail provide developed
opportunities in the area, as does the Ravens Roost Cabin. The rolling
nature and vegetation of the landform generally allows a visitor to feel
remote from the sights and sounds of human activity. The area is readily
accessible from the community of Petersburg

(5) Special Features (Ecologic, Geologic, Scientific, Cultural): The
municipal watershed makes portions of the area extremely valuable   The
area has long been a popular recreation and hiking area for the town of
Petersburg.

c. **Availability for Management as Wilderness or in an Unroaded Condition**

   (1) Resource Potentials

      (a) **Recreation Potential:** There is potential for outfitter and guide
      permits and for additional ski and summer trails. Potential also
      exists for additional cabins, shelters, and roaded recreation
      activities, such as sightseeing, and downhill ski development

      (b) **Fish Resource:** No fish habitat enhancement projects were
      identified in the Tongass Land Management Plan, amended Winter
      1985-86.

      (c) **Wildlife Resource:** The Tongass Land Management Plan, amended
      Winter 1985-86 schedules some habitat improvement within the VCU's,
      but it is unlikely to occur within the roadless area.

      (d) **Timber Resource:** There are 1,879 acres inventoried as
      tentatively suitable for harvest. This includes 120 acres of riparian
      old growth, and 1,739 acres of non-riparian old growth.

      (e) **Land Use Authorizations:** There are no special uses in the area

      (f) **Minerals:** The area has low minerals potential.

      (g) **Areas of Scientific Interest:** The area has not been identified
      as a candidate Research Natural Area, or for any other scientific
      purpose.

(2) **Management Considerations**

(a) The potential for managing timber in this roadless area is dependent on market values. A road system and/or logging systems capable of harvesting the area would be necessary Nearby roads could be extended to accomplish some of this

(b) Maintenance of the area in a roadless condition enhances opportunities for certain wildlife, recreation activities, and continuation of watershed use by the city

(c) Fire: The area has no significant fire history

(d) **Insects and Disease:** Endemic tree diseases common to Southeast Alaska are present; there are no know epidemic disease occurrences

(e) **Land Status:** The area is surrounded on three sides by State land. The most recent selection deleted about 2,000 acres from the northern end of the roadless area.

d. **Relationship to Communities and Other Roadless and Wilderness Areas**

(1) **Nearby Roadless and Wilderness Areas and Uses:** The nearest roadless area is East Mitkof which is located about two miles to the southeast The Petersburg Creek-Duncan Salt Chuck Wilderness lies just to the west of Petersburg, across Wrangell Narrows.

(2) **Distance From Population Centers (Accessibility):** Approximate distances from population centers are as follows:

Community		Air Miles	Water Miles
Juneau	(Pop. 23,729)	123	133
Petersburg	(Pop. 4,040)	1	3
Wrangell	(Pop. 2,836)	26	32
Ketchikan	(Pop 12,705)	115	146

Petersburg is the nearest stop on the Alaska Marine Highway.

(3) **Interest by Proponents:**

(a) **Moratorium areas:** The area has not been identified as a "moratorium" area or proposed as Wilderness in legislative initiatives to date.

(b) **Local users/residents:** Portions of the area are identified for community expansion and development. Other portions of the area are traditional and/or popular recreation areas.

e. **Environmental Consequences**

ALTERNATIVE ANALYSIS TO BE DONE LATER

INDIVIDUAL ROADLESS AREA DESCRIPTION

NAME: East Mitkof (220)   ACRES (GROSS): 10,350   ACRES (NFS): 10,250

GEOZONE: S04
GEOGRAPHIC PROVINCE: Central Interior Islands

1989 WILDERNESS ATTRIBUTE RATING: 16

a. Description

(1) **Relationship to RARE II areas:** The table below displays the VCU 1/ names, VCU numbers, original WARS 2/ rating, and comments. This enables the reader to compare the roadless areas evaluated in Appendix C with previous analyses.

VCU Name	VCU No.	1979 WARS Rating	Comments
Narrows	447*	20	
Mitkof	450*	-	Not Rated in 1979
Ideal	453*		Not Rated in 1979

*--The roadless area includes only part of this VCU

(2) **History:** The area was inhabited by several clans of the Stikine Tlingit. An abandoned village site and petroglyphs are reported in the vicinity of Ideal Cove.. A saltery operated in Ideal Cove during the late 19th - early 20th century, and there appear to be some remnants of cabins

(3) **Location and Access:** This roadless area is located on the eastern side of Mitkof Island, adjacent to the southern end of Frederick Sound. The area is eight miles southeast of the city of Petersburg Forest roads and harvest units generally make up the irregular shaped western, southern. and northern boundaries, while Frederick Sound defines the eastern side The roads and Frederick Sound provide access to portions of this roadless area   Trails in the Three Lakes area provide good access to that portion of the roadless area. Petersburg is served by the Alaska Marine Highway and daily jet service.

1/ A VCU (Value Comparison Unit) is one of 867 watersheds which make up the Forest and were differentiated for planning purposes in the Tongass Land Management Plan.
2/ Wilderness Attribute Rating System (WARS) was the nationwide system used to rate the wilderness attributes of roadless areas in the Roadless Area Review and Evaluation (RARE II).

(4) Geography and Topography: The area generally slopes to the east in a gentle manner Terrain in the northern portion is nearly flat Terrain in the southern portion exhibits some relief, but is only gently rolling The highest point is just over 1,000 feet in elevation and the lowest point is at sea level. The area contains approximately 14 miles of shoreline on saltwater The majority of the area (8,368 acres) is covered by forest Muskeg covers about 1,781 acres, and freshwater lakes cover about 100 acres The major lakes are Sand, Shelter, Hill, and Crane

(5) Ecosystem:

(a) Classification: The area is classified as being in the Central Interior Islands Geographic Province. This province is generally characterized by rolling, subdued topography and extensive muskeg areas. This roadless area displays the characteristics of this province, with few hills reaching 600 feet in elevation. Much of the area is low lying and poorly drained. There are four lakes and many small muskeg ponds. Two medium-sized streams drain the hills to the west of the area, and several smaller streams drain the lowlands of the area itself. Landform variety is low and the shoreline on saltwater is fairly regular with Ideal Cove the only notable indentation.

(b) Vegetation: Vegetation of the lower, poorly-drained portions of this roadless area consists of large areas of peat moss "muskegs" with scattered lodgepole pine and scrub cedar. The better-drained hills support more typical spruce-hemlock and Alaska-cedar

There are 8,368 acres of forested land, of which 4,324 acres are commercial forest land. Of the commercial forest land, 3,704 acres are non-riparian old growth and 500 acres are riparian old growth

(c) Soils: Soils in this area are formed in a wide variety of parent material, including bedrock and glacial drift. In general, well- or moderately-well-drained soils are on moderate to steep mountain slopes with permeable parent materials. These soils are very acidic, have cold soil temperatures, and are very high in organic matter Rooting is largely limited to the surface organic layers and the top few inches of mineral soil. These soils are usually moist, sometimes wet, but are never dry.

More-poorly-drained soils developed on less-sloping areas and/or areas with impermeable soil materials. These soils have deep accumulations of organic matter and range from scrubby forested wetlands to open muskeg.

Alpine soils, generally above 2,000 feet elevation, are mostly shallow, very wet organic soils or are extremely shallow and rocky

(d) Fish Resource: VCU 450 was rated "high" for sport and commercial fish as part of the Tongass Land Management Plan (1979) and by the Alaska Department of Fish and Game in its Forest Habitat Integrity Program (1983) VCU 453 was highly rated for estuarine values

(e) **Wildlife Resource:** A small population of Sitka black-tailed deer and black bear range over the roadless area. There are also a few moose in the area

(f) **Threatened and Endangered Species:** The area contains no known threatened or endangered species

(6) **Current Use and Management:** VCU 453 and 453 are allocated to Land Use Designation (LUD) 3 (3,885 acres) in the Tongass Land Management Plan   LUD 3 allows the land to be managed for a variety of uses, with the emphasis on managing for uses in a compatible and complementary manner to provide the greatest combination of benefits   VCU 450 is allocated to LUD 4, (6,364) which provides for intensive resource use and development. The State has recently selected the land around Ideal Cove, an area of about 900 acres .

Due to its proximity to Petersburg and easy accessibility, the East Mitkof Roadless Area receives relatively-heavy recreational use. This use is centered around the Three Lakes area, which has a system of interconnecting trails, which in itself is unique to Southeast Alaska. The trails are short and gentle, adding to their popularity. Each of the lakes has a boat for general public use, and an old Civilian Conservation Corps shelter exists at Shelter Lake. Wintertime use of the area, mainly snowmobile use, is growing. Cross-country ski use also occurs, and is related to accessibility of the roads in winter to vehicles. The area around Ideal Cove receives a moderate amount of marine recreation use

The roads which bound three sides of the area bring in other uses as well. Hunting, fishing, and woodcutting are all popular activities   There is some subsistence use in the area.

(7) **Appearance (Apparent Naturalness):** The majority of the area appears unmodified. Exceptions are the trails and shelter, and areas adjacent to clearcuts and roads.

Seventeen percent of the acreage was inventoried Variety Class B (possessing landscape diversity that is common for the character type) The remaining 83 percent was inventoried in Variety Class C (possessing a low degree of landscape diversity)

Most of the roadless area (84 percent) is in Existing Visual Condition (EVC) I; these areas appear to be untouched by human activity Nine percent of the area is in EVC III, in which changes to the landscape are noticed by the average person, but they do not attract attention. The natural appearance of the landscape still remains dominant. About three percent is in EVC IV, in which changes to the landscape are easily noticed by the average person and may attract some attention. They appear to be disturbances but resemble natural patterns. EVC V accounts for the remaining four percent. These are areas in which changes to the landscape are obvious to the average person, and appear to be major disturbances

(8) **Surroundings (External Influences):** Roads and timber management activities occur on three sides of the roadless area. Noise and sights of vehicles and active timber sales may occur periodically, being greatest in magnitude near the roads and lessening as one moves away. Along Frederick Sound, fishing and pleasure craft may be visible and heard. Low-flying aircraft may temporarily distract visitors in the area at times.

(9) **Attractions and Features of Special Interest:** The proximity to Petersburg to roaded access makes portions of this roadless area attractive for recreation. The prime attractions are the complex of freshwater lakes and trails, and Ideal Cove. Ideal Cove has been selected by the State, and could serve as a gateway for small boats, such as canoes and kayaks, to the Stikine-LeConte Wilderness. It provides a sheltered route and channel through the mudflats. The area contains five inventoried recreation places totaling 5,285 acres.

b. **Capability of Management as Wilderness or in an Unroaded Condition**

(1) **Manageability and Management Area Boundaries:** The area is bounded on three sides by roads and timber management activities. There are few topographic breaks or other features to define the area. Feasibility of management in a Wilderness condition is low due to the amount of managed activities adjacent to this relatively narrow strip of roadless area. The level of development of planked trails and the amount of use in the Three Lakes area is also inconsistent with Wilderness designation. Feasibility of management in an unroaded condition is high, as it maintains traditional opportunities.

(2) **Natural Integrity:** Except for the plank trails and minor development at the lakes, the area is unmodified, and has maintained its overall integrity. However, adjacent management activities have likely impacted some of the natural integrity of this area, though this impact is not considered high.

(3) **Opportunity for Solitude:** There is a moderate to low opportunity for solitude within the area. Air traffic and marine traffic pass nearby and may be heard and observed by people in this roadless area. The trails and lakes also concentrate users, lessening the probability of solitude. Overall recreation use levels are moderate, except along the trail corridor and some easily-accessible locales, which are high. Generally, a person camped or traveling inland is unlikely to see others. Timber harvest or periodic activities in the adjacent areas would have a significant impact on the opportunity for solitude when they are occurring.

(4) **Opportunity for Primitive Recreation:** The area provides primarily Semi-Primitive Recreation opportunity as inventoried with the Recreation Opportunity Spectrum (ROS) System.

ROS Class	Acres
Semi-Primitive Non-Motorized (SPNM)	5,724
Semi-Primitive Motorized (SPM)	2,923
Roaded Natural (RN)	260
Roaded Modified (RM)	340

The area contains five inventoried recreation places

ROS CLASS	# OF REC. PLACES	TOTAL ACRES	CAPACITY BY RVD
SPNM	2	3,022	2,684
SPM	1	1,001	385
RN	2	260	325

The Three Lakes Trails system provides developed opportunities in the area. as does the shelter at Shelter Lake. The rolling nature and vegetation of the landform generally allows a visitor to feel remote from the sights and sounds of human activity The area is readily accessible from the community of Petersburg.

(5) **Special Features (Ecologic, Geologic, Scientific, Cultural):** There are few freshwater lakes on Mitkof Island. The clustering and accessibility of these lakes are a special feature The area has long been a popular recreation and hiking area for the town of Petersburg

c. **Availability for Management as Wilderness or in an Unroaded Condition**

(1) **Resource Potentials**

(a) **Recreation Potential:** There is potential for outfitter and guide permits, winter trails, and for additional summer trails Potential also exists for additional cabins, shelters, and roaded recreation activities, such as sightseeing and interpretation. In cooperation with the State, Ideal Cove could provide an important trail access to the Stikine-LeConte Wilderness and be used more extensively by watercraft , and be used for other marine activities, in cooperation with the state if appropriate development occurs

(b) **Fish Resource:** The Tongass Land Management Plan, amended Winter 1985-86, does not identify any fish habitat enhancement projects

(c) **Wildlife Resource:** As identified in the Tongass Land Management Plan, amended Winter 1985-86, no wildlife enhancement projects are planned.

(d) **Timber Resource:** There are 3,083 acres inventoried as tentatively suitable for harvest. This includes 320 acres of riparian old growth, and 2,663 acres of non-riparian old growth

(e) **Land Use Authorizations:** There are no special uses in the area

(f) **Minerals:** The area has low minerals potential

(g) **Areas of Scientific Interest:** The area has not been identified as a candidate Research Natural Area or for any other scientific purpose.

(2) Management Considerations

(a) The potential for managing timber in this roadless area is dependent on market values. A road system and/or logging systems capable of harvesting the area would be necessary   Nearby roads could be extended to accomplish some of this

(b) Maintenance of the area in a roadless condition enhances opportunities for certain wildlife and traditional recreation activities

(c) Fire: The area has no significant fire history

(d) Insects and Disease: Endemic tree diseases common to Southeast Alaska are present; there are no know epidemic disease occurrences

(e) Land Status: Ideal Cove, an area of about 900 acres, was selected by the State.

d. Relationship to Communities and Other Roadless and Wilderness Areas

(1) Nearby Roadless and Wilderness Areas and Uses: The nearest roadless areas are North Mitkof, and Manzanita. All are within two to four miles distance, and are separated by roads and harvest areas. The nearest Wilderness is the Stikine-LeConte, portions of which are about one to six miles away, across Frederick Sound and Dry Strait

(2) Distance From Population Centers (Accessibility): Approximate distances from population centers are as follows

Community		Air Miles	Water Miles
Juneau	(Pop. 23,729)	125	135
Petersburg	(Pop. 4,040)	8	12
Wrangell	(Pop. 2,836)	16	18
Ketchikan	(Pop. 12,705)	105	140

Petersburg is the nearest stop on the Alaska Marine Highway

(3) Interest by Proponents:

(a) Moratorium areas: The area has not been identified as a "moratorium" area or proposed as Wilderness in legislative initiatives to date

(b) Local users/residents: Portions of the area are traditional and/or popular recreation areas.

e. Environmental Consequences

ALTERNATIVE ANALYSIS TO BE DONE LATER

INDIVIDUAL ROADLESS AREA DESCRIPTION

NAME: Manzanita (223)   ACRES (GROSS): 8,070   ACRES (NFS): 7,850

GEOZONE: S04
GEOGRAPHIC PROVINCE: Central Interior Islands

1989 WILDERNESS ATTRIBUTE RATING: 18

a. Description

   (1) Relationship to RARE II areas: The table below displays the VCU 1/
   names, VCU numbers, original WARS 2/ rating, and comments This enables
   the reader to compare the roadless areas evaluated in Appendix C with
   previous analyses.

VCU Name	VCU No.	1979 WARS Rating	Comments
Sumner	452*	20	
Ideal	453*	0	Not Rated in 1979
Dry	454*	0	Not Rated in 1979

   *--The roadless area includes only part of this VCU

   (2) History: The area was claimed by the Stikine Tlingit clans, although
   no aboriginal sites have been recorded within this area. A mild-cure fish
   plant reportedly operated along the shores of Dry Strait in the early
   1900's.

   (3) Location and Access: This roadless area is located on the southeast
   corner of Mitkof Island The area is 18 miles southeast of the city of
   Petersburg Forest roads, harvest units, and the Mitkof Highway generally
   make up the irregularly-shaped boundaries. There is a small portion
   bounded by saltwater on the eastern side. The roads provide access to
   portions of this roadless area. Petersburg is served by the Alaska Marine
   Highway and daily jet service.

   (4) Geography and Topography: The area exhibits great relief, as the core
   is made up of a ridge system, with drainages oriented in all directions
   Slopes are moderate to steep. Elevation is from sea level to about 2,500
   feet. The area contains one mile of shoreline on saltwater The majority
   of the area (7,349 acres) is covered by forest Muskeg covers about 20
   acres. There is one small pond near the southwest corner.

1/ A VCU (Value Comparison Unit) is one of 867 watersheds which make up the
    Forest and were differentiated for planning purposes in the Tongass Land
    Management Plan.
2/ Wilderness Attribute Rating System (WARS) was the nationwide system used to
    rate the wilderness attributes of roadless areas in the Roadless Area
    Review and Evaluation (RARE II).

(5) Ecosystem:

   (a) Classification: The area is classified as being in the Central
   Interior Islands Geographic Province   This province is generally
   characterized by subdued, rolling topography and extensive muskegs,
   but may have rugged terrain in localized areas   This roadless area
   displays the mountainous characteristics of the province   The area is
   essentially a mountaintop and ridge system, with the boundaries on the
   lower slopes

   Drainage from this area forms the high gradient headwaters for several
   moderate-sized streams.

   (b) Vegetation: Vegetation of this roadless area primarily consists
   of typical spruce-hemlock forests on the mountain sides, and minor
   amounts of subalpine scrub on top

   There are 7,349 acres of forested land, of which 4,486 acres are
   commercial forest land. Of the commercial forest land, 4,026 acres
   are non-riparian old growth and 461 acres are riparian old growth

   (c) Soils: Soils in this area are formed in a wide variety of parent
   materials, including bedrock and glacial drift   In general, well- or
   moderately-well-drained soils are on moderate to steep mountain slopes
   with permeable parent materials. These soils are very acidic, have
   cold soil temperatures, and are very high in organic matter   Rooting
   is largely limited to the surface organic layers and the top few
   inches of mineral soil. These soils are usually moist, sometimes wet
   but are never dry

   More-poorly-drained soils developed on less-sloping areas and/or areas
   with impermeable soil materials   These soils have deep accumulations
   of organic matter and range from scrubby forested wetlands to open
   muskeg

   Alpine soils, generally above 2,000 feet elevation, are mostly
   shallow, very wet organic soils or are extremely shallow and rocky

   (d) Fish Resource: None of the streams within the area contain fish
   habitat   Water from the area does not flow into any highly-rated
   sport fish streams or commercially-important fish streams   There are
   no important estuarine values in the area.

   (e) Wildlife Resource: A population of Sitka black-tailed deer and
   black bear range over the roadless area. A few moose may use the
   area.

   (f) Threatened and Endangered Species: The area contains no known
   threatened or endangered species.

(6) Current Use and Management: Two VCU's which make up portions of the
area are allocated to Land Use Designation (LUD) 3 (2,182 acres)   LUD 3
allows the land to be managed for a variety of uses, with the emphasis on
managing for uses in a compatible and complementary manner to provide the
greatest combination of benefits. The third VCU is allocated to LUD 4

(5,108 acres), which provides for intensive resource use and development.
Some State land selections have occurred along the southern portion of this
roadless area

Due to its proximity to Petersburg and accessibility by road, the Manzanita
Roadless Area receives light to moderate recreational use   Most use is
concentrated along the outside edges which are accessible by roads   Uses
along the roads, which bound three sides of the area, are primarily
hunting, berry picking, snowmobiling and woodcutting. Some of the use is
likely for subsistence

(7) Appearance (Apparent Naturalness): The majority of the area appears
unmodified   Exceptions are areas adjacent to clearcuts and roads

One-hundred percent of the area was inventoried as Variety Class B
(possessing landscape diversity that is common for the character type)

Most of the roadless area (68 percent) is in Existing Visual Condition
(EVC) I; these areas appear to be untouched by human activity   About 20
percent is in EVC IV, in which changes to the landscape are easily noticed
by the average person and may attract some attention   They appear to be
disturbances but resemble natural patterns. EVC V accounts for the
remaining 12 percent. These are areas in which changes to the landscape are
obvious to the average person, and appear to be major disturbances

(8) Surroundings (External Influences): Roads and timber management
activities occur on all sides of the roadless area   Noise and sights of
vehicles and active timber sales may occur periodically, being greatest in
magnitude near the roads and lessening as one moves away. The Tyee
Powerline skirts the western side of the area and is visible from many
places within the roadless area. Low-flying aircraft may temporarily
distract visitors in the area fairly frequently

(9) Attractions and Features of Special Interest: The proximity to
Petersburg by roaded access make portions of this roadless area attractive
for recreation   The prime attractions are hunting, woodcutting and
gathering areas, and the system of ridges in the center, which provides
views and excellent snow machine travel. Saltwater access is also an
attraction. The area contains two inventoried recreation places totaling
321 acres.

b. Capability of Management as Wilderness or in an Unroaded Condition

(1) Manageability and Management Area Boundaries: The area is bounded on
all sides by roads and timber management activities. There are few
topographic breaks or other natural features to define the area
Feasibility of management in a Wilderness condition is low to moderate, due
to the amount of managed activities adjacent to this roadless area.
Feasibility of management in an unroaded condition is moderate, due to the
steepness of the terrain.

(2) **Natural Integrity:** The area is unmodified, however its overall integrity is not considered pristine. Adjacent management activities have likely impacted some of the natural integrity of this area, such as wildlife. The irregular shape of the area also lessens its natural integrity

(3) **Opportunity for Solitude:** There is a low opportunity for solitude within the area Air traffic and vehicle traffic pass nearby and may be heard and observed by people in this roadless area Overall recreation use levels are low, except along the fringes near road access Generally, a person camped or traveling away from the roads is unlikely to encounter other people nearby Timber harvest or periodic activities in the adjacent areas would have a significant impact on the opportunity for solitude when they are occurring.

(4) **Opportunity for Primitive Recreation:** The area provides some Semi-Primitive Recreation opportunity as inventoried with the Recreation Opportunity Spectrum (ROS) System.

ROS Class	Acres
Semi-Primitive Non-Motorized (SPNM)	3,143
Semi-Primitive Motorized (SPM)	280
Roaded Modified (RM)	4,426

The area contains two inventoried recreation places.

ROS CLASS	# OF REC. PLACES	TOTAL ACRES	CAPACITY BY RVD
SPM	1	280	129
RM	1	40	39

There are no developed recreation opportunities in this area The steep nature of the landforms allows a visitor to feel remote from the sights and sounds of human activity. The area is readily accessible from the community of Petersburg.

(5) **Special Features (Ecologic, Geologic, Scientific, Cultural):** The system of ridgelines and the minor saltwater access attract recreationists

c. **Availability for Management as Wilderness or in an Unroaded Condition**

(1) **Resource Potentials**

(a) **Recreation Potential:** There is little potential for outfitter and guide permits. There is potential for trails, and possibly shelters, to access the ridgelines and saltwater. There is some potential for interpretive activities due to its accessibility and proximity to the existing interpretive tour of the Mitkof Highway and Three Lakes Road. A State boat ramp and unmaintained picnic area exist nearby

(b) Fish Resource: No fish habitat enhancement projects were identified in the Tongass Land Management Plan, amended Winter 1985-86

(c) Wildlife Resource: As identified in the Tongass Land Management Plan, amended Winter 1985-86, no wildlife habitat improvement projects are planned within the roadless area.

(d) Timber Resource: There are 2,684 acres inventoried as tentatively suitable for harvest. This includes 260 acres of riparian old growth, and 2,423 acres of non-riparian old growth

(e) Land Use Authorizations: There are no special uses in the area

(f) Minerals: The area has low minerals potential.

(g) Areas of Scientific Interest: The area has not been identified as an Inventoried Potential Research Natural Area, or for any other scientific purpose.

(2) Management Considerations

(a) The potential for managing timber in this roadless area is dependent on market values. A road system and/or logging systems capable of harvesting the area would be necessary. Nearby roads could be extended to accomplish some of this

(b) Maintenance of the area in a roadless condition enhances opportunities for certain wildlife and traditional recreation activities.

(c) Fire: The area has no significant fire history.

(d) Insects and Disease: Endemic tree diseases common to Southeast Alaska are present; there are no know epidemic disease occurrences

(e) Land Status: All National Forest System land.

d. Relationship to Communities and Other Roadless and Wilderness Areas

(1) Nearby Roadless and Wilderness Areas and Uses: The nearest roadless areas are North Mitkof, East Mitkof, and Crystal. All are within two to twelve miles distance, and are separated by roads and harvest areas The nearest Wilderness is the Stikine-LeConte, portions of which are about one mile away across Dry Strait.

(2) Distance From Population Centers (Accessibility): Approximate distances from population centers are as follows:

Community		Air Miles	Water Miles
Juneau	(Pop 23,729)	130	140
Petersburg	(Pop 4,040)	17	20
Wrangell	(Pop. 2,836)	11	16
Ketchikan	(Pop. 12,705)	100	115

Petersburg is the nearest stop on the Alaska Marine Highway

(3)   Interest by Proponents:

(a) Moratorium areas: The area has not been identified as a "moratorium" area or proposed as Wilderness in legislative initiatives to date

(b) Local users/residents: Portions of the area are used for recreation.

e.   Environmental Consequences

ALTERNATIVE ANALYSIS TO BE DONE LATER

INDIVIDUAL ROADLESS AREA DESCRIPTION

NAME: Crystal (224)   ACRES (GROSS): 21,794   ACRES (NFS): 19,293

GEOZONE. S04
GEOGRAPHIC PROVINCE: Central Interior Islands

1989 WILDERNESS ATTRIBUTE RATING: 20

a   Description

    (1) **Relationship to RARE II areas:** The table below displays the VCU 1/
names, VCU numbers, original WARS 2/ rating, and comments This enables
the reader to compare the roadless areas evaluated in Appendix C with
previous analyses.

VCU Name	VCU No.	1979 WARS Rating	Comments
Narrows	447*	20	
Woewodski	448*	24	
Crystal	451*	-	Not Rated in 1979
Sumner	452*	20	

*--The roadless area includes only part of this VCU

    (2) **History:** The area was claimed be several Stikine Tlingit clans and
used for hunting and gathering of subsistence items. Evidence of their use
is indicated by the remains of temporary camps, fish weirs, petroglyphs
and bark-stripped trees. The area was also important in historic times

    (3) **Location and Access:** This roadless area is located on the southwest
corner of Mitkof Island. The area is 15 miles southwest of the city of
Petersburg. Forest roads, harvest units, the Mitkof Highway, and saltwater
make up the irregularly-shaped boundaries. The roads provide access to
portions of this roadless area. Petersburg is served by the Alaska Marine
Highway and daily jet service.

1/ A VCU (Value Comparison Unit) is one of 867 watersheds which make up the
Forest and were differentiated for planning purposes in the Tongass Land
Management Plan.
2/ Wilderness Attribute Rating System (WARS) was the nationwide system used to
rate the wilderness attributes of roadless areas in the Roadless Area
Review and Evaluation (RARE II).

(4) Geography and Topography: Two mountainous areas dominate the
landform   To the north lies Crystal Peak and associated ridgelines   To
the south lies the northern portion of the Sumner Mountains   A river
valley separates the two mountain areas. Elevation ranges from sea level
to 3,317 feet at Crystal Peak   The area contains six miles of shoreline on
saltwater   Slopes are fairly steep overall, except in the northwest
portion where they lessen as they approach saltwater   Crystal Lake is a
significant water body to the north, and a somewhat smaller lake exists to
the northwest   The majority of the area, 17,432 acres, is covered by
forest   Muskeg covers about 40 acres, and alpine covers about 660 acres.
Rock outcrops and faces cover another 340 acres   The lakes cover a
combined area of 240 acres.

(5) Ecosystem:

(a) Classification: The area is classified as being in the Central
Interior Islands Geographic Province. This province is generally
characterized by subdued, rolling topography and extensive muskeg
areas, but may have rugged terrain in localized areas   The roadless
area exhibits landforms fairly typical of the province.

The area contains several small streams and forms the headwaters of
two medium-sized streams.

(b) Vegetation: Vegetation of this roadless area primarily consists
of typical spruce-hemlock forests on the mountain sides, alpine
vegetation at elevations above 2,000 feet, and low-lying,
poorly-drained portions of the area are often covered with muskeg

There are 17,432 acres of forested land, of which 9,387 acres are
commercial forest land. Of the commercial forest land, 6,825 acres
are non-riparian old growth and 881 acres are riparian old growth

(c) Soils: Soils in this area are formed in a wide variety of parent
materials, including bedrock and glacial drift. In general, well- or
moderately-well-drained soils are on moderate to steep mountain slopes
with permeable parent materials   These soils are very acidic, have
cold soil temperatures, and are very high in organic matter   Rooting
is largely limited to the surface organic layers and the top few
inches of mineral soil. These soils are usually moist, sometimes wet
but are never dry

More-poorly-drained soils developed on less-sloping areas and/or areas
with impermeable soil materials   These soils have deep accumulations
of organic matter and range from scrubby forested wetlands to open
muskeg.

Alpine soils, generally above 2,000 feet elevation, are mostly
shallow, very wet organic soils or are extremely shallow and rocky

(d) Fish Resource: Fish resources have been rated as part of the
Tongass Land Management Plan (1979) and by the Alaska Department of
Fish and Game in its Forest Habitat Integrity Program (1983) These
ratings describe the value of VCU's for sport fish, commercial fish,
and estuaries.

VCU 447 was rated high for sport fish and commercial fish values, although that small portion of VCU 447 in this roadless area did not contribute significantly to that rating   VCU 451 was also rated high for sport fish values   VCU's 447 and 452 were rated as moderately-high value for commercial fish and VCU 451 was rated as having high commercial fish value   VCU's 448 and 452 were rated as having highly valued estuaries.

(e) Wildlife Resource: A population of Sitka black-tailed deer and black bear range over the roadless area, as do some moose

(f) Threatened and Endangered Species: The area contains no known threatened or endangered species.

(6) Current Use and Management: All VCU's of which this roadless area is composed are allocated to Land Use Designation (LUD) 3. LUD 3 allows the land to be managed for a variety of uses, with the emphasis on managing for uses in a compatible and complementary manner to provide the greatest combination of benefits. Some State land selections have occurred or are pending in the southern portion of this roadless area. The western portion of this roadless area has been selected by the State, and selections are pending which encompass Crystal Lake. Crystal Lake provides a water source for the State's Crystal Lake Fish Hatchery and for domestic use by the residents at the hatchery   There is a concrete dam on the outlet of Crystal Lake and a penstock which brings water down the mountain where it is used to generate electricity for the city of Petersburg. The top of Crystal Peak is currently being studied for a possible communications site

Due to its proximity to Petersburg and accessibility by road and water, the Crystal Roadless Area receives moderate recreational use. Most of the use, consisting primarily of hunting, berry picking and woodcutting, is concentrated along the outside edges which are accessible by the roads which bound three sides of the area. Crystal Lake and the alpine ridges above attract recreationists despite the lack of extensive improved access. There is a trail from the hatchery to Crystal Lake. There is some subsistence use in the area.

(7) Appearance (Apparent Naturalness): The majority of the area appears unmodified. Exceptions are areas adjacent to clearcuts and roads, and the dam and penstock from Crystal Lake.

Twenty-nine percent of this roadless area was inventoried in Variety Class A (possessing landscape diversity that is unique for the character type), and 71 percent of the acreage was inventoried Variety Class B (possessing landscape diversity that is common for the character type)   None was inventoried in Variety Class C.

Most of the roadless area (86 percent) is in Existing Visual Condition (EVC) I; these areas appear to be untouched by human activity. EVC II accounts for two percent, in which changes to the landscape are not noticed by the average person unless pointed out   About five percent of the area is in EVC III, in which changes to the landscape are noticed by the average person, but they do not attract attention. The natural appearance of the landscape still remains dominant   About four percent is in EVC IV, in

which changes to the landscape are easily noticed by the average person and
may attract some attention They appear to be disturbances but resemble
natural patterns EVC V accounts for the remaining three percent These
are areas in which changes to the landscape are obvious to the average
person, and appear to be major disturbances

(8) **Surroundings (External Influences):** Roads and timber management
activities occur on three sides of the roadless area Noise and sights of
vehicles and active timber sales may occur periodically, being greatest in
magnitude near the roads and lessening as one moves away Wrangell
Narrows, which receives heavy boat traffic, is adjacent to the west
Low-flying aircraft may temporarily distract visitors in the area fairly
frequently

(9) **Attractions and Features of Special Interest:** The proximity to
Petersburg by roaded access make portions of this roadless area attractive
for recreation. The prime attractions are hunting, woodcutting and
gathering areas, and the system of ridges in alpine terrain which provides
outstanding views. Saltwater access is also an attraction The area
contains five inventoried recreation places totaling 6,865 acres

b. **Capability of Management as Wilderness or in an Unroaded Condition**

(1) **Manageability and management area boundaries:** The area is bounded on
three sides by roads and timber management activities Private land occurs
on the other side, and there are pending State land selections in the core
of the area, at Crystal Lake. There are few topographic breaks or other
natural features to define the area. Feasibility of management in a
Wilderness condition is low to moderate, due to the amount of cultural
activities adjacent to this roadless area Feasibility of management in an
unroaded condition is moderate, as it maintains traditional opportunities,
and the domestic water source.

(2) **Natural Integrity:** The area is unmodified, however its overall
integrity is not considered pristine. Adjacent management activities have
likely impacted some of the natural integrity of this area, such as
wildlife The irregular shape of the area and inclusion of private land
also lessen its natural integrity.

(3) **Opportunity for Solitude:** There is a low to moderate opportunity for
solitude within the area. Air traffic and vehicle traffic pass nearby and
may be heard and observed by people in this roadless area Overall
recreation use levels are moderate, being higher along the fringes near
road access. Generally, a person camped or traveling within the area away
from the roads is unlikely to encounter others nearby. Timber harvest or
periodic activities in adjacent areas would have a significant impact on
the opportunity for solitude when they are occurring.

(4) **Opportunity for Primitive Recreation:** The area provides some
Semi-Primitive Recreation opportunity as inventoried with the Recreation
Opportunity Spectrum (ROS) System

ROS Class	Acres
Semi-Primitive Non-Motorized (SPNM)	5,724
Roaded Natural (RN)	1,021
Roaded Modified (RM)	12,549

The area contains five inventoried recreation places

ROS CLASS	# OF REC. PLACES	TOTAL ACRES	CAPACITY BY RVD
SPNM	1	5,724	256
RN	2	920	9,649
RM	2	220	211

The only developed recreation facility in the area is the trail from the
hatchery up to Crystal Lake The steep nature of the landforms and
relationship to external influences allow a visitor to feel somewhat remote
from the sights and sounds of human activity The area is readily
accessible from the community of Petersburg.

(5) **Special Features (Ecologic, Geologic, Scientific, Cultural):** The
system of ridgelines, which comprises the greatest amount of alpine setting
on Mitkof Island, is an important feature. Crystal Lake, road access from
Petersburg, and saltwater access also attract recreationists

c. **Availability for Management as Wilderness or in an Unroaded Condition**

   (1) **Resource Potentials**

   (a) **Recreation Potential:** There is little potential for outfitter
   and guide permits Potential trails and shelters have been identified
   to access the ridgelines. There is some potential for interpretive
   activities due to the areas accessibility and proximity to the
   existing interpretive tour of the Mitkof Highway and Three Lakes Road,
   and the popular Blind Slough recreation site

   (b) **Fish Resource:** No fish habitat enhancement projects are
   identified in the Tongass Land Management Plan, amended Winter 1985-86
   for this area.

   (c) **Wildlife Resource:** As identified in the Tongass Land Management
   Plan, amended Winter 1985-86, no wildlife enhancement projects are
   planned in the roadless area.

   (d) **Timber Resource:** There are 5,764 acres inventoried as
   tentatively suitable for harvest. This includes 460 acres of riparian
   old growth, and 4,663 acres of non-riparian old growth

   (e) **Land Use Authorizations:** There are three special uses in the
   area

   (f) **Minerals:** The area has low minerals potential

(g) **Areas of Scientific Interest:** The area has not been identified as an Inventoried Potential Research Natural Area, or for any other scientific purpose

(2) **Management Considerations**

(a) The potential for managing timber in this roadless area is dependent on market values. A road system and/or logging systems capable of harvesting the area would be necessary Nearby roads could be extended to accomplish some of this

(b) Maintenance of the area in a roadless condition enhances opportunities for certain wildlife, and traditional and potential recreation activities. The extensive alpine area is an attraction for recreationists.

(c) **Fire:** The area has no significant fire history

(d) **Insects and Disease:** Endemic tree diseases common to Southeast Alaska are present, there are no know epidemic disease occurrences

(e) **Land Status:** An extensive area along Wrangell Narrows, and the basin and area around Crystal Lake have been selected by the State About 160 acres of private land exist along Wrangell Narrows

d. **Relationship to Communities and Other Roadless and Wilderness Areas**

(1) **Nearby Roadless and Wilderness Areas and Uses:** The nearest roadless areas are North Mitkof, East Mitkof, and Manzanita. All are within two to twelve miles distance, and are separated by roads and harvest areas The nearest Wilderness is the Stikine-LeConte, portions of which are about 12 miles away

(2) **Distance From Population Centers (Accessibility):** Approximate distances from population centers are as follows:

Community ·		Air Miles	Water Miles
Juneau	(Pop 23,729)	130	140
Petersburg	(Pop 4,040)	15	17
Wrangell	(Pop. 2,836)	20	30
Ketchikan	(Pop. 12,705)	90	105

Petersburg is the nearest stop on the Alaska Marine Highway

(3) **Interest by Proponents:**

(a) **Moratorium areas:** The area has not been identified as a "moratorium" area or proposed as Wilderness in legislative initiatives to date.

(b) **Local users/residents:** Portions of the area are traditional and/or popular recreation areas. Support for a trail to the ridgeline and alpine terrain above Crystal Lake has evolved from several recreation public meetings.

INDIVIDUAL ROADLESS AREA DESCRIPTION

NAME: Kadin (225)   ACRES (GROSS): 1,623   ACRES (NFS): 1,623

GEOZONE: S14
GEOGRAPHIC PROVINCE: Central Interior Islands

1989 WILDERNESS ATTRIBUTE RATING: 24

a. Description

(1) **Relationship to RARE II areas:** The table below displays the VCU 1/
names, VCU numbers, original WARS 2/ rating, and comments. This enables
the reader to compare the roadless areas evaluated in Appendix C with
previous analyses

VCU Name	VCU No.	1979 WARS Rating	Comments
Vank	455*	17	Rating included other islands in the group

*--The roadless area includes only part of this VCU

(2) **History:** Kadin Island was claimed by the Stikine Tlingit and evidence
of their use is indicated by the presence of petroglyphs The island was
named in 1863 for an Aleut member of a Russian surveying party   The island
was likely visited by early fur traders traveling between the Stikine River
and Fort Wrangell   Kadin is known locally as High Island, in reference to
its height relative to nearby islands.

(3) **Location and Access:** This roadless area consists of one small island
located off the mouth of the Stikine River. At low tides it is nearly
surrounded by tideflats formed by the sediments of the Stikine River   It
is north and slightly west of the town of Wrangell   Sumner Strait, Stikine
Strait and Eastern Passage all converge in this area   Access is by way of
boat or floatplane. There are no sites suitable for landing wheeled
aircraft.

(4) **Geography and Topography:** The island rises fairly steeply and
uniformly to a height just above 1,000 feet. Kadin Island is basically
kidney shaped, and the landform is heavily influenced by its location at
the mouth of the Stikine River. High winds moving down the Stikine River
canyon pick up silt from the unvegetated glacial river floodplain and
deposit it as loess on islands at the river's mouth, including Kadin
Island. The island is completely covered by forest, and contains six miles
of shoreline on saltwater.

1/ A VCU (Value Comparison Unit) is one of 867 watersheds which make up the
Forest and were differentiated for planning purposes in the Tongass Land
Management Plan.
2/ Wilderness Attribute Rating System (WARS) was the nationwide system used to
rate the wilderness attributes of roadless areas in the Roadless Area
Review and Evaluation (RARE II).

(5) Ecosystem:

(a) Classification: The area is classified as being in the Central Interior Island Geographic Province   This province is characterized by generally subdued, rolling topography and extensive muskeg areas, but may have rugged terrain in localized areas   This island exhibits the typical rounded landform, but because of its small size it lacks the characteristic land and waterform variety   •

There are no significant streams on the island   The small drainages are steep and short to saltwater

(b) Vegetation: The island is heavily vegetated with spruce-hemlock and spruce-devil's club forest types.

There are 1,603 acres of forested land, all of which is commercial forest land. Of the commercial forest land, 1,483 acres are non-riparian old growth and 120 acres are riparian old growth

(c) Soils: Soils are unique because of the influence of the Stikine River. High winds moving down the Stikine River canyon pick up silt from the unvegetated glacial river floodplain and deposit it as loess on islands at the river's mouth. The continuing rain of loess onto the upper soil layers provides a supply of unleached, nutrient-rich soil material to the forests of the island   The loess deposition overcomes the process of acid bog formation (paludification) that overtakes most stable sites of moderate topographic relief in the Tongass National Forest. Few areas in the world have a combination of high rainfall and recent loess deposition, so the properties of the soils here are of special interest   Thick loess soils also have a high water storage capacity, so the hydrology of the island is of interest too.

(d) Fish Resource: There are no fish streams on the island

(e) Wildlife Resource: A small population of Sitka black-tailed deer and black bear range over the roadless area

(f) Threatened and Endangered Species: The area contains no known threatened or endangered species

(6) Current Use and Management: The VCU in which this island is located is allocated to Land Use Designation (LUD) 3   LUD 3 allows the land to be managed for a variety of uses, with the emphasis on managing for uses in a compatible and complementary manner to provide the greatest combination of benefits. There is some subsistence use in the area. The island is at the mouth of the Stikine River. Recreationists traveling into the Stikine-LeConte Wilderness up the river must pass by this area

(7) **Appearance (Apparent Naturalness):** The area appears unmodified

The entire island was inventoried Variety Class B (possessing landscape diversity that is common for the character type) and all of it is in Existing Visual Condition (EVC) I, these areas appear to be untouched by human activity

(8) **Surroundings (External Influences):** The area is at the mouth of the Stikine River Several nearby islands, especially Liesnoi, and Sokolof, have been impacted by management activities, mainly clearcutting and road building These management activities and their effects are visible from this roadless area Areas of past timber harvest are also visible to the north on Mitkof Island. When harvesting activities occur near the roadless area, their sights and sounds may create an impact. Boats frequent the nearby saltwater as the Stikine River is a major destination. The proximity to Wrangell and Petersburg also contribute many pleasure craft to the vicinity. Boats may sometimes be visible from parts of the roadless area This island is located on the final approach to the Wrangell airport and low-flying aircraft may temporarily distract visitors in the area at times

(9) **Attractions and Features of Special Interest:** The unique soil associations of the island result in the occurrence of a unique form of high-productivity Sitka spruce/devil's club forest type. The fringe of the island is subject to tidal influence and changes in water level due to shifts of the river. The island contains one inventoried recreation place of about 1,623 acres.

b. Capability of Management as Wilderness or in an Unroaded Condition

(1) **Manageability and Management Area Boundaries:** The area is bounded on all sides by saltwater. The island by itself does not lend itself well to being managed as a Wilderness due to its small size and the amount of marine traffic in the area and activities in the nearby adjacent areas However, this area is adjacent to the existing Stikine-LeConte Wilderness, and visitors traveling up the river generally pass by this "gateway". Thus its addition as Wilderness, would simply extend that management philosophy. Overall manageability in the roadless state is considered moderately high.

(2) **Natural Integrity:** The area is unmodified, and has maintained its overall integrity.

(3) **Opportunity for Solitude:** There is a low to moderate opportunity for solitude within the area. Airplanes landing at or leaving the Wrangell airport often fly low over the island. Frequent marine traffic passing nearby will likely be observed by people on the island due to a lack of topographic screening. Present recreation use levels are low Generally, a person camped or traveling inland is unlikely to encounter others Timber harvest or other activities in the adjacent areas, which occur periodically, would have a significant impact on the opportunity for solitude when they are occurring.

(4) **Opportunity for Primitive Recreation:** The area provides primarily Semi-Primitive Recreation opportunity as inventoried with the Recreation Opportunity Spectrum (ROS) System

ROS class	Acres
Semi-Primitive Motorized (SPM)	1,623

The area contains one inventoried recreation place

ROS CLASS	# OF REC. PLACES	TOTAL ACRES	CAPACITY BY RVD
SPM		1,623	180

There are no developed recreation opportunities in the area The character of the landforms generally does not allow the visitor to feel remote from the sights and sounds of human activity. The area is accessible by boat from the community of Petersburg in about two hours, and from Wrangell in less than one hour.

(5) **Special Features (Ecologic, Geologic, Scientific, Cultural):** The unique soil associations of the island, the hydrology, and the occurrence of a unique form of high-productivity Sitka spruce/devil's club forest type are special features of this area. The fringe of the island is subject to tidal influence and changes in water level due to shifts of the river, and may also be of scientific interest. The island forms part of the gateway for the majority of visitors traveling up the Stikine River

c. **Availability for Management as Wilderness or in an Unroaded Condition**

(1) Resource Potentials

(a) **Recreation Potential:** There is some potential for outfitter and guide permits, or for developed trails, cabins, or shelters

(b) **Fish Resource:** No fish habitat enhancement projects are identified in the Tongass Land Management Plan, amended Winter 1985-86.

(c) **Wildlife Resource:** As identified in the Tongass Land Management Plan, amended Winter 1985-86, wildlife enhancement projects are not planned for this area.

(d) **Timber Resource:** There are 1,122 acres inventoried as tentatively suitable for harvest. This includes 80 acres of riparian old growth, and 1,042 acres of non-riparian old growth.

(e) **Land Use Authorizations:** There are no special uses in the area

(f) **Minerals:** The area has low minerals potential.

(g) **Areas of Scientific Interest:** The area has been inventoried as a Potential Research Natural Area (RNA) by the RNA Task Force

(2) Management Considerations

(a) The potential for managing timber in this roadless area is
dependent on high market values. A road system and/or logging systems
capable of harvesting the island would be necessary   Development of
beach access and log transfer sites would also be required, both of
which would be difficult

(b) Maintenance of the area in a roadless condition enhances
opportunities for certain wildlife, and for further consideration as a
Research Natural Area. It could also be added to the existing
adjacent Stikine-LeConte Wilderness

(c) Fire: The area has no significant fire history.

(d) Insects and Disease: Endemic tree diseases common to Southeast
Alaska are present; there are no know epidemic disease occurrences

(e) Land Status: All National Forest System land

d. Relationship to Communities and Other Roadless and Wilderness Areas ·

(1) Nearby Roadless and Wilderness Areas and Uses: Another small roadless
island (Greys Island) lies within a mile to the west. The Stikine-LeConte
Wilderness lies just to the east. Recreational use is moderate in the
immediate area.

(2) Distance From Population Centers (Accessibility): Approximate
distances from population centers are as follows

Community		Air Miles	Water Miles
Juneau	(Pop 23,729)	135	150
Petersburg	(Pop. 4,040)	27	44
Wrangell	(Pop. 2,836)	4	4
Ketchikan	(Pop. 12,705)	85	100

Wrangell is the nearest stop on the Alaska Marine Highway

(3) Interest by Proponents:

(a) Moratorium areas: The area has not been identified as a
"moratorium" area or proposed as Wilderness in legislative initiatives
to date.

(b) Local users/residents: Most use of the area is recreational, and
is marine oriented.

e. Environmental Consequences

ALTERNATIVE ANALYSIS TO BE DONE LATER

INDIVIDUAL ROADLESS AREA DESCRIPTION

NAME: Greys (226)   ACRES (CROSS): 361   ACRES (NFS): 361

GEOZONE: S14
GEOGRAPHIC PROVINCE. Central Interior Islands

1989 WILDERNESS ATTRIBUTE RATING: 22

a. Description

(1) **Relationship to RARE II areas:** The table below displays the VCU 1/ names, VCU numbers, original WARS 2/ rating, and comments. This enables the reader to compare the roadless areas evaluated in Appendix C with previous analyses.

VCU Name	VCU No.	1979 WARS Rating	Comments
Vank	455*	17	

*--The roadless area includes only part of this VCU.

(2) **History:** The Stikine Tlingit claimed this island. The island was named for a Russian ship used to transport land surveyors The waters west of the island were evidently used as an anchorage by the Russians The island was likely visited by early fur traders traveling between the Stikine River and Fort Wrangell. The only site currently recorded is the remains of a fox farm begun in 1923

(3) **Location and Access:** This roadless area consists of one small island located off the mouth of the Stikine River At low tides, one side is bounded by tideflats formed by the sediments of the Stikine River It is north and slightly west of the town of Wrangell. Sumner Strait, Stikine Strait, and Eastern Passage all converge in this area. Access is by way of boat or floatplane. There are no sites suitable for landing wheeled aircraft.

(4) **Geography and Topography:** The island rises fairly gently to a height just above 400 feet, being slightly steeper on the northern side than the southern side. The island and landform are basically oval shaped The landform is heavily influenced by its location at the mouth of the Stikine River. High winds moving down the Stikine River canyon pick up silt from the unvegetated glacial river floodplain and deposit it as loess on islands at the river's mouth, including Greys Island The area is completely covered by forest, and contains three miles of shoreline on saltwater

---

1/ A VCU (Value Comparison Unit) is one of 867 watersheds which make up the Forest and were differentiated for planning purposes in the Tongass Land Management Plan.

2/ Wilderness Attribute Rating System (WARS) was the nationwide system used to rate the wilderness attributes of roadless areas in the Roadless Area Review and Evaluation (RARE II).

(5) Ecosystem:

(a) Classification: The area is classified as being in the Central
Interior Island Geographic Province. This province is characterized
by generally subdued, rolling topography and extensive muskeg
areas,but may have rugged terrain in localized areas While the
island displays the typical rounded, mountainous landform, because of
its small size, it lacks the land and water form variety
characteristic of the region. There are no significant streams on the
island.

(b) Vegetation: Vegetation on this island is primarily typical
spruce/hemlock and spruce/devil's club forest types.

There are 361 acres of forested land, all of which is commercial
forest land. Of the commercial forest land, 341 acres are
non-riparian old growth and 20 acres are riparian old growth

(c) Soils: Soils are unique because of the influence of the Stikine
River. High winds moving down the Stikine River canyon pick up silt
from the unvegetated glacial river floodplain and deposit it as loess
on islands at the river's mouth. The continuing rain of loess onto
the upper soil layers provides a supply of unleached, nutrient-rich
soil material to the forests of the island. The loess deposition
overcomes the process of acid bog formation (paludification) that
overtakes most stable sites of moderate topographic relief in the
Tongass National Forest. Few areas in the world have a combination of
high rainfall and recent loess deposition, so the properties of the
soils here are of special interest. Thick loess soils also have a
high water storage capacity, so the hydrology of the island is of
interest too

(d) Fish Resource: There are no fish streams on the island

(e) Wildlife Resource: A small population of Sitka black-tailed deer
and black bear range over the roadless area

(f) Threatened and Endangered Species: The area contains no known
threatened or endangered species.

(6) Current Use and Management: The VCU in which this island is located
is allocated to Land Use Designation (LUD) 3. LUD 3 allows the land to be
managed for a variety of uses, with the emphasis on managing for uses in a
compatible and complementary manner to provide the greatest combination of
benefits. There is some subsistence use in the area.

(7) Appearance (Apparent Naturalness): The area appears unmodified

The whole island was inventoried as Variety Class B (possessing landscape
diversity that is common for the character type) and as being in Existing
Visual Condition (EVC) I. EVC I areas appear to be untouched by human
activity.

(8) Surroundings (External Influences): The area is at the mouth of the
Stikine River   Several nearby islands, Liesnoi, Vank, and Sokolof, have
been impacted by visible management activities, mainly clearcutting and
road building   Areas of past timber harvest are also visible to the south
on Woronkofski and Wrangell Islands, and the town of Wrangell can be seen
When harvesting activities occur near the roadless area, their sights and
sounds may create an impact. Boats frequent the nearby saltwater as the
Stikine River is a major destination. The proximity to Wrangell and
Petersburg also contributes many pleasure craft to the vicinity which may
be visible from parts of the roadless area. Low-flying aircraft may
temporarily distract visitors in the area at times.

(9) Attractions and Features of Special Interest: The unique soil
associations of the island result in the occurrence of a unique form of
high-productivity Sitka spruce/devil's club forest type. Part of the
fringe of the island is subject to tidal influence and changes in water
level due to shifts of the river. There is one inventoried recreation
place on the island totaling 140 acres.

b. Capability of Management as Wilderness or in an Unroaded Condition

(1) Manageability and Management Area Boundaries: The area is bounded on
all sides by saltwater. The island does not lend itself well to being
managed as a Wilderness because of its small size and lack of insulation
from the marine traffic in the area, and activities in the nearby adjacent
areas   However, this area is near the existing Stikine-LeConte
Wilderness. Continued management in an unroaded condition is likely
because of its small size, steep topography, and shoreline which does not
provide a practical location for a log transfer facility   Overall
manageability is considered moderate.

(2) Natural Integrity: The area is unmodified, and has maintained its
overall integrity

(3) Opportunity for Solitude: There is a low to moderate opportunity for
solitude within the area. Low-flying airplanes and frequent marine traffic
pass nearby and may be observed by people in this roadless area. Present
recreation use levels are low. Generally, a person camped or traveling
inland is unlikely to encounter others. Timber harvest or other activities
in the adjacent areas, which occur periodically, would have a significant
impact on the opportunity for solitude when they are occurring

(4) Opportunity for Primitive Recreation: The area provides
Semi-Primitive Recreation opportunity as inventoried with the Recreation
Opportunity Spectrum (ROS) System.

ROS Class	Acres
Semi Primitive Motorized (SPM)	361

The area contains one inventoried recreation place

ROS CLASS	# OF REC. PLACES	TOTAL ACRES	CAPACITY BY RVD
SPM	1	140	270

There are no developed recreation opportunities in the area The character
of the landform generally does not allow the visitor to feel remote from
the sights and sounds of human activity around the island The area is
accessible by boat from the community of Petersburg in about two hours, and
from Wrangell in less than one hour During the salmon fishing season, the
area adjacent to Greys Island is a very popular fishing location

(5) Special Features (Ecologic, Geologic, Scientific, Cultural) The
unique soil associations of the island, the hydrology, and the occurrence
of a unique form of high-productivity Sitka spruce/devil's club forest type
are special features of this area Part of the fringe of the island is
subject to tidal influence and changes in water level due to shifts of the
river, and may also be of scientific interest.

c. **Availability for Management as Wilderness or in an Unroaded Condition**

(1) **Resource Potentials**

(a) **Recreation Potential:** There is some potential for outfitter and
guide permits or for developed trails, cabins, or shelters

(b) **Fish Resource:** No fish habitat enhancement projects are
identified in the Tongass Land Management Plan, amended Winter
1985-86

(c) **Wildlife Resource:** As identified in the Tongass Land Management
Plan, amended Winter 1985-86, no wildlife enhancement projects are
planned

(d) **Timber Resource:** There are 300 acres inventoried as tentatively
suitable for harvest This includes 20 acres of riparian old growth,
and 280 acres of non-riparian old growth.

(e) **Land Use Authorizations:** There are no special uses in the area.

(f) **Minerals:** The area has low minerals potential

(g) **Areas of Scientific Interest:** The area has not been identified
for any scientific value However nearby Kadin Island has been
identified as a candidate Research Natural Area, as it best represents
the influence of the Stikine River on soils and plant associations

(2) **Management Considerations**

(a) The potential for managing timber in this roadless area is
dependent on high market values. A road system and/or logging systems
capable of harvesting the island would be necessary Development of
beach access and log transfer sites would also be required and are
likely to be difficult.

(b) Maintenance of the area in a roadless condition enhances opportunities for certain wildlife. The area could be a substitute for Kadin Island as a candidate Research Natural Area, however the overall qualities are not as good in meeting the objectives It could also fit in with the existing management of the adjacent Stikine-LeConte Wilderness

(c) Fire: The area has no significant fire history

(d) Insects and Disease: Endemic tree diseases common to Southeast Alaska are present, there are no know epidemic disease occurrences

(e) Land Status: All National Forest System land.

d. Relationship to Communities and Other Roadless and Wilderness Areas

(1) Nearby Roadless and Wilderness Areas and Uses: One other roadless area exists nearby on Kadin Island to the east. The Stikine-LeConte Wilderness is also to the east, beyond Kadin Island Recreational use is moderate in the immediate area except during the salmon fishing season when the area around Greys Island is heavily used.

(2) Distance From Population Centers (Accessibility): Approximate distances from population centers are as follows:

Community		Air Miles	Water Miles
Juneau	(Pop. 23,729)	135	150
Petersburg	(Pop. 4,040)	27	42
Wrangell	(Pop. 2,836)	5	5
Ketchikan	(Pop. 12,705)	90	116

Wrangell is the nearest stop on the Alaska Marine Highway

(3) Interest by Proponents:

(a) Moratorium areas: The area has not been identified as a "moratorium" area or proposed as Wilderness in legislative initiatives to date.

(b) Local users/residents: Most use of the area is marine oriented recreation.

e. Environmental Consequences

ALTERNATIVE ANALYSIS TO BE DONE LATER

INDIVIDUAL ROADLESS AREA DESCRIPTION

NAME: North Wrangell (227)   ACRES (GROSS): 14,460   ACRES (NFS): 11,624

GEOZONE: S07
GEOGRAPHIC PROVINCE: Central Interior Islands

1989 Wilderness Attribute Rating: 17

a. Description

(1) **Relationship to RARE II areas:** The table below displays the VCU 1/ names, VCU numbers, original WARS 2/ rating, and comments. This enables the reader to compare the roadless areas evaluated in Appendix C with previous analyses.

VCU Name	VCU No.	1979 WARS Rating	Comments
Wrangell	475*	19	
Eastern	476*	21	
Nemo	477*	18	

*--The roadless area includes only part of this VCU.

(2) **History:** The area was used by the Stikine Tlingit in prehistoric times, however only a few sites have been recorded. Tlingit sites include a former camp and a possible burial site. A historical homestead site is present along the shoreline

(3) **Location and Access:** The area is located on Wrangell Island and is bounded on the east by Eastern Passage, on the south by Forest Road 6259, on the west by the Zimovia Highway, and on the north by development associated with the city of Wrangell. The boundary roads connect to the city of Wrangell. The area is accessed by saltwater and by the Wrangell Island roads There are no sites suitable for landing wheeled aircraft

(4) **Geography and Topography:** The area is basically a mountain ridge forming the northern tip of Wrangell Island, with four somewhat rounded peaks ranging in elevation from 2,000 to 2,600 feet. On both sides of the mountains are rather short, steep drainages containing small streams emptying into salt water There is no saltwater shoreline in federal ownership.

1/ A VCU (Value Comparison Unit) is one of 867 watersheds which make up the Forest and were differentiated for planning purposes in the Tongass Land Management Plan.
2/ Wilderness Attribute Rating System (WARS) was the nationwide system used to rate the wilderness attributes of roadless areas in the Roadless Area Review and Evaluation (RARE II).

(5) Ecosystem:

(a) **Classification:** The area is classified as being in the Central
Interior Islands Geographic Province. This province in generally
characterized by rolling, subdued topography and extensive muskeg
areas, but may have rugged terrain in localized areas   In this
roadless area there are no known areas of unique or uncommon
plant/soils associations or geologic formations.

(b) **Vegetation:** Alpine vegetation dominates above 2,500 feet
elevation. Poorly-drained areas between the peaks, and flater areas
on the ridgetop are generally covered with muskeg and scrub lodgepole
pine. Steeper, more-well-drained mountain sides support heavy stands
of Sitka spruce, western hemlock, redcedar and Alaska cedar.

There are approximately 11,304 acres of forested land of which 6,843
acres are commercial forest land. Of the commercial forest land,
6,163 acres are non-riparian old growth and 660 acres are riparian old
growth.

(c) **Soils:** Soils in this area are formed in a wide variety of parent
material, including bedrock and glacial drift. In general, well- or
moderately-well-drained soils are on moderate to steep mountain slopes
with permeable parent materials. These soils are very acidic, have
cold soil temperatures, and are very high in organic matter   Rooting
is largely limited to the surface organic layers and the top few
inches of mineral soil   These soils are usually moist, sometimes wet,
but are never dry

More-poorly-drained soils developed on less-sloping areas and/or areas
with impermeable soil materials   These soils have deep accumulations
of organic matter and range from scrubby forested wetlands to open
muskeg.

Alpine soils, generally above 2,000 feet elevation, are mostly
shallow, very wet organic soils or are extremely shallow and rocky

(d) **Fish Resource:** Fish resources have been rated as part of the
Tongass Land Management Plan (1978) and by the Alaska Department of
Fish and Game in its Forest Habitat Integrity Program (1983)   These
ratings describe the value of VCU's for sport fish, commercial fish
and estuaries. VCU 475 rated as having highly valued estuaries

(e) **Wildlife Resource:** Important species include Sitka black-tailed
deer, wolves, black bear, pine marten and a small population of moose

(f) **Threatened and Endangered Species:** The area contains no known
threatened or endangered species.

(6) **Current Use and Management:** All of the area was allocated to Land Use
Designation 3 in the Tongass Land Management Plan, which allows road
construction and timber harvest in conjunction with strong protection
measures to meet other resource objectives   Eastern Passage receives
moderately-heavy use by commercial and pleasure boats. The entire

shoreline in the area was selected by the State and currently receives
little recreation use. Areas closely associated with the roads, especially
where they cross the larger streams, receive higher use during the summer
Two trails access parts of the area The Institute Trail accesses the area
from the northwest, ending at the Shoemaker Bay shelter An alpine trail
comes into the area from the southeast. There is some subsistence use in
the area, primarily associated with roadside wood and berry gathering In
1984, a 138 KV powerline was constructed through the area.

(7) Appearance (Apparent Naturalness): Land access roads and closely
associated clearcut timber harvest units adjoin the area on three sides,
and a 138 KW powerline crosses the area near its center Most of the area
away from the roads appears natural and undisturbed. The powerline and
right-of-way clearing are visible and often obvious from the water and from
some areas within the roadless area. Clearcuts associated with the roads,
and portions of the City are obvious from some parts of the roadless area
The rest of the roadless area is unmodified.

The majority of this roadless area (49 percent) is natural appearing, where
only ecological change has occurred (Existing Visual Condition (EVC) Type
I). Six percent of the area appears to be untouched by human activity (EVC
Type II). Nine percent of this roadless area is EVC Type III, where
changes in the landscape are noticed by the average forest visitor The
natural appearance of the landscape remains dominant. Thirty-six percent
is in EVC Type V where changes in the landscape are obvious to the average
person, and appear to be major disturbances

The entire area is inventoried Variety Class B (possessing landscape
diversity that is common for the character type)

(8) Surroundings (External Influences): Boats plying the waters of
Eastern Passage and Zimovia Strait may be visible from within parts of the
area but usually are not intrusive. It is possible to see clearcuts and
portions of the city of Wrangell, and hear automobiles on the roads and
other noises of the community from some locations within this roadless
area. Low-flying aircraft traveling to and from Wrangell may, at times,
fly over the area The State has selected lands along the Zimovia Strait
and Eastern Passage shorelines Future uses of that land is uncertain,
however some development is likely

(9) Attractions and Features of Special Interest: The fact that the area
is accessible by road from Wrangell may be an attraction for some There
are no special or unique features. The area contains five inventoried
recreation places totaling 9,924 acres.

b. Capability of Management as Wilderness or in an Unroaded Condition

(1) Manageability and Management Area Boundaries: On three sides, the
area boundary is defined by mostly roads and clearcut timber harvest
units. The fourth side is defined by the saltwater shore, which is now
State land The powerline crossing near the central part of the area is an
inconsistent inclusion. Except for several minor valleys, there is very
little geographic containment of the space within the area or physical
screening from outside influences There is little reason to build

additional roads in this area, unless access to the timber on the lower
mountain slopes or to the State land along Zimovia Strait is desired

(2) Natural Integrity: The area is bounded on three sides by land access
roads and clearcut timber harvest units   A 138 KV powerline crosses near
the center of the area.

(3) Opportunity for Solitude: There is a good opportunity for solitude
within the area, especially after one has gone a short distance from the
roads. Present recreation use levels are low except near the roads
Generally, a person camped or traveling away from the roads is unlikely to
see others.

(4) Opportunity for Primitive Recreation: The area provides primarily
semi-primitive recreation opportunities:

ROS Class	Acres
Semi-Primitive Non-Motorized (SPNM)	8,823
Semi-Primitive Motorized (SPM)	2,741
Roaded Modified (RM)	60

The area contains five recreation places.

ROS CLASS	# OF REC. PLACES	TOTAL ACRES	CAPACITY BY RVD
SPNM	1	8,823	2,605
SPM	3	1,080	1,360
RM	1	20	217

Two trails and a shelter are the only facilities in the area   The
character of the landforms and vegetation generally allows the visitor to
feel remote from the sights and sounds of human activity   The area is
accessible by boat and automobile from the community of Wrangell in less
than two hours. Travel within the area is not especially challenging,
requiring only moderate woods skills and experience. The presence of black
bears does present a degree of challenge and a need for caution

(5) Special Features (Ecologic, Geologic, Scientific, Cultural): There
are no known unique features in the area. The Institute Trail is one of
the few trails easily accessible to a major population center on the
Stikine Area. Beginning on the south end of the city of Wrangell, the
trail receives relatively heavy use.

c. Availability for Management as Wilderness or in an Unroaded Condition

(1) Resource Potentials

(a) Recreation Potential: There is potential for development of a
trail system, and cabins or shelters. Because of the area's
accessibility from the city of Wrangell, there is potential for use of
off-road vehicles and snowmobiles, and for cross-country skiing

(b) **Fish Resource:** No specific fish habitat enhancement projects are identified for this area in the Tongass Land Management Plan, amended Winter 1985-86

(c) **Wildlife Resource:** As identified in the Tongass Land Management Plan, amended 1985-86, moose and deer winter range habitat improvement projects are planned in the area. These projects typically consist of planting, thinning, and seeding.

(d) **Timber Resource:** There are 4,522 acres inventoried as tentatively suitable for harvest. This includes 440 acres of riparian old growth, and 4,062 acres of non-riparian old growth Some parts ofthis area are highly prone to strong winds which blow down standing timber left exposed by cutting adjacent stands.

(e) **Land Use Authorizations:** Near the middle of this roadless area, a 138 KV powerline, under special use permit, crosses from one side to the other

(f) **Minerals:** The area generally has a low minerals rating and there are no known current claims.

(g) **Areas of Scientific Interest:** The area contains no inventoried potential Research Natural Areas. The area has not been identified for any other scientific value.

(2) **Management Considerations**

(a) The potential for managing timber in this roadless area is high as roads could be extended from the existing system and much of the area could be logged without constructing a camp or additional log transfer facilities.

(b) The area is readily accessible by sheltered waters and by road from the city of Wrangell. Maintenance of the area in a roadless condition enhances opportunities for residents of the city of Wrangell who do not have a boat to have a semi-primitive recreation experience. It also maintains opportunities for wildlife, such as wolves, bears, and moose, to move freely through the area

(c) **Fire:** The area has no significant fire history.

(d) **Insects and Disease:** Endemic tree diseases common to Southeast Alaska are present; there are no know epidemic disease occurrences

(e) **Land Status:** The State owns all of the land along the east side of the area, including all of the land along the beach, and lands adjacent to the south and west sides of the area.

d. **Relationship to Communities and Other Roadless and Wilderness Areas**

(1) **Nearby Roadless and Wilderness Areas and Uses:** There are two other roadless areas on Wrangell Island, separated from the North Wrangell Roadless Area by roads. Additional roadless areas are located nearby, across narrow saltwater channels, on Etolin Island and on the mainland

The nearest Wilderness is the Stikine-LeConte, approximately ten miles to
the north The area currently receives light to moderate use inland, away
from saltwater or road access

(2) **Distance From Population Centers (Accessibility):** Approximate
distances from population centers are as follows.

Community			Air Miles	Water Miles
Juneau	(Pop	23,729)	155	170
Petersburg	(Pop	4,040)	50	80
Wrangell	(Pop	2,836)	2	2
Ketchikan	(Pop	12,705)	60	75

Wrangell is the nearest stop on the Alaska Marine Highway and is
approximately two road miles from this area.

(3) **Interest by Proponents:**

(a) **Moratorium areas:** The area has not been identified as a
"moratorium" area or proposed as Wilderness in legislative initiatives
to date.

(b) **Local users/residents:** There have been no local initiatives or
public sentiment expressed to have the area remain roadless   There
has been interest by some residents of Wrangell in developing
additional roads in the area to facilitate additional logging and
roaded recreation opportunities

e. **Environmental Consequences**

ALTERNATIVE ANALYSIS TO BE DONE LATER

INDIVIDUAL ROADLESS AREA DESCRIPTION

NAME: South Wrangell (229)   ACRES (GROSS): 75,990   ACRES (NFS): 71,173

GEOZONE: S07
GEOGRAPHIC PROVINCE: Central Interior Islands

1989 WILDERNESS ATTRIBUTE RATING· 20

a. Description

(1) **Relationship to RARE II areas:** The table below displays the VCU 1/ names, VCU numbers, original WARS 2/ rating, and comments This enables the reader to compare the roadless areas evaluated in Appendix C with previous analyses.

VCU Name	VCU No.	1979 WARS Rating	Comments
Nemo	477*	18	
Venus	478*	22	
Thoms	479*	23	
Fools	480*	24	
Madan	504*	21	
Blake	505*	22	

*--The roadless area includes only part of this VCU.

(2) **History:** The area was inhabited by the Tlingit in prehistoric and historic times. While the area has likely been prospected for minerals. there are no known mining claims. In 1984, a 138 KV powerline was constructed through part of the area along Blake Channel

(3) **Location and Access:** The area is located on Wrangell Island and is bounded on the east by Blake Channel, on the south by Ernest Sound. and on the west by Zimovia Strait. On the north it is bounded by roads which connect to the city of Wrangell. The area is accessed by the surrounding saltwater and by the Wrangell Island roads There are no sites suitable for landing wheeled aircraft.

1/ A VCU (Value Comparison Unit) is one of 867 watersheds which make up the forest and were differentiated for planning purposes in the Tongass Land Management Plan.
2/ Wilderness Attribute Rating System (WARS) was the nationwide system used to rate the wilderness attributes of roadless areas in the Roadless Area Review and Evaluation (RARE II).

(4) **Geography and Topography:** The area is generally characterized by moderately-diverse, rounded to occasionally-blocky terrain, with many mountains reaching elevations of over 2,000 feet The tallest is almost 3,000 feet in elevation Between the mountains are rather broad, U-shaped valleys containing several sizable streams The mountain ridge on the east side of the area contains numerous small cirque lakes and short, steep streams There are approximately 49 miles of shoreline on saltwater which are--except for Fools Inlet, Southeast Cove, and the complex around Thoms Place--rather regular and uniform. Freshwater lakes cover about 540 acres, alpine covers 140 acres, and rock occupies another 100 acres

(5) **Ecosystem:**

    (a) **Classification:** The area is in the Central Interior Islands Geographic Province This province is generally characterized by rolling, subdued topography and extensive muskeg area, but may have localized, rugged terrain. This roadless area is more characteristic of the rugged, mountainous terrain. There are no known areas of unique or uncommon plant/soils associations or geologic formations in the area.

    (b) **Vegetation:** Alpine vegetation dominates above 2,500 feet elevation. The valley floors and poorly-drained areas between hills are generally covered with muskeg (40 acres) and scrub lodgepole pine. Steeper, more-well-drained hillsides support heavy stands of Sitka spruce, western hemlock, redcedar and Alaska-cedar There are small grass flats at the head of Fools Inlet and at Thoms Place

There are approximately 68,833 acres of forested land of which 34,256 acres are commercial forest land Of the commercial forest land, 31,177 acres are non-riparian old growth and 2,760 acres are riparian old growth

    (c) **Soils:** Soils in this area are formed in a wide variety of parent materials, including bedrock and glacial drift. In general, well- or moderately-well-drained soils are on moderate to steep mountain slopes with permeable parent materials These soils are very acidic, have cold soil temperatures, and are very high in organic matter Rooting is largely limited to the surface organic layers and the top few inches of mineral soil. These soils are usually moist, sometimes wet, but are never dry

More-poorly-drained soils developed on less-sloping areas and/or areas with impermeable soil materials. These soils have deep accumulations of organic matter and range from scrubby forested wetlands to open muskeg.

Alpine soils, generally above 2,000 feet elevation, are mostly shallow, very wet organic soils or are extremely shallow and rocky

(d) **Fish Resource:** Fish resources have been rated as part of the Tongass Land Management Plan (1979) and by the Alaska Department of Fish and Game in its Forest Habitat Integrity Program (1983)   These ratings describe the value of VCU's for sport fish, commercial fish and estuaries

VCU 479 rated as highly valued for sport fish, commercial fish, and estuaries

Three ADF&G numbered salmon producing streams are present   Fools Creek and Thoms Creek are substantial producers of salmon   Average annual peak escapement of pink salmon is 8,300 for Fools Creek and 4,900 for Thoms Creek   Thoms Creek is a popular sport fishing stream and there is a run of sockeye salmon which is used for subsistence fishing.

(e) **Wildlife Resource:** Important species include Sitka black-tailed deer, wolves, black bear, pine marten, and small populations of brown bear and moose.

(f) **Threatened and Endangered Species:** The area contains no known threatened or endangered species.

(6) **Current Use and Management:** Three drainages in the area (VCU's 477, 479, and 504, which total 23,576 acres) were allocated to Land Use Designation (LUD) 3 in the Tongass Land Management Plan, which allows road construction and timber harvest in conjunction with protection measures to meet other resource objectives. The other three drainages (VCU's 478, 480, and 505, which total 47,517 acres) were allocated to LUD 4 which places stronger emphasis on timber management   Blake Channel, Zimovia Strait and Ernest Sound receive moderately-heavy use by commercial and pleasure boats   The shoreline along the Blake Channel is mostly rocky and receives little recreation use   The areas around Thoms Place and in Fools Inlet receive higher use, especially during the salmon runs. There is a public recreation cabin on Thoms Lake. There is some subsistence use in the area, particularly use of salmon in Thoms Creek.

(7) **Appearance (Apparent Naturalness):** An access road and associated clearcut timber harvest units practically bisects the area   The roadless area itself, with the exception of the cabin at Thoms Lake, the private cabins at Thoms Place, and the powerline near Blake Channel, is unmodified. The powerline is well located to minimize its visibility from the water and from elsewhere within the roadless area. Clearcuts associated with the roads are obvious from some parts of the roadless area

The majority of this roadless area (88 percent) is natural appearing, where only ecological change has occurred (Existing Visual Condition (EVC) Type I). Less than one percent of the area appears to be untouched by human activity (EVC Type II). Six percent of this roadless area is EVC Type III, where changes in the landscape are noticed by the average forest visitor   The natural appearance of the landscape remains dominant   One percent of the area is in EVC Type IV, where changes in the landscape are easily noticed by the average person and may attract some attention   They appear to be disturbances but resemble natural patterns   Five percent is in EVC

Type V where changes in the landscape are obvious to the average person, and appear to be major disturbances.

Twenty-three percent of this roadless area is inventoried Variety Class A (possessing landscape diversity that is unique for the character type), 32 percent is inventoried Variety Class B (possessing landscape diversity that is common for the character type) and the remaining 45 percent is inventoried Variety Class C (possessing a low degree of landscape diversity)

(8) Surroundings (External Influences): Boats plying the waters of Blake Channel, Zimovia Strait, and Ernest Sound may be visible from within parts of the area but usually are not intrusive. It is possible to see clearcuts and hear automobiles on the roads from some locations within this roadless area.

(9) Attractions and Features of Special Interest: Thoms Lake, Thoms Creek, and Thoms Place are all attractions, especially during the salmon run. Thoms Place and Thoms Lake were selected by the State Thoms Place is now a State Marine Park. The area contains 27 inventoried recreation places totaling 22,399 acres. There are no improved trails in the area

b. Capability of Management as Wilderness or in an Unroaded Condition

(1) Manageability and management area boundaries: The area is generally well defined by saltwater on the west and south. The northern boundary along the roads is not well defined and the powerline along the eastern and northeastern part of the area would either have to be included or will form a very poor boundary Feasibility of managing the southeastern portion of this area in a roadless condition is moderately high, but is very low in the rest of the area.

(2) Natural Integrity: The area is nearly bisected by a land access road, almost isolating the northwestern portion. A 138 KV powerline crosses the eastern and northeastern edges of the area.

(3) Opportunity for Solitude: There is a good opportunity for solitude within the area, especially after one has gone a short distance from the roads Present recreation use levels are low except around Thoms Lake, at streams and lakes near the roads, and occasionally at the mouths of some streams Generally, a person camped or traveling inland is likely to see others only occasionally

(4) Opportunity for Primitive Recreation: The area provides primarily primitive non-motorized opportunity·

ROS Class	Acres
Semi-Primitive Non-Motorized (SPNM)	45,536
Semi-Primitive Motorized (SPM)	18,857
Roaded Natural (RN)	2,360
Roaded Modified (RM)	4,420

The area contains 27 recreation places

ROS CLASS	# OF REC. PLACES	TOTAL ACRES	CAPACITY BY RVD
SPNM	2	9,181	2,843
SPM	11	7,118	4,379
RN	6	1,320	4,855
RM	8	4,400	5,020

There are two recreation cabins in the area, both on State land   There is
a picnic area and trail at Long Lake. The character of the landforms
generally allows the visitor to feel remote from the sights and sounds of
human activity   The area is accessible by boat from the community of
Wrangell in less than two hours, and from Ketchikan in approximately seven
hours. Access on land is by road from the city of Wrangell. Travel within
the area is not especially challenging, requiring only moderate woods
skills and experience. The presence of both black and brown bears,
especially around salmon streams in the fall, does present a degree of
challenge and a need for caution.

(5) Special Features (Ecologic, Geologic, Scientific, Cultural): There
are opportunities to observe and study historic and prehistoric cultural
features along Zimovia Strait. The area's accessibility by road makes it
attractive for many recreation opportunities

c. Availability for Management a Wilderness or in an Unroaded Condition

(1) Resource Potentials

(a) Recreation Potential: There is potential for additional
outfitter and guide permits and for developed trails and additional
cabins or shelters   Because of the area's accessibility from the city
of Wrangell, there is also potential for use of off-road vehicles and
snowmobiles.

(b) Fish Resource: The Tongass Land Management Plan, amended Winter
1985-86 identifies fish habitat enhancement projects in this area
Fish enhancement projects continue to surface, however none are
planned at this time

(c) Wildlife Resource: As identified in the Tongass Land Management
Plan, amended 1985-86, moose and winter range habitat improvement
projects are planned in the area. These projects typically consist of
browse enhancement involving seeding, planting, and releasing

(d) Timber Resource: There are 22,697 acres inventoried as
tentatively suitable for harvest. This includes 1,740 acres of
riparian old growth, and 20,717 acres of non-riparian old growth
Some areas are highly prone to strong winds which blow down standing
timber left exposed by cutting adjacent stands.

(e) Land Use Authorizations: A 138 KV powerline under special use
permit crosses along the eastern edge of the area   There is a radio
repeater located on a mountaintop between Fools Inlet and Blake
Channel, and a lighthouse withdrawal near Blake Island   The State has
selected lands around Thoms Lake and Thoms Place   The Sealaska Native
Corporation has selected several small historic sites along the coast.

(f) **Minerals:** The area generally has a low minerals rating and there are no known current claims

(g) **Areas of Scientific Interest:** The area contains no inventoried potential Research Natural Areas, and has not been identified for any other scientific value

(2) **Management Considerations**

(a) The potential for managing timber in this roadless area is high, as roads could be extended from the existing system and the area could be logged without constructing a camp or additional log transfer facilities.

(b) The area is readily accessible by sheltered waters and by road from the city of Wrangell. With this good access potential, there is higher potential for recreation opportunities, both dispersed and developed. Maintenance of the area or parts thereof in a roadless condition, enhances primitive recreation opportunities for those residents of the city of Wrangell without boats. It also enhances the opportunities for residents of Thoms Place to maintain their current lifestyles. Opportunities for wildlife, such as wolves, bears, and moose, to move freely through the area are also maintained

(c) **Fire:** The area has no significant fire history

(d) **Insects and Disease:** Endemic tree diseases common to Southeast Alaska are present; there are no know epidemic disease occurrences.

(e) **Land Status:** Several Native land selections have occurred adjacent to this roadless area Venus Cove (3,565 acres), Thoms Lake (1,760 acres), and Thoms Place (2,525 acres) have all been selected by the State

d. **Relationship to Communities and Other Roadless and Wilderness Areas**

(1) **Nearby Roadless and Wilderness Areas and Uses:** There are two other smaller roadless areas on Wrangell Island, separated from South Wrangell Roadless Area by roads. Additional roadless areas are located nearby, across narrow saltwater channels, on Etolin Island and on the mainland The nearest Wilderness is the Stikine-LeConte, approximately twenty-five miles to the north. The area currently receives light to moderate use inland, away from saltwater or road access.

(2) **Distance From Population Centers (Accessibility):** Approximate distances from population centers are as follows·

Community		Air Miles	Water Miles
Juneau	(Pop. 23,729)	150	200
Petersburg	(Pop. 4,040)	50	80
Wrangell	(Pop 2,836)	20	30
Ketchikan	(Pop 12,705)	60	75

Wrangell is the nearest stop on the Alaska Marine Highway.

(3) Interest by Proponents:

(a) Moratorium areas: The area has not been identified as a
"moratorium" area or proposed as Wilderness in legislative initiatives
to date.

(b) Local users/residents: Some residents and landholders of Thoms
Place have expressed the desire to have the immediate area around
Thoms Place remain roadless and undeveloped to maintain the current
environment   There has been interest by some residents of Wrangell in
developing additional roads in the area to facilitate additional
logging and roaded recreation opportunities.

Environmental Consequences

ALTERNATIVE ANALYSIS TO BE DONE LATER

INDIVIDUAL ROADLESS AREA DESCRIPTION

NAME: Woronkofski (231)   ACRES (GROSS): 9,773   ACRES (NFS): 9,773

GEOZONE: S14
GEOGRAPHIC PROVINCE: Central Interior Islands

1989 WILDERNESS ATTRIBUTE RATING: 22

a. Description

(1) Relationship to RARE II areas: The table below displays the VCU 1/
names, VCU numbers, original WARS 2/ rating, and comments. This enables
the reader to compare the roadless areas evaluated in Appendix C with
previous analyses.

VCU Name	VCU No.	1979 WARS Rating	Comments
Woronkofski	461*	12	

*--The roadless area includes only part of this VCU.

(2) History: The island was apparently used by several groups of the
Stikine Tlingit as a hunting and fishing area. They harvested deer,
salmon, clams, seaweed, cockles and mussels. Evidently there were Tlingit
fort sites on the northern and southern ends of the island. Several gold
mine claims were made in 1900 in a cove near Elephants Nose, a local
feature.

(3) Location and Access: The area is located on Woronkofski Island, and
is bounded by Stikine Strait on the west, Zimovia Strait on the east,
Sumner Strait to the north, and Chichagof Pass to the south. The city of
Wrangell lies five miles to the northeast, and is served by the Alaska
Marine Highway and jet service. There are no sites suitable for landing
wheeled aircraft. A small road system and log transfer facility exist on
the island. The island is accessible from saltwater by boat, and several
moorage sites exist

(4) Geography and Topography: The area is generally characterized by
steeply rising mountains reaching elevations of over 2,000 feet The
tallest is over 3,000 feet in elevation. Also included in this area is
about 220 acres in alpine. Two drainages which originate in glacial
cirques flow to the north. Freshwater lakes make up about 120 acres
There are approximately nine miles of shoreline on saltwater within the
roadless area

1/ A VCU (Value Comparison Unit) is one of 867 watersheds which make up the
Forest and were differentiated for planning purposes in the Tongass Land
Management Plan.
2/ Wilderness Attribute Rating System (WARS) was the nationwide system used to
rate the wilderness attributes of roadless areas in the Roadless Area
Review and Evaluation (RARE II).

(5) Ecosystem:

(a) Classification: The area is in the Central Interior Islands Geographic Province This province is generally characterized by rolling, subdued topography and extensive muskeg areas, but may have localized, rugged terrain

(b) Vegetation: Alpine vegetation dominates above 2,500 feet elevation The valley floors and poorly-drained areas between hills are generally covered with muskeg and scrub lodgepole pine Steeper, more-well-drained hillsides support heavy stands of Sitka spruce, western hemlock, redcedar and Alaska-cedar

There are approximately 9,092 acres of forested land of which 5,027 acres are commercial forest land. Of the commercial forest land, 4,266 acres are non-riparian old growth and 581 acres are riparian old growth.

(c) Soils: Soils in this area are formed in a wide variety of parent materials, including bedrock and glacial drift. In general, well- or moderately-well-drained soils are on moderate to steep mountain slopes with permeable parent materials. These soils are very acidic, have cold soil temperatures, and are very high in organic matter Rooting is largely limited to the surface organic layers and the top few inches of mineral soil. These soils are usually moist, sometimes wet, but are never dry.

More-poorly-drained soils developed on less-sloping areas and/or areas with impermeable soil materials. These soils have deep accumulations of organic matter and range from scrubby forested wetlands to open muskeg.

Alpine soils, generally above 2,000 feet elevation, are mostly shallow, very wet organic soils or are extremely shallow and rocky

(d) Fish Resource: Fish resources have been rated as part of the Tongass Land Management Plan (1979) and by the Alaska Department of Fish and Game in its Forest Habitat Integrity Program (1983) These ratings describe the value of VCU's for sport fish, commercial fish and estuaries.

The one VCU, 461, is highly valued for commercial fish.

(e) Wildlife Resource: Important species include Sitka black-tailed deer and black bear.

(f) Threatened and Endangered Species: The area contains no known threatened or endangered species

(6) Current Use and Management: The entire island, which includes the roadless area, was allocated to Land Use Designation (LUD) 3 in the Tongass Land Management Plan, which allows road construction and timber harvest in conjunction with strong protection measures to meet other resource objectives The north and east sides of the island have been logged and

partially roaded, and a narrow strip on the west side has also been
harvested. The saltwater bodies surrounding the island receive
moderately-heavy use by commercial and pleasure boats. The shoreline
receives moderate recreation use. Some recreation use occurs on the road
system, generally from residents of Wrangell who sometimes transport small
motorcycles and all-terrain vehicles. There is some subsistence use in the
area.

(7) Appearance (Apparent Naturalness): The roadless area itself, is
unmodified. It is surrounded on three sides by clearcut harvest areas,
which also penetrate the drainages toward the interior of the island. A
person in a boat approaching the roadless area would see a combination of
managed and natural scenery

The majority of this roadless area (85 percent) is natural appearing, where
only ecological change has occurred (Existing Visual Condition (EVC) Type
I). Two percent of this roadless area is EVC Type III, where changes in
the landscape are noticed by the average forest visitor. The natural
appearance of the landscape remains dominant. Two percent of the area is
in EVC Type IV, where changes in the landscape are easily noticed by the
average person and may attract some attention. They appear to be
disturbances but resemble natural patterns. Eleven percent is in EVC
Type V where changes in the landscape are obvious to the average person,
and appear to be major disturbances.

About 22 percent of this roadless area is inventoried Variety Class A
(possessing landscape diversity that is unique for the character type), and
78 percent is inventoried Variety Class B (possessing landscape diversity
that is common for the character type).

(8) Surroundings (External Influences): Boats plying the adjacent
saltwaters may be visible from within parts of the area, but usually are
not intrusive. It is possible to see clearcuts and roads from some
locations within this roadless area Sights and sounds from the town of
Wrangell are also apparent from some locations within the roadless area
The Alaska Marine Highway passes within one-half mile along the west and
north sides of the roadless area.

(9) Attractions and Features of Special Interest: Elephants Nose is a
prominent rocky feature on the north end of the island at the edge of the
roadless area. Sunrise Lake is one of three small subalpine lakes
Fishing is popular off the northern portion of the island. The area
contains nine inventoried recreation places totaling 9,613 acres There
are no improved trails in the area.

b. Capability of Management as Wilderness or in an Unroaded Condition

(1) Manageability and management area boundaries: The area is generally
defined by saltwater on the west, east, and south, however harvest
activities have occurred in several places from the beach along these
boundaries. Roads and cutting units which follow a drainage penetrating
the roadless area define the northern boundary Feasibility of managing
the southern portion of this area in a roadless condition is moderately
high, but maintaining the rest of the area in a roadless condition would be
difficult.

(2) **Natural Integrity:** Timber harvest activities are evident along parts of the southern, eastern, and western portions of the island, and dominate the northern portion of the area The remaining core of the island is the roadless area, but timber harvest and roads which follow one of the drainages, penetrate this core In other portions of this roadless area, natural integrity is high.

(3) **Opportunity for Solitude:** There is a good opportunity for solitude within the area, especially after one has gone a short distance from the roads. Present recreation use levels are low except at the mouths of some streams. Generally, a person camped or traveling inland is likely to only occasionally see others

(4) **Opportunity for Primitive Recreation:** The area provides primarily semi-primitive motorized recreation opportunity·

ROS Class	Acres
Semi-Primitive Non-Motorized (SPNM)	3,164
Semi-Primitive Motorized (SPM)	6,389
Roaded Modified (RM)	60

The area contains nine recreation places

ROS CLASS	# OF REC. PLACES	TOTAL ACRES	CAPACITY BY RVD
SPNM	1	3,164	314
SPM	5	6,389	891
RM	3	60	25

The character of the area generally allows the visitor to feel remote from the sights and sounds of human activity. The area is accessible by boat from the community of Wrangell in less than one-half hour, and from Ketchikan in approximately seven hours. Visitors from Wrangell sometimes bring motorcycles or small all-terrain vehicles by boat to the road system, and then access portions of the roadless area by foot Travel within the area is not especially challenging, requiring only moderate woods skills and experience The presence of black bears, especially around salmon streams in the fall, does present a degree of challenge and a need for caution.

(5) **Special Features (Ecologic, Geologic, Scientific, Cultural):** Elephants Nose is a prominent rocky feature on the northern end of the island.

c. **Availability for Management a Wilderness or in an Unroaded Condition**

(1) **Resource Potentials**

(a) **Recreation Potential:** There is potential for additional outfitter and guide permits, developed trails, and cabins or shelters Because of the areas accessibility from the city of Wrangell, there is also potential for use of off-road vehicles and snowmobiles.

(b) **Fish Resource:** No fish habitat enhancement projects are identified for this area in the Tongass Land Management Plan, amended Winter 1985-86.

(c) **Wildlife Resource:** As identified in the Tongass Land Management Plan, amended 1985-86, habitat improvement projects are planned in the area. These projects typically consist of thinning and planting

(d) **Timber Resource:** There are 3,545 acres inventoried as tentatively suitable for harvest This includes 381 acres of riparian old growth, and 3,084 acres of non-riparian old growth Some areas are highly prone to strong winds which blow down standing timber left exposed by cutting adjacent stands.

(e) **Land Use Authorizations:** No special uses are authorized in this area. Two lighthouse reservations exist.

(f) **Minerals:** The area generally has a low minerals rating and there are no known current claims.

(g) **Areas of Scientific Interest:** The area does not contain any inventoried potential Research Natural Areas, and has not been identified for any other scientific value.

(2) Management Considerations

(a) The potential for managing timber in this roadless area is high. as roads could be extended from the existing system and much of the area could be logged without constructing a camp or additional log transfer facilities

(b) The area is readily accessible by sheltered waters from the city of Wrangell. Maintenance of the area in a roadless condition enhances opportunities for residents of the city of Wrangell to have a semi-primitive recreation experience. It also maintains opportunities for wildlife to move freely through the area.

(c) **Fire:** The area has no significant fire history

(d) **Insects and Disease:** Endemic tree diseases common to Southeast Alaska are present; there are no know epidemic disease occurrences

(e) **Land Status:** All National Forest System lands

d. **Relationship to Communities and Other Roadless and Wilderness Areas**

(1) **Nearby Roadless and Wilderness Areas and Uses:** Only one roadless area lies adjacent to the Woronkofski Roadless Area This is the North Etolin Island Roadless Area, located to the south. Additional roadless areas are located nearby, across narrow saltwater channels, on Etolin Island and on Wrangell Island. The nearest Wilderness is the Stikine-LeConte, approximately twenty miles to the north. The area currently receives light use inland, away from saltwater or road access

(2) Distance From Population Centers (Accessibility): Approximate distances from population centers are as follows:

Community		Air Miles	Water Miles
Juneau	(Pop 23,729)	145	165
Petersburg	(Pop 4,040)	32	42
Wrangell	(Pop. 2,836)	5	5
Ketchikan	(Pop 12,705)	78	90

Wrangell is the nearest stop on the Alaska Marine Highway.

(3) Interest by Proponents:

(a) **Moratorium areas:** The area has not been identified as a "moratorium" area or proposed as Wilderness in legislative initiatives to date.

(b) **Local users/residents:** Most of the area use is by residents of Wrangell for recreation purposes. There has been no formal support for or opposition to maintaining this area in a roadless condition

e. Environmental Consequences

ALTERNATIVE ANALYSIS TO BE DONE LATER

INDIVIDUAL ROADLESS AREA DESCRIPTION

NAME: North Etolin (232)   ACRES (GROSS): 46,887   ACRES (NFS): 46,887

GEOZONE: S06
GEOGRAPHIC PROVINCE: Central Interior Islands

1989 WILDERNESS ATTRIBUTE RATING: 25

a. Description

(1) Relationship to RARE II areas: The table below displays the VCU 1/
names, VCU numbers, original WARS 2/ rating, and comments This enables
the reader to compare the roadless areas evaluated in Appendix C with
previous analyses

VCU Name	VCU No.	1979 WARS Rating	Comments
Chichagof	462	19	
Kunk	463	24	
Anita	464*	23	
Quiet	465*	21	
Mosman	467*	26	

*--The roadless area includes only part of this VCU

(2) History: North Etolin Island was claimed by the Tansaqwedi and Nokedi
clans of the Stikine Tlingit Their use is evidenced by the remains of
villages, fish camps, fort sites, petroglyphs, and fish weirs Historic
uses included hunting, trapping, and commercial fishing

(3) Location and Access: The area is located on the north end of Etolin
Island and is bounded by Stikine Strait on the northwest, Zimovia Strait on
the east, and Anita Bay to the south. The city of Wrangell lies 10 miles
to the north, and is served by the Alaska Marine Highway and jet service
There are no sites suitable for landing wheeled aircraft. A small road
system and Log Transfer Facility exist on the island immediately south of
the roadless area The island is accessible from saltwater by boat, and
good moorage sites exist.

1/ A VCU (Value Comparison Unit) is one of 867 watersheds which make up the
Forest and were differentiated for planning purposes in the Tongass Land
Management Plan.
2/ Wilderness Attribute Rating System (WARS) was the nationwide system used to
rate the wilderness attributes of roadless areas in the Roadless Area
Review and Evaluation (RARE II).

(4) Geography and Topography: The area is generally characterized by steeply-rising mountains reaching elevations of over 3,000 feet. The tallest in this area is over 3,900 feet. Alpine covers 2,143 acres and rock another 841 acres. There is much landform variety. Mountains less than 3,500 feet in elevation were overridden by glaciers in the past and have rounded, hummocky summits, knobs, and ridges. Higher mountains are sometimes sharp crested. Two drainages flow to the north, and a major drainage flows to the south through the roadless area. Kunk Lake and several small lakes exist between the mountain peaks, and account for 541 acres. There are 36 miles of shoreline on saltwater.

(5) Ecosystem:

(a) Classification: The area is in the Central Interior Islands Geographic Province. This province is generally characterized by rolling, subdued topography and extensive muskegs, but may have localized rugged terrain.

(b) Vegetation: Alpine vegetation dominates above 2,500 feet elevation. The valley floors and poorly-drained areas between hills are generally covered with muskeg (160 acres), and scrub lodgepole pine. Steeper, more-well-drained hillsides support heavy stands of Sitka spruce, western hemlock, redcedar and Alaska-cedar.

There are approximately 41,741 acres of forested land of which 23,317 acres are commercial forest land. Of the commercial forest land, 20,113 acres are non-riparian old growth and 2,664 acres are riparian old growth.

(c) Soils: Soils in this area are formed in a wide variety of parent materials, including bedrock and glacial drift. In general, well- or moderately-well-drained soils are on moderate to steep mountain slopes with permeable parent materials. These soils are very acidic, have cold soil temperatures, and are very high in organic matter. Rooting is largely limited to the surface organic layers and the top few inches of mineral soil. These soils are usually moist, sometimes wet, but are never dry.

More-poorly-drained soils developed on less-sloping areas and/or areas with impermeable soil materials. These soils have deep accumulations of organic matter and range from scrubby forested wetlands to open muskeg.

Alpine soils, generally above 2,000 feet elevation, are mostly shallow, very wet organic soils or are extremely shallow and rocky.

(d) Fish Resource: Fish resources have been rated as part of the Tongass Land Management Plan (1979) and by the Alaska Department of Fish and Game in its Forest Habitat Integrity Program (1983). These ratings describe the value of VCU's for sport fish, commercial fish and estuaries.

One VCU, 463, is rated as high value for sport fish. VCU 467 is rated as highly valued for commercial fish.

(e) **Wildlife Resource:** Important species include Sitka black-tailed deer, black bear, and elk. Elk were introduced to the island in 1986 as a cooperative effort to establish elk in Southeast Alaska Subsequent elk transplants have occurred and are planned Survival so far has been described as marginal.

(f) **Threatened and Endangered Species:** The area contains no known threatened or endangered species

(6) **Current Use and Management:** The northern and western portions of the roadless area, 24,381 acres, were allocated to Land Use Designation (LUD) 2 in the Tongass Land Management Plan, which allows road construction and timber harvest in conjunction with strong protection measures to meet other resource objectives. The southern and eastern portions, 22,327 acres, were allocated to LUD 4, which provides for intensive resource use and development. The area south of the roadless area has been logged and partially roaded, and a small area on the northeast side has also been harvested. The saltwater bodies surrounding the island receive moderately heavy use by commercial and pleasure boats. A one and one-third mile trail exists to Kunk Lake and receives light recreation use There is subsistence use in the area.

(7) **Appearance (Apparent Naturalness):** The roadless area itself is unmodified. It is bounded on one side by clearcut harvest areas. A person in a boat approaching the roadless area would see natural scenery

The majority of this roadless area (92 percent) is natural appearing, where only ecological change has occurred (Existing Visual Condition (EVC) Type I). Two percent of the area is in EVC Type IV, where changes in the landscape are easily noticed by the average person and may attract some attention. They appear to be disturbances but resemble natural patterns Six percent is in EVC Type V where changes in the landscape are obvious to the average person, and appear to be major disturbances

About 45 percent of this roadless area is inventoried Variety Class A (possessing landscape diversity that is unique for the character type). 45 percent is inventoried Variety Class B (possessing landscape diversity that is common for the character type) and the remaining 10 percent is inventoried Variety Class C (possessing a low degree of landscape diversity).

(8) **Surroundings (External Influences):** Boats plying the adjacent saltwaters may be visible from within parts of the area, but usually are not intrusive. It is possible to see clearcuts and roads from some southern locations within this roadless area. Sights and sounds from the town of Wrangell may be apparent from some locations, especially with development of private land across from Zimovia Strait. The Alaska Marine Highway passes within one-half mile along the west side of the roadless area.

(9) **Attractions and Features of Special Interest:** The landform variety, including subalpine peaks, stream drainages, and lakes, is an attraction as is the presence of elk Kunk Lake is a popular recreation destination accessible by trail. The area contains 11 inventoried recreation places totaling 21,209 acres

b. Capability of Management as Wilderness or in an Unroaded Condition

   (1) Manageability and management area boundaries: The area is well
   defined by saltwater on the west, east, and north, however a small
   beach-logged area exists on the northeast side. The southern boundary is
   defined by flat land running east to west, which contains roads and cutting
   units. Feasibility of managing the southern portion of this area in a
   roadless condition is moderate, and is high for the rest of the area

   (2) Natural Integrity· Timber harvest activities dominate the southern
   boundary of the area A small beach-logged area on the northwest portion
   has regrown. Within the roadless area, the natural integrity is
   unmodified, except for the trail to Kunk Lake.

   (3) Opportunity for Solitude: There is a good opportunity for solitude
   within the area. Present recreation use levels are low except at the
   mouths of some streams and along the Kunk Lake Trail. Generally, a person
   camped or traveling inland is unlikely to see others. Low-flying aircraft
   may, at times, pass over the roadless area, and the State ferry and boaters
   may pass next to the roadless area, but all are generally non-intrusive

   (4) Opportunity for Primitive Recreation: The area provides primarily
   semi-primitive motorized and non-motorized, as well as primitive,
   recreation opportunities:

ROS Class	Acres
Primitive (P)	15,799
Semi-Primitive Non-Motorized (SPNM)	15,239
Semi-Primitive Motorized (SPM)	14,508
Roaded Modified (RM)	1,342

The area contains 11 recreation places.

ROS CLASS	# OF REC. PLACES	TOTAL ACRES .	CAPACITY BY RVD
P	2	13,136	2,317
SPNM	8	7,052	3,300
SPM	1	1,021	200

The character of the area generally allows the visitor to feel remote from
the sights and sounds of human activity. The area is accessible by boat
from the community of Wrangell in less than one hour, and from Ketchikan in
approximately seven hours. Travel within the area is challenging,
requiring a high degree of woods skills and experience. The presence of
black bears, especially around salmon streams in the fall, presents a
degree of challenge and a need for caution. The Kunk Lake Trail provides
access to a portion of the interior of this roadless area, and to a remote
lake basin.

   (5) Special Features (Ecologic, Geologic, Scientific, Cultural): There
   are opportunities to observe a variety of ecological and landform settings
   The Kunk Lake Trail provides recreational opportunities Elk were
   transplanted on the island and are not native to Alaska

c. Availability for Management as Wilderness or in an Unroaded Condition

   (1) Resource Potentials

      (a) Recreation Potential: There is potential for additional
      outfitter and guide permits, developed trails, and cabins or
      shelters If the elk population grows, a harvest may occur at some
      point in the future

      (b) Fish Resource: The Tongass Land Management Plan, amended Winter
      1985-86 does not identify any specific fish habitat enhancement
      projects

      (c) Wildlife Resource: As identified in the Tongass Land Management
      Plan, amended 1985-86, deer range habitat improvement projects are
      planned in the area. Elk projects may be proposed in the future

      (d) Timber Resource: There are 17,188 acres inventoried as
      tentatively suitable for harvest This includes 2,003 acres of
      riparian old growth, and 14,885 acres of non-riparian old growth
      Some areas are highly prone to strong winds which blow down standing
      timber left exposed when adjacent stands are cut

      (e) Land Use Authorizations: Their are no special use authorizations
      in this area.

      (f) Minerals: The area generally has a low minerals rating and there
      are no known current claims.

      (g) Areas of Scientific Interest: The area contains no inventoried
      potential Research Natural Areas The area has not been identified
      for any other scientific value.

   (2) Management Considerations

      (a) The potential for managing timber in this roadless area is
      moderate, as roads could be extended from the existing system and much
      of the area could be logged without constructing a camp or additional
      log transfer facilities.

      (b) The area is readily accessible by sheltered waters from the city
      of Wrangell. Maintenance of the area in a roadless condition enhances
      opportunities for visitors to and residents of the city of Wrangell to
      have a semi-primitive recreation experience. It also maintains
      opportunities for wildlife to move freely through the area.

      (c) Fire: The area has no significant fire history.

      (d) Insects and Disease: Endemic tree diseases common to Southeast
      Alaska are present, there are no know epidemic disease occurrences

      (e) Land Status: Entirely National Forest Systems land

d. Relationship to communities and other roadless and Wilderness areas
    (1) Nearby Roadless and Wilderness Areas and Uses: There are two other
    roadless areas on Etolin Island   Additional roadless areas are located
    nearby, across narrow saltwater channels, on Woronkofski Island and on
    Wrangell Island   The nearest Wilderness is the Stikine-LeConte,
    approximately twenty miles to the north   The area currently receives light
    use inland, away from saltwater or road access

    (2) Distance From Population Centers (Accessibility): Approximate
    distances from population centers are as follows·

Community		Air Miles	Water Miles
Juneau	(Pop 23,729)	160	175
Petersburg	(Pop. 4,040)	32	42
Wrangell	(Pop. 2,836)	5	5
Ketchikan	(Pop. 12,705)	78	94

Wrangell is the nearest stop on the Alaska Marine Highway

    (3) Interest by Proponents:

        (a) Moratorium areas: The area has not been identified as a
        "moratorium" area or proposed as Wilderness in legislative initiatives
        to date

        (b) Local users/residents: The area is primarily used for
        recreational purposes by the citizens of Wrangell. There has been no
        formal support for or opposition to maintaining this area in a
        roadless condition. There has been general support for the elk
        transplant program on the island.

e. Environmental Consequences

    ALTERNATIVE ANALYSIS TO BE DONE LATER

INDIVIDUAL ROADLESS AREA DESCRIPTION

NAME: Mosman (233)   ACRES (GROSS): 57,974   ACRES (NFS): 57,974

GEOZONE: S06
GEOGRAPHIC PROVINCE: Central Interior Islands

1989 WILDERNESS ATTRIBUTE RATING: 24

a. Description

(1) Relationship to RARE II areas: The table below displays the VCU 1/
names, VCU numbers, original WARS 2/ rating, and comments. This enables
the reader to compare the roadless areas evaluated in Appendix C with
previous analyses.

VCU Name	VCU No.	1979 WARS Rating	Comments
Anita	464*	23	
Quiet	465*	21	
Steamer	466	25	
Mosman	467*	26	
Burnett	468*	24	

*--The roadless area includes only part of this VCU.

(2) History: This area was claimed by several Stikine Tlingit clans
during prehistoric times. Evidence includes the remains of villages, fish
camps, fish weirs, petroglyphs, and bark-stripped trees Evidence of
historic use includes fox farms, trapping cabins, homesteads, canneries and
temporary camps

(3) Location and Access: The area is located in the middle of Etolin
Island. It is bounded by Clarence Strait on the west, the South Etolin
Roadless Area on the south and east, and an area of roads and harvest units
to the north. The city of Wrangell lies 22 miles to the north, and is
served by the Alaska Marine Highway and jet service There are no sites
suitable for landing wheeled aircraft. A small road system and log
transfer facility exist on the island immediately north of the roadless
area. The island is accessible from saltwater by boat, and good moorage
sites exist.

1/ A VCU (Value Comparison Unit) is one of 867 watersheds which make up the
Forest and were differentiated for planning purposes in the Tongass Land
Management Plan.
2/ Wilderness Attribute Rating System (WARS) was the nationwide system used to
rate the wilderness attributes of roadless areas in the Roadless Area
Review and Evaluation (RARE II).

(4) Geography and Topography: The area is generally characterized by a series of mountains oriented nearly in a north-south alignment, separated by the long, narrow waterways of Mosman and Burnett Bays There is much landform variety as some of the mountains are gentle, while others, such as the Keating Range, rise steeply. Alpine covers 1,842 acres, and rock 1,602 acres The highest peaks attain elevations of about 3,000 feet Numerous short streams drain the area Several lakes exist in the area, the major ones being Streets Lake to the west, and Navy and Burnett Lakes on the east side of the roadless area. These lakes cover about 661 acres Small islands make up another 1,743 acres There is 104 miles of shoreline on saltwater

(5) Ecosystem:

(a) Classification: The area is in the Central Interior Islands Geographic Province. This province is generally characterized by rolling, subdued topography and extensive muskeg areas, but may have localized, rugged terrain. This roadless area displays a great deal of landform variety

(b) Vegetation: Alpine vegetation dominates above 2,500 feet in elevation. A few poorly-drained areas between hills (20 acres) are generally covered with muskeg and scrub lodgepole pine Steeper, more-well-drained hillsides support heavy stands of Sitka spruce, western hemlock, redcedar and Alaska-cedar

There are approximately 52,806 acres of forested land of which 28,960 acres are commercial forest land. Of the commercial forest land, 24,550 acres are non-riparian old growth and 3,367 acres are riparian old growth.

(c) Soils: Soils in this area are formed in a wide variety of parent materials, including bedrock and glacial drift. In general, well- or moderately-well-drained soils are on moderate to steep mountain slopes with permeable parent materials. These soils are very acidic, have cold soil temperatures, and are very high in organic matter Rooting is largely limited to the surface organic layers and the top few inches of mineral soil These soils are usually moist, sometimes wet, but are never dry

More-poorly-drained soils developed on less-sloping areas and/or areas with impermeable soil materials. These soils have deep accumulations of organic matter and range from scrubby forested wetlands to open muskeg.

Alpine soils, generally above 2,000 feet elevation, are mostly shallow, very wet organic soils or are extremely shallow and rocky

(d) Fish Resource: Fish resources have been rated as part of the Tongass Land Management Plan (1979) and by the Alaska Department of Fish and Game in its Forest Habitat Integrity Program (1983) These ratings describe the value of VCU's for sport fish, commercial fish and estuaries.

One VCU, 466, is rated as high value for sport fish   VCU's 476 and
468 are rated as highly valued for commercial fish

(e) **Wildlife Resource:** Important species include Sitka black-tailed
deer, black bear, and elk. The elk were introduced on the island in
1986 as a cooperative project.

(f) **Threatened and Endangered Species:** The area contains no known
threatened or endangered species.

(6) **Current Use and Management:** The majority of the roadless area, 55,008
acres, was allocated to Land Use Designation (LUD) 3 in the Tongass Land
Management Plan, which allows road construction and timber harvest in
conjunction with strong protection measures to meet other resource
objectives. A small portion in the northeast portion, 1,702 acres, was
allocated to LUD 4, which provides for intensive resource use and
development. The area north of the roadless area has been logged and
partially roaded. The saltwater bodies surrounding the island receive
moderately-heavy use by commercial and pleasure boats. The shoreline and
bays receive light recreation use. Steamer Bay Cabin is located in the
northwest corner of the roadless area. There is subsistence use in the
area. Other facilities exist within or immediately adjacent to this area
and include a fish hatchery, oyster farm, electronic sites, shelter cabin.
a fish pass, a research cabin and a fish weir

(7) **Appearance (Apparent Naturalness):** The roadless area is unmodified,
except for the recreation cabin and other improvements mentioned above   It
is bounded inland on one side by clearcut harvest areas   A person in a
boat approaching the roadless area would see natural scenery.

The majority of this roadless area (93 percent) is natural appearing, where
only ecological change has occurred (Existing Visual Condition (EVC)
Type I). Less than one percent of this roadless area is EVC Type III.
where changes in the landscape are noticed by the average forest visitor.
The natural appearance of the landscape remains dominant   Less than one
percent of the area is in EVC Type IV, where changes in the landscape are
easily noticed by the average person and may attract some attention   They
appear to be disturbances but resemble natural patterns. Six percent is in
EVC Type V where changes in the landscape are obvious to the average
person, and appear to be major disturbances.

About 31 percent of this roadless area is inventoried Variety Class A
(possessing landscape diversity that is unique for the character type), 55
percent is inventoried Variety Class B (possessing landscape diversity that
is common for the character type) and the remaining 14 percent is
inventoried Variety Class C (possessing a low degree of landscape
diversity).

(8) **Surroundings (External Influences):** Boats plying the adjacent
saltwaters may be visible from within parts of the area but usually are not
intrusive   It is possible to see clearcuts and roads from some northern
locations within this roadless area   The Alaska Marine Highway passes
within two miles along the west side of the roadless area

(9) **Attractions and Features of Special Interest:** The landform variety, including subalpine peaks, stream drainages, and lakes, is an attraction The bays provide sheltered moorages and a sense of remoteness The elk population is unique to Alaska. The area contains 16 inventoried recreation places totaling 17,824 acres

b **Capability of Management as Wilderness or in an Unroaded Condition**

(1) **Manageability and Management Area Boundaries:** The area is well defined by saltwater on the west, and south The northern boundary is defined by flat land running east to west, which contains roads and cutting units The eastern boundary is defined by the drainage break of the mountains, which separates this area from the South Etolin Roadless Area Feasibility of managing the northern portion of this area in a roadless condition is moderate, and is high in the rest of the area

(2) **Natural Integrity:** Timber harvest activities dominate the northern boundary of the area. Within the roadless area, the natural integrity is unmodified, except for the recreation cabin and facilities mentioned

(3) **Opportunity for Solitude:** There is a good opportunity for solitude within the area away from improvements and facilities. Present recreation use levels are low except at the mouths of some streams and at the Steamer Bay Cabin. Generally, a person camped or traveling inland is unlikely to see others Low-flying aircraft may, at times, pass over, and the State ferry and boaters may pass next to the roadless area, but all are generally non-intrusive.

(4) **Opportunity for Primitive Recreation:** The area provides primarily semi-primitive motorized and non-motorized recreation opportunities

ROS Class	Acres
Primitive (P)	7,047
Semi-Primitive Non-Motorized (SPNM)	24,982
Semi-Primitive Motorized (SPM)	23,322
Roaded Modified (RM)	2,623

The area contains 16 recreation places.

ROS CLASS	# OF REC. PLACES	TOTAL ACRES	CAPACITY BY RVD
P	1	20	2
SPNM	1	20	3
SPM	12	14,461	7,904
RM	2	440	1,040

The character of the area generally allows the visitor to feel remote from the sights and sounds of human activity. The area is accessible by boat from the community of Wrangell in one to two hours, and from Ketchikan in approximately seven hours Travel within the area is challenging. requiring a high degree of woods skills and experience The presence of black bears, especially around salmon streams in the fall, presents a degree of challenge and a need for caution The long bays penetrate the area and provide access to portions of the interior, as well as protect users from the open waters and traffic of Clarence Strait

(5) Special Features (Ecologic, Geologic, Scientific, Cultural): There are opportunities to observe a variety of ecological and landform settings The Steamer Bay Cabin facilitates recreation activities in the area Elk are also a unique attraction.

c. Availability for Management as Wilderness or in an Unroaded Condition

(1) Resource Potentials

(a) Recreation Potential: There is potential for additional outfitter and guide permits, developed trails, and cabins or shelters. Elk hunting may be possible at some point in the future

(b) Fish Resource: The Tongass Land Management Plan, amended Winter 1985-86 does not identify any specific fish habitat enhancement projects for this area.

(c) Wildlife Resource: As identified in the Tongass Land Management Plan, amended 1985-86, deer range habitat improvement projects are planned in the area. Elk projects may surface in the future

(d) Timber Resource: There are 21,564 acres inventoried as tentatively suitable for harvest This includes 2,205 acres of riparian old growth and 18,157 acres of non-riparian old growth Some areas are highly prone to strong winds which blow down standing timber left exposed when adjacent stands are cut.

(e) Land Use Authorizations: There are five special use authorizations, and lighthouse reservations

(f) Minerals: The area generally has a low minerals rating and there are no known current claims.

(g) Areas of Scientific Interest: The area contains no inventoried potential Research Natural Areas and has not been identified for any other scientific value

(2) Management Considerations

(a) The potential for managing timber in this roadless area is moderate, as roads could be extended from the existing system and much of the area could be logged without constructing a camp or additional log transfer facilities.

(b) Maintenance of the area in a roadless condition enhances opportunities for visitors to and residents of the city of Wrangell to have a semi-primitive recreation experience It also maintains opportunities for wildlife to move freely through the area, and could compliment management of the adjacent roadless area

(c) Fire: The area has no significant fire history

(d) Insects and Disease: Endemic tree diseases common to Southeast Alaska are present, there are no know epidemic disease occurrences

(e) Land Status: Entirely National Forest System land

d. Relationship to Communities and Other Roadless and Wilderness Areas

(1) Nearby Roadless and Wilderness Areas and Uses: The only roadless area adjacent is South Etolin which is located to the south The North Etolin Roadless Area, located to the north, is separated from the Mosman Roadless Area by a valley and roaded area Additional roadless areas are located nearby, across narrow saltwater channels, and include Kashavarof and South Zarembo. The nearest Wilderness is the Stikine-LeConte, approximately twenty-five miles to the north. The area currently receives light use inland, away from saltwater or road access.

(2) Distance From Population Centers (Accessibility): Approximate distances from population centers are as follows:

Community		Air Miles	Water Miles
Juneau	(Pop. 23,729)	170	185
Petersburg	(Pop 4 040)	44	60
Wrangell	(Pop. 2,836)	22	30
Ketchikan	(Pop. 12,705)	63	84

Wrangell is the nearest stop on the Alaska Marine Highway

(3) Interest by Proponents:

(a) Moratorium areas: The area has not been identified as a "moratorium" area or proposed as Wilderness in legislative initiatives to date, but is adjacent to one, South Etolin.

(b) Local users/residents: The area is primarily used for recreational purposes by the citizens of Wrangell. There has been no formal support for or opposition to maintaining this area in a roadless condition. The elk transplants have generally been supported.

e. Environmental Consequences

ALTERNATIVE ANALYSIS TO BE DONE LATER

INDIVIDUAL ROADLESS AREA DESCRIPTION

NAME: South Etolin (234)   ACRES (GROSS): 113,031   ACRES (NFS): 113,031

GEOZONE: S06
GEOGRAPHIC PROVINCE: Central Interior Islands

1989 WILDERNESS ATTRIBUTE RATING: 27

a. Description

(1) Relationship to RARE II areas: The table below displays the VCU 1/
names, VCU numbers, original WARS 2/ rating, and comments This enables
the reader to compare the roadless areas evaluated in Appendix C with
previous analyses.

| | | 1979 | |
VCU Name	VCU No.	WARS Rating	Comments
Anita	464*	23	
Olive	469*	22	
Zimovia	470*	20	
Menefee	471	23	
McHenry	472	27	
Onslow	473	26	
Canoe	474	20	

*--The roadless area includes only part of this VCU

(2) History: The area was inhabited by several clans of the Stikine
Tlingit. Evidence of their use includes several village sites and numerous
fort sites, temporary camps, fish weirs, petroglyphs and bark-stripped
trees. Historic use of this area was also considerable and is represented
by the remains of the first salmon hatchery in Alaska as well as salteries
canneries, fox farms, trapping cabins, and other temporary camps

(3) Location and Access: The area encompasses the southern end of Etolin
Island. It is bounded by Clarence Strait on the west, the Mosman Roadless
Area to the north, and Ernest Sound to the south and east The city of
Wrangell lies 22 miles to the north, and is served by the Alaska Marine
Highway and jet service. There are no sites suitable for landing wheeled
aircraft. A small road system and log transfer facility exist on the
island immediately north of the roadless area. The island is accessible
from saltwater by boat, and there are good moorage sites.

1/ A VCU (Value Comparison Unit) is one of 867 watersheds which make up the
Forest and were differentiated for planning purposes in the Tongass Land
Management Plan.
2/ Wilderness Attribute Rating System (WARS) was the nationwide system used to
rate the wilderness attributes of roadless areas in the Roadless Area
Review and Evaluation (RARE II).

(4) Geography and Topography: The area is generally characterized by a series of rugged mountains, subalpine ridges, and glacial cirque lakes. Several of the mountains rise to over 3,700 feet, with the mountains on the southern end of this area being slightly gentler and rising to 2,000 feet. Alpine accounts for 3,099 acres and rock for 4,260 acres. There is much landform variety as some of the mountains are gentle, while others rise steeply. Numerous short streams drain the area, with several longer streams draining the southern portion. There are numerous lakes in the area which cover a total of 2,178 acres. Several large islands separated by narrow bodies of water lie off the southern end of Etolin Island and are included in this roadless area, as are numerous smaller islands in this vicinity. Combined, these islands account for 6,911 acres. About 180 miles of shoreline on saltwater exist.

(5) Ecosystem:

   (a) Classification: The area is classified as being in the Central Interior Islands Geographic Province. This province is generally characterized by rolling, subdued topography and extensive muskeg areas, but may have rugged terrain in localized areas. This roadless area has much landform variety, including great variety of island forms of all sizes. '

   (b) Vegetation: Alpine vegetation dominates above 2,500 feet elevation. The valley floors and poorly-drained areas between hills are generally covered with muskeg (396 acres) and scrub lodgepole pine. Steeper, more-well-drained hillsides support heavy stands of Sitka spruce, western hemlock, redcedar and Alaska-cedar.

   There are approximately 100,148 acres of forested land of which 49,270 acres are commercial forest land. Of the commercial forest land, 44,539 acres are non-riparian old growth and 3,653 acres are riparian old growth.

   (c) Soils: Soils in this area are formed in a wide variety of parent materials, including bedrock and glacial drift. In general, well- or moderately-well-drained soils are on moderate to steep mountain slopes with permeable parent materials. These soils are very acidic, have cold soil temperatures, and are very high in organic matter. Rooting is largely limited to the surface organic layers and the top few inches of mineral soil. These soils are usually moist, sometimes wet, but are never dry.

   More-poorly-drained soils developed on less-sloping areas and/or areas with impermeable soil materials. These soils have deep accumulations of organic matter and range from scrubby forested wetlands to open muskeg.

   Alpine soils, generally above 2,000 feet elevation, are mostly shallow, very wet organic soils or are extremely shallow and rocky.

   (d) Fish Resource: Fish resources have been rated as part of the Tongass Land Management Plan (1979) and by the Alaska Department of Fish and Game in its Forest Habitat Integrity Program (1983). These ratings describe the value of VCU's for sport fish, commercial fish and estuaries.

One VCU, 469, is rated as highly value for sport fish. VCU's 469 and 472 rated as highly valued for commercial fish VCU's rated as highly valued estuaries include 469, 470, and 473.

(e) Wildlife Resource: Important species include Sitka black-tailed deer, black bear, and elk The elk were introduced to the area in 1986 in a cooperative project.

(f) Threatened and Endangered Species: The area contains no known threatened or endangered species

(6) Current Use and Management: The majority of the roadless area, 90,127 acres, was allocated to Land Use Designation (LUD) 1 in the Tongass Land Management Plan. This area was considered by Congress for Wilderness designation, but Congress later decided not to include these lands in the National Wilderness Preservation System, thus directing their release from LUD 1. The future allocation of this area is to be determined. A small portion of the northern tip of this roadless area, 21,504 acres, is allocated to LUD 4, which provides for intensive resource use and development. The area north of the roadless area has been logged and partially roaded. The saltwater bodies surrounding the island receive moderately-heavy use by commercial and pleasure boats The shoreline and bays receive light recreation use. There is subsistence use in the area

(7) Appearance (Apparent Naturalness): The roadless area is unmodified It is bounded inland on one side by clearcut harvest areas A person in a boat approaching the roadless area would see natural scenery

The majority of this roadless area (98 percent) is natural appearing, where only ecological change has occurred (Existing Visual Condition (EVC) Type I). One percent of this roadless area is EVC Type III, where changes in the landscape are noticed by the average forest visitor. The natural appearance of the landscape remains dominant. One percent is in EVC Type V where changes in the landscape are obvious to the average person, and appear to be major disturbances.

Forty-one percent of this roadless area is inventoried Variety Class A (possessing landscape diversity that is unique for the character type) Forty-eight percent is inventoried Variety Class B (possessing landscape diversity that is common for the character type) The remaining 11 percent is inventoried Variety Class C (possessing a low degree of landscape diversity).

(8) Surroundings (External Influences): Boats plying the adjacent saltwaters may be visible from within parts of the area, but usually are not intrusive. It is possible to see clearcuts and roads from some northern locations within this roadless area. The Alaska Marine Highway passes within two miles of the roadless area along the west side

(9) Attractions and Features of Special Interest: The landform variety, including subalpine peaks, stream drainages, and lakes, is an attraction The bays provide sheltered moorages and a sense of remoteness   The presence of elk is unique to Alaska   The area contains 16 inventoried recreation places totaling 30,169 acres

b   Capability of Management as Wilderness or in an Unroaded Condition

(1) Manageability and Management Area Boundaries: The area is well defined by saltwater on the west, east, and south   The northern boundary is irregular, and is defined by ridgelines separating drainages Feasibility of managing the northern portion of this area in a roadless condition is moderate to high depending on management of the adjacent roadless area (Mosman). Management of the remaining area as roadless is high.

(2) Natural Integrity: The area is unmodified, and has maintained its natural integrity

(3) Opportunity for Solitude: There is a good opportunity for solitude within the area. Present recreation use levels are low except at the mouths of some streams and at good anchorages   Generally, a person camped or traveling inland is unlikely to see others   At times, low-flying aircraft may pass over, and the State ferry and boaters may pass next to the roadless area. All are generally non-intrusive

(4) Opportunity for Primitive Recreation: The area provides primarily semi-primitive motorized and non-motorized recreation opportunity

ROS Class	Acres
Primitive (P)	34,764
Semi-Primitive Non-Motorized (SPNM)	37,432
Semi-Primitive Motorized (SPM)	38,234
Roaded Natural (RN)	1,739
Roaded Modified (RM)	860

The area contains 16 recreation places.

ROS CLASS	# OF REC. PLACES	TOTAL ACRES	CAPACITY BY RVD
P	1	2,923	228
SPNM	2	2,723	460
SPM	10	23,503	11,625
RN	1	740	163
RM	2	280	465

The character of the area generally allows the visitor to feel remote from the sights and sounds of human activity. The area is accessible by boat from the community of Wrangell in one to two hours, and from Ketchikan in approximately seven hours. Travel within the area is challenging, requiring a high degree of woods skills and experience The presence of black bears, especially around salmon streams in the fall, presents a degree of challenge and a need for caution Anchorages around the roadless area provide access to portions of the interior, as well as remove users from the open waters and traffic of Clarence Strait

(5) Special Features (Ecologic, Geologic, Scientific, Cultural): There are opportunities to observe a variety of ecological and landform settings. Elk are unique to Alaska, and are present on the island.

c. **Availability for Management as Wilderness or in an Unroaded Condition**

   (1) **Resource Potentials**

       (a) **Recreation Potential:** There is potential for additional outfitter and guide permits, developed trails, and cabins or shelters. The elk population may offer a unique hunting experience in the future.

       (b) **Fish Resource:** The Tongass Land Management Plan, amended Winter 1985-86 does not identify any fish habitat enhancement projects in this area

       (c) **Wildlife Resource:** As identified in the Tongass Land Management Plan, amended 1985-86, deer range habitat improvement projects are planned in the area Elk projects may occur in the future as well

       (d) **Timber Resource:** There are 36,356 acres inventoried as tentatively suitable for harvest. This includes 2,435 acres of riparian old growth and 33,122 acres of non-riparian old growth Some areas are highly prone to strong winds which blow down standing timber left exposed when adjacent stands are cut.

       (e) **Land Use Authorizations:** There are two special use authorizations.

       (f) **Minerals:** The area generally has a low minerals rating and there are no known current claims.

       (g) **Areas of Scientific Interest:** The area does not contain any inventoried potential Research Natural Areas and has not been identified for any other scientific value.

   (2) **Management Considerations**

       (a) The potential for managing timber in this roadless area is low due to the rugged nature of the terrain An exception is in the southern portion where the potential is moderate due to the more-gently sloping terrain Harvesting the timber, however, would require construction of transportation facilities and additional log transfer facilities

(b) Maintenance of the area in a roadless condition enhances opportunities for visitors to and residents of the city of Wrangell to have a semi-primitive recreation experience It also maintains opportunities for wildlife to move freely through the area, and could compliment management of the adjacent roadless area

(c) Fire: The area has no significant fire history

(d) Insects and Disease: Endemic tree diseases common to Southeast Alaska are present, there are no know epidemic disease occurrences

(e) Land Status: The State has selected approximately 805 acres near McHenry Anchorage.

d. Relationship to Communities and Other Roadless and Wilderness Areas

(1) Nearby Roadless and Wilderness Areas and Uses: There is one other roadless area adjacent to the west (Mosman). The area currently receives light use inland, away from saltwater

(2) Distance From Population Centers (Accessibility): Approximate distances from population centers are as follows:

Community		Air Miles	Water Miles
Juneau	(Pop 23,729)	170	185
Petersburg	(Pop 4,040)	46	65
Wrangell	(Pop. 2,836)	22	30
Ketchikan	(Pop 12,705)	61	82

Wrangell is the nearest stop on the Alaska Marine Highway

(3) Interest by Proponents:

(a) Moratorium areas: The area has been identified as a "moratorium" area and proposed as Wilderness in H.R. 987.

(b) Local users/residents: Most use of the area is for recreational purposes by the citizens of Wrangell. There has been support for maintaining this area in a roadless condition. The elk transplant program is generally supported

e. Environmental Consequences

ALTERNATIVE ANALYSIS TO BE DONE LATER

INDIVIDUAL ROADLESS AREA DESCRIPTION

NAME: West Zarembo (235)   ACRES (GROSS): 6,945   ACRES (NFS): 6,945

GEOZONE: S05
GEOGRAPHIC PROVINCE: Central Interior Islands

1989 WILDERNESS ATTRIBUTE RATING: 19

a. Description

   (1) **Relationship to RARE II areas:** The table below displays the VCU 1/
   names, VCU numbers, original WARS 2/ rating, and comments This enables
   the reader to compare the roadless areas evaluated in Appendix C with
   previous analyses.

		1979	
VCU Name	VCU No.	WARS Rating	Comments
St. John	457*	-	Not rated in 1979
Snow	458*	13	

   *--The roadless area includes only part of this VCU.

   (2) **History:** Zarembo Island was evidently used by all of the Stikine
   Tlingit clans for hunting and gathering. Their use is evidenced by several
   fish weirs and petroglyph sites along the west coast of the island
   Historic use of the area is evidenced by the remains of a log cabin site

   (3) **Location and Access:** The area is located on the west side of Zarembo
   Island. Zarembo Island is south of Mitkof Island, and ten miles west of
   the town of Wrangell and Wrangell Island. Sumner Strait lies to the north
   and Clarence Strait to the west. Saltwater access is by boat or
   floatplane. There are no sites suitable for landing wheeled aircraft The
   road system on Zarembo Island accesses the eastern portion of this roadless
   area.

   (4) **Geography and Topography:** The area is generally flat and slightly
   rolling. Two streams drain the area, and small freshwater lakes account
   for about 100 acres. The flat muskegs rise to the east to timbered
   hillsides of elevations of about 1,000 feet. The area contains ten miles
   of shoreline on saltwater.

1/ A VCU (Value Comparison Unit) is one of 867 watersheds which make up the
    Forest and were differentiated for planning purposes in the Tongass Land
    Management Plan.
2/ Wilderness Attribute Rating System (WARS) was the nationwide system used to
    rate the wilderness attributes of roadless areas in the Roadless Area
    Review and Evaluation (RARE II).

·(5) Ecosystem:

(a) Classification: The area is in the Central Interior Islands Geographic Province This province is generally characterized by rolling, subdued topography and extensive muskeg areas, but may have rugged terrain in localized area There are no known areas of unique or uncommon plant/soils associations or geologic formations in the area.

(b) Vegetation: Vegetation of this roadless area primarily consists of typical spruce/hemlock forests Low-lying, poorly-drained portions of the area are muskeg, and cover about 80 acres

There are 6,745 acres of forested land of which 3,652 acres are commercial forest land. Of the commercial forest land, 2,774 acres are non-riparian old growth and 499 acres are riparian old growth

(c) Soils: Soils in this area are formed in a wide variety of parent materials, including bedrock and glacial drift. In general, well- or moderately-well-drained soils are on moderate to steep mountain slopes with permeable parent materials. These soils are very acidic, have cold soil temperatures, and are very high in organic matter Rooting is largely limited to the surface organic layers and the top few inches of mineral soil. These soils are usually moist, sometimes wet. but are never dry

More-poorly-drained soils developed on less-sloping areas and/or areas with impermeable soil materials These soils have deep accumulations of organic matter and range from scrubby forested wetlands to open muskeg.

Alpine soils, generally above 2,000 feet elevation, are mostly shallow, very wet organic soils or are extremely shallow and rocky.

(d) Fish Resource: Fish resources have been rated as part of the Tongass Land Management Plan (1979) and by the Alaska Department of Fish and Game in its Forest Habitat Integrity Program (1983) These ratings describe the value of VCU's for sport fish, commercial fish. and estuaries.

VCU's with highly valued estuaries include VCU 457.

(e) Wildlife Resource: A small population of Sitka black-tailed deer and black bear range over the roadless area.

(f) Threatened and Endangered Species: The area contains no known threatened or endangered species.

(6) Current Use and Management: Both VCU's in the area were allocated to Land Use Designation 4 in the Tongass Land Management Plan, which allows for intensive resource use and development Salvage beach logging has occurred in the past on portions of the area There is some subsistence use in the area

(7) **Appearance** (Apparent Naturalness): The area appears unmodified, however adjacent clearcut harvest units have impacted parts of the area's natural appearance. The visual character type of this area is Kupreanof Lowland, characterized by islands of rolling terrain exhibiting gradual relief separated by an intricate network of waterways Numerous small rocky islands, shorelines and rock reefs are evident

None of this roadless area was inventoried in Variety Class A (possessing landscape diversity that is unique for the character type) and nine percent of the acreage was inventoried Variety Class B (possessing landscape diversity that is common for the character type). The majority of the area, 91 percent, was inventoried in Variety Class C (possessing a low degree of landscape diversity)

The vast majority (86 percent) of the roadless area is in Existing Visual Condition (EVC) I; these areas appear to be untouched by human activity The remaining 14 percent is in EVC IV, in which changes to the landscape are easily noticed by the average person.

(8) **Surroundings** (External Influences): The roadless area is on Zarembo Island where timber management activities occur, and a road network is located. Clearcut harvest areas and reforested plantations are adjacent to the roadless area on the east side. When harvesting activities occur adjacent to or near the roadless area, their sights and sounds may create an impact. Boats plying the adjacent saltwater may be visible from within parts of the roadless area but usually are not intrusive Low-flying aircraft may temporarily distract visitors in the area

(9) **Attractions and Features of Special Interest:** The scenery of the area is typical of much of the lowlands of Southeast Alaska. The area contains one inventoried recreation place totaling 100 acres

b. **Capability of Management as Wilderness or in an Unroaded Condition**

(1) **Manageability and Management Area Boundaries:** The area is bounded on one side by land managed for timber. The other side is primarily beachfront, some of which has been salvaged logged in the past Feasibility of management in a roadless condition is low

(2) **Natural Integrity:** The area is unmodified. Logging outside of the roadless area, but within higher reaches of the drainage, may have altered some of the natural processes. This impact, however, is considered low

(3) **Opportunity for Solitude:** There is a moderate opportunity for solitude within the area. Low-flying airplanes and recreational boaters may at times pass nearby and be observed by people in this roadless area Present recreation use levels are low. Generally, a person camped or traveling inland is unlikely to see others. Periodic timber harvest activities in the adjacent areas would have a significant impact on the opportunity for solitude.

(4) **Opportunity for Primitive Recreation:** The area provides primarily primitive non-motorized opportunity as inventoried with the Recreation Opportunity Spectrum (ROS) System.

ROS Class	Acres
Semi-Primitive Non-Motorized (SPNM)	5,907
Roaded Modified (RM)	1,038

The area contains one inventoried recreation place

ROS CLASS	# OF REC. PLACES	TOTAL ACRES	CAPACITY BY RVD
RM		100	15

There are no developed recreation opportunities in the area The character
of the landforms generally allows the visitor to feel remote from the
sights and sounds of human activity. The area is accessible by boat from
the community of Petersburg in about three hours, and from Wrangell in
approximately two hours.

(5) **Special Features (Ecologic, Geologic, Scientific, Cultural):** There
are no known special features in this roadless area.

c. **Availability for Management as Wilderness or in an Unroaded Condition**

(1) **Resource Potentials**

(a) **Recreation Potential:** There is potential for outfitter and guide
permits and for developed trails, cabins, or shelters

(b) **Fish Resource:** The Tongass Land Management Plan, amended Winter
1985-86 identifies fish habitat enhancement projects for VCU's 457 and
458.

(c) **Wildlife Resource:** As identified in the Tongass Land Management
Plan, amended Winter 1985-86, deer mitigation projects are planned in
both VCU's, but are unlikely to occur within the roadless area

(d) **Timber Resource:** There are 2,355 acres inventoried as
tentatively suitable for harvest. This includes 359 acres of riparian
old growth, and 1,656 acres of non-riparian old growth

(e) **Land Use Authorizations:** There are no special uses in the area,
except for a Coast Guard reservation.

(f) **Minerals:** The area has moderate minerals potential.

(g) **Areas of Scientific Interest:** The area does not contain any
inventoried potential Research Natural Areas and has not been
identified for any other scientific value.

(2) **Management Considerations**

(a) The potential for managing timber in this roadless area is
dependent on high market values A road system is already present
nearby and could be extended into parts of this area A site for
transferring logs to saltwater is already present on Zarembo Island

(b) Maintenance of the area in a roadless condition enhances opportunities for wildlife to move freely through the area

(c) Fire: The area has no significant fire history

(d) Insects and Disease: Endemic tree diseases common to Southeast Alaska are present, there are no know epidemic disease occurrences

(e) Land Status: Entirely National Forest System lands

d. Relationship to Communities and Other Roadless and Wilderness Areas

(1) **Nearby Roadless and Wilderness Areas and Uses:** Two other roadless areas exist on Zarembo Island--East Zarembo Roadless Area and South Zarembo Roadless Area. These roadless areas are not adjacent to each other, but are separated by timber management areas. Recreational use is light in all of the roadless areas on Zarembo Island.

(2) **Distance From Population Centers (Accessibility):** Approximate distances from population centers are as follows·

Community		Air Miles	Water Miles
Juneau	(Pop. 23,729)	140	160
Petersburg	(Pop 4,040)	28	34
Wrangell	(Pop 2,836)	24	28
Ketchikan	(Pop. 12,705)	88	95

Petersburg and Wrangell are the nearest stops on the Alaska Marine Highway.

(3) **Interest by Proponents:**

(a) **Moratorium areas:** The area has not been identified as a "moratorium" area or proposed as Wilderness in legislative initiatives to date

(b) **Local users/residents:** Most use of the area is recreational and occurs along the beach fringe

e. Environmental Consequences

ALTERNATIVE ANALYSIS TO BE DONE LATER

INDIVIDUAL ROADLESS AREA DESCRIPTION

NAME: East Zarembo (236)   ACRES (GROSS): 8,990   ACRES (NFS). 8,990

GEOZONE: S05
GEOGRAPHIC PROVINCE: Central Interior Islands

1989 WILDERNESS ATTRIBUTE RATING: 19

a. Description

(1) Relationship to RARE II areas: The table below displays the VCU 1/ names, VCU numbers, original WARS 2/ rating, and comments. This enables the reader to compare the roadless areas evaluated in Appendix C with previous analyses.

| | | 1979 | |
VCU Name	VCU No.	WARS Rating	Comments
Baht	456*	-	Not rated in 1979
Meter	459*	13	

*--The roadless area includes only part of this VCU

(2) History: Zarembo Island was shared by all of the Stikine Tlingit clans for hunting and gathering of subsistence items There are, however, no sites currently recorded for this area. , The absence of sites may reflect the low number of cultural resource inventories conducted in this area.

(3) Location and Access: This roadless area is located on the east side of Zarembo Island. Zarembo Island is south of Mitkof Island, and ten miles west of the town of Wrangell and Wrangell Island. Sumner Strait lies to the north, and Clarence Strait to the west Access is by boat or floatplane to Zarembo Island, then by traveling cross-country on foot or by using the road system to access the roadless area. There are no sites suitable for landing wheeled aircraft. The road system on Zarembo Island surrounds the roadless area.

(4) Geography and Topography: The terrain is generally rolling Several streams drain the area, and about 140 acres of small ponds and lakes exist. Elevation ranges from 1,000 to 2,000 feet. The area does not contain any miles of shoreline on saltwater. The majority of the area is covered by forest, with about 20 acres considered alpine, and 60 acres of muskeg.

1/ A VCU (Value Comparison Unit) is one of 867 watersheds which make up the Forest and were differentiated for planning purposes in the Tongass Land Management Plan.
2/ Wilderness Attribute Rating System (WARS) was the nationwide system used to rate the wilderness attributes of roadless areas in the Roadless Area Review and Evaluation (RARE II).

(5) Ecosystem:

(a) Classification: The area is in the Central Interior Islands
Geographic Province This province is generally characterized by
rolling, subdued topography and extensive muskeg areas, but may have
localized, rugged terrain. There are no known areas of unique or
uncommon plant/soils associations or geologic formations in the area

(b) Vegetation: Vegetation of this roadless area primarily consists
of typical spruce/hemlock forests Low-lying, poorly-drained portions
of the area are muskeg

There are 8,690 acres of forested land of which 3,856 acres are
commercial forest land. Of the commercial forest land, 3,476 acres
are non-riparian old growth and 380 acres are riparian old growth

(c) Soils: Soils in this area are formed in a wide variety of parent
materials, including bedrock and glacial drift In general, well- or
moderately-well-drained soils are on moderate to steep mountain slopes
with permeable parent materials. These soils are very acidic, have
cold soil temperatures, and are very high in organic matter. Rooting
is largely limited to the surface organic layers and the top few
inches of mineral soil These soils are usually moist, sometimes wet,
but are never dry

More-poorly-drained soils developed on less-sloping areas and/or areas
with impermeable soil materials. These soils have deep accumulations
of organic matter and range from scrubby forested wetlands to open
muskeg.

Alpine soils, generally above 2,000 feet elevation, are mostly
shallow, very wet organic soils or are extremely shallow and rocky

(d) Fish Resource: Fish resources have been rated as part of the
Tongass Land Management Plan (1979) and by the Alaska Department of
Fish and Game in its Forest Habitat Integrity Program (1983) These
ratings describe the value of VCU's for sport fish, commercial fish,
and estuaries

VCU 459 is rated as having a highly valued estuary, though this
roadless area contributes little to that rating.

(e) Wildlife Resource: A small population of Sitka black-tailed deer
and black bear range over the roadless area.

(f) Threatened and Endangered Species: The area contains no known
threatened or endangered species.

(6) Current Use and Management: Both VCU's in the area were allocated to
Land Use Designation 3 in the Tongass Land Management Plan, which
emphasizes managing for a variety of uses and activities in a compatible
and complementary manner to provide the greatest combination of benefits
There is some subsistence use in the area.

(7) **Appearance (Apparent Naturalness):** The area appears unmodified, however adjacent management activities have affected the apparent naturalness of this roadless area

The visual character type of this area is Kupreanof Lowland, characterized by islands of rolling terrain exhibiting gradual relief separated by an intricate network of waterways   Numerous small rocky islands, shorelines and rock reefs are evident   One-hundred percent of the acreage was inventoried Variety Class B (possessing landscape diversity that is common for the character type)

The vast majority (67 percent) of the roadless area is in Existing Visual Condition (EVC) I; these areas appear to be untouched by human activity Three percent of the area is in EVC IV, in which changes to the landscape are easily noticed by the average person and may attract some attention They appear to be disturbances but resemble natural patterns   EVC V accounts for the remaining 30 percent. These are areas in which changes to the landscape are obvious to the average person, and appear to be major disturbances.

(8) **Surroundings (External Influences):** This roadless area is located on Zarembo Island where timber management activities occur, and a road network is found   Clearcut harvest areas and reforested plantations generally surround the roadless area. When harvesting activities occur adjacent to or near the roadless area, their sights and sounds may create an impact Boats plying the nearby saltwater may be visible from within parts of the roadless area but usually are not intrusive. Low-flying aircraft may temporarily distract visitors in the area

(9) **Attractions and Features of Special Interest:** The scenery of the area is typical of much of the lowlands of Southeast Alaska   The area contains three inventoried recreation places totaling 1,139 acres

Capability of Management as Wilderness or in an Unroaded Condition

(1) **Manageability and management area boundaries:** The area is bounded on all sides by land managed for timber. Harvesting patterns and road development resulted in no readily defined roadless area boundary, such as a ridgeline, drainage, or road. Feasibility of management in a roadless condition is low.

(2) **Natural Integrity:** The area is unmodified. Logging outside of the roadless area, but within higher reaches of the drainage, may have altered some of the natural processes. This impact, however, is considered low

(3) **Opportunity for Solitude:** There is a moderate opportunity for solitude within the area. Low-flying airplanes and recreational boaters may at times pass nearby and be observed by people in this roadless area Present recreation use levels are low. Generally, a person camped or traveling inland is unlikely to see others   Periodic timber harvest activities in the adjacent areas would have a significant impact on the opportunity for solitude when they are occurring

(4) **Opportunity for Primitive Recreation:** The area provides primarily semi-primitive recreation opportunity as inventoried with the Recreation Opportunity Spectrum (ROS) System.

ROS Class	Acres
Semi-Primitive Non-Motorized (SPNM)	6,972
Roaded Modified (RM)	2,018

The area contains three inventoried recreation places

ROS CLASS	# OF REC. PLACES	TOTAL ACRES	CAPACITY BY RVD
RM	3	1,139	279

There are no developed recreation opportunities in the area. The character of the landforms generally allows the visitor to feel remote from the sights and sounds of human activity The area is accessible by boat from the community of Petersburg in about three hours, and from Wrangell in approximately two hours.

(5) **Special Features (Ecologic, Geologic, Scientific, Cultural):** There are no known special features in this roadless area.

c. **Availability for Management as Wilderness or in an Unroaded Condition**

(1) **Resource Potentials**

(a) **Recreation Potential:** There is potential for outfitter and guide permits and for developed trails, cabins, or shelters

(b) **Fish Resource:** The Tongass Land Management Plan, amended Winter 1985-86 identifies fish habitat enhancement projects in this area Though identified, it is unlikely that these projects will occur

(c) **Wildlife Resource:** As identified in the Tongass Land Management Plan, amended Winter 1985-86, deer mitigation projects are planned

(d) **Timber Resource:** There are 2,937 acres inventoried as tentatively suitable for harvest This includes 340 acres of riparian old growth, and 2,597 acres of non-riparian old growth

(e) **Land Use Authorizations:** There are no special uses in the area

(f) **Minerals:** The area has moderate minerals potential

(g) **Areas of Scientific Interest:** The area contains no inventoried potential Research Natural Areas and has not been identified for any other scientific value.

(2) **Management Considerations**

(a) The potential for managing timber in this roadless area is
dependent on high market values. A road system is already present
nearby and could be extended into parts of this area   A site for
transferring logs to saltwater is already present on Zarembo Island

(b) Maintenance of the area in a roadless condition enhances
opportunities for wildlife to move freely through the area

(c) Fire: The area has no significant fire history

(d) **Insects and Disease:** Endemic tree diseases common to Southeast
Alaska are present; there are no know epidemic disease occurrences

(e) **Land Status:** Entirely National Forest System lands

d. **Relationship to Communities and Other Roadless and Wilderness Areas**

(1) **Nearby Roadless and Wilderness Areas and Uses:** Two other roadless
areas exist on Zarembo Island. These are West Zarembo and South Zarembo
None of these roadless areas are adjacent to each other, but are separated
by areas managed for timber. Recreational use is light in all of the
roadless areas on the island

(2) **Distance From Population Centers (Accessibility):** Approximate
distances from population centers are as follows

Community		Air Miles	Water Miles
Juneau	(Pop. 23,729)	140	160
Petersburg	(Pop 4,040)	28	34
Wrangell	(Pop. 2,836)	22	25
Ketchikan	(Pop 12,705)	88	95

Petersburg and Wrangell are the nearest stops on the Alaska Marine Highway.

(3) **Interest by Proponents:**

(a) **Moratorium areas:** The area has not been identified as a
"moratorium" area or proposed as Wilderness in legislative initiatives
to date

(b) **Local users/residents:** Most use of the area is recreational, and
occurs along the beach fringe.

e. **Environmental Consequences**

ALTERNATIVE ANALYSIS TO BE DONE LATER

INDIVIDUAL ROADLESS AREA DESCRIPTION

NAME: South Zarembo (237)   ACRES (GROSS): 32,288   ACRES (NFS): 32,288

GEOZONE: S05
GEOGRAPHIC PROVINCE: Central Interior Islands

1989 WILDERNESS ATTRIBUTE RATING: 21

a Description

(1) **Relationship to RARE II areas:** The table below displays the VCU 1/
names, VCU numbers, original WARS 2/ rating, and comments This enables
the reader to compare the roadless areas evaluated in Appendix C with
previous analyses.

		1979	
VCU Name	VCU No.	WARS Rating	Comments
St. John	457*	-	Not rated in 1979
Snow	458*	13	
Meter	459*	13	

*--The roadless area includes only part of this VCU

(2) **History:** Zarembo Island was used by all of the Stikine Tlingit clans
for hunting and gathering of subsistence items. Their use of southern
Zarembo Island is indicated by the reported remains of a village site as
well as recorded burial sites, fish weirs, petroglyphs and pictographs
Historic use is evidenced by the remains of several cabins

(4) **Geography and Topography:** The area has moderately-rolling terrain
Several streams drain the area, and about 80 acres of small ponds and lakes
exist. Elevation ranges from sea level to 2,500 feet. The area contains
11 miles of shoreline on saltwater. The majority of the area is covered by
forest, with about 300 acres considered alpine, and 180 acres of muskeg

(3) **Location and Access:** The area is located on the south side of Zarembo
Island. Zarembo Island is south of Mitkof Island, and ten miles west of
the town of Wrangell and Wrangell Island. Sumner Strait lies to the north.
Stikine Strait to the south, and Clarence Strait to the west. Access is by
boat or floatplane to Zarembo Island, then by traveling cross-country on
foot or by using the road system to access the roadless area A portion of
the roadless area is also accessible from saltwater There are no sites
suitable for landing wheeled aircraft. The road system on Zarembo Island
accesses northern portions of the roadless area.

1/ A VCU (Value Comparison Unit) is one of 867 watersheds which make up the
Forest and were differentiated for planning purposes in the Tongass Land
Management Plan.
2/ Wilderness Attribute Rating System (WARS) was the nationwide system used to
rate the wilderness attributes of roadless areas in the Roadless Area
Review and Evaluation (RARE II).

(5) **Ecosystem:**

(a) **Classification:** The area is in the Central Interior Islands Geographic Province. This province is characterized by rolling, subdued topography and extensive muskeg areas, but may have localized, rugged terrain. There are no known areas of unique or uncommon plant/soils associations or geologic formations in the area.

(b) **Vegetation:** Vegetation of this roadless area primarily consists of typical spruce/hemlock forests. Low-lying, poorly-drained portions of the area are muskeg

There are 31,167 acres of forested land of which 13,648 acres are commercial forest land. Of the commercial forest land, 11,411 acres are non-riparian old growth and 1,738 acres are riparian old growth

(c) **Soils:** Soils in this area are formed in a wide variety of parent materials, including bedrock and glacial drift. In general, well- or moderately-well-drained soils are on moderate to steep mountain slopes with permeable parent materials. These soils are very acidic, have cold soil temperatures, and are very high in organic matter Rooting is largely limited to the surface organic layers and the top few inches of mineral soil These soils are usually moist, sometimes wet, but are never dry.

More-poorly-drained soils developed on less-sloping areas and/or areas with impermeable soil materials These soils have deep accumulations of organic matter and range from scrubby forested wetlands to open muskeg.

Alpine soils, generally above 2,000 feet elevation, are mostly shallow, very wet organic soils or are extremely shallow and rocky.

(d) **Fish Resource:** Fish resources have been rated as part of the Tongass Land Management Plan (1979) and by the Alaska Department of Fish and Game in its Forest Habitat Integrity Program (1983) These ratings describe the value of VCU's for sport fish, commercial fish, and estuaries.

VCU's with highly valued estuaries include 457 and 459

(e) **Wildlife Resource:** A small population of Sitka black-tailed deer and black bear range over the roadless area.

(f) **Threatened and Endangered Species:** The area contains no known threatened or endangered species.

(6) **Current Use and Management:** One VCU in the area (16,544 acres) was allocated to Land Use Designation (LUD) 3 in the Tongass Land Management Plan. LUD 3 emphasizes managing for a variety of uses and activities in a compatible and complementary manner to provide the greatest combination of benefits. Two VCU's in the area (15,703 acres) were allocated to LUD 4 where opportunities are provided for intensive resource use and development. There is some subsistence use in the area

(7) **Appearance (Apparent Naturalness):** The area appears unmodified, however adjacent management activities have affected the apparent naturalness of this roadless area

The visual character type of this area is Kupreanof Lowland, characterized by islands of rolling terrain exhibiting gradual relief separated by an intricate network of waterways. Numerous small rocky islands, shorelines and rock reefs are evident.

Ninety-two percent of the acreage was inventoried Variety Class B (possessing landscape diversity that is common for the character type) The remaining eight percent was inventoried in Variety Class C (possessing a low degree of landscape diversity).

The vast majority (70 percent) of the roadless area is in Existing Visual Condition (EVC) I, these areas appear to be untouched by human activity Twelve percent of the area is in EVC IV, in which changes to the landscape are easily noticed by the average person and may attract some attention. They appear to be disturbances but resemble natural patterns. EVC V accounts for the remaining 18 percent. These are areas in which changes to the landscape are obvious to the average person, and appear to be major disturbances

(8) **Surroundings (External Influences):** The area is on Zarembo Island which is an area of timber management activities, and includes a road network. Clearcut harvest areas and reforested plantations generally surround the roadless area, except for a small section of shoreline adjacent to Stikine Strait. When harvesting activities occur adjacent to or near the roadless area, their sights and sounds may create an impact Boats plying the nearby saltwater may be visible from within parts of the roadless area but usually are not intrusive. Low-flying aircraft may temporarily distract visitors in the area.

(9) **Attractions and Features of Special Interest:** The scenery of the area is typical of much of the lowlands of Southeast Alaska   The area contains two inventoried recreation places totaling 2,282 acres.

b. **Capability of Management as Wilderness or in an Unroaded Condition**

(1) **Manageability and management area boundaries:** The area is bounded on most sides by land managed for timber. Harvesting patterns and road development resulted in no readily defined roadless area boundary, such as a ridgeline, drainage, or road   Feasibility of management in a roadless condition is low

(2) **Natural Integrity:** The area is unmodified. Logging outside of the roadless area, but within higher reaches of the drainage, may have altered some of the natural processes. This impact, however, is considered low

(3) Opportunity for Solitude: There is a moderate opportunity for
solitude within the area. Low-flying airplanes and recreational boaters
may at times pass nearby and be observed by people in this roadless area
Present recreation use levels are low. Generally, a person camped or
traveling inland is unlikely to see others Periodic timber harvest
activities in the adjacent areas would have a significant impact on the
opportunity for solitude when they are occurring

(4) Opportunity for Primitive Recreation: The area provides primarily
semi-primitive recreation opportunity as inventoried with the Recreation
Opportunity Spectrum (ROS) System

ROS Class	Acres
Semi-Primitive Non-Motorized (SPNM)	23,093
Semi-Primitive Motorized (SPM)	2,778
Roaded Modified (RM)	6,416

The area contains two inventoried recreation places.

ROS CLASS	# OF REC. PLACES	TOTAL ACRES	CAPACITY BY RVD
SPM	1	1,198·	490
RM	1	1,083	162

There are no developed recreation opportunities in the area. The character
of the landforms generally allows the visitor to feel remote from the
sights and sounds of human activity. The area is accessible by boat from
the community of Petersburg in about three hours, and from Wrangell in
approximately two hours

(5) Special Features (Ecologic, Geologic, Scientific, Cultural)· There
are no known special features in this roadless area.

c. Availability for Management as Wilderness or in an Unroaded Condition

(1) Resource Potentials

(a) Recreation Potential: There is potential for outfitter and guide
permits and for developed trails, cabins, or shelters

(b) Fish Resource: The Tongass Land Management Plan, amended Winter
1985-86 identifies some fish habitat enhancement projects for the
VCU's which encompass this area.

(c) Wildlife Resource: As identified in the Tongass Land Management
Plan, amended Winter 1985-86, deer mitigation projects are planned

(d) Timber Resource: There are 10,333 acres inventoried as
tentatively suitable for harvest. This includes 1,318 acres of
riparian old growth, and 8,334 acres of non-riparian old growth

(e) Land Use Authorizations: There are no special uses in the area,
except for a Coast Guard electronics site

(f) **Minerals:** The area has moderate minerals potential

(g) **Areas of Scientific Interest:** The area contains no inventoried potential Research Natural Areas, and has not been identified for any other scientific value

(2) **Management Considerations**

(a) The potential for managing timber in this roadless area is dependent on high market values. A road system is already present nearby and could be extended into this area. A site for transferring logs to saltwater is already present

(b) Maintenance of the area in a roadless condition enhances opportunities for wildlife to move freely through the area.

(c) **Fire:** The area has no significant fire history

(d) **Insects and Disease:** Endemic tree diseases common to Southeast Alaska are present; there are no know epidemic disease occurrences

(e) **Land Status:** Entirely National Forest System lands

d. **Relationship to Communities and Other Roadless and Wilderness Areas**

(1) **Nearby Roadless and Wilderness Areas and Uses:** Two other roadless areas exist on Zarembo Island--West Zarembo and East Zarembo   None of these roadless areas are adjacent to each other, but are separated by areas managed for timber. Recreational use is light in all of them

(2) **Distance From Population Centers (Accessibility):** Approximate distances from population centers are as follows

Community		Air Miles	Water Miles
Juneau	(Pop. 23,729)	140	160
Petersburg	(Pop 4,040)	32	46
Wrangell	(Pop. 2,836)	26	31
Ketchikan	(Pop 12,705)	86	91

Petersburg and Wrangell are the nearest stops on the Alaska Marine Highway

(3) **Interest by Proponents:**

(a) **Moratorium areas:** The area has not been identified as a "moratorium" area or proposed as Wilderness in legislative initiatives to date.

(b) **Local users/residents:** Most use of the area is recreational, and occurs along the beach fringe.

e. **Environmental Consequences**

ALTERNATIVE ANALYSIS TO BE DONE LATER

INDIVIDUAL ROADLESS AREA DESCRIPTION

NAME: Kashevarof (238)   ACRES (GROSS): _____   ACRES (NFS): 5,725

GEOZONE: S14
GEOGRAPHIC PROVINCE: Central Interior Islands

1989 WILDERNESS ATTRIBUTE RATING: 22

a. Description

(1) **Relationship to RARE II areas:** The table below displays the VCU 1/
names, VCU numbers, original WARS 2/ rating, and comments This enables
the reader to compare the roadless areas evaluated in Appendix C with
previous analyses

VCU Name	VCU No.	1979 WARS Rating	Comments
	460*	16	

*--The roadless area includes only part of this VCU.

(2) **History:** The Tihitan clan of the Stikine Tlingit claimed this area
which was used chiefly for hunting seals and gathering seaweed Their use
is evidenced by the remains of temporary camps, fish weirs, and
petroglyphs Historic use is indicated by the remains of numerous fox
farms, trapping cabins, and temporary camps.

(3) **Location and Access:** This roadless area consists of a series of small
islands located in Clarence Strait, between the southwest side of Zarembo
Island and the northeast corner of Prince of Wales Island. Sumner Strait
is to the north. The two northern most islands in the Kashevarof Island
group, Bushy and Shrubby, are not included in this roadless area as they
have been logged. Access is by way of boat or floatplane. There are no
sites suitable for landing wheeled aircraft.

(4) **Geography and Topography:** The islands in this roadless area have
little relief and are flat to slightly rolling with a high point of 482
feet on one of the Blashke Islands. Two island groups, Middle Islands and
Bashke Islands, are in a basically north-south orientation with Clarence
Strait. On either flank are the West and East Islands, and several other
smaller ones. There are ___ miles of shoreline on saltwater. The majority
of the area is covered by forest.

1/ A VCU (Value Comparison Unit) is one of 867 watersheds which make up the
forest and were differentiated for planning purposes in the Tongass Land
Management Plan.

2/ Wilderness Attribute Rating System (WARS) was the nationwide system used to
rate the wilderness attributes of roadless areas in the Roadless Area
Review and Evaluation (RARE II).

(5) **Ecosystem:**

(a) **Classification:** The area is in the Central Interior Islands Geographic Province This province is generally characterized by rolling, subdued topography and extensive muskeg areas, but may have localized rugged terrain There are no known areas of unique or uncommon plant/soils associations or geologic formations in the area

(b) **Vegetation:** Vegetation of this roadless area primarily consists of typical spruce/hemlock forests Low-lying, poorly-drained portions of the area are muskeg

There are _____ acres of forested land of which _____ acres are commercial forest land. Of the commercial forest land, _____ acres are non-riparian old growth and ___ acres are riparian old growth.

(c) **Soils:** Soils in this area are formed in a wide variety of parent material, including bedrock and glacial drift. In general, well- or moderately-well-drained soils are on moderate to steep mountain slopes with permeable parent materials. These soils are very acidic, have cold soil temperatures, and are very high in organic matter Rooting is largely limited to the surface organic layers and the top few inches of mineral soil. These soils are usually moist, sometimes wet, but are never dry

More-poorly-drained soils developed on less-sloping areas and/or areas with impermeable soil materials. These soils have deep accumulations of organic matter and range from scrubby forested wetlands to open muskeg.

Alpine soils, generally above 2,000 feet elevation, are mostly shallow, very wet organic soils or are extremely shallow and rocky

(d) **Fish Resource:** Fish resources have been rated as part of the Tongass Land Management Plan (1978) and by the Alaska Department of Fish and Game in its Forest Habitat Integrity Program (1983) These ratings describe the value of VCU's for sport fish, commercial fish, and estuaries. The one VCU for this area is not rated high for any of these values.

(e) **Wildlife Resource:** A small population of Sitka black-tailed deer and black bear range over the roadless area.

(f) **Threatened and Endangered Species:** The area contains no known threatened or endangered species.

(6) **Current Use and Management:** The one VCU in the area is allocated to Land Use Designation 4, however no major resource activities have occurred in the roadless area. There is some subsistence use in the area

(7) **Appearance (Apparent Naturalness):** The area appears unmodified, except in one small portion where adjacent management activities have affected the apparent naturalness.

The visual character type of this area is Kupreanof Lowland, characterized
by islands of rolling terrain exhibiting gradual relief separated by an
intricate network of waterways   Numerous small, rocky islands, shorelines,
and rock reefs are evident   The character type is largely covered with
spruce/hemlock forest except at infrequent higher elevations where
scattered muskeg and alpine deciduous species occur. There are also
significant areas of muskeg/lodgepole pine association

____ percent of this roadless area was inventoried in Variety Class A
(possessing landscape diversity that is unique for the character type) and
___ percent of the acreage was inventoried Variety Class B (possessing
landscape diversity that is common for the character type)   The remaining
acreage of ___ percent was inventoried in Variety Class C (possessing a low
degree of landscape diversity).

The vast majority (__ percent) of the roadless area is in Existing Visual
Condition (EVC) I; these areas appear to be untouched by human activity
___ percent of the area is in EVC III, in which changes to the landscape
are noticed by the average person, but they do not attract attention   The
natural appearance of the landscape still remains dominant   EVC V accounts
for the remaining __ percent. These are areas in which changes to the
landscape are obvious to the average person, and appear to be major
disturbances

(8) Surroundings (External Influences): The area is between Zarembo
Island and Prince of Wales Island, and evidence of management activities,
mainly clearcutting and road building, is visible   Harvest is also visible
on Shrubby Island which is located to the north of this roadless area
When harvesting activities occur adjacent to or near the roadless area,
their sights and sounds may create an impact. Boats frequent the nearby
saltwater, as Clarence Strait is a major passage for cruiseships, barges,
ferries, and pleasure craft. They may be visible from parts of the
roadless area. Low-flying aircraft may temporarily distract visitors in
the area at times.

(9) Attractions and Features of Special Interest: The numerous small
islands and sheltered bays provide opportunities for discovery, day use
activities, and anchorage   The area contains ____ inventoried recreation
places totaling _____ acres.

b. Capability of Management as Wilderness or in an Unroaded Condition

(1) Manageability and Management Area Boundaries: The area is bounded on
all sides by saltwater. The island clusters lend all or part of this
roadless area to be managed either as Wilderness or in an unroaded
condition. Manageability in a Wilderness condition is less feasible due to
the amount of marine traffic in the area and activities in the nearby
adjacent areas. Overall manageability is considered moderate

(2) Natural Integrity: The area is unmodified, and has maintained its
overall integrity

(3) Opportunity for Solitude: There is moderate opportunity for solitude within the area   Low-flying airplanes and frequent marine traffic pass nearby and may be observed by people in this roadless area   Present recreation use levels are low   Generally, a person camped or traveling inland is unlikely to see others   Timber harvest or other periodic activities in the adjacent areas would have a significant impact on the opportunity for solitude when they are occurring.

(4) Opportunity for Primitive Recreation: The area provides primarily semi-primitive recreation opportunity as inventoried with the Recreation Opportunity Spectrum (ROS) System

ROS class	Acres
Primitive (P)	_____
Semi-Primitive Non-Motorized (SPNM)	_____
Semi-Primitive Motorized (SPM)	_____

The area contains __ inventoried recreation places.

ROS CLASS	# OF REC. PLACES	TOTAL ACRES	CAPACITY BY RVD
P	x	xXXXXXXX	XX
SPNM	X	XXXXXXXX	XX
SPM	X	XXXXXXXX	XXX
RN	X	XXXXXXXX	XXX
RM	X	XXXXXXXX	XXX

There are no developed recreation opportunities in the area   The character of the landforms generally allows the visitor to feel remote from the sights and sounds of human activity. The area is accessible by boat from the community of Petersburg in about four hours, and from Wrangell in approximately two hours.

(5) Special Features (Ecologic, Geologic, Scientific, Cultural): There are no special features in this roadless area. Their location and the array of islands make them attractive for recreational pursuits

c. Availability for Management as Wilderness or in an Unroaded Condition

(1) Resource Potentials

(a) Recreation Potential: There is potential for outfitter and guide permits and for developed trails, cabins, or shelters

(b) Fish Resource: No fish habitat enhancement projects are identified in the Tongass Land Management Plan, amended Winter 1985-86.

(c) Wildlife Resource: As identified in the Tongass Land Management Plan, amended Winter 1985-86, wildlife enhancement projects are not planned in the roadless area

(d) Timber Resource: There are _____ acres inventoried as tentatively suitable for harvest. This includes ___ acres of riparian old growth, and _____ acres of non-riparian old growth

(e) Land Use Authorizations: There are four special use permits in the area, and a Coast Guard reservation

(f) Minerals: The area has low minerals potential

(g) Areas of Scientific Interest: The area does not contain any inventoried potential Research Natural Areas, and has not been identified for any scientific purpose.

(2) **Management Considerations**

(a) The potential for managing timber in this roadless area is dependent on high market values. A road system and/or logging systems capable of harvesting the numerous small islands would be necessary. Development of beach access and log transfer sites would also be required.

(b) Maintenance of the area in a roadless condition enhances opportunities for certain wildlife, as some of the islands in this group have been logged and the timber stands converted for even-age management.

(c) Fire: The area has no significant fire history

(d) Insects and Disease: Endemic tree diseases common to Southeast Alaska are present; there are no know epidemic disease occurrences

(e) Land Status: Entirely National Forest Systems land

d. Relationship to Communities and Other Roadless and Wilderness Areas

(1) **Nearby Roadless and Wilderness Areas and Uses:** Other roadless areas are separated by extensive bodies of water. Recreational use is light in all of them.

(2) **Distance From Population Centers (Accessibility):** Approximate distances from population centers are as follows:

Community		Air Miles	Water Miles
Juneau	(Pop. 23,729)	160	195
Petersburg	(Pop. 4,040)	44	54
Wrangell	(Pop 2,836)	30	35
Ketchikan	(Pop. 12,705)	72	86

Hollis, on Prince of Wales Island, and Wrangell are the nearest stops on the Alaska Marine Highway

(3) Interest by Proponents:

(a) Moratorium areas: The area has not been identified as a
"moratorium" area or proposed as Wilderness in legislative initiatives
to date

(b) Local users/residents: Most use of the area is recreational, and
is marine oriented

e   Environmental Consequences

ALTERNATIVE ANALYSIS TO BE DONE LATER

INDIVIDUAL ROADLESS AREA DESCRIPTION

NAME: Keku (239)   ACRES (GROSS): 12,146   ACRES (NFS): 12,126

GEOZONE: S01
GEOGRAPHIC PROVINCE: Central Interior Islands

1989 WILDERNESS ATTRIBUTE RATING: 22

a. Description

   (1) Relationship to RARE II areas: The table below displays the VCU 1/
   names, VCU numbers, original WARS 2/ rating, and comments This enables
   the reader to compare the roadless areas evaluated in Appendix C with
   previous analyses.

VCU Name	VCU No.	1979 WARS Rating	Comments
Keku	398	23	
Saginaw Bay	399	21	

   (2) History: Keku Straits and nearby islands were used by the Tlingit
   The area was claimed by several clans of the Kake Tlingit and there is a
   rich assortment of cultural resources. These sites include the remains of
   villages, temporary camps, cave shelters, fish weirs, burial sites,
   pictographs, petroglyphs, and garden sites. A historic cannery was located
   in Saginaw Bay, and numerous fox farms and temporary camps on the Keku
   Islets

   In modern times, this area has been a contingency area of the Alaska Pulp
   Corporation Long-term Timber Sale Contract since 1960 A logging camp was
   developed at nearby Rowan Bay and is still active with up to 130 seasonal
   occupants Road development has occurred to the south, along the head of
   Saginaw Bay. Forest Road 6415 connects Rowan Bay to Security Bay and
   Saginaw Bay, and is used as a major route for hauling logs to the log
   transport facility in Rowan Bay However, a large slide has since blocked
   this connection.

   (3) Location and Access: Keku Roadless Area is located on the northern
   end of Kuiu Island It lies east of the Security Roadless Area, also on
   Kuiu Island, and is bordered by Rocky Pass and Keku Strait It is accessed
   primarily by saltwater via boat or floatplane. Several good anchorages are
   located in Saginaw Bay and Halleck Harbor. There are no sites suitable for
   landing wheeled aircraft. There is no ferry service to Kuiu Island There
   is a regularly scheduled mail flight to Rowan Bay, but there are no visitor
   services such as rental vehicles or boats.

1/ A VCU (Value Comparison Unit) is one of 867 watersheds which make up the
    Forest and were differentiated for planning purposes in the Tongass Land
    Management Plan.
2/ Wilderness Attribute Rating System (WARS) was the nationwide system used to
    rate the wilderness attributes of roadless areas in the Roadless Area
    Review and Evaluation (RARE II).

(4) Geography and Topography: Landforms in this area are characterized by gently-sloping to moderately-steep hills that are abruptly broken by prominent limestone cliffs The cliffs generally parallel each other, and are oriented in a northwest-southeast direction. Orientation of the landscape makes development of a road system challenging The area contains 36 miles of shoreline on saltwater Offshore islands total 1,483 acres, and lakes make up another 120 acres.

(5) Ecosystem:

  (a) Classification: The area is in the Central Interior Islands Geographic Province This province is generally characterized by rolling, subdued topography and extensive muskeg areas, but may have localized, rugged terrain.

  (b) Vegetation: Muskeg/scrub timber complexes (120 acres), are interspersed with mixed conifer plant communities on better-drained sites. Timbered hill slopes are dominated by western hemlock, Sitka spruce, and Alaska-cedar plant communities

  There are approximately 11,444 acres of forested land of which 7,015 acres are commercial forest land. Of the commercial forest land, 6,373 acres are non-riparian old growth and 461 acres are riparian old growth.

  (c) Soils: Soils are generally shallow to moderately deep and well drained on forested hill slopes. Well- to somewhat poorly-drained soils developed on the footslope below the limestone cliffs within Saginaw Bay. Areas of muskeg soils occupy nearly level positions along the ridgetops and in the valleys

  (d) Fish Resource: Fish resources have been rated as part of the Tongass Land Management Plan (1979) and by the Alaska Department of Fish and Game in its Forest Habitat Integrity Program (1983) These ratings describe the value of VCU's for sport fish, commercial fish and estuaries

  VCU 399 is rated as highly valued for commercial fish.

  Two ADF&G numbered salmon producing streams are present Neither are large producers and no escapement data is available.

  (e) Wildlife Resource: The 1979 Tongass Land Management Plan Environmental Impact Statement indicates that this area is highly rated for wildlife values.

  (f) Threatened and Endangered Species: The area contains no known threatened or endangered species.

(6) Current Use and Management: The entire area was allocated to Land Use Designation (LUD) 4 in the Tongass Land Management Plan; however, to date, no developments or resource management activities have occurred within the area. This area is part of a contingency area for the Alaska Pulp Corporation long-term timber sale contract There were independent sales throughout and just outside of this area before the long-term contract began operation in 1973 in Saginaw Bay. A logging camp was established in Saginaw Bay until the camp was pulled out. Logging operations on Kuiu Island now center on Rowan Bay The road systems of Rowan and Saginaw were connected in 1976, and traverse the area A large slide in November 1988 blocked off the road about one-quarter mile from Saginaw Bay Because of the size of the slide and the diminished need for access to Saginaw Bay, it is doubtful that the road link will be reconstructed soon

Sealaska Corporation has identified up to 5,000 acres for potential selection. Status of that selection is still pending

The area is popular for black bear hunting.

(7) Appearance (Apparent Naturalness): Most of the area appears unmodified. Exceptions exist near the old cannery and the former logging camp sites, along shorelines where beach logging occurred, and in those portions of the roadless area which are adjacent to logged areas

The majority of this roadless area (89 percent) is natural appearing, where only ecological change has occurred (Existing Visual Condition (EVC) Type I) One percent of the area appears to be untouched by human activity (EVC Type II) Less than one percent of this roadless area is EVC Type III, where changes in the landscape are noticed by the average forest visitor The natural appearance of the landscape remains dominant One percent of the area is in EVC Type IV, where changes in the landscape are easily noticed by the average person and may attract some attention They appear to be disturbances but resemble natural patterns Eight percent is in EVC Type V where changes in the landscape are obvious to the average person, and appear to be major disturbances.

Fourteen percent of this roadless area is inventoried Variety Class A (possessing landscape diversity that is unique for the character type), eight percent is inventoried Variety Class B (possessing landscape diversity that is common for the character type) and the remaining 78 percent is inventoried Variety Class C (possessing a low degree of landscape diversity).

(8) Surroundings (External Influences): Keku Strait and Saginaw Bay border this area on three sides. Management activities have been continuing along the head of Saginaw Bay, where road construction and timber harvesting have been extensive. Forest Road 6415, which connects Rowan Bay to Security and Saginaw Bays, will likely continue to serve as a major access route for hauling logs Modifications on lands adjacent to this route will continue to occur under current management direction as the area is designated LUD 4 and is a part of the long-term timber sale contract area. Logging on adjacent islands has affected the setting of adjacent roadless islands as well as the area as a whole

(9) **Attractions and Features of Special Interest:** Several historical and aboriginal sites attract visitors to the area. Beachcombing is also popular in this area. The area contains five inventoried recreation places totaling 842 acres. There are no developed trails. The presence of good anchorage sites in Saginaw Bay and Halleck Harbor allow visitors to "boat camp" overnight. Sport fishing for king salmon is considered good.

b. **Capability of Management as Wilderness or in an Unroaded Condition**

(1) **Manageability and Management Area Boundaries:** Saltwater surrounds this roadless area on three sides. Road access has been developed to the head of Saginaw Bay, with the potential to extend into the Keku Strait area (VCU 398)

(2) **Natural Integrity:** The area is essentially unmodified, except for some evidence of past occupancy, beach logging, and other logging and roading which has somewhat fragmented this roadless area.

(3) **Opportunity for Solitude:** Generally, there is a high opportunity for solitude in the Keku Roadless Area. Exceptions would be along the road to Saginaw Bay when logging and other activities are occurring. Use of floatplanes and motorboats may disrupt visitors for brief periods. Present recreation use levels are low. Persons camped along the shore are generally unlikely to encounter other recreationists, but they might be seen by or may be able to see an occasional fishing boat offshore.

(4) **Opportunity for Primitive Recreation:** The area provides primarily semi-primitive recreation opportunity.

ROS Class	Acres
Semi-Primitive Non-Motorized	7,075
Semi-Primitive Motorized	4,529
Roaded Modified	521

The area contains five recreation places

ROS CLASS	# RECREATION PLACES	TOTAL ACRES	CAPACITY BY RVD
SPM	2	761	469
RM	3	80	139

There are no developed recreation facilities.

(5) **Special Features (Ecologic, Geologic, Scientific, Cultural):** Fossil hunting occurs within Halleck Harbor which directly adjoins the area. Sport fishing and bear hunting occur throughout the area.

c. **Availability for Management as Wilderness or in an Unroaded Condition**

(1) **Resource Potentials**

(a) **Recreation Potential:** Recreation potential for Keku is moderate, as there is potential for additional outfitter and guide permits, cabins, and opportunities associated with roaded access

(b) **Fish Resource:** The Tongass Land Management Plan, amended Winter 1985-86, identifies fish habitat enhancement projects

(c) **Wildlife Resource:** As identified in the Tongass Land Management Plan, amended 1985-86, habitat improvement projects are planned in the area. These projects typically consist of seeding, planting, and thinning

(d) **Timber Resource:** There are 5,311 acres inventoried as tentatively suitable for timber harvest This includes 341 acres of riparian old growth and 4,790 acres of non-riparian old growth None of the area is second growth, except for small patches along the shores that were beach logged.

(e) **Land Use Authorizations:** One year-long, residence special use permit exists in the head of Saginaw Bay.

(f) **Minerals:** There are no inventoried sites with high mineral development potential in the area.

(g) **Areas of Scientific Interest:** The area contains no inventoried potential Research Natural Areas and has not been identified for any other scientific value.

(2) Management Considerations

(a) In general, long-term timber sales on Kuiu Island will result in · further road development, thus increasing access to parts of the Keku Roadless Area

(b) Maintenance of the area in a roadless condition would have no direct beneficial effect on nearby roadless areas To the south and east are Pillars, Security, East Kuiu and South Kuiu Roadless Areas. and the Tebenkof Bay Wilderness. Some of these areas will incur road construction and timber harvesting in the next one to two years. as indicated in the Supplemental Environmental Impact Statement for the area.

(c) **Fire:** The area has no significant fire history

(d) **Insects and Disease:** Endemic tree diseases common to Southeast Alaska are present; there are no know epidemic disease occurrences

(e) **Land Status:** One aboriginal site, a former village site. has been selected by Sealaska Corporation under 14(H)(1) provisions of ANGSA. Up to 5,000 acres have been selected in Saginaw Bay This selection is pending. Much of this overlaps into this roadless area The State has selected lands in Security Bay, which affects some of this area.

d. Relationship to Communities and Other Roadless and Wilderness Areas

(1) **Nearby Roadless and Wilderness Areas and Uses:** This area does not
directly adjoin any other roadless areas. Separation generally occurs
across bodies of saltwater or roads and timber harvest areas   Tebenkof Bay
Wilderness lies about 24 miles to the south. This area receives light
recreational use

(2) **Distance From Population Centers (Accessibility):** Approximate
distances from population centers are as follows:

Community		Air Miles	Water Miles
Juneau	(Pop.23,729)	100	128
Petersburg	(Pop. 4,040)	44	78
Wrangell	(Pop. 2,836)	72	124
Ketchikan	(Pop.12,705)	135	160

Kake and Petersburg are the nearest stops on the Alaska Marine Highway.

(3) **Interest by Proponents:**

(a) **Moratorium areas:** The area has not been proposed as a
"moratorium" area in legislative initiatives to date

(b) **Local users/residents:** This area has cultural and traditional
use value to the residents of Kake. It was identified as being part
of the lands "subject to existing rights under provisions of ANILCA",
although land conveyance has never officially occurred.

e. Environmental Consequences

ALTERNATIVE ANALYSIS TO BE DONE LATER

INDIVIDUAL ROADLESS AREA DESCRIPTION

NAME: Security (240)   ACRES (GROSS): 41,585   ACRES (NFS): 41,105

GEOZONE: S01
GEOGRAPHIC PROVINCE: Central Interior Islands

1989 WILDERNESS ATTRIBUTE RATING: 25

a. Description

    (1) Relationship to RARE II areas: The table below displays the VCU 1/
    names, VCU numbers, original WARS 2/ rating, and comments   This enables
    the reader to compare the roadless areas evaluated in Appendix C with
    previous analyses

VCU Name	VCU No.	1979 WARS Rating	Comments
Saginaw	399*	21	
Security Bay	400*	26	Eastern half of VCU is roaded extensively Several small islands located in bay
Washington Bay	401	24	Steeply-sloping and highly-dissected terrain Almost impossible to road
Rowan Bay ▾	402*	21	Most of VCU has been roaded extensively. Mouth of Rowan Bay has several small islands

    *--The roadless area includes only part of this VCU

    (2) History: North Kuiu Island was claimed by several clans of the Kake
    Tlingit. Evidence of their use is indicated by the remains of village
    sites, temporary camps, fort sites, garden sites, fish weirs, pictographs,
    petroglyphs and bark-stripped trees   Security and Saginaw Bays were
    heavily used prior to 1870   These bays are still important for gathering
    subsistence items. Historic use of the area is evidenced by the remains of
    a herring reduction plant in Washington Bay, and fox farms and troller
    camps in Security and Saginaw Bays.

    Since 1960, North Kuiu Island, which includes this roadless area. has been
    a contingency area for the Alaska Pulp Corporation long-term timber sale
    A logging camp was developed at nearby Rowan Bay in support of logging
    operations, and is still active with up to 130 seasonal occupants
    Extensive road development and logging has occurred east of this area

1/ A VCU (Value Comparison Unit) is one of 867 watersheds which make up the
    Forest and were differentiated for planning purposes in the Tongass Land
    Management Plan.
2/ Wilderness Attribute Rating System (WARS) was the nationwide system used to
    rate the wilderness attributes of roadless areas in the Roadless Area
    Review and Evaluation (RARE II).

(3) **Location and Access:** The Security Roadless Area is located on the northwest side of Kuiu Island bordering on Chatham Strait It is accessed primarily by saltwater and by air. Along the west-facing slope, a secure anchorage is available within Washington Bay, the remaining coastline is rocky and open to marine weather Both Security and Rowan Bays have good anchorages. It is possible to land floatplanes within Washington Bay and also in adjacent Security and Rowan Bays. There are no sites suitable for landing wheeled aircraft There is no ferry service to Kuiu Island Access is possible by road and boat from Rowan Bay for local residents of the Rowan Bay logging camp There is a regularly scheduled mail flight to Rowan Bay, but there are no visitor services such as rental vehicles or boats.

(4) **Geography and Topography:** The coastal area is characterized by steep, heavily-dissected slopes, rocky beaches, and numerous streams cascading directly into saltwater. Security and Rowan Bays have terrain more gently sloping to the water, which is characteristic of glaciated valleys Elevations range from sea level to 3,000 feet. This area is classified as part of the Kupreanof Lowlands character type, but displays some distinctive characteristics similar to those of the Baranof Highlands along the exposed coastline. Small islands account for 339 acres of this area, while freshwater lakes make up another 279 acres. Alpine covers 637 acres, and rock covers 2,789 acres. The area contains 56 miles of shoreline on saltwater

(5) **Ecosystem:**

   (a) **Classification:** The area is in the Central Interior Islands Geographic Province This province is generally characterized by rolling, subdued topography and extensive muskeg areas, but may have localized, rugged terrain. The west-facing side of Security Roadless Area is typical of the exposed, moderate-energy shoreline facing west and south along major waterways of Southeast Alaska. There are no known areas of unique or uncommon plant/soils associations or geologic formations in the area.

   (b) **Vegetation:** The area is typical of a mountain hemlock plant community above an elevation of 2,000 feet, with relatively little interspersed muskeg (40 acres).

   There are approximately 35,485 acres of forested land of which 28,762 acres are commercial forest land. Of the commercial forest land, 24,256 acres are non-riparian old growth and 4,307 acres are riparian old growth.

   (c) **Soils:** Soils in this area are formed in a wide variety of parent materials, including bedrock and glacial drift. In general, well- or moderately-well-drained soils are on moderate to steep mountain slopes with permeable parent materials. These soils are very acidic, have cold soil temperatures, and are very high in organic matter Rooting is largely limited to the surface organic layers and the top few inches of mineral soil. These soils are usually moist, sometimes wet but are never dry.

More-poorly-drained soils developed on less-sloping areas and/or areas
with impermeable soil materials. These soils have deep accumulations
of organic matter and range from scrubby forested wetlands to open
muskeg.

Alpine soils, generally above 2,000 feet elevation, are mostly
shallow, very wet organic soils or are extremely shallow and rocky

(d) Fish Resource: Fish resources have been rated as part of the
Tongass Land Management Plan (1979) and by the Alaska Department of
Fish and Game in their Forest Habitat Integrity Program (1983) These
ratings describe the value of VCU's for sport fish, commercial fish
and estuaries.

VCU's rated high in commercial fish values include 399, 400, and 402
Those rated in high in estuary values include 400 and 402.

Rowan Bay includes Rowan Creek which is a popular sport fishing stream
and is regularly used by residents of the Rowan Bay logging camp
Security Creek, Rowan Creek, and Browns Creek are primary contributors
to fish production in Rowan and Security Bays.

Nine ADF&G numbered salmon producing streams are present in the area
Security Creek is the best producer with an average annual peak
escapement of 15,200 pink and 9,200 chum salmon. The stream also has
good runs of coho and steelhead. The other streams are minor
producers in comparison.

(e) Wildlife Resource: The salt chuck at the head of Security Bay is
known for high-quality waterfowl hunting. Black bear populations on
Kuiu attract numerous hunters.

(f) Threatened and Endangered Species: The area contains no known
threatened or endangered species.

(6) Current Use and Management: The area was allocated to Land Use
Designation (LUD) 4 in the Tongass Land Management Plan, however, no
resource management activities have occurred in the area to date. This is
primarily due to the difficulty in developing access into the upper
mountain slopes. Access development is being planned It is likely that
road construction will occur along both sides of previously unroaded
portions of Security Bay. Personal resource use by logging camp residents
currently occurs in the vicinity of Rowan Bay and Security Bay

Kake residents also favor waterfowl hunting in Security Bay Boating and
sport fishing are popular. Lack of cabins or commercial overnight
facilities limits use by fly-in recreationists. Security Bay is a popular
anchorage for commercial fishermen. A fish buying station is normally
established there every year

(7) Appearance (Apparent Naturalness): The west-facing slope in this area
appears unmodified from a major travelway used by both cruiseships and the
Alaska Marine Highway ferry system (Sensitivity Level 1 travel route)
Several clearcuts are visible from within Rowan and Security Bays

About 97 percent of this roadless area is natural appearing, where only ecological change has occurred (Existing Visual Condition (EVC) Type I) The remaining three percent is in EVC Type V where changes in the landscape are obvious to the average person, and appear to be major disturbances

Fifty percent of this area is inventoried Variety Class A (possessing landscape diversity that is unique for the character type), 37 percent is inventoried Variety Class B (possessing landscape diversity that is common for the character type), and the remaining 13 percent is in Variety Class C (possessing a low degree of landscape diversity)

(8) **Surroundings (External Influences):** Areas east of and adjacent to Security Roadless Area are heavily modified by past and present timber harvest activities centered around Rowan Bay. Forest Road 6402, which runs north from Rowan Bay, connects with Security and Saginaw Bays   It continues to serve as a major access route for hauling logs Modifications on lands adjacent to this route will continue to occur under current management direction as the area is in LUD 4 and is a part of the Alaska Pulp Corporation long-term timber sale contract area. The State has selected land in Security Bay for a future marine park. A private residence also exists there.

(9) **Attractions and Features of Special Interest:** The area includes all of Security Bay, Washington Bay, a portion of Rowan Bay and two Lighthouse Reserves--one south of Washington Bay and one near Kingsmill Point   The area contains seven inventoried recreation places totaling 6,371 acres The most important of these recreation places includes the salt chuck at the head of Security Bay which is known particularly for good waterfowl hunting. The presence of anchorage sites within Washington Bay and along shorelines in Security Bay and Rowan Bay are noteworthy.

b. **Capability of Management as Wilderness or in an Unroaded Condition**

(1) **Manageability and Management Area Boundaries:** The northeastern, northern, western and southern boundaries of this area are surrounded by saltwater. The remaining portions border highly-roaded and modified terrain. Feasibility of management of the lower slopes adjacent to Rowan and Security Bays in an unroaded condition is low. The remaining area with steep slopes and dissected terrain will likely remain unroaded, regardless of this classification, due to infeasibility of road construction Forest Road 6425 runs parallel to the eastern shore of Security Bay, and clearcut units directly adjoin the roadless boundary. Potential for development of private land or land within the State marine park could also influence future manageability.

(2) **Natural Integrity:** The area is essentially unmodified Some evidence of past occupancy is present at the abandoned fox farms located on adjacent islands, and at the fish camps and the cannery sites at the mouths of both Washington and Rowan Bays.

(3) **Opportunity for Solitude:** There is a low opportunity for solitude within the area Use of floatplanes and motorboats may disrupt visitors for brief periods Noise from logging trucks on the adjacent road can be heard during periods of harvest activity Present recreation use levels are low, and generally a person camped along the shore would have moderate chance of seeing others

(4) **Opportunity for Primitive Recreation:** The area provides primarily primitive and semi-primitive non-motorized recreation opportunity.

ROS Class	Acres
Primitive (P)	15,884
Semi-Primitive Non-Motorized (SPNM)	14,414
Semi-Primitive Motorized (SPM)	7,825
Roaded Natural (RN)	219
Roaded Modified (RM)	2,660
Rural (R)	100

The area contains seven recreation places.

ROS CLASS	# OF REC. PLACES	TOTAL ACRES	CAPACITY BY RVD
SPNM	1	1,122	140
SPM	3	4,849	3,423
RN	1	219	11
RM	2	180	127

There are no developed recreation facilities This area opens onto water features, generally allowing the visitor to feel remote from the sights and sounds of human activity. Traveling by boat into the area requires extended boating time in exposed waters, challenging the skills of even experienced skippers.

(5) **Special Features (Ecologic, Geologic, Scientific, Cultural):** The abandoned cannery sites, fish camps, and fish traps attract some visitors If facilities are developed in the State marine park, it is expected that use will increase.

c. **Availability for Management as Wilderness or in an Unroaded Condition**

   (1) Resource Potentials

   (a) **Recreation Potential:** If a ferry route were established to Rowan or Saginaw Bays, there would be the potential for construction of a boat launch directly into the inner bay. This would open up a new array of recreation opportunities. Potential sites exist for one or more recreation cabins or shelters. There is potential for additional outfitter and guide permits.

   (b) **Fish Resource:** The Tongass Land Management Plan, amended Winter 1985-86 identifies fish habitat enhancement projects in this area Fish enhancement projects continue to surface and there is potential for additional projects in this area. The chum salmon population in

Security Bay may be enhanced by construction of egg incubation boxes at a unique supply of spring water.

(c) **Wildlife Resource:** As identified in the Tongass Land Management Plan, amended 1985-86, several habitat improvement projects are planned in the area. These projects typically consist of seeding, planting, and thinning.

(d) **Timber Resource:** There are 15,849 acres inventoried as tentatively suitable for timber harvest. This includes 2,375 acres of riparian old growth and 13,355 acres of non-riparian old growth. None of the area is second growth except small patches near the cannery site where pilings and fuel were obtained from 1930-1950.

(e) **Land Use Authorizations:** None.

(f) **Minerals:** There are no inventoried areas with high mineral development potential in the area.

(g) **Areas of Scientific Interest:** This area contains no inventoried potential Research Natural Areas and has not been identified for any other scientific value.

(2) **Management Considerations**

(a) Activities under the Alaska Pulp Corporation long-term sale contract will increase road access into parts of this roadless area.

(b) Maintenance of the area in a roadless condition would have little effect on adjacent roadless areas such as Bay of Pillars and the Tebenkof Wilderness, since Security is separated by saltwater from these areas. Maintaining portions in a roadless condition enhances some recreational opportunities.

(c) **Fire:** The area has no significant fire history.

(d) **Insects and Disease:** Endemic tree diseases common to Southeast Alaska are present; there are no know epidemic disease occurrences.

(e) **Land Status:** The State of Alaska selected an area along the eastern shore of Security Bay as a State marine park. Currently, this park has no developments. Land has also been selected in Rowan Bay just west of the present logging camp. Private land, including a private residence, is located along the eastern shore of Security Bay.

d. **Relationship to Communities and Other Roadless and Wilderness Areas**

(1) **Nearby Roadless and Wilderness Areas and Uses:** South and adjacent to a small portion of this roadless area are the Bay of Pillars Roadless Area and the Tebenkof Bay Wilderness. Essentially all of south and east Kuiu Island is unroaded. Across Chatham Strait, about 10 miles to the west, is the South Baranof Wilderness. These areas receive light use.

(2) Distance From Population Centers (Accessibility): Approximate
distances from population centers are as follows:

Community		Air Miles	Water Miles
Juneau	(Pop 23,729)	100	128
Petersburg	(Pop 4,040)	46	86
Ketchikan	(Pop 12,705)	130	160

Kake and Petersburg are the nearest stops on the Alaska Marine Highway.

(3) Interest by Proponents:

(a) Moratorium areas: The area has not been identified as a
"moratorium" area or proposed in Wilderness legislation initiatives to
date

(b) Local users/residents: With the exception of the head of
Security Bay, there has been little interest expressed in retaining
the roadless character of unroaded parts of Kuiu Island

e. Environmental Consequences

ALTERNATIVE ANALYSIS TO BE DONE LATER

INDIVIDUAL ROADLESS AREA DESCRIPTION

NAME: North Kuiu (241)   ACRES (GROSS): 9,741   ACRES (NFS): 9,741

GEOZONE: S01
GEOGRAPHIC PROVINCE: Central Interior Islands

1989 WILDERNESS ATTRIBUTE RATING: 19

a. Description

    (1) Relationship to RARE II areas: The table below displays the VCU 1/
    names, VCU numbers, acres, original WARS 2/ rating, and comments   This
    enables the reader to compare the roadless areas evaluated in Appendix C
    with previous analyses.

| | | 1979 | |
VCU Name	VCU No.	WARS Rating	Comments
Saginaw	399*	23	
Security	400*	26	
Kadak	421*	22	

    *--The roadless area includes only part of this VCU.

    (2) History: The area was within the territory of the Kake Tlingit,
    however no cultural resources are currently recorded. This is probably due
    to the absence of cultural resource inventories within this area   The
    probability of cultural resources being found within this area appears to
    be low, as it does not lie along the shore

    (3) Location and Access: This roadless area is located near the center of
    the northern portion of Kuiu Island. Roads surround the area and provide
    access. Rowan Bay, a logging camp, is the only community on Kuiu Island
    and is connected to this road system. Kake, the nearest town, is located
    on nearby Kupreanof Island. Access to the roadless area is by chartered
    floatplane or boat to Kuiu Island, then by land   There is no regularly
    scheduled transportation to this area.

    (4) Geography and Topography: This roadless area is characterized by
    rolling terrain with drainages in all directions. The area consists mostly
    of the ridges and upper reaches of these drainages   Elevations range
    between 1,000 and 2,000 feet. Generally, slopes are gentle with little
    relief. The roadless area does not connect with saltwater   About 20 acres
    of freshwater lakes are found in the area. The majority of the area, 9,641
    acres, is covered by forest. Rock outcrops and faces cover another 20
    acres.

1/ A VCU (Value Comparison Unit) is one of 867 watersheds which make up the
    Forest and were differentiated for planning purposes in the Tongass Land
    Management Plan.
2/ Wilderness Attribute Rating System (WARS) was the nationwide system used to
    rate the wilderness attributes of roadless areas in the Roadless Area
    Review and Evaluation (RARE II).

(5) Ecosystem:

(a) Classification: The area is in the Central Interior Islands Geographic Province   This province is generally characterized by rolling, subdued topography and extensive muskeg areas, but may have rugged terrain in localized areas

(b) Vegetation: Vegetation of this roadless area primarily consists of typical spruce/hemlock forests. Low-lying, poorly-drained portions of the area are muskeg

There are 9,641 acres of forested land, of which 8,739 acres are commercial forest land. Of the commercial forest land, 7,536 acres are non-riparian old growth and 1,042 acres are riparian old growth

(c) Soils: Soils in this area are formed in a wide variety of parent materials, including bedrock and glacial drift   In general, well- or moderately-well-drained soils are on moderate to steep mountain slopes with permeable parent materials   These soils are very acidic, have cold soil temperatures, and are very high in organic matter   Rooting is largely limited to the surface organic layers and the top few inches of mineral soil. These soils are usually moist, sometimes wet, but are never dry.

More-poorly-drained soils developed on less-sloping areas and/or areas with impermeable soil materials   These soils have deep accumulations of organic matter and range from scrubby forested wetlands to open muskeg.

Alpine soils, generally above 2,000 feet in elevation, are mostly shallow, very wet organic soils or are extremely shallow and rocky

(d) Fish Resource: Fish resources have been rated as part of the Tongass Land Management Plan (1979) and by the Alaska Department of Fish and Game in its Forest Habitat Integrity Program (1983)   These ratings describe the value of VCU's for sport fish, commercial fish, and estuaries

The one VCU in this area rated high for sport fish is 421   VCU's rated as high value for commercial fish are 399, 400 and 421   VCU's rated as highly valued estuaries include 400 and 421

(e) Wildlife Resource: A population of Sitka black-tailed deer and black bear range over the roadless area.

(f) Threatened and Endangered Species: The area contains no known threatened or endangered species

(6) Current Use and Management: All three VCU's (9,741 acres) are allocated to Land Use Designation 4, which provides for intensive resource use and development.

Road systems and timber management activities surround this roadless area
Hunting is the primary recreational use. Most use is concentrated along
the road-accessible outside edges of the roadless area. Overall use levels
are low   There is some subsistence use in the area.

(7) **Appearance (Apparent Naturalness):** The majority of the area appears
unmodified   The remainder of the area has been heavily influenced by
adjacent management activities, mainly clearcuts and roads

Forty percent of this roadless area was inventoried in Variety Class B
(possessing landscape diversity that is common for the character type)
The remaining 60 percent was inventoried in Variety Class C (possessing a
low degree of landscape diversity).

Most of the roadless area 75 percent, is in Existing Visual Condition (EVC)
I, these areas appear to be untouched by human activity, EVC V accounts
for the remaining 25 percent. These are areas in which changes to the
landscape are obvious to the average person, and appear to be major
disturbances.

(8) **Surroundings (External Influences):** Roads and timber management
activities occur on all sides of the roadless area. Noise and sights of
vehicles and active timber sales may occur periodically, being greatest in
magnitude near the roads and lessening as one moves away   Low-flying
aircraft may temporarily distract visitors in the area.

(9) **Attractions and Features of Special Interest:** There are no special
attractions or features in this roadless area. The area contains no
inventoried recreation places.

b. Capability of Management as Wilderness or in an Unroaded Condition

(1) **Manageability and Management Area Boundaries:** The area is bounded on
all sides by roads and timber management activities. Some of the cutting
units have impacted parts of the core of the roadless setting   There are
few topographic breaks or other natural features to define the area
Feasibility of management in a Wilderness condition is low to moderate, due
to the amount of timber harvest activity adjacent to this roadless area
Feasibility of management in an unroaded condition is moderate, as it
maintains traditional opportunities.

(2) **Natural Integrity:** The area is unmodified, however its overall
integrity is not considered pristine. Adjacent management activities have
likely impacted some of the natural integrity of this area. The irregular
shape of the area, patterns of adjacent timber management, and roading have
also impacted the area's natural integrity.

(3) **Opportunity for Solitude:** There is a moderate opportunity for
solitude within the area. Vehicle and logging traffic occasionally pass
nearby and may be heard and observed by people in this roadless area
There may also be long periods where no vehicle traffic exists, as traffic
is generally a function of adjacent or nearby timber management
activities   Overall recreation use levels are low, being higher along the
fringes near roads   Generally, a person camped or traveling inland is

unl'ikely to see others   Timber harvest or other activities in the adjacent
areas, which occur periodically, would have a significant impact on the
opportunity for solitude when they are occurring

(4) **Opportunity for Primitive Recreation:** The area provides
semi-primitive recreation opportunity as inventoried with the Recreation
Opportunity Spectrum (ROS) System.

ROS Class	Acres
Semi-Primitive Non-Motorized (SPNM)	5,031
Roaded Modified (RM)	4,710

No inventoried recreation places are found within this roadless area

There are no developed recreation opportunities in this area.   The
vegetation and the rolling nature of the landform do allow a visitor to
feel remote from the sights and sounds of human activity   The area is
difficult to access due to the logistics of getting to Kupreanof Island,
and then having to travel inland.

(5) **Special Features (Ecologic, Geologic, Scientific, Cultural):** The area
contains no known features of special interest.

c. **Availability for Management as Wilderness or in an Unroaded Condition**

(1) **Resource Potentials**

(a) **Recreation Potential:** There is some potential for outfitter and
guide permits.   There is also potential for some off-road vehicles to
enter the roadless area

(b) **Fish Resource:** No fish habitat enhancement projects are
identified in the Tongass Land Management Plan, amended Winter
1985-86.

(c) **Wildlife Resource:** As identified in the Tongass Land Management
Plan, amended Winter 1985-86, wildlife habitat improvement projects
are planned.   These projects typically consist of seeding, planting,
and thinning for browse species.

(d) **Timber Resource:** There are 6,514 acres inventoried as
tentatively suitable for harvest.   This includes 802 acres of riparian
old growth, and 5,612 acres of non-riparian old growth

(e) **Land Use:** There are no special uses in the area

(f) **Minerals:** The area has low minerals potential.

(g) **Areas of Scientific Interest:** The area has not been identified
as an Inventoried Potential Research Natural Area or for any other
scientific purpose

(2) **Management Considerations**

(a) The potential for managing timber in this roadless area is dependent on market values. A road system and/or logging systems capable of harvesting the area would be necessary Nearby roads could be extended to accomplish much of this

(b) Maintenance of the area in a roadless condition enhances opportunities for certain wildlife and traditional recreation activities

(c) Fire: The area has no significant fire history

(d) **Insects and Disease:** Endemic tree diseases common to Southeast Alaska are present; there are no know epidemic disease occurrences

(e) **Land Status:** Entirely National Forest Systems land

d. **Relationship to Communities and Other Roadless and Wilderness Areas**

(1) **Nearby Roadless and Wilderness Areas and Uses:** The nearest roadless areas are Keku, Security, Camden, and Bay of Pillars. All are within one to eight miles distance. The Tebenkof Bay Wilderness also located on Kuiu Island, is about 15 miles to the south of the North Kuiu Roadless Area

(2) **Distance From Population Centers (Accessibility):** Approximate distances from population centers are as follows.

Community		Air Miles	Water Miles
Juneau	(Pop. 23,729)	100	128
Petersburg	(Pop. 4,040)	46	80
Wrangell	(Pop. 2,836)	68	124
Ketchikan	(Pop. 12,705)	130	160

Kake is the nearest stop on the Alaska Marine Highway

(3) **Interest by Proponents:**

(a) **Moratorium areas:** The area has not been identified as a "moratorium" area or proposed as Wilderness in legislative initiatives to date.

(b) **Local users/residents:** Portions of the area are traditional and/or popular recreation areas.

e. **Environmental Consequences**

ALTERNATIVE ANALYSIS TO BE DONE LATER

INDIVIDUAL ROADLESS AREA DESCRIPTION

NAME: Camden (242)   ACRES (GROSS): 54,730   ACRES (NFS): 54,730

GEOZONE: S01
GEOGRAPHIC PROVINCE: Central Interior Islands

1989 WILDERNESS ATTRIBUTE RATING: 25

a. Description

(1) Relationship to RARE II areas: The table below displays the VCU 1/ names, VCU numbers, original WARS 2/ rating, and comments This enables the reader to compare the roadless areas evaluated in Appendix C with previous analyses.

VCU Name	VCU No.	1979 WARS Rating	Comments
Rowan Bay	402*	21	
Pillar	403*	23	
Threemile Arm	419*	22	
Port Camden	420*	24	
Kadake·Bay	421*	22	

*--The roadless area includes only part of this VCU

(2) History: Evidently the Port Camden area was claimed by the Saqtunedi clan of the Kake Tlingit. It was an important subsistence area and sites include a village, several temporary camps, portage trails, fish weirs petroglyphs, and bark-stripped trees. Historic period activities include a log dump and several trapping cabins. This area has been part of the Alaska Pulp Corporation long-term timber sale area since 1960 A logging camp was developed at nearby Rowan Bay which is still active Up to 130 seasonal occupants reside there. Road development has occurred south of this area. The roads which connect Rowan Bay, across the isthmus, to Port Camden and Threemile Arm are primarily used for hauling logs to the log transfer facility at Rowan Bay. Forest Road 6402 was constructed in 1986

(3) Location and Access: Camden Roadless Area is primarily located on a peninsula on the northeast corner of Kuiu Island and borders Keku Strait and Rocky Pass. It is accessible by saltwater (from the community of Kake or the Rowan Bay logging camp) by road (from Rowan Bay logging camp) or by air. Both shores of Port Camden have good anchorages, as does the mouth of Kadake Bay. Floatplane landing is possible within both Kadake and Rowan Bays. There are no sites suitable for landing wheeled aircraft There is no ferry service Kuiu Island. Mail flights to Rowan Bay occur regularly. but no visitor services such as rental vehicles or boats are available

1/ A VCU (Value Comparison Unit) is one of 867 watersheds which make up the Forest and were differentiated for planning purposes in the Tongass Land Management Plan.

2/ Wilderness Attribute Rating System (WARS) was the nationwide system used to rate the wilderness attributes of roadless areas in the Roadless Area Review and Evaluation (RARE II).

(4) Geography and Topography: Landforms along this area are characterized
by gently-rolling hills that are typically short, extremely broken and
benched, making development of a road system challenging. Steeper slopes
are forested, but muskegs and scrub timber are very common on
gently-sloping to moderately-steep hills. The area contains 53 miles of
shoreline on saltwater Freshwater lakes occupy 340 acres and small
islands account for 180 acres

(5) Ecosystem:

    (a) Classification: The area is in the Central Interior Islands
    Geographic Province This province is generally characterized by
    rolling, subdued topography and extensive muskeg areas Rugged
    terrain may be found in localized areas. The coastline area
    represents a richly varied ecosystem. The isthmus area between Port
    Camden, Bay of Pillars, and Threemile Arm includes several naturally
    occurring springs, which adds diversity to the habitat

    (b) Vegetation: Muskeg/scrub timber complexes (120 acres) are
    interspersed with mixed conifer plant communities on excessively-wet
    sites. Timbered hill slopes are dominantly western hemlock, Sitka
    spruce, and Alaska-cedar plant communities.

    There are approximately 53,791 acres of forested land of which 30,470
    acres are commercial forest land. Of the commercial forest land,
    27,284 acres are non-riparian old growth and 2,936 acres are riparian
    old growth.

    (c) Soils: Soils in this area are formed in a wide variety of parent
    material, including bedrock and glacial drift In general, well- or
    moderately-well-drained soils are on moderate to steep mountain slopes
    with permeable parent materials. These soils are very acidic, have
    cold soil temperatures, and are very high in organic matter Rooting
    is largely limited to the surface organic layers and the top few
    inches of mineral soil These soils are usually moist, sometimes wet
    but are never dry

    More-poorly-drained soils developed on less-sloping areas and/or areas
    with impermeable soil materials. These soils have deep accumulations
    of organic matter and range from scrubby forested wetlands to open
    muskeg.

    Alpine soils, generally above 2,000 feet elevation, are mostly
    shallow, very wet organic soils or are extremely shallow and rocky.

    (d) Fish Resource: There are eight ADF&G numbered salmon producing
    streams within the area. Kadake Creek borders the western boundary of
    this area and constitutes the largest single drainage on Kuiu Island
    It has average annual escapements of 12,600 pink and 1,000 chum, and
    good runs of coho and steelhead. It supports both commercial and
    sport fishing Slippery Creek, on the west side of Port Camden Bay,
    has been enhanced with a fish ladder, providing access for stocked
    Coho to the upper watershed. Kadake Creek is also a popular sport
    fishing stream and is regularly used by residents of the Rowan Bay

logging camp, as well as supporting an outfitter guide   Egg boxes
have been placed in Port Camden Creek

Fish resources have been rated as part of the Tongass Land Management
Plan (1978) and by the Alaska Department of Fish and Game in its
Forest Habitat Integrity Program (1983)   These ratings describe the
value of VCU's for sport fish, commercial fish and estuaries

Two VCU's, 403 and 421, are rated as high value for sport fish   VCU's
402, 403, 419, 420, and 421 were rated as highly valued for commercial
fish   VCU's rated as highly valued estuaries include 402, 419, and
421

(e) **Wildlife Resource:** Port Camden Bay represents a rich ecosystem
It supports quality waterfowl hunting at the head of the bay, as well
as quality habitat for black bear, fur bearers, marine mammals and
bald eagle. The Camden area is .readily accessible by boat from Kake.
and has a tradition of high subsistence use

(f) **Threatened and Endangered Species:** The area contains no known
threatened or endangered species

(6) **Current Use and Management:** The entire area was allocated to Land Use
Designation (LUD) 4 in the Tongass Land Management Plan, however, only
limited Forest Service resource management activities have occurred in the
area, such as fisheries enhancement projects   The area has low-value
timber stands and roading is difficult in the eastern half of the Camden
VCU. The Supplemental EIS for the 1986-90 operating plan has identified
roading the remaining portion of Kadake Creek (VCU 421) and initiating
roading and management on the western side of Port Camden (VCU 420)   The
area receives high subsistence use from the residents of Kake

Both Port Camden and Threemile Arm receive light to moderate recreation
use. A Forest Service public recreation cabin is located at the mouth of
Kadake Creek. Two portage trails provide opportunities for canoeists and
kayakers to access additional recreation areas   The Threemile Arm portage
is 1.25 miles long and connects Port Camden with Threemile Arm   The Bay of
Pillars portage is one mile long and connects Port Camden with the Bay of
Pillars. Both portages receive light recreation use and are considered
difficult

(7) **Appearance (Apparent Naturalness):** The roadless area appears
natural. Few management activities are visible within Port Camden and from
Frederick Sound, a major travelway used by both cruiseships and Alaska
Marine Highway ferries.

The majority of this roadless area (94 percent) is natural appearing, where
only ecological change has occurred (Existing Visual Condition (EVC)
Type I)   Less than one percent of the area appears to be untouched by
human activity (EVC Type II)   Less than one percent of this roadless area
is EVC Type III, where changes in the landscape are noticed by the average
forest visitor. The natural appearance of the landscape remains dominant.
Less than one percent of the area is in EVC Type IV, where changes in the
landscape are easily noticed by the average person and may attract some
attention. They appear to be disturbances but resemble natural patterns

Four percent is in EVC Type V where changes in the landscape are obvious to the average person, and appear to be major disturbances

Fifty-five percent is inventoried Variety Class B (possessing landscape diversity that is common for the character type) and the remaining 45 percent is inventoried Variety Class C (possessing a low degree of landscape diversity)

(8) **Surroundings (External Influences):** Areas west and adjacent to Camden Roadless Area are heavily modified by past and present timber harvest activities along Kadake Creek Forest Road 6402, which connects Rowan Bay to Port Camden and Three Mile Arm, was constructed in about 1986 It continues to serve as a major access route for hauling logs and timber harvest, and vehicles can be heard and seen in parts of the roadless area Occasional marine and air traffic can also be observed.

(9) **Attractions and Features of Special Interest:** The area includes all of Port Camden, Kadake Bay and a portion of Three Mile Arm. Attractions in this area include a Forest Service public recreation cabin at the mouth of Kadake Bay; and two trails used to portage between Threemile Arm, Port Camden, and the Bay of Pillars. There is a total of 2.25 miles of trail in the area. The unique feature of upwelling springs at the head of Port Camden in the area known as "the isthmus" provides unique habitat and adds to good waterfowl hunting. The presence of good anchorage sites along both shores of Port Camden allows visitors to stay overnight Portage trails between three major bodies of water allow hikers and kayakers recreation opportunities not found elsewhere on this island. The area contains 10 inventoried recreation places totaling 15,440 acres.

b. Capability of Management as Wilderness or in an Unroaded Condition

(1) **Manageability and Management Area Boundaries:** Frederick Sound forms the northern boundary of this roadless area. The southern boundary is formed by Forest Road 6402 and Threemile Arm. The eastern boundary borders Rocky Pass Roadless Area, and the western boundary directly adjoins the roaded portion of Kadake Creek. It is likely that the area will be roaded in conjunction with timber harvesting.

(2) **Natural Integrity:** The area is essentially unmodified Roading and timber harvesting adjacent to this area have likely had an effect on the areas natural integrity, however the impact is not considered great

(3) **Opportunity for Solitude:** There is moderate to high opportunity for solitude within the Kadake Creek, Port Camden, and isthmus areas. Use of floatplanes and motorboats may disrupt visitors for brief periods in all regions of Camden Roadless Area. Noise from logging trucks on the adjacent road system may be audible during periods of harvest activity. Present recreation use levels are low.

(4) **Opportunity for Primitive Recreation:** The area provides primarily primitive and semi-primitive non-motorized recreation opportunity·

ROS Class	Acres
Primitive (P)	17,677
Semi Primitive Non-Motorized (SPNM)	15,334
Semi Primitive Motorized (SPM)	5,882
Roaded Natural (RN)	2,290
Roaded Modified (RM)	12,533

The area contains ten recreation places

ROS CLASS	# OF REC. PLACES	TOTAL ACRES	CAPACITY BY RVD
P	2	6,800	914
SPNM	1	1,000	400
SPM	3	3,987	3,926
RN	1	657	468
RM	3	2,996	1,465

There is a recreation cabin at the mouth of Kadake Creek and two portage trails. The general character of the landscape and water features allows visitors to feel remote from the sights and sounds of human activity Access by boat into the area requires extended boating time in exposed waters, challenging the skills of even experienced skippers.

(5) **Special Features (Ecologic, Geologic, Scientific, Cultural):** The highly-productive estuarine habitat at the head of Port Camden and Threemile Arm in combination with natural upwelling springs provide a unique combination of wildlife species and habitat. Fossil hunting and the presence of petrified tree species no longer indigenous to Alaska are of special scientific interest along the eastern shore of Port Camden Bear hunting, crabbing, and fishing occur throughout the area

c. **Availability for Management as Wilderness or in an Unroaded Condition**

(1) **Resource Potentials**

(a) **Recreation Potential:** Recreation potential for the Camden area is high, access being the primary limiting factor for increased recreation use Several potential sites exist for recreation cabins There is potential for additional outfitter and guide permits Kayaking and canoeing are increasing in connection with the recent establishment of portage trails and an brochure on kayaking/canoeing opportunities in the area.

(b) **Fish Resource:** The Tongass Land Management Plan, amended Winter 1985-86 identifies fish habitat enhancement projects in this area Potential exists for a substantial increase in the number of coho salmon returning to habitat above the Slippery Creek fishway Stocking of this stream has begun.

(c) **Wildlife Resource:** As identified in the Tongass Land Management Plan, amended 1985-86, habitat improvement projects are planned in the area. These projects typically consist of deer range improvement

(d) Timber Resource: There are 23,973 acres inventoried as
tentatively suitable for timber harvest. This includes 2,097 acres of
riparian old growth, and 21,636 acres of non-riparian old growth
None of the area is second growth except for small patches along the
west shore of Port Camden where beach logging occurred

(e) Land Use Authorizations: There are no land use authorizations in
this area

(f) Minerals: There are no inventoried areas with high mineral
development potential in the area.

(g) Areas of Scientific Interest: The site along the eastern shore
of Port Camden, where fossils have been located, is an inventoried
potential Research Natural Area, and is of special scientific
interest.

(2) **Management Considerations**

(a) Long-term timber sales on Kuiu Island may result in increased
roading of Kuiu Island, which may provide additional access to parts
of the Camden Roadless Area.

(b) Maintenance of the area in a roadless condition would likely
benefit the adjacent Rocky Pass and Bay of Pillars Roadless Areas, and
existing recreation opportunities. It is most likely, however, that
this will not occur.

(c) Fire: The area has no significant fire history

(d) Insects and Disease: Endemic tree diseases common to Southeast
Alaska are present; there are no know epidemic disease occurrences

(e) Land Status: Entirely National Forest Systems land

d. **Relationship to Communities and Other Roadless and Wilderness Areas**

(1) **Nearby Roadless and Wilderness Areas and Uses:** The Rocky Pass
Roadless Area, to the east, directly adjoins the Camden Roadless Area   Bay
of Pillars Roadless Area and the Tebenkof Bay Wilderness adjoin the Camden
area to the southwest, separated by one logging road. These areas receive
light use.

(2) **Distance From Population Centers (Accessibility):** Approximate
distances from population centers are as follows:

Community		Air Miles	Water Miles
Juneau	(Pop. 23,729)	100	128
Petersburg	(Pop. 4,040)	46	80
Wrangell	(pop. 2,836)	72	95
Ketchikan	(pop 12,705)	140	170

Kake and Petersburg are the nearest stops on the Alaska Marine Highway.

(3) Interest by Proponents:

(a) **Moratorium areas:** The area has not been identified as a "moratorium" area in legislative initiatives to date

(b) **Local users/residents:** Port Camden is a high interest area. Previous attempts to road and develop a log transfer facility along the eastern side of Port Camden met with high public resistance

c. Environmental Consequences

ALTERNATIVE ANALYSIS TO BE DONE LATER

INDIVIDUAL ROADLESS AREA DESCRIPTION

NAME: Rocky Pass (243)   ACRES (GROSS): 79,556   ACRES (NFS): 78,976

GEOZONE: S01 and S10
GEOGRAPHIC PROVINCE: Central Interior Islands

1989 WILDERNESS ATTRIBUTE RATING: 26

a. Description

(1) Relationship to RARE II areas: The table below displays the VCU 1/ names, VCU numbers, original WARS 2/ rating, and comments This enables the reader to compare the roadless areas evaluated in Appendix C with previous analyses.

VCU Name	VCU No.	1979 WARS Rating	Comments
Keku	398*	23	
Cathedral	425*	14	
Big John	427	26	
Rocky Pass	428	25	

*--The roadless area includes only part of this VCU

(2) History: The Keku Strait area was used by both the Kake and Kuiu Tlingit. Former sites include temporary camps, garden areas, fish weirs and fort sites A Tlingit site at Irish Creek has been radiocarbon dated to about 300 B C The area was used in historic times for fox farms, trapping cabins and temporary camps The portion of this roadless area on Kuiu Island has been part of the Alaska Pulp Corporation long-term timber sale area since 1960, although no activities have ever been scheduled A logging camp was developed at nearby Rowan Bay, and is still active Up to 130 seasonal occupants reside there Road development has occurred to the south, along the northern shore of Threemile Arm. Forest Road 6434 is scheduled to be extended along this shore to the end of Threemile Arm with one of the Alternatives in the Supplemental EIS for 1981-90 APC operating period. This road would reach within one-half mile of the lower end of the Rocky Pass Roadless Area.

1/ A VCU (Value Comparison Unit) is one of 867 watersheds which make up the Forest and were differentiated for planning purposes in the Tongass Land Management Plan.
2/ Wilderness Attribute Rating System (WARS) was the nationwide system used to rate the wilderness attributes of roadless areas in the Roadless Area Review and Evaluation (RARE II).

(3) Location and Access: Rocky Pass Roadless Area lies east of the Camden
Roadless Area on Kuiu Island, and west of the South Kupreanof Roadless Area
on Kupreanof Island   It is accessed primarily by saltwater via boat or by
float plane   Several good anchorages are located along the pass   There
are no sites suitable for landing wheeled aircraft. Forest Road 6040
adjoins Rocky Pass Roadless Area near the head of McNaughton Bay,
connecting to Kake, approximately 15 miles away. There is no ferry service
to Kuiu Island, although a ferry stops in Kake, which is on Kupreanof
Island. There is a regularly scheduled mail flight to Rowan Bay but there
are no visitor services such as rental vehicles or boats

(4) Geography and Topography: Landforms along this area are characterized
by rolling to moderately steep hills, typically less than 1,500 feet in
elevation. Hill slopes are short and extremely broken or benched   Unlike
most roadless areas which are separated by waterways, this roadless area
encompasses a waterway   The narrow and often shallow waterway has scores
of small islands and rocks. In addition, the surrounding landform is an
important backdrop in this setting. The area contains 171 miles of
saltwater shoreline. Small islands account for a total of 1,853 acres,
while lakes cover another 180 acres. Alpine covers about 20 acres

(5) Ecosystem:

   (a) Classification: The area is in the Central Interior Islands
   Geographic Province. This province is generally characterized by
   rolling, subdued topography and extensive muskeg areas, but may have
   localized, rugged terrain. This area is classified as being in the
   Kupreanof Lowlands character type which is noted for the diversity of
   shoreline and associated groups of small islands

   (b) Vegetation: Muskeg/scrub timber complexes (2,849 acres) on
   excessively-wet areas are interspersed with mixed conifer plant
   communities on better-drained sites. Timbered hill slopes are
   dominated by western hemlock, sitka spruce, and Alaska-cedar plant
   communities.

   There are approximately 74,591 acres of forested land of which 39,531
   acres are commercial forest land. Of the commercial forest land,
   36,077 acres are non-riparian old growth and 3,014 acres are riparian
   old growth.

   (c) Soils: Soils in this area are formed in a wide variety of parent
   material, including bedrock and glacial drift   In general, well- or
   moderately-well-drained soils are on moderate to steep mountain slopes
   with permeable parent materials. These soils are very acidic, have
   cold soil temperatures, and are very high in organic matter   Rooting
   is largely limited to the surface organic layers and the top few
   inches of mineral soil. These soils are usually moist, sometimes wet,
   but are never dry.

   More-poorly-drained soils developed on less-sloping areas and or areas
   with impermeable soil materials. These soils have deep accumulations
   of organic matter and range from scrubby forested wetlands to open
   muskeg.

Alpine soils, generally above 2,000 feet elevation, are mostly
shallow, very wet organic soils or are extremely shallow and rocky

(d) Fish Resource: Thirteen ADF&G numbered salmon producing streams
are present. Many of the streams have upper watersheds outside of the
area. The largest salmon producers are Big John Creek, Irish Creek,
and Tunehean Creek   Average peak escapement for pink salmon is 1,100
for Big John Creek, and 23,600 for Tunehean Creeks   Escapements of
chum are 1,000 Tunehean Creek, 1,500 for Irish Creek, and 600 for Big
John Creek   A fish ladder was constructed on Irish Creek to allow
passage of pink, coho, chum, and steelhead to the upper watershed
Streams in the area also have good runs of coho

Fish resources have been rated as part of the Tongass Land Management
Plan (1978) and by the Alaska Department of Fish and Game in its
Forest Habitat Integrity Program (1983). These ratings describe the
value of VCU's for sport fish, commercial fish and estuaries

There are two VCU's which are rated as high value for sport fish
These are 425 and 428   VCU's rated as highly valued for commercial
fish are 425, 427, and 428. VCU's rated as highly valued estuaries
include 425, 427, and 428.

(e) Wildlife Resource: Several eagle nest trees dot the shores from
Big John Bay south through Rocky Pass. Large flocks of ducks and
geese use this area during their fall migrations. Many of the small
islands show sign of otter activity

(f) Threatened and Endangered Species: The area contains no known
threatened or endangered species

(6) Current Use and Management: Most of the area (74,162 acres) was
allocated to Land Use Designation (LUD) 2 in the Tongass Land Management
Plan. Another 4,654 acres was allocated to LUD 4, and a small amount
allocated to LUD 3, 159 acres. A fish pass, two recreation cabins, a short
trail, and an offshore oyster farm are the only major management activities
in the area. There is State land on High Island   The Coast Guard once
maintained navigation aids for smaller vessels, but these have since been
removed. A high degree of challenge and skill is needed to navigate
amongst the scenic array of rocks and islands.

At one time it was proposed that a road be built across Rocky Pass waterway
at High Island, which would then tie together Kuiu and Kupreanof Islands.
This is still a possibility, but not likely in the near future

(7) Appearance (Apparent Naturalness): Most of the area appears
unmodified from travel routes in Rocky Pass.

The majority of this roadless area (97 percent) is natural appearing, where
only ecological change has occurred (Existing Visual Condition (EVC)
Type I)   Less than one percent appears in EVC types II, III, IV and V.

Nine percent of this roadless area is inventoried Variety Class A
(possessing landscape diversity that is unique for the character type). 24

percent is inventoried Variety Class B (possessing landscape diversity that
is common for the character type) and the remaining 67 percent is
inventoried Variety Class C (possessing a low degree of landscape
diversity).

(8) **Surroundings (External Influences):** A road from Kake and timber
harvest areas lies along the northern boundary of this roadless area
Light marine and air traffic occur within the area

(9) **Attractions and Features of Special Interest:** This area is prized for
its geologic diversity, and is a prime area for rock hounds to visit   Big
John and Devil's Elbow recreation cabins are located within this roadless
area   The unmodified nature of the waterway makes this area attractive for
explorers with small boats. Overall use levels are light. There are 12
inventoried recreation places totaling 16,462 acres   There is one
developed trail, Big John, in the area. Bear hunting and sport fishing
occur throughout Rocky Pass. .

b. **Capability of Management as Wilderness or in an Unroaded Condition**

(1) **Manageability and management area boundaries:** Rocky Pass is
surrounded by land on two sides and opens onto Sumner Strait to the south
and Keku Strait to the north. Forest Road 6040 currently approaches the
northern boundary from Kake. Forest Road 6434, which connects Rowan Bay
thru the isthmus to Port Camden and Threemile Arm is planned to be extended
to within one-half mile of the southern end of Rocky Pass.

(2) **Natural Integrity:** The area is essentially unmodified

(3) **Opportunity for Solitude:** There is a high opportunity for solitude in
the Rocky Pass area. Use of floatplanes and powerboats may disrupt
visitors for brief periods   Present recreation use levels are moderate
Persons camped along the shore are generally unlikely to encounter another
person, but might see or be visible to the occasional fishing boat

(4) **Opportunity for Primitive Recreation:** The area provides primarily
primitive and semi-primitive opportunities.

ROS Class	Acres
Primitive (P)	51,155
Semi-Primitive Non-Motorized (SPNM)	12,783
Semi-Primitive Motorized (SPM)	11,238
Roaded Natural (RN)	40
Roaded Modified (RM)	597

The area contains 12 recreation places.

ROS CLASS	# OF REC. PLACES	TOTAL ACRES	CAPACITY BY RVD
P	4	8,725	3,772
SPM	5	7,558	5,078
RN	1	40	71
RM	2	139	222

There are two Forest Service recreation cabins and one developed trail in the Rocky Pass Roadless Area.

(5) **Special Features (Ecologic, Geologic, Scientific, Cultural):** Rock hounding for agates and geodes, or other semi-precious stones, as well as looking for petrified wood and fossils are popular in Rocky Pass Grassflats and waterfowl hunting in the major estuaries are popular, as are sport fishing for steelhead and salmon in Tunehean and Kushneahin Creeks Bear hunting occurs throughout the area.

One of the main features of the Rocky Pass area is the shallow body of water that is only navigable on high tides by larger boats It is one of the few areas in which nautical charts measures feet instead of fathoms

c. **Availability as Wilderness or in an Unroaded Condition**

   (1) **Resource Potentials**

      (a) **Recreation Potential:** Recreation potential for Rocky Pass is high, as there are opportunities for additional recreation cabins, trails, and outfitter and guide permits.

      (b) **Fish Resource:** No additional fish habitat enhancement projects are identified in the Tongass Land Management Plan, amended Winter 1985-86 for this area.

      (c) **Wildlife Resource:** As identified in the Tongass Land Management Plan, amended 1985-86, deer mitigation habitat improvement projects are planned in the area.

      (d) **Timber Resource:** There are 28,356 acres inventoried as tentatively suitable for timber harvest. This includes 1,518 acres of riparian old growth and 26,599 acres of non-riparian old growth None of the area is second growth.

      (e) **Land Use Authorizations:** None

      (f) **Minerals:** There are no inventoried areas with high mineral development potential in the area.

      (g) **Areas of Scientific Interest:** The area contains no inventoried potential Research Natural Areas and has not been identified for any other scientific value.

   (2) **Management Considerations**

      (a) Long-term timber sales may result in increased roading of Kuiu Island, which may provide additional access to the Rocky Pass Roadless Area. Continued development of road system south of Kake would parallel Rocky Pass and could make future management of the area in primitive settings more challenging.

(b) Maintenance of the area in a roadless condition would be
beneficial to both Camden and South Kupreanof Roadless Areas   To the
south and east are the Tebenkof Bay Wilderness, and East and South
Kuiu Roadless Areas   Some of the East Kuiu area may incur road
construction and timber harvesting in the next one to two years

(c) Fire: The area has no significant fire history

(d) Insects and Disease: Endemic tree diseases common to Southeast
Alaska are present; there are no know epidemic disease occurrences

(e) Land Status: The State has selected 605 acres on High Island

d. Relationship to Communities and Other Roadless and Wilderness Areas

(1) **Nearby Roadless and Wilderness Areas and Uses:** This area adjoins the
Port Camden and South Kupreanof Roadless Areas. Other roadless areas are
contiguous to these, including the Tebenkof Bay Wilderness to the west, and
the Petersburg Creek-Duncan Salt Chuck Wilderness to the east   Use in all
of these areas is generally light.

(2) **Distance From Population Centers (Accessibility):** Approximate
distances from population centers are as follows:

Community		Air Miles	Water Miles
Juneau	(Pop. 23,729)	120	143
Petersburg	(Pop. 4,040)	30	70
Wrangell	(Pop. 2,836)	70	75
Ketchikan	(Pop. 12,705)	145	175

Kake and Petersburg are the nearest stops on the Alaska Marine Highway

(3) **Interest by Proponents:**

(a) **Moratorium areas:** The area has been identified as a "moratorium"
area in legislative initiatives.

(b) **Local users/residents:** Residents of Kake have a cultural,
traditional interest in the Rocky Pass area. Recreationists from
Wrangell and Petersburg frequent the area.

e. Environmental Consequences

ALTERNATIVE ANALYSIS TO BE DONE LATER

INDIVIDUAL ROADLESS AREA DESCRIPTION

NAME: Pillars (244)   ACRES (GROSS): 28,610   ACRES (NFS): 28,570

GEOZONE: S01
GEOGRAPHIC PROVINCE: Central Interior Islands

1989 WILDERNESS ATTRIBUTE RATING: 25

a. Description

(1) **Relationship to RARE II areas:** The table below displays the VCU 1/
names, VCU numbers, original WARS 2/ rating, and comments. This enables
the reader to compare the roadless areas evaluated in Appendix C with
previous analyses.

VCU Name	VCU No.	1979 WARS Rating	Comments
Rowan Bay	402*	21	
Pillar	403*	23	
Camden	420*	--	Not rated in 1979

*--The roadless area includes only part of this VCU.

(2) **History:** The Bay of Pillars area was claimed by the Kake Tlingit
Evidence of their use include the remains of a village site, garden areas,
a portage trail, temporary camps, and bark-stripped trees A cannery
operated at Pillar Bay from about 1930 to 1950, and employed Native people
from Kake and Port Camden Several fox farms were located on the islands
during the 1940's, all of which are abandoned, as is the cannery Other
historic sites include a salmon hatchery, trapping cabins, and temporary
camps. There is some evidence of previous habitation or use, such as beach
logged areas, at the inner bay. A logging camp was developed at nearby
Rowan Bay in about 1973 and is still active with up to 130 seasonal
occupants. Forest Road 6402, which is the north boundary of the area, was
constructed in 1980 to haul logs to Rowan Bay

1/ A VCU (Value Comparison Unit) is one of 867 watersheds which make up the
Forest and were differentiated for planning purposes in the Tongass Land
Management Plan.
2/ Wilderness Attribute Rating System (WARS) was the nationwide system used to
rate the wilderness attributes of roadless areas in the Roadless Area
Review and Evaluation (RARE II).

(3) Location and Access: The Bay of Pillars area is located on the west side of Kuiu Island bordering Chatham Strait. It abuts the Tebenkof Bay Wilderness to the south It is accessed primarily by water from Pillar Bay and the portage trail from Port Camden, and by air. Anchorages are available at several points in both the outer and inner bays, and both the inner and outer bays have accessible shorelines suitable for landing small craft Floatplane landing is possible on the inner bay and Kutlaku Lake, there are no sites suitable for landing wheeled aircraft There is no ferry service to Kuiu Island. Access is possible by road and boat from Rowan Bay for local residents of the Rowan Bay logging camp There is a regularly scheduled mail flight to Rowan Bay, but there are no visitor services such as rental vehicles or boats.

(4) Geography and Topography: The Bay of Pillars area is characterized by a large, open bay with numerous small islands, and a large inner bay connected to the outer bay by a narrow, rocky, but navigable channel The inner and outer bays are surrounded by peaks and ridges which average about 1,800 feet; some peaks reach over 3,000 feet. The outer bay is subject to occasional strong wave action. Kutlaku Lake is a major feature accessed from the south arm of the inner bay The area contains 42 miles of shoreline on saltwater. Alpine covers 1,135 acres and rock another 1,035 acres. The lakes account for 199 acres, and small islands another 776 acres.

(5) Ecosystem:

   (a) Classification: This area is in the Central Interior Islands Geographic Province This province is generally characterized by rolling, subdued topography and extensive muskeg areas, but may have localized, rugged terrain. The area is part of the Kupreanof Lowlands physiographic region, which is typical of Mitkof, Kupreanof and Kuiu Islands This region is noted for its rolling terrain, glacial outwash character underlain by limestone. The area also includes some 20 small islands and exposed rocks which, along with the seven miles of tidal shoreline, is typical of the exposed, moderate-energy shoreline facing west and south along major waterways There are no known areas of unique or uncommon plant/soils associations or geologic formations in the area.

   (b) Vegetation: The area is heavily covered by spruce and hemlock to an elevation of 2,000 feet. There is relatively little interspersed muskeg (100 acres)

There are approximately 24,568 acres of forested land of which 20,586 acres are commercial forest land. Of the commercial forest land, 18,556 acres are non-riparian old growth and 1,712 acres are riparian old growth.

   (c) Soils: Bedrock types are non-calcareous sedimentary rocks, such as mudstone, sandstones and graywackes. Bedrock generally weathers to silty or loamy texture soils This geographic area, the Sedimentary Hills, comprises one of the most productive forest areas on Kuiu Island.

Soils in this area are formed in a wide variety of parent material,
including bedrock and glacial drift. In general, well- or
moderately-well-drained soils are on moderate to steep mountain slopes
with permeable parent materials. These soils are very acidic, have
cold soil temperatures, and are very high in organic matter Rooting
is largely limited to the surface organic layers and the top few
inches of mineral soil These soils are usually moist, sometimes wet,
but are never dry

More-poorly-drained soils developed on less-sloping areas and/or areas
with impermeable soil materials These soils have deep accumulations
of organic matter and range from scrubby forested wetlands to open
muskeg.

Alpine soils, generally above 2,000 feet elevation, are mostly
shallow, very wet organic soils or are extremely shallow and rocky

(d) Fish Resource: Six ADF&G numbered salmon producing streams are
within the area. The most important are Katlaku and Kwatahein
Creeks. Kutlaku has an annual average peak escapement of 1,200
sockeye, 16,800 pink, and 200 chum. Kwatahein has an annual average
escapement of 3,900 pink and good runs of coho and steelhead.
Subsistence fishermen, mostly from Kake, harvest sockeye at the mouth
of Katlaku, and sport anglers are beginning to fish steelhead in
Kwatahein. Kutlaku Lake contains cutthroat trout and Dolly Varden
char.

Fish resources have been rated as part of the Tongass Land Management
Plan (1978) and by the Alaska Department of Fish and Game in its
Forest Habitat Integrity Program (1983) These ratings describe the
value of VCU's for sport fish, commercial fish and estuaries

One VCU, 403, is rated as high value for sport fish. VCU's rated as
highly valued for commercial fish are 403 and 420

(e) Wildlife Resource: Habitat for black bear, deer, furbearers,
land birds and waterfowl is highly valued in the Pillars area This
area has been identified as an important wintering area and migration
resting area for waterfowl. There are no known concentrations of
marine wildlife or sea lion haul-out sites. A large black bear
population on Kuiu Island attracts numerous hunters to this area

(f) Threatened and Endangered Species: The area contains no known
threatened or endangered species

(6) Current Use and Management: All of the area was allocated to LUD 2 in
the Tongass Land Management Plan, however few Forest Service management
activities have occurred in the area The outer bay is frequently used as
an anchorage by commercial fishermen. Personal resource use by logging
camp residents occurs in the vicinity of Rowan Bay. Some of this resource
use occurs within the Pillars Roadless Area Boating and sport fishing are
popular. Lack of cabins or commercial overnight facilities limits use by
fly-in recreationists The Bay of Pillars Portage Trail connects the inner
bay with Port Camden This one mile canoe/kayak route receives light

recreational use, but use is increasing slowly since its establishment a few years back. The area, especially Katlaku Creek, is used heavily for subsistence by Kake residents

(7) **Appearance (Apparent Naturalness):** The area appears unmodified except for the remains of an abandoned cannery on the south side of the outer bay   Two clearcuts outside the area are visible from portions of the surface of the inner bay   To the west, the steep-sided bays frame views of islands and trees in the foreground, with Baranof Island's snowcapped peaks in the background   The enclosed nature of the area tends to minimize views of modified areas outside the roadless area   The area is not visible from present ferry and cruiseship routes

The majority of this roadless area (97 percent) is natural appearing, where only ecological change has occurred (Existing Visual Condition (EVC) Type I). Less than one percent of the area appears to be untouched by human activity (EVC Type II). One percent of this roadless area is EVC Type III, where changes in the landscape are noticed by the average forest visitor   The natural appearance of the landscape remains dominant. One-half percent of the area is in EVC Type IV, where changes in the landscape are easily noticed by the average person and may attract some attention. They appear to be disturbances but resemble natural patterns. Less than one percent is in EVC Type V where changes in the landscape are obvious to the average person, and appear to be major disturbances.

Twenty-two percent of this roadless area is inventoried Variety Class A (possessing landscape diversity that is unique for the character type), 53 percent is inventoried Variety Class B (possessing landscape diversity that is common for the character type), and the remaining 25 percent is inventoried Variety Class C (possessing a low degree of landscape diversity)

(8) **Surroundings (External Influences):** The region north of the Bay of Pillars area is heavily modified by past and present timber harvest activities centered around Rowan Bay   Forest Road 6402, extending southeast from Rowan Bay, (the Isthmus Road) was constructed in about 1980, and skirts the north side of the inner bay. Traffic noise is apparent in the bay when the road is in use   Visually, however, the road is mostly screened. Other modifications on lands to the north will likely occur under current management direction as the area is in LUD 4 and subject to long-term timber contracts.

(9) **Attractions and Features of Special Interest:** The area contains 10 inventoried recreation places totaling 11,568 acres. These recreation places include Kutlaku Lake, the Cannery site, and the inner bay   Fishing opportunity on Kwatahein Creek is an important attraction for recreation   The presence of good anchorage sites attracts boating use to the inner bay. A canoe/kayak portage trail connects the Inner Bay to Port Camden (uninhabited) on the east coast of Kuiu Island. Rocky pillar formations can be found in the bay   The tidal rip between the inner and outer bay is noted for producing whitewater wave action, a thrill for canoeists and kayakers

b. Capability of Management as Wilderness or in an Unroaded Condition

(1) **Manageability and management area boundaries:** The area is relatively
enclosed by topographic divides and feasibility of management in a roadless
condition is high   Forest Road 6402 comes to within a few hundred feet
distance of the Inner Bay and has reduced the manageability of the area in
a primitive setting   Development of private land on the cannery site could
influence future management

(2) **Natural Integrity:** The area is essentially unmodified   Evidence of
old structures include several abandoned fox farms on islands in the outer
bay, and the cannery site   The Pillar Bay-Port Camden Trail has a minor
impact on the area's natural integrity. The road on the north side of the
inner bay has also impacted the area's natural integrity.

(3) **Opportunity for Solitude:** There is a high opportunity for solitude
within the area   At times, use of floatplanes and powerboats may disrupt
visitors for brief periods. Noise from logging trucks on the adjacent road
is audible during periods of harvest activity. Present recreation use
levels are low, and generally a person camped in either the inner or outer
bay is unlikely to see others.

(4) **Opportunity for Primitive Recreation:** The area provides primarily
primitive, and semi-primitive motorized recreation opportunities.

ROS Class	Acres
Primitive (P)	22,358
Semi-Primitive Motorized (SPM)	4,718
Roaded Natural (RN)	60
Roaded Modified (RM)	1,434

The area contains ten recreation places.

ROS CLASS	# OF REC. PLACES	TOTAL ACRES	CAPACITY BY RVD
P	5	8,222	1,870
SPM	2	2,210	1,126
RN	1	60	43
RM	2	1,076	992

There are no developed recreation facilities except for the canoe portage
trail. The enclosed character of the water features in the area generally
allows the visitor to feel remote from the sights and sounds of human
activity. Access by boat into the area requires extended boating time in
exposed waters, and entering the Inner Bay requires boating skill and may
present great risk. The presence of black bears also presents a degree of
challenge and a need for woods skills and experience.

(5) **Special Features (Ecologic, Geologic, Scientific, Cultural):** The
abandoned cannery site attracts some visitors   Sockeye salmon spawning in
Kutlaku Lake are a seasonal, ecologic feature. The enclosed setting of the
bay and the rocky pillar formations are also attractions

c. Availability for Management as Wilderness or in an Unroaded Condition

   (1) Resource Potentials

      (a) Recreation Potential: A potential trail corridor exists from saltwater to Kutlaku Lake Potential sites exist at Kutlaku Creek for one or more recreation cabins or shelters. There is potential for additional outfitter and guide permits A potential shelter location has been identified to provide safe to kayakers traveling between this area and the Tebenkof Bay Wilderness, through the open waters of Chatham Strait If a ferry route were established to Rowan Bay, there would be the potential for the construction of a boat launch directly into the inner bay from existing roads This would open up other recreation opportunities.

      (b) Fish Resource: Fisheries enhancement at Kwatahein Creek occurred in 1989 with construction of a fish ladder to make the upper watershed accessible to pink and chum salmon.

      (c) Wildlife Resource: As identified in the Tongass Land Management Plan, amended 1985-86, deer habitat improvement projects are planned in the area.

      (d) Timber Resource: There are 16,684 acres inventoried as tentatively suitable. This includes 1,334 acres of riparian old growth, and 15,250 acres of non-riparian old growth Very little of the area is second growth. Small patches of second growth exist near the cannery site where pilings and fuel were obtained from 1930-1950. and near Katlaku Creek

      (e) Land Use Authorizations: Two electronics sites are located adjacent to or just within the roadless area.

      (f) Minerals: There are no inventoried areas with high mineral development potential in this roadless area.

      (g) Areas of Scientific Interest: The area contains no inventoried potential Research Natural Areas, and has not been identified for any other scientific value.

   (2) Management Considerations

      (a) Long-term timber sales on Kuiu Island may increase road access on Kuiu Island, and in particular to the Bay of Pillars area

      (b) Maintenance of the area in a roadless condition enhances management of the adjacent Tebenkof Bay Wilderness. It would provide enhanced opportunities for solitude and primitive recreation in the Wilderness and in the general area.

      (c) Fire: The area has no significant fire history

      (d) Insects and Disease: Endemic tree diseases common to Southeast Alaska are present, there are no know epidemic disease occurrences

    (e) Land Status: There are 80 acres of private land within the area. This site contains the remains of a cannery abandoned in about 1950.

d. Relationship to Communities and Other Roadless and Wilderness Areas

    (1) Nearby Roadless and Wilderness Areas and Uses: The Tebenkof Bay Wilderness is adjacent to the southern boundary of the Pillar Roadless Area. The Port Camden Roadless Area is just across Forest Road 6402 to the north. South Baranof Wilderness is across Chatham Strait about 10 miles to the west. These areas receive light use.

    (2) Distance From Population Centers (Accessibility): Approximate distances from population centers are as follows:

Community		Air Miles	Water Miles
Juneau	(Pop. 23,729)	110	148
Petersburg	(Pop. 4 040)	56	100
Wrangell	(Pop. 2,836)	72	145
Ketchikan	(Pop. 12,705)	130	170

Kake, Petersburg, and Wrangell are the nearest stops on the Alaska Marine Highway.

    (3) Interest by Proponents:

        (a) Moratorium areas: The area has been identified as a "moratorium" area and has been proposed as Wilderness in legislative initiatives.

        (b) Local users/residents: There is strong interest on the part of inhabitants of some local communities to retain the roadless character of unroaded parts of Kuiu Island.

e. Environmental Consequences

    ALTERNATIVE ANALYSIS TO BE DONE LATER

INDIVIDUAL ROADLESS AREA DESCRIPTION

NAME: East Kuiu (245)   ACRES (GROSS): 46,271   ACRES (NFS): 46,271

GEOZONE: S01
GEOGRAPHIC PROVINCE: Southern Outer Islands

1989 WILDERNESS ATTRIBUTE RATING: 26

a   Description

(1) Relationship to RARE II areas: The table below displays the VCU 1/
names, VCU numbers, original WARS 2/ rating, and comments This enables
the reader to compare the roadless areas evaluated in Appendix C with
previous analyses

VCU Name	VCU No.	1979 WARS Rating	Comments
Alvin Bay	416	21	
No Name Bay	417	20	Scheduled for roading in Supplemental EIS
Seclusion Hbr.	418	24	Scheduled for roading in Supplemental EIS
Three Mile Arm	419*	22	Partially roaded VCU

*--The roadless area include's only part of this VCU

(2) History: The area was used by both the Kake and Kuiu Tlingits Few
cultural resource inventories have been conducted Recorded sites include
temporary camps, garden areas, fish weirs and petroglyphs In 1793,
Captain Vancouver's ended his first explorations in Southeast Alaska at
Conclusion Island Historic uses of the area included fox farming, and
trapping. This area has been part of the Alaska Pulp Corporation long-term
timber sale area since 1960. A logging camp was developed at nearby Rowan
Bay which still active, having up to 130 seasonal occupants Road
development has occurred to the north, along the southern shore of
Threemile Arm. Forest Road 6402 interconnects Rowan Bay across the
isthmus to Port Camden and Threemile Arm, primarily for hauling logs to the
log transfer facility in Rowan Bay The road was constructed in 1986

1/ A VCU (Value Comparison Unit) is one of 867 watersheds which make up the
Forest and were differentiated for planning purposes in the Tongass Land
Management Plan.
2/ Wilderness Attribute Rating System (WARS) was the nationwide system used to
rate the wilderness attributes of roadless areas in the Roadless Area
Review and Evaluation (RARE II).

(3) Location and Access: East Kuiu Roadless Area lies directly east of
the Tebenkof Bay Wilderness on Kuiu Island, and borders Keku Strait It is
accessed primarily by saltwater via boat or by floatplane Several good
anchorages can be found in Reid, Alvin, and No Name Bays, as well as at the
head of Seclusion Harbor There are no sites suitable for landing wheeled
aircraft There is no ferry service to Kuiu Island. There is a regularly
scheduled mail flight to Rowan Bay, but there are no visitor services such
as rental vehicles or boats

(4) Geography and Topography: Landforms along this area are characterized
by gently-rolling hills that are typically short, extremely broken and
benched, making development of a road system challenging Steeper slopes
are forested, intermixed with scrub timber on gently-sloping hills and
benches. The area contains 91 miles of shoreline on saltwater Small
islands make up 3,791 acres and lakes account for 220 acres Alpine covers
about 600 acres, ice and snow 80 acres, and rock another 439 acres.

(5) Ecosystem:

    (a) Classification: The area is in the Southern Outer Islands
    Geographic Province This province is generally characterized by
    rolling, subdued topography, and localized, rugged terrain Highly
    productive forests are often found in this province, especially on
    limestone and marble soils derived form ancient coral reefs

    (b) Vegetation: Muskeg/scrub timber complexes (100 acres) are
    interspersed with mixed conifer plant communities on better-drained
    sites. Timbered hill slopes are dominantly western hemlock, Sitka
    spruce, and Alaska-cedar plant communities.

    There are approximately 43,973 acres of forested land of which 31,288
    acres are commercial forest land. Of the commercial forest land,
    26,895 acres are non-riparian old growth and 3,035 acres are riparian
    old growth

    (c) Soils: Soils in this area are formed in a wide variety of parent
    material, including bedrock and glacial drift In general, well- or
    moderately-well-drained soils are on moderate to steep mountain slopes
    with permeable parent materials These soils are very acidic, have
    cold soil temperatures, and are very high in organic matter Rooting
    is largely limited to the surface organic layers and the top few
    inches of mineral soil These soils are usually moist, sometimes wet,
    but are never dry

    More-poorly-drained soils developed on less-sloping areas and/or areas
    with impermeable soil materials These soils have deep accumulations
    of organic matter and range from scrubby forested wetlands to open
    muskeg.

    Alpine soils, generally above 2,000 feet elevation, are mostly
    shallow, very wet organic soils or are extremely shallow and rocky

(d) **Fish Resource:** This area has 16 ADF&G numbered salmon producing
streams. It is know to produce coho, pink, and chum salmon. The best
producer may be the stream at the head of Seclusion Harbor with
average annual peak escapements of 4,700 pink salmon Generally, the
area does not produce large numbers of salmon, and sport fishing
pressure is low.

Fish resources have been rated as part of the Tongass Land Management
Plan (1978) and by the Alaska Department of Fish and Game in its
Forest Habitat Integrity Program (1983) These ratings describe the
value of VCU's for sport fish, commercial fish and estuaries

VCU 419 was rated as highly valued for commercial fish VCU's rated
as having highly valued estuaries include 416, 417, 418, 419

(e) **Wildlife Resource:** Salt Lagoon-Seclusion Harbor has a unique
combination of freshwater and saltwater, making it valuable habitat
for waterfowl, black bear, furbearers, marine mammals and bald
eagles. This is also true for estuarine habitat found in Alvin Bay,
Reid Bay and at the head of Threemile Arm.

(f) **Threatened and Endangered Species:** The area contains no known
threatened or endangered species.

(6) **Current Use and Management:** The majority of the area (44,512 acres)
was allocated to Land Use Designation (LUD) 4 in the Tongass Land
Management Plan, however few management activities have occurred within the
area. The Supplemental EIS for the 1981-90 operating plan has identified
road construction into No Name Bay (through VCU 418 and 417) in one of the
alternatives, from Threemile Arm A small portion of the area is LUD 1
release (1,751 acres) to allow for transportation system development The
Alecks Creek Portage Trail is four miles long and connects the Tebenkof Bay
Wilderness to Keku Straits on the other side of the island This allows
passage by canoes and kayaks in relatively sheltered waters There is also
evidence of past beach logging in the area. A Forest Service radio
repeater site is also present.

(7) **Appearance (Apparent Naturalness):** Most of the area appears
unmodified from major travel routes in Keku Straight and Sumner Strait,
with the exception of areas beach logged in the 1960's

The majority of this roadless area (88 percent) is natural appearing, where
only ecological change has occurred (Existing Visual Condition (EVC)
Type I). Less then one percent of the area appears to be untouched by
human activity (EVC Type II). About one percent of the area is in EVC
Type IV, where changes in the landscape are easily noticed by the average
person and may attract some attention. They appear to be disturbances but
resemble natural patterns Eleven percent is in EVC Type V where changes
in the landscape are obvious to the average person, and appear to be major
disturbances.

Ten percent of this roadless area is inventoried Variety Class A
(possessing landscape diversity that is unique for the character type), 76
percent is inventoried Variety Class B (possessing landscape diversity that
is common for the character type), and the remaining 14 percent is
inventoried Variety Class C (possessing a low degree of landscape
diversity).

(8) **Surroundings (External Influences):** Adjacent and to the west of the
East Kuiu Roadless Area is the Tebenkof Bay Wilderness area   To the south,
no management activities have been initiated; but to the north road
construction and timber harvesting have been extensive   Forest Road 6402
which connects Rowan Bay through the isthmus to Port Camden and Threemile
Arm, was constructed about 1986. It will continue to serve as a major
access route for hauling logs, and has the potential to be extended into No
Name Bay. Timber harvest on lands adjacent to this route will continue to
occur under current management direction.

(9) **Attractions and Features of Special Interest:** The area includes all
of Alvin, Reid and No Name Bays, and Seclusion Harbor. Attractions in this
area include the south-facing sand beaches in Reid and Alvin Bays, and the
Alecks Creek portage trail which connects No Name Bay with the Tebenkof
Wilderness. There is a total of four miles of improved trail in the area
The presence of good anchorage sites within each of the bays and in
Seclusion Harbor allows visitors to "boat camp" overnight. Seclusion
Harbor-Salt Lagoon is a known sport fishing area for pink and chum salmon
The area contains 14 inventoried recreation places totaling 13,880 acres

b. **Capability of Management as Wilderness or in an Unroaded Condition**

(1) **Manageability and Management Area Boundaries:** The northern boundary
is the roaded portion of Threemile Arm, the western boundary is Tebenkof
Bay Wilderness, and the eastern boundary consists of Keku and Sumner
Straits. South Kuiu Roadless Area is to the south. The alternatives
designed in the Supplemental EIS for the 1986-90 operating period identify
continued roading and harvesting, possibly into Salt Lagoon and No Name
Bay.

(2) **Natural Integrity:** The majority of the area is essentially
unmodified. Some evidence of past occupancy is present at the abandoned
fox farms on islands in this area, as well as past beach logging

(3) **Opportunity for Solitude:** There is a high opportunity for solitude in
the East Kuiu Roadless Area. Use of floatplanes and powerboats may disrupt
visitors for brief periods. Present recreation use levels are low
Persons camped along the shore are generally unlikely to encounter other
recreationists, but may see or be seen by the occasional fishing boat
offshore.

(4) Opportunity for Primitive Recreation: The area provides primarily primitive recreation opportunity

ROS Class	Acres
Primitive (P)	36,397
Semi Primitive Non-Motorized (SPNM)	2,440
Roaded Modified (RM)	7,434

The area contains 14 recreation places

ROS CLASS	# OF REC. PLACES	TOTAL ACRES	CAPACITY BY RVD
P	6	8,086	2,670
RM	8	5,795	9,560.

There are no developed recreation facilities. The Alecks Creek Trail allows the visitors the opportunity to enter the Tebenkof Wilderness from the east side of Kuiu Island, affording extended canoe and kayak opportunities

(5) Special Features (Ecologic, Geologic, Scientific, Cultural): The south-facing sand beaches found in Reid and Alvin Bays are unusual for southeast Alaska, and provide for good beach combing and picnicking Sport fishing, and bear hunting occur throughout the area

c. Availability for Management as Wilderness or in an Unroaded Condition

(1) Resource Potentials

(a) Recreation Potential: Recreation potential for East Kuiu is moderate. A potential recreation cabin site has been identified at the head of the Salt Lagoon. There is potential for additional outfitter and guide permits.

(b) Fish Resource: No fish habitat enhancement projects are identified for this area in the Tongass Land Management Plan, amended Winter 1985-86

(c) Wildlife Resource: The Tongass Land Management Plan, amended 1985-86 did not identify any habitat improvement projects in the area

(d) Timber Resource: There are 23,880 acres inventoried as tentatively suitable for timber harvest. This includes 2,117 acres of riparian old growth, and 20,705 acres of non-riparian old growth Some of the area is second growth; such as small patches along the shores in Reid Bay, No Name Bay, and Alvin Bay that were beach logged in the 1960's.

(e) Land Use Authorizations: None.

(f) Minerals: There are no inventoried areas with high mineral development potential in the area.

(g) Areas of Scientific Interest: The area contains no inventoried potential Research Natural Areas and has not been identified for any other scientific value

(2) Management Considerations

(a) Long-term timber sales on Kuiu Island may result in increased road development on Kuiu Island, which may increase access to portions of the East Kuiu Roadless Area

(b) Maintenance of the area in a roadless condition would have a beneficial effect on the adjacent Tebenkof Bay Wilderness and South Kuiu Roadless Area by maintaining primitive recreation settings

(c) Fire: The area has no significant fire history.

(d) Insects and Disease: Endemic tree diseases common to Southeast Alaska are present; there are no know epidemic disease occurrences

(e) Land Status: No Name Bay is a proposed State land selection

d. Relationship to Communities and Other Roadless and Wilderness Areas

(1) Nearby Roadless and Wilderness Areas and Uses: This area adjoins the Tebenkof Bay Wilderness on the west, and South Kuiu Roadless Area to the south. These areas receive light recreational use

(2) Distance From Population Centers (Accessibility): Approximate distances from population centers are as follows:

Community		Air Miles	Water Miles
Juneau	(Pop. 23,729)	110	150
Petersburg	(Pop 4,040)	56	75
Wrangell	(Pop 2,836)	72	135
Ketchikan	(Pop. 12,705)	130	160

Kake and Petersburg are the nearest stops on the Alaska Marine Highway

(3) Interest by Proponents:

(a) Moratorium areas: The area has been identified as a "moratorium" area for Wilderness consideration in recent legislative initiatives.

(b) Local users/residents: Residents of Point Baker/Port Protection use the area for subsistence crabbing and shellfish harvesting There is a fair level of public resistance to developing a road system into No Name Bay

e. Environmental Consequences
   ALTERNATIVE ANALYSIS TO BE DONE LATER

INDIVIDUAL ROADLESS AREA DESCRIPTION

NAME: South Kuiu (246)   ACRES (GROSS): 124,085   ACRES (NFS): 124,065

GEOZONE: S02
GEOGRAPHIC PROVINCE: Southern Outer Islands

1989 WILDERNESS ATTRIBUTE RATING: 28

a. Description

    (1) Relationship to RARE II areas: The table below displays the VCU 1/
names, VCU numbers, original WARS 2/ rating, and comments. This enables
the reader to compare the roadless areas evaluated in Appendix C with
previous analyses

VCU Name	VCU No.	1979 WARS Rating	Comments
Malmesbury	408	27	
Bear	409	27	
Table	410	23	
Kell	411	27	
McArthur	412	22	
Affleck	413	21	
Amelius	414	22	
Beauclerc	415	27	

    *--The roadless area includes only part of this VCU

    (2) History: The area was claimed by the Kuiu Tlingit who eventually
settled in Klawock. Evidence of former occupation includes remains of
villages, fort sites, cave shelters, temporary camps, fish weirs, and
petroglyphs. Historic period sites include a saltery in Port Malmesbury, a
cannery in Kell Bay, a few fox farms, temporary camps, and remains of Coast
Guard occupancy when the lighthouse at the southern end of the roadless
area was still manned

    (3) Location and Access: South Kuiu Roadless Area is directly south of
the Tebenkof Bay Wilderness area on Kuiu Island, and borders on Chatham and
Sumner Straits. It is accessed primarily by saltwater via boat or by
floatplane. Several good anchorages can be found in the numerous bays and
inlets. There are no sites suitable for landing wheeled aircraft There is
no ferry service to Kuiu Island. There is a regularly scheduled mail
flight to Rowan Bay, but there are no visitor services such as rental
vehicles or boats.

1/ A VCU (Value Comparison Unit) is one of 867 watersheds which make up the
    Forest and were differentiated for planning purposes in the Tongass Land
    Management Plan.
2/ Wilderness Attribute Rating System (WARS) was the nationwide system used to
    rate the wilderness attributes of roadless areas in the Roadless Area
    Review and Evaluation (RARE II).

(4) Geography and Topography: Landforms within this area are varied and represent all geomorphic types found on Kuiu Island Gently-rolling hills that are typically short, extremely broken and benched, are in stark contrast to the sharply-rising, heavily-dissected mountain slopes at the head of Port Malmesbury and Crowley Bight. Deep islets and broken terrain make development of a road system, which would interconnect bays and islets to a primary log transfer facility, challenging and unfeasible The area contains 226 miles of shoreline on saltwater. Islands make up 1,238 acres, lakes 703 acres, alpine 381 acres, and rock 1,445 acres.

(5) Ecosystem:

(a) Classification: The area is in the Southern Outer Islands Geographic Province. This province is generally characterized by rolling, subdued topography, but may have localized, rugged terrain This area displays much greater relief and landform variety than is typical of the region

(b) Vegetation: Muskeg/scrub timber complexes (320 acres) cover a good portion of the South Kuiu Roadless Area. Ridges of mixed conifer plant communities are interspersed on better drained sites Timbered hill slopes are dominantly Sitka spruce/western hemlock, and more-poorly-drained slopes consist of western hemlock/Alaska-cedar plant communities.

There are approximately 118,364 acres of forested land of which 76,929 acres are commercial forest land. Of the commercial forest land, 68,670 acres are non-riparian old growth and 6,774 acres are riparian old growth.

(c) Soils: Soils in this area are formed in a wide variety of parent material, including bedrock and glacial drift. In general, well- or moderately-well-drained soils are on moderate to steep mountain slopes with permeable parent materials. These soils are very acidic, have cold soil temperatures, and are very high in organic matter Rooting is largely limited to the surface organic layers and the top few inches of mineral soil. These soils are usually moist, sometimes wet but are never dry.

More-poorly-drained soils developed on less-sloping areas and/or areas with impermeable soil materials. These soils have deep accumulations of organic matter and range from scrubby forested wetlands to open muskeg.

Alpine soils, generally above 2,000 feet elevation, are mostly shallow, very wet organic soils or are extremely shallow and rocky

(d) Fish Resource: This large area has 34 ADF&G numbered salmon producing streams. In general the area is a good producer of anadromous fish Two of the best known streams are at the head of Bear Harbor and Kell Bay. Bear Harbor Creek has an annual average peak escapement of 33,200 pink salmon Kell Bay Creek has an escapement of 21,400 pink and 1,000 chum salmon. All the streams have runs of coho

Fish resources have been rated as part of the Tongass Land Management Plan (1978) and by the Alaska Department of Fish and Game in its Forest Habitat Integrity Program (1983). These ratings describe the value of VCU's for sport fish, commercial fish and estuaries

VCU 409 was rated as highly valued for commercial fish   VCU's rated as having highly valued estuaries include 409 and 412

(e) **Wildlife Resource:** The area displays the typical array of wildlife found on Kuiu Island, including black bears, deer, furbearers and waterfowl.

(f) **Threatened and Endangered Species:** The area contains no known threatened or endangered species.

(6) **Current Use and Management:** The area was allocated to Land Use Designation LUD 3 (83,814 acres), and LUD 4 (40,251 acres) in the Tongass Land Management Plan. No road development has occurred within the area In the past, some beach logging occurred in Port Malmesbury, along the Affleck Canal, and in Port Beauclerc. The Affleck Canal portage trail connects Petrof Bay in Tebenkof Bay Wilderness with Affleck Canal. This 1.5 mile route is difficult. The Coast Guard maintains navigation aids in the area, and once maintained an access trail for supplies

(7) **Appearance (Apparent Naturalness):** Most of the area appears unmodified from major travel routes in Keku Straight and Sumner Strait. with the exception of areas beach logged in the 1960's

The majority of this roadless area (97 percent) is natural appearing, where only ecological change has occurred (Existing Visual Condition (EVC) Type I). Two percent of the area appears to be untouched by human activity (EVC Type II). Less then one percent of this roadless area is EVC Type III, where changes in the landscape are noticed by the average forest visitor. The natural appearance of the landscape remains dominant

Six percent of this roadless area is inventoried Variety Class A (possessing landscape diversity that is unique for the character type), 87 percent is inventoried Variety Class B (possessing landscape diversity that is common for the character type) and the remaining seven percent is inventoried Variety Class C (possessing a low degree of landscape diversity).

(8) **Surroundings (External Influences):** Tebenkof Bay Wilderness and East Kuiu Roadless Areas lie north and adjacent to South Kuiu Roadless Area Occasional aircraft and marine traffic are present. The Affleck Canal portage trail provides access into the Tebenkof Wilderness from Affleck Canal.

(9) **Attractions and Features of Special Interest:** The area includes numerous bays and inlets, which provide many anchorages, and beach combing opportunities Sport fishing and a limited number of outfitter guides operate from within the roadless area. The area contains 12 inventoried recreation places totaling 26,684 acres There is a total of 1 5 miles of improved trail in the area. The presence of numerous anchorage sites throughout the area allows visitors to "boat camp" overnight

b. Capability of Management as Wilderness or in an Unroaded Condition

(1) **Manageability and Management Area Boundaries:** The northern boundary of the South Kuiu Roadless Area is formed by Tebenkof Wilderness and the East Kuiu Roadless Area. To the south, east and west, it is bordered by Sumner Strait and Chatham Strait. Due to the dissected terrain, it is highly unlikely for a road system to be developed or interconnected between this area and the remaining portions of Kuiu Island

(2) **Natural Integrity:** The area is essentially unmodified. Some evidence of past beach log harvest is visible.

(3) **Opportunity for Solitude:** There is a high opportunity for solitude in the South Kuiu Roadless Area. Use of floatplanes and powerboats may disrupt visitors for brief periods, but this occurrence is infrequent Present recreation use levels are low. Persons camped along the shore are generally unlikely to encounter other recreationists, but might be seen by or are able to see the occasional fishing boat offshore

(4) **Opportunity for Primitive Recreation:** The area provides primarily primitive and semi-primitive motorized recreation opportunity.

ROS Class	Acres
Primitive (P)	110,662
Semi-Primitive Motorized (SPM)	13,403

The area contains 12 recreation places

ROS CLASS	# OF REC. PLACES	TOTAL ACRES	CAPACITY BY RVD
P	8	22,233	3,787
SPM	4	4,450	2,140

There are no developed recreation facilities. The Afflecks Creek Trail allows the visitors the opportunity to enter the Tebenkof Wilderness from the east side of Kuiu Island.

(5) **Special Features (Ecologic, Geologic, Scientific, Cultural):** The prime attraction in this area is the close proximity to the Tebenkof Wilderness area and the combined primitive settings of the Wilderness and the roadless area. The numerous bays, islets, and mountainous terrain provide ample opportunity for isolated, undeveloped forms of recreation

c. Availability for Management as Wilderness or in an Unroaded Condition

   (1) Resource Potentials

      (a) Recreation Potential: Recreation potential for South Kuiu is
      moderate   There is potential for additional outfitter and guide
      permits, trails, cabins and shelters

      (b) Fish Resource: No fish habitat enhancement projects are
      identified for this area in the Tongass Land Management Plan, amended
      Winter 1985-86   Fish enhancement projects continue to surface and
      there is potential for additional projects in this area

      (c) Wildlife Resource: As identified in the Tongass Land Management
      Plan, amended 1985-86, no habitat improvement projects are planned in
      the area.

      (d) Timber Resource: There are 54,469 acres inventoried as
      tentatively suitable for timber harvest. This includes 4,670 acres of
      riparian old growth, and 48,977 acres of non-riparian old growth
      Very little of this area is in second growth. Second growth is found
      only in small patches where beach logging previously occurred

      (e) Land Use Authorizations: A special use permit exists for a
      waterline.

      (f) Minerals: There are no inventoried areas with high mineral
      development potential in the area.

      (g) Areas of Scientific Interest: The area contains no inventoried
      potential Research Natural Areas and has not been identified for any
      other scientific value

   (2) Management Considerations

      (a) Long-term timber sales on Kuiu Island may result in increased
      road development on Kuiu Island which may increase access to
      individual bays of the South Kuiu Roadless Area

      (b) Maintenance of the area in a roadless condition would have aid in
      in maintaining the primitive settings on the adjacent Tebenkof Bay
      Wilderness and East Kuiu Roadless Area.

      (c) Fire: The area has no significant fire history.

      (d) Insects and Disease: Endemic tree diseases common to Southeast
      Alaska are present; there are no know epidemic disease occurrences

      (e) Land Status: All National Forest Systems land.

d. Relationship to Communities and Other Roadless and Wilderness Areas

   (1) Nearby Roadless and Wilderness Areas and Uses: This area adjoins the
   Tebenkof Bay Wilderness and East Kuiu roadless areas to the north These
   areas receive light recreational use

   (2) Distance From Population Centers (Accessibility): Approximate
   distances from population centers are as follows

Community			Air Miles	Water Miles
Juneau	(Pop	23,729)	145	170
Petersburg	(Pop	4,040)	55	65
Wrangell	(Pop.	2,836)	60	65
Ketchikan	(Pop.	12,705)	135	165

Kake and Petersburg are the nearest stops on the Alaska Marine Highway

   (3) Interest by Proponents:

      (a) Moratorium areas: The area has been identified as a "moratorium"
      area in current legislative proposals for consideration as Wilderness

      (b) Local users/residents: Residents of Point Baker/Port Protection
      use the area for subsistence crabbing and shellfish harvesting

e. Environmental Consequences ·

   ALTERNATIVE ANALYSIS TO BE DONE LATER

INDIVIDUAL ROADLESS AREA DESCRIPTION

NAME: Skagway-Juneau (301)   ACRES (GROSS): 1,209,259   ACRES (NFS): 1,209,199
            Icefield   .

GEOZONE. C23
GEOGRAPHIC PROVINCE: Lynn Canal and Coast Range

1989 WILDERNESS ATTRIBUTE RATING: 24

a. Description

    (1) Relationship to RARE II areas: The table below displays the VCU 1/
    names, VCU numbers, original WARS 2/ rating, and comments. This enables
    the reader to compare the roadless areas evaluated in Appendix C with
    previous analyses.

VCU Name	VCU No.	1979 WARS Rating	Comments
White Pass	001	--	Not rated in 1979.
Denver Glacier	002	22	
Skagway	003	19	
Kasidaya Creek	004	20	
Taiya	005	19	
Wishbone Gl.	006	22	
Mt. Bagot	007	22	
Dayebas Creek	008	20	
Meade Glacier	009	26	
Yeldagalga Cr.	010	22	
Sinclair Mt.	011	23	
Berners River	012	25	
Lace River	013	28	
Antler River	014	24	
Gilkey River	015	28	
Berners Bay	016	23	
W.Sinclair	018	20	
Kakuhan	019	20	
Comet	020	21	
Gilkey Glacier	021	25	
Taku Glacier	022	25	
Nugget Creek	030	21	
Ptarmigan Gl.	031	20	
Boundary Creek	049	23	

1/ A VCU (Value Comparison Unit) is one of 867 watersheds which make up the
    forest and were differentiated for planning purposes in the Tongass Land
    Management Plan.
2/ Wilderness Attribute Rating System (WARS) was the nation-wide system used
    to rate the wilderness attributes of roadless areas in the Roadless Area
    Review and Evaluation (RARE II).

(2) **History:**   Past uses on the Juneau Icefield include personal sporting
ventures and commercially guided ventures related to technical ice and rock
climbing, ski touring, photography, and camping. Commercial helicopter
landing tours and numerous fixed-wing craft conduct "flightseeing" tours
over the Icefield and glaciers   The Oceanographic Division of the U S
Army had conducted research on the Gilkey Glacier and its tributaries
Dr Maynard Miller has conducted glacial research through the Foundation of
Glacier Research across the entire Icefield for approximately forty years
and is continuing this research to date

The Berners Bay area has evidence of gold mining activities from the early
1900's, and several old farming homesteads   Two mines, the Kensington and
Jualin, have recently reopened. There are five people with cabins in the
Berners Bay area that are currently applying for authorization of those
cabins in the pre-ANILCA cabin program.

In the Denver Glacier Trail area, there is an old recreation residence
cabin that was under special use permit, but it is no longer being used

(3) **Location and Access:** The area is located on the Juneau mainland and
is bordered by the Canadian Border to the east and north, and by Lynn Canal
to the west. The southern boundary is defined by the southern edge of the
Juneau Icefield above the Taku River drainage. Access to this vast area is
by a variety of means. Railroad access is possible from Skagway north to
the border of the Yukon Territory, helicopter and airplane (both floatplane
and occasional ski and wheeled planes) are used to access many parts of the
area, and boats are used to access those portion of the roadless area
bordered by saltwater. There is a primitive landing strip at a public
recreation cabin near the Katzehin River.

Recreationists can also access portions of the area by foot from trails off
the Juneau Road System, particularly from above the Mendenhall Glacier and
from near the Lemon Creek area by Camp 17 of the Juneau Icefield Research
Project. Two trails provide access from the White Pass and Yukon Railroad
in Skagway.

The Alaska Marine Highway ferries provide access to the communities of
Juneau and Skagway but there are no stops within the roadless area   Lynn
Canal is considered a major travel route.

(4) **Geography and Topography:** The area is generally characterized by a
great variety of geological features with large, massive landforms
Uplands are generally 5,000 to 7,000 feet in elevation. The Juneau
Icefield is the predominant landform in this area along with the resultant
glaciers. In the Skagway area, the Icefield gives way to dramatic rock
mountains with deep, steep-walled, U-shaped valleys. Along Lynn Canal,
several tidewater glaciers tumble down to the saltwater between precipitous
cliffs and mountain walls   Hanging glaciers are the source of many
beautiful waterfalls. Ice and snow total 506,813 acres, and rock covers
263,858 acres of this roadless area. Another 5,434 acres are inventoried
as alpine environment, and 998 acres as muskeg. Freshwater lakes comprise
3,699 total acres   There are 60 miles of shoreline on saltwater

Major river systems in the area include the Skagway River; the Katzehin
River, and the Berners, Lace, Antler, and Gilkey Rivers flowing into
Berners Bay The Berners Bay area is characterized by these
moderately-large streams whose deltas form a broad intertidal flat and flow
into the shallow, sandy bay

(5) Ecosystem:

(a) Classification: The area is classified as being primarily in the
Lynn Canal Geographic Province which is generally characterized by
rugged, scoured terrain with large vertical relief This province is
the driest and one of the most continental environments in Southeast
Alaska. Extreme rain shadow from the Chilkat Mountains and St Elias
Range allows extensive development of fire-dependent forests
(lodgepole and birch), and the southern and westward extension of
boreal forest and tundra plant species. The southern portion of this
roadless area (approximately from the Taku and Lemon Glaciers south to
the Taku River) is in the Coast Range Geographic Province This
designation is characterized by rugged, heavily-glaciated terrain with
extensive alpine and ice field environments Productive forest land
is usually confined to river valleys and marine terraces

(b) Vegetation: For much of this area, vegetation is not present in
any form because of the Icefield. In areas that have been
deglaciated, the land is in various stages of plant colonization
Much of the vegetation occurs in valley bottoms and at lower
elevations Lush alpine meadows, western hemlock/Sitka spruce
forests, some cottonwood, birch and subalpine fir/mountain hemlock
forests are typical, depending on elevation.

There are approximately 131,826 acres of forested land of which 64,823
acres are commercial forest land. Of the commercial forest land,
9,724 acres are riparian old growth and 50,897 acres are non-riparian
old growth.

(c) Soils: The bare rock exposed on the east side of Lynn Canal is
metamorphic rock--slate, schist, and marble This rock type is
visible from Berners Bay north to Skagway Soils in the Skagway area
are characterized generally as being shallow to bedrock soils
primarily of organic and mineral origin, while those in the Berners
Bay area may range from well-developed, deep, colluvial soils on
moderate to steep slopes to poorly-drained, mineral and/or organic
soils on benches and moderate slopes. Occurrences of muskegs with
reduced productivity occur on these benches. The entire area has been
overridden by glaciers with a predominance of glacial materials
throughout but especially on mid to lower slopes.

(d) Fish Resource: Fish resources have been rated as part of the
Tongass Land Management Plan (1979) and by the Alaska Department of
Fish and Game in its Forest Habitat Integrity Program (1983) These
ratings describe the value of VCU's for sport fish, commercial fish,
and estuaries

Two VCU's were rated as having the highest value for sport fish in the
roadless area. These two VCU's are Berners River (VCU 12) and Gilkey
River (VCU 15). Berners River (VCU 12), Berners Bay (VCU 16), Nuggett
Creek (VCU 30), and Boundary Creek (VCU 49) were all rated highly for
commercial fish. There were no VCU's in this area inventoried as
having highly valued estuaries.

(e) Wildlife Resource: Populations of black and brown bear range
primarily at the lower elevations and in timbered river drainages.
Moose are also present, especially in the Berners Bay and Katzehin
drainages. Good mountain goat habitat and goat populations exist on
the steeper cliffs and mountains in the entire area. Populations of
wolf and wolverine also exist in the area. Portions of this roadless
area are important for migratory waterfowl.

(f) Threatened and Endangered Species: The area contains no known
threatened or endangered species, although it may receive some
migratory use from the peregrine falcon. The bald eagle, a protected
species, is found along the coastlines and river drainages.

(6) ·Current Use and Management: This entire roadless area was allocated
to Land Use Designation 2 in the Tongass Land Management Plan (1979) which
provides for management of the area in a roadless state to retain the
wildland character. This designation permits wildlife and fish habitat
improvement and primitive recreational facilities.

In 1987, a Decision Notice and Finding of No Significant Impact for the
Management Guidelines for Helicopter Landing Tours on the Juneau Icefield
was signed and issued by the Juneau Ranger District. These management
guidelines authorize helicopter landing tours in certain zones on the
Juneau Icefield at varying levels of use and disallow landing tours in
other zones. These management guidelines were only for helicopter landing
tours and did not serve to provide guidelines for flightseeing tours or
charter tours solely intended for point-to-point transportations.
Helicopter landing tours are also occurring out of Skagway on the Denver
Glacier.

Dr Maynard Miller continues his research on the Juneau Icefield through
the Foundation of Glacier Research.

A fish weir and tent camp site were recently authorized to Alaska
Department of Fish and Game, Commercial Fisheries Division, on the Berners
River.

Several trails provide direct access into the area. The Laughton Glacier
Trail (to Laughton Glacier Recreation Cabin) and the Denver Glacier Trail
are in the Skagway area; the Lemon Creek and Nugget Creek trails, and
Heintzleman Ridge Route are in the Juneau area. Most Icefield use occurs
in the Juneau area and is accessed by helicopter or by foot from the
Mendenhall Glacier or Lemon Glacier areas.

(7) **Appearance (Apparent Naturalness):** The vast majority of the Icefield's area appears unmodified and pristine except for the occasional camps of the Juneau Icefield Research Project. The Berners Bay area is essentially unmodified except for the adjacent mining operations at Kensington and Jualin, and the few well-screened cabins in the area

The visual character type of this roadless area is Coast Range   Scale of landforms are generally large, massive, and give an impression of great bulk   Uplands are generally 5,000 to 7,000 feet in elevation dissected by deep, steep-walled, U-shaped valleys. Mountain ridges are generally rounded summits but are surmounted, at times, by aretes and horns rising 8,000 to 9,000 feet

Fifty-five percent of this roadless area was inventoried in Variety Class A (possessing landscape diversity that is unique for the character type) with 44 percent in Variety Class B (possessing landscape diversity that is common for the character type)

Almost 100 percent of this area is in Existing Visual Condition (EVC) I, these areas appear to be untouched by human activity

(8) **Surroundings (External Influences):** Much of this vast area is comprised of the Juneau Icefield and receives little influence from external factors. The Juneau Icefield receives some visual and auditory impacts from flightseeing tours, regular aircraft travel routes and occasional helicopter charters   When on the Icefield, the only human influence would be primarily from air traffic or the infrequent camps of the Juneau Icefield Research Project.

Lynn Canal serves as a major travel corridor for flights, ferries, ships and boats but much of the immediate area along Lynn Canal is unavailable for much human activity because of the steepness of the terrain   The Katzehin public recreation cabin is accessed by wheeled aircraft on a primitive air strip near the Katzehin River. The Berners Bay area does receive a variety of uses - recreation, mining, boating, fish enhancement projects, and hunting to name a few

(9) **Attractions and Features of Special Interest:** The natural features of the area, the scenery, and the opportunity to see wildlife and to study the processes which formed this country may all be considered attractions   The Icefield and numerous glaciers offer unparalleled scenery and opportunities for mountaineering, skiing, ice and rock climbing, camping, and scenic viewing.

Fishing opportunities in the streams are a minor attraction   The area contains 21 inventoried recreation places totaling 151,420 acres   There are two improved trails and one public recreation cabin in the Skagway area

b. **Capability of Management as Wilderness or in an Unroaded Condition**

(1) **Manageability and management area boundaries** The area is well defined by international borders on two sides and the Lynn Canal on one side   Feasibility of management in a roadless condition is high

(2) **Natural Integrity:** The area is generally unmodified and natural, long-term ecological processes operate unimpeded. The two active mining claims adjacent to this roadless area in the Berners Bay area have potentially the greatest impact on modification of ecological systems of the surrounding area

(3) **Natural Appearance:** This roadless area is basically unmodified and so vast that the area is perceived to be pristine, natural, and free from disturbances of any kind The few recreation facilities in this area serve to focus use near those facilities

(4) **Opportunity for Solitude:** There is a great opportunity for solitude within the area.   Solitude may be affected by flight paths of small planes, jets or helicopters for short periods of time. When on the Icefield, the sense of solitude and remoteness can be dramatic Along the shoreline of Lynn Canal, one can expect to see frequent air and water traffic, including large ships such as cruiseships and the Alaska Marine Highway ferries. Within Berners Bay, there is less of a chance for solitude Recreational boaters and kayakers frequent the area, and there are two active mining claims on the north side of the bay. In the area north of Skagway, the terrain is such that it offers a high degree of solitude once one leaves the influence of the railroad tracks of the White Pass and Yukon Railroad.

(5) **Opportunity for Primitive Recreation:** The area provides primarily Primitive and Pristine recreation opportunities.

ROS Class	Acres
Pristine (P1)	392,259
Primitive (P2)	689,644
Semi-Primitive Non-Motorized (SPNM)	110,731
Semi-Primitive Motorized (SPM)	7,945
Roaded Natural (RN)	6,739

The area contains 21 recreation places.

ROS CLASS	# OF REC. PLACES	TOTAL ACRES	CAPACITY BY RVD
P1	2	85,570	19,389
P2	2	6,620	4,313
SPNM	9	49,224	28,216
SPM	2	5,427	12,624

There are two public recreation cabins in this roadless area - Laughton Glacier Cabin accessible by trail from the White Pass Railroad approximately 17 miles north of Skagway, and Katzehin Cabin near the Katzehin River/Lynn Canal area.

This roadless area offers unparalleled opportunity for dispersed recreation --viewing spectacular scenery, hiking, mountaineering, ski touring, hunting, and boating

(6) **Special Features (Ecologic, Geologic, Scientific, Cultural):** There
are opportunities to observe and study fish and wildlife and the various
forces which formed these mountains The glaciers and Icefield are the
most significant features Four Research Natural Areas have been
identified in this area because of the uniqueness and scientific values of
the ecosystems represented

c   Availability for Management as Wilderness or in an Unroaded Condition

(1) Resource Potentials

(a) **Recreation Potential:** The unique terrain, scenery, and wildlife
populations of this area provide unlimited recreation potential. The
Tongass Land Management Plan, amended Winter 1985-86 identifies
additional trails and cabins and shelters throughout the area
Interest has been expressed for heli-hiking opportunities

(b) **Fish Resource:** No fisheries habitat improvement opportunities
have been identified in the amended Tongass Land Management Plan,
1985-86.

(c) **Wildlife Resource:** Opportunities for both moose and swan habitat
enhancement were identified in the Berners Bay area in the amended
Tongass Land Management Plan, 1985-86.

(d) **Timber Resource:** There are 32,571 acres inventoried as
tentatively suitable for harvest. This includes 5,501 acres of
suitable riparian old growth and 24,829 acres of suitable non-riparian
old growth

(e) **Land Use Authorizations:** Currently, there are no long-term
special use permits issued for the area, although five people with
cabins in the Berners Bay area are applying for authorization
Occasionally, the topic of building a road from Juneau to the
"outside" road system of Skagway, Haines, or Canada resurfaces A
bill has been proposed in the Alaska State Legislature to fund an
environmental impact statement for analysis of proposals to construct
a road to Haines or up the Taku River Valley to Canada

(f) **Minerals:** The area generally has a low minerals rating except
for the Berners Bay area. That area has a high mineral development
potential, priority-one minerals rating, and two mines have currently
re-opened north of Berners Bay.

(g) **Areas of Scientific Interest:** This roadless area contains four
inventoried potential research natural areas. The Juneau Icefield has
also been under study by Dr. Maynard Miller in the Juneau Icefield
Research Project for the last forty years.

(2) Management Considerations

(a) The potential for managing timber in this roadless area is
limited, and extremely localized, as the majority of this area is ice
fields and glaciers

(b) If a road to Skagway or Haines becomes a reality, there would be the possibility that it may cross the portion of this roadless area in the Berners Bay area   It is unfeasible that a road north would run the entire length of the east side of Lynn Canal because of the steepness of the slopes north of Berners Bay, the numerous rivers of considerable magnitude, and the tidewater glaciers found on the that side of the Canal

(c) Management of this area is a roadless state maintains opportunities for wildlife, such as wolves, bears, and moose, to move freely through the area.

(d) Fire: The area has no significant fire history, although fires have occurred in the Skagway vicinity and actually may be the closest that forest fires and glaciers in North America have simultaneously occurred!

(e) Insects and Disease: Endemic tree diseases common to Southeast Alaska are present; there are no know epidemic disease occurrences

(f) Land Status: A proposed State land selection in the Katzehin River area may occur   This selection contains a Forest Service public recreation cabin with airstrip access. Another selection on the west side of Berners Bay was proposed as a State selection but the recommendation was not to select   The patented mining claims just north of Berners Bay area are the only private lands within this analysis area.

d. Relationship to Communities and Other Roadless and Wilderness Areas

(1) Nearby Roadless and Wilderness Areas and Uses: The Skagway-Juneau Icefield is part of a larger mainland unroaded landmass which runs from the international border north of Skagway, to Misty Fiords National Monument Wilderness and the international border to the south.

(2) Distance From Population Centers (Accessibility): Approximate distances from population centers are as follows:

Community		Air Miles	Water Miles
Juneau	(Pop. 23,729)	Adjacent	25
Petersburg	(Pop. 4,040)	100	170
Skagway	(Pop. 583)	Adjacent	Adjacent
Haines	(Pop. 1,838)	3	3

The nearest stops on the Alaska Marine Highway to access any portion of this area are either Juneau, Haines, or Skagway.

(3) Interest by Proponents:

(a) Moratorium areas: The area in the immediate vicinity of Berners Bay has been identified as a proposed "moratorium" area or proposed as Wilderness in legislative initiatives to date

(b) Local users/residents: Use of the area is divided into at least three separate factions Use in the Berners Bay area is relatively high because of its proximity to Juneau and the end of the Juneau Road System at Echo Cove Boating and kayaking occur frequently in the bay In 1985 a group called Friends of Berners Bay formed to halt proposed logging in the area and in Sawmill Cove adjacent to this roadless area

In the portion of the roadless area that is accessed from Skagway, local users are primarily hunters and recreationists Many tourists view the spectacular scenery of this roadless area from the White Pass and Yukon Railroad without actually entering the roadless area

Icefield use is low in terms of recreation visitor days (RVD's), yet thousands view the Icefield from flightseeing or helicopter landing tours. Some individuals, and outfitters and guides with small groups have traversed the Icefield from Atlin, British Columbia to Juneau.

e. Environmental Consequences

ALTERNATIVE ANALYSIS TO BE DONE LATER

INDIVIDUAL ROADLESS AREA DESCRIPTION

NAME: Taku-Snettisham (302)   ACRES (GROSS): 736,271   ACRES (NFS): 736,112

GEOZONE: C23 and C21
GEOGRAPHIC PROVINCE: Coast Range

1989 WILDERNESS ATTRIBUTE RATING: 22

a. Description

    (1) Relationship to RARE II areas: The table below displays the VCU 1/
    names, VCU numbers, original WARS 2/ rating, and comments This enables
    the reader to compare the roadless areas evaluated in Appendix C with
    previous analyses

VCU Name	VCU No.	1979 WARS Rating	Comments
Rhine Creek	038	19	
Carlson Creek	039	22	
Annex Lake·	040	17	
Taku Inlet	041	19	
Lake Dorothy	042	23	
Turner Lake	043	25	
Davidson Creek	044	21	
Glory Lake	045	23	
Taku River·	046	27	
Mt. Swineford	047	24	
Wright Glacier	048	22	
Long Lake	050	22	
Slocum Inlet	051	18	
Taku Harbor	052	--	Not rated in 1979
Limestone Inlet	053	22	
Webster Park	054	--	Not rated in 1979.
Port Snettisham	055	20	
Mfigs Peak	056	21	
Gilbert Bay	057	23	
Speel Arm	058	22	
Lower Speel River	059	24	
Upper Speel River	060	28	
Whiting River	061	23	
Williams Cove	064	22	

1/ A VCU (Value Comparison Unit) is one of 867 watersheds which make up the
    Forest and were differentiated for planning purposes in the Tongass Land
    Management Plan.
2/ Wilderness Attribute Rating System (WARS) was the nationwide system used to
    rate the wilderness attributes of roadless areas in the Roadless Area
    Review and Evaluation (RARE II).

(2) History: This large area has a long and varied history of use, dating from Tlingit use in prehistoric and historic times to the present use by a variety of Alaska residents and visitors The Taku River is a travel corridor that has been used continually since the earliest human occupation of the area Uses of the area since the 1800's include mining, fox farming, logging and milling, and settling Remains of structures and other human cultural activity, in varying degrees of deterioration, can still be found

(3) Location and Access: This roadless area is located on the Juneau mainland, and includes and runs south of the Taku River corridor to the Tracy Arm-Fords Terror Wilderness' northern boundary This area is bordered by Stephens Passage on the west with two major river inlets Taku Inlet and Port Snettisham. A portion of Holkam Bay directly outside of Tracy Arm-Fords Terror Wilderness is also included in the southern border The Taku River-Port Snettisham Roadless Area is contiguous with both the Skagway-Juneau Icefield Roadless Area and the Tracy Arm-Fords Terror Wilderness

This large area is accessed by a variety of means. The Taku River serves as a major river corridor for recreational boats to access the Forest Service recreation cabins, several recreation residences, some private inholdings, and a commercial restaurant lodge located on the river Floatplanes also land on the Taku River, the inland lakes, and the ports and bays included in the area. A hiking trail departs from the Juneau Road System in Thane and provides hike-in access to Point Bishop, a distance of approximately 9 6 miles Another trail that receives considerable use is located in Taku Inlet to access West Turner Lake and recreation cabin from saltwater.

Helicopters are used to access various interior points, although they are used less frequently than floatplanes or wheeled planes.

(4) Geography and Topography: The area is typical of recently glaciated mainlands of Southeast Alaska. It is mountainous with deep fiords and inshore islands characteristic of a submerged coastline Many of the shorelines are rocky and difficult to access - especially in Stephens Passage. There are 206 miles of shoreline on saltwater, with 12,462 acres of beach. A large part of the area is alpine tundra (16,538 acres), ice and snow (86,505 acres) and rock (174,109 acres). There are 20 acres of small islands and 16,745 acres of freshwater lakes in the area Large lakes in the area include Turner Lake, Lake Dorothy, Twin Glacier Lake, Sweetheart Lakes, Crater Lake and Crescent Lake

(5) Ecosystem:

(a) Classification: The area is classified as being in the Coast Range Geographic Province. The region is generally characterized by rugged, heavily glaciated terrain with extensive alpine and ice field environments Productive forest lands are usually confined to river valleys and marine terraces Alpine lakes, young, dynamic rivers, and deep, U-shaped troughs are characteristically present in this area Major river systems include the Taku, Speel, and Whiting Rivers

(b) Vegetation: Vegetation of this roadless area primarily consists
of typical spruce/hemlock forests Western hemlock and Sitka spruce
dominate the overstory while the understory is composed of shrubs such
as red huckleberry, rusty menziesia, and devil's club The forest
floor is covered with a mat of mosses, liverworts, and plants such as
deerheart, bunchberry dogwood, single delight, and skunk cabbage
Streamside riparian vegetation is characterized by salmonberry,
devil's club, alder, grasses, ferns, and currants Vegetation
classified as muskegs are not abundant (2,475 acres); however, muskeg
is interspersed within other types in units too small to map
Therefore, the acreage for muskeg may be substantially understated
These areas, dominated by sphagnum mosses, sedges, and shrubs of the
heath family, are interspersed among low-elevation timber stands where
drainage is restricted. Trees within the muskegs are sparse and
consist mainly of stunted hemlock, lodgepole pine, and Alaska-cedar

There are approximately 266,691 acres of forested land of which
119,370 acres are commercial forest land. Of the commercial forest
land, 96,819 acres are non-riparian old growth and 15,221 acres are
riparian old growth. Alpine tundra totals 16,538 acres.

(c) Soils: Shallow mineral soils (less than four inches deep) on
steep, V-notched, dissected sideslopes are common in the
glacially-formed, U-shaped valleys of Southeast Alaska and in this
particular analysis area. Small areas of organic soils (muskegs) are
found on sideslope benches where subsurface drainage is impaired
Inclusion of fine-textured (clay) soils of glacial origin occur
infrequently along lower sideslopes, posing potential hazard Slides
are not uncommon.

(d) Fish Resource: Fish resources have been rated as part of the
Tongass Land Management Plan (1979) and by the Alaska Department of
Fish and Game in its Forest Habitat Integrity Program (1983) These
ratings describe the value of VCU's for sport fish, commercial fish.
and estuaries.

There are four VCU's which are rated as high value for sport fish
These are Turner Lake (43) and the Taku River (46) which are popular
fishing areas for Juneau residents, and the Lower Speel River (59) and
Whiting River (61).

VCU's rated as highly valued for commercial fish are:

Taku Inlet	41
Davidson Creek	44
Taku River	46
Mt. Swineford	47
Slocum Inlet	51
Lower Speel River	59
Upper Speel River	60
Whiting River	61

VCU's rated as highly valued estuaries include Taku Inlet (41),
Davidson Creek (44) and Taku River (46)

The glacial Taku River is significant for fish production on an international scale - primarily for king, coho, sockeye and chum salmon   The commercial fishery is regulated under the United States-Canada Pacific Salmon Treaty as one of the three major transboundary river fisheries on the Tongass National Forest

Snettisham Fish Hatchery is a major State fish hatchery adjacent to the roadless area.

(e) Wildlife Resource: Generally, the roadless area provides good moose and goat habitat and these species are present within it   Other large mammal species include both black and brown bear   Furbearers such as mink, marten, and beaver are also present.

(f) Threatened and Endangered Species: The area contains no known threatened or endangered species.

(6) Current Use and Management: Twelve VCU's (313,408 acres) were allocated to Land Use Designation 2 in the Tongass Land Management Plan, which provides for management of the area in a roadless state to retain the wildland character. Ten other VCU's (313,408 acres) were allocated to Land Use Designation 3 which allows the land to be managed for a variety of uses.   The emphasis is on managing for uses and activities in a compatible and complementary manner to provide the greatest combination of benefits in these VCU's. These areas have either high use or high amenity values in conjunction with high commodity values. Two VCU's (26,297 acres) were designated in Land Use Designation 4 where opportunities are provided for intensive resource use and development. The emphasis is primarily on commodity or market resources in these two VCU's subject to provisions which protect physical and biological productivity.

Trails found in this roadless area include Turner Lake Trail, Twin Glacier Trail, Taku Harbor Trail, and Crater Lake Trail, but several of these trails do not receive regular maintenance and may be in disrepair   There are three recreation residences under special use permit

The Whiting River has been used in the past for guided rafting trips. Cruiseships and tour boats entering Tracy Arm pass by Holkum Bay

A utility corridor (under a Memorandum of Understanding with Alaska Power Authority) parallels the coastline from the Snettisham hydroelectric plant at the head of Port Snettisham north to Juneau.

Several fisheries projects found within this roadless area are primarily within the Taku River watershed.

Limestone Inlet (within VCU 53) has been identified as an area of scientific research value and was designated a Research Natural Area

(7) Appearance (Apparent Naturalness): A vast majority of the area is considered unmodified except for those areas primarily located near the shoreline with evidence of use   That use includes the existing powerlines that run from Juneau to Snettisham, private inholdings (consisting of residential and recreation residences and a commercial lodge) on the Taku

River, two public recreation cabins on Turner Lake, and historic sites of old fox farms, mining claims, settlements, and cabins. Snettisham hydroelectric plant and adjacent fish hatchery, although outside of the roadless area, affect the immediate area at the head of Port Snettisham in terms of apparent naturalness.

The visual character type of this roadless area is Coast Range. Landforms are generally large, massive and give an impression of great bulk Uplands are generally 5,000 to 7,000 feet in elevation dissected by deep, steep-walled, U-shaped valleys Mountains ridges are generally rounded summits but are surmounted, at times, by aretes and horns rising 8,000 to 9,000 feet The large, saltwater fiords protruding into this character type are sometimes extremely steep-sided, affording great visual relief because of the abrupt differences in elevation.

Sixty-three percent of this roadless area was inventoried in Variety Class B (possessing landscape diversity that is common for the character type) and 32 percent of the acreage was inventoried Variety Class A (possessing landscape diversity that is unique for the character type)

The majority (95.5 percent) of this roadless area is in Existing Visual Condition (EVC) I; these areas appear to be untouched by human activity 0 3 percent of the acreage is in EVC IV, which are areas in which changes in the landscape are easily noticed by the average person and may attract some attention. There appears to be disturbances but they resemble natural patterns. EVC V, where changes in the landscape are obvious to the average person, accounts for 1.2 percent. Changes in EVC V appear to be major disturbances.

(8) **Surroundings (External Influences):** External influences in the area are primarily localized In the Taku River corridor, boat traffic should be expected, and during the summer months, there is frequent air traffic Flightseeing tours are offered over such glaciers as the Taku, Hole-in-the Wall, and Twin Glaciers near the Taku River. Taku Lodge also generates floatplane traffic.

The utility corridor (powerlines) running from Snettisham hydroelectric power plant to Juneau is a visual influence that is difficult to ignore particularly when accessing that area from saltwater Snettisham Power Plant and adjacent fish hatchery, and associated air and boat traffic impact the Port Snettisham area.

(9) **Attractions and Features of Special Interest:** The natural features of the area, the scenery, and the opportunity to see wildlife are all considered attractions. High-quality fishing opportunities in the streams and lakes also provide attractions. The area contains 27 inventoried recreation places totaling 156,723 acres. There are several trails and three public recreation cabins in this roadless area

b. **Capability of Management as Wilderness or in an Unroaded Condition**

(1) **Manageability and Management Area Boundaries:** The area is well defined by saltwater to the west and the international border with British Columbia, Canada, to the east The southern boundary is the Tracy Arm-Fords Terror Wilderness boundary The northern boundary of this

roadless area is approximately the ridgeline north above the Taku River,
this roadless area is contiguous with the Skagway-Juneau Icefields Roadless
Area   Because of the private land and activities on the Taku River, and
the presence of a fish hatchery and power plant in Snettisham Inlet, it may
be less feasible to manage in a wilderness condition in those areas

(2) Natural Integrity: The area is unmodified except for the areas
mentioned above - Taku River and Snettisham power plant and fish hatchery,
and three public recreation cabins and associated trails   The overall
influence of these developments on the natural integrity of the area is
very low

(3) Opportunity for Solitude: There is a high opportunity for solitude
within much of the area but one should expect to see occasional air traffic
and boat traffic, especially in the Stephens Passage area. The character
of the landforms generally allows visitors to feel remote from the sights
and sounds of human activity with several exceptions. Impacts from
motorized traffic are confined primarily to saltwater corridors, and those
inland locations overflown by floatplanes accessing the recreation cabins

(4) Opportunity for Primitive Recreation: The area provides primarily
primitive recreation opportunity as inventoried with the Recreation
Opportunity Spectrum (ROS) system.

ROS Class	Acres
Primitive I (P1)	344,413
Primitive II (P2)	136,528
Rural (R)	1,492
Roaded Natural (RN)	15,696
Semi-Primitive Non-Motorized (SPNM)	196,021
Semi-Primitive Motorized (SPM)	35,360
No ROS	6,345

The area contains 27 recreation places.

ROS CLASS	# OF REC. PLACES	TOTAL ACRES	CAPACITY BY RVD
P1	3	9,559	1,008
P2	6	22,564	18,811
RN	4	11,612	42,096
SPNM	7	93,989	67,101
SPM	7	18,997	49,296

There are three public recreation cabins in the area   Two of these cabins
are located on Turner Lake and are extremely popular.

(5) Special Features (Ecologic, Geologic, Scientific, Cultural): There
are opportunities to observe and study fish and wildlife and the various
forces which formed the mountains in the area. Limestone Inlet has been
designated a Research Natural Area since 1971. The minor and major
glaciers visible throughout the area are also significant attractions

c. Availability for Management as Wilderness or in an Unroaded Condition

   (1) Resource Potentials

      (a) **Recreation Potential:** The values that attract users to this area are a sense of solitude, natural beauty, viewing and/or harvesting fish and wildlife, and relatively-easy accessibility from Juneau   The area provides unlimited primitive and semi-primitive recreation opportunities   Because of the rugged terrain, use is concentrated but additional trails and recreation cabins would disperse, and possibly increase, use of the area

      (b) **Fish Resource:** The Tongass Land Management Plan, amended Winter 1985-86 identifies numerous fish habitat enhancement projects   Fish enhancement projects continue to surface and there is potential for additional projects in this area. A fisheries enhancement project (establishment of a salmon fishery) was recently approved at Turner Lake but, because of several appeals, the decision to approve the project was rescinded.

      (c) **Wildlife Resource:** As identified in the Tongass Land Management Plan, amended 1985-86, several moose and swan habitat improvement projects are planned for the area in the future. These projects typically consist of willow manipulation and the construction of swan nesting structures.

      (d) **Timber Resource:** There are 71,884 acres inventoried as tentatively suitable for harvest. This includes 10,112 acres of riparian old growth, and 58,703 acres of non-riparian old growth

      Past planning resulted in offered timber sales in the Gilbert Bay-Williams Cove area, but those activities were halted when two different purchasers defaulted on the sales. There is potential for timber harvest activity in the area, primarily in this portion of the roadless area.

      (e) **Land Use Authorizations:** A powerline authorized under a Memorandum of Understanding between the Forest Service and the City and Borough of Juneau parallels the shoreline from the Snettisham Power Plant north to Juneau, to provide electric power to our capital city.

      (f) **Minerals:** The area has been identified as having mineral development potential. There are currently several known claims in the area.

      (g) **Areas of Scientific Interest:** This roadless area contains one designated Research Natural Area in Limestone Inlet   The Yehring Creek area has been identified as a potential Research Natural Area

(2) **Management Considerations**

(a) The potential for managing timber in this roadless area is dependent on the development of high market values and harvest methods which will allow extraction without need for extensive roading

(b) **Fire:** The area has no significant fire history

(c) **Insects and Disease:** Endemic tree diseases common to Southeast Alaska are present, there are no know epidemic disease occurrences

(d) Proposals occasionally surface to build a road from Juneau to an "outside" road system in Haines, Skagway, or Canada. A bill has recently been proposed in the Alaska State Legislature to fund an environmental impact statement to analyze such a proposal to construct a road to Canada through the Taku River Valley or a road to Haines

(e) **Land Status:** The Snettisham Hydroelectric project and reservoirs area has been proposed as State land selection. This proposal encompasses 2,666 acres. Another proposed State selection is near Dorothy Lake. There are several private inholdings within this roadless area, primarily on the Taku River.

d. **Relationship to Communities and Other Roadless and Wilderness Areas**

(1) **Nearby Roadless and Wilderness Areas and Uses:** Because the Taku-Snettisham Roadless Area is contiguous with the Skagway-Juneau Icefield Roadless Area and Tracy Arm-Fords Terror Wilderness, the three in their entirety make up a larger mainland unroaded landmass of approximately 2,500,000 acres.

(2) **Distance From Population Centers (Accessibility):** Approximate distances from population centers are as follows:

Community		Air Miles	Water Miles
Juneau	(Pop. 23,729)	Adjacent	Adjacent
Petersburg	(Pop. 4,040)	75	85
Sitka	(Pop. 8,041)	180	75

The nearest stop on the Alaska Marine Highway is Juneau

(3) **Interest by Proponents:**

(a) **Moratorium areas:** A small portion of the area (Williams Cove outside Tracy Arm-Fords Terror Wilderness) has been identified as part of a proposed moratorium area or proposed as Wilderness in legislative initiatives to date.

(b) **Local users/residents:** Most use of the area is associated with recreational boating, hunting, viewing scenery and wildlife, and fishing. Some mining activities are also occurring The majority of use occurs within one-quarter mile from the shoreline

e. Environmental Consequences

   ALTERNATIVE ANALYSIS TO BE DONE LATER

INDIVIDUAL ROADLESS AREA DESCRIPTION

NAME: Sullivan (303)   ACRES (GROSS): 66,677   ACRES (NFS): 66,657

GEOZONE: C23
GEOGRAPHIC PROVINCE: Lynn Canal

1989 WILDERNESS ATTRIBUTE RATING: 25

a   Description

     (1) Relationship to RARE II areas: The table below displays the VCU 1/
     names, VCU numbers, original WARS 2/ rating, and comments. This enables
     the reader to compare the roadless areas evaluated in Appendix C with
     previous analyses.

VCU Name	VCU No.	1979 WARS Rating	Comments
Sullivan Island	094	18	
Sullivan Mt.	095	24	
S.Davidson Gl.	096	25	
W Sullivan	097	21	
Sullivan Delta	098	26	
Point Can	099	23	
Lower Endicott	105*	24	Most of this VCU is designated Wilderness Portion near Lynn Canal is not

     *--The roadless area includes only part of this VCU.

     (2) History: Any documented historical use of this roadless area has been
     minimal. Native use of the area was probably limited to hunting or
     trapping mink, lynx and other animals including goat and bear, and
     gathering berries. Others cultivated garden plots, gathered seaweed and
     mussels, and hunted seal on the shore of Lynn Canal. Mining began in more
     recent history, and some mining activities continue into the present   A
     fox farm was present in the 1930's

1/ A VCU (Value Comparison Unit) is one of 867 watersheds which make up the
    forest and were differentiated for planning purposes in the Tongass Land
    Management Plan.
2/ Wilderness Attribute Rating System (WARS) was the nationwide system used to
    rate the wilderness attributes of roadless areas in the Roadless Area
    Review and Evaluation (RARE II).

(3) Location and Access: The area is located on west side of Lynn Canal
and extends from the National Forest boundary on the north to the Endicott
River Wilderness boundary to the south   The portion of VCU 105 that is
adjacent to Lynn Canal is not designated Wilderness, and a harvest unit
from the 1960's serves as the continuation of the southern boundary of this
roadless area   There are two other cut areas from the 1960's along Lynn
Canal in VCU's 95 and 97/98   The western boundary abuts Glacier Bay
National Park and Preserve

(4) Geography and Topography: The area is generally characterized by
rugged, scoured terrain with large, vertical relief. The mountain peaks
are often snow-covered and reach elevations up to 4,700 feet   Glaciers
have scraped steep, rugged slopes and formed glacial bowls. Alluvial fans
are formed from the glacial rivers that feed into Lynn Canal but these are
the primary areas that were cut in the 1960's. The area contains 37 miles
of shoreline on saltwater and at two river mouths, the shoreline is flat
and accessible. There are 19,422 acres inventoried as rock, and 14,961
acres inventoried as ice and snow. Alpine encompasses 1,120 acres   Only
40 acres of freshwater lakes are found in this area.

(5) **Ecosystem:**

    (a) **Classification:** The area is classified as being in the Lynn
    Canal Geographic Province. This province is generally characterized
    as one of the driest and most continental environments in Southeast
    Alaska. Rain shadow from the Chilkat Mountains and St Elias Range
    allows extensive development of fire-dependent forests (lodgepole and
    birch), and the southern and westward extension of boreal forest and
    tundra plant species

    (b) **Vegetation:** Vegetation is interspersed with spruce/hemlock rain
    forest typical of Southeast Alaska and contains frequently scoured,
    well-drained alluvial deposits supporting willow and alder   There are
    approximately 19,422 acres of forested land of which 15,710 acres are
    commercial forest land. Of the commercial forest land, 1,701 acres
    are riparian old growth and 11,106 acres are non-riparian old growth

    (c) **Soils:** Shallow mineral soils (less than four inches thick) on
    steep, V-notched, dissected side slopes are common in the area   Small
    organic soils (muskegs) occur on infrequent benches and at subalpine
    elevations. Of concern are soils and vegetation occurring on
    recently-deglaciated areas. These soils are fragile and slight
    disturbance can eliminate or significantly set back the vegetative
    succession.

    (d) **Fish Resource:** Fish resources have been rated as part of the
    Tongass Land Management Plan (1979) and by the Alaska Department of
    Fish and Game in its Forest Habitat Integrity Program (1983)   These
    ratings describe the value of VCU's for sport fish, commercial fish,
    and estuaries.

No VCU's were highly valued in these ratings for sport or commercial
fish. Lower Endicott (VCU 105) received a high estuarine rating

(e) Wildlife Resource: Mountain goats, moose, bear and wolves, and some deer are the wildlife species of most general interest in this area   Smaller wildlife include mink and lynx

(f) Threatened and Endangered Species: The area contains no known threatened or endangered species

(6) Current Use and Management: All of the VCU's in this roadless area were allocated to Land Use Designation 3 in the Tongass Land Management Plan. This designation allows for management of these lands for a variety of uses and activities in a compatible and complementary manner to provide the greatest combination of benefits. These areas have either high use or high amenity values in conjunction with high commodity values.

There are no developed trails within this area, but an airstrip is located adjacent to the Sullivan Roadless Area on an alluvial fan along Lynn Canal within a cut area from the 1960's and receives use primarily from hunters and occasional miners

(7) Appearance (Apparent Naturalness): This area is basically unmodified except for small mining claims in the area. An airstrip is directly adjacent to the roadless area within an older harvest area mentioned above, and provides access for users.

The visual character type of this roadless area is primarily Coast Range Much of the area is characterized by moderately complex to complex terrain dominated by angular profiles and sharply defined crests often penetrated by prominent inlets and bays. Thirty-one percent of this area was inventoried in Variety Class A (possessing landscape diversity that is unique for the character type) with 67 percent in Variety Class B (possessing landscape diversity that is common for the character type) The remaining two percent is in Variety Class C (possessing a low degree of landscape diversity)

The Existing Visual Condition (EVC) of 93 percent of this roadless area is EVC I. These areas appear to be untouched by human activity   Seven percent was inventoried in EVC III. These are areas in which changes in the landscape are notice by the average person, but they do not attract attention. The natural appearance of the landscape still remains dominant

(8) Surroundings (External Influences): This area is bounded by Lynn Canal which serves as a major travel corridor for flights, ferries, ships and boats. To the south is an adjacent clearcut from 1966   Three additional cut areas from the 1960's are found along the alluvial fans formed by glacial rivers flowing into Lynn Canal. Currently, thinning activities are occurring in those harvest units.

(9) Attractions and Features of Special Interest: Of primary interest in this area is the opportunity to hunt for both moose and bear, although people also hunt within the adjacent Endicott River Wilderness   The area contains four inventoried recreation places which contains 12,291 acres These are no improved trails or public recreation cabins in the area

b. Capability of Management as Wilderness or in an Unroaded Condition

(1) **Manageability and Management Area Boundaries:** The area is generally
well defined by topographic features   Lynn Canal serves as the western
boundary and Endicott River Wilderness serves as the southern boundary
The forest boundary is the northern limit of this area and that boundary
transects Mt Sullivan. The adjacent four harvest units on Lynn Canal were
cut in the 1960's along flat alluvial fans, and revegetation has occurred
so this does not serve as a strong detraction near the roadless area

(2) **Natural Integrity:** The area is basically unmodified except for the
mining claims within the area. No other disturbances are known

(3) **Opportunity for Solitude:** There is a high opportunity for solitude
within the area. Present use of the area is low which is undoubtedly
related to poor access opportunities. Much of the access is
weather-dependent. There are no regularly scheduled small plane or ferry
stops within this area. Along the shoreline of Lynn Canal, there is a
greater opportunity for seeing or hearing others--primarily small planes,
ferries, small boats or cruiseships--but Sullivan Island screens much of
the water traffic. Some thinning is occurring within the adjacent harvest
units and some drilling may be occurring on some of the current mining
claims.

(4) **Opportunity for Primitive Recreation:** The area provides primarily
pristine and semi-primitive recreation opportunities.

ROS Class	Acres
Pristine (P)	35,823
Semi-Primitive Non-Motorized (SPNM)	27,572
Semi-Primitive Motorized (SPM)	7,165

The area contains four recreation places.

ROS CLASS	# OF REC. PLACES	TOTAL ACRES	CAPACITY BY RVD
SPNM	2	6,907	2,779
SPM	2	5,384	117,778

There are no public recreation facilities in the area and the character of
the landforms generally allows the visitor to feel remote from the sights
and sounds of human activity, except when on the shoreline

(5) **Special Features (Ecologic, Geologic, Scientific, Cultural):** There
are no known special features in this area. The area has not been
identified as an area of potential scientific value.

c. Availability for Management as Wilderness or in an Unroaded Condition

(1) Resource Potentials

(a) **Recreation Potential:** There is a possibility to develop public
recreation cabins within the area but because of the difficulty and
cost of access, the potential remains low. Outfitter and guide

services may be increased in the future, especially in relation to big game hunting

(b) Fish Resource   The potential remains low for fish enhancement projects within this area.

(c) Wildlife Resource: No habitat improvements have been identified in the Tongass Land Management Plan, amended Winter 1985-86

(d) Timber Resource: There are 11,547 acres inventoried as tentatively suitable for harvest   This includes 1,340 acres of riparian old growth and 7,944 acres of non-riparian old growth

(e) Land Use Authorizations: There are no long-term special use permits issued for this area. Numerous mining claims exist and two Plans of Operation have been submitted.

(f) Minerals: The area generally has Priority Two and Three mineral development potential ratings, and there are numerous known current claims.

(g) Areas of Scientific Interest: This roadless area contains no designated or inventoried potential Research Natural Areas

(2) **Management Considerations**

(a) This area is adjacent to Endicott River Wilderness and there would be opportunity to manage this area in conjunction with that Wilderness.

(b) Occasionally, the topic of building a road to Haines surfaces, and most potential proposals indicate the west side of Lynn Canal as the route of choice.

(c) Fire: The area has no significant fire history

(d) Insects and Disease: Endemic tree diseases common to Southeast Alaska are present; there are no know epidemic disease occurrences

(e) Land Status: A small parcel of private land is located on the southern tip of Sullivan Island

d. Relationship to Communities and Other Roadless and Wilderness Areas

(1) **Nearby Roadless and Wilderness Areas and Uses:** The Sullivan Roadless Area is part of a larger mainland unroaded landmass of approximately 383,799 acres located between the northern National Forest boundary at Point Sullivan to the southern tip of the Chilkat Peninsula at Point Couverden. That larger acreage total includes Endicott Wilderness and Chilkat-West Lynn Roadless Area (304). Additionally, this area is adjacent to Glacier Bay National Monument

(2) **Distance From Population Centers (Accessibility)** Approximate distances from population centers are as follows.

Community			Air Miles	Water Miles
Juneau	(Pop	23,729)	50	50
Haines	(Pop	1,838)	14	14
Skagway	(Pop.	583)	28	28

The nearest stop on the Alaska Marine Highway is Haines

(3) Interest by Proponents:

(a) **Moratorium areas:** Sullivan Island has been identified as a proposed "moratorium" area or proposed as Wilderness in legislative initiatives to date

(b) **Local users/residents:** Most use of the area is associated with moose or bear hunting

e. **Environmental Consequences**

ALTERNATIVE ANALYSIS TO BE DONE LATER

INDIVIDUAL ROADLESS AREA DESCRIPTION

E: Chilkat-West (304)   ACRES (GROSS): 211,517   ACRES (NFS): 207,277
              Lynn Canal
ZONE: C19
GRAPHIC PROVINCE   Northern Interior Islands and Lynn Canal

9 WILDERNESS ATTRIBUTE RATING: 23

Description

(1) Relationship to RARE II areas: The table below displays the VCU 1/
names, VCU numbers, original WARS 2/ rating, and comments. This enables
the reader to compare the roadless areas evaluated in Appendix C with
previous analyses.

| | | 1979 | |
VCU Name	VCU No.	WARS Rating	Comments
Lower Endicott	105*	24	VCU is partial Wilderness
Upper St. James	106*	23	
Wm. Henry Bay	107	18	
Pt. Danger	108	18	
Boat Harbor	109*	18	State Land Selection
Middle St.James	110	- -	Not rated in 1979.
St.James Bay	111	23	
Nun Mountain	112	23	
Lynn Sisters	113	22	
No Name Basin	114	22	
Earth Station	115	18	
Couverden Lake	116	24	
Couverden Is.	117	24	
Ansley Basin	118	19	
Humpy Creek	119	23	
Porpoise Is.	120	19	
Excursion In.	121	18	
122 Creek	122	- -	Not rated in 1979
Ripoff	123		Not rated in 1979

*--The roadless area includes only part of this VCU.

(2) History: The southern end of the Chilkat Peninsula has been suitable
for human occupation for at least the last 11,000 years, and documented
prehistoric sites have been recorded there. Tlingit tribes were the
primary inhabitants of the area.

A VCU (Value Comparison Unit) is one of 867 watersheds which make up the
Forest and were differentiated for planning purposes in the Tongass Land
Management Plan.
Wilderness Attribute Rating System (WARS) was the nationwide system used to
rate the wilderness attributes of roadless areas in the Roadless Area
Review and Evaluation (RARE II).

More recent history includes mining activities, significant black bear
hunting in the southern Chilkat area, and a timber sale (the Couverden
Timber Sale)   Two previous operators defaulted on the sale and currently
the third purchaser is progressing with the sale

(3) Location and Access: The Chilkat-Lynn Roadless Area, located on the
mainland, is bordered on the east by Lynn Canal   Icy Strait into Excursion
Inlet borders the southern tip of this area, as does the Couverden Timber
Sale area. The roadless area is adjacent to Endicott River Wilderness to
the north and Glacier Bay National Park and Preserve to the west

The communities closest to the roadless area are Gustavus (approximately 10
miles west), Juneau (approximately 20 miles directly east of the southern
tip), Hoonah (across Icy Strait by 10 miles), and Haines (35 miles directly
north of the northern portion of the area).

No regularly-scheduled airplane or Alaska Marine Highway ferry service
provide access to this area.

(4) Geography and Topography: The Chilkat-West Lynn Canal Roadless Area
is characterized by rugged topography. The Chilkat Mountain Range runs the
entire north-south length of the roadless area; its lateral,
glacially-formed valleys are typically U-shaped. Highland elevations range
from 2,000 to 4,500 feet with alpine covering 36,741 acres, rock covering
27,190 acres, and ice and snowfields covering 9,749 acres   The entire area
has been extensively glaciated and contains many glacial features,
including glacial cirques and tarns. The Endicott terraced alluvial plain
is significant topographically in the northern portion of this area   The
side walls of many of the valleys have been scoured by ancient ice sheets,
and bedrock outcroppings are common throughout the area.

The southern coastline, along Excursion Inlet, is comprised of moderate to
steeply-sloping forest terrain supporting relatively small drainage
systems. Swanson Harbor and the Couverden Island group form the
southernmost tip of the peninsula and are basically low and wooded   The
area's southern slopes are, for the most part, gently rolling and uniformly
forested, particularly in foreground situations   Rugged, snow-clad peaks
form an impressive backdrop panorama. There are 74 miles of shoreline on
saltwater, with 4,513 acres of beach in this roadless area, and 300 acres
of small islands. Freshwater lakes comprise only 599 acres in the area

(5) Ecosystem:

     (a) Classification: The northern portion of this area is classified
     as being in the Lynn Canal Geographic Province. That region is
     generally characterized by rugged, scoured terrain with large,
     vertical relief. The southern portion of this area is classified as
     being in the Northern Interior Islands Geographic Province   This area
     is protected from the full force of storms off of the outer coast but
     with colder climate and more rugged topography than the central
     interior islands

     (b) Vegetation: Timber stands within this area are composed
     primarily of western hemlock and Sitka spruce. The forest understory

varies in density and composition depending on the percent of canopy
closure which, in turn, is affected by soil type, incidence of
blowdown, and soil drainage. Understory vegetation of blueberry,
huckleberry, rusty menziesia and devil's club is typical   Muskeg
areas are dominated by sphagnum mosses, sedges, rushes and ericacious
shrubs and comprise 799 acres of this area. Muskeg is interspersed
within other types in units too small to map, therefore, the acreage
for muskeg may be substantially understated   Grass-sedge meadows are
located at lower elevations along the coast   Low mat-forming
vegetation adapted to snowpack and wind abrasion dominates alpine
areas, heaths, grasses and low plants, such as deer cabbage, are
typical.

There are approximately 99,409 acres of forested land of which 61,303
acres are commercial forest land. Of the commercial forest land,
51,401 acres are non-riparian old growth and 6,909 acres are riparian
old growth.

(c) **Soils:**   Glacial till from local glacial origin is the
predominant soil parent material and has been deposited on valley side
walls to approximately 1,500 feet in elevation. The glacial till
thins as it reaches higher elevations. Deeper, well-drained, forested
soils occur along the lower slopes and valley bottoms   The valley
bottoms are alluvial with outwash materials of stratified sands,
gravels, and silts of glacial or recent stream origin   Through the
natural erosion processes, some landslides have occurred   Snow
avalanche paths are present, reaching valley bottoms in many cases
Timbered, organic, muskeg soils are found throughout the area

(d) **Fish Resource:** Fish resources have been rated as part of the
Tongass Land Management Plan (1979) and by the Alaska Department of
Fish and Game in its Forest Habitat Integrity Program (1983)   These
ratings describe the value of VCU's for sport fish, commercial fish,
and estuaries.

There were no VCU's rated as having the highest value for sport fish
in this area. There are seven rated as highly valued for commercial
fish. These seven VCU's are

Lower Endicott	105
Upper St. James	106
Middle St.James	110
St. James Bay	111
Couverden Island	117
Humpy Creek	119
Porpoise Island	120

VCU's rated as highly valued estuaries include Boat Harbor (109) and
St. James Bay (111).

In addition, many streams support runs of Dolly Varden, steelhead and
cutthroat trout

(e) **Wildlife Resource:** This roadless area commonly supports goats, black and brown bear, Sitka black-tailed deer, bald eagles, and wolves Moose are also present Sea mammal rookeries are found throughout the area.

(f) **Threatened and Endangered Species:** The area contains no known threatened or endangered species.

(6) **Current Use and Management:** Twelve VCU's (164,007 acres) were allocated to Land Use Designation 3 in the Tongass Land Management Plan. which designates that these lands will be managed for a variety of uses and activities in a compatible and complementary manner to provide the greatest combination of benefits These areas have either high use or high amenity values in conjunction with high commodity values The other four VCU's (49,282 acres) were allocated to Land Use Designation 2 which allows for management in a roadless state to retain the wildland character, but permits wildlife and fish habitat improvements and primitive recreational facility development.

Current recreation uses within this roadless area are, for the most part, dispersed; with hunting, fishing (fin and shellfish), and pleasure boating adjacent to the roadless area the most popular pursuits. The highland core of the southern Chilkat Peninsula remains a remote and challenging environment for the backpacker, mountaineer, and hunter. All-weather anchorages and interesting coves and beaches within the Point Couverden/St James Bay area offer excellent opportunities for beachcombing, camping, and picnicking. There are no public recreation cabins or trails within the area. The National Guard, in recent years, has conducted maneuvers in this area.

(7) **Appearance (Apparent Naturalness):** The Chilkat-West Lynn Roadless Area appears basically unmodified The visual character type of this roadless area is Coast Range Landforms are generally large, massive, and give an impression of great bulk. Uplands are generally 5,000 to 7,000 feet in elevation dissected by deep, steep-walled, U-shaped valleys Mountain ridges are generally rounded summits but are surmounted, at times, by aretes and horns rising 8,000 to 9,000 feet

Twelve percent of this roadless area was inventoried in Variety Class A (possessing landscape diversity that is unique for the character type), 75 percent in Variety Class B (possessing landscape diverstiy that is common for the character type), and 13 percent in Variety Class C (possessing a low degree of landscape diversity).

The vast majority of the roadless area (94 percent) is in Existing Visual Condition (EVC) I; these areas appear to be untouched by human activity Only 0.5 percent of the acreage is in EVC II. These are areas in which changes in the landscape are not noticed by the average person unless pointed out. Three and one-half percent of the acreage is in EVC III where changes in the landscape are noticed by the average person but they do not attract attention The natural appearance of the landscape still remains dominant. Approximately 1 5 percent of this roadless area is in EVC IV where changes in the landscape are easily noticed by the average person and may attract some attention They appear as disturbances but resemble

natural patterns   One percent of the area is in EVC V, where changes in
the landscape are in glaring contrast to the natural condition   The
changes appear to be drastic disturbance

(8) **Surroundings (External Influences):** Logging may occur in the
Couverden Timber Sale area, and that activity may affect the adjacent
roadless area in terms of noise and visual impacts

Lynn Canal serves as a major travel corridor for flights, ferries, ships
and boats   In addition, air and water traffic to both Gustavus (Glacier
Bay National Park) and Hoonah utilize Icy Strait   Popular commercial
fishing grounds are adjacent to the southern portion of this area also
Solitude is frequently absent along the shore of this peninsula in view of
the substantial boating activity in Lynn Canal and Icy Strait during the
summer months.

(9) **Attractions and Features of Special Interest:** The complexities of
alpine tundra, scrub and old-growth forest, numerous small lakes,
snowfields, steeply-walled glacial valleys and waterfalls offer a variety
of visual and sensory experiences. In reasonable proximity to Juneau,
recreation and hunting opportunities serve to draw people to the southern
portion of this roadless area. An equally important asset of the southern
Chilkat Peninsula, from a more passive standpoint, relates to the
Peninsula's importance as a scenic backdrop for those traveling Lynn Canal
(Juneau/Haines/Skagway) and Chatham and Icy Straits aboard the
ever-increasing number of cruiseships and State ferries

The area contains 13 inventoried recreation places totaling 53,607 acres
There are no improved trails or public recreation cabins in the area

b. **Capability of Management as Wilderness or in an Unroaded Condition**

(1) **Manageability and Management Area Boundaries:** The area is generally
well-defined by adjacent bodies of water and the adjacent roadless areas of
Glacier Bay National Park and Monument, and Endicott River Wilderness
There are some State-selected or private parcels of land in St James Bay
and at the north end of Excursion Inlet. For the majority of the area, the
feasibility of management in a roadless condition is good

(2) **Natural Integrity:** The roadless area is unmodified and, therefore
maintains the natural integrity well. Long-term ecological processes are
generally intact and operating.

(3) **Opportunity for Solitude:** There is a high opportunity for solitude
within the interior of the area, but the element of solitude is affected
along the shore of the area because of the substantial boating activities
and flight corridors.

(4) **Opportunity for Primitive Recreation:** The area provides primarily
primitive and semi-primitive, non-motorized recreation opportunities

ROS Class	Acres
Primitive I (P1)	121,604
Rural (R)	20
Roaded Natural (RN)	1,037
Roaded Modified (RM)	2,361
Semi-Primitive Non-Motorized (SPNM)	80,043
Semi-Primitive Motorized (SPM)	9,426

The area contains 13 recreation places

ROS CLASS	# OF REC. PLACES	TOTAL ACRES	CAPACITY BY RVD
P1	1	26,902	15,969
R	1	20	40,880
RN	2	956	8,394
RM	3	2,361	7,094
SPNM	2	15,382	4,450
SPM	4	7,986	75,900

There are no public recreation facilities within this area and recreation remains primarily dispersed. The majority of use occurs along the coastline. Access is from private boats or private or chartered aircraft

(5) **Special Features (Ecologic, Geologic, Scientific, Cultural):** Moose and black bear hunting activities are increasing in popularity in this area.

c. **Availability for Management as Wilderness or in an Unroaded Condition**

(1) **Resource Potentials**

(a) **Recreation Potential:** There is great potential to provide a variety of recreation opportunities within this roadless area. High wildlife values coincide with high-quality dispersed recreation areas. The rugged interior of the Chilkat Peninsula offers the hiker backpacker and mountaineer diverse and imposing scenery, a high degree of challenge, and unlimited opportunities to experience solitude All-weather anchorages and interesting coves and beaches offer excellent opportunities for beachcombing, camping, and picnicking   As populations rise in nearby communities, use of this area will undoubtedly increase.

(b) **Fish Resource:** One fish habitat improvement project was identified in the Tongass Land Management Plan, amended Winter 1985-86.

(c) **Wildlife Resource:** No wildlife habitat enhancement projects have been identified for this area.

(d) **Timber Resource:** There are 46,896 acres inventoried as tentatively suitable for harvest This includes 5,502 acres of riparian old growth and 38,510 acres of non-riparian old growth

(e) Land Use Authorizations: Alascom has a special use permit for a repeater station in William Henry Bay.

(f) Minerals: Mineral activity and prospecting have been concentrated along the coast and more accessible areas inland Locations of copper and silver have been made on small, weakly-mineralized areas on the west side of Point Howard Generally, the area has low mineral potential As a result, it has not been heavily prospected, but there are numerous known current claims.

(g) Potential Research Areas: One site, located in the lower Endicott River area, has been identified as an inventoried potential Research Natural Area.

(2) **Management Considerations**

(a) Periodically, the idea of a proposed highway north to Haines surfaces Some discussions, including a draft environmental statement in 1973, proposed a possible ferry and highway terminal in St James Bay. Since that time, the State selected the area immediately around the bay If indeed a highway was constructed north, the Chilkat Peninsula-West Lynn Canal area would be one logical route

(b) Fire: The area has no significant fire history

(c) Insects and Disease: Endemic tree diseases common to Southeast Alaska are present; there are no know epidemic disease occurrences

(d) Land Status: The area around St James Bay has been conveyed to the State Swanson Harbor, at the southern tip of Chilkat Peninsula has been proposed for State selection. There is one small inholding in VCU 107 and several small parcels of private land adjacent to this roadless area.

d. Relationship to Communities and Other Roadless and Wilderness Areas

(1) **Nearby Roadless and Wilderness Areas and Uses:** The Chilkat-West Lynn Canal Roadless Area is part of a larger mainland unroaded landmass which includes Endicott River Wilderness and Glacier Bay National Park and Monument.

(2) **Distance From Population Centers (Accessibility)** Approximate distances from population centers are as follows

Community		Air Miles	Water Miles
Juneau	(Pop. 23,729)	20	20
Haines	(Pop. 1,838)	20	20
Gustavus	(Pop. 218)	10	10
Hoonah	(Pop 960)	10	10

The Alaska Marine Highway provides service to Juneau, Haines and Hoonah

(3) Interest by Proponents:

(a) Moratorium areas: The area has not been identified as a "moratorium" area or proposed as Wilderness in legislative initiatives to date

(b) Local users/residents: Most use of the area is associated with recreational, hunting, and some mining. Commercial fisheries occur on saltwater outside the southern and western sides of this roadless area, and the area is heavily fished

e   Environmental Consequences

ALTERNATIVE ANALYSIS TO BE DONE LATER

INDIVIDUAL ROADLESS AREA DESCRIPTION

E: Juneau Urban (305)   ACRES (GROSS)· 105,669   ACRES (NFS)   105,110

ZONE: C21
GRAPHIC PROVINCE: Lynn Canal and Coast Range

9 WILDERNESS ATTRIBUTE RATING: 17

Description

(1) Relationship to RARE II areas: The table below displays the VCU 1/
names, VCU numbers, original WARS 2/ rating, and comments This enables
the reader to compare the roadless areas evaluated in Appendix C with
previous analyses.

VCU Name	VCU No.	1979 WARS Rating	Comments
Sawmill Creek	017*	18	
Canyon Creek	023	21	
Cowee Creek	024	16	
Echo Cove	025*	--	Not rated in 1979
Herbert-Eagle	026	22	
Auke Bay	027*	--	Not rated in 1979.
Montana Creek	028*	13	
Mendenhall	029	19	
Nugget Creek	030*	21	

*--The roadless area includes only part of this VCU

(2) History: The Juneau Urban area has a long history of inhabitation
Tlingit Natives lived in the area long before the Gold Rush days which
began in 1880 and spurred the rapid establishment of Juneau. Mining
activities that flourished in that era diminished during World War II
because of fixed gold prices, wartime inflation, and labor shortages.
Increased participation in outdoor recreational pursuits and tourism
opportunities began to take place in those areas which were originally
accessed and developed, in previous years, by mining ventures Currently,
recreation use is generally high in this area and activities include
hiking, fishing, hunting, picnicking, viewing scenery, mountaineering on
glaciers, and other recreational activities. A recent surge in mineral
exploration and development is currently underway

A VCU (Value Comparison Unit) is one of 867 watersheds which make up the
Forest and were differentiated for planning purposes in the Tongass Land
Management Plan.
Wilderness Attribute Rating System (WARS) was the nationwide system used to
rate the wilderness attributes of roadless areas in the Roadless Area
Review and Evaluation (RARE II).

(3) Location and Access: The area is located on the Juneau mainland and
includes land from Echo Bay, north to City and Borough of Juneau land
boundaries, and south to the Lemon Creek area   The boundary to the east is
the geozone boundary between Juneau Goldbelt (C21) and Juneau Icefield
(C23). Generally, this analysis area falls below the 3,000-4,000 foot
elevation of the Juneau Icefield. The Juneau Urban Roadless Area is
contiguous with the Skagway-Juneau Icefields Roadless Area on the east
side   The western and southern boundaries of this roadless area are
formed by City and Borough of Juneau-owned land which is urban in nature
and much of it roaded   Glacier Highway runs generally north to south from
Juneau to Echo Cove and provides easy access to this entire area

(4) Geography and Topography: The area is generally characterized as
being mountainous, forested, and, in places, deeply incised with
steep-walled, glacially-scoured valleys that extend from sea level to the
Juneau Icefield. Glaciers and icefalls are the most dramatic features and
combined with the surrounding ridges of over 3,000-4,000 feet, provide
topographic relief of extraordinary beauty.

The area contains only three miles of saltwater shoreline, as practically
all coastline is either City and Borough land or privately owned and/or
roaded. A large part of the area is either ice and snow (12,309 acres),
rock (15,262 acres), or alpine (1,958 acres). Muskeg encompasses 1,043
acres. There are 1,499 acres of freshwater lakes in this area

(5) Ecosystem:

(a) Classification: The northern portion of this area is classified
as being in the Lynn Canal Geographic Province   This province is
generally characterized by rugged, scoured terrain with large
vertical relief. The southern portion of this area is classified in
the Coast Range Geographic Province which includes rugged,
heavily-glaciated terrain with extensive alpine and ice field
environments.

(b) Vegetation: Hemlock/spruce rain forests, muskegs, alder
thickets, alpine slopes, and riparian zones all can be found in this
diverse area   There are approximately 63,167 acres of forested land
of which 45,325 acres are classified as commercial forest land   Of
this commercial forest land, 5,317 acres are riparian old growth and
34,032 acres are non-riparian old growth

(c) Soils: Alpine portions of this area consist of shallow to
bedrock soils primarily of organic and mineral origin   The majority
of the area's soils range from well-developed, deep, colluvial soils
on moderate to steep slopes; shallow to bedrock colluvial soils that
are well-drained and developed on very steep slopes; and
poorly-drained, mineral and/or organic soils on benches and moderate
slopes. Occurrences of muskegs with reduced productivity occur on
some of these benches

The entire area has been overridden by glaciers with a predominance of
glacial materials throughout but especially on mid to lower slopes.

(d) **Fish Resources:** Fish resources have been rated as part of the
Tongass Land Management Plan (1979) and by the Alaska Department of
Fish and Game in its Forest Habitat Integrity Program (1983)   These
ratings describe the value of VCU's for sport fish, commercial fish,
and estuaries

There are seven VCU's which are rated as high value for sport fish.
They are listed below, those with an asterisk indicate that only part
of the VCU is within this roadless area

Canyon Creek	023
Cowee Creek	024
Echo Cove	025*
Herbert-Eagle	026
Auke Bay	027*
Montana Creek	028*
Mendenhall	029

Of those, three VCU's were rated as highly valued for commercial
fish. They are Auke Bay (27), Mendenhall (29), and Nugget Creek
(30). Auke Bay (27) is also highly valued in its estuarine rating

(e) **Wildlife Resource:** Wildlife populations are typical of the
mainland areas surrounding Juneau and contain numerous waterfowl and
upland birds. Deer populations are impacted because of severe winter
conditions, and generally high predator populations. Mountain goats
occupy the higher elevations during summer months, generally moving to
lower elevations during heavy snow periods. Furbearers are found
throughout the area, as are both black and brown bear

(f) **Threatened and Endangered Species:** The area contains no known
threatened or endangered species. Two species of peregrine falcon may
migrate through this area; both are on the Federal Threatened and
Endangered Species List.

(6) **Current Use and Management:** Seven VCU's (74,881 acres) were allocated
to Land Use Designation (LUD) 3 in the Tongass Land Management Plan   These
areas are to be managed for a variety of uses and activities in a
compatible and complementary manner to provide the greatest combination of
benefits. These areas have either high use or high amenity values in
conjunction with high commodity values. Three of those VCU's were
designated to be managed with a LUD 3 emphasis but excluded from
calculation of timber yield. Two VCU's (30,229 acres) were allocated to
Land Use Designation 2 which allows management in a roadless state to
retain the wildland character of the area but permit wildlife and fish
habitat improvements and primitive recreation facility development

Numerous trails departing from the Juneau Road System transect this
roadless area, and there are two extremely popular public recreation cabins
accessible by trails in this area   The Mendenhall Glacier Recreation Area
is included in this roadless area and includes some of the most used trails
on the Chatham Area. A major visitor center and large campground are
within the Recreation Area and adjacent to this roadless area

Many of the special use permits in the area are associated with recreational outfitters and guides activities   In 1987, management guidelines for helicopter landing tours on the Juneau Icefield were developed and several helicopter companies are currently authorized to conduct landing tours on the Icefield and glaciers within this roadless area. Guided rafting trips are permitted across Mendenhall Lake to access Mendenhall River

(7) Appearance (Apparent Naturalness): The area offers spectacular scenery and opportunities to view wildlife and vegetation, yet users will perceive that historically, the area has been modified and impacted   The modifications that have occurred in the area (such as trails, recreation cabins, historic mining remains) and activities such as helicopter landing tours affect the natural appearance of this area.

The visual character type of this roadless area is Coast Range. Landforms are generally large, massive and give an impression of great bulk   Uplands are generally 5,000 to 7,000 feet in elevation, dissected by deep, steep-walled, U-shaped valleys. Mountain ridges are generally rounded summits but are surmounted, at times, by aretes and horns rising 8,000 to 9,000 feet.

Forty-three percent of the area was inventoried in Variety Class A (possessing landscape diversity that is unique for the character type) and 42 percent of the acreage was inventoried in Variety Class B (possessing landscape diversity that is common for the character type)   The remaining acreage was categorized in Variety Class C (possessing a low degree of landscape diversity).

The vast majority (96 percent) of this roadless area is in Existing Visual Condition (EVC) I; these areas appear to be untouched by human activity   Approximately one percent is in EVC III. These areas are where changes in the landscape are noticed by the average person but they do not attract attention. The natural appearance of the landscape still remains dominant

(8) Surroundings (External Influences): External influences that affect this roadless area are the Juneau Road System, numerous flight paths and air traffic in the area, and an urban population who utilizes the area extensively. From vistas and vantage points, users of the area also can view Gastineau Channel and Lynn Canal, both busy waterways for ferries, cruiseships, and private and commercial vessels

(9) Attractions and Features of Special Interest: The natural features of the area, the scenery, and the opportunity to see wildlife and to study the processes which formed this country are all attractions. The proximity to the Juneau Icefield and the numerous glaciers offer unparalleled scenery and opportunities for mountaineering, skiing, ice and rock climbing, camping, and scenic viewing.

High-quality fishing opportunities in the streams and lakes are also an attraction   The area contains 18 inventoried recreation places encompassing 56,634 acres   These are numerous improved trails in the area and two popular public recreation cabins

b. Capability of Management as Wilderness or in an Unroaded Condition

(1) **Manageability and Management Area Boundaries:** The area is contiguous with the Skagway-Juneau Icefield Roadless Area and, because of the nature of the glaciers and Icefield, the areas covered with glaciers and ice at the higher elevations will undoubtedly remain roadless Boundaries formed by City and Borough of Juneau lands may not be well defined and easily locatable on the ground The lower elevation area is impacted by easy access from the Juneau Road System and would be more difficult to manage as wilderness

(2) **Natural Integrity:** The area is modified by public recreation cabins, numerous trails, and past and present mining claims. In addition, air traffic by regularly-scheduled air operators, flightseeing tours, and helicopter landing tours all contribute to impacting the ecological processes in the area.

(3) **Opportunity for Solitude:** There is not a high opportunity for solitude in this area. Frequent air traffic by jets, small planes, and helicopters is usually present. Noise from the Juneau Road System can be heard in much of the area. The trails and public recreation cabins in the area are generally considered to be highly used, and contact with other users is not uncommon.

(4) **Opportunity for Primitive Recreation:** The area provides primarily Primitive and Semi-Primitive Non-Motorized recreation opportunity

ROS Class	Acres
Pristine (P1)	461
Primitive (P2)	38,838
Semi-Primitive Non-Motorized (SPNM)	42,906
Semi-Primitive Motorized (SPM)	15,244
Rural (R)	561
Roaded Natural (RN)	6,540
Urban	559

The area contains 18 recreation places.

ROS CLASS	# OF REC. PLACES	TOTAL ACRES	CAPACITY BY RVD
SPNM	5	37,731	14,450
SPM	4	14,245	881
RN	6	4,117	10,086
R	3	542	26,596

As mentioned previously, there are two public recreation cabins in the area, and numerous trails which tend to focus recreational use in the area. Hunters and fishers also use the area quite extensively

(5) **Special Features (Ecologic, Geologic, Scientific, Cultural):** The glaciers and surrounding scenery are the most significant special features of the area.

c. Availability for Management as Wilderness or in an Unroaded Condition

   (1) Resource Potentials

      (a) Recreation Potential: The spectacular scenery, relatively-easy access to the area and opportunity to view and/or harvest fish and wildlife serve to make this roadless area attractive and recreation potential seemingly infinite   Recreation opportunities include both developed and dispersed projects

      (b) Fish Resource: Several fish habitat improvement projects have been identified in the Tongass Land Management Plan, amended 1985-86 for this analysis area.

      (c) Wildlife Resource: The amended Tongass Land Management Plan, 1985-86, identified several waterfowl habitat improvement projects

      (d) Timber Resource: There are 32,153 acres inventoried as tentatively suitable for harvest. This includes 3,838 acres of suitable riparian old growth and 24,838 acres of suitable non-riparian old growth.

      (e) Land Use Authorizations: Special use permits for this area are issued primarily for outfitters and guides activities. Recently, there has been renewed interest in mineral exploration as evidenced by eighteen new Plans of Operation received by the Juneau Ranger District in the summer of 1988.

      (f) Minerals: This area encompasses much of what is known as the Juneau Gold Belt and is recognized as an area of high mineral development potential, priority one.

      (g) Areas of Scientific Research: This roadless area does not contain any designated or inventoried potential Research Natural Areas.

  (2) Management Considerations

      (a) The Cowee-Davies Timber Sale, located in this roadless area, was halted during the appeal process because the court deemed an environmental impact statement necessary. Timber sales within this area would be controversial because of its close proximity to Juneau and the high recreation use of the area.

      (b) Because of its proximity to Juneau, interest is high regarding any management decisions made for this area.

      (c) Juneau was founded because of the discovery of gold. Because much of the current outdoor recreational pursuits and tourism opportunities take place in those areas that were originally accessed and developed by mining ventures of the past, the recent surge in mineral exploration and development is being met with mixed emotions

      (d) Fire: The area has no significant fire history

(e) Insects and Disease: Endemic tree diseases common to Southeast Alaska are present, there are no known epidemic disease occurrences

(f) Land Status: A parcel of 48 acres has been recently selected by the State in the Eagle River area, and a larger parcel has been proposed. The Auke Cape/Lena Cove parcel of 653 acres is also a proposed State selection. Two small patented mining claims are within the area.

d. Relationship to Communities and Other Roadless and Wilderness Areas

(1) **Nearby Roadless and Wilderness Areas and Uses:** The Juneau Urban Roadless Area is contiguous with the Skagway-Juneau Icefield Roadless Area (301) and forms a larger mainland unroaded landmass of approximately 1,314,309 acres.

(2) **Distance From Population Centers (Accessibility)·** Approximate distances from population centers are as follows:

Community		Air Miles	Water Miles
Juneau	(Pop. 23,729)	Adjacent	Adjacent
Petersburg	(Pop 4,040)	120	125
Skagway	(Pop 583)	56	65
Haines	(Pop. 1,838)	45	45

The nearest stop on the Alaska Marine Highway is the Auke Bay Ferry Terminal in Juneau.

(3) Interest by Proponents:

(a) **Moratorium areas·** The area has not been identified as a "moratorium" area or proposed as Wilderness in legislative initiatives to date.

(b) Local users/residents: Most use of the area is associated with a variety of recreational activities, both motorized and non-motorized, which includes hunting, fishing, viewing scenery, and activities in support of tourism. There is local interest and concern regarding availability of firewood.

e. **Environmental Consequences**

ALTERNATIVE ANALYSIS TO BE DONE LATER

INDIVIDUAL ROADLESS AREA DESCRIPTION

NAME: Mansfield Peninsula (306) ACRES (GROSS): 53,054   ACRES (NFS): 52,994

GEOZONE: C20
GEOGRAPHIC PROVINCE: Northern Interior Islands

1989 WILDERNESS ATTRIBUTE RATING: 20

a. Description

(1) **Relationship to RARE II areas:** The table below displays the VCU 1/ names, VCU numbers, original WARS 2/ rating, and comments. This enables the reader to compare the roadless areas evaluated in Appendix C with previous analyses.

VCU Name	VCU No.	1979 WARS Rating	Comments
Barlow Cove	125	18	
Funter Bay	126*	17	
Calm Station	127	19	
Hawk Inlet	128	15	
Lone Mountain	129	19	
Horse Island	130	14	
Fowler Creek	131*	18	

*--The roadless area includes only part of this VCU

(2) **History:** The Mansfield Peninsula has had a long history of use Undoubtedly, Native use of the area focused on fishing and hunting. More recent history reveals the importance of mining in the area; much of the peninsula contains active or historic mining claims in evidence today An old cannery site is located on the south side of Hawk Inlet adjacent to this roadless area.

(3) **Location and Access:** The area is located on Mansfield Peninsula which is the northernmost portion of Admiralty Island It is surrounded by Stephens Passage to the east and Lynn Canal/Chatham Strait to the west The southern boundary of this roadless area is adjacent to the recent road constructed from Young Bay to Green's Creek Mine. It is approximately three miles from the eastern shore of the peninsula to the west side of Douglas Island and seven miles to Auke Bay/Juneau

1/ A VCU (Value Comparison Unit) is one of 867 watersheds which make up the Forest and were differentiated for planning purposes in the Tongass Land Management Plan.
2/ Wilderness Attribute Rating System (WARS) was the nationwide system used to rate the wilderness attributes of roadless areas in the Roadless Area Review and Evaluation (RARE II).

The area is accessed primarily by private boats, and private or chartered planes or helicopters Several excellent anchorages are found adjacent to the peninsula, including Funter Bay, Hawk Inlet, and Barlow Cove As of 1987, regular service for employees of Green's Creek Mine has been provided by boat shuttle There is no public transportation to the area

(4) Geography and Topography: The area is generally characterized by low-elevation, relatively-flat topography with two rugged mountain peaks over 3,100 feet The area contains 76 miles of shoreline on saltwater. Only 100 acres are inventoried as alpine and 1,400 acres as rock Muskeg comprises 2,066 acres, and freshwater lakes 140 acres

(5) Ecosystem:

(a) Classification: The area is classified as being in the Northern Interior Islands Geographic Province. Islands in this province are generally protected from the full force of storms off of the outer coast but have colder climate, more rugged topography, and more distinctive fauna than the Central Interior Islands Province

(b) Vegetation: Lower slopes are generally densely forested with typical spruce/hemlock forest, but sometimes exhibit a combination of muskeg openings, brush, and scattered tree cover up to approximately 2,500 feet in elevation. There are approximately 49,688 acres of forested land of which 28,409 acres are commercial forest land Of the commercial forest land, 25,587 acres are non-riparian old growth and 1,401 are riparian old growth

(c) Soils: Much of the area's soils range from well-developed, deep colluvial soils on moderate to steep slopes, shallow to bedrock colluvial soils that are well-drained and developed on very steep slopes; and poorly-drained, mineral and/or organic soils on benches and moderate slopes. Occurrences of muskegs with reduced productivity occur in this area also.

(d) Fish Resources: Fish resources have been rated as part of the Tongass Land Management Plan (1979) and by the Alaska Department of Fish and Game in its Forest Habitat Integrity Program (1983) These ratings describe the value of VCU's for sport fish, commercial fish, and estuaries.

No VCU's were rated of highest value for either sport or commercial fish in this roadless area. Funter Bay (VCU 126) and Hawk Inlet (VCU 128) are highly valued estuaries.

(e) Wildlife Resource: The Mansfield Peninsula supports a large population of brown bear as well as Sitka black-tailed deer Smaller animals include furbearers such as mink, marten, and beaver

(f) Threatened and Endangered Species: The area does not contain any known threatened or endangered species

(6) **Current Use and Management:** All VCU's (54,094 acres) in this roadless area were allocated to Land Use Designation 3 in the Tongass Land Management Plan with emphasis on managing for uses and activities in a compatible and complementary manner to provide the greatest combination of benefits   These areas have either high use or high amenity values in conjunction with high commodity values

Approximately ten to thirteen isolated hunter or recreation residence cabins are under special use permit in this area, and most are accessed from the eastern shoreline which is closest to Juneau. A special use permit in the past authorized heli-hiking opportunities in the alpine areas, but that permit was never exercised.

Active mining claims and associated patented land are found within this roadless area to a large extent.

Hunting is the primary activity in the area, other than mining   There are no public recreation cabins but there are several minor trails to access recreation residences.

(7) **Appearance (Apparent Naturalness):** The visual character of this roadless area is Admiralty-Chichagof. For the most part, landforms are generally rounded. This visual character type can exhibit great diversity. The majority (68 percent) of this roadless area is found in Variety Class B (possessing landscape diversity that is common for the character type) with 32 percent in Variety Class C (possessing a low degree of landscape diversity)

Ninety-seven percent of this roadless area is in Existing Visual Condition (EVC) I; these areas appear to be untouched by human activity   Two percent is inventoried in EVC III. These areas have changes in the landscaped that are noticed by the average person but they do not attract attention   The natural appearance of the landscape still remains dominant. These small areas appear modified by mining claims and historic mines in the area

(8) **Surroundings (External Influences):** External influences include activities around mining claims, and associated traffic to and from Greens Creek's mining operation located just south of this roadless area   Jets and small planes fly over Mansfield Peninsula on regular flight paths and often at low altitudes. The Alaska Marine Highway ferry route includes both Stephens Passage and Lynn Canal/Chatham Strait so vessels are visible from areas within this roadless area.

(9) **Attractions and Features of Special Interest:** Primary attractions to this area include good anchorages, and high-quality hunting and fishing opportunities in a location easily accessible from the capital city of Juneau. The area contains 14 inventoried recreation places totaling 34.744 acres. There are minor improved trails in the area.

b. Capability of Management as Wilderness or in an Unroaded Condition

(1) Manageability and Management Area Boundaries: The area is well defined by shorelines but may be more difficult to manage in a wilderness condition because of the numerous existing mining claims on the peninsula The southern border of this roadless area is adjacent to a road authorized under an easement to access Greens Creek Mine, and traffic and activities in this area are expected to increase as the Greens Creek mine swings into full operation

(2) Natural Integrity   The area has been modified by mining claims, and access routes to these claims, for many years

(3) Opportunity for Solitude: There is not a high opportunity for solitude within the area because of the numerous floatplanes, helicopters, boats, ferries, and cruiseships traveling to, near, or over this peninsula

(4) Opportunity for Primitive Recreation: The area provides primarily a Semi-Primitive Non-Motorized recreation opportunity.

ROS Class	Acres
Primitive II (P2)	2,961
Semi-Primitive Non-Motorized (SPNM)	38,999
Semi-Primitive Motorized (SPM)	5,865
Roaded Natural (RN)	6,189

The area contains 14 recreation places

ROS CLASS	# OF REC. PLACES	TOTAL ACRES	CAPACITY BY RVD
P2	1	2,580	1,564
SPNM	2	15,978	3,523
SPM	2	3,840	6,293
RN	5	2,780	4,994

(5) Special Features (Ecologic, Geologic, Scientific, Cultural)': No known special features exist in this roadless area

c. Availability for Management as Wilderness or in an Unroaded Condition

(1) Resource Potentials

(a) Recreation Potential: Recreation potential for this peninsula is moderately high because of its close proximity to a large population center. Public recreation cabins that can be accessed by saltwater are desired. Heli-hiking opportunities in the alpine may become more popular.

(b) Fish Resource: No fish habitat enhancement projects are projected for the future

(c) Wildlife Resource: No projects for the future are identified

(d) **Timber Resource:** There are 23,584 acres inventoried as
tentatively suitable for harvest This includes 1,201 acres of
suitable riparian old growth and 21,102 acres of suitable non-riparian
old growth

(e) **Land Use Authorizations:** There is a right-of-way for an old
tractor trail to the Williams Mine departing from the south shore of
Funter Bay This area is not technically within the roadless area but
is adjacent to it

(f) **Minerals:** The area generally has a priority-one high mineral
development potential rating, and there are currently numerous known
claims within the area.

(g) **Areas of Scientific Interest:** This roadless area contains no
designated or inventoried potential Research Natural Areas.

(2) **Management Considerations**

(a) **Fire:** The area has no significant fire history.

(b) **Insects and Disease:** Endemic tree diseases common to Southeast
Alaska are present; there are no know epidemic disease occurrences

(c) **Land Status:** A parcel at Hawk Inlet was nominated but not
recommended for State selection, as was a parcel near Young Bay A
parcel at Funter Bay has been proposed as well as a parcel on the east
side of the peninsula south of Colt Island. No selections or
conveyances have occurred to date

d. **Relationship to Communities and Other Roadless and Wilderness Areas**

(1) **Nearby Roadless and Wilderness Areas and Uses:** Nearby roadless areas
to Mansfield Peninsula include only the Greens Creek-Young Bay Roadless
Area (307) but they are separated by the road and easement that traverses
the peninsula to access the Greens Creek Mine.

(2) **Distance From Population Centers (Accessibility):** Approximate
distances from population centers are as follows:

Community		Air Miles	Water Miles
Juneau	(Pop. 23,729)	7	7
Sitka	(Pop. 8,041)	75	110
Skagway	(Pop. 583)	74	74
Haines	(Pop. 1,838)	63	63

The nearest stop on the Alaska Marine Highway is Auke Bay/Juneau

(3) **Interest by Proponents:**

(a) **Moratorium areas:** The area has not been identified as a proposed
"moratorium" area or proposed as Wilderness in legislative initiatives
to date

      (b) Local users/residents: Most use of the area is associated with mining, hunting and fishing.

o   Environmental Consequences

   ALTERNATIVE ANALYSIS TO BE DONE LATER

INDIVIDUAL ROADLESS AREA DESCRIPTION

NAME: Greens Creek (307)   ACRES (GROSS): 48,917   ACRES (NFS): 48,078

GEOZONE: C20 and C15
GEOGRAPHIC PROVINCE: Northern Interior Islands

1989 WILDERNESS ATTRIBUTE RATING: 21

a   Description

(1) **Relationship to RARE II areas:** The table below displays the VCU 1/
names, VCU numbers, original WARS 2/ rating, and comments This enables
the reader to compare the roadless areas evaluated in Appendix C with
previous analyses.

VCU Name	VCU No.	1979 WARS Rating	Comments
Hawk Inlet	128*	15	
Fowler Creek	131*	18	
Young Bay	132	00	
Eagle Peak	133	23	
Green Creek	144	22	

*--The roadless area includes only part of this VCU.

(2) **History:** Evidence of prehistoric and historic use of this roadless
area is documented Historically, Tlingit clans have used the area as a
seasonal subsistence procurement area, and seasonal camps and at least one
village site have been noted. Trapper cabins have been found in the area,
along with evidence of hunting and fishing camps. On the eastern shore of
Hawk Inlet adjacent to this roadless area, the evidence of an old cannery
which burned in 1976 still remains. That cannery was constructed in 1911
Today, those remaining buildings are owned by the Bristol Bay Native
Corporation.

A cabin was constructed in the Young Bay area by the Civilian Conservation
Corps in the late 1930's as a shelter and was later converted into a
recreation cabin. A corduroy trail from the cabin to Young Lake is thought
to have been constructed in conjunction with the shelter

1/ A VCU (Value Comparison Unit) is one of 867 watersheds which make up the
   Forest and were differentiated for planning purposes in the Tongass Land
   Management Plan.
2/ Wilderness Attribute Rating System (WARS) was the nationwide system used to
   rate the wilderness attributes of roadless areas in the Roadless Area
   Review and Evaluation (RARE II).

(3) **Location and Access:** The area is located on Admiralty Island and is directly north of Admiralty Island National Monument Wilderness   VCU 144 is within Admiralty Island National Monument but is not designated Wilderness   The northern boundary of this roadless area is formed by the access road to Greens Creek Mine that traverses Mansfield Peninsula from Young Bay to Hawk Inlet.

The Greens Creek Roadless Area is accessed primarily by private boats and private or chartered aircraft   As of 1987, regular service for employees of Greens Creek Mine has been provided by boat shuttle   There is no public transportation to the area.   .

(4) **Geography and Topography:** This area's terrain ranges from hummocky and blocky landforms to complex terrain dominated by angular profiles and sharply-defined crests. Geologic features range from minor peaks to prominent escarpments, craggy peaks, and rock outcrops that tend to dominate the view. Level plains and foothills along Hawk Inlet and Young Bay include pocket clearings of meadows, muskegs, and lakes   There are 11 miles of shoreline on saltwater   About 4,085 acres are inventoried as alpine and 1,902 acres as rock. Freshwater lakes comprise 160 acres and there are 40 acres of small islands.

(5) **Ecosystem:**

    (a) **Classification:** The area is classified as being in the Northern Interior Islands Geographic Province. This province is generally characterized as being protected from the full force of storms off of the outer coast, but with colder climate and more rugged topography than in the Central Interior Islands province

    (b) **Vegetation:** Vegetation of this area is dominated by spruce/hemlock forest. The understory is composed of shrubs such as blueberry, huckleberry, rusty menziesia, and devil's club   Common groundcover plants are trailing raspberry, bunchberry, foamflower, and twisted stalk. Various cryptogams carpet the forest floor; mosses are dominant but liverworts and lichens are also abundant

There are approximately 37,386 acres of forested land of which 28,157 acres are commercial forest land. Of the commercial forest land, 25,495 acres are non-riparian old growth and 1,782 acres are riparian old growth.

    (c) **Soils:** Soils in the area are largely a result of the movement of glaciers that covered the area 5,000 to 10,000 years ago, and from erosion of glacial deposits since then. Soil types vary considerably depending upon their distance from Hawk Inlet, major streams, and Young Bay   Bedrock underlies the entire area

    (d) **Fish Resource:** Fish resources have been rated as part of the Tongass Land Management Plan (1979) and by the Alaska Department of Fish and Game in their Forest Habitat Integrity Program (1983)   These ratings describe the value of VCU's for sport fish, commercial fish, and estuaries

One VCU was rated as having the highest value for sport fish in this area. This is VCU 133, Eagle Peak This VCU was also rated as highly valued for commercial fish VCU's rated as highly valued estuaries include Hawk Inlet (128), Eagle Peak (133), and Green Creek (144)

(e) **Wildlife Resource:** Important populations of wildlife in this roadless area include brown bear, Sitka black-tailed deer, bald eagles, waterfowl/shorebirds, and furbearers such as mink, marten, river otter, and beaver

(f) **Threatened and Endangered Species:** The area contains no known threatened or endangered species. Two species of peregrine falcon may migrate through this area; both are on the Federal Endangered and Threatened Species List

(6) **Current Use and Management:** All of the VCU's except VCU 144 were allocated to Land Use Designation 3 in the Tongass Land Management Plan, with an emphasis on managing for uses and activities in a compatible and complementary manner to provide the greatest combination of benefits Total acreage for these LUD 3 VCU's is 31,028 acres. These areas have either high use or high amenity values in conjunction with high commodity values. The other drainage (VCU 144) is' designated Non-Wilderness National Monument Lands, LUD 1, with 16,710 acres. Although not subject to the provisions and requirements of the National Wilderness Preservation System, it is to be managed to protect objects of ecological, cultural, geological, historical, prehistorical, and scientific interest. Harvesting of timber for commercial purposes is not permitted. The Alaska National Interest Lands Conservation Act (ANILCA) has recognized the mineral values in these locations and has provided for mineral development. Although withdrawn from entry, ANILCA makes provisions for continued prospecting on lands within three-quarters of a mile of valid mineral claims.

Within this roadless area are three public recreation cabins and a trail Because of the close proximity to Juneau, this roadless area receives considerable use for recreational, hunting, and fishing pursuits.

Of utmost impact to this roadless area is the adjacent Greens Creek Mining operation located in VCU 144. The access road forms a "cherry stem" boundary within the roadless area and the activities found here have the greatest impacts on the adjacent roadless area.

Young Bay Experimental Forest is located in VCU 133

(7) **Appearance (Apparent Naturalness):** Several activities and facilities within or adjacent to this roadless area affect its apparent naturalness The three recreation cabins and trail, the adjacent Greens Creek Mine and associated road, and the adjacent fire-gutted cannery facility on Hawk Inlet all provide evidence of human alteration.

The visual character type of this roadless area is Admiralty-Chichagof For the most part, landforms in this unit are generally rounded Notable exceptions exist, however, especially on the northern portions of Admiralty Island where mountainous terrain tends to be rugged and snow-covered most of the year. Numerous tidal meadows of varying sizes are found in this

unit and lower slopes are generally densely forested but can exhibit a
combination of muskeg openings, brush, and scattered tree cover up to
approximately 2,500 feet in elevation

Thirty-five percent of this roadless area was inventoried in Variety
Class A (possessing landscape diversity that is unique for the character
type) and 30 percent in Variety Class B (possessing landscape diversity
that is common for the character type) The remaining 35 percent is in
Variety Class C (possessing a low degree of landscape diversity)

The majority of this area (96 percent) is inventoried in EVC I   These
areas appear to be untouched by human activity Approximately three
percent (1,520 acres) are inventoried in EVC III, where changes in the
landscape are noticed by the average person but do not attract attention
The natural appearance of the landscape still remains dominant

(8) **Surroundings (External Influences):** Primary external influences to
this roadless area include the Greens Creek Mine, and road and traffic
associated with that operation. Other influences may be aircraft passing
over the roadless area, boats in both Hawk Inlet and Young Bay, and
firearms discharged by hunters.

(9) **Attractions and Features of Special Interest:** The natural features of
the area, the scenery, and the opportunity to see and hunt wildlife are all
considered attractions High-quality fishing opportunities in the streams
and lakes are also an attraction The area contains twelve inventoried
recreation places encompassing 29,509 acres There is one improved trail
in the area providing hike-in access to Young Lake where two public
recreation cabins are located Another very popular cabin is located in
Admiralty Cove

. **Capability of Management as Wilderness or in an Unroaded Condition**

(1) **Manageability and management area boundaries:** The area is generally
well defined by a combination of topographic features, existing roads and
adjacency to Admiralty Island National Monument Wilderness The
feasibility of management of this area in a roadless condition is
relatively good except in VCU 144 The largest impacts to wilderness
values would be activities and traffic associated with the mining operation
and the impact of those activities within that VCU

(2) **Natural Integrity:** The three public recreation cabins, the trail
mining operations, and past historic activities are in or are visible from
this roadless area; therefore, the roadless area appears modified to some
extent.

(3) **Opportunity for Solitude:** Opportunities for solitude vary depending
upon one's location. Along any of the coastlines of this roadless area
opportunities for solitude decrease as aircraft, pleasure boats,
cruiseships, and Alaska State ferries pass Within the Greens Creek
drainage, traffic increases in the form of both aircraft and motorized
vehicles along the access road

The three public recreation cabins on Admiralty Cove and Youngs Lake are
extremely popular and generally in use for much of the year
Recreationists and/or hunters will probably be in evidence near those
areas   Away from these developed facilities or shorelines   much of the
area is not accessible by boat or floatplane, and the opportunity for
solitude increases dramatically

(4) Opportunity for Primitive Recreation: The area provides primarily a
semi-primitive non-motorized recreation opportunity.

ROS Class	Acres
Primitive (P)	480
Semi-Primitive Non-Motorized (SPNM)	38,956
Semi-Primitive Motorized (SPM)	4,801

The area contains twelve recreation places.

ROS CLASS	# OF REC. PLACES	TOTAL ACRES	CAPACITY BY RVD
P1	1	220	6
P2	1	260	14
SPNM	2	24,246	2,138
SPM	4	1,121	2,766

As mentioned previously, there are three public recreation cabins and one
trail within this roadless area.

(5) Special Features (Ecologic, Geologic, Scientific, Cultural): Young
Bay Experimental Forest is located in VCU 133.

c. Availability for Management as Wilderness or in an Unroaded Condition

    (1) Resource Potentials

        (a) Recreation Potential: This area has been recognized for the
        numerous recreation opportunities and potential it provides   The
        Tongass Land Management Plan, amended Winter 1985-86, identifies
        several recreation projects such as construction of a water-trail or
        National Recreation Trail, and public recreation cabins

        (b) Fish Resource: No fish habitat enhancement projects have been
        identified in this roadless area; therefore, unroaded or wilderness
        designation would have little effect on this resource.

        (c) Wildlife Resource: No wildlife enhancement projects are planned
        for this roadless area.

        (d) Timber Resource: There are 15,472 acres inventoried as
        tentatively suitable for harvest   This includes 1,782 acres of
        riparian old growth and 13,590 acres of non-riparian old growth

        (e) Land Use Authorizations: None

(f) **Minerals:** The area generally has a high mineral development potential, priority-one minerals rating, in the vicinity of Greens Creek mining operation (VCU 144) There are known current claims in the area

(g) **Areas of Scientific Interest:** There are no designated or inventoried potential Research Natural Areas in this roadless area Young Bay Experimental Forest is located in VCU 133

(2) Management Considerations

(a) The impacts of the Greens Creek mine and associated developments in VCU 144 significantly impact that entire drainage

(b) **Fire:** The area has no significant fire history

(c) **Insects and Disease:** Endemic tree diseases common to Southeast Alaska are present; there are no know epidemic disease occurrences

(d) **Land Status:** The State had nominated 841 acres near Young Bay for selection but did not propose selection of this parcel This is because State ownership would be perceived as a conflict with the Greens Creek Mine non-development concept for the Hawk Inlet and Young Bay areas. This non-development concept is to last thirty years, the expected life of the mine.

d. **Relationship to Communities and Other Roadless and Wilderness Areas**

(1) **Nearby Roadless and Wilderness Areas and Uses:** Greens Creek-Young Bay Roadless Area is part of a larger unroaded landmass of approximately 985,474 acres which includes Admiralty Island National Monument Wilderness. Mansfield Peninsula Roadless Area (306) is in close proximity to this roadless area but is separated only by the access road from Young Bay to Hawk Inlet

(2) **Distance From Population Centers (Accessibility):** Approximate distances from population centers are as follows:

Community		Air Miles	Water Miles
Juneau	(Pop. 23,729)	10	20
Hoonah	(Pop 960)	28	32
Sitka	(Pop. 8,041)	71	105
Ketchikan	(Pop. 12,705)	210	240
Angoon	(Pop. 639)	43	43

The closest Alaska Marine Highway ferry terminals to this roadless area are Auke Bay/Juneau, Hoonah, and Angoon.

(3) Interest by Proponents:

(a) **Moratorium areas:** A portion of this roadless area has been identified as a potential moratorium area or proposed as Wilderness in legislative initiatives to date   The proposed area is primarily in the Young Bay/Admiralty Cove area

(b) **Local users/residents:** Most use of the area is associated with hunting although camping, boating, fishing, and shellfish gathering are also important.

e   Environmental Consequences

ALTERNATIVE ANALYSIS TO BE DONE LATER

INDIVIDUAL ROADLESS AREA DESCRIPTION

NAME: Windham-Port (308)   ACRES (GROSS): 240,777   ACRES (NFS)· 240,294
         Houghton

GEOZONE: C25
GEOGRAPHIC PROVINCE: Coast Range

1989 WILDERNESS ATTRIBUTE RATING. 23

⌐   Description

    (1) **Relationship to RARE II areas:** The table below displays the VCU 1/
    names, VCU numbers, original WARS 2/ rating, and comments This enables
    the reader to compare the roadless areas evaluated in Appendix C with
    previous analyses.

VCU Name	VCU No.	1979 WARS Rating	Comments
Sandford Cove	066	21	
Sand Bay	068	20	
Dry Bay	069	21	
Pt. Windham	070	21	
Windham Bay	071	20	
Windham Creek	072	18	
Sunset Island	073	20	
Libby Creek	074*	20	
Hobart Bay	075*	24	
Chuck River	076	23	
Hobart Creek*	077	21	
Salt Chuck	079	27	
Alice Lake	080*	20	
Pt. Hot	081*	19	
Negro Creek	082	22	
Port Houghton	083	21	
Sandborn Canal	084	22	

    *--The roadless area includes only part of this VCU

    (2) **History:** There is evidence that portions of this area have been used
    since prehistoric times. In more recent history, evidence of small
    homesteads, logging, mining activities, and fox farms can still be found
    dating back to the 1800's and early 1900's.

1/ A VCU (Value Comparison Unit) is one of 867 watersheds which make up the
    Forest and were differentiated for planning purposes in the Tongass Land
    Management Plan.
2/ Wilderness Attribute Rating System (WARS) was the nationwide system used to
    rate the wilderness attributes of roadless areas in the Roadless Area
    Review and Evaluation (RARE II).

(3) Location and Access: The area is located directly south of
Tracy Arm-Fords Terror Wilderness and is bordered to the west by Stephens
Passage   The southern and eastern boundaries lie along the administrative
boundary between the Chatham and Stikine Areas of the Tongass National
Forest

The area is accessed primarily by boat and occasionally by floatplane,
although there are no regularly-scheduled flights into the area

(4) Geography and Topography: The topography of the area is typical of
glaciated valleys in Southeast Alaska   The area contains U-shaped valleys
with steep, glacially-scoured sidewalls and mountainous ridgetops
Elevations range from sea level to over 5,000 feet   There are 140 miles of
shoreline on saltwater, and 320 acres of small islands within this roadless
area. Rock comprises 12,977 acres of this area and alpine 2,399 acres
Ice and snow total 2,062 acres. Muskeg totals 601 acres and there are 582
acres of freshwater lakes.

(5) Ecosystem:

   (a) Classification: The area is classified as being in the Coast
   Range Geographic Province. This province is generally characterized
   by rugged, heavily-glaciated terrain with extensive alpine
   environments. Productive forest lands are usually confined to river
   valleys and marine terraces   Alpine lakes; young, dynamic rivers and
   deep, U-shaped troughs are characteristically present in this area

   (b) Vegetation: Most forest timber stands are composed primarily of
   western hemlock and Sitka spruce, although Alaska-cedar is
   occasionally found scattered throughout the spruce/hemlock stands, and
   lodgepole pine can be found on poorly-drained sites   Red alder and
   Sitka alder line some streams and shorelines, and dominate landslides
   and other areas where soil disturbance has occurred   There are
   approximately 195,808 acres of forested land of which 155,010 acres
   are commercial forest land. Of the commercial forest land, 15,430
   acres are riparian old growth and 139,460 acres are non-riparian old
   growth.

   (c) Soils: Soils on the sideslopes are predominantly shallow
   residuals which have developed from metasediments. Rooting strength
   is an important factor in slope stability, because of its anchoring
   effect on the shallow soil mantle. Valley bottom soils on floodplains
   and terraces are composed primarily of alluvial silts, sands, and
   gravel.

   (d) Fish Resource: Fish resources have been rated as part of the
   Tongass Land Management Plan (1979) and by the Alaska Department of
   Fish and Game in its Forest Habitat Integrity Program (1983)   These
   ratings describe the value of VCU's for sport fish, commercial fish
   and estuaries.

Only one VCU (76) was rated as having the highest value for sport fish
in this area   The VCU's rated as highly valued for commercial fish
are 71, 76, 77, and 84   VCU's rated as highly valued estuaries
include 79, 80, 81, 82, 83, and 84

(e) **Wildlife Resource.** The area supports a rich wildlife
population   Larger mammal species include both black and brown bear
as well as moose, Sitka black-tailed deer, wolves, and at the higher
elevations, mountain goats   Smaller animals include furbearers such
as mink, marten, and beaver

(f) **Threatened and Endangered Species:** The area contains no known
threatened or endangered species.

(6) Current Use and Management: VCU 66 (13,867 acres) was allocated to
Land Use Designation (LUD) 2 in the Tongass Land Management Plan, which
provides for management of the area in a roadless state to retain the
wildland character   Two other drainages (VCU's 71 and 79) and part of VCU
75 were allocated to LUD 3 which allows the land to be managed for a
variety of uses   The emphasis is on managing for uses and activities in a
compatible and complementary manner to provide the greatest combination of
benefits in these VCU's   These areas have either high use or high amenity
values in conjunction with high commodity values. A total of 66,311 acres
were allocated to LUD 3   Seven entire VCU's (VCU 68, 69, 70, 72, 82, 83
and 84) and six partial VCU's (73, 74, 76, 77, 80, and 81) were allocated
to LUD 4 which is to provide for intensive resource use and development
where emphasis is primarily on commodity or market resources   A total of
160,219 acres were allocated to LUD 4. The identification of partial VCU's
in all of the Land Use Designations above reflect the fact that the
remaining portions of each VCU are privately owned (Native land selection
at Hobart Bay)

There are only two minor trails in this roadless area. Most use is focused
along shorelines and at several upland mining claims.

(7) Appearance (Apparent Naturalness): The area appears unmodified except
for the occasional remains of old fox farms, cabins, or evidence of mining
claims. Within Windham Bay, there are several inholdings and mining
claims, and private cabins may be occasionally visible   Hobart Bay is
being actively logged at the present time by Goldbelt, Inc.; and in the
immediate vicinity of their land, harvest units are visible which affect
the apparent naturalness of the area. Those units extend around and in to
the north side of the entrance to Port Houghton, so viewsheds from areas
appear highly modified where logging is occurring.

Of the area inventoried, eight percent is considered Variety Class A
(possessing landscape diversity that is unique for the character type) with
57 percent in Variety Class B (possessing landscape diversity that is
common for the character type)   Thirty-three percent is in Variety Class C
(possessing a low degree of landscape diversity)

Almost 98 percent of this roadless area is in Existing Visual Condition (EVC) I, these areas appear to be untouched by human activity. Less than one percent is inventoried in EVC II. These areas are those in which changes in the landscape are not noticed by the average person unless pointed out

(8) Surroundings (External Influences): The northern portion of this
· analysis area is adjacent to Endicott Arm of Tracy Arm-Fords Terror wilderness and the associated tour boats may occasionally be seen.

Windham Bay is a popular bay for fishing, crabbing, and other recreational and commercial activities, and the bay provides access routes to some of the mining claims to the east. Floatplanes and boats may be seen in Windham Bay more frequently than in the other bays of this roadless area

The area located between Hobart Bay and Tracy Arm-Fords Terror Wilderness is steep and remote; access is difficult. That area may be impacted by the active logging and roading by Goldbelt, Inc. on their private land both in a visual and auditory sense

Port Houghton is a large bay with no permanent facilities within Commercial fishing and crabbing boats use the bay; and to the north, at the mouth of the bay, logging is occurring on private land. The area is vast enough to minimize the external influences of these activities

The Alaska Marine Highway ferries travel Stephens Passage on a regular basis, but because of the vastness of the area, usually appear only as small ships in the distance

(9) Attractions and Features of Special Interest: The areas immediately adjacent to saltwater or major creeks are highly valued for recreation uses such as bear and deer hunting, camping, beach combing and viewing wildlife. Fishing opportunities in both the streams and saltwater is also an attraction as well as crabbing opportunities in the bays. The area contains 17 inventoried recreation places encompassing 99,107 acres. There are few improved trails in the area and no public recreation cabins

b. Capability of Management as Wilderness or in an Unroaded Condition

(1) Manageability and Management Area Boundaries: The Windham-Port Houghton Roadless Area is contiguous with Tracy Arm-Fords Terror Wilderness to the north and east, and with Fanshaw (201) and Spires (202) Roadless Areas to the south. The western boundary is primarily Stephens Passage, except for the area adjacent to Hobart Bay which is privately owned. This analysis area could easily be managed in a roadless condition, but in that area adjacent to Hobart Bay, boundaries may be more difficult to manage and impacts from private activities would affect a user's experience there

(2) Natural Integrity: The area is unmodified except for the fox farms, cabins, and mining claims mentioned above. Generally, long-term ecological processes operate intact throughout the area

(3) Opportunity for Solitude   There are vast opportunities for solitude within a large portion of the area   The Alaska Marine Highway has only slight impact on one's feelings of solitude, and there is no regular air traffic into or over the area   The area directly adjacent to Goldbelt Inc land in Hobart Bay would be most affected by external influences.

(4) Opportunity for Primitive Recreation. The area provides primarily Pristine and Semi-Primitive Non-Motorized recreation opportunities

ROS Class	Acres
Pristine (P1)	126,133
Primitive (P2)	2,762
Semi-Primitive Non-Motorized (SPNM)	85,738
Semi-Primitive Motorized (SPM)	14,886

The area contains 16 recreation places

ROS CLASS	# OF REC. PLACES	TOTAL ACRES	CAPACITY BY RVD
P1	3	35,581	2,972
P2	2	2,762	3,444
SPNM	8	36,640	32,833
SPM	3	12,223	52,698

There are no public recreation cabins in the area. The vastness of the area generally allows the visitor to feel remote from the sights and sounds of human activity, except in the immediate vicinity of Hobart Bay   Access is primarily gained from commercial fishing boats or private recreational boats, or floatplanes

(5) Special Features (Ecologic, Geologic, Scientific, Cultural): There are opportunities to observe and study fish and wildlife throughout the area. Historic and prehistoric sites are special features within this area including petroglyphs in Windham Bay   Within Port Houghton, the salt chuck at the head of the bay is an attraction to many

. Availability for Management as Wilderness or in an Unroaded Condition

(1) Resource Potentials

(a) Recreation Potential   The recreation values of this area are primarily associated with the sense of solitude one can find, and the opportunity to view and/or harvest fish and wildlife   There is potential for developing recreation facilities such as public recreation cabins in the area, but because of the distance from any population center, use may be low   Recreation potential focuses primarily on primitive and semi-primitive opportunities

(b) Fish Resource: The Tongass Land Management Plan, amended Winter 1985-86 identified one habitat improvement project in Port Houghton.

(c) Wildlife Resource: No wildlife habitat improvement projects are identified for the future in this roadless area

(d) Timber Resource. There are 114,049 acres inventoried as
tentatively suitable for harvest   This includes 12,328 acres of
riparian old growth and 101,641 acres of non-riparian old growth

(e) Land Use Authorizations: A land exchange was completed in 1988
with Colabelt, Inc in which the U S Forest Service received parcels
in Port Houghton in exchange for land near Libby Creek This exchange
enabled the Forest Service to manage Port Houghton in its entirety,
except for the private land on the north side of the bay at the mouth
of Port Houghton. Sealaska retains subsurface rights on portions of
that Port Houghton tract

(f) Minerals: Portions of this area, especially in the Windham Bay
area, are considered to have high mineral development potential,
priority three. There are known current claims near Endicott Arm and
Windham Bay.

(g) Areas of Scientific Interest: This roadless area contains no
designated or inventoried potential Research Natural Areas

(2) **Management Considerations**

(a) **Timber:** The potential for managing timber in this roadless area
is good

(b) **Fire:** The area has no significant fire history

(c) **Insects and Disease:** Endemic tree diseases common to Southeast
Alaska are present; there are no know epidemic disease occurrences

(d) **Land Status:** There are 481 acres of private land within the
area. These acres are primarily located in Dry Bay, or consist of
patented mining claims east of Windham Bay.

d. **Relationship to Communities and Other Roadless and Wilderness Areas**

(1) **Nearby Roadless and Wilderness Areas and Uses:** The Tracy Arm-Fords
Terror Wilderness is adjacent to this roadless area to the north and east
To the south lies the Fanshaw (201) and Spires (202) Roadless Areas in the
Stikine Area of the Tongass National Forest.

(2) **Distance From Population Centers (Accessibility):** Approximate
distances from population centers are as follows:

Community		Air Miles	Water Miles
Juneau	(Pop. 23,729)	50	50
Petersburg	(Pop 4,040)	35	50
Wrangell	(Pop. 2,836)	70	70

The closest stops on the Alaska Marine Highway are Petersburg (south of the
area) and Juneau (north of the area)

(3) Interest by Proponents:

(a) Moratorium areas: A large portion of this area has been identified as a proposed "moratorium," area or proposed as Wilderness in legislative initiatives to date

(b) Local users/residents: Most use of the area is associated with fishing (both commercial and sport), hunting, beachcombing, mining, and crabbing Much of the use in the Port Houghton area originates from Petersburg Residents of Hobart Bay logging camp also recreate in the area

e. Environmental Consequences

ALTERNATIVE ANALYSIS TO BE DONE LATER

INDIVIDUAL ROADLESS AREA DESCRIPTION

NAME. Juneau Islands (309)   ACRES (GROSS): 7,190   ACRES (NFS)· 7.051

GEOZONE: C21
GEOGRAPHIC PROVINCE: Lynn Canal

1989 WILDERNESS ATTRIBUTE RATING. 17

a. Description

(1) Relationship to RARE II areas: The table below displays the VCU 1/
names, VCU numbers, original WARS 2/ rating, and comments This enables
the reader to compare the roadless areas evaluated in Appendix C with
previous analyses.

VCU Name	VCU No.	· 1979 WARS Rating	Comments
Shelter Island	124	18	
Auke Bay	27*	-.-	Not rated in 1979
Echo Cove	25*		Not rated in 1979

+--The roadless area includes only part of this VCU

(2) History: These islands, located within the vicinity of Juneau, have
had a long history of human occupation and activity. Tlingit Natives lived
in the area long before the Gold Rush days of the 1890's which brought a
large population of white settlers to Juneau. Because of their close
proximity to Juneau, these islands have received significant associated
use Many of the islands contained fox farms earlier in this century
More recent use focuses on recreational and gathering opportunities of the
islands - picnicking and camping, hunting, trapping, and viewing scenery in
conjunction with the boating necessary to access the islands

(3) Location and Access: This roadless area is comprised of the islands
directly adjacent to the City and Borough of Juneau urban area in Lynn
Canal and Auke Bay They are separated by the larger unroaded landmass of
Skagway-Juneau Icefield and Juneau Urban Roadless Areas by Juneau City and
Borough lands and roads, and by private roads and developments The
primary islands are Shelter Island, Lincoln Island, Benjamin Island,
Coghlan Island, Portland Island, and Spuhn Island. These islands are
accessed primarily by private boats and kayaks.

1/ A VCU (Value Comparison Unit) is one of 867 watersheds which make up the
Forest and were differentiated for planning purposes in the Tongass Land
Management Plan.
2/ Wilderness Attribute Rating System (WARS) was the nationwide system used to
rate the wilderness attributes of roadless areas in the Roadless Area
Review and Evaluation (RARE II).

(4) Geography and Topography· These islands are generally characterized as small, low-lying islands with insignificant geologic features   Minor peaks and promontories, and small, singular, wave-cut formations are typical examples   Shorelines usually offer some opportunities for landing boats and going ashore.

The area contains 36 miles of shoreline on saltwater and 6,851 acres classified as small islands   Freshwater lakes comprise 60 acres and muskegs. 100 acres

(5) Ecosystem:

(a) **Classification:** The area is classified as being in the Lynn Canal Geographic Province. This province is generally characterized by rugged, scoured terrain with large, vertical relief   As islands. this roadless area contains somewhat-less-significant features and is characterized by diverse, hummocky, occasionally-blocky terrain often penetrated by secondary bays and coves   Water features are also insignificant in that shorelines and associated saltwater features offer little diversity   Streams, ponds or bogs are typically minor

(b) **Vegetation:** These islands are typically covered with spruce/hemlock forest with some cedar   Western hemlock and Sitka spruce dominate the overstory, while the understory is composed of shrubs such as red huckleberry, rusty menziesia, and devil's club. The forest floor is covered with a mat of mosses, liverworts, and plants such as deerheart, bunchberry dogwood, single delight, and skunk cabbage. The occasional muskegs are dominated by sphagnum mosses, sedges, and shrubs of the heath family   Trees within the muskegs are sparse and consist mainly of stunted hemlock, lodgepole pine, and Alaska-cedar.

There are approximately 7,090 acres of forested land of which 4,808 acres are commercial forest land. Of the commercial forest land 4,227 acres are non-riparian old growth and 60 acres riparian old growth.

(c) **Soils:** Soils are primarily poorly-drained, mineral and or organic soils on benches and moderate slopes with some occurrence of muskegs with reduced productivity or well-developed, deep colluvial soils on moderate to steep slopes.

(d) **Fish Resource:** Fish resources have been rated as part of the Tongass Land Management Plan (1979) and by the Alaska Department of Fish and Game in its Forest Habitat Integrity Program (1983)   These ratings describe the value of VCU's for sport fish, commercial fish and estuaries.

Both Auke Bay (VCU 27) and Echo Cove (VCU 25) were evaluated as having the highest value for sport fish in this area   This evaluation includes mainland shoreline outside of this roadless analysis area. VCU 27 is also highly valued for commercial fish and estuaries.

(e) Wildlife Resource: Sitka black-tailed deer are found on these islands as are small furbearers such as mink and marten

(f) Threatened and Endangered Species: The area contains no known threatened or endangered species

(6) Current Use and Management: Shelter and Lincoln Islands (and the associated smaller islands adjacent to these two islands) were allocated to Land Use Designation (LUD) 2 in the Tongass Land Management Plan, which are to be managed in a roadless state to retain their wildland character. This designation permits wildlife and fish habitat improvement and primitive recreational facility development   LUD 2 acreage totals 6,091 acres   The remaining islands, 1,260 acres, were allocated to Land Use Designation 3 which allows management for a variety of uses. The emphasis is on managing for uses and activities in a compatible and complementary manner to provide the greatest combination of benefits. These areas have either high use or high amenity values in conjunction with high commodity values

All of these islands receive recreational use from the population of adjacent Juneau. There is a dispersed picnic ground (with buoy) on Portland Island.

(7) Appearance (Apparent Naturalness): These islands have sustained use for many years and evidence of that use can easily be found   Camps, remnants of old fox farms, and cut trees all affect the apparent naturalness of the islands

The visual character type of this roadless area is Admiralty-Chichagof. For the most part, landforms are generally rounded   Lower slopes are often densely forested, but sometimes exhibit a combination of muskeg openings brush, and scattered tree cover up to approximately 2,500 feet in elevation. Approximately 84 percent of the acreage in this roadless area was inventoried in Variety Class B (possessing landscape diversity that is common for the character type), 16 percent was inventoried in Variety Class A (possessing landscape diversity that is unique for the character type).

The entire area (except for 40 acres) was inventoried in Existing Visual Condition I, these areas appear to be untouched by human activity

(8) Surroundings (External Influences): Lynn Canal and Auke Bay are both extremely busy waterways   Cruiseships, Alaska Marine Highway Ferries, and private recreational and commercial boats all ply these waters regularly. The islands within this roadless area are influenced by this activity and by the overhead air traffic from the Juneau Airport. Sights and sounds of the nearby urban area are also noticeable from these islands

(9) Attractions and Features of Special Interest: These islands are popular because of their close proximity to and easy access from Juneau. The area contains six inventoried recreation places totaling 3,306 acres. There are no improved trails on the islands nor public recreation cabins but Portland Island has a dispersed picnic ground that is used on a regular basis by local boaters and kayakers

b   Capability of Management as Wilderness or in an Unroaded Condition

(1) **Manageability and Management Area Boundaries:** This roadless area
consists of small islands within Lynn Canal and Auke Bay   The
feasibility of management in a roadless condition is good, but the
surrounding activities of Juneau would make management of these islands as
a designated wilderness difficult

(2) **Natural Integrity:** The islands in this roadless area have been
modified throughout the years by the activities occurring on them   These
activities have compromised the natural integrity of the islands

(3) **Opportunity for Solitude:** There is little opportunity for solitude
within the area because of the the amount of both air and marine traffic
associated with the City and Borough of Juneau and Lynn Canal

(4) **Opportunity for Primitive Recreation:** The area provides primarily
Roaded Natural and Semi-primitive Non-motorized recreation opportunities

ROS Class	Acres
Semi-Primitive Non-Motorized (SPNM)	3,207
Semi-Primitive Motorized (SPM)	20
Roaded Natural (RN)	4,303
Rural (R)	40

The area contains six recreation places.

ROS CLASS	# OF REC. PLACES	TOTAL ACRES	CAPACITY BY RVD
SPM	1	20	100
RN	4	3,246	17,848
R	1	40	195

Portland Island has one dispersed picnic site; there are no other
recreation facilities in this roadless area. When on these islands, it is
impossible for a visitor to feel remote from the sights and sounds of human
activity   Access is limited to boats   Floatplanes may be able to access
some of the islands, but landings would be dependent upon weather and
location.

(5) **Special Features (Ecologic, Geologic, Scientific, Cultural):**   The
easy proximity to a population center and the opportunity to view marine
wildlife serve as attractions to these islands

c. Availability for Management as Wilderness or in an Unroaded Condition

(1) Resource Potentials

(a) **Recreation Potential:** There is great potential for increased
recreation opportunities on these islands and for this reason   the
State has proposed selection of all of these islands for State
acquisition

(b) Fish Resource: There is no identified potential for fish resource enhancement on these islands.

(c) Wildlife Resource: No projects are identified in the Tongass Land Management Plan, Amended Winter 1985-86.

(d) Timber Resource: There are 3,947 acres inventoried as tentatively suitable for harvest. This includes 3,606 acres of suitable non-riparian old growth and 20 acres of riparian old growth.

(e) Land Use Authorizations: A youth wilderness camp, organized through the City and Borough of Juneau, is authorized on Portland Island.

(f) Minerals: The area generally has a low minerals rating; there are no known current claims.

(g) Areas of Scientific Interest: This roadless area contains no designated or inventoried potential Research Natural Areas

(2) Management Considerations

(a) Timber: The potential for managing timber in this roadless area is low.

(b) Fire: The area has no significant fire history, although very small, human-caused fires occur occasionally throughout the summer months.

(c) Insects and Disease: Endemic tree diseases common to Southeast Alaska are present; there are no known epidemic disease occurrences.

(d) Land Status: All of the islands from Auke Bay/Fritz Cove northwest to Bridge Cove, generally lying between Stephens Passage and Lynn Canal, have been proposed for selection by the State of Alaska. At this time, Spuhn Island has been tentatively approved The southern tip and a portion of the northern tip of Shelter Island are privately owned.

d. Relationship to Communities and Other Roadless and Wilderness Areas

(1) Nearby Roadless and Wilderness Areas and Uses: The Juneau Islands Roadless Area is not contiguous with any other roadless area The two largest islands (Shelter and Lincoln Islands) are near Mansfield Peninsula Roadless Area, and are only separated from the peninsula by two miles of saltwater. The entire area is separated from the Skagway-Juneau Roadless Area and Juneau Urban Roadless Area by saltwater.

(2) Distance From Population Centers (Accessibility): Approximate distances from population centers are as follows·

Community			. Air Miles	Water Miles
Juneau	(Pop	23,729)	2	2
Petersburg	(Pop	4,040)	120	135
Skagway	(Pop	583)	63	63
Haines	(Pop	1,838)	56	56

The nearest stop on the Alaska Marine Highway is Auke Bay Ferry Terminal in Juneau   .

(3) Interest by Proponents:

(a) **Moratorium areas:** The area has not been identified as a proposed "moratorium" area or proposed as Wilderness in legislative initiatives to date.   .

(b) **Local users/residents:** Most use of the area is associated with pleasure boating and saltwater fishing

e. **Environmental Consequences**

ALTERNATIVE ANALYSIS TO BE DONE LATER

INDIVIDUAL ROADLESS AREA DESCRIPTION

NAME: Douglas Island (310)   ACRES (GROSS): 27,430   ACRES (NFS): 27,390

GEOZONE: C21
GEOGRAPHIC PROVINCE: Coast Range

1989 WILDERNESS ATTRIBUTE RATING: 18

Description

(1) Relationship to RARE II areas: The table below displays the VCU 1/
names, VCU numbers, original WARS 2/ rating, and comments. This enables
the reader to compare the roadless areas evaluated in Appendix C with
previous analyses.

| | | 1979 | |
VCU Name	VCU No.	WARS Rating	Comments
Douglas	033*		Not rated in 1979.
Fish Creek	034*		Not rated in 1979
Peterson Creek	035*	--	Not rated in 1979.
Inner Point	036*	18	
McDonough Peak	037*	18	

+--The roadless area includes only part of this VCU

(2) History: Douglas Island is directly across Gastineau Channel from
Juneau, the capital city of Alaska The history of Douglas Island has been
linked to that of Juneau since the discovery of gold in the area in the
1860's Historical remains found in this area include the Treadwell Ditch
and ditch tenders' cabin More recent history from the 1930's include
remains from a ski tow and two cabins, one of which has been restored and
is in the public recreation cabin reservation system.

(3) Location and Access: Douglas Island is located directly across
Gastineau Channel from Juneau. This roadless area under analysis includes
only a portion of this island. City and Borough of Juneau lands border
this roadless area on all sides except to the west which is Native-selected
land. Eagle Crest Road and Ski Area serve to access the "doughnut hole" of
private or roaded land in the center of this analysis area

The Douglas Island Roadless Area can be easily accessed from the
Juneau-Douglas road system or by using several trails that enter the area
Snowmobiles are used during winter months when 12 inches or more of snow
are on the ground.

1/ A VCU (Value Comparison Unit) is one of 867 watersheds which make up the
   Forest and were differentiated for planning purposes in the Tongass Land
   Management Plan.
2/ Wilderness Attribute Rating System (WARS) was the nationwide system used to
   rate the wilderness attributes of roadless areas in the Roadless Area
   Review and Evaluation (RARE II).

(4) Geography and Topography: The area is generally characterized by rounded landforms and moderately-significant geologic features   Elevations range from several hundred feet to over three thousand feet

The area contains 12 miles of shoreline on saltwater on the southeast side of the island   There are 500 acres of alpine in this small roadless area and 580 acres of rock   There are no inventoried acres of ice and snow, muskeg, or freshwater lakes

(5) Ecosystem.

   (a) Classification: The area is classified as being in the Coast Range Geographic Province. This province is generally characterized by heavily-glaciated terrain with extensive alpine environments

   (b) Vegetation: The area is characterized by a moderately-varied vegetative pattern of typical spruce/hemlock forest   Natural forest openings occur in the form of small, frequent muskegs

   There are approximately 23,973 acres inventoried as forested land of which 16,314 acres are commercial forest land. Of the commercial forest land, 13,475 acres are non-riparian old growth and 1,700 acres are riparian old growth.

   (c) Soils: Alpine portions of this area consists of shallow to bedrock soils, primarily of organic and mineral origin. The majority of the area's soils range from well-developed, deep, colluvial soils on moderate to steep slopes, and poorly-drained, mineral and/or organic soils on benches and moderate slopes   Occurrences of muskegs with reduced productivity occur on these benches   The entire area has been overridden by glaciers, with a predominance of glacial till throughout the Island, especially on mid- to lower slopes.

   (d) Fish Resource: Fish resources have been rated as part of the Tongass Land Management Plan (1979) and by the Alaska Department of Fish and Game in its Forest Habitat Integrity Program (1983)   These ratings describe the value of VCU's for sport fish, commercial fish, and estuaries

   VCU 34, which is partially contained in this roadless area, is rated as having the highest value for sport fish in this area   That same VCU is highly valued for commercial fish. There are no VCU's inventoried as highly valued for estuaries

   (e) Wildlife Resource: Larger mammals include black bear and Sitka black-tailed deer. Furbearers include marten, mink and ermine

   (f) Threatened and Endangered Species: The area contains no known threatened or endangered species

(6) Current Use and Management: All Value Comparison Units (VCU's),
totaling 27,910 acres, were allocated to Land Use Designation 3 in the
Tongass Land Management Plan and are to be managed for a variety of uses.
The emphasis is on managing for uses and activities in a compatible and
complementary manner to provide the greatest combination of benefits At
the time of the designation the area was excluded from calculation of
timber yield

The area, with its immediate proximity to Juneau and Douglas, receives
heavy use Hunting is popular as are hiking, camping, climbing,
cross-country skiing, and snowmobiling Two trails are included in the
area and one public recreation cabin

(7) Appearance (Apparent Naturalness): The area is essentially unmodified
except in the area of the trails and cabin. The "ski bowl" around the
cabin contains remains of the old downhill ski tow

The visual character type is Admiralty-Chichagof. For the most part,
landforms are generally rounded. Lower slopes are generally densely
forested, but sometimes exhibit a combination of muskeg openings, brush,
and scattered tree cover up to approximately 2,500 feet in elevation
Upper slopes and summits appear barren from a distance, but usually offer a
variety of alpine vegetation as well as numerous rock outcroppings.

The majority of this area (25,512 acres) was inventoried in Variety Class B
(possessing landscape diversity that is common for the character type) with
only 1,838 acres inventoried in Variety Class C (possessing a low degree of
landscape diversity)

Ninety-six percent of the area is in Existing Visual Condition (EVC) I.
These areas appear to be untouched by human activity. The remaining
acreage (four percent) is in either EVC II or III There are areas in
which changes in the landscape are noticed but may or may not attract some
attention.

(8) Surroundings (External Influences): Because of its proximity to
Juneau and Douglas, many external activities influence this area The City
and Borough of Juneau operates a downhill ski operation, and a road
provides access to the ski area Because it is directly across from the
downtown area of Juneau, it is possible to view residential and business
buildings, cruiseships, numerous boats, and frequent air traffic by both
floatplanes, jets, and helicopters from the ridges within the roadless
area. The south and west sides of the island are popular hunting and
fishing areas, and boat traffic should be expected.

(9) Attractions and Features of Special Interest: Primary attractions are
good hunting, hiking, beautiful scenery, high alpine meadows, and
relatively-easy access. The area contains three inventoried recreation
places totaling 21,772 acres. There are two improved trails in the area
and one public recreation cabin The cabin is popular year-round

b   Capability of Management as Wilderness or in an Unroaded Condition

(1) Manageability and Management Area Boundaries: This roadless area
would be difficult to manage and define because of the mixed ownership of
the island   City and Borough of Juneau ownership boundaries and Native
land selection boundaries add complexity in defining area boundaries on the
ground   Also, the activities on land of other ownership may not be
complementary with roadless area management

(2) Natural Integrity· The area is modified by trails and a recreation
cabin   It is also affected by its close proximity to roads and to an urban
environment

(3) Opportunity for Solitude: There is little opportunity for solitude,
especially on the northeast side of the island which faces the
Juneau-Douglas urban area. Other users, floatplanes, helicopters, boats,
cruiseships, snowmobiles, and traffic noise all contribute to the lack of
sense of solitude. The south and southwest sides of the island receive a
reduced impact from the urban area of Juneau and Douglas, but air and boat
traffic are generally present

(4) Opportunity for Primitive Recreation: The area provides primarily
semi-primitive recreation opportunities:

ROS Class	Acres
Roaded Natural (RN) .	2,000
Semi-Primitive Non-Motorized (SPNM)	22,554
Semi-Primitive Motorized	3,357

ROS CLASS	# OF REC. PLACES	TOTAL ACRES	CAPACITY BY RVD
RN	1	240	1,831
SPNM	1	18,175	9,155
SPM	1	3,357	16,480

There is one public recreation cabin in the area. Because much of the use
occurs either on the coastline, trails or in the alpine, one is generally
not outside of the sights and sounds of other human activity

(5) Special Features (Ecologic, Geologic, Scientific, Cultural): There is
high interest in providing recreational opportunities, on this roadless
area and Douglas Island as a whole, for the community of Juneau. Winter
sports such as cross-country skiing, snowmobiling, and recreation cabin use
are all important to local residents   Historic remains such as the
Treadwell Ditch also serve as attractors to the area

c. Availability for Management as Wilderness or in an Unroaded Condition

(1) Resource Potentials

(a) Recreation Potential: The easily-accessible alpine environment
is perhaps the primary recreation attractor, and there is great
potential for increased recreation opportunities in this area.

Additional trails for hikers, cross-country skiers, and snowmobilers are possibilities, and there has been discussion about a trail/hut system in conjunction with a trail circumnavigating Douglas Island

(b) **Fish Resource:** There is little opportunity for fish enhancement projects in this area

(c) **Wildlife Resource:** No projects are proposed in the way of wildlife resource management

(d) **Timber Resource:** There are 9,956 acres inventoried as tentatively suitable for harvest This includes 1,040 acres of riparian old growth, and 13,475 acres of non-riparian old growth.

(e) **Land Use Authorizations:** None.

(f) **Minerals:** The island has been identified as an area of potential mineral development. Currently, there are several claims in the southwest portion of the Douglas Island Roadless Area.

(g) **Areas of Scientific Interest:** The area has not been identified as an area of scientific interest.

(2) **Management Considerations**

(a) **Timber:** The potential for managing timber in this roadless area is poor because of the extensive alpine/muskeg environment and lack of appropriate timber to make such activity financially feasible Also, its close proximity to Juneau would most likely create controversy of such actions. Douglas Island is valued primarily for the recreational and hunting opportunities it provides Local residents depend on Douglas Island, to some extent, for firewood

(b) **Fire:** The area has no significant fire history

(c) **Insects and Disease:** Endemic tree diseases common to Southeast Alaska are present; there are no known epidemic disease occurrences

(d) **Land Status:** This roadless area is adjacent to conveyed Native land selections primarily located on the coastline Douglas Island in its entirety, was nominated for State selection by the U S Forest Service. The recommendation by the State was to not select most of this land. A three-hundred-acre parcel on the north side of the island was also proposed, as was a portion encompassing the road which provides access to Eagle Crest Ski Area. At this time, none of these proposals has been accepted or conveyed.

d. **Relationship to Communities and Other Roadless and Wilderness Areas**

(1) **Nearby Roadless and Wilderness Areas and Uses:** This area is not part of a larger unroaded landmass. It is surrounded either by City and Borough of Juneau lands, Native lands or the North Douglas Highway on the south shore. The City and Borough-managed ski area is located directly in the center of this roadless area

(2) Distance From Population Centers (Accessibility): Approximate distances from population centers are as follows

Community			Air Miles	Water Miles
Juneau	(Pop	23,729)	0	0
Petersburg	(Pop	4,040)	120	125
Sitka	(Pop	8,041)	85	155
Haines	(Pop	1,838)	70	70
Skagway	(Pop	563)	84	84

The nearest stop on the Alaska Marine Highway is the Auke Bay Terminal in Juneau.

(3) Interest by Proponents:

(a) **Moratorium areas:** The area has not been identified as a "moratorium" area or proposed as Wilderness in legislative initiatives to date.

(b) **Local users/residents:** Most use of the area is associated with either recreational or hunting uses by local users and residents Snowmobilers are concerned that they will be prevented from using the area, and there is need for a higher elevation access for them in the winter. Some local residents would like to see additional cabins built in the area or a hut/trail system built and implemented

e. Environmental Consequences

ALTERNATIVE ANALYSIS TO BE DONE LATER

INDIVIDUAL ROADLESS AREA DESCRIPTION

NAME: Chichagof (311)   ACRES (GROSS): 969,439   ACRES (NFS): 637.228

GEOZONE: C01, C02, C04, C05, and C06
GEOGRAPHIC PROVINCE: Northern Outer Islands and Northern Interior Islands

1989 WILDERNESS ATTRIBUTE RATING   29

a   Description

(1) Relationship to RARE II areas: The table below displays the VCU 1/ names, VCU numbers, original WARS 2/ rating, and comments This enables the reader to compare the roadless areas evaluated in Appendix C with previous analyses.

VCU Name	VCU No.	1979 WARS Rating	Comments
Lemesurier Is.	186	17	
Elfin Cove	187	19	
Mount Althrop	188	19	
Port Althrop	189*	21	
Idaho Inlet	190	25	
Gull Cove	191	19	
Goose Island	192	22	
Mud Bay	193*	--	Not rated in 1979
Loon Lakes	194	24	
Point Adolphus	195	21	
Chicken Creek	196	22	
Eagle Creek	197*	18	
Flynn Cove	198*	21	
Humpback Creek	200*	22	
Neka Bay	201*	--	Not rated in 1979
Port Frederick	202*	22	
Tenakee Inlet	224*	22	
Ltle Goose Flats	225	24	
Goose Flats	226	24	
Hub Station	227	18	
Long Bay	228	23	
Seal Bay	229*	23	
Bech Station	230*	--	Not rated in 1979
Saltery Bay	231*	22	
Crab Bay	232*	20	
S. Crab Bay	233*	0	

*--The roadless area includes only part of this VCU

1/ A VCU (Value Comparison Unit) is one of 867 watersheds which make up the Forest and were differentiated for planning purposes in the Tongass Land Management Plan.
2/ Wilderness Attribute Rating System (WARS) was the nationwide system used to rate the wilderness attributes of roadless areas in the Roadless Area Review and Evaluation (RARE II).

VCU Name	VCU No.	1979 WARS Rating	Comments
Inbetween	234*	- -	Not rated in 1979
Kadashan River	235*	22	
Corner Bay	236*	- -	Not rated in 1979
Kook Lake	239*	- -	Not rated in 1979
Ltle Basket Bay	240	20	
Do 2 Station	241*	- -	Not rated in 1979
White Rock	242*		Not rated in 1979
Sitkoh Bay	243*		Not rated in 1979
False Island	245*	- -	Not rated in 1979
Broad Island	246*	21	
Finger Mountain	247*	21	
916 Lake	248	21	
Lisianski River	249*	22	
Phonograph Creek	250*	21	
Pelican	251*	18	
Tarn Mountain	252	20	
Mite Cove	253*	20	
Takanis Lake	256	21	
Bohlemia Basin	257*	0	
Lisianski Strait	258*	20	
Apex-El Nido	260*	20	
Lisianski Ridge	262*	24	

/(2) **History:** Many prehistoric sites have been identified on the Chatham area, including two major sites. One site is located at Ground Hog Bay on the Chilkat Peninsula, and the other is located at Hidden Falls, on Baranof Island Both of these sites indicate human occupation of Southeast Alaska dates back more than 9,000 years. Ground Hog Bay is approximately 15 miles north of the northern portion of the Chichagof Roadless Area, and Hidden Falls is about 28 miles from the southern portion of this roadless area It is very probable the Chichagof Roadless Area was used by the same Natives.

The Tenakee/Hoonah Portage has been used since precontact times and is still used today for recreation purposes Tlingit oral history tells that the portage was found by very early Natives when they observed killer whales swimming across the isthmus. This tale very likely dates back to when this lowland was submerged The Tenakee/Hoonah portage was commonly used by the Natives for canoe travel. It was used by John Muir in 1880 during his exploration of the area. In the 1920's and 1930's, the Tenakee/Hoonah Portage was commonly used by hand trollers They traveled in groups and hand-carried their boats across this small piece of land between Port Frederick and Tenakee Inlet.

A stream flows from Kook Lake, disappears underground in spots, and flows from a cave into Basket Bay. This closed-in area was used by the Natives to hunt seal and to fish An abandoned Native village site has been identified here

At the time of Euroamerican contact, the Hoonah and Angoon Tlingit used
this area of Chichagof Island. Villages, and sites for seasonal hunting
fishing, and collecting activities were located throughout the Chichagof
Roadless Area. The Forest Archaeologist has surveyed sites in VCU's 201
and 202, which include two Native villages and a historical site

The Port Althorp area was surveyed by Captain Vancouver in 1794, where he
found a native burial box just south of Point Adolphus He also explored
and named Port Frederick

Salteries were established at Idaho Inlet in 1884, and at Basket and
Saltery Bays in the early 1900's A salmon cannery, built by Alaska
Pacific Salmon Company at Port Althorp, burned in 1940 and was never
rebuilt.

Homesteads were established at Kadashan Bay in 1915 In 1936, one
homestead was established at Idaho Inlet. This homestead, Gull Cove, was a
trading post that operated for years The community of Pelican was
established in 1938.

(3) **Location and Access:** The Chichagof Roadless Area is located on
Chichagof Island, and includes the Lemesurier and Inian Island groups
Orientation is from the northwest to the southeast and includes most of the
central portion of Chichagof Island. The southern and southwestern
boundaries lie along the West Chichagof-Yakobi Wilderness, Hoonah Sound
and Peril Straits, from Soapstone Cove to False Island The southeastern
boundary is defined by harvest units and roads from False Island to Little
Basket Bay on Chatham Strait, and Chatham Strait itself

The northern and eastern boundaries lie along harvest units from Basket
Bay/Kook Lake to the Kadashan River, then along Tenakee Inlet to a point
approximately five miles southeast of the Tenakee-Hoonah Portage The
boundaries lie along Port Frederick to Neka Bay, north along private land
to Icy Strait and along Icy Strait and Cross Sound to Soapstone Cove

Two towns are surrounded by Chichagof Roadless Evaluation Area--Pelican on
Lisianski Inlet, and Elfin Cove at Port Althorp' Two logging camps, one at
Eight Fathom Bight and the other at Corner Bay, are encompassed by the
roadless area. Two communities near but not within the roadless area are
Tenakee Springs (directly across Tenakee Inlet) and Hoonah (located to the
northeast, across Port Frederick).

Access to the Chichagof Roadless Area is by regular or chartered plane
service, the Alaska Marine Highway (to Pelican) or by private boat

(4) **Geography and Topography:** Most of this area is very mountainous The
flatter areas are primarily around the estuaries and tidal flats There
are high mountain lakes in the northern portion of the area. Muskeg is
found throughout. The evaluation unit is typical of recently glaciated
terrain with rugged mountains dissected by steep-sided, U-shaped valleys
and streamcourses

There are many creeks and rivers, lakes, bays and fiords Many large lakes
such as Kook Lake, and lake chains such as those in the Meadow Creek area
are found throughout the roadless area Streams are generally larger and
longer here than on other islands of Southeast Alaska Major streams
include Lisianski, Trail, Neka, Kadashan and Mud Bay Rivers, and Chicken
Humpback, Gallagher and Tonalite Creeks Saltwater bays and estuaries are
numerous and exhibit much variety The shoreline is rocky and difficult to
access

Elevations range from sea level to 3,770 feet at the highest point
approximately two miles north of Tarn Mountain Scattered throughout the
unit are peaks exceeding 3,000 feet Elevations on the small islands are
less, ranging to about 2,100 feet.

There are 450 miles of shoreline on saltwater and 27,273 acres of beach
Also included are 12,017 acres of small islands, 3,358 acres of freshwater
lakes, 340 acres of snow and ice, 65,631 acres of alpine tundra, and 66,459
acres of rock

(5) **Ecosystem:**

   (a) **Classification:** The area is classified as being in the Northern
   Outer Islands and Northern Interior Islands Geographic Provinces The
   Northern Outer Island province is characterized by rugged,
   highly-dissected topography with an exposed, extremely-wet outer
   coastal environment. There are extensive alpine environments combined
   with productive forested areas, often highly fragmented and generally
   concentrated on oversteepened slopes and on valley bottoms.

   In the Northern Interior Island province, the coastline is protected
   from the full force of storms, unlike the outer coast These islands
   have a colder climate and more rugged topography than in the Central
   Interior Islands Province

   Rocky islands, reefs and rock bluffs are frequently found on the outer
   coast of Chichagof Island Rocky shorelines interspersed with small
   gravel beaches are found throughout the unit.

   Numerous tidal meadows of varying sizes are found in this unit Lower
   slopes are generally densely forested, but often exhibit a combination
   of muskeg openings, brush and scattered trees to approximately 1,500
   feet in elevation. Upper slopes and summits may appear barren from a
   distance, but usually offer a variety of alpine vegetation as well as
   numerous rock outcroppings.

   (b) **Vegetation:** Dense western hemlock/Sitka spruce forests dominate
   the overstory of the Chichagof Roadless Area The understory is
   composed of shrubs such as red huckleberry, rusty menziesia, and
   devil's club The forest floor is covered with a mat of mosses,
   liverworts, and plants such as deerheart, bunchberry dogwood, single
   delight, and skunk cabbage Streamside riparian vegetation is
   characterized by salmonberry, devil's club, alder grasses, ferns, and
   currants.

Muskegs are dominated by sphagnum mosses, sedges, and shrubs of the heath family, and are interspersed among low-elevation timber stands where drainage is restricted. Trees are sparse and consist mainly of stunted hemlock, lodgepole pine, and Alaska-cedar.

Common marine plants in the near-shore waters include brown, red, and green algae, and eelgrass. Tideflats are found at the heads of many of the bays and are usually associated with stream estuaries. The tideflats generally support sea milkwort, glasswort, and algae. Sedge meadows like Mud Bay, occur between the shore and the forest. Low beach meadows are composed of beach ryegrass, reed bent grass, hairgrass, fescue grass, beach lovage, goose tongue, and sedges. Upper beach meadow plants include yarrow, bedstraw, starwort, ferns, western columbine, and cow parsnip. Oregon crabapple, alder, devil's club, and blueberry occur along the border of the beach meadow and the forest.

At elevations above 2,000 feet, the plant communities are generally characterized by low shrubs, grasses, and sedges. Subalpine forests and meadows occur at the interface between the forested communities and the alpine tundra.

There are approximately 447,379 acres of forested lands, of which 270,220 acres are classified as commercial forest land. There are 34,168 acres classified as riparian old growth and 214,972 acres as non-riparian old growth. Approximately 65,631 acres are alpine tundra vegetation, and 32,596 acres are classed as muskeg. Muskeg is interspersed within other types in units too small to map. Therefore, the acreage for muskeg may be substantially understated.

(c) Soils: In the Chichagof Roadless Area, soil development is influenced by high levels of rainfall, cool summer temperatures, a short growing season and moderately-low soil temperatures. Under such conditions, organic matter decomposes slowly and tends to accumulate in areas where it is being produced or deposited. Because of the high rainfall, the available nutrients can be leached rapidly and exposed mineral soils are subject to erosion.

In general, due to the rapid loss of material by erosion and efficient rainwater runoff, shallow soils with good drainage tend to develop on steeper slopes. Examples of these unstable soil conditions exist from Point Adolphus to Mud Bay and on the ridge west of the Eight Fathom Bight road system. Deep, well-drained soils commonly occur on gentler slopes where transported soil materials have collected.

Deep organic soils (muskegs) tend to develop where drainage is poor. This situation occurs where the soil material fails to provide sufficient internal drainage or where topography prevents external drainage. These areas are generally not well suited for road construction since the soil materials tend to be wet and have low bearing strengths. Drainage improves with increased slope gradient, however, as slopes become oversteepened, soil depths become much shallower. Riparian area soils tend to contain flood-deposited sands and gravels.

(d) Fish Resource. The evaluation area is highly valued for fish
production   The Kadashan River is recognized as the highest pink
salmon producer in northern Southeast Alaska and the third best
producer of all of Southeast Alaska   The streams running into Sitkoh
Bay and Seal Bay are also considered high producing streams

Many streams throughout the roadless evaluation area are highly rated
for salmonid production   These include the Mud Bay River and Chicken
Creek (pink salmon with smaller runs of chum salmon), and Humpback
Creek (a large odd-year run of pink salmon and a moderate run of chum
salmon)   The Neka River, Portage Creek, Chum Creek, and Homestead
Creek are also important salmon streams   Streams noted for their coho
salmon producing ability are the three streams running into Crab Bay
and the streams at the heads of Long Bay and North Hoonah Sound
Many of the these streams provide anadromous trout and char habitat,
but the level of production is unknown.

Fish resources have been rated as part of the Tongass Land Management
Plan (1979) and by the Alaska Department of Fish and Game (ADF&G) in
its Forest Habitat Integrity Program (1983)   These ratings describe
the value of VCU's for sport fish, commercial fish and estuaries

The following table lists 29 VCU's rated high to very high for sport
and/or commercial fisheries values

		Spt.	Com.			Spt	Com
Port Althrop	189	X	X	S Crab Bay	233	-	X
Idaho Inlet	190	X	X	Inbetween	234	X	
Mud Bay	193	X	X	Kadashan River	235	X	X
Loon Lakes	194	X	-	Corner Bay	236	X	
Chicken Creek	196	X	X	Kook Lake	239		
Flynn Cove	198	X	-	White Rock	242	X	
Humpback Creek	200	X	X	Sitkoh Bay	243	X	
Neka Bay	201	X	X	Finger Mountain	247	-	X
Tenakee Inlet	224	X	-	916 Lake	248		
Ltle. Goose Flats	225	X	-	Lisianski River	249	X	X
Goose Flats	226	X	X	Phonograph Creek	250	X	X
Long Bay	228	X	X	Pelican	251		
Seal Bay	229	X	X	Tarn Mountain	252	X	X
Saltery Bay	231	X	X	Lisianski Ridge	262	X	X
Crab Bay	232	-	X				

The 30 VCU's listed below are rated as containing highly valuable
estuaries.

Lemesurier Is.	186	Tenakee Inlet	224	Inbetween	234
Elfin Cove	187	Ltle Goose Flats	225	Kadashan River	235
Idaho Inlet	190	Goose Flats	226	Corner Bay	236
Gull Cove	191	Hub Station	227	Sitkoh Bay	243
Goose Island	192	Long Bay	228	False Island	245
Mud Bay	193	Seal Bay	229	Finger Mountain	247
Flynn Cove	198	Beth Station	230	916 Lake	248
Humpback Creek	200	Saltery Bay	231	Lisianski River	249
Neka Bay	201	Crab Bay	232	Mite Cove	253
Port Frederick	202	S. Crab Bay	233	Lisianski Strait	258

(e) Wildlife Resource: Diverse wildlife species exist in the
Chichagof Roadless Area. Birds, and waterfowl rearing and nesting
areas are abundant   Some of the most noted are Mud Bay, the whole
Neka Bay area, Lemesurier Island, and Goose Island   Bald eagle
habitat, including nesting and roosting trees, is found along the
shorelines

North Hoonah Sound and Mud, Long, Seal, Saltery, Crab, and Kadashan
Bays are good examples of high-quality brown bear habitat   The north
end of Hoonah Sound is also desirable seal habitat

There are many areas designated critical deer winter range   This
includes all of Goose Island, along the shoreline and estuary of Mud
Bay, all around the lake system northeast of Mud Bay, Chicken Creek,
the whole Neka Bay and river valley area, and all of the area around
Tenakee/Hoonah Portage. Other areas are the Kadashan drainage and
shoreline, Corner Bay, the Basket Bay area including Kook Lake,
intermittently along the Peril Strait shoreline, and the heads of
North Hoonah Sound and Lisianski Inlet.

There are 684,245 acres of brown bear habitat and 677,467 acres of
marten habitat. Habitat for other management indicator species
include black bear (9,979 acres), Sitka black-tailed deer (684,245
acres) and red squirrel (684,245 acres).

(f) Threatened and Endangered Species: The Chichagof Roadless Area
contains no known resident threatened or endangered plant or animal
species. The area has been identified as having habitats for two
migrating endangered species   The Peale's peregrine falcon passes
through the forests during spring and fall migration flights, and the
humpback whale inhabits nearby waters   The bald eagle, a protected
species, heavily uses the coastline.

(6) Current Use and Management: Four VCU's (102,337 acres) were
designated Land Use Designation (LUD) 2 in the Tongass Land Management Plan
in 1979   These lands are to be managed in a roadless state to retain their
wildland character, but wildlife and fish habitat improvement and primitive
recreational facility development are permitted. This designation excludes
roads, except for specifically authorized uses, timber harvesting except
for controlling insect infestations or to protect other resource values
and major concentrated recreational facilities.

The LUD 3 allocation was given to 13 VCU's (224,534 acres)   The emphasis
is on managing for uses and activities in a compatible and complementary
manner to provide the greatest combination of benefits   These areas have
either high use or high amenity values in conjunction with high commodity
values. Allowances in calculated potential timber yield have been made to
meet multiple objectives. These lands may include concentrated
recreational developments   Two VCU's (187 and 251) were allocated to LUD
3, but remain withdrawn from forms of entry, appropriation or disposal.

Thirty-one VCU's (356,173 acres) were designated as a LUD 4 These lands
will be managed for a variety of uses Opportunities will be provided for
intensive resource use and development where emphasis is primarily on
commodity or market resources Allowances in calculated potential timber
yield have been made to provide for protection of physical and biological
productivity

The roadless area is included in the Alaska Pulp Corporation Long-term
Timber Sale Contract Area VCU's 187 and 251 contain the communities of
Elfin Cove and Pelican The timber in these VCU's has been excluded from
the calculation of timber yield because of the close proximity of the
townsite boundaries

There are 60 identified recreation places throughout this roadless area,
totalling 297,305 acres. There is an eight-mile long, unmaintained trail
between Lisianski Inlet and North Hoonah Sound, and the Basket Bay Trail
(451) between Basket Bay and Kook Lake

There are a number of recreation activities taking place within the area
include hiking, dispersed camping, big game hunting, marine viewing,
beachcombing, saltwater kayaking, and saltwater shore'fishing Other
activities include stream fishing, picnicking, nature study, viewing
scenery, small game hunting, lake fishing, flightseeing, waterfowl hunting,
beach related waterplay, canoeing, viewing wildlife and fish, powerboat
use, gathering of forest products, and cross-country skiing

Floatplane trips to area lakes are common, these provide access for work
and recreation activities There is a great deal of small powerboat use
from all surrounding communities including Tenakee Springs, Kennel Creek
logging camp, Baranof Hot Springs, Hoonah, Angoon, Sitka, and Juneau

There are 11 special use permits for activities such as electronic sites,
isolated cabins, an agriculture residence, a resort, a cabin and weir for
research studies, and a helicopter site A number of outfitter and guide
permittees on the Chatham Area use the Chichagof Roadless Area
Lemesurier, Inian, Three Hill and George Islands, Mud Bay, Idaho Inlet
Point Althrop, Lisianski Inlet, and Lisianski Strait all have identified
use There is a shelter at Little Saltery Bay and a hunter's cabin at Crab
Bay There are ten unpatented mining claims in VCU's 240 and 241 (the Lori
claims) and ten in VCU's 258 and 260 (the Apex-El Nido mine)

(7) Appearance (Apparent Naturalness): The Chichagof Roadless Area has
been modified throughout the years by human influence, however, considering
the vastness of the area, the effects have been insignificant Most of the
change has been along the shoreline areas and many of the human occupancy
sites are deteriorated and have been overgrown by the forest

The visual character type is the Admiralty-Chichagof Landforms are
generally rounded, but include steep, rugged mountains on the west side of
the unit These mountains are snowcapped much of the year Rocky
shorelines, interspersed with gravel beaches, are found along most of the
coast. Streams are often short and swift, flowing directly to saltwater
however, some of the largest and longest of the Southeast Alaska island
rivers are also found here Bays and estuaries are common and show a wide

range of visual characteristics   Other significant water features include
large lakes and lake chains

Lower slopes are densely vegetated and are interspersed with muskeg and
small lakes   Upper slopes appear bare from a distance, but often contain
muskeg, alpine-tundra vegetation, and scattered tree cover

The evaluation area is inventoried as 15 percent Variety Class A
(possessing landscape diversity that is unique for the character type) 58
percent Variety Class B (possessing landscape diversity that is common for
the character type) and 27 percent Variety Class C (possessing a low degree
of landscape diversity)

The majority of the area (87 percent) is inventoried as an Existing Visual
Condition (EVC) I, which appears untouched by human activity.
Approximately 0.2 percent is inventoried as EVC II, ares in which changes
in the landscape are not noticeable to the average visitor unless pointed
out. Lands inventoried as EVC III (0 3 percent) are those areas in which
changes in the landscape are noticed by the average person, but they do not
attract attention There is 1 2 percent in an EVC IV, or areas in which
changes in the landscape are easily noticed by the average visitor, and may
attract some attention   EVC V, in which changes to the landscape are
obvious to the average visitor, totals 9 7 percent. The balance of the
area (1.6 percent) is in EVC VI, where changes in the landscape are in
glaring contrast to the natural landscape.

(8) Surroundings (External Influences): External influences affecting
Lemesurier and Inian Islands primarily come from Elfin Cove, Pelican and
Gustavus. Gustavus lies to the northeast across Icy Strait, while the
communities of Pelican and Elfin Cove are located in Lisianski Inlet and
Port Althorp respectively

The north-northeast corner of the Chichagof Roadless Area borders Sealaska
and Huna Totem Corporation lands. The eastern portions of these private
lands have been completely harvested and roaded. In the next three years
the western portion is scheduled to be harvested to the same extent   There
is an operating private log transfer facility located at Westport, on the
southern end of these private lands

The West Chichagof-Yakobi Wilderness: The West Chichagof-Yakobi Wilderness
is approximately 65 miles long and averages eight miles in width   It
borders the entire southwestern side of the roadless area   Though this
Wilderness is remote, it is frequently used by small boat and plane
owners. Many people are drawn to this area by the natural thermal hot
springs located in the Wilderness. Three public use cabins are also
located in the Wilderness.

Eight Fathom Bight Area: The Eight Fathom Bight road system is a major
external influence   It extends from the Eight Fathom Bight logging camp on
Port Frederick, ten miles through the Neka River valley to Otter Lake, and
then two miles along Mud Bay River   A lateral road system, approximately
three and one-half miles long, is located in the Mud Bay River drainage.
Harvest operations, begun in the mid-1970's and completed in the early
1980's, cut timber within one-half mile of either side of the road systems
in these drainages.

Eight Fathom Bight is the location of a log transfer facility (LTF) and a logging camp   The camp and LTF are usually open from March until November   During the nine months the camp is open, approximately 80 people reside there   The winter population is normally 12 to 15 people   The road system continues approximately one mile west of the camp and LTF   This lower, flatter area was originally logged in the mid 1960's, with the foothills harvested in the mid 1980's   The Eight Fathom Bight logging camp was slated to close in the summer of 1989, however, current plans include logging in the area, requiring the camp to be kept open   In addition, the Mud Bay area is scheduled for harvest activities, requiring the use of the existing camp facilities, and loghaul to the Eight Fathom Bight LTF

Salt Lake Bay/Port Frederick/Tenakee Inlet Area. The Salt Lake Bay roaded area and the townsite of Tenakee Springs are located in the Port Frederick-Tenakee Inlet area. Tenakee Inlet and Port Frederick are commonly used by small boats   The Salt Lake Bay area (outside of, but adjacent to the roadless unit) contains about eleven miles of road, harvest operations will continue under current plans   Operations of the Salt Lake Bay LTF will continue   There is one public recreation cabin at Salt Lake Bay

Corner Bay Area: The Corner Bay road system and associated harvest units located in the northwest of the Kook Lake road system and extending into the roadless area for approximately nine miles, were completed in the early 1970's. A logging camp and Forest Service Work Center are located at Corner Bay   The camp was established in the mid-1970's and the population varies, depending on the type of work and the season   During the spring, summer and fall the camp averages 60 to 70 people and during winters it may drop to as low as one family, who act as caretakers for the camp

Corner Bay-Kadashan Road System. The Chichagof Roadless Area borders the southern shore of Tenakee Inlet, which includes Long, Seal, Saltery, Crab and Kadashan Bays   The Corner Bay road system connects Kadashan Bay to the Corner Bay logging camp   The cutting units in the Corner Bay/Kadashan area were logged in the early 1960's   The Operating Plan for the Alaska Pulp Corporation Long-term Timber Sale proposed a road to connect the Kadashan road with the Sitkoh Bay/False Island road system   After eight miles of this road were built, construction was halted by litigation. The area adjacent to Crab Bay was logged from the beach in the mid-1950's, while the southern drainages of Crab Cove were extensively logged in 1977   In 1968, Saltery Bay was beach logged, and Seal Bay tractor logged. Between these two bays is the Inbetween Timber Sale, harvested in 1983

Peril Strait. The Chichagof Roadless Area lies along Peril Strait for 28 miles. There is evidence of beach logging in much of the area   A drainage northwest of Moore Mountain was extensively logged in the mid-1970's   The southeast corner of the Chichagof Roadless Area is surrounded by the False Island/Sitkoh Bay/White Rock road system and logging   Logging operations were started in the 1960s and completed in the late 1970's.

Basket Bay-Kook Lake   The roadless area bounds Chatham Strait for about four miles   Located within this area are Little Basket Bay, Basket Lake, the eastern and southern shorelines of Kook Lake and the southern shoreline

of Basket Bay   The Corner Bay/Kook Lake road system and harvest units form
the northeastern boundaries of the Chichagof Roadless Area   Construction
of the Kook Lake road has been completed past Basket Bay but may be
extended if the courts approve the Supplemental 1981-86 and 1986-90 Alaska
Pulp Corporation Long-Term Timber Sale plan   Harvest activities will
continue under current plans

(9) Attractions and Features of Special Interest: The northern portion of
the Chichagof Roadless Area contains several high alpine lakes used for
fly-in fishing trips   The lakes, originally stocked in the 1930's provide
a unique recreation opportunity   Although big game hunting occurs in all
parts of the roadless area, Point Adolphus to Gull Cove is considered
important for this activity

Because of its sheer size and pristine land and water mass, the Neka Bay
area is considered an attraction and special interest feature within the
Chichagof Roadless Area. The Kadashan area and the area between Lisianski
Inlet and North Hoonah Sound are of special interest because they contain
two of the few remaining intact Sitka spruce old-growth ecosystems outside
of wilderness on the northern half of the Forest. These groves, between
400-500 years old, are considered to have some of the highest fish and
wildlife significance on the Chatham Area.

Tenakee/Hoonah Portage is a quarter-mile-long piece of land that separates
Tenakee Inlet from Port Frederick. A trail, laid with sticks at the
portage, is a special feature that allows people to push their skiffs and
kayaks over the portage.

b. Capability of Management as Wilderness or in an Unroaded Condition

(1) Manageability and Management Area Boundaries: Manageability as
wilderness is high. Most boundaries are defined by the coastline or are
not critical because they adjoin Wilderness. Other areas are bound by
physical characters, such as roads or harvest units   Effects of most
current activities in adjoining areas are minimal because such activities
which are saltwater-based or wilderness related, are transitory   While
activities associated with road construction and logging operations are
highly distracting, they affect a relatively small portion of the roadless
area. Past activities may detract from portions of the roadless area,
however, they have provided better access into the interior of the roadless
area via an existing road system.   Were the Chichagof evaluation area left
unroaded, it would complement the West Chichagof-Yakobi Wilderness
Conversely, the presence of the Wilderness enhances the wilderness
character of the Chichagof Roadless Area.

Exceptions to the ease of manageability as wilderness would be in areas
where there are no physical boundaries. Making up only a small portion of
the total length of the boundary, these areas include all private
ownerships such as Cape Bingham/Mite Cove, Huna Totem/Sealaska lands on
Port Frederick and Icy Strait, private parcels at Mud Bay, and the lands at
Pelican, Elfin Cove, Port Althrop, and Bohlemia Basin   All other
non-federal ownerships are very small and offer no problems for
manageability as wilderness

(2) Natural Integrity: The Chichagof Roadless Area is unmodified except for isolated areas Located within, but excluded from this roadless area are the heavily-modified Eight Fathom Bight/Neka River logging camp, roaded and harvested areas, roads and logging at Kadashan and Crab Bays, mining operations at Cape Bingham/Mite Island, and the communities of Pelican and Elfin Cove These modifications are distinct when considered individually but would not have much of an influence on the overall roadless area

(3) Opportunity for Solitude: The opportunity for solitude in the Chichagof Roadless Area is very high Over the vast majority of the area there are no impacts from humans The proximity of the Chichagof Roadless Area to the West Chichagof-Yakobi Wilderness enhances the opportunity for solitude

In the northern portion of the roadless area, ongoing logging activities and roading on adjacent Huna Totem and Sealaska private lands will adversely affect the opportunity for solitude during the next three years, until timber harvest ceases After cessation of harvest, the opportunity for solitude will be restored

The area near Kook Lake/Corner Bay is presently being logged Equipment noise, logging activities, the logging camp, and LTF would adversely affect the opportunity for solitude Recreational use occurs around Kadashan Bay from the Kadashan/Corner Bay road system and the Corner Bay logging camp Because the road system is not continuously used, solitude is broken only when use is occurring. Because the road is incomplete and will probably be used for recreation purposes only, the solitude of the area would be restored easily

The former False Island logging camp is under special use permit to the Southeast Alaska Regional Health Corporation for its Adolescent Treatment Program. The agency operates a youth camp at False Island, using the contiguous area for their programs The likelihood of an interruption to solitude in this area is higher here, but is not significant The False Island/Sitkoh Bay/White Stone road systems are mainly used for hunting access, but may receive some use by youth camp members

In addition to the ongoing logging operations, an alternative in the Supplemental EIS for the 1981-86 and 1986-90 APC Long-term Timber Sale Plan, proposes continuation of roading and timber harvesting in the areas around Eight Fathom Bight, Kook Lake/Corner Bay and Kadashan Bay This alternative was selected and these areas are planned for entry in 1990. The logging camps at Corner Bay, Eight Fathom Bight, and False Island will be maintained Maintenance of the camps will result in a continued high level of charter plane service, small boat use, and recreation traffic on area road systems. These would be in addition to the impacts on solitude from harvest activities

There is, and would continue to be, interruption to the solitude around the townsites of Pelican and Elfin Cove These interruptions would increase around the patented mines, should they to come into production

Small aircraft overflights for recreation access and service to the various communities and camps will continue   This use would occur primarily over the coastal zone and along the major valleys   There are several daily, commercial, high-altitude overflights, these are primarily to the south of the roadless area, or to the north over Icy Straits   Small boats use most of the coastal waters for commercial or sport fishing and hunting access The Alaska Marine Highway ferries use Peril, Chatham, and Icy Straits, and Cross Sound   All of these activities provide interruption to solitude however, they are transitory and short term in nature .

(4) Opportunity for Primitive Recreation: The Chichagof Roadless Area provides primarily primitive and semi-primitive non-motorized opportunities; however, because of existing use patterns, it is evident that both off-road and highway vehicles use portions of the area   The following areas are as inventoried with the Recreation Opportunity Spectrum System:

ROS Class	Acres
Primitive I (P1)	284,898
Primitive II (P2)	12,577
Rural (R)	240
Roaded Natural (RN)	3,037
Roaded Modified (RM)	41,707
Semi-Primitive Non-Motorized (SPNM)	292,070
Semi-Primitive Motorized (SPM)	47,513
No ROS	1,942

The area contains 56 recreation places, totalling 297,305 acres

ROS CLASS	# OF REC. PLACES	TOTAL ACRES	CAPACITY BY RVD
P1	7	34,060	3,480
P2	5	7,521	7,849
RN	3	1,359	12,538
RM	8	38,108	16,826
SPNM	14	156,888	56,061
SPM	19	37,457	62,510

There are no public recreation cabins in the Chichagof Roadless Area, however, cabins in adjacent areas are located at Salt Lake Bay, White Sulfur Springs, Goulding Lake, Kook Lake, and two at Sitkoh Lake

This area can be accessed by boat or by plane, or may be accessed by foot off of one of several road systems.

(5) Special Features (Ecologic, Geologic, Scientific, Cultural) · Lemesurier Island was not glaciated during the last ice advance from Glacier Bay. This provides an area to study geological and ecological features in contrast to the norm   The mouth of Basket Bay has formations of grey, grey and white, white, dark blue, and black marble   There are reports, dating from 1917, of a hot spring area near the head of North Hoonah Sound.

c   Availability for Management as Wilderness or in an Unroaded Condition

   (1) Resource Potentials

      (a) Recreation Potential: The following recreation projects are
      proposed in the Tongass Land Management Plan, as Amended 1985-86.

         Lemesurier Island - leave undeveloped and emphasize its scenery,
         wildlife and back country features

         George Islands - restore and maintain the World War II shore gun
         site as a visitors site

         Elfin Cove to Port Althorp - construct a trail and public
         recreation cabin.

         Pelican - construct a trail system around the townsite

         Idaho Inlet - construct public recreation cabins, shelters and a
         trail to Tenakee Inlet.

         Mud Bay - construct a public recreation cabin and a trail to
         Otter Lake.

         Neka Bay - construct a marine park and public recreation cabin.

         Tenakee/Hoonah Portage - construct a public recreation shelter.

         Long Bay - construct a public recreation cabin

         Crab Bay - construct a public recreation cabin

         Little Saltery Bay - construct a public recreation cabin and
         shelters.

         North Hoonah Sound to Pelican - construct a trail through the
         Lisianski River valley

         Kook Lake - construct a trail.

      Freshwater fishing use of the high mountain lakes in the northern
      portion of the Chichagof Roadless Area will increase Outfitter and
      guide use will probably increase throughout the area, especially
      around Elfin Cove, Neka Bay, Pelican, Lisianski Inlet and Strait
      Access will be mainly by boat.

      (b) Fish Resource: There are no identified fishery projects

      (c) Wildlife Resource: The amended Tongass Land Management Plan
      identified the following wildlife habitat management projects

         Neka Lake - nest platforms for various waterfowl

Kadashan drainage - road closure device for seasonal traffic control.

(d) **Timber Resource:** There are 182,549 acres inventoried as tentatively suitable for harvest (27 percent of the evaluation area). This includes 26,472 acres of riparian old growth and 132,228 acres of non-riparian old growth The emphasis for much of the area is to continue timber harvest and related road construction (including replacement of several bridges) for the Alaska Pulp Corporation 1986-90 and 1991-95 planning periods The potential for managing timber in this roadless area is high in those areas with operable timber stands The large areas of mature/overmature timber that are operable and accessible, combined with the existing road systems and log transport facilities, makes timber management feasible and likely in those areas

Areas not included in timber management emphasis are Lemesurier Island, the Elfin Cove and Port Althrop areas, all of Lisianski Inlet and Strait, all of the Idaho Inlet area, and all of the area on Tenakee Inlet from north of Tenakee Springs to about the end of the inlet (including Long Bay)

(e) **Land Use Authorizations:** The current special use permits will probably continue. The potential for more frequent use of the area by outfitters and guides is high.

(f) **Minerals:** In 1984, several areas within the Chichagof Roadless Area were identified as having a high potential for development of locatable minerals These include the area from Idaho Inlet east to the private lands of the Huna Totem and Sealaska Corporations, along the eastern and southwestern shoreline of Lisianski Inlet, and all of the northern shore of Peril Strait and the southern shore of Tenakee Inlet. Mineral development potential along the western shoreline of Lisianski Inlet is high, similar potential exists just south of this shoreline. Several mining operations have occurred or are occurring presently within the Chichagof Roadless Area.

(g) **Areas of Scientific Interest:** There are two inventoried potential Research Natural Areas in the Chichagof Roadless Area. These are Upper Tenakee Inlet Hot Springs, located in VCU 224, and Tonalite Creek, located in VCU 235

(2) **Management Considerations**

(a) **Timber:** Because the entire area is within the primary sale area for the Alaska Pulp Corporation (APC) Long-term Timber Sale, the potential for timber management in the Chichagof Roadless Area is very high.

The roaded areas being considered in the Supplemental EIS for the 1981-86 and 1986-90 APC Long-term Timber Sale plan are Neka River Mud Bay River, Salt Lake Bay, the head of Sitkoh Bay, Corner Bay Kook Creek and Kadashan Because of the noise and traffic caused by timber harvesting, harvest activities in these areas will affect the Chichagof Roadless Area Some of the logging units will be within the

Chichagof Roadless Area boundaries, accessed from the existing road
systems

Unroaded areas being considered for harvest are Neka Bay Flats, the
two southwestern drainages closest to Mud Bay, Gallagher Creek, and
Humpback Creek (which may or may not be accessed through private
Native lands), the northwestern portion of Salt Lake Bay, the drainage
between Corner Bay and Kadashan, the Kadashan drainage, and the Hook
Creek drainage off of Kadashan.

(b) Fire: The area has no significant fire history

(c) Insects and Disease: Endemic tree diseases common to Southeast
Alaska are present, there are no know epidemic disease occurrences.

(d) Land Status: Several parcels of non-Federal lands are located in
the area. Most are on saltwater and are located within the area being
analyzed as roadless, but are excluded from it. These include lands
on Inian and Lemesurier Islands, Mud Bay, Gull Cove, a village site
and a private parcel on Idaho Inlet, the community of Elfin Cove, Port
Althrop, Cape Bingham to Mite Cove, the community of Pelican and
surrounding lands, a parcel on Hoonah Sound northwest of Broad Island
and the Tenakee Inlet/Port Frederick Portage Lands away from
saltwater, and more difficult to exclude, are the two holdings in
Bolhemia Basin.

There are no outstanding (unconveyed) Native land selections or State
selections Several unconveyed Native allotments are located along
the various coastlines

d. Relationship to Communities and Other Roadless and Wilderness Areas

(1) Nearby Roadless and Wilderness Areas and Uses: There are two area
Wildernesses These are the West Chichagof-Yakobi to the south and west
(on Chichagof Island) and the Admiralty Island National Monument Wilderness
(on Admiralty Island) to the east across Chatham Strait. The West
Chichagof-Yakobi and the Chichagof Roadless Area share a common boundary.
Other roadless analysis areas within the immediate vicinity are Hoonah
Sound (across Hoonah Sound to the west), North Baranof (across Peril Strait
to the south), Point Craven (to the southeast and separated by roads and
harvest units), Trap Bay (to the east and separated by roads and harvest
units), Tenakee Ridge (to the north and east across Tenakee Inlet), Game
Creek (to the east across Port Frederick), and Pleasant Island (in Icy
Strait to the north). Other evaluation areas on Chichagof Island include
Pavlof/East Point, Point Augusta, Whitestone, and Freshwater Bay Glacier
Bay National Park and Monument is located across Icy Strait to the north

(2) Distance From Population Centers (Accessibility): Approximate
distances from population centers are as follows.

Community			Air Miles	Water Miles
Juneau	(Pop	23,729)	42	55
Pelican	(Pop	238)	Adjacent	Adjacent
Elfin Cove	(Pop	61)	Adjacent	Adjacent
Hoonah	(Pop	960)	8	8
Tenakee Spr	(Pop	95)	4	4
Gustavus	(Pop	218)	8	8
Angoon	(Pop	639)	10	10
Sitka	(Pop	8,041)	35	42

Gustavus has regular jet service in the summer and scheduled small plane service in the winter. Hoonah and Pelican have year-round scheduled small aircraft service. There is charter service to Tenakee Springs, Elfin Cove, and the Eight Fathom Bight and Corner Bay logging camps. The Alaska Marine Highway serves Hoonah and Tenakee Springs on a regular basis, and Pelican on a monthly basis.

(3) Interest by Proponents:

(a) Moratorium areas: Portions of the Chichagof Roadless Area have been designated as "moratorium" areas or have been proposed as wilderness in legislative initiatives to date. These include the areas identified as Lemesurier Island, Point Adolphus/Mud Bay, Chichagof (the area from Idaho Inlet south to Tenakee Inlet, around the southern shore of Seal Bay, west to the Moore Mountains ridge system and south along North Hoonah Sound, west and south through Sergius Narrows, and north along the West Chichagof/Yakobi Wilderness boundary), and Kadashan

(b) Local users/residents: The people using the analysis area are from all of the surrounding towns and logging camps These population concentrations include Pelican, Elfin Cove, Hoonah, Gustavus, Tenakee Springs, Eight Fathom Bight, Corner Bay, Juneau, Sitka and Angoon Almost all methods of transportation access the area including boats, all-terrain vehicles, and planes. Use from outfitter/guides occurs throughout the area. Subsistence uses take place throughout most of the area and includes hunting, fishing, and gathering

(c) Concern of Local Residents: Each community has its own emphasis issues. Elfin Cove, Pelican, and Tenakee Springs would like to see roading and logging techniques now being used changed so the impacts to the land are not so great, and a change to the amount of logs being taken off the land. Hoonah's opinions vary; they would like to see a sustained cut for economic reasons, but would also like the land protected for subsistence use, and for preservation of the Native way of life. There has been opposition to logging the Kadashan drainage from the communities of Tenakee Springs, Juneau, and Sitka They advocate leaving it in a natural state because of the many complete ecosystems and the number of years the drainage has been used as a research area

Local issues include the continuing harvesting and roading of the timberlands, the continuation of jobs in a local area, the effects of logging on fisheries and wildlife habitat, maintaining the visual quality of high-interest areas, maintaining lifestyles, location of log transfer facilities, the distribution of harvest volume classes and the tradeoffs between environmental protection measures and the economics of the harvest activities

e. Environmental Consequences

ALTERNATIVE ANALYSIS TO BE DONE LATER

INDIVIDUAL ROADLESS AREA DESCRIPTION

NAME: Trap Bay (312)   ACRES (GROSS): 22,028   ACRES (NFS): 22 008

GEOZONE: C06
GEOGRAPHIC PROVINCE: Northern Interior Islands

1989 WILDERNESS ATTRIBUTE RATING: 14   .

a. Description

(1) **Relationship to RARE II areas:** The table below displays the VCU 1/
names, VCU numbers, acres, original WARS 2/ rating, and comments This
enables the reader to compare the roadless areas evaluated in Appendix C
with previous analyses.

		1979	
VCU Name	VCU No.	WARS Rating	Comments
Corner Bay	236*	--	Not rated in 1979
Trap Bay	237	21	
South Passage	238	21	
Kook Lake	239*	--	Not rated in 1970

*--The roadless area includes only part of this VCU

(2) **History:** There have been archaeological sites found at Ground Hog Bay
on the Chilkat Peninsula, and Hidden Falls on Baranof Island Evidence at
these sites indicates that occupation of Southeast Alaska dates to over
9,000 years ago The Trap Bay Roadless Area is located approximately 32
miles south of Ground Hog Bay, and 50 miles north of Hidden Falls Because
of the proximity of these two prehistoric sites to this roadless area it
is probable that this roadless area was used by Native peoples in the same
time frame.

Tlingit tradition includes stories about the area, such as the fishermen of
Angoon using the clouds at the top of Trap Bay Mountain as a weather
barometer to tell the direction of the wind on Chatham Strait Another
story concerns an underground stream which flows from Kook Lake to Basket
Bay and has a salmon run. Before entering Basket Bay, the stream passes
through a cave into which the Natives would climb to hunt seals and to
fish.

1/ A **VCU (Value Comparison Unit) is one of 867 watersheds which make up the
   Forest and were differentiated for planning purposes in the Tongass Land
   Management Plan.**
2/ **Wilderness Attribute Rating System (WARS) was the nationwide system** used to
   rate the wilderness attributes of roadless areas in the Roadless Area
   Review and Evaluation (RARE II).

The Hoonah and Angoon Tlingit were using this area of Chichagof Island at the time of Euroamerican contact Villages and sites for seasonal hunting, fishing, and collecting activities were located throughout the area The forest archaeologist has identified a burial site and petroglyphs near Corner Bay, as well as an abandoned village site in the area of Basket B y

(3) Location and Access· The Trap Bay Roadless Area is located on the east side of Chichagof Island Tenakee Inlet forms the northern boundary and Chatham Strait borders on the east Kook Lake and Basket Bay form the southern boundary, and the Corner Bay road system and harvest units form the western boundary

Tenakee Springs and the Corner Bay logging camp are the two closest communities. Both have regular charter plane service, and Tenakee Springs is on the Alaska Marine Highway ferry route. One may use the extensive road system out of Corner Bay to access this roadless area, and then travel inland on foot The area may also be accessed by boat

(4) Geography and Topography: The Trap Bay Roadless Area has four well-defined ridge systems and three large drainages. About 80 percent of this area is mountainous with 40 percent being very rough and steep The streamside zones total about 20 percent of the area Elevations range from sea level to 3,870 feet in the west-central portion of the unit The evaluation area adjoins Kook Lake to the south, however, there are no sizeable lakes within the roadless area itself

There are 17 miles of shoreline on saltwater and 1,038 acres of beach Other terrain features are 619 acres of alpine tundra 230 acres of freshwater lakes, 20 acres of ice and snow, and 919 acres of rock

(5) Ecosystem:

(a) Classification: The Trap Bay Roadless Area is in the Northern Interior Islands Geographic Province Unlike the outer coast the coastline in this province is protected from the full force of storms. This being the case, the area has a colder climate, a more rugged topography, and more distinctive fauna than the Outer Coast Geographic Province. Mountains elevations vary from 2,015 to 3,870 feet.

Rocky shorelines interspersed with small gravel beaches are found throughout the character type Saltwater bays and estuaries are numerous and exhibit much variety There are tidal meadows of varying sizes found in this unit.

Lower slopes are generally densely forested, but sometimes exhibit a combination of muskeg openings, brush, and scattered tree cover up to elevations of approximately 2,500 feet in this area Upper slopes and summits appear barren from a distance, but usually offer a variety of alpine vegetation as well as numerous rock outcroppings.

(b) Vegetation: Dense western hemlock/Sitka spruce forests dominate
the timbered overstory, with an understory of shrubs such as red
huckleberry, rusty menziesia, and devil's club The forest floor is
covered with a mat of mosses, liverworts, deerheart, bunchberry
dogwood, single delight, and skunk cabbage Streamside riparian
vegetation is characterized by salmonberry, devil's club alder
grasses, ferns, and currants

The muskegs are dominated by sphagnum mosses, sedges, and shrubs in
the heath family and are interspersed among low-elevation forest
stands where drainage is restricted Trees are sparse in these areas
and consist mainly of stunted hemlock, lodgepole pine, and
Alaska-cedar

Tideflats, found at the heads of the bays and estuaries, generally
support sea milkwort, glasswort, and algae. Beach meadows occur
between the shore and the forest. Lower beach meadows are composed of
beach ryegrass, reed bent grass, hairgrass, fescue grass, beach
lovage, goose tongue, and sedges. Upper beach meadow plants include
yarrow, bedstraw, starwort, ferns, western columbine, and cow
parsnip. Oregon crabapple, alder, devil's club, and blueberry occur
along the border of the beach meadow and the forest

At elevations above 2,000 feet, the plant communities are
characterized by low shrubs, grasses, and sedges. Subalpine forests
and meadows occur at the interface between the forested communities
and the alpine tundra.

There are approximately 16,877 acres of forested lands, of which
13,825 acres are classified as commercial forest land   There are
2,214 acres classified as riparian old growth and 11,317 acres as
non-riparian old growth. Approximately 619 acres are alpine tundra
vegetation, and 120 acres are classed as muskeg. Muskeg is
interspersed within other types of vegetation in units too small to
map. Therefore, the acreage for muskeg may be substantially
understated.

(c) Soils: Glaciers played an important part in the placement and
character of soil parent material in this area. The development of
soils is influenced by high levels of rainfall, cool summer
temperatures, a short growing season, and moderately-low soil
temperatures. Shallow soils with good drainage develop on steeper
slopes due to rapid loss of material by erosion and efficient
rainwater runoff. Deep, well-drained soils commonly occur below
shallow soils on gentler slopes where transported soil materials have
collected. Poorly-drained soils are associated with low relief and
impermeable subsurface layers.

In locations with poor drainage, deep organic soils (muskegs) tend to
form. This situation occurs where the soil material fails to provide
sufficient internal drainage or where topography prevents external
drainage

Drainage improves with increased slope gradient, however, as slopes become oversteepened, soil depths become much shallower In riparian areas, soil zones tend to contain sand and gravels as a result of flood deposition

(d) **Fish Resource:** Fishing, especially for salmon, is a major resident subsistence activity Abundant streams in the area provide spawning and rearing habitat for pink, chum, coho, and sockeye salmon Sport and commercial fishing in area waters is common Other species include cutthroat trout, steelhead trout, Dolly Varden char, stickleback, and smelt Important saltwater fisheries include crab, sablefish, and rockfishes

Fish resources have been rated as part of the Tongass Land Management Plan (1979) and by the Alaska Department of Fish and Game (ADF&G) in its Forest Habitat Integrity Program (1983). These ratings describe the value of VCU's for sport fish, commercial fish and estuaries

VCU's rated as highly valued for sport fish are 236, 237, and 239 VCU's 236 and 239 were rated as highly valued for commercial fish Those VCU's rated as having highly valued estuaries are 236 and 237

(e) **Wildlife Resource:** Wildlife is high in numbers and species diversity Species include brown bear, Sitka black-tailed deer, pine marten, mink, and land otter, as well as smaller mammals and several amphibians. There are few resident bird species, however the area is used by many migratory species Eagles are common in the coastal zone. Sport and subsistence deer hunting are very important in this area

The entire area (22,008 acres) has been identified as habitat for the management indicator species of Sitka black-tailed deer, brown bear pine marten, and red squirrel

(f) **Threatened and Endangered Species:** The area contains no known threatened or endangered species This area has been identified as providing temporary habitats for two migrating endangered species. The American peregrine falcon passes through the forests during the spring and fall migration flights. The humpback whale inhabits nearby waters, but there is no designated critical habitat near areas of existing or planned log transfer facilities The bald eagle, a protected species, uses the area for nesting and roosting

(6) **Current Use and Management:** The Trap Bay Roadless Area is completely encompassed in the Alaska Pulp Corporation Long-term Timber Sale Contract Area.

One VCU (3,688 acres) was designated as a Land Use Designation (LUD) 3 in the Tongass Land Management Plan The emphasis is on managing for uses and activities in a compatible and complementary manner to provide the greatest combination of benefits These areas have either high use or high amenity values in conjunction with high commodity values Allowances in calculated potential timber yield have been made to meet multiple objectives These lands may include concentrated recreational developments

Three VCU's (18,320 acres) were allotted to LUD 4   These lands will be
managed for a variety of uses   Opportunities will be provided for
intensive resource use and development where emphasis is primarily on
commodity or market resources   Allowances in calculated potential timber
yield have been made to provide for protection of physical and biological
productivity

There are three research cabins located in the Trap Bay area   Two belong
to federal agencies, the Forestry Science Lab (Forest Service), and the
National Marine Fisheries Service, and one belongs to the Alaska Department
of Fish and Game

There is an identified anchorage in Trap Bay. The recreation activities
taking place in this area are waterfowl and big game hunting, hiking,
viewing wildlife/fish, saltwater shore recreation, stream and lake fishing,
cross-country skiing, and powerboat use.

The roadless area can be accessed from the Hoonah/Corner Bay road system on
the western and southern boundaries. The north side faces Tenakee Inlet
and the east side borders Chatham Strait   These two sides are easily
accessed by boats

There is a special use permit in VCU 238 for an electronic site   There are
a number of outfitters and guides holding Chatham Area special use permits
that use this area.

•(7) Appearance (Apparent Naturalness): Other than the areas adjacent to
timber harvest activities (much of the boundary), the Trap Bay evaluation
area appears natural and unmodified. The boundaries adjacent to timber
harvest units and roads appears highly modified   There are some minor
developments (three research cabins constructed in the 1960's), these are
unobtrusive and do not generally detract from the naturalness   There are
no other readily apparent signs of human activities.

The visual character type is the Admiralty-Chichagof. Landforms for the
type are generally rounded, low mountains. However, Trap Bay Mountain is a
tall, steep, very-rugged mountain with craggy peaks and steep,
sharply-defined ridgelines. Rocky shorelines, interspersed with gravel
beaches are found along the coastline. Streams are short and swift,
flowing directly to saltwater. Small bays and estuaries are present and
show a range of visual characteristics. Lower slopes are densely
vegetated, and are interspersed with muskeg and small lakes   Upper slopes
appear bare from a distance, but often contain muskeg, alpine tundra
vegetation, and scattered tree cover.

The evaluation area is inventoried as 21 percent Variety Class A
(possessing landscape diversity that is unique for the character type), 47
percent Variety Class B (possessing landscape diversity that is common for
the character type) and 32 percent Variety Class C (possessing a low degree
of landscape diversity).

The majority of the area (88 percent) is inventoried as an Existing Visual Condition (EVC) I, which appears untouched by human activity The balance is inventoried as an EVC V, in which changes to the landscape are obvious to the average visitor

(8) Surroundings (External Influences): Most of the Trap Bay Roadless Area is isolated from the rest of Chichagof Island by a strongly-defined ridge system, close to the southern and western roadless unit boundaries To the north of this area is Tenakee Inlet The townsite of Tenakee Springs is located approximately three and one half miles to the northwest, across the Inlet Tenakee Springs is on the regular Alaska Marine Highway route and has regularly scheduled small plane service Chatham Strait lies to the east, with Admiralty Island located six miles across the saltwater

To the south of the Trap Bay Roadless Area is the Kook Lake road system and timber harvest units. The road construction has been completed past Basket Bay; the cutting units were completed in summer 1989 This road system is approximately five miles long and connects with the Corner Bay road system.

South of the harvest area are Kook Lake and Basket Bay These areas are used heavily for subsistence and recreation. A Forest Service public recreation cabin is located on the western end of Kook Lake, south of the harvest area which is the roadless area boundary. There is an unmaintained trail from Basket Bay to the southern shore of Kook Lake Another, from the Kook Lake road to the cabin and lake, is heavily used by the people living at the Corner Bay logging camp

The western boundary of this roadless area adjoins with the Corner Bay road system and harvest units This area was heavily harvested in the early 1970's.

Corner Bay logging camp is located at Corner Bay and is approximately one mile west of the Trap Bay Roadless Area. This camp is open seasonally from March until November. The population can fluctuate from 60 to 70 people during the working period, to one or two families caretaking the camp in the winter This camp is accessed by year-round small plane charter service and by boat.

(9) Attractions and Features of Special Interest: Trap Mountain is very rugged and imposing. The area to the north of the mountain is a large cirque. Fishermen fishing Chatham Strait use Trap Bay as an overnight anchorage. Trap Mountain was special to the Natives because they used the clouds around the top of the mountain to see which way the wind was blowing on Chatham Strait.

The chances of seeing bear and deer in this area are very good

There are six recreation places, totaling 5,772 acres

b   Capability of Management as Wilderness or in an Unroaded Condition

(1) **Manageability and Management Area Boundaries:** Manageability as wilderness is high   The coastline along Chatham Strait to the east and Tenakee Inlet to the north provide easily-defined boundaries   There are strong ridge systems to the south and west that separate the Kook Lake and Corner Bay road systems from the Trap Bay Roadless Area   Activities on the southern boundary (along Kook Lake) detract somewhat from the manageability, as the boundary is defined by active harvest units

(2) **Natural Integrity:** Little human modification has occurred in this area. The integrity of the area is basically intact; the only intrusions within the evaluation unit are the three research cabins

(3) **Opportunity for Solitude:** There is a moderate opportunity for solitude in this area around the shorelines because of the constant activities of the Corner Bay logging camp and the town of Tenakee Springs Boats and small planes use this area regularly   Because of lack of access and use, solitude would be easier to find further into the center of this area.

(4) **Opportunity for Primitive Recreation:** Eighty-five percent of the area provides the opportunity for Semi-Primitive Non-Motorized recreation   The balance is in Semi-Primitive Motorized and Roaded Modified.

ROS Class	Acres
Roaded Modified (RM)	380
Semi-Primitive Non-Motorized (SPNM)	18,635
Semi-Primitive Motorized (SPM)	2,974

The area contains six recreation places.

ROS CLASS	# OF REC. PLACES	TOTAL ACRES	CAPACITY BY RVD
RM	2	380	56
SPNM	2	3,974	2,014
SPM	2	1,418	2,382

There are no public recreation cabins in the Trap Bay Roadless Area   The character of the landforms provide a feeling of remoteness away from the shoreline. The Trap Bay Roadless Area is readily accessed by boat or small plane.

(5) **Special Features (Ecologic, Geologic, Scientific, Cultural):** Trap Mountain is an impressive mountain with an exposed rock top, continuing into different types of alpine vegetation and finally in to a heavy old-growth forest at the base. These features of exposed rock, different alpine vegetation types and heavy timber growth are found all along the ridge systems in this area   The autumn colors in the alpine zone are spectacular in this area

c   Availability for Management as Wilderness or in an Unroaded Condition

   (1)   Resource Potentials

      (a) Recreation Potential: The recreation opportunities at Sitkoh and
      Kook Lakes are to be emphasized in accordance with the Tongass Land
      Management Plan, as Amended 1985-86   There will be a trail
      constructed in the Kook Lake area

      (b) Fish Resource: There are no fisheries enhancement projects
      planned for this area.

      (c) Wildlife Resource: There is potential for the introduction of
      mountain goats in the Trap Bay Mountain area and on the adjoining
      ridge systems.

      (d) Timber Resource: There are 10,074 acres inventoried as
      tentatively suitable for harvest. This includes 1,815 acres of
      riparian old growth and 7,880 acres of non-riparian old growth   The
      area is located within the Alaska Pulp Corporation Long-term Contract
      Area. The potential for managing timber in this roadless area is
      high. While there is much of the area that is not suitable for timber
      management, the evaluation area is roaded on two sides and does have
      reasonable potential for future road development   Large areas of
      mature/overmature timber that meet operability criteria, coupled with
      accessibility from existing road systems, make timber harvest a viable
      proposition.

      (e) Land Use Authorizations: The current special use permits will
      probably continue   The potential for more outfitters and guides using
      the area more frequently is probable with the increase of need

      (f) Minerals: The potential for mineral development is low

   (2)   Management Considerations

      (a) Timber: The viability of timber management in the unit increases
      the potential for harvest activities

      (b) Fire: The area has no significant fire history

      (c) Insects and Disease: Endemic tree diseases common to Southeast
      Alaska are present; there are no know epidemic disease occurrences

      (d) Land Status: There are no non-Federal lands or withdrawals nor
      or there any encumbrances or use restrictions.

d   Relationship to Communities and Other Roadless and Wilderness Areas

   (1)   Nearby Roadless and Wilderness Areas and Uses: Other roadless areas
   in the immediate area include the Pavlof/East Point (located to the north
   across Tenakee Inlet), and the Chichagof (to the south and west)   Others
   in the general area are Point Craven, Game Creek, North Baranof, and Salt
   Lake Bay

Admiralty Island National Monument Wilderness is to the east across Chatham
Strait (approximately six miles away) The West Chichagof-Yakobi
Wilderness is located across Chichagof Island, approximately 48 miles away.

(2) Distance From Population Centers (Accessibility): Approximate
distances from population centers are as follows

Community			Air Miles	Water Miles
Juneau	(Pop	23,729)	42	65
Tenakee Spr	(Pop	95)	7	7
Angoon	(Pop.	639)	22	22
Hoonah	(Pop.	960)	28	54
Sitka	(Pop.	8,041)	47	90

Tenakee Springs is the closest town that is on the regularly-scheduled
route of the Alaska Marine Highway system. Other terminals are located at
Hoonah and Angoon. Commercial airline service is available at Sitka and
Juneau.

(3) Interest by Proponents:

(a) Moratorium areas: The Trap Bay Roadless Area includes the Trap
Bay Moratorium Area as proposed for study as a wilderness area as
described in Senate Bill S 341 ("Wirth Bill"), and as proposed for
wilderness in House Bill HR 987 ("Mrazek Bill")

(b) Local users/residents: Much of the use within the unit is
associated with the Tenakee Springs and Corner Bay logging camp
populations There is boat use to Trap Bay from the surrounding
towns, and transit fishermen fishing on Chatham Strait

(c) Concerns of Local Residents: The local issues include the
continuing roading and harvesting of the timber lands, the effects of
logging on fisheries and wildlife habitat, maintaining the visual
quality of high-interest areas, maintaining lifestyles, location of
log transfer facilities, the distribution of harvest volume classes
and the tradeoffs between environmental protection measures and the
economics of the harvest activities.

e Environmental Consequences

ALTERNATIVE ANALYSIS TO BE DONE LATER

INDIVIDUAL ROADLESS AREA DESCRIPTION

NAME: Point Craven (314)   ACRES (GROSS): 11,847   ACRES (NFS) 11,937

GEOZONE: C08
GEOGRAPHIC PROVINCE: Northern Interior Islands

1989 WILDERNESS ATTRIBUTE RATING: 21

a. Description

   (1) Relationship to RARE II areas: The table below displays the VCU 1/
   names, VCU numbers, original WARS 2/ rating, and comments This enables
   the reader to compare the roadless areas evaluated in Appendix C with
   previous analyses.

VCU Name	VCU No.	1979 WARS Rating	Comments
Sitkoh Bay	243C*	0	LUD 4
Sitkoh Lake	244C*	0	LUD 4
False Island	245C*	0	LUD 4

   *--The roadless area includes only part of this VCU

   (2) History: It is believed that Southeast Alaska was settled about
   10,000 to 11,000 years ago   There are human occupancy sites seven miles to
   the south of the evaluation area that date to more than 9,000 years before
   present (BP)   The oldest known site within the Point Craven Roadless Area
   dates to approximately 3,000 BP   This date may be pushed back by future
   field investigations. The area was apparently used by Native peoples from
   the Sitka, Hoonah, and Angoon areas   A permanent village was located at
   Point Craven, with seasonal sites located in Sitkoh Bay and on the coast
   Tlingits fleeing Sitka after the 1804 battle, retreated to the Point Craven
   area, where a community of up to 1,000 people was established

   Early European entries were tied to hunting and exploration   Lt Lisiansky
   of the Russian Navy mapped the Peril Strait area in 1805   Peril Strait was
   important then, as now, for access to the inland waterways which provided
   protected north-south water travel, as well as access to the inland
   islands   The primary activities have remained fishing, hunting, and
   furgathering. Fish canneries and traps were important in whole area in the
   early 20th Century, generally replacing furgathering as furs became both
   more scarce and less of an economic factor. A cannery was located within
   the evaluation area on Sitkoh Bay.

1/ A VCU (Value Comparison Unit) is one of 867 watersheds which make up the
   forest and were differentiated for planning purposes in the Tongass Land
   Management Plan.
2/ Wilderness Attribute Rating System (WARS) was the nationwide system used to
   rate the wilderness attributes of roadless areas in the Roadless Area
   Review and Evaluation (RARE II).

Recent activities include logging and road construction in the Sitkoh Bay,
Peril Strait, and Sitkoh Creek areas   Sitkoh Bay and Sitkoh Creek are
heavily used by sport and subsistence fishers   Two sawmill sites are
located outside the roadless to the north and east on Sitkoh Bay.

(3) **Location and Access:** The Point Craven Roadless Evaluation Area is
located on Chichagof Island, north of Peril Strait, south of Sitkoh Creek
and west of Sitkoh Bay   The community of Hoonah is approximately 40 miles
to the north and the city of Sitka is about 32 miles to the south   Access
is by boat or floatplane. There are roads in exclusion areas along the
coast in Sitkoh Bay and Peril Strait that provide foot or vehicle access to
the associated river valleys   All-terrain vehicles (ATV) use these to as
as well as some off-road vehicles

(4) **Geography and Topography:** The topography is typical of most of the
island areas. It is characterized by narrow river valleys, surrounded by
mountains. Terrain relief ranges from sea level to more than 2,600 feet in
elevation at the southeast corner of VCU 244   The mountains are steep and
highly dissected by streams. Terrain features are such that stream runs
are relatively short, with a high gradient. Because of this, broad river
valleys have not developed. The one exception is Sitkoh Creek and the
lower reaches of its tributaries on the northern boundary of the evaluation
area. There are several small lakes scattered about the area, generally
above the 1,000 foot elevation   While there are no large lakes within the
roadless area, Sitkoh Lake lies to the north, immediately outside the Point
Craven Roadless Area.

Other terrain features are 220 acres of alpine tundra, and 20 acres of
freshwater lakes

(5) **Ecosystem:**

(a) **Classification:** The area is classified as being in the Northern
Interior Islands geographic province. This province is characterized
by a colder climate and steeper, more rugged terrain than either the
Northern Outer Islands or the Central Interior Islands provinces   It
is protected from the full force of outer coastal storms   The
roadless area is typical of the province.

(b) **Vegetation:** Dense western hemlock-Sitka spruce forests dominate
the overstory, with an understory of shrubs such as red huckleberry
rusty menziesia, and devil's club, and a forest floor is covered with
a mat of mosses, liverworts, and plants such as deerheart, bunchberry
dogwood, single delight, and skunk cabbage. Streamside riparian
vegetation is characterized by salmonberry, devil's club, alder,
grasses, ferns, and currants.

Muskegs, dominated by sphagnum mosses, sedges, and shrubs of the heath
family, are interspersed among low elevation timber stands where
drainage is restricted   Trees are sparse and consist mainly of
stunted hemlock, lodgepole pine, and Alaska-cedar

At elevations above about 2,000 feet, the plant communities are characterized by low shrubs, grasses, and sedges Subalpine forests and meadows occur at the interface between the forested communities and the alpine tundra

There are approximately 10,637 acres of forested lands, of which 7,5?? acres are classified as commercial forest land (CFL) There are ?5? acres classified as riparian old growth and 6,737 acres as non riparian old growth Approximately 220 acres are alpine tundra vegetation, and 400 acres are classed as muskeg Muskeg is interspersed within other types in units too small to map Therefore, the acreage for muskeg may be substantially understated

(c) Soils: Glacial activity, combined with a basically sedimentary bedrock, are primary factors in soil development in the evaluation area. Other factors are high rainfall, cool summer temperatures and a short growing season. Because of rainfall, many soils are highly leached. Dense vegetative growth, combined with a slow breakdown of organic matter leaves a thick duff layer on most of the subalpine soils

The soils are highly variable and range from exposed bedrock and very shallow, poorly developed soils in the higher elevations to fluvial and colluvial deposits in the river bottoms There are large areas of deep supersaturated or inundated organic soils (muskeg) over much of the area, particularly at elevations above 1,000 feet The steeper slopes are generally well drained, shallow, moderately productive soils The stream bottoms are generally better soils, well to poorly drained and are highly productive

(d) Fish Resource. There are four Pacific salmon (sockeye cono pink and chum) valuable for commercial, subsistence and sport fishing that spawn and rear in these waters. In addition, steelhead trout is a favored sportfishing species The steelhead run in Sitkoh Creek is one of the few in Southeast Alaska and is considered very valuable Other species include Dolly Varden char, stickleback and smelt Important saltwater fisheries include crab, sablefish and rockfishes.

Fish resources have been rated as part of the Tongass Land Management Plan (1979) and by the Alaska Department of Fish and Game (ADF&G) in their Forest Habitat Integrity Program (1983) These ratings describe the value of VCU's for sport fish, commercial fish and estuaries Two VCU's, Sitkoh Bay (243C) and Sitkoh Lake (244) are highly rated for commercial and sport fisheries values

There are two VCU's containing highly valued estuaries These are Sitkoh Bay (243) and False Island (245)

(e) **Wildlife Resource:** Wildlife is high both in numbers and species
diversity They include brown bear, Sitka black-tailed deer, pine
marten, mink, and land otter, as well as smaller mammals and several
amphibians There are few resident bird species; however, the area is
used by many migratory species Eagles are common in the coastal
zone. Sport and subsistence deer hunting is very important in this
area.

The entire area (11,837 acres) has been identified as habitat for the
management indicator species of Sitka black-tailed deer, brown bear,
pine marten and red squirrel

(f) **Threatened and Endangered Species:** There are no known threatened
or endangered plant or animal species within the roadless area. The
area may receive some migratory use by the peregrine falcon The bald
eagle, a protected species, uses the area for nesting and rearing

(6) **Current Use and Management:** The entire area (three VCU's, 11,837
acres) is allocated as Land Use Designation (LUD) 4 in the Tongass Land
Management Plan (1979) This allocation provides for intensive resource
management and development, consistent with provisions to protect physical
and biological productivity.

Forest Service management activities within the roadless evaluation area
have been limited to permit administration. A Forest Service recreation
cabin is located at Sitkoh Lake, just to the northwest of the roadless
area. Timber harvest and road construction along the coastline in Sitkoh
Bay have been excluded from the roadless area. Other logging activities
have occurred to the south and west on the majority of the evaluation unit
boundary The entire evaluation area is within Management Area 6 of the
Alaska Pulp Corporation (APC) Long-term Timber Sale Contract area, however,
no activities outside of those mentioned have occurred or are currently
planned. There are no special use permits specific to the roadless area
however, the area is used by outfitters and guides for sport fishing and
hunting activities.

(7) **Appearance (Apparent Naturalness):** Other than the areas adjacent to
timber harvest activities (much of the boundary), the Point Craven
evaluation area appears natural and unmodified. The boundaries adjacent to
timber harvest units and roads (about 60 percent of the boundary) appear
highly modified. There is some minor development along the coastline,
these are unobtrusive and do not generally detract from the naturalness
There are no other readily apparent signs of human activities

The visual character type is the Admiralty-Chichagof. Landforms are
generally rounded, low mountains. Rocky shorelines, interspersed with
gravel beaches, are found along Sitkoh Bay and Peril Straits Streams are
short and swift, flowing directly to saltwater The exception is Sitkoh
Creek. Small bays and estuaries are present and show a range of visual
characteristics Lower slopes are densely vegetated and are interspersed
with muskeg and small lakes Upper slopes appear bare from a distance but
often contain muskeg, alpine tundra vegetation and scattered tree cover

The evaluation area is inventoried as 81 percent Variety Class B (Common) and 19 percent Variety Class C (Minimal) The majority of the area (71 percent) is inventoried as an Existing Visual Condition (EVC) I, which appears untouched by human activity Twenty-four percent is inventoried as an EVC V, in which changes to the landscape are obvious to the average visitor Three percent are in an EVC IV, or areas in which changes in the landscape are easily noticed by the average visitor, and may attract some attention The balance of the area (2 percent) is in EVC VI, areas where changes in the landscape are in glaring contrast to the natural landscape.

(8) Surroundings (External Influences): There are two small privately owned tracts within, but excluded from, the roadless area These are located on Sitkoh Bay at Chatham and just northwest of Chatham. Peril Strait is the Alaska Marine Highway route connecting Sitka with the rest of Southeast Alaska. During the summer months there are approximately ten weekly ferry passages that pass the evaluation area.   This strait is also used by cruiseships and tourboats The Strait is the major connecting corridor between the west side of Baranof and Chichagof Islands and the inland waterways Therefore, it is popular with sport and commercial fishing boats, as well as supporting barge traffic Sitkoh Bay gets pleasure and commercial fishing craft use.

(9) Attractions and Features of Special Interest: Although the wildlife and natural beauty of the area are attractions, there is little to distinguish the Point Craven Roadless Area from many other areas Basic attractions are the opportunity to "get away from it all" (solitude), sportfishing and hunting There are no Forest Service recreation facilities, such as cabins, nor are there any developed/maintained trails. Access incidental to use of the Sitkoh Lake Recreation Cabin (adjacent to the northwestern corner of the roadless area) and Sitkoh Lake itself may occur. Of special interest may be the diverse cultural resource sites in the general area, however, there are no interpretative or information programs at present.

b. Capability of Management as Wilderness or in an Unroaded Condition

   (1) Manageability and Management Area Boundaries: Manageability as wilderness is moderate The boundaries are defined by the coastline and Sitkoh Creek to the north, logging areas on the east, Peril Strait and logging areas to the south and a major ridgeline to the west Effects of current activities are minimal because these activities are transitory in nature. Past activities may detract from the majority of the boundary of the roadless area, however, they may provide better access, via an existing road system, into the interior of the area.

   (2) Natural Integrity: The evaluation area is unmodified except for minor activities, such as tent frames, and for early cabin and campsites, including those where Native activity occurred Most of the early sites have now deteriorated and grown over, making them apparent only with close examination Existing cabins/camps are fairly unobtrusive and infrequent and do not detract from the natural integrity of the total area

(3) Opportunity for Solitude   The opportunity for solitude is high   Once away from the coastal areas, the rugged terrain provides for protection from surrounding activities   High altitude overflights by commercial airliners (approximately six per day) and occasional small aircraft flights may provide some distraction

(4) Opportunity for Primitive Recreation: The area provides primarily semi-primitive non-motorized opportunities

ROS Class	Acres
Rural (R)	20
Roaded Modified (RM)	760
Semi-Primitive Non-Motorized (SPNM)	10,517
Semi-Primitive Motorized (SPM)	480

The area contains 3 recreation places, totaling 1,757 acres   A Forest Service recreation cabin is located at Sitkoh Lake, just outside the northwestern corner of the evaluation area.

ROS CLASS	# OF REC. PLACES	TOTAL ACRES	CAPACITY BY RVD
RM	2	320	4,623
SPNM	1	1,437	3,380

(5) Special Features (Ecologic, Geologic, Scientific, Cultural): Although a high probability for numerous cultural resource sites exists, little study has been done   There are five known or suspected (unconfirmed) sites, dating back about 3,000 years. Future surveys may find sites contemporary with older sites in the general area and may add substantially to knowledge of pre-European culture Most known sites are located in the coastal zone   Further field investigation may reveal an opportunity to add to the pool of scientific or ecological knowledge for other resources, however, current indications are that there is nothing unique about the area.

c. Availability for Management as Wilderness or in an Unroaded Condition

(1) Resource Potentials

(a) Recreation Potential: The potential exists to enhance primitive and/or semi-primitive recreation opportunities However, the opportunity for development of anything other than a trail system seems to be low. The presence of the Sitkoh Lake cabin, and the absence of any distinguishing features, would limit management needs for development in the area. There are opportunities for interpretative activities associated with the cultural and historical sites.

The Tongass Land Management Plan, as amended in 1985-86 (TLMP) does not identify recreation facilities development for the evaluation area.

(b) Fish Resource: No habitat improvement projects are identified in the Tongass Land Management Plan, Amended Winter 1985-86

(c) Wildlife Resource: The Tongass Land Management Plan, as amended does not identify any habitat improvement projects

(d) Timber Resource: There are 4,095 acres inventoried as tentatively suitable for harvest This includes 340 acres of ripari.. ' old growth and 3,675 acres of non-riparian old growth The area is located within the APC Long-term Timber Sale contract area The potential for managing timber in this roadless area is high The evaluation area is roaded on three sides and has a reasonable potential for future road development. Large areas of mature-overmature timber that meet operability criteria, coupled with accessibility from existing road systems, make timber harvest a viable proposition.

(e) Land Use Authorizations: No special use permits have been issued for use of the evaluation area However, the area is commonly used by outfitter/guides There is one structure, located on private land on Sitkoh Bay, that is partially on the National Forest Probable future permits would be for subsistence or recreational facilities or for outfitter/guide services. Potential is high for a significant increase in permits for outfitter/guides in the Sitkoh Creek area

(f) Minerals: The development potential for locatable minerals is estimated to be low or non-existent on the entire area

(g) Areas of Scientific Interest: There are no inventoried potential Research Natural Areas within the evaluation unit

(2) Management Considerations

(a) Fire: The area has no significant fire history

(b) Insects and Disease: Endemic tree diseases common to Southeast Alaska are present, there are no know epidemic disease occurrences

(c) Land Status: There are no patented private lands in the roadless area. There are two parcels of private land located within the boundaries, but are excluded from the roadless area There are two unconveyed Native allotments on Sitkoh Bay There are no other non-Federal lands or withdrawals.

d. Relationship to Communities and Other Roadless and Wilderness Areas

(1) Nearby Roadless and Wilderness Areas and Uses: The West Chichagof-Yakobi Wilderness is located approximately 45 miles to the west, with Admiralty Island National Monument Wilderness located 15 miles away across Chatham Strait Adjacent roadless evaluation areas are the Chatham #311 (to the north, and separated by timber harvest units and roads) and North Baranof #330 (across Peril Strait to the south) Others in the general area are Trap Bay, #312, North Kruzof, #326, Hoonah Sound, #328 and Sitka Urban, #331

(2) Distance From Population Centers (Accessibility): Approximate distances from population centers are as follows

Community			Air Miles	Water Miles
Juneau	(Pop.	23,729)	60	95
Hoonah	(Pop	960)	50	70
Sitka	(Pop	8,041)	30	65

The closest Alaska Marine Highway terminals are at Angoon, Tenakee Springs Hoonah, and Sitka Commercial airline service is available in Sitka

(3) Interest by Proponents:

(a) **Moratorium areas:** The Point Craven Roadless Evaluation Area is not in a moratorium area, nor is it proposed for wilderness in current legislative initiatives

(b) **Local users/residents:** The nearest communities are Tenakee Springs (population 156), about 25 water miles to the north and Angoon (population 635) 12 miles to the east. Sitkoh Bay is the primary site for use in the general area. Heaviest subsistence use is indicated to be from Angoon. Activities are primarily subsistence hunting and fishing; there is some sport fishing, particularly for steelhead trout. These activities do not necessarily take place in the roadless area.

(c) **Concerns of local residents:** There has been strong concern expressed about the ability to maintain subsistence use in the Sitkoh Bay area. This concern is tied to a desire to restrict timber harvest around Sitkoh Bay and the adjacent outside coastline

e. **Environmental Consequences**

ALTERNATIVE ANALYSIS TO BE DONE LATER

INDIVIDUAL ROADLESS AREA DESCRIPTION

NAME: Point Augusta (317)   ACRES (GROSS): 19,479   ACRES (NFS): 19,479

GEOZONE: C02
GEOGRAPHIC PROVINCE: Northern Interior Islands

1989 WILDERNESS ATTRIBUTE RATING. 22

a   Description

(1) Relationship to RARE II areas: The table below displays the VCU 1/ names, VCU numbers, original WARS 2/ rating, and comments This enables the reader to compare the roadless areas evaluated in Appendix C with previous analyses.

VCU Name	VCU No.	1979 WARS Rating	Comments
Suntaheen Creek	209*	22	
False Bay	210*	21	
Point Augusta	211	19	

*--The roadless area includes only part of this VCU

(2) History: Prehistoric sites like Ground Hog Bay on the Chilkat Peninsula and Hidden Falls on Baranof Island indicate that this area of Southeast Alaska was occupied by humans over 9,000 years ago The Point Augusta Roadless Area is located approximately 13 miles south of the Ground Hog Bay and 60 miles north of the Hidden Falls All three of these areas are located on Icy and Chatham Straits It is probable that the area that is now a roadless area was used by these prehistoric peoples

At the time of Euroamerican contact, the Hoonah and Angoon Tlingit used this area of Chichagof Island Villages and sites for seasonal hunting, fishing and collecting activities were located throughout Point Augusta was named after the King of England's daughter in 1794 by Captain Vancouver

Forest archaeologists have identified a burial site in VCU 210

(3) Location and Access: The Point Augusta Roadless Area is located on the northeastern coast of Chichagof Island. Whitestone Harbor is adjacent to its northwestern corner. Icy and Chatham Straits are to the north and the east respectively False Bay and the Hoonah road system border to the south and west.

1/ A VCU (Value Comparison Unit) is one of 867 watersheds which make up the forest and were differentiated for planning purposes in the Tongass Land Management Plan.
2/ Wilderness Attribute Rating System (WARS) was the system used to rate the wilderness attributes of roadless areas in the Roadless Area Review and Evaluation (RARE II).

• Hoonah, the community associated with this roadless area, has regularly
  scheduled small plane and Alaska Marine Highway ferry service

(4) Geography and Topography: The Point Augusta Roadless Area has rounded
mountains and long flowing streams   There are 14 miles of shoreline on
saltwater, with 820 acres of beach and 320 acres of alpine tundra   There
are no large lakes are located here

(5) Ecosystem:

   (a) Classification. The Point Augusta Roadless Area is classified in
   the Northern Interior Island geographic province   Unlike the outer
   coast, the coastline is protected from full force of storms   These
   islands have a colder climate, a highly dissected topography and an
   extensive alpine environment with productive forested areas which are
   highly fragmented and usually concentrated on oversteepened slopes and
   on valley bottoms.

   (b) Vegetation: Western hemlock-Sitka spruce forests dominate the
   overstory of this area. There are approximately 18,039 acres of
   forested land of which 14,359 acres are commercial forest land   Of
   the commercial forest land, 11,359 acres are non-riparian old growth
   and 840 acres are riparian old growth.

   The understory is composed of shrubs such as red huckleberry, rusty
   menziesia, and devil's club   The forest floor is covered with a mat
   of mosses, liverworts, deerheart, bunchberry.dogwood, single delight,
   and skunk cabbage. Streamside riparian vegetation is characterized by
   salmonberry, devil's club, alder, grasses, ferns, and currants

   There are 640 acres of muskeg in the Point Augusta Roadless Area.
   They are dominated by sphagnum mosses, sedges, and shrubs of the heath
   family and are interspersed among low elevation timber stands where
   drainage is restricted   Trees are sparse and consist mainly of
   stunted hemlock, lodgepole pine, and Alaska-cedar.

   The tide flats generally support sea milkwort, glasswort, and algae.
   Lower beach meadows are composed of beach ryegrass, reed bent grass,
   hairgrass, fescue grass, beach lovage, goose tongue, and sedges
   Upper beach meadow plants include yarrow, bedstraw, starwort, ferns,
   western columbine, cow parsnip, Oregon crabapple, alder, devil's club
   and blueberry

   At elevations generally above 2,000 feet, the plant communities are
   characterized by low shrubs, grasses, and sedges. Subalpine forests
   and meadows occur at the interface between the forested communities
   and the alpine tundra.

   (c) Soils: In the Point Augusta Roadless Area, the development of
   soils is influenced by high levels of rainfall, cool summer
   temperatures, a short growing season and moderately low soil
   temperatures   Under such conditions, organic matter decomposes slowly
   and tends to accumulate in areas where it is being produced or
   deposited

Shallow soils with good drainage in this roadless area develop on steeper slopes due to rapid loss of material by erosion and efficient rainwater runoff   Deep, well drained soils occur below shallow soils on gentler slopes where transported soil materials have collected

Poorly drained soils are associated with low relief and impermeable subsurface layers   In locations with poor drainage, deep organic soils (muskegs) tend to form   This situation occurs where the soil material fails to provide sufficient internal drainage or where topography prevents external drainage   Drainage improves with increased slope gradient, however, as slopes become oversteepened soil depths become much shallower   In riparian areas, soil zones tend to contain sand and gravels as a result of floods depositing them.

(d) **Fish Resource:** Fish resources have been rated as part of the Tongass Land Management Plan (1979) and by the Alaska Department of Fish and Game in their Forest Habitat Integrity Program (1983)   These ratings describe the value of VCU's for sport fish, commercial fish and estuaries.

False Bay (VCU 210) is the only VCU rated as high value for commercial fish   None of the VCU's in the Point Augusta Roadless Area are rated as high value for sport fish or estuaries

Iyouktug Creek is an anadromous stream for pink and chum salmon   The headwater tributary channels for this large fish-producing stream are found here   Resident Dolly Varden and anadromous trout and char have a minor occurrence.

(e) **Wildlife Resource:** Critical deer winter habitat exists in this roadless area. Bald Eagle nesting and roosting trees are located along the shoreline and into the major drainages.

(f) **Threatened and Endangered Species:** The area contains no known resident threatened or endangered species, Peale's peregrine falcon which is on the threatened list, passes through the forests during the spring and fall migration flights

(6) **Current Use and Management:** VCU's 209-211 (9,798 acres) were designated as a LUD 4 in TLMP in 1979   These lands will be managed for a variety of uses   Opportunities will be provided for intensive resource use and development where emphasis is primarily on commodity or market resources. Allowances in calculated potential timber yield have been made to provide for protection of physical and biological productivity.

Anchorages have been identified in Whitestone Harbor and False Bay   The recreation activities include big game hunting, hiking, cross-country skiing, dispersed camping, saltwater-shore fishing, beachcombing, viewing wildlife/fish and kayaking

There are a number of outfitter and guides under special use permit on the Chatham Area that use the area   There is also a special use permit for lighthouse reserve within the roadless area

(7) Appearance (Apparent Naturalness): The visual character type of this roadless area is Admiralty-Chichagof   The coastline, unlike the outer coast, is protected from full force of storms   Therefore, these islands have a colder climate, a more rugged topography and a distinctive fauna. Mountains elevations vary from 1,800-2,400 feet

Rocky shorelines are interspersed with small gravel beaches and the streams are quite large and long   There are some saltwater bays and estuaries in this area and they exhibit much variety

The lower slopes are densely forested and exhibit a combination of muskeg openings   Brush and scattered tree cover may be found up to approximately 2,400 feet in elevation.

One percent of the acreage was inventoried Variety Class A (Distinctive). 28 percent was in Variety Class B (Common) and 71 percent of this acreage was inventoried in Variety Class C (Minimal Variety). The majority (90 percent) of this roadless area is in Existing Visual Condition (EVC) I. these areas appear to be untouched by human activity. Approximately 1 percent of the acreage is in EVC II, in which changes in the landscape are not noticed by the average person unless pointed out   The balance of the area, or 9 percent, is in EVC V where changes in the landscape are obvious to the average person. The changes appear to be major disturbances

(8) Surroundings (External Influences): The two large bodies of water. Icy Strait and Lynn Canal, are to the north of the Point Augusta Roadless Area. Their average width is' ten miles. The eastern boundary is Chatham Strait and approximately five miles across the water is Admiralty Island National Monument   The Hoonah road system designates the southern and eastern boundaries

The northern and eastern portion of the Point Augusta Roadless Area is viewed from the Alaska Marine Highway ferry route on Chatham and Icy Straits. The flight path for regularly scheduled small plane service to Hoonah is over this area.

(9) Attractions and Features of Special Interest: The northwest corner of the Point Augusta Roadless Area is part of Whitestone Harbor, a protected harbor, used regularly for day and overnight use. There is a panoramic view of Icy Strait, Chatham Strait and Lynn Canal from Whitestone Harbor. The Point Augusta Roadless area contains five inventoried recreation places which contains 5,339 acres.

b. Capability of Management as Wilderness or in an Unroaded Condition

(1) Manageability and Management Area Boundaries: The Point Augusta Roadless Area has a definable northern and eastern boundary. Icy Strait and Chatham Strait. False Bay/Hoonah roaded area is the barrier to the south The Suntaheen roaded and harvested area, approximately two to four miles wide, is to the west

Point Augusta could be managed as a wilderness or a roadless area but the areas near the roads and harvesting boundaries would have to be moved to the top of the nearest ridge system for solitude and visual reasons. As a consequence, the roadless area would become much smaller in size with the ridge-designated boundaries

(2) Natural Integrity: The Point Augusta Roadless Area has had little human modification to the land base and is natural appearing.

(3) Opportunity for Solitude. Because of its size, the Point Augusta Roadless Area offers an opportunity for solitude. It is approximately five miles square with Icy Strait and Chatham Strait to the north and east. The western and southern borders are designated by the roading and harvesting. These two areas would be disruptive to this roadless areas solitude during timber operations

(4) Opportunity for Primitive Recreation: The Point Augusta Roadless Area provides primarily an opportunity for semi-primitive non-motorized recreation.

ROS Class	Acres
Primitive I (P1)	4,119
Roaded Natural (RN)	3,560
Semi-Primitive Non-Motorized (SPNM)	9,299
Semi-Primitive Motorized (SPM)	2,480

The area contains five recreation places

ROS CLASS	# OF REC. PLACES	TOTAL ACRES	CAPACITY BY RVD
RN	1	3,560	2,016
SPNM	2	9,300	6,049
SPM	2	2,480	6,157

There are no recreation cabins in this area. People access this roadless area from the Hoonah/False Bay road systems and by small boats using Whitestone Harbor and False Bay. The possibility of meeting another group of people is likely especially around the saltwater bay

(5) Special Features (Ecologic, Geologic, Scientific, Cultural). None

c. Availability for Management as Wilderness or in an Unroaded Condition

(1) Resource Potentials

(a) Recreation Potential: In the original Tongass Land Management Plan (TLMP), written in 1979, there was a proposal to build an alpine trail system. A marine park is programmed for the Whitestone Harbor area after harvesting has been completed and the log transfer facility closed

(b) Fish Resource. TLMP also programmed a fish passage in the upper portions of Suntaheen Creek

(c) **Wildlife Resource:** TLMP proposed boxes for cavity nesters, riparian cover planting, and second-growth timber management wildlife habitat improvement in all VCU's if the area was harvested

(d) **Timber Resource:** The emphasis in this area was to continue timber harvest and related access road construction for the APC Long-Term timber sale

There are 11,259 acres inventoried as tentatively suitable for harvest This includes 620 acres of riparian old growth, and 8 759 acres of non-riparian old growth

(e) **Land Use Authorizations** The current special use permits will probably continue. An increase in outfitter/guide use is probable.

(f) **Minerals:** The 1984 U S Geological Survey did not identify the Point Augusta Roadless Area as having mineral development potential.

(g) **Areas of Scientific Interest:** There are no potential or inventoried Research Natural Areas in the Point Augusta Roadless Area.

(2) **Management Considerations**

(a) **Timber:** The potential for managing timber in the Point Augusta Roadless Area is high because the whole area falls into the APC Long-term Timber Sale area. The existing nearby road systems log transfer facility, and the logging camp at Hoonah make the management timber harvest economical

(b) **Wildlife:** Wildlife management would not change except for the possibility of enhancement projects

(c) **Fire:** The area has no significant fire history

(d) **Insects and Disease:** Endemic tree diseases common to Southeast Alaska are present; there are no know epidemic disease occurrences

(e) **Land Status:** There is one Native land selection in this roadless area.

d. **Relationship to Communities and Other Roadless and Wilderness Areas**

(1) **Nearby Roadless and Wilderness Areas and Uses:** To the north of the Point Augusta Roadless Area are Icy Strait and Lynn Canal. Approximately ten miles across Icy Strait is the Chilkat-West Lynn Canal Roadless Area (#304) on the Chilkat Peninsula.

Admiralty Island National Monument and Wilderness is east of this area approximately five miles across Chatham Strait. The Freshwater Bay Roadless Area (#325) is south of the Point Augusta area The two roadless areas are separated by the Hoonah/Suntaheen/False Bay road systems which are 1/2 mile to two miles wide

Whitestone Roadless Area (#318) is to the west and is divided from the
other roadless area by the Hoonah/Whitestone Harbor road system and
harvesting

(2) Distance From Population Centers (Accessibility). Approximate
distances from population centers are as follows.

Community			Air Miles	Water Miles
Juneau	(Pop	23,729)	24	42
Hoonah	(Pop	960)	10	20
Tenakee Spr	(Pop	95)	18	28
Gustavus	(Pop	218)	35	35

Hoonah is the nearest community to this area that has Alaska Marine Highway
ferry service.   People accessing this area will use the Hoonah road system
or a privately-owned boat

(3) Interest by Proponents:

(a) Moratorium areas: This area has not been identified as a
proposed moratorium area or Wilderness in legislative initiatives to
date.

(b) Local users/residents: Most use of the Point Augusta Roadless
Area is associated with the Hoonah population. There is boat use to
Whitestone Harbor and False Bay from the surrounding towns
Outfitter/guide use in this area has been identified as well as the
subsistence use   People use this area to hunt and gather such forest
products as roots and berries

(c) Concerns of local residents: The local issues concerning this
area are continuing harvesting and roading of the timber lands, the
effects on fisheries and wildlife habitat caused by logging,
maintaining the visual quality of high interest areas, maintaining
lifestyles, location of log transfer facilities, the distribution of
harvest volume classes and the tradeoffs between environmental
protection measures and the economics of the harvest activities.

e. Environmental Consequences

ALTERNATIVE ANALYSIS TO BE DONE LATER

INDIVIDUAL ROADLESS AREA DESCRIPTION

NAME: Whitestone (318)   ACRES (GROSS): 6,140   ACRES (NFS): 6,100

GEOZONE: C02
GEOGRAPHIC PROVINCE. Northern Interior Islands

1989 WILDERNESS ATTRIBUTE RATING. 21

a   Description

(1) Relationship to RARE II areas: The table below displays the VCU 1/
names, VCU numbers, original WARS 2/ rating, and comments This enables
the reader to compare the roadless areas evaluated in Appendix C with
previous analyses.

VCU Name	VCU No.	1979 WARS Rating	Comments
First No 2	208*	19	
Suntaheen Creek	209*	22	

*--The roadless area includes only part of this VCU.

(2) History: In the Whitestone Roadless Area cultural resources include
the evidence of past human activity, dating from the first occupation of
Southeast Alaska to the recent past. Some sites in the region, including
the Ground Hog Bay site on the Chilkat Peninsula and the Hidden Falls site
on Baranof Island, indicate that the occupation of Southeast Alaska dates
to over 9,000 years ago This roadless area is nine miles south of the
Ground Hog Bay site and 65 miles north of the Hidden Falls sites

Petroglyphs have been found by the Forest archeologist at Whitestone Harbor
and there is evidence of the Russians traders using the harbors around this
roadless area during the 1800's.

(3) Location and Access: The Whitestone Roadless Area is on Chichagof
Island   Directly north of this roadless area is Icy Strait (averaging
eight to nine miles across). Whitestone Harbor borders the eastern section
of this roadless area, harvested and roaded areas bound the southern edge.

The nearest community is Hoonah. The town has regular charter plane
service and is on the Alaska Marine Highway route   The Whitestone Roadless
Area may be accessed from the Hoonah road system by vehicle and walking.
Powerboats are frequently used to access the northern portions of the
roadless area.

1/ A VCU (Value Comparison Unit) is one of 867 watersheds which make up the
    forest and were differentiated for planning purposes in the Tongass Land
    Management Plan.
2/ Wilderness Attribute Rating System (WARS) was the nationwide system used to
    rate the wilderness attributes of roadless areas in the Roadless Area
    Review and Evaluation (RARE II).

(4) Geography and Topography: The Whitestone Roadless Area is a flat
expanse of land that is approximately seven miles long and three miles
wide   Muskeg accounts for 1,600 acres of this area   There are 13 miles of
shoreline on saltwater and 760 beach acres

(5) Ecosystem:

(a) Classification: The area is classified as being in the Northern
Interior Islands geographic province   Unlike the outer coast, the
coastline is protected from full force of storms   These islands have
a colder climate, more rugged topography and a distinctive fauna than
in the Central Interior Islands Province   This particular area is
very flat with elevations up to 200 feet. Rocky shorelines
interspersed with small gravel beaches are found throughout the
character type. Streams are generally larger and longer in this
area. Saltwater bays and estuaries are numerous and exhibit much
variety, from small sheltered coves to the large bay at Whitestone
Harbor   Numerous tidal meadows of varying sizes are found in this
unit. Whitestone is densely forested and exhibits a combination of
muskeg openings, brush and scattered tree cover

(b) Vegetation: Western hemlock-Sitka spruce forests dominate the
overstory of the Southeast Alaska rain forest. The understory is
composed of such shrubs as red huckleberry, rusty menziesia, and
devil's club, and the forest floor is covered with a mat of mosses
liverworts, and plants such as deerheart, bunchberry dogwood, single
delight, and skunk cabbage   Streamside riparian vegetation is
characterized by salmonberry, devil's club, alder, grasses, ferns, and
currants

Muskegs, dominated by sphagnum mosses, sedges, and shrubs of the heath
family, are interspersed among low elevation timber stands where
drainage is restricted. Trees are sparse and consist mainly of
stunted hemlock, lodgepole pine, and Alaska-cedar

Common marine plants in the near-shore waters include brown, red and
green algae, and eelgrass   Tideflats are found at the heads bays and
estuaries and are usually associated with stream estuaries   The
tideflats generally support sea milkwort, glasswort, and algae   Beach
meadows occur between the shore and the forest   Lower beach meadows
are composed of beach ryegrass, reed bent grass, hairgrass, fescue
grass, beach lovage, goose tongue, and sedges   Upper beach meadow
plants include yarrow, bedstraw, starwort, ferns, western columbine
and cow parsnip   Oregon crabapple, alder, devil's club, and blueberry
occur along the border of the beach meadow and the forest

There are 4,480 acres of forested land of which 3,220 acres are
commercial forest land. Of the commercial forest land, 220 acres are
riparian old growth and 2,780 acres are non-riparian old growth

(c) Soils: The Whitestone Roadless Area has poorly drained soils
because of low relief and impermeable subsurface layers   In locations
with poor drainage, deep organic soils (muskegs) tend to form   This
situation occurs where the soil material fails to provide sufficient

internal drainage or where topography prevents external drainage
These areas are generally not well suited for road construction since
the soil materials tend to be wet and have associated low bearing
strengths   In riparian areas, soil zones tend to contain sand and
gravels as a result of flood deposition.

(d) Fish Resource: Fish resources have been rated as part of the
Tongass Land Management Plan (1979) and by the Alaska Department of
Fish and Game in their Forest Habitat Integrity Program (1983) These
ratings describe the value of VCU's for sport fish, commercial fish,
and estuaries

Neither VCU in this roadless area was rated as having the highest
value for sport or commercial fish nor for estuarine values

(e) Wildlife Resource: The Whitestone Roadless Area shoreline is
considered critical deer habitat and the entire roadless area is Sitka
black-tailed deer and brown bear habitat   Small mammals include
marten and red squirrel.

(f) Threatened and Endangered Species: The Whitestone Roadless Area
contains no known inventoried resident threatened or endangered
species. The Peale's peregrine falcon passes through the forests
during the spring and fall migration flights, this falcon is on the
Federal Endangered and Threatened Species.

(6) Current Use and Management: Both VCU's 208 and 209 (6,100 acres) have
been designated as a LUD 4 in the TLMP in 1979   These lands are to be
managed for a variety of uses   Opportunities will be provided for
intensive resource use and development where emphasis is primarily on
commodity or market resources   Allowances in calculated potential timber
yield have been made to provide for protection of physical and biological
productivity

An anchorage is located in the northwest corner of Whitestone Harbor
Recreation activities identified are big game hunting, hiking,
cross-country skiing, dispersed camping, saltwater shore fishing,
beachcombing, viewing wildlife/fish, and kayaking

Except for permits for outfitter and guides, there are no other special use
permits in this area.

(7) Appearance (Apparent Naturalness): This roadless area appears
unmodified. The visual character type of this area is
Admiralty-Chichagof. This character type, particularly in this area, is
characterized by somewhat insignificant geologic features, features (if
present) are usually subordinate to other objects of the visual field
This roadless area is characterized by somewhat insignificant water
features such as featureless shorelines, streams and minor lakes, ponds and
bogs. Seventy-eight percent of all acreage was inventoried in Variety
Class C (Minimal)   The remaining 22 percent is in Variety Class A
(Distinctive)

The majority of this roadless area (66 percent) is in Existing Visual Condition (EVC) I, these areas appear to be untouched by human activity. Thirty-four percent of the area is in EVC V. In these areas, changes in the landscape are obvious to the average person and appear to be major disturbances.

(8) **Surroundings (External Influences):** To the north of the Whitestone Roadless Area are Icy Strait and the Alaska Marine Highway route. This passage is also heavily used by private boat owners.

Whitestone Harbor, to the east of this roadless evaluation area, has an identified recreation anchorage in its northwest corner. A log transfer facility (LTF) is located on the southern shore of Whitestone harbor and a road runs along the south shore. The road travels west adjacent to the Whitestone Roadless Area for approximately 3 miles and branches to the north and south into major timber harvesting areas.

The northernmost harvest area continues for five miles along the southern boundary of the Whitestone Roadless Area. At that point, the land ownership changes from Forest Service to Huna Totem Corporation lands. The National Forest System lands were logged in the early 1980's. The corporation lands extend west for approximately another five miles to Hoonah and have also been extensively harvested. A small western portion of the Whitestone Roadless Area borders on private Huna Totem lands.

- This roadless area is easily accessible from all these road systems with minimal walking involved.

(9) **Attractions and Features of Special Interest:** Whitestone Harbor is considered a desirable harbor; it receives constant use from the Hoonah population and transient mariners. From Whitestone Harbor there is a panoramic view of Icy Strait, Lynn Canal and Chatham Strait. Five recreation places have been inventoried in this roadless area totaling 6,060 acres.

b. Capability of Management as Wilderness or in an Unroaded Condition

(1) **Manageability and Management Area Boundaries:** The entire roadless area (approximately two miles wide and six miles long) is lowlying and exhibits little terrain relief. Icy Strait borders the roadless area to the north and east. The Hoonah road system, the road to the log transfer facility at Whitestone Harbor and the private lands of Huna Totem Corporation bound the south and east portion of the Whitestone Roadless Area. Because of the relative smallness of this roadless area and the immediate external influences, management in a wilderness condition may be difficult to accomplish.

(2) **Natural Integrity:** The Whitestone Roadless Area has been unmodified by human development.

(3) **Opportunity for Solitude:** A high opportunity for solitude exists in this area along the northern shoreline and in the interior of this roadless area but along the boundaries formed by roads and harvesting, opportunity for solitude diminishes.

(4) Opportunity for Primitive Recreation: The area provides primarily semi-primitive non-motorized and semi-primitive motorized opportunities

ROS Class	Acres
Semi-Primitive Non-Motorized (SPNM)	2,020
Semi-Primitive Motorized (SPM)	3,800
Roaded Natural (RN)	220

The area contains five recreation places.

ROS CLASS	# OF REC. PLACES	TOTAL ACRES	CAPACITY BY RVD
SPMN	1	2,020	486
SPM	1	3,800	8,091
RN	3	240	462

There are no public recreation cabins in the Whitestone Roadless Area. The area is used heavily by the residents of Hoonah and the possibility of encountering people is high especially along the shoreline. The area can be accessed by walking from a vehicle or boat. Entry into this area can be accomplished by floatplane along any of the beaches on the northern portion of this area.

(5) Special Features (Ecologic, Geologic, Scientific, Cultural): There are several memorial sites in this area for people who have drowned along this coastline.

c. Availability for Management as Wilderness or in an Unroaded Condition

(1) Resource Potentials

(a) Recreation Potential: Because of the area's easy accessibility to Hoonah residents, there is increased recreational hunting and gathering potential. In the Tongass Land Management Plan (TLMP) proposed a marine park for the Whitestone Harbor log transfer facility after logging has been completed. This marine park would be equipped with an outdoor recreation vehicle (ORV) facilities

(b) Fish Resource: In lower Suntaheen Creek, there are proposed log weirs for rearing and spawning habitat.

(c) Wildlife Resource: TLMP identified cavity nest boxes, second-growth management for wildlife habitat improvement, and riparian cover plantings projects in future years

(d) Timber Resource: The management emphasis for this area is to continue timber harvest, related access road construction, and replacement of bridges on several of the roads for the APC 1986-90 and 1991-95 timber sale

Within this roadless area, there are 2,380 acres inventoried as tentatively suitable for harvest. This includes 80 acres of riparian old growth and 2,240 acres of non-riparian old growth

(e) Land Use Authorizations: The current special use permits will probably continue   Increased use by outfitter/guides is probable with an increased need

(f) Minerals· The 1984 U S Geological Survey did not identify the Whitestone Roadless Area as having potential for mineral development.

(2) Management Considerations

(a) Timber: The potential for managing timber in the Whitestone Roadless Area is very high because area is entirely within the APC Long-term Timber Sale area   The Whitestone Harbor area and the portion to the south and west of this roadless area are being considered in the Supplemental Environmental Impact Statement for the 1981-86 and 1986-90 Alaska Pulp Corporation Long-term Timber Sale Plan. The existing nearby road systems make the management of this area for timber harvest economical

(b) Wildlife: The wildlife management would not change   If the area was harvested, enhancement projects would probably occur

(c) Fire: The area has no significant fire history.

(d) Insects and Disease: Endemic tree diseases common to Southeast Alaska are present, there are no know epidemic disease occurrences.

(e) Land Status: There are two Native withdrawals within this roadless area.

d. Relationship to Communities and Other Roadless and Wilderness Areas

(1) Nearby Roadless and Wilderness Areas and Uses: There are no other roadless areas contiguous with Whitestone Roadless Area   Both Chilkat-West Lynn Canal (#304) and Mansfield Peninsula (#306) Roadless Areas are across major bodies of water   Separated by the Hoonah road system and the associated harvesting are the Point Augusta (#317) and Freshwater (#325) Roadless Areas

(2) Distance From Population Centers (Accessibility): Approximate distances from population centers are as follows

Community			Air Miles	Water Miles
Juneau	(Pop	23,729)	28	45
Hoonah	(Pop.	960)	12	14
Tenakee Spr	(Pop.	95)	21	35
Gustavus	(Pop	218)	27	34

The closest Alaska Marine Highway service to the Whitestone Roadless Area is to Hoonah

(3) Interest by Proponents:

(a) Moratorium areas: This area has not been identified as a proposed "moratorium" area or proposed as Wilderness in legislative initiatives to date

(b) Local users/residents: Most use of the area is from Hoonah Whitestone Harbor receives heavy boat use from Hoonah and from surrounding communities   Some private floatplane operators use this area.

The local issues concerning this area are continuing harvesting and roading of the timber lands, the effects on fisheries and wildlife habitat caused by logging, maintaining the visual quality of high interest areas, maintaining lifestyles, location of log transfer facilities, the distribution of harvest volume classes and the tradeoffs between environmental protection measures and the economics of the harvest activities.

The people of Hoonah use this area for subsistence gathering for roots, berries and hunting. The Natives feel these natural products are becoming scarce in their local area.

e. Environmental Consequences

ALTERNATIVE ANALYSIS TO BE DONE LATER

INDIVIDUAL ROADLESS AREA DESCRIPTION

NAME. Pavlof/East Point (319)   ACRES (GROSS): 10,900   ACRES (NFS) 10,900

GEOZONE: C02 and C04
GEOGRPAHIC PROVINCE: Northern Interior Islands

1989 WILDERNESS ATTRIBUTE RATING: 22

a   Description

(1) Relationship to RARE II areas: The table below displays the VCU 1/ names, VCU numbers, original WARS 2/ rating, and comments This enables the reader to compare the roadless areas evaluated in Appendix C with previous analyses.

VCU Name	VCU No.	1979 WARS Rating	Comments
Kennel Creek	217*		Not rated in 1979
Pavlof River	218*		Not rated in 1979
Point Cannery	219*		Not rated in 1979

*--The roadless area includes only part of this VCU

(2) History: Cultural resource information, especially prehistoric information, in the Pavlof/East Point Roadless Area is limited Some sites in the region, including the Ground Hog Bay site on the Chilkat Peninsula and the Hidden Falls site on Baranof Island, indicate that the occupation of Southeast Alaska dates to over 9,000 years ago This area is located approximately 32 miles to the south of Ground Hog Bay and 46 miles to the north of Hidden Falls. It is very probable that Pavlof Harbor area was used by the people who inhabited the area at that time

At the time of Euroamerican contact, the Hoonah and Angoon Tlingit used this area of Chichagof Island. Villages and sites for seasonal hunting fishing, and collecting activities were located throughout the area. Pavlof Harbor was used as a fish station by the early Native cultures   The Hudson Bay Trading Company conducted illegal trading with the Tlingit in Pavlof Bay from 1859-65 The Astoria and Alaska Packing Company had a fish packing plant here until 1889 and a saltery was established by 1900. Recent historical activities in this area have included commercial fishing and logging.

The forest archaeologists have located Native sites in all of the VCU's in this area. They have documented the Freshwater Bay village site, garden spots, an old smokehouse, and a pictograph.

1/ A VCU (Value Comparison Unit) is one of 867 watersheds which make up the forest and were differentiated for planning purposes in the Tongass Land Management Plan.
2/ Wilderness Attribute Rating System (WARS) was the system used to rate the wilderness attributes of roadless areas in the Roadless Area Review and Evaluation (RARE II).

(3) Location and Access: The Pavlof/East Point Roadless Area is bounded by Chatham Strait, Tenakee Inlet and Freshwater Bay Timber harvest units and roads form the inland boundary of this roadless area The nearest communities are the Kennel Creek logging camp, located immediately to the northwest on Freshwater Bay and Tenakee Springs, located five miles to the South on Tenakee Inlet

Access from the Kennel Creek/Hoonah Road System and the community of Tenakee Springs is mainly by privately-owned boats and walking Kennel Creek has charter plane service and Tenakee Springs has Alaska Marine Highway service and regular small plane service

(4) Geography and Topography: The Pavlof/East Point Roadless Area is characterized by mountains varying from 1,700 feet in the Pavlof Ridge system to 2,880 feet near the Tenakee Springs townsite boundary The large Pavlof draining inclues a river, lake, waterfalls and a bay There are seventeen miles of saltwater shoreline on saltwater and 1,040 acres of beach, 200 acres of alpine tundra, and 40 acres of rock. There are 160 acres of small islands and 100 acres of freshwater lakes in the area Pavlof Lake is the largest lake in the area.

(5) Ecosystem:

(a) Classification: The Pavlof/East Point Roadless Area is in the Northern Interior Island geographic province. The coastline is protected from the full force of storms, has a colder climate and a highly dissected topography than the outer coast. This province typically has an extensive alpine environment with productive forested areas which are highly fragmented and usually concentrated on oversteepened slopes and on valley bottoms

(b) Vegetation: In this roadless area, Western hemlock-Sitka spruce forests dominate. There are approximately 9,760 acres of forested land of which 7,900 acres are commercial forest land. Of the commercial forest land, 7,480 acres are non-riparian old growth and 140 acres are riparian old growth

The understory is composed of shrubs such as red huckleberry rusty menziesia, and devil's club The forest floor is covered with a mat of mosses, liverworts, deerheart, bunchberry dogwood, single delight and skunk cabbage Streamside riparian vegetation is characterized by salmonberry, devil's club, alder, grasses, ferns, and currants

Muskeg comprises 240 acres in this area. They are dominated by sphagnum mosses, sedges, and shrubs of the heath family, are interspersed among low elevation timber stands where drainage is restricted. Trees are sparse and consist mainly of stunted hemlock lodgepole pine, and Alaska-cedar

The tideflats support sea milkwort, glasswort, and algae Lower beach meadows are composed of beach ryegrass, reed bent grass, hairgrass, fescue grass, beach lovage, goose tongue, and sedges Upper beach meadow plants include yarrow, bedstraw, starwort, ferns, western columbine, and cow parsnip Oregon crabapple, alder, devil's club, and blueberry occur along the border of the beach meadow and the forest

At elevations generally above 2,000 feet, the plant communities are characterized by low shrubs, grasses, and sedges Subalpine forests and meadows occur at the interface between the forested communities and the alpine tundra.

(c) **Soils:** There are unstable soils in the Pavlof/East Point Roadless Area on the north side of Pavlof Ridge and along the area called East Point. Because of the high rainfall, the available nutrients can be leached rapidly and exposed mineral soils are subject to erosion. Due to rapid loss of material by erosion and efficient rainwater runoff, the shallow soils with good drainage develop on steeper slopes.

The Pavlof drainage has poorly drained and deep organic soils (muskegs) Drainage improves with increased slope, however, as slopes become oversteepened, soil depths become more shallow The riparian areas in this area tend to contain sand and gravels resulting from soil deposit during floods   .

(d) **Fish Resource:** Fish resources have been rated as part of the Tongass Land Management Plan (1979) and by the Alaska Department of Fish and Game in their Forest Habitat Integrity Program (1983) These ratings describe the value of VCU's for sport fish, commercial fish, and estuaries.

One VCU has been rated as high value for sport and commercial fish, Pavlof River (218) VCU's rated as highly valued for estuaries include Pavlof River (218) and Cannery Point (219)

Pavlof River and Lake have a significant salmon run Fish ladders have been constructed on Pavlof River and one Pavlof Falls Many of these streams provide habitat for anadromous trout and char but the level of production is unknown

(e) **Wildlife Resource:** Designated deer winter range is found from lower Pavlof Ridge to Cedar Cove, around Pavlof Lake and lower part of the Pavlof River. Outer Point and all of Wachusett Cove are also considered deer winter range Deer winter range can also be found northwest of East Point and continuing southwest to Coffee Cove Bald eagle, roosting and nesting habitat, exists along the shoreline of the roadless area

(f) Threatened and Endangered Species: The Pavlof/East Point
Roadless Area contains no known resident threatened or endangered
species However, the area does provide habitat for the Peale's
peregrine falcon as it passes through the forests during the spring
and fall migration flights This falcon is currently on the Federal
Endangered and Threatened Species List

(6) Current Use and Management: The Pavlof/East Point Roadless Area is
completely within the Alaska Pulp Corporation Long-term Timber Sale
contract area The Tongass Land Management Plan (1979) allocated 2 VCU's
(8,200 acres) to Land Use Designation 3 The emphasis in LUD 3 is on
managing for uses and activities in a compatible and complementary manner
to provide the greatest combination of benefits. These areas have either
high use or high amenity values in conjunction with high commodity values
Allowances in calculated potential timber yield have been made to meet
multiple objectives. These lands may include concentrated recreational
developments.

There is one VCU (2,700 acres) designated as a Land Use Designation (LUD) 4
in the Tongass Land Management Plan (TLMP) in 1979. These lands will be
managed for a variety of uses. Opportunities will be provided for
intensive resource use and development where emphasis is primarily on
commodity or market resources Allowances in calculated potential timber
yield have been made to provide for protection of physical and biological
productivity

Recreation places have been identified in the Pavlof/East Point Roadless
Area People anchor their boats and use the area around Pavlof Harbor and
Pavlof Lake for dispersed camping Trails run from Pavlof Harbor to the
north and south shore of Pavlof Lake and from the Tenakee Springs townsite
boundary townsite boundary of Tenakee Springs to private land at Coffee
Cove. Activities occurring in the Pavlof/East Point Roadless Area are
marine viewing, stream and lake fishing, kayaking, hiking, and big game
hunting. A number of outfitter and guides use this area

A State selection is located at Pavlof Lake and special use permits have
been issued for cabins north of Pavlof Harbor and at Wachusett Cove

The Forest Service manages two fish passes on the Pavlof River As a
wildlife improvement project, nesting boxes for general waterfowl with
emphasis on ducks and geese, have been placed along Pavlof Lake

(7) Appearance (Apparent Naturalness): This roadless area is classified
as being in the Admiralty-Chichagof character type Rocky shorelines are
interspersed with small gravel beaches. Streams are generally larger and
longer on the east side of the Chichagof Island There are some saltwater
bays and they exhibit much variety and size.

The lower slopes are densely forested, but sometimes exhibit a combination
of muskeg openings, brush, and scattered tree cover up to approximately
2,500 feet. Upper slopes and summits appear barren from a distance but
offer a variety of alpine vegetation as well as numerous rock outcroppings

Thirteen percent of this roadless area is inventoried in Variety Class A
(Distinct), 31 percent in Variety Class B (Common) and 56 percent of the
acreage is in Variety Class C (Minimal Variety)

The majority (65 percent) of this roadless area is in Existing Visual
Condition (EVC) I, these areas appear to be untouched by human activity
One percent of the acreage is in EVC II, which changes are not noticed by
the average person unless pointed out   Approximately 3 percent of the
acreage is in EVC IV, where changes in the landscape are easily noticed by
the average person and may attract some attention   There appear to be
disturbances but they resemble natural patterns   Thirty-one percent is in
EVC V where changes in the landscape are obvious to the average person.
and appear to be major disturbances.

The area has been modified by a two recreation cabins, trails around the
Pavlof Lake area, and a trail from the Tenakee Springs townsite boundary to
Coffee Cove

(8) Surroundings (External Influences): The Kennel Creek road system,
built in the early 1960's, borders the northwest corner of the roadless
area. This system continues past the Kennel Creek logging camp, built at
the same time as the road system, and turns into the Hoonah road system   A
Forest Service work center is located at Kennel Creek is used year round
but most heavily during the summer months

The Kennel Creek system runs southeast into the Pavlof River drainage   In
the early 1980's the Wast Point and Pavlof River roads were connected.
Because this road comes within one-half mile of the beach, harvesting on
both of these areas and the East Point roading almost cuts the roadless
area in two. The Pavlof/East Point area can be accessed from either of
these road systems

The southwest corned of the Roadless Area is bordered by a small parcel of
private land at Coffee Cove and the Tenakee Springs townsite boundary   The
actual town of Tenakee is five miles distant   Tenakee Springs receives
regular Alaska Marine Highway service   The roadless area can be accessed
by the Forest Service trail that emerges from the townsite boundary and
ends at the private land at Coffee Cove.

(9) Attractions and Features of Special Interest: Pavlof Harbor is
unique because it is offers protection from the weather on four sides   It
is noted on the nautical charts as a safe harbor and, as such, is used
consistently by transit vessels   An easy trail, which parallels the
waterfalls between the lake and the bay, accesses the north and south
shores of Pavlof Lake   The Pavlof/East Point Roadless Area contains four
inventoried recreation places which contains 3,220 acres.

In the Pavlof drainage, there are significant runs of salmon from the
harbor into the lake and river   Two fish ladders have been constructed in
this drainage to enhance these fisheries

b. Capability of Management as Wilderness or in an Unroaded Condition

(1) **Manageability and Management Area Boundaries:** Because the northwest corned of the roadless area is separated from the rest of it by Pavlof Ridge, Cedar Cove, Cedar and Little Cedar Islands are isolated from the rest of the area.

The Pavlof/East Point Roadless Area continues south into the Pavlof Harbor area which includes Pavlof Lake and Wachusett Cove Small hills in this area separate the lake and bays from the harvested and roaded areas to the north, west and south. The average distance from the harvest areas is approximately 3/4 of a mile

The roadless area extends around East Point and is well-defined by a heavy ridge system to the southwest. The western boundary extends to a harvested drainage and the townsite boundaries of Tenakee Springs.

Due to the large roaded areas which intrude into it, this area could not be easily defined or managed as roadless or wilderness.

(2) **Natural Integrity:** The natural integrity of the Pavlof/East Point Roadless Area has not been modified heavily by human activities. It appears natural except for the two fish passes constructed in the Pavlof drainage and the old mechanical equipment around Pavlof Lake left from the saltery and fish packing plant in the early 1900's

(3) **Opportunity for Solitude:** This area as a whole does not offer a high opportunity for solitude The activities associated with the Forest Service work center, the Kennel Creek road system and logging camp, and the year-round population of Tenakee Springs all affect the solitude of this area. The Alaska Marine Highway route passes on two sides of the area, and floatplanes and powerboats land along its shoreline Only at Pavlof Harbor and Lake would one experience a protected opportunity for solitude.

(4) **Opportunity for Primitive Recreation:** The Pavlof/East Point Roadless Area provides primarily semi-primitive non-motorized opportunity.

ROS Class	Acres
Semi-Primitive Non-Motorized (SPNM)	7,141
Semi-Primitive Motorized (SPM)	2,120

The area contains four recreation places.

ROS CLASS	# OF REC. PLACES	TOTAL ACRES	CAPACITY BY RVD
SPNM	1	1,660	1,097
SPM	3	340	3,668

There are no public recreation cabins in this area

(5) Special Features: Pavlof Harbor is the special feature of this Roadless Area. It has ecological attraction because of the significant salmon runs each year, geologic interest because of the shape and protection the harbor provides, and cultural importance because of the continuous historical use the area has received

c Availability for Management as Wilderness or in an Unroaded Condition

(1) Resource Potentials

(a) Recreation Potential. The Tongass Land Management Plan (1979) proposed construction of a public recreation cabin at Pavlof Lake with a trail connection to the existing Kennel Creek/Hoonah road system There was also the potential for a campground on the lake.

(b) Fish Resource: Pavlof Lake is being considered for a fertilization program.

(c) Wildlife Resource: Wildlife habitat improvement riparian cover planting is planned for VCU's 217 and 218 if the area is logged

(d) Timber Resource: The emphasis in this area is to continue timber harvest and related access road construction for the APC 1986-90 and 1991-95 timber sale

There are 7,100 acres of timber inventoried as tentatively suitable for harvest This includes 80 acres of riparian old growth, and 6,500 acres of non-riparian old growth

(e) Land Use Authorizations: The current special use permits will continue. The potential for increased outfitter and guide use is probable as need increases

(f) Minerals: In 1984, this area was identified as having mineral development potential for magmatic oxide or sulfide, copper and molybdenum porphyry

(g) Areas of Scientific Interest: There are no Research Natural Areas in this area and no potential inventoried Research Natural Areas have been identified.

(2) Management Considerations

(a) Timber: The potential for managing timber in the Pavlof/East Point Roadless Area is high because the entire area is in the APC Long-term Timber Sale area. The existing nearby road systems and logging camp make the management for timber harvest economical

(b) Wildlife: Wildlife enhancement projects would be a possibility.

(c) Fire: The area has no significant fire history.

(d) Insects and Disease: Endemic tree diseases common to Southeast Alaska are present, there are no know epidemic disease occurrences

(e) Land Status: There is one State selection located north of, and adjacent to, Pavlof Lake and west Pavlof Harbor

d   Relationship to Communities and Other Roadless and Wilderness Areas

(1) Nearby Roadless and Wilderness Areas and Uses· Tenakee Ridge Roadless Area is to the west   The Indian River roaded area varies one to four miles in width and separates these two roadless areas   The Freshwater Bay Roadless Area is located two to three miles north of the Pavlof-East Point Roadless Area across Freshwater Bay   Trap Bay Roadless Area is north across two to three mile wide Tenakee Inlet

(2) Distance From Population Centers (Accessibility): Approximate distances from population centers are as follows

Community		Air Miles	Water Miles
Juneau	(Pop. 23,729)	43	65
Sitka	(Pop 8,041)	50	100
Tenakee Spr	(Pop 95)	10	10
Hoonah	(Pop. 960)	25	42
Angoon	(Pop. 639)	25	25

Tenakee Springs is the closest town to this area that has Alaska Marine Highway service

(3) Interest by Proponents:

(a) Moratorium areas: The area has not been identified as a proposed moratorium area or Wilderness in legislative initiatives

(b) Local users/residents: The area's use is associated with Tenakee Springs population, the people at Kennel Creek logging camp and Hoonah. Boats, planes, and outfitter/guides from all the communities in northern Southeast Alaska use at Pavlof Harbor and Lake

The local issues concerning this area are continuing harvesting and roading of the timber lands, the effects on fisheries and wildlife habitat caused by logging, maintaining the visual quality of high interest areas, maintaining lifestyles, location of log transfer facilities, the distribution of harvest volume classes and the tradeoffs between environmental protection measures and the economics of the harvest activities

e. Environmental Consequences

ALTERNATIVE ANALYSIS TO BE DONE LATER

INDIVIDUAL ROADLESS AREA DESCRIPTION

NAME. Tenakee Ridge (321)   ACRES (GROSS): 30,405   ACRES (NFS). 24,202

GEOZONE: CO2 and CO4
GEOGRAPHIC PROVINCE· Northern Interior Islands

1989 WILDERNESS ATTRIBUTE RATING   24

a. Description

(1) **Relationship to RARE II areas:** The table below displays the VCU 1/ names, VCU numbers, original WARS 2/ rating, and comments This enables the reader to compare the roadless areas evaluated in Appendix C with previous analyses.

VCU Name	VCU No.	1979 WARS Rating	Comments
Freshwater Bay	215*	25	
Freshwater Ck.	216*		Not rated in 1979
Kennel Creek	217*		Not rated in 1979
Pavlof River	218*		Not rated in 1979
Point Cannery	219*		Not rated in 1979
Tenakee Springs	220*		Not rated in 1979

*--The roadless area includes only part of this VCU.

(2) **History:** Some sites in the region, including the Ground Hog Bay site on the Chilkat Peninsula and the Hidden Falls site on Baranof Island indicate that the occupation of Southeast Alaska dates to over 9 000 years ago The Tenakee Ridge Roadless Area is halfway between Ground Hog Bay and Hidden Falls sites, approximately 50 miles from either site The natural mineral hot springs in this area could suggest use by these early peoples.

At the time of Euroamerican contact, the Hoonah and Angoon Tlingit used this area of Chichagof Island   Forest archaeologists have identified petroglyphs and pictographs in VCU's 215 and 219 The pictographs are reported to commemorate an early Native battle scene

There are Native garden sites in VCU's 217, 218, 219 The remains of a Native smokehouse, the Freshwater Bay village site and a Native site are all located in VCU 218. Native burial sites have also been identified in VCU 220. There was a working salmon cannery in Tenakee Springs in 1942

1/ A VCU (Value Comparison Unit) is one of 867 watersheds which make up the forest and were differentiated for planning purposes in the Tongass Land Management Plan.
2/ Wilderness Attribute Rating System (WARS) was the nation-wide system used to rate the wilderness attributes of roadless areas in the Roadless Area Review and Evaluation (RARE II).

It is assumed that the roadless area north of this community was being used for recreational opportunities such as hunting

(3) **Location and Access.** Tenakee Ridge Roadless Area is located on Chichagof Island   The southern boundary is the small town of Tenakee Springs located on Tenakee Inlet   This roadless area is bounded on all other sides by harvesting activities and associated roads   Access is primarily through the Tenakee Springs townsite or from these adjacent roads   These road systems connect to the Hoonah road system   Tenakee Springs has regular scheduled plane service and is on the Alaska ...... Highway route   The roadless area itself contains no shorelines for boat access.

(4) **Geography and Topography:** This roadless area is a rugged, mountainous area with ridges and peaks reaching over 3,500 feet. The area is basically the ridge system left between two heavily harvested areas which are accessed by the adjacent Kennel Creek and Indian River road systems   Lower slopes are generally densely forested, while upper slopes and summits may appear barren with various rock outcroppings, but a variety of alpine vegetation also exists. Alpine comprised 3,320 acres and rock 1,740 acres. There are only 420 acres of muskeg and 20 acres of freshwater lakes in this area.

(5) **Ecosystem:**

   (a) **Classification:** The Tenakee Ridge Roadless Area is in the Northern Interior Island geographic province   Coastlines in this geographic province, unlike the outer coast that are in the Northern Outer Islands, are protected from full force of storms   These islands have a colder climate, more rugged topography, and also a more distinctive fauna than the Central Interior Islands province

   Mountain elevations in this roadless area vary from 2,300 - 3,800 feet. Streams are generally larger and longer in this area than on the other islands of Southeast Alaska. Upper slopes and summits appear barren from a distance, but many of the peaks offer a variety of alpine vegetation as well as numerous rock outcropping

   (b) **Vegetation:** Western hemlock-Sitka spruce forests dominate the overstory of this roadless area. The understory is composed of shrubs such as red huckleberry, rusty menziesia, and devil's club, and the forest floor is covered with a mat of mosses, liverworts, and plants such as deerheart, bunchberry dogwood, single delight, and skunk cabbage. Streamside riparian vegetation is characterized by salmonberry, devil's club, alder, grasses, ferns, and currants

   At elevations generally above 2,000 feet, the plant communities are characterized by low shrubs, grasses, and sedges   Subalpine forests and meadows occur at the interface between the forested communities and the alpine tundra

(c) **Soils:** Glacier history in Southeast Alaska has played an
important part in the placement and character of soil parent material
in many places   In this roadless area, development of soils is
influenced by high levels of rainfall, cool summer temperatures, a
short growing season and moderately low soil temperatures   Under such
conditions, organic matter decomposes slowly and tends to accumulate
in areas where it is being produced or deposited   Due to the rapid
loss of material by erosion and efficient rainwater runoff, shallow
soils with good drainage develop on steeper slopes

Deep, well drained soils commonly occur below shallow soils on gentler
slopes where transported soil materials have collected   Drainage
improves with increased slope gradient; however, as slopes become
steeper, soil depths become much shallower   In riparian areas, soil
zones tend to contain sand and gravels as a result of flood
deposition.

(d) **Fish Resource:** Fish resources have been rated as part of the
Tongass Land Management Plan (1979) and by the Alaska Department of
Fish and Game in their Forest Habitat Integrity Program (1983)   These
ratings describe the value of VCU's for sport fish, commercial fish
and estuaries.

There were two VCU's rated as having the highest value for sport fish
in this area   They were Pavlof River (#218) and Tenakee Springs
(#220)   Three VCU's were highly valued for commercial fisheries
Freshwater Bay (#215), Freshwater Creek (#216), and Pavlof River
(#218)   Those VCU's rated highly in estuarine values were Pavlof
River (#218), Point Cannery (#219), and Tenakee Springs (#220).

The Tenakee Ridge Roadless Area possesses the headwaters and tributary
channels for some of the large fish-producing streams that flow through
adjacent roaded areas   Examples are the North and South Fork of
Freshwater Creek, Kennel Creek, Indian and Pavlof Rivers

(e) **Wildlife Resource:** The entire area is inventoried as brown bear
and Sitka black-tailed deer habitat. Small mammals include marten and
red squirrel.

(f) **Threatened and Endangered Species:** This roadless area contains
no known resident threatened or endangered species   The Peale's
peregrine falcon may migrate through this area during the spring and
fall migration flights; this falcon is on the Federal Endangered and
Threatened Species List.

(6) **Current Use and Management:** The entire Tenakee Ridge Roadless Area is
included in the Alaska Pulp Corporation Long-term Timber Sale contract
area. VCU's 215, 218, 219, and 220 have been designated as a LUD 3 in TLMP
in 1979   Acreage totals 31,163. The emphasis is on managing for uses and
activities in a compatible and complementary manner to provide the greatest
combination of benefits   These areas have either high use or high amenity
values in conjunction with high commodity values in conjunction with high
commodity values   These lands may include concentrated recreational
developments   Allowances in calculated potential timber yield have been

made to meet multiple objectives in all those VCU's except VCU 220   VCU
220 encompasses the community of Tenakee Springs   Part of this VCU has
been excluded from the timber yield calculation because of the close
proximity of the townsite boundary

VCU's 216 and 217 have been designated as LUD 4 in the TLMP in 1979   Tot. l
acreage for LUD 4 designation in this roadless area is 13,200 acres   These
lands will be managed for a variety of uses   Opportunities will be
provided for intensive resource use and development where emphasis is
primarily on commodity or market resources. Allowances in calculated
potential timber yield have been made to provide for protection of physic l
and biological productivity

The recognized recreation activities are hiking, dispersed camping, big
game hunting, small game hunting, upland bird hunting, ice fishing,
cross-country skiing, viewing wildlife/fish, stream fishing, waterfowl
hunting, kayaking and lake fishing. Except for outfitter and guide use in
the Tenakee Ridge area, there are no other special use permits

(7) **Appearance (Apparent Naturalness):** This area appears unmodified at
this time. The visual character type is Admiralty-Chichagof   This
character type exhibits great diversity   For the most part, landforms in
this character type are generally rounded but notable exceptions exist
especially on the northern portions of Admiralty and Chichagof Islands
where mountainous terrain tends to be rugged and snow-covered   Fifty-two
percent of this area is inventoried in Variety Class B (Common) with 30
percent considered Variety Class C (Minimal)   The remaining 18 percent is
in Variety Class A (Distinctive).

Almost 72 percent of this area is in Existing Visual Condition (EVC) V
This classification indicates that changes in the landscape are visible and
obvious to the average person. These changes appear to be major
disturbances   Twenty-seven percent (27 percent) of the area is in EVC I
these areas appear to be untouched by human activities

(8) **Surroundings (External Influences):** The Tenakee Ridge Roadless Area
is completely land bound. Adjacent to this roadless area to the north and
west is the Kennel Creek logging camp and road system   This area was
extensively harvested in 1962 and 1981-1982. The Hoonah and Kennel Creek
road systems connect at the Kennel Creek logging camp

Kennel Creek logging camp was constructed in the mid-1960s. The population
in the camp varies with the seasons. In the summer between 60-80 people
reside there and in the winter, 6-12 people. This camp periodically opens
and closes every three years depending on the timber work load. A Forest
Service work station is also located at the Kennel Creek logging camp
Charter plane service provides access to the Kennel Creek logging camp

The Tenakee Springs townsite is to the south of this roadless area
Tenakee Springs is served by the Alaska Marine Highway system and regular
scheduled small plane service

The Indian River road system borders the western section of the Tenakee Ridge Roadless Area   This area also was intensively harvested in 1977 The Indian River and the Hoonah roaded harvest areas intersect at the northwest boundary of this roadless area.

(9) Attractions and Features of Special Interest· There are no specific attractions or special features in this roadless area

b   Capability of Management as Wilderness or in an Unroaded Condition

(1) Manageability and Management Area Boundaries: The boundaries of the Tenakee Ridge Roadless Area are defined by the roading and harvesting on the west, north, and east sides of this area. The Tenakee Springs townsite boundary is the southern border of this roadless area.

(2) Natural Integrity: The Tenakee Ridge Roadless Area has had no modification, and natural integrity of the area is maintained

(3) Opportunity for Solitude: Tenakee Ridge Roadless Area has a high opportunity for solitude   The area is approximately nine miles long and between one and three miles wide and is remote with no formal trails or recreation developments to concentrate use.

(4) Opportunity for Primitive Recreation: The area provides primarily semi-primitive non-motorized opportunity·

ROS Class	Acres
Semi-Primitive Non-Motorized (SPNM)	21,822
Semi-Primitive Motorized (SPM)	3,720
Roaded Natural (RN)	980
Roaded Modified (RM)	17,901

The area contains eight recreation places.

ROS CLASS	# OF REC. PLACES	TOTAL ACRES	CAPACITY BY RVD
SPNM	2	260	7,452
SPM	1	3,700	3,203
RN	3	600	3,062
RM	2	3,659	1,714

There are no public recreation cabins in this area   The chief access into the Tenakee Ridge Roadless Area is walking from roaded and private lands

(5) Special Features (Ecologic, Geologic, Scientific, Cultural): There are no specific special features in this roadless area

c. Availability for Management as Wilderness or in an Unroaded Condition

   (1) Resource Potentials

      (a) Recreation Potential: In the Tongass Land Management Plan
      (TLMP), there is an alpine trail planned in VCU 215   The potential
      exists for an increase in big game hunting   If the population of
      Tenakee increases, the probability of personal use of wood products
      will expand

      (b) Fish Resource: There are plans to install incubator boxes in
      underutilized rearing areas of the South Fork of Freshwater Creek

      (c) Wildlife Resource: There are no wildlife enhancement projects
      planned for the Tenakee Ridge Roadless Area.

      (d) Timber Resource: There will be a contined emphasis on timber
      harvest, related access road construction, and replacement of bridges
      on several of the roads for the APC 1986-90 and 1991-95 operating
      periods.

      (e) Land Use Authorizations: Special use permits are expected to
      continue their current status. An increase in outfitter/guides using
      the area is probable

      (f) Minerals: The US Geological survey of 1984, identified the area
      as having mineral development potential   There are epigenetic
      (changes in rocks due to external influences) and disseminated and
      polymetallic veins identified in this area.

      (g) Areas of Scientific Interest: No Research Natural Areas exist in
      the Tenakee Ridge Roadless Area nor any proposed

   (2) Management Considerations

      (a) Timber: The potential for managing timber in the Tenakee Ridge
      Roadless Area is very high because the whole area falls into the APC
      Long-term Timber Sale area. The existing nearby road systems and
      logging camp make the management of this area for timber harvest
      economical.

      (b) Wildlife: In the event of timber harvest, wildlife management of
      this area would not change except for the possibility of enhancement
      projects.

      (c) Fire: The area has no significant fire history

      (d) Insects and Disease: Endemic tree diseases common to Southeast
      Alaska are present; there are no know epidemic disease occurrences

      (e) Land Status: Entirely National Forest Systems land

d   Relationship to Communities and Other Roadless and Wilderness Areas

(1) **Nearby Roadless and Wilderness Areas and Uses:** Tenakee Ridge Roadless Area is not contiguous to any other roadless or wilderness area Freshwater Bay Roadless Area (#325) is located approximately one mile away to the north on the other side of the Hoonah/Kennel harvest and road system The Kennel Creek-East Point harvest units and road system separ the Pavlof/East Point Roadless Area (#319) from the Tenakee Ridge Roadless Area   Game Creek Roadless Area (323) is approximately one-half to three-quarters of a mile away and separated by roads and harvest units in the Indian River drainage

(2) **Distance From Population Centers (Accessibility):** Approximate distances from population centers are as follows:

Community		Air Miles	Water Miles
Juneau	(Pop 23,729)	42	70
Tenakee Spr	(Pop 95)	1	0
Hoonah	(Pop. 960)	22	58
Angoon	(Pop. 639)	28	32

Tenakee Springs is adjacent to the Tenakee Ridge Roadless Area and has regular Alaska Marine Highway service

(3) **Interest by Proponents:**

(a) **Moratorium areas:** The area has not been identified as a proposed "moratorium" area or proposed as Wilderness in legislative initiatives to date

(b) **Local users/residents:** Most use of the area is associated with the Tenakee Springs population, the residents of Kennel Creek logging camp, and community of Hoonah. The residents of Tenakee Springs has an interest in this area because subsistence use is highly valued in the area and this roadless area is used for collecting wood locally.

The local issues concerning this area are the continued harvesting and roading of the forest lands, the effects on fisheries and wildlife habitat caused by logging, maintaining the visual quality of high-interest areas, maintaining lifestyles, the location of log transfer facilities, the distribution of harvest volume classes and the tradeoffs between environmental protection measures and the economics of the harvest activities.

e. Environmental Consequences

ALTERNATIVE ANALYSIS TO BE DONE LATER

INDIVIDUAL ROADLESS AREA DESCRIPTION

NAME: Game Creek (323)   ACRES (GROSS): 88,612   ACRES (NFS) 67.040

GEOZONE: C02 and C04
GEOGRAPHIC PROVINCE: Northern Interior Islands

1989 WILDERNESS ATTRIBUTE RATING: 24

a. Description

(1) **Relationship to RARE II areas:** The table below displays the VCU 1/ names, VCU numbers, original WARS 2/ rating, and comments. This enables the reader to compare the roadless areas evaluated in Appendix C with previous analyses.

VCU Name	VCU No.	1979 WARS Rating	Comments
Pt. Frederick	202*	22	
Seagull Creek	203*	21	
Game Creek	204*	23	
Freshwater Bay	215*	25	
Freshwater Ck.	216*	--	Not rated in 1979
Tenakee Springs	220*		Not rated in 1979
Whip Station	221*	--	Not rated in 1979
Sand Station	222*	18	

*--The roadless area includes only part of this VCU

(2) **History:** Port Frederick is adjacent to Game Creek Roadless Area and was named in 1794 by Captain Vancouver. At the time of Euroamerican contact, the Hoonah and Angoon Tlingit used this area of Chichagof Island Villages and sites for seasonal hunting, fishing, and collecting activities were located throughout the area. The forest archaeologist has identified a Native village site, cache pits, shell middens piles, and an old smokehouse/cabin in VCU's 203 and 204 Petroglyphs and Native burial sites can be found in VCU's 215 and 220

(3) **Location and Access:** The Game Creek Roadless Area is located in the middle of Chichagof Island To the north are Huna Totem and Sealaska Corporation lands and the town of Hoonah. To the south and southeast areTenakee Inlet and a small portion of the Tenakee Springs townsite boundary. The western side of this roadless area is bounded by Port Frederick.

1/ A VCU (Value Comparison Unit) is one of 867 watersheds which make up the forest and were differentiated for planning purposes in the Tongass Land Management Plan.
2/ Wilderness Attribute Rating System (WARS) was the system used to rate the wilderness attributes of roadless areas in the Roadless Area Review and Evaluation (RARE II).

Tenakee Springs and Hoonah are the closest communities to the Game Creek
Roadless Area Both communities have Marine Highway and regular scheduled
plane service   Access into the area from these communities is primarily
through using the road system from Hoonah and then walking, or by walking
from Tenakee Springs

(4) Geography and Topography· The Game Creek Roadless Area is mountainous
with one large U-shaped valley in the northwest corner and many U-shaped
valleys   The northern area is mostly mountain ridges but Upper Game and
Seagull drainages provide wide, open areas with heavy ridge systems to the
southeast and west in the central portion of this roadless area. The Game
Creek Roadless Area also contains part of the Freshwater drainage A heavy
ridge system running northwest to southeast with some associated flat
ground is located in the southern portion of this roadless area. Most of
the valleys have streams that flow year round. There are 44 miles of
saltwater shoreline and 2,679 acres of beach. A portion of the area is
alpine tundra (3,298 acres) and rock (1,419 acres)   There are 60 acres of
small islands and 20 acres of freshwater lakes

(5) Ecosystem:

   (a) Classification: The Game Creek Roadless Area is in the Northern
   Interior Islands geographic province. In this province, the coastline
   is protected from the full force of the storms, unlike the outer
   coast. These islands have a colder climate, highly dissected
   topography, and an extensive alpine environment   Productive forested
   areas are highly fragmented and usually concentrated on oversteepened
   slopes and on valley bottoms.

   (b) Vegetation: Western hemlock-Sitka spruce forests dominate the
   overstory of the Game Creek Roadless Area   The understory is composed
   of shrubs such as red huckleberry, rusty menziesia, and devil's club.
   The forest floor is covered with a mat of mosses, liverworts.
   deerheart, bunchberry dogwood, single delight, and skunk cabbage.
   Streamside riparian vegetation is characterized by salmonberry,
   devil's club, alder, grasses, ferns, and currants

   There are 1,419 acres of muskegs in the Game Creek Roadless Area.
   These areas are dominated by sphagnum mosses, sedges, and shrubs of
   the heath family, and are interspersed among low elevation timber
   stands where drainage is restricted. Trees are sparse and consist
   mainly of stunted hemlock, lodgepole pine, and Alaska-cedar.

   Common marine plants in the near-shore waters include brown, red and
   green algae, and eelgrass. Tideflats are found at the heads of many
   of the bays and are usually associated with stream estuaries   The
   tideflats generally support sea milkwort, glasswort, and algae   Beach
   meadows occur between the shore and the forest. Lower beach meadows
   are composed of beach ryegrass, reed bent grass, hairgrass, fescue
   grass, beach lovage, goose tongue, and sedges   Upper beach meadow
   plants include yarrow, bedstraw, starwort, ferns, western columbine
   and cow parsnip Oregon crabapple, alder, devil's club, and blueberry
   occur along the border of the beach meadow and the forest

There are approximately 51,121 acres of forested land of which 34,157 acres are commercial forest land Of the commercial forest land 29,111 acres are non-riparian old growth and 6,657 acres are riparian old growth

'At elevations generally above 2,000 feet, the plant communities are characterized by low shrubs, grasses, and sedges Subalpine forests and meadows occur at the interface between the forested communities and the alpine tundra

(c) Soils: In this roadless area, glacial history has played an important part in the placement and character of soil parent material. The development of soils is influenced by high levels of rainfall, cool summer temperatures, a short growing season and moderately low soil temperatures. Because of the high rainfall in this area, the available nutrients can be leached rapidly and exposed mineral soils are subject to erosion.

There are shallow soils with good drainage on the steeper slopes The upper soils tend to be eroded by rainwater runoff. Deep, well-drained soils occur below shallow soils on gentler slopes where transported soil materials have collected.

The poorly-drained soils in Seagull Creek and Upper Game Creek are associated with low relief and impermeable subsurface layers In locations with poor drainage, deep organic soils (muskegs) tend to form. This situation occurs where the soil material fails to provide sufficient internal drainage or where topography prevents external drainage

Since these soil materials tend to be wet and have been associated with lower bearing strengths, these areas are generally not well-suited for road construction. Drainage improves with increased slope gradient. However, as slopes become oversteepened, soil depths become much shallower. In riparian areas, soils tend to contain sand and gravels as a result of flood deposition.

(d) Fish Resource: Fish resources have been rated as part of the Tongass Land Management Plan (1979) and by the Alaska Department of Fish and Game in their Forest Habitat Integrity Program (1983) These ratings describe the value of VCU's for sport fish, commercial fish and estuaries

One VCU which is rated as high value for sport fish, Tenakee Springs (220). VCU's rated as highly valued for commercial fish are Game Creek (204), Freshwater Bay (215), and Freshwater Creek (216) VCU's rated as highly valued estuaries include Tenakee Springs (220), Whip Station (221) and Sand Station (222).

Game Creek is a major anadromous stream. Seagull Creek has some pink and coho production. There are many headwater tributaries within this roadless area for the large fish-producing streams located in adjacent roaded areas These include North and South Fork of Freshwater Creek and Indian River Dolly Varden may occur in this area

(e) Wildlife Resource: The Upper Game Creek area has been identified as having important wildlife habitat   Critical deer winter range is located along Port Frederick on the western boundary of the Game Creek Roadless Area   Bald eagles use this shoreline to roost and nest

(f) Threatened and Endangered Species: This roadless area contains no known resident threatened or endangered species   However, it provides habitat for the Peale's peregrine falcon as it passes through the forests during the spring and fall migration flights   This falcon is currently on the Federal Endangered and Threatened Species List.

(6) Current Use and Management: This roadless area is completely within in the Alaska Pulp Corporation Long-term Timber Sale Contract Area   VCU's 202, 215, and 220 (totaling 18,715 acres) were designated as a LUD 3 in the Tongass Land Management Plan in 1979. The emphasis is on managing for uses and activities in a compatible and complementary manner to provide the greatest combination of benefits. These areas have either high use or high amenity values in conjunction with high commodity values   These lands may include concentrated recreational developments   Allowances in calculated potential timber yield have been made to meet multiple objectives   Part of VCU 220 was excluded from the timber yield calculation because of the close proximity to the townsite boundary of Tenakee Springs

Five VCU's (57,730 acres) were designated as LUD 4. These lands are managed for a variety of uses   Opportunities are to be provided for intensive resource use and development where emphasis is primarily on commodity or market resources   Allowances in calculated potential timber yield have been made to provide for protection of physical and biological productivity

No public recreation cabins are located within this roadless area   although there is a cabin at nearby Salt Lake Bay   No formal trails are located within the roadless area.

Recreation activities taking place in this roadless area are waterfowl hunting, hiking, saltwater shore fishing, beachcombing, kayaking, stream fishing, dispersed camping, picnicking, viewing wildlife/fish, viewing scenery, big game hunting, nature study, viewing from marine access boating, gathering forest products, cross-country skiing, small game hunting, upland bird hunting, and powerboat use   Outfitter/guides also use this area.

(7) Appearance (Apparent Naturalness): The Game Creek Roadless Area has not been heavily modified. The visual character type of this area is Admiralty-Chichagof. The landforms in this area are generally rounded with mountain elevations vary from 2,300-3,400 feet. Upper slopes and summits appear barren from a distance, but offer a variety of alpine vegetation as well as numerous rock outcroppings.

The Game Creek Roadless Area has rocky shorelines interspersed with small gravel beaches   Streams are larger and longer in this area than on other islands of Southeast Alaska   Tidal meadows associated with estuaries are common in this roadless area

Fourteen percent of the acreage in the Game Creek Roadless Area was inventoried Variety Class A (Distinctive), 57 percent of this roadless area was inventoried in Variety Class B (Common) and 29 percent of was inventoried in Variety Class C (Minimal Variety).

The majority (55 percent) of this roadless area is in Existing Visual Condition (EVC) I, these areas appear to be untouched by human activity. Two percent of the acreage is in EVC III, where changes to the landscape are noticed by the average person but the natural appearance of the landscape remains dominant. Six percent of the acreage is in EVC IV, these are areas in which changes in the landscape are easily noticed by the average person and may attract some attention. There appear to be disturbances but they resemble natural patterns. Thirty-seven percent is in EVC V where changes in the landscape are obvious to the average person and those changes appear to be major disturbances.

(8) **Surroundings (External Influences):** To the north of this area are Huna Totem and Sealaska private lands. These lands have been and are being roaded and harvested. To the northeast, the roadless area borders the Hoonah road system and harvesting in the North Fork of Freshwater Creek. The Hoonah road system continues east and south to the Kennel Creek logging camp and the Indian River drainage. This road system is the boundary of the southeast corner of the Game Creek Roadless Area where the townsite of Tenakee Springs begins. Tenakee Inlet bounds the southern shoreline of this roadless area. Past beach logging has occurred from the Tenakee Springs townsite boundary northwest to the end of VCU 221. The roadless area boundary in adjacent VCU 222 is formed by the Salt Lake Bay road system. This road system accessed units harvested in the mid-1980's.

Hoonah and Tenakee Springs are on the Alaska Marine Highway route. The Game Creek Roadless Area can easily be accessed from both of these towns by using existing road systems and/or walking. There is also scheduled plane service into Hoonah, Tenakee Springs, Kennel Creek, and Eight Fathom Bight logging camps. Direct access by powerboat and walking is possible from Port Frederick and Tenakee Inlet.

(9) **Attractions and Features of Special Interest:** The Game Creek Roadless Area, Seagull Creek and Upper Game Creek basins have unusually large muskegs. These substantial openings create an environment for many and varied recreation opportunities, especially hunting and hiking. Game Creek is a major anadromous and resident fishing stream. The area contains 11 inventoried recreation places which contains 26,760 acres.

b. **Capability of Management as Wilderness or in an Unroaded Condition**

(1) **Manageability and Management Area Boundaries:** The Game Creek Roadless Area is bounded by road systems on all sides: Hoonah, Game Creek, Indian River and Salt Lake Bay. Huna Totem private lands, Port Frederick, and Tenakee Inlet are also adjacent to this area. Management in a roadless state or wilderness is feasible.

(2). **Natural Integrity:** The Game Creek Roadless Area has not been heavily modified and the natural integrity of the area is maintained.

(3) Opportunity for Solitude: There is high opportunity for solitude in
this area between centers of human activity   Even though there are road
systems surrounding this roadless area, two of the systems are not readily
accessible from populated areas and vehicles must be brought in by boats
The recreation activities taking place in this roadless area are dispersed
and encounters with other parties are infrequent   The Game Creek Roadless
Area is being considered for logging and roading in the Supplemental
Environmental Impact Statement for 1981-85 and 1986-90 Alaska Pulp
Corporation Long-term Timber Sale Contract   If this EIS is approved, the
noise from those operations would definitely effect this area

(4) Opportunity for Primitive Recreation: The area provides primarily
Semi-Primitive Non-Motorized recreation opportunities as inventoried with
the Recreation Opportunity Spectrum (ROS) system.

ROS Class	ACRES
Primitive I (PI)	21,204
Roaded Natural (RN)	1,641
Semi-Primitive Non-Motorized (SPNM)	38,784
Semi-Primitive Motorized (SPM)	4,159

The area contains ten recreation places.

ROS CLASS	# OF REC. PLACES	TOTAL ACRES	CAPACITY BY RVD
RN	3	1,681	7,914
SPNM	3	10,782	7,331
SPM	4	4,399	2,377

The nearest public recreation cabin to the Game Creek Roadless Area is at
Salt Lake Bay. The Seagull drainage landform allows easy walking access to
this roadless area from Port Frederick. The large muskegs in the Game
Creek Roadless Area provide a feeling of expanse for miles   Once accessed,
the ridge system to the north and south provides a very isolated
experience

(5) Special Features (Ecologic, Geologic, Scientific, Cultural): The
Seagull Creek and Upper Game Creek areas are geologically interesting
because of their obvious glacially caused U-shaped valleys   The valley is
very wide in the bottom and has steep side walls to the north and south

c. Availability for Management as Wilderness or in an Unroaded Condition

(1) Resource Potentials

(a) Recreation Potential: The Tongass Land Management Plan proposed
the construction of an alpine trail in VCU 204   Increased hunting,
fishing, and dispersed camping are possible in the Game Creek Roadless
Area. Because the Game Creek Road system is closed to vehicles
dispersed camping in that area may increase   Bear hunters will not be
able to access this area by driving

(b) Fish Resource: TLMP proposed building of a fish passage in Freshwater Creek drainage

Lake Creek, identified as underutilized fisheries habitat, is being considered for sockeye salmon incubation boxes A possible woody debris enhancement project also exists in the Game Creek Drainage

(c) Wildlife Resource: TLMP proposed that if logging occured in VCU's 203, 204, 215, and 216, riparian cover would be planted to improve wildlife habitat

(d) Timber Resource: There are 29,131 acres inventoried as tentatively suitable for harvest. This includes 5,398 acres of riparian old growth, and 20,375 acres of non-riparian old growth

The emphasis in this area continues to be timber harvest, related access road construction, and replacement of bridges on several of the roads for the APC 1986-90 and 1991-95 harvest areas

(e) Land Use Authorizations: The current special use permits will probably continue An increased in outfitter/guide use of this area is predicted.

(f) Minerals: The Geological Survey conducted in 1984 identified the Game Creek Roadless Area as having mineral development potential There are epigenetic and disseminated and polymetallic veins identified in this area

(g) Areas of Scientific Interest: No Research Natural Areas exist or are proposed for the Game Creek Roadless Area

(2) Management Considerations

(a) Timber: Because the entire Game Creek Roadless Area falls into the APC Long-term Timber Sale Area, the potential for managing timber in this roadless area is very high. The existing nearby road systems and logging camp at Kennel Creek make the management of this area for timber harvest economical.

(b) Wildlife: The wildlife management would not change except for the possibility of enhancement projects.

(c) Fire: The area has no significant fire history

(d) Insects and Disease: Endemic tree diseases common to Southeast Alaska are present; there are no know epidemic disease occurrences

(e) Land Status: There is one native selection in the Game Creek Roadless Area.

d   Relationship to Communities and Other Roadless and Wilderness Areas

(1) Nearby Roadless and Wilderness Areas and Uses: No roadless or
wilderness areas are contiguous to Game Creek Roadless Area   Nearby
roadless areas are Freshwater Bay (#325) and Tenakee Ridge (#321) but these
two areas are separated from Game Creek Roadless Area by roaded and
harvested areas

(2) Distance From Population Centers (Accessibility)· Approximate
distances from population centers are as follows

Community		Air Miles	Water Miles
Juneau	(Pop. 23,729)	40	58
Hoonah	(Pop. 960)	7	7
Tenakee Spr	(Pop. 95)	0	1

The nearest Alaska Marine Highway service is at Tenakee Springs   Hoonah
also has ferry service and this roadless area can be accessed from the
Hoonah road system.

(3) Interest by Proponents:

(a) Moratorium areas: The Game Creek Roadless Area has not been
identified as a proposed moratorium area or as Wilderness in .
legislative initiatives to date.

(b) Local users/residents: Most of the use in this roadless area is
associated with the populations of Tenakee Springs and Hoonah.
Boating, driving and walking are all used to hunting access from these
communities   The outfitter and guides use Game and Seagull Creeks for
hunting purposes and therefor has concerns about their businesses.

The local issues concerning this area are continuing harvesting and
roading of the timber lands, the effects on fisheries and wildlife
habitat caused by logging, maintaining the visual quality of high
interest areas, maintaining lifestyles, location of log transfer
facilities, the distribution of harvest volume classes and the
tradeoffs between environmental protection measures and the economics
of the harvest activities.

The majority of the people in Tenakee Springs and a significant
portion of people in Hoonah consider this section of land as a
subsistence area. People from these communities hunt and gather
forest products for everyday use as well as for native arts and
crafts. Both communities feel there has been a reduction of these
types of natural resources   These feelings are caused by the
extensive roading and harvesting around their communities by Alaska
Pulp Corporation on National Forest system lands and the native
corporations of Huna Totem and Sealaska on their lands

Another concern of Tenakee Springs is the connecting of the Indian
River road system to the Hoonah road system. Tenakee Springs a small
community accessed by the Alaska Marine Highway system, small boats
and regularly scheduled plane service. The people fear they will lose
their isolated lifestyles with the connections of these two road
systems

There is also a significant group of people in Hoonah that would like
to see the Game Creek Roadless Area developed   These people feel
developing this area would stabilize the economy of their town by
providing work for the existing logging camp at Hoonah

e.   Environmental Consequences

ALTERNATIVE ANALYSIS TO BE DONE LATER

INDIVIDUAL ROADLESS AREA DESCRIPTION

NAME: Pleasant Island (324)   ACRES (GROSS): 12,239   ACRES (NFS): 12,239

GEOZONE: C07
GEOGRAPHIC PROVINCE: Northern Interior Islands

1989 WILDERNESS ATTRIBUTE RATING: 22

a   Description

(1) Relationship to RARE II areas: The table below displays the VCU 1/
names, VCU numbers, original WARS 2/ rating, and comments This enables
the reader to compare the roadless areas evaluated in Appendix C with
previous analyses.

VCU Name	VCU No.	1979 WARS Rating	Comments
Porpoise Is.	120C	19	
Pleasant Is.	185C	18	

(2) **History:**   There is no recorded pre-European use of the Pleasant
Island/Porpoise Islands area. However, considering the resources
available, probable early uses were hunting and gathering. Temporary camps
were likely. Pleasant Island was named in 1879 by S. Hall Young who was
traveling with naturalist John Muir en route from Hoonah to Glacier Bay
Steve Kane operated a fox farm on Porpoise Island in about 1923. During
World War II, Porpoise Island was found to have the most toxic clams in
Southeast Alaska; these toxins were extracted for use during the war

(3) **Location and Access:** The evaluation area consists of Pleasant Island
and the Porpoise Islands, located north of Chichagof Island and
approxiamtely two miles south of the mainland. It is surrounded by Icy
Strait and Icy Passage. The town of Gustavus and Glacier Bay National
Monument (GBNM) lie to the north across Icy Passage. Excursion Inlet is to
the northeast and the Chilkat Peninsula to the east.

The closest communities to this evaluation area are Gustavus and Hoonah
Both of these towns have regular charter plane service and Hoonah is on the
the Alaska Marine Highway ferry route.

1/ A VCU (Value Comparison Unit) is one of 867 watersheds which make up the
    forest and were differentiated for planning purposes in the Tongass Land
    Management Plan.
2/ Wilderness Attribute Rating System (WARS) was the nation-wide system used
    to rate the wilderness attributes of roadless areas in the Roadless Area
    Review and Evaluation (RARE II).

(4) Geography and Topography: The islands in the Pleasant Island Roadless
Area are somewhat different from the larger islands in Southeast Alaska
The coastline is protected from full force of storms, unlike the outer
coast. Terrain relief is not great; it is characterized by flat
streamcourses and rolling hills, with a maximum elevation of about 800 feet
at the Knob on Pleasant Island. Terrain features have been highly modified
by glaciation. The short streamcourses follow meandering courses, in
broad, flat floodplains to saltwater. Their headwaters lay in somewhat
steeper, narrower valleys. There are several small lakes scattered about
the area.

Pleasant Island consists of a relatively young lava flow overlaying a much
older formation. Pleasant Island was not glaciated in the neoglacial
advance on the mainland and serves as a contrast with the more recently
glaciated area around Glacier Bay. Several tidal meadows of varying sizes
are found in this area. The islands generally exhibit a combination of
muskeg openings, brush and scattered tree cover.

The Porpoise Islands are of the same origin and share general features
The terrain is flat and reaches little more than 200 feet at the highest
points.

There are 20 miles of saltwater shoreline, 1,220 acres of beach, and 100
acres of freshwater lakes.

(5) Ecosystem:

    (a) Classification: The roadless area is in the Northern Interior
    Island Geographic Province. These islands have a colder climate than
    the outer islands and have a distinctive fauna. Pleasant Island and
    the Porpoise Islands are not typical of the province. Mountains
    elevations are very different from the geotype in that they do not
    reach above 800 feet. Rocky shorelines interspersed with small gravel
    beaches are found within this area. Streams within the province are
    generally larger and longer than on other islands of Southeast Alaska.
    this characteristic is not shown because of the small size of the
    islands involved. Saltwater estuaries are present, but do not exhibit
    much variety in shapes and sizes. Tidal meadows of varying sizes are
    found in this area.

    (b) Vegetation: Western hemlock and Sitka spruce dominate the
    overstory of the Pleasant Island Roadless Area. The understory is
    composed of shrubs such as red huckleberry, rusty menziesia, and
    devil's club. The forest floor is covered with a mat of mosses,
    liverworts, deerheart, bunchberry dogwood, single delight, and skunk
    cabbage. Streamside riparian vegetation is characterized by
    salmonberry, devil's club, alder, grasses, ferns, and currants

    Muskegs, dominated by sphagnum mosses, sedges, and shrubs of the heath
    family, are interspersed among low elevation timber stands where
    drainage is restricted Trees are sparse and consist mainly of
    stunted hemlock, lodgepole pine, and Alaska-cedar.

Tide flats in the Pleasant Island Roadless Area are found at the heads
of the bays and estuaries, and support sea milkwort, glasswort, and
algae   Beach meadows occur between the shore and the forest   Lower
beach meadows are composed of beach ryegrass, reed bent grass
hairgrass, fescue grass, beach lovage, goose tongue, and sedges
Upper beach meadow plants include yarrow, bedstraw, starwort ferns,
western columbine, and cow parsnip   Oregan crabapple alder, devil's
club, and blueberry occur along the border of the beach meadow and the
forest

There are approximately 12,099 acres of forested lands, of which 3,713
acres are classified as commercial forest land (CFL)   There are 1,240
acres classified as riparian oldgrowth and 3,440 acres as nonriparian
oldgrowth Approximately 20 acres are classified as muskeg, however,
muskeg may be interspersed within other types in units too small to
map. Therefore, the acreage for muskeg may be substantially
understated.

(c) Soils: The development of soils is influenced by high levels of
rainfall, cool summer temperatures, a short growing season and
moderately low soil temperatures. Under such conditions, organic
matter decomposes slowly and tends to accumulate in areas where it is
being produced or deposited.

The island was not covered in the last ice advance from Glacier Bay
The ecosystems of the island and mainland are markedly different
because of this phenomena   The Forest Service, National Park Service,
and a number of university systems have cooperative field research
projects on the island   Radiocarbon dating suggests some of the bog
basins may be greater than 14,000 years old.

The roadless area has generally poorly-drained soils which are
associated with low relief and impermeable subsurface layers   In
locations with poor drainage, deep organic soils (muskegs) tend to
form. This situatin occurs where the soil material fails to provide
sufficient internal drainage or where topography prevents external
drainage

(d) Fish Resource: There are four Pacific salmon (sockeye, coho,
pink and chum) valuable for commercial, subsistence and sport fishing
that spawn and rear in these waters. Other species include steelhead
trout, Dolly Varden char, stickleback and smelt   King salmon are
important in Icy Strait. Near-shore saltwater fisheries include crab
clams, sablefish and rockfishes.

Fish resources have been rated as part of the Tongass Land Management
Plan (1979) and by the Alaska Department of Fish and Game (ADF&G) in
their Forest Habitat Integrity Program (1983)   These ratings describe
the value of VCU's for sport fish, commercial fish and estuaries

VCU 120C rated high for sport fish values   VCU's 120C and 185C rated
high for commercial fisheries values   There are no highly rated
estuaries

(e) Wildlife Resource   Pleasant Island supports a significant
population of Sitka Black-tailed deer, bald eagles and Vancouver
Canada geese   Habitat types identified for the evaluation area
include old growth, forested, deer winter range, inland wetland beach
fringe, estuarine fringe, and streamside riparian

Other wildlife species include pine marten, land otter and mink, as
well as smaller mammals and several amphibians   There are few
resident bird species, however, the area is used by many migratory
species, including waterfowl   Sport and subsistence deer hunting is
very important in this area

Habitat for black-tailed deer, brown bear and red squirrel totals
12,239 acres. Inventoried habitat for other management indicator
species include mountain goat, black bear and pine marten (180 acres
each).

(f) **Threatened and Endangered Species:** The area contains no known
resident threatened or endangered species   This area has been
identified as having habitats for two migrating endangered species
The American peregrine falcon passes through the forests during the
spring and fall migration flights and the humpback whale inhabits
nearby waters. A sensitive species, the bald eagle, commonly uses the
islands for roosting and nesting.

(6) **Current Use and Management:** VCU 185 (12,059 acres) was designated
Land Use Designation (LUD) 2 in the Tongass Land Management Plan (TLMP) in
1979   These lands are to be managed in a roadless state to retain their
wildland character, but this would permit wildlife and fish habitat
improvement and primitive recreational facility development   This
designation excluded· roads, except for specifically authorized uses
timber harvesting, except for controlling insect infestations or to protect
other resource values; and major concentrated recreational facilities

VCU 120 (180 acres) was designated as a LUD 3 in TLMP in 1979   The
emphasis was on managing for uses and activities in a compatible and
complementary manner to provide the greatest combination of benefits
These areas have either high use or high amenity values in conjunction with
high commodity values. Allowances in calculated potential timber yield
have been made to meet multiple objectives   These lands may include
concentrated recreational developments

The recreation activities taking place in this area include marine wildlife
and scenery viewing, beachcombing, saltwater kayaking, hiking, dispersed
camping, picnicking and big game hunting.

No special use permits have been issued for specific use of the evaluation
area; however, the area is used by several outfitter/guides, such as
sea-kayakers

(7) **Appearance (Apparent Naturalness)**· This area has been basically
unmodified by human influence

The evaluation area is inventoried as 13 percent Variety Class A
(Distinctive), and 87 percent Variety Class C (Minimal) The entire
evaluation area is inventoried as an Existing Visual Condition (EVC) I,
which appears untouched by human activity

(8) Surroundings (External Influences): Gustavus is located to the north,
three miles across Icy Passage, Glacier Bay National Park is north of the
town Gustavus has regular jet service in the summer season and regular
small plane service during the winter

Four miles to the east is the Chilkat-West Lynn Canal Roadless Area, and
the small community of, Excursion Inlet. The town has year-round small
plane charter service. A logged and roaded area is located south of
Excursion Inlet.

To the south, across Icy Strait, is the Chichagof Roadless Area and Huna
Totem and Sealaska Native Lands. The town of Hoonah is located 17 miles to
the southeast of the Pleasant Island area, it has regular Alaska Marine
Highway ferry service

(9) Attractions and Features of Special Interest: Pleasant Island's
terrain is extremely flat, caused by old glaciation Early white explorers
used this island heavily because of its easy access and considered it a
place to reprovision and rest in the Icy Strait area The Porpoise Islands
have old cabins left from a fox farm established in 1923

b. Capability of Management as Wilderness or in an Unroaded Condition

(1) Manageability and Management Area Boundaries: The management of this
area as wilderness would be easily accomplished The boundaries are easily
definable and manageable. The evaluation area, being totally surrounded by
saltwater, would not be subject to permanent influences from outside it.
All external influences would be transitory in nature.

(2) Natural Integrity: Although the area has had long-time use by the
residents of Gustavus, the area shows very little human influence

(3) Opportunity for Solitude: Commercial jets serving Gustavus fly over a
portion of the Pleasant Island Roadless Area between June and August The
regular charter service planes fly over the area year-round A small
fishing fleet from Gustavus uses the coastlines of these islands Pleasant
Island is heavily used by residents of Gustavus for deer hunting, berry
picking, wood gathering, and general recreation. All of these activities
detract from the opportunity for solitude.

(4) Opportunity for Primitive Recreation: The entire area (12,239 acres)
provides for a semi-primitive, motorized recreation opportunity

The area contains two recreation places

ROS CLASS	# OF REC. PLACES	TOTAL ACRES	CAPACITY BY RVD
SPM	2	12,239	2,890

There are no public recreation cabins in the Pleasant Island Roadless Area   The landforms would allow people to feel remote, but air and water traffic is too apparent for this area to be considered a primitive experience

(5) Special Features (Ecologic, Geologic, Scientific, Cultural): There are geological and scientific research projects being done on Pleasant Island by the Forest Service Research Lab and the National Park Service

ε   Availability for Management as Wilderness or in an Unroaded Condition

(1) Resource Potentials

(a) **Recreation Potential:** The management objective for recreation management, as stated in the Amended 1985-86 Tongass Land Management Plan, is to promote no development but to emphasize scenic, wildlife and backcountry features

(b) **Fish Resource:** There are no identified fisheries improvement projects.

(c) **Wildlife Resource:** There were no habitat improvement projects identified in the Tongass Land Management Plan, as amended.

(d) **Timber Resource:** There are 3,020 acres inventoried as tentatively suitable for harvest. This includes 200 acres of riparian oldgrowth and 2,820 acres of nonriparian oldgrowth. The potential for managing timber in this roadless area is estimated to be low   The large areas of non-commercial timber and timber which is marginally operable because of accessibility limits management potential   Timber management is possible, but may not be economically feasible, because the timber stands are not high volume-per-acre nor of high quality. No suitable log transfer facility locations exist.

(e) **Land Use Authorizations:** No special use permits have been issued for specific use of the evaluation area. However, the area is used by several outfitter/guides. Possible future permits would be for subsistence or recreational facilities or for outfitter/guide services, such as sea-kayakers. Potential is low for a significant increase in special use permits other than for incidental use.

(f) **Minerals:** This area has been identified as having no mineral development potential.

(g) **Areas of Scientific Interest:**   One potential Research Natural Area is located on Pleasant Island; it encompasses the entire island The island is important as a field site for research concerning ecosystem development on recently glaciated land surfaces in Glacier Bay National Park (GBNP)   The island is one of the closest areas with old-growth forest, lake and muskeg ecosystems to compare with the successional surfaces in GBNP

(2) Management Considerations

(a) Fire: The area has no significant fire history

(b) Insects and Disease: Endemic tree diseases common to Southeast Alaska are present, there are no know epidemic disease occurrences

(c) Land Status: There are no patented private lands within the roadless area, nor are there any encumbrances, withdrawals or restrictions on National Forest Systems lands

d. Relationship to Communities and Other Roadless and Wilderness Areas

(1) **Nearby Roadless and Wilderness Areas and Uses:** Glacier Bay National Park is located just north of the Pleasant Island Roadless Area, across Icy Passage. The Chilkat - West Lynn Canal (#304) Roadless Area lies four miles to the east across Icy Strait   The Chichagof (#311) Roadless Area is seven miles to the south of Pleasant Island. Eleven miles to the west is a second portion of Glacier Bay National Monument.

(2) **Distance From Population Centers (Accessibility):** Approximate distances from population centers are as follows:

Community		Air Miles	Water Miles
Juneau	(Pop. 23,729)	32	68
Gustavus	(Pop 218)	2	2
Hoonah	(Pop 960)	17	21

The nearest stop for the Alaska Marine Highway is in Hoonah   The nearest commercial air service is in Gustavus and Juneau.

(3) Interest by Proponents:

(a) **Moratorium areas:** The evaluation area is a part of the Pleasant/Lemesurier Islands moratorium area proposed for study as a wilderness area as described in S 341 ("Wirth Bill"), and as proposed for wilderness in HR 987 ("Mrazek Bill")

(b) **Local users/residents:** Most use of the area is associated with Gustavus and Hoonah populations   Subsistence is a major use of these islands; users are from both communities   There are outfitter guides who use this group of islands for recreation tourism.

(c) **Concerns of Local Residents:** Local issues involve keeping Pleasant Island in a natural state for subsistence uses and for recreation. Gustavus is surrounded by National Park on three sides Pleasant Island is considered their "backyard" for subsistence and as an unregulated playground

e. Environmental Consequences

ALTERNATIVE ANALYSIS TO BE DONE LATER

INDIVIDUAL ROADLESS AREA DESCRIPTION

NAME: Freshwater Bay (325)   ACRES (GROSS): 72,029   ACRES (NFS)   63,200

GEOZONE: C02
GEOGRAPHIC PROVINCE: Northern Interior Islands

1989 WILDERNESS ATTRIBUTE RATING: 24

a. Description

(1) **Relationship to RARE II areas:** The table below displays the VCU 1/
names, VCU numbers, original WARS 2/ rating, and comments. This enables
the reader to compare the roadless areas evaluated in Appendix C with
previous analyses.

VCU Name	VCU No.	1979 WARS Rating	Comments
Game Creek	204*	23	
Gartina Creek	205*	20	
Spasski Creek	207*	23	
First No. 2	208*	19	
Suntaheen Creek	209*	22	
False Bay	210*	21	
Gypsum Creek	212*	18	
Iyoukeen Peninsula	213*	18	
Seal Creek	214*	22	
Freshwater Bay	215*	25	

*--The roadless area includes only part of this VCU.

(2) **History:** Some sites in the region, including the Ground Hog Bay site
on the Chilkat Peninsula and the Hidden Falls site on Baranof Island,
indicate that the occupation of Southeast Alaska dates to over 9,000 years
ago The Freshwater Bay Roadless Area is located 35 miles south of the
Ground Hog Bay site and 50 miles north of the Hidden Falls site

At the time of Euroamerican contact, the Hoonah and Angoon Tlingit were
using this area of Chichagof Island. Villages and sites for seasonal
hunting, fishing, and collecting activities were located   The forest
archaeologists have identified cache pits, bear shell midden and a
smokehouse/cabin in VCU 204 on Long Island. There are native burial sites
in VCU's 205 and 210 and petroglyphs in VCU's 209 and 215

1/ A VCU (Value Comparison Unit) is one of 867 watersheds which make up the
Forest and were differentiated for planning purposes in the Tongass Land
Management Plan.
2/ Wilderness Attribute Rating System (WARS) was the nationwide system used to
rate the wilderness attributes of roadless areas in the Roadless Area
Review and Evaluation (RARE II).

Some of the most recent historical activities taking place in this roadless area include the Gypsum Camel mining operation In the early 1900's, there was a gypsum mining operation in Gypsum Creek The stone was moved one mile to the Iyoukeen Cove by rail A trestle was built over the water for 2,000 feet to access the ships for loading

(3) Location and Access This area is located on the northeast corner of Chichagof Island Included in this area is the northern shore of Freshwater Bay To the northwest are Huna Totem and Sealaska Corporation lands, and the town of Hoonah. The southeast portion of the roadless area is bordered by Chatham Strait.

This area can be access from the Hoonah road system, small boats and charter flights The nearest Alaska Marine Highway into this area is at Hoonah.

(4) Geography and Topography: This area is quite mountainous with large deep stream drainages. Terrain relief ranges sealevel to more than 3 400 feet in the far western corner of the evaluation unit. Several peaks north of Seal Creek reach 3,000 feet or higher. There are some flat areas at the head of Freshwater Bay. The area contains 31 miles of shoreline on saltwater, with 1,900 acres of beach. A large part of the area is alpine tundra (6,780 acres), and rock (3,120 acres) There are 20 acres of freshwater lakes in the area.

(5) Ecosystem:

(a) Classification: In the Northern Interior Island province the coastline is protected from full force of storms, unlike the outer coast. These islands have a colder climate, a highly dissected topography, and an extensive alpine environments with productive forested areas, highly fragmented and usually concentrated on oversteepened slopes and on valley bottoms

(b) Vegetation: Western hemlock-Sitka spruce forests dominate the overstory of this roadless area. The understory is composed of shrubs such as red huckleberry, rusty menziesia, and devil's club The forest floor is covered with a mat of mosses, liverworts, deerheart bunchberry dogwood, single delight, and skunk cabbage Streamside riparian vegetation is characterized by salmonberry, devil's club, alder, grasses, ferns, and currants

Muskegs, dominated by sphagnum mosses, sedges, and shrubs of the heath family, are interspersed among low elevation timber stands where drainage is restricted. Trees are sparse and consist mainly of stunted hemlock, lodgepole pine, and Alaska-cedar There is 1,480 acres of muskeg in this area. Muskeg is interspersed within other types in units too small to map, therefore, the acreage for muskeg may be substantially understated

Tideflats are found at the heads of the bays and estuaries and are
usually associated with stream estuaries   The tideflats generally
support sea milkwort, glasswort, and algae   Beach meadows occur
between the shore and the forest   Lower beach meadows are composed of
beach ryegrass, reed bent grass, hairgrass, fescue grass beach
lovage, goose tongue, and sedges   Upper beach meadow plants include
yarrow, bedstraw, starwort, ferns, western columbine, and cow
parsnip   Oregon crabapple, alder, devil's club and blueberry ve...
along the border of the beach meadow and the forest.

At elevations generally above 2,000 feet, the plant communities ...
characterized by low shrubs, grasses, and sedges   Subalpine forests
and meadows occur at the interface between the forested communities
and the alpine tundra.

There are approximately 49,383 acres of forested land of which 38,831
acres are commercial forest land. Of the commercial forest land,
32,541 acres are non-riparian old growth and 4,360 acres are riparian
old growth.

(c) **Soils:** The development of soils in the roadless area is
influenced by high levels of rainfall, cool summer temperatures, a
short growing season, and moderately low soil temperatures   In the
Freshwater Bay Roadless Area, shallow soils with good drainage develop
on steeper slopes due to rapid loss of material by erosion and
efficient rainwater runoff   This is obvious on the steep slopes that
face Freshwater Bay. Deep, well drained soils occur below shallow
soils on gentler slopes where transported soil materials have
collected

The poorly drained soils in this area are associated with low relief
and impermeable subsurface layers   In locations with poor drainage
deep organic soils (muskegs) tend to form   Drainage improves with
increased slope gradient, however, as slopes become oversteepened
soil depths become much shallower   In riparian areas, soil zones tend
to contain sand and gravels as a result of flood deposition

(d) **Fish Resource:** Fishing, especially for salmon, is a major source
of subsistence for local residents   Abundant streams in the unit
provide spawning and rearing habitat for pink, chum, coho, and sockeye
salmon. Sport and commercial fishing in area waters is common   Other
species include cutthroat trout, steelhead trout, Dolly Varden char,
stickleback and smelt.   Important saltwater fisheries include crab,
sablefish and rockfishes

Wukuklook and Gypsum Creek are major anadromous streams. There are
many headwater tributaries for the large fish producing streams
located within roaded areas, these include the North Fork of
Freshwater Creek, Seal Creek, and Iyoukeen Creek.

Fish resources have been rated as part of the Tongass Land Management
Plan (1979) and by the Alaska Department of Fish and Game in their
Forest Habitat Integrity Program (1983)   These ratings describe the
value of VCU's for sport fish, commercial fish, and estuaries

There are no VCU's rated as having a high value for sport fish in the
Freshwater Bay Roadless Area. VCU's rated as highly valued for
commercial fish are Game Creek (204), False Bay (210) and Freshwater
Bay (215)   One VCU, Spasski Creek (207), is rated as containing a
highly valued estuary

(e) **Wildlife Resource:** In the Freshwater Bay Roadless Area, Iyoukeen
Peninsula. most of the shorelines, and into some of the drainages are
designated critical deer winter range   Hippoback Ridge is considered
good deer habitat   This area has high quality bear habitat, as well
as Vancouver Canada geese use   There are bald eagle nesting and
roosting trees in this area.

(f) **Threatened and Endangered Species:** The Freshwater Bay Roadless
Area contains no known threatened or endangered species. This area
has been identified as having habitats for two migrating endangered
species. The Peale's peregrine falcon passes through the forests
during the spring and fall migration flights and the humpback whale
inhabits nearby waters. A sensitive species, the bald eagle, commonly
uses the coastline for nesting and roosting

(6) **Current Use and Management:** The roadless area is completely within
the Alaska Pulp Corporation Long Term Timber Sale Contract area. There are
two VCU's (13,981 acres) designated as a Land Use Designation (LUD) 3 in
the Tongass Land Management Plan (TLMP) in 1979   The emphasis is on
managing for uses and activities in a compatible and complementary manner
to provide the greatest combination of benefits   These areas have either
high use or high amenity values in conjunction with high commodity values
Allowances in calculated potential timber yield have been made to meet
multiple objectives

Eight VCU's (40,404 acres) were designated as LUD 4   These lands will be
managed for a variety of uses   Opportunities will be provided for
intensive resource use and development where emphasis is primarily on
commodity or market resources   Allowances in calculated potential timber
yield have been made to provide for protection of physical and biological
productivity

There is an identified anchorage in False Bay, providing access to the
roadless area. There are many identified recreation places   Recreation
activities taking place include viewing of wildlife/fish, beachcombing,
saltwater shore fishing, steam fishing, hiking dispersed camping. big game
hunting, waterfowl hunting, small game hunting, upland bird hunting.
viewing scenery, cross-country skiing, and saltwater kayaking

There are a block of unpatented mining claims known as the Gypsum Claims in
VCU 212. A special use permit for a shelter has been issued at Iyoukeen
Cove in VCU's 212/213   There are a number of outfitter/guides who use this
area

(7) Appearance (Apparent Naturalness): Other than the gypsum mining
operations area, the Freshwater Bay Roadless Area has not been
significantly modified and appears entirely natural   The visual character
type of this area is Admiralty-Chichagof   The landforms in this area ar
generally rounded with mountain elevations vary from 2,055-3,395 feet   The
Freshwater Bay Roadless Area has rocky shorelines interspersed, with small
gravel beaches   Streams are generally larger and longer in this character
type than on other islands of Southeast Alaska   Saltwater bays and
estuaries are present and exhibit much variety   Several tidal meadows of
varying sizes are found in this unit

Lower slopes are densely forested, but exhibit a combination of muskeg
openings, brush and scattered tree cover up to approximately 2,500 feet
elevation. Upper slopes and summits appear barren from a distance, but
offer a variety of alpine vegetation as well as numerous rock outcroppings.

The evaluation area is inventoried as 38 percent of the acreage in a
Variety Class A (Distinctive), 34 percent was in Variety Class B (Common)
and 28 percent of this roadless area was in Variety Class C (Minimal
Variety)

The majority (68 percent) of this roadless area is in Existing Visual
Condition (EVC) I, these areas appear to be untouched by human activity.
One percent of the acreage is in EVC II, where changes to the landscape are
not noticed by the average person unless pointed out   Four percent is in
an EVC IV, which are areas in which changes in the landscape are easily
noticed by the average person and may attract some attention   There
appears to be disturbances but they resemble natural patterns   The balance
of the area, or 27 percent, is in EVC V where changes in the landscape are
obvious to the average person. The changes appear to be major
disturbances

(8) Surroundings (External Influences): To the northwest of this area are
Huna Totem and Sealaska private lands. These lands have been, and are
being, roaded and logged. The Cartina Creek drainage is the municipal
watershed for Hoonah; part of the watershed is within the evaluation area.

The northeast corner borders on a harvested and roaded area that was logged
in the early 1980's. The roading in this area extends east and south to
Flints Point. The Point Augusta Roadless Area is located northeast of the
roaded area. An active log transfer facility (LTF) is located in False Bay
to the east of the Freshwater Bay Roadless Area. Chatham Strait borders
the southeast corner of the Freshwater Bay Roadless Area. The width of
Chatham Strait in this area is eight to nine miles across to Admiralty
Island.

Seal Creek, in the southern portion of the roadless area, also has an LTF
and a road system. Freshwater Bay bounds the evaluation area to the
south. Kennel Creek logging camp and Pavlof/East Point Roadless Area are
on the south side of Freshwater Bay   There is an active log transfer
facility (LTF) at the Kennel Creek camp   The North Fork of Freshwater

Creek is located northwest of the Kennel Creek camp   This area has been
extensively logged and roaded   The southwest corner of Freshwater Bay
Roadless Area borders this harvested area   Immediately to the west of the
logged area is the Game Creek Roadless Area

The road systems to the northeast and southwest of the Freshwater Bay
evaluation area are interconnected through the Hoonah road system   The
southwestern road system is also connected to the Kennel Creek road system.

The ferry route to Hoonah passes the southeast corner of the roadless
area   There are regularly scheduled flights to Hoonah and charter flight
service to Kennel Creek logging camp   Access to this area from the road
systems is readily available, with minimal walking involved.

(9) Attractions and Features of Special Interest: The Iyoukeen Peninsula
is of special interest. The peninsula is approximately four miles long and
1/8 of a mile wide   There is no undergrowth and walking the length is like
being in a park.

The natural features of the area, the scenery, and the opportunity to see
wildlife are all attractions. High quality fishing opportunities in the
streams and lakes also provide attractions   The area contains 11
inventoried recreation places which contains 20,083 acres   There are no
recreation cabins in this area.

b. **Capability of Management as Wilderness or in an Unroaded Condition**

(1) Manageability and Management Area Boundaries: The northern boundaries
of Freshwater Bay Roadless Area are the Huna Totem Native Corporation Lands
and Forest Service managed lands   Both areas have been extensively
logged. The Hoonah road system and harvest units continue to the east and
combines with the False Bay road system and units in the southeast corner
of the area. The southeast corner of this area is bordered by Freshwater
Bay and Chatham Strait. On the southwestern corner of this roadless area
is the Kennel Creek road system and harvest units. This system joins with
the Hoonah road systems and harvest units   The western boundary is defined
by the Huna Totem and Sealaska private lands

The boundaries of this area are not hard to manage because of the clear cut
definition of human activity (roads and logged units), and the saltwater
passages that adjoin the unit. The lands that lay next to private and
Forest Service harvested lands would be difficult to manage for a
wilderness experience.

(2) Natural Integrity: The Freshwater Bay Roadless Area has had little
modification by humans. The overall appearance is natural except for some
evidences in the forest and near the water of the gypsum mining operation
from the early 1900's.

(3) Opportunity for Solitude: The opportunity for solitude in the
Freshwater roadless area is rated high because of the area's size   The
area measures approximately twelve by seven miles across

Because this area is within the APC Long-term Timber Sale program area, as
well as bordering private lands that are being harvested, there is the
possibility of noise from the surrounding road systems

(4) Opportunity for Primitive Recreation: The area provides primarily
Primitive and Semiprimitive Non-motorized recreation opportunities, as
inventoried with the Recreation Opportunity Spectrum (ROS) system

ROS Class	Acres
Primitive I (PI)	26,263
Roaded Natural (RN)	5,760
Semi-Primitive Non-Motorized (SPNM)	25,303
Semi-Primitive Motorized (SPM)	9,140

The area contains 11 recreation places.

ROS CLASS	# OF REC. PLACES	TOTAL ACRES	CAPACITY BY RVD
RN	3	5,100	7,578
RM	3	5,560	4,576
SPNM	3	8,802	7,985
SPM	2	620	6,192

The nearest public recreation cabin to the Freshwater Bay Roadless Area is
at Salt Lake Bay   There is a remote chance of meeting other recreation
groups in this area because of the proximity to Hoonah and Tenakee Springs
and the use this area is receiving now   Access into this area is by boat,
using the road system from Hoonah or taking the ferry to Tenakee Springs
and walking into the area.

(5) Special Features (Ecologic, Geologic, Scientific, Cultural): The
Sonyakay Ridge is a geological form of special interest   Sonyakay Ridge is
a very prominent ridge system, between located Iyouktug and Wukuklook
Creeks The land form is very steep and very rugged. The peaks vary in
height from 2200 to 2500 feet along this ridgeline.

The abandoned gypsum mine on Gypsum Creek is a special feature of
historical interest.

c. Availability for Management as Wilderness or in an Unroaded Condition

(1) Resource Potentials

(a) Recreation Potential: In the original Tongass Land Management
Plan (1979), there was a proposal for alpine trails near the head of
Freshwater Bay, on to the ridge system of Elephant Mountain and
Sonyakay Ridge. There were also alpine shelters planned for the
Sonyakay Ridge area. Outfitter and guide use has the potential to
increase in this area

(b) Fish Resource: The TLMP, as Amended, identifies fish passage
projects for Freshwater and Suntaheen Creeks

(c) Wildlife Resource: Projects planned in TLMP, as Amended, include nesting platforms in Upper Freshwater Creek, and cavity- nester nest boxes in VCU 204, 213, 214, and 215 Wildlife habitat improvement riparian cover planting and habitat improvement for second growth management debris reduction is also planned if the area is logged There is the potential to promote Peale's peregrine falcon nesting habitat in the Elephant Mountain area

(d) Timber Resource: The potential for managing timber within the roadless area is very high because the entire area falls into the APC Long-term timber sale area The existing road systems and communities make the management for timber harvest economical The management emphasis is to continue timber harvest, related access road construction, and replacement of bridges on several of the roads for the APC 1986-90 and 1991-95 timber sales.

Road construction and harvesting has been initiated in this roadless area. The Seal Creek road system is under construction, with logging to be completed by 1992. Wukuklook Creek road construction is to be extended approximately five miles into the drainage and four miles into the Gypsum Creek drainage. Logging is to be completed by 1995

There are 30,221 acres inventoried as tentatively suitable for harvest This includes 3,560 acres of riparian old growth, and 24,541 acres of non-riparian old growth Potential timber volume is _____.

(e) Land Use Authorizations: The current special use permits will continue The potential for more outfitters and guides using the area more frequently is probable with the increase of need

(f) Minerals: The area was identified as having a moderate potential for mineral development in 1984

(g) Potential Research Area: There are no potential or inventoried Research Natural Areas in the Freshwater Bay Roadless Area

(2) Management Considerations

(a) Wildlife: Wildlife management would not change except for the possibility of enhancement projects

(b) Fire: The area has no significant fire history.

(c) Insects and Disease: Endemic tree diseases common to Southeast Alaska are present; there are no know epidemic disease occurrences

(d) Land Status: There are two Native land selections in the Freshwater Roadless Area. Private lands include the patented Gypsum Mines within the roadless area

d   Relationship to Communities and Other Roadless and Wilderness Areas

(1) **Nearby Roadless and Wilderness Areas and Uses:** To the north and
northeast are the Whitestone (#318) and Point Augusta (#317) roadless
evaluation areas Directly to the south, across Freshwater Bay, is the
Pavlof/East Point (#323) Roadless Area. The Game Creek (#323) Roadless
area is located to the west, across the Hoonah-Kennel Creek road system
The Admiralty Island National Monument Wilderness is located to the west,
across Chatham Strait

The nearest communities to the Freshwater Bay Roadless Area are Hoonah the
Kennel Creek logging camp and Tenakee Springs The Huna Totem Corporation
lands lay to the northwest

To the south of the Freshwater Bay Roadless Area is the saltwater inlet,
Freshwater Bay. Two miles across the bay is the Pavlof/East Point Roadless
Area. The Kennel Creek/Hoonah road and harvesting system borders the
southwest corner of the Freshwater Roadless Area. This area is
approximately 3/4 of a mile wide and is the northern boundary of the Game
Creek Roadless Area. The western edge of this roadless area is designated
by the private lands of Huna Totem and Sealaska. On the other side of
these private lands is the water inlet Port Frederick.

(2) **Distance From Population Centers (Accessibility):** Approximate
distances from population centers are as follows:

Community			Air Miles	Water Miles
Juneau	(Pop	23,729)	32	58
Hoonah	(Pop	960)	10	50
Tenkee Spr	(Pop	95)	12	23
Angoon	(Pop.	639)	32	32

The nearest towns to Freshwater Bay Roadless Area that are served by the
Alaska Marine Highway system are Tenakee Springs, Hoonah and Angoon The
closest commercial airline service is at Sitka and Juneau

(3) **Interest by Proponents:**

(a) **Moratorium areas:** This roadless area is not been proposed as a
"moratorium" area nor as Wilderness in legislative initiatives to
date.

(b) **Local users/residents:** Most use of the area is associated with
residents of Tenakee Springs, Kennel Creek logging camp, and Hoonah
There is boat use in Freshwater Bay from all the surrounding towns
Subsistence use in the area is considered a priority among the local
residents. Outfitter/guide use is by boat via the Kennel Creek/Hoonah
and False Bay/Hoonah road systems

(c) Concerns of Local Residents: Local issues include the continuing harvesting and roading of the timber lands, the effects on fisheries and wildlife habitat caused by logging, maintaining the visual quality of high interest areas, maintaining lifestyles, location of log transfer facilities, the distribution of harvest volume classes and the tradeoffs between environmental protection measures and the economics of the harvest activities

e. Environmental Consequences

ALTERNATIVE ANALYSIS TO BE DONE LATER

INDIVIDUAL ROADLESS AREA DESCRIPTION

NAME: North Kruzof (326)   ACRES (GROSS): 31,190   ACRES (NFS): 31,170

GEOZONES: C10
GEOGRAPHIC PROVINCE. Northern Outer Islands

1989 WILDERNESS ATTRIBUTE RATING: 21

a. Description

    (1) Relationship to RARE II areas: The table below displays the VCU 1/
    names, VCU numbers, original WARS 2/ rating, and comments This enables
    the reader to compare the roadless areas evaluated in Appendix C with
    previous analyses.

| | | 1979 | |
VCU Name	VCU No	WARS Rating	Comments
Neva Strait	302*	18	
Sukoi Strait	303*	--	Not rated in 1979
Sinitsin Bay	304	18	
Sealion Cove	305	26	
Gilmer Bay	306*	20	
Krestof Sound	309*	20	

    (2) History: This large area has a long and varied history of use dating
    from Tlingit use in prehistoric and historic times to the present use by a
    variety of Alaska residents and visitors. Use of the area has been
    primarily for hunting, fishing, recreation, and temporary occupancy
    Remains of structures and other human cultural activity in varying degrees
    of deterioration can still be found

    *--The roadless area includes only part of this VCU.

    (3) Location and Access: The area is located on the northern end of
    Kruzof Island. The area also includes Partofshikof Island on the eastern
    side of Kruzof Island and a number of offshore islands and rocks It is
    bounded on the north by Salisbury Sound, on the west by the Pacific Ocean
    and on the south by the road system and timber harvesting in the area
    between Gilmer Bay and Krestof Sound The eastern boundary of the area is
    formed by Neva Strait and Krestof Sound.

1/ A VCU (Value Comparison Unit) is one of 867 watersheds which make up the
   Forest and were differentiated for planning purposes in the Tongass Land
   Management Plan.
2/ Wilderness Attribute Rating System (WARS) was the nationwide system used to
   rate the wilderness attributes of roadless areas in the Roadless Area
   Review and Evaluation (RARE II).

The primary form of access to the area is by saltwater along all
coastlines Access to the area is generally good This is due to the
numerous bays and fiords that provide sheltered anchorage for boats and
the proximity to Sitka There is only one National Forest System Trail
within the area, the Sealion Cove Trail. It is 2 5 miles in length
beginning at Kalinin Bay and ending at Sealion Cove.

(4) Geography and Topography· The area is generally characterized by
small irregular mountains or ridges 1,000 to 2 000 feet in elevation   an
steep slopes Numerous rocky crests and sharp ridges are found scattered
throughout the area The coastline is scalloped with bays   ed w ...
encompasses Sukoi Strait between Kruzof Island and Partofshikof Island.
The shoreline is characterized by forested lowlands with a relatively
gentle slope Rocky islands, reefs, and rock bluffs dominate the coast
along northern and western sides of the area. The rocky shoreline is
interspersed with small gravel or sandy beaches.

Streams are generally short and flow directly to saltwater, and the area
contains one named lake, Surprise Lake A dominant feature of the area is
the rugged ridge that runs the width of Kruzof Island along the southern
boundary of the area. With an elevation of 2,000 feet, it effectively
forms a wall between this roadless area and the rest of Kruzof Island

Approximately 4 percent of the area consists of alpine tundra, ice, snow
and rock. This includes 759 acres of alpine tundra, and 479 acres of
rock. There are 80 acres of small islands located along the coastline and
1,843 acres of freshwater lakes in the area. The only large lake in the
area is Surprise Lake.

(5) Ecosystem:

    (a) Geographic Province: The area is classified as being in the
    Northern Outer Islands Geographic Province This province is
    generally characterized by rugged highly dissected topography exposed
    extremely wet outer coastal environment, and extensive alpine
    environments with productive forested areas highly fragmented and
    usually concentrated on oversteepened slopes and on valley bottoms.

    (b) Vegetation: The proximity of this area to the open North Pacific
    Ocean and the unimpeded movement of storms into the area from the
    southwest results in a high rainfall. Conifer cover density varies
    widely even on low slopes near saltwater and is usually interspersed
    with muskeg and other lower forms of vegetation. Larger intertidal
    grass and associated meadows species are infrequent. The effects of
    wind and salt spray affect the character and, to some extent, the
    species on the west side of this unit.

    The vegetation of this roadless area consists primarily of typical
    spruce-hemlock forests. Western hemlock-Sitka spruce dominate the
    overstory while the understory is composed of shrubs such as red
    huckleberry, rusty menziesia, and devil's club The forest floor is
    covered with a mat of mosses, liverworts, and plants such as
    deerheart, bunchberry dogwood, single delight, and skunk cabbage.
    Streamside riparian vegetation is characterized by salmonberry,
    devil's club, alder, grasses, ferns, and currants

Muskegs are abundant within this area, however due to their small size and association with forested sites, accurate acreage estimates are difficult These areas, dominated by sphagnum mosses, sedges, and shrubs of the heath family, are interspersed among low elevation timber stands where drainage is restricted Trees within the muskegs are sparse and consist mainly of stunted hemlock, lodgepole pine, and Alaska cedar

Small tide flats are found at the heads of Kalinin Bay and Sinitsin Cove and are associated with stream estuaries The tideflats generally support sea milkwort, glasswort, and algae Beach meadows occur between the shore and the forest Lower beach meadows are composed of beach ryegrass, reed bent grass, hairgrass, fescue grass, beach lovage, goose tongue, and sedges. Upper beach meadow plants include yarrow, bedstraw, starwort, ferns, western columbine, and cow parsnip. Oregon crabapple, alder, devil's club, and blueberry occur along the border of the beach meadow and the forest.

There are approximately 27,170 acres of forested land of which 15,702 acres are commercial forest land. Of the commercial forest land, 13,744 acres are non-riparian old growth and 719 acres are riparian old growth.

(c) Soils: Shallow mineral soils with good drainage can be found on steeper slopes due to rapid loss of material by erosion and efficient rainwater runoff. Deep, well drained soils commonly occur below the shallow soils on the gentler slopes where transported soil materials have collected. Poorly drained soils are found associated with low relief and impermeable subsurface layers In locations with poor drainage, deep organic soils (muskegs) tend to form In riparian areas, soil zones tend to contain sand and gravels as a result of flood deposition.

(d) Fish Resource: Fish resources have been rated as part of the Tongass Land Management Plan (1979) and by the Alaska Department of Fish and Game in their Forest Habitat Integrity Program (1983) These ratings describe the value of VCU's for sport fish, commercial fish and estuaries.

There is one VCU which is rated as high value for sport fish, Krestof Sound (309) There is also only one VCU rated as highly valued for commercial fish, Krestof Sound (309). There are four VCU's rated as having highly valued estuaries. These are Neva Strait (302), Sinitsin Bay (304), Sealion Cove (305), and Krestof Sound (309).

(e) Wildlife Resource: There are many varied wildlife resources in this roadless area. Birds and waterfowl rearing and nesting areas are abundant in this area. Generally, the area provides good habitat for deer and brown bear. Bald eagle habitat, nesting and roosting trees encompasses this roadless area along the shorelines

(f) Threatened and Endangered Species: The area contains no known
resident threatened or endangered species   This area has been
identified as having habitats for two migrating endangered species
The Peale's peregrine falcon passes through the forests during the
spring and fall migration flights and the humpback whale inhabits
nearby waters

(6) Current Use and Management. The majority of this area (All of VCU 305
and those portions of VCU's 302, 303, and 309 located within this roadless
area) was allocated to Land Use Designation (LUD) 3 in the Tongass Land
Management Plan

Units allocated to LUD 3 are to be managed for a variety of uses. The
emphasis is on managing for both amenity and commodity oriented uses in a
compatible manner to provide the greatest combination of benefits   These
areas usually have high amenity values in conjunction with high commodity
values. Allowances in calculated potential timber yield have been made to
meet multiple use coordination objectives

The other two VCU's in this area were allocated to Land Use Designation
(LUD) 4 in the Tongass Land Management Plan. This includes all of VCU 304,
Sinitsin Bay, and a portion of VCU 306, Gilmer Bay

Units allocated to LUD 4 provide opportunities for intensive development of
resources   Emphasis is primarily on commodity, or market resources and
their use   It also provides for amenity values. When conflicts over
competing resource uses arise, conflicts would most often be resolved in
favor of commodity values   Allowances in calculated potential timber yield
have been made to provide for protection of physical and biological
productivity.

There are a number of authorized special uses existing within the area.
The following are the major uses at this time   Sitka Sound Seafoods has a
special use permit for use of facilities at Kalinin Bay in support of a
temporary fish buying scow   The Federal Aviation Agency has an interagency
agreement for use of facilities on top of the ridge in the southern portion
of the area as a radio site for air to ground communications between pilots
of general aviation aircraft and personnel in Flight Service Stations   A
Forest Service radio repeater site is located on the same ridge and is used
for intra-agency radio communications.

Recreational use of the area is primarily for hunting and fishing, and
enjoying the scenery   This use is scattered across the area and with the
usual concentrations near lakes, streams, and shorelines

There is no private land in the roadless area.

(7) Appearance (Apparent Naturalness): A vast majority of the area is
considered unmodified except for those areas primarily located near the
shoreline with evidence of current or historic use   Evidence of historic
use includes old fish cold storage facilities in Kalinin Bay, old cabins,
and other historic occupancies   Current use includes the temporary fish
buying scow and facilities, various short-term occupancies, and other

evidence of the use of the area and the surrounding waters   All of this
evidence is readily apparent to visitors that visit the specific sites.

The visual character type of this roadless area is classified as
Admiralty-Chichagof Landforms in this unit are generally rounded   Rocky
islands, reef, and rock bluffs are found frequently on the outer coast
Rocky shorelines interspersed with small gravel beaches are found
throughout the character type   Streams are generally short and swift on
the west side of the roadless area   The streams are clear and many offer
considerable visual variety, e g , pools, rapids, cascades, riffles falls,
and meandering forms   Saltwater bays and estuaries are numerous and
exhibit much variety, from small sheltered coves to large exposed for s.
Often dramatic high energy seas occur on the outer coast

Approximately 16 percent of this roadless area was inventoried in 1984 as
being Visual Variety Class B (Common), and approximately 62 percent as
Variety Class C (Minimal Variety). The remaining 22 percent of the acreage
was inventoried Variety Class A (Distinctive).

The majority (82 percent) of this roadless area was inventoried in 1984 as
having an Existing Visual Condition (EVC) I; these areas appear to be
untouched by human activity   Approximately 6 percent of the acreage is in
EVC IV, which are areas in which changes in the landscape are easily
noticed by the average person and may attract some attention. There appear
to be disturbances but they resemble natural patterns   Twelve percent is
in EVC V where changes in the landscape are obvious to the average person.
The changes appear to be major disturbances

(8) Surroundings (External Influences): The area is bordered by saltwater
on three sides. As a result, external influences on those sides are
limited to the sights and sounds of motorized boats   The southern boundary
adjoins an area of timber activity and its associated road system   Due to
the effects of topographic screening by a ridge of mountains at the
southern end of the roadless area, this development has had only local
impact on the roadless area

(9) Attractions and Features of Special Interest: Two features of special
interest in the North Kruzof Roadless Area are Sealion Cove and the
National Forest System Trail leading to it. A beautiful mile-long white
sandy beach is at Sealion Cove, a wonderful place for beachcombing,
camping, watching sealions, and viewing the open Pacific Ocean   The small
lake midway along the trail has a sandy bottom and is good swimming,
although the water is very cold.

The natural features of the area, the scenery, and the opportunity to see
wildlife are all considered attractions. High quality fishing
opportunities in the streams and lakes also provide attractions. The area
contains 10 inventoried recreation places which contains 21,141 acres
These is one National Forest System Trail in this roadless area, but no
public recreation cabins.

b. Capability of Management as Wilderness or in an Unroaded Condition

(1) **Manageability and Management Area Boundaries·** The North Kruzof
Roadless Area is generally well defined by topographic features   The
boundaries determined by Gilmer Bay, the Pacific Ocean, Salisbury Sound
Neva Strait, and Krestof Sound are easily described and recognized   Even
the southern boundary, which is result of a road system and timber
activity, roughly parallels one steeply sloped ridge of mountains over
2,000 feet in elevation and a second one over 1,500 feet   The poorest
boundary occurs in the area of Sukoi Inlet, and even that is reasonably
secure

The feasibility of management of this area as Wilderness or in an unroaded
condition is good as there is no significant motorized access or other
current nonconforming uses.

(2) **Natural Integrity:** The area is unmodified except for the evidence of
current and historic use of the area. This evidence, although locally
significant, has a very low overall effect on the natural integrity of the
area. Both the relative size of the developments and their location along
the shoreline contribute to that low impact, The long-term ecological
processes are intact and operating with the effect of human influences on
natural processes unmeasurable.

(3) **Opportunity for Solitude:** There is a moderate to high opportunity for
solitude within the area. Both the size of the area and the screening
offered by the topography and vegetation increase the opportunity for
solitude   Recreational use of the area is relatively limited and
dispersed, so that encounters with other visitors are unlikely   The sight
or sound of airplanes overhead and boats along the coastlines can
occasionally intrude on a visitor's solitude   On Partofshikof Island along
Neva Strait, ferries of the Alaska Marine Highway system, and other ships,
boats, and floatplanes can be observed or heard in this major water
transportation corridor

(4) **Opportunity for Primitive Recreation:** The area provides a moderate to
high opportunity for primitive recreation as a result of its size,
topographic and vegetative screening, diversity of primitive recreational
opportunities, and physical challenges   This area has a highly irregular
topography and diverse vegetation that combine to offer a setting capable
of providing a variety of primitive recreation opportunities   There are
lakes, ponds, streams, bays, rugged mountains, and a varied coastline that
contribute to these opportunities   The absence of developed recreational
facilities further enhances the opportunity for primitive recreation

The area provides primarily a Primitive recreation opportunity as
inventoried with the Recreation Opportunity Spectrum (ROS) system   The
acreage of each ROS class within the Roadless Area are listed below

ROS Class	Acres
Roaded Natural (RN)	4,038
Roaded Modified (RM)	1,998
Semi,Primitive Non-Motorized (SPNM)	23,952
Semi-Primitive Motorized (SPM)	4,038
No ROS	1,788

The area contains ten recreation places

ROS CLASS	# OF REC. PLACES	TOTAL ACRES	CAPACITY BY RVD
RN	1	1,858	3,039
RM	3	2,418	10,220
SPNM	2	13,366	2,220
SPM	4	3,499	7,003

There is one National Forest System Trail in the area, the Sealion Cove
Trail, and no recreation cabins.

(5) **Special Features (Ecologic, Geologic, Scientific, Cultural):** There
are no known features of ecologic, geologic, scientific, or cultural
significance.

c. **Availability for Management as Wilderness or in an Unroaded Condition**

(1) **Resource Potentials**

(a) **Recreation Potential:** The Tongass Land Management Plan, Amended
Winter 1985-86 identified opportunities for Recreation Cabins in
Sealion Cove and Gilmer Bay No potential trail locations or
developed recreation sites have been identified at this time

The varied terrain, diverse vegetation, and attractive scenery of this
area provide unlimited recreation potentials for dispersed
recreation. Additional trails and cabins or shelters are possible.

(b) **Fish Resource:** The Tongass Land Management Plan, Amended Winter
1985-86 identified opportunities for fish stocking in the unnamed lake
one mile east of Sealion Cove.

(c) **Wildlife Resource:** The Tongass Land Management Plan Amended
Winter 1985-86 identified opportunities for wildlife habitat
improvement on the southwest side of Partofshikof Island through
management of second-growth forest.

(d) **Timber Resource:** The Tongass Land Management Plan, Amended
Winter 1985-86 did not identify any opportunities for management of
the timber resource in this roadless area. There are 9,531 acres
inventoried as tentatively suitable for harvest This includes 480
acres of riparian old growth, and 8,172 acres of non-riparian old
growth.

(e) **Land Use Authorizations:** Other than for the Forest Service and the Federal Aviation Agency Radio sites in the southern portion of the area, no major land use authorizations exist

(f) **Minerals:** The area does not have a high mineral development potential and there are no known claims

(g) **Areas of Scientific Interest:** There are no known areas of scientific interest in the roadless area

(2) Management Considerations

(a) **Timber:** The potential for managing timber in this roadless area is dependent on the development of high market values and harvest methods which will allow extraction without need for extensive roading.

(b) **Fire:** The area has no significant fire history

(c) **Insects and Disease:** Endemic tree diseases common to Southeast Alaska are present in the area, however, there are no know epidemic disease occurrences

(d) Land Status: INFORMATION NOT YET AVAILABLE

d. Relationship to Communities and Other Roadless and Wilderness Areas.

(1) **Nearby Roadless and Wilderness Areas and Uses:** The nearest Wilderness is the West Chichagof-Yakobi Wilderness that lies north of Salisbury Sound. Two other nearby Wildernesses are the Admiralty National Monument Wilderness, which lies east of Chatham Strait, and the South Baranof Wilderness south of Sitka.

Nearby roadless areas include Middle Kruzof and South Kruzof, both on Kruzof Island, and North Baranof, which lies east of Neva Strait on Baranof Island.

(2) **Distance From Population Centers (Accessibility):** Approximate distances from population centers are as follows

Community		Air Miles	Water Miles
Juneau	(Pop. 23,729)	80	140
Sitka	(Pop. 8,041)	20	20
Angoon	(Pop. 639)	50	70

The nearest stop on the Alaska Marine Highway is Sitka.

(3) Interest by Proponents:

(a) Moratorium areas: This area has not been identified as a "moratorium" area or proposed as Wilderness in legislative initiatives to date

(b) Local users/residents: Most use of the area is associated with recreational boating, hunting and fishing, and viewing wildlife and the scenery of the area.

e   Environmental Consequences

ALTERNATIVE ANALYSIS TO BE DONE LATER

INDIVIDUAL ROADLESS AREA DESCRIPTION

NAME: Middle Kruzof (327)   ACRES (GROSS): 15,540   ACRES (NFS): 15,540

GEOZONES: C10
GEOGRAPHIC PROVINCE: Northern Outer Islands

1989 WILDERNESS ATTRIBUTE RATING: 22

a. Description

(1) Relationship to RARE II areas: The table below displays the VCU 1/
names, VCU numbers, original WARS 2/ rating, and comments This enables
the reader to compare the roadless areas evaluated in Appendix C with
previous analyses.

| | | 1979 | |
VCU Name	VCU No	WARS Rating	Comments
Sukoi Strait	303*	- -	Not rated in 1979
Gilmer Bay	306*	20	
Cuvacan Cove	307*	- -	Not rated in 1979
Krestof Sound	309*	20	

*--The roadless area includes only part of this VCU

(2) History: This large area has a long and varied history of use dating
from Tlingit use in prehistoric and historic times to the present use by a
variety of Alaska residents and visitors Use of the area has been
primarily for hunting, fishing, recreation, and temporary occupancy.
Remains of structures and other human cultural activity in varying degrees
of deterioration can still be found.

(3) Location and Access: The area is located in the middle of Kruzof
Island. It runs from Point Mary at the northern end of Shelikof Bay, north
along the coast to the head of Gilmer Bay From there it runs across
Kruzof Island to Krestof Sound. It is bounded on the north by the roads
and timber activity that cross the Island from Gilmer Bay to Sukoi Inlet.
It is bounded on the south by the roads and timber activity that cross the
island from Shelikof Bay to Mud Bay The area also includes the Nedezhda
Islands in Krestof Sound and a number of small offshore islands and rocks.

The primary form of access to the area is by saltwater along both the
Pacific Ocean and the Krestof Sound coastlines. Access to the area is
generally good. This is due to the bays that provide sheltered anchorage
for boats, and the roadless areas' proximity to Sitka. There are no
National Forest System Trails within the area.

1/ A VCU (Value Comparison Unit) is one of 867 watersheds which make up the
Forest and were differentiated for planning purposes in the Tongass Land
Management Plan.

2/ Wilderness Attribute Rating System (WARS) was the nationwide system used to
rate the wilderness attributes of roadless areas in the Roadless Area
Review and Evaluation (RARE II).

(4) Geography and Topography: The area is generally characterized by small irregular mountains or ridges 1,000 to 2,000 feet in elevation having steep slopes   Rocky crests and sharp ridges are found scattered throughout the area   The eastern portion of the area is gently sloping   The rock shoreline is characterized by forested lowlands with a relatively gentle slope and interspersed with small gravel or sandy beaches   The few streams in the area are generally short and flow directly to saltwater

There are _____ miles of shoreline along saltwater   There are 60 acres of alpine tundra and 180 acres of rock. There are 240 acres of freshwater lakes in the area, although none of the lakes are large

(5) **Ecosystem:**

(a) **Classification:** The area is classified as being in the Northern Outer Islands Geographic Province. This province is generally characterized by rugged highly dissected topography, exposed extremely wet outer coastal environment, and extensive alpine environments with productive forested areas highly fragmented and usually concentrated on oversteepened slopes and on valley bottoms.

(b) **Vegetation:** The vegetation of this roadless area consists primarily of typical spruce-hemlock forests   Western hemlock-Sitka spruce dominate the overstory while the understory is composed of shrubs such as red huckleberry, rusty menziesia, and devil's club. The forest floor is covered with a mat of mosses, liverworts, and plants such as deerheart, bunchberry dogwood, single delight, and skunk cabbage   Streamside riparian vegetation is characterized by salmonberry, devil's club, alder, grasses, ferns, and currants.

Muskegs are abundant within this area, however due to their small size and association with forested sites, accurate acreage estimates are difficult   These areas, dominated by sphagnum mosses, sedges, and shrubs of the heath family, are interspersed among low elevation timber stands where drainage is restricted. Trees within the muskegs are sparse and consist mainly of stunted hemlock, lodgepole pine, and Alaska cedar.

At elevations generally above 2,000 feet, the plant communities are characterized by low shrubs, grasses, and sedges   Subalpine forests and meadows occur at the interface between the forested communities and the alpine tundra.

There are approximately 24,616 acres of forested land of which 16,906 acres are commercial forest land. Of the commercial forest land, 10,575 acres are non-riparian old growth and 901 acres are riparian old growth.

(c) **Soils:** Shallow mineral soils with good drainage can be found on steeper slopes due to rapid loss of material by erosion and efficient rainwater runoff   Deep, well drained soils commonly occur below the shallow soils on the gentler slopes where transported soil materials have collected   Poorly drained soils are found associated with low relief and impermeable subsurface layers   In locations with poor

drainage, deep organic soils (muskegs) tend to form   In riparian
areas, soil zones tend to contain sand and gravels as a result of
flood deposition

(d) **Fish Resource**   Fish resources have been rated as part of the
Tongass Land Management Plan (1979) and by the Alaska Department of
Fish and Game in their Forest Habitat Integrity Program (1983). These
ratings describe the value of VCU's for sport fish, commercial fish
and estuaries

The Krestof Sound (200) VCU rated as high value for sport fish
commercial fish, and estuaries   No other VCU's rated highly.

(e) **Wildlife Resource:** There are many varied wildlife resources in
this roadless area. Birds and waterfowl rearing and nesting areas are
abundant   Generally, the area provides deer and brown bear habitat.
Bald eagle habitat, nesting and roosting trees, encompasses this
roadless area along the shorelines

(f) **Threatened and Endangered Species:** The area contains no known
resident threatened or endangered species. This area has been
identified as having habitats for two migrating endangered species.
The Peale's peregrine falcon passes through the forests during the
spring and fall migration flights and the humpback whale inhabits
nearby waters.

(6) **Current Use and Management:** The majority of this area was allocated
to Land Use Designation (LUD) 3 in the Tongass Land Management Plan   This
includes those portions of VCU's 303, 307, and 309 contained within this
roadless area

Areas allocated to LUD 3 are to be managed for a variety of uses   The
emphasis is on managing for both amenity and commodity oriented uses in a
compatible manner to provide the greatest combination of benefits   These
areas usually have high amenity values in conjunction with high commodity
values. Allowances in calculated potential timber yield have been made to
meet multiple use coordination objectives

The other VCU in this area was allocated to Land Use Designation (LUD) 4 in
the Tongass Land Management Plan. This includes a portion of VCU 306
Gilmer Bay

Areas allocated to LUD 4 provide opportunities for intensive development of
resources. Emphasis is primarily on commodity, or market resources and
their use, while also providing for amenity values. When conflicts over
competing resource uses arise, conflicts would most often be resolved in
favor of commodity values. Allowances in calculated potential timber yield
have been made to provide for protection of physical and biological
productivity

Recreational use of the area is primarily for hunting, fishing, and
enjoying the scenery   This use is scattered across the area and with the
usual concentrations near lakes, streams, and shorelines

(7) **Appearance (Apparent Naturalness)**· A vast majority of the area is considered unmodified except for those areas primarily located near the boundary with evidence of current or historic use   Evidence of historic use includes clearcut timber sales outside the boundary of the area Current use includes various short-term occupancies and other evidence of · the use of the area and the surrounding waters   All of this evidence is readily apparent to visitors that visit the specific sites

The visual character type of this roadless area is classified as Admiralty-Chichagof. Landforms in this character type are generally rounded   Rocky islands. reefs, and rock bluffs are found frequently on the outer coast   Rocky shorelines interspersed with small gravel beaches are found throughout the character type. Streams are generally short and swift on the west side of the roadless area. The streams are clear and many offer considerable visual variety, e.g., pools, rapids, cascades, riffles. falls, and meandering forms. Saltwater bays and estuaries are numerous and . exhibit much variety, from small sheltered coves to large exposed forms Often dramatic high energy seas occur on the outer coast.

The Middle Kruzof Roadless Area is a poor example of this visual character class as it has few of the described features, or the features are limited or poorly represented.

Approximately 10 percent of this roadless area was inventoried in 1984 as being Visual Variety Class B (Common), and approximately 78 percent as Variety Class C (Minimal Variety)   The remaining 12 percent of the acreage was inventoried Variety Class A (Distinctive)

Approximately 40 percent of this roadless area was inventoried in 1984 as having an Existing Visual Condition (EVC) I; these areas appear to be untouched by human activity   There is 60 percent of the area in EVC V where changes in the landscape are obvious to the average person   The changes appear to be major disturbances.

(8) **Surroundings (External Influences)**: The area is bordered by saltwater on two sides   As a result, external influences on those sides are limited to the sights and sounds of motorized boats. The northern and southern boundaries adjoin areas of timber activity and the associated road systems. These developments have not only had local impact on the roadless area, the sights and sounds of timber harvests and motorized use of the roads affect the entire area due to its narrow shape and the way it wraps around the old timber harvests.

(9) **Attractions and Features of Special Interest**: The natural features of the area, the scenery, and the opportunity to see wildlife are all considered attractions. The area contains eight inventoried recreation places which contains 24,639 acres. These are no National Forest System Trails in this roadless area, and no public recreation cabins. There are no other attractions or features of special interest.

b   Capability of Management as Wilderness or in an Unroaded Condition

(1) Manageability and Management Area Boundaries: The Middle Kruzof
Roadless Area generally does not have a boundary that is well defined by
topographic features The majority of the boundary for this L-shaped area
is defined by road systems and timber activity The boundaries determined
by Gilmer Bay, the Pacific Ocean, Shelikof Bay, and Krestof Sound are
easily described and recognized Both the northern boundary and the
southern boundary of the area follow road systems and timber activity over
hills and though valleys.

The feasibility of management of this area as Wilderness or in an unroaded
condition is reduced due to significant motorized access along both the
northern and southern boundaries. The manageability is also affected by
the fact that the area is only one mile wide along the western leg, and not
much over two miles wide along the northern leg.

(2) Natural Integrity: The area is unmodified except for the evidence of
current and historic use of the area. This evidence although locally
significant, has a very low overall effect on the natural integrity of the
area. Both the relative size of the developments and their location along
the shoreline or boundary contribute to that low impact. The long-term
ecological processes are intact and operating with the effect of human
influences on natural processes unmeasurable However, the narrow shape of
the area and the fact that it wraps around a large area of timber activity,
makes it difficult to ignore the adjacent development, when viewing the
roadless area.

(3) Opportunity for Solitude: There is a moderate opportunity for
solitude within the area Recreational use of the area is relatively
limited and dispersed, so that encounters with other visitors are
unlikely. The sight or sound of airplanes overhead and boats along the
coastlines can occasionally intrude on a visitor's solitude There is
motorized recreation occurring both on the adjacent road system and in some
off-road locations that can be heard.

(4) Opportunity for Primitive Recreation: The area provides a only a
moderate opportunity for primitive recreation as a result of its size, lack
of topographic screening, and physical challenges. There are few lakes,
ponds, or stream that contribute to the opportunities The absence of
developed recreational facilities enhances the opportunity for primitive
recreation.

The area provides primarily a Primitive recreation opportunity as
inventoried with the Recreation Opportunity Spectrum (ROS) system. The
acreage of each ROS class within the Roadless Area are listed below

ROS Class	Acres
Roaded Natural (RN)	1,382
Roaded Modified (RM)	9,315
Semi-Primitive Non-Motorized (SPNM)	16,645
Semi-Primitive Motorized (SPM)	640

The area contains eight recreation places.

ROS CLASS	# OF REC. PLACES	TOTAL ACRES	CAPACITY BY RVD
R-NAT	3	1,382	4,458
SPNM	2	14,985	11,124
SPM	3	8,273	5,939

No National Forest System Trails or recreation cabins exist in the area.

(5) Special Features (Ecologic, Geologic, Scientific, Cultural): There are no known features of ecologic, geologic, scientific, or cultural significance

c. **Availability for Management as Wilderness or in an Unroaded Condition**

(1) Resource Potentials

(a) **Recreation Potential:** The current Tongass Land Management Plan, Amended Winter 1985-86 identified opportunities for a Recreation Cabin in Gilmer Bay. No potential trail locations or developed recreation sites have been identified at this time.

The motorized recreation use on the Kruzof Island Road and the attraction of the Shelikof Recreation Cabin and Shelikof Bay will continue to draw visitors to the roaded area south of this roadless area. The topography, shape, and size will restrict the opportunities for managing this area for recreational opportunities in an unroaded condition.

(b) **Fish Resource:** The current Tongass Land Management Plan Amended Winter 1985-86 did not identify any opportunities for enhancement of the fish resources within this roadless area.

(c) **Wildlife Resource:** The current Tongass Land Management Plan Amended Winter 1985-86 did not identify any opportunities for enhancement of the wildlife resources within this roadless area

(d) **Timber Resource:** The current Tongass Land Management Plan, Amended Winter 1985-86 did not identify any opportunities for management of the timber resource in this roadless area. There are 11,797 acres inventoried as tentatively suitable for harvest. This includes 581 acres of riparian old growth, and 7,510 acres of non-riparian old growth.

(e) **Land Use Authorizations:** No significant land use authorizations exist within the roadless area.

(f) **Minerals:** The area does not have a high mineral development potential and there are no known claims

(g) **Areas of Scientific Interest:** There are no known areas of scientific interest in the roadless area

(2) **Management Considerations**

    (a) **Timber:** The potential for managing timber in this roadless area is dependent on the development of high market values and harvest methods which will allow extraction without need for extensive roading

    (b) **Fire·** The area has no significant fire history.

    (c) **Insects and Disease:** Endemic tree diseases common to Southeast Alaska are present in the area, however, there are no know epidemic disease occurrences

    (d) **Land Status:** NOT YET AVAILABLE

d. **Relationship to Communities and Other Roadless and Wilderness Areas**

(1) **Nearby Roadless and Wilderness Areas and Uses:** The nearest Wilderness is the West Chichagof-Yakobi Wilderness that lies north of Salisbury Sound Two other nearby Wildernesses are the Admiralty National Monument Wilderness, which lies east of Chatham Strait, and the South Baranof Wilderness south of Sitka.

Nearby roadless areas include North Kruzof and South Kruzof, both on Kruzof Island, North Baranof, which lies east of Neva Strait on Baranof Island, and Sitka Sound, which includes islands and Whitestone Peninsula in Sitka Sound.

(2) **Distance From Population Centers (Accessibility):** Approximate distances from population centers are as follows

Community		Air Miles	Water Miles
Juneau	(Pop. 23,729)	90	150
Sitka	(Pop 8,041)	10	10
Angoon	(Pop. 639)	50	80

The nearest stop on the Alaska Marine Highway is Sitka

(3) **Interest by Proponents:**

    (a) **Moratorium areas:** The area has not been identified as a "moratorium" area or proposed as Wilderness in legislative initiatives to date

    (b) **Local users/residents:** Most use of the area is associated with recreational boating, hunting and fishing, and viewing the wildlife and the scenery of the area.

e. Environmental Consequences

    ALTERNATIVE ANALYSIS TO BE DONE LATER

INDIVIDUAL ROADLESS AREA DESCRIPTION

NAME: Hoonah Sound (328)   ACRES (GROSS)· 97,277   ACRES (NFS): 97,257

GEOZONE: C05
GEOGRAPHIC PROVINCE: Northern Outer Islands

1989 WILDERNESS ATTRIBUTE RATING: 19

a. Description

(1) Relationship to RARE II areas: The table below displays the VCU 1/ names, VCU numbers, original WARS 2/ rating, and comments. This enables the reader to compare the roadless areas evaluated in Appendix C with previous analyses.

VCU Name	VCU No.	1979 WARS Rating	Comments
Rapids Point	279C	17	LUD 3
Deep Bay	280C	22	LUD 4
Ushk Bay	281C*	20	LUD 4
Fick Cove	282C	18	LUD 4
Patterson Bay	283C	22	LUD 4
South Arm	285C*	22	LUD 3
Moser Island	286C	19	LUD 3

*--The roadless area includes only part of this VCU

(2) History: Southeast Alaska is believed to have been settled about 10,000 to 11,000 years ago There are human occupancy sites in the general vicinity of the Hoonah Sound roadless area that date to 9,000+ years before present (BP). The oldest known site within the Hoonah Sound evaluation area dates to approximately 3,000 BP This date may be pushed back by future field investigations

Tlingit oral history indicates that the upper areas of Hoonah Sound were not used except for seasonal hunting, fishing and gathering The northernmost known permanent village site in the Hoonah Sound area is located at Poison Cove. Seasonal villages have been located along Hoonah Sound to Patterson Bay. The area was apparently used by Native peoples from the Sitka, Hoonah and Angoon areas. In 1799 100 to 150 of Alexandre Baranov's Aleut hunters died at Poison Cove from eating "mussels" from the tideflats.

1/ A VCU (Value Comparison Unit) is one of 867 watersheds which make up the forest and were differentiated for planning purposes in the Tongass Land Management Plan.
2/ Wilderness Attribute Rating System (WARS) was the nation-wide system used to rate the wilderness attributes of roadless areas in the Roadless Area Review and Evaluation (RARE II).

Early European entries were for trade, hunting and exploration   Lt.
Lisiansky of the Russian Navy mapped the Peril Strait area in 1805   Peril
Strait was important thEn, as now, for access to the inland waterways which
provided protected north-south water travel, as well as access to the
inland islands

The primary activities have remained fishing, hunting and furgathering.
Although fish canneries and traps were important in Hoonah Sound in the
early 20th Century, none have been found in the roadless area   Emmons . 3x
vixon Islands were used for fox farming from 1920 to 1925   Rodgers Point
was the site of a Federal Aviation Administration VHF radio site from 1950
to 1966 and an Alaskan Coastal Airlines "Radio-H" station from 1953 to
1960   Recent activities include logging and road construction activities
in Ushk Bay and Patterson Bays and Fick Cove.

(3) **Location and Access:** The Hoonah Sound roadless evaluation area is
located on Chichagof Island, west of Hoonah Sound and North of Peril
Strait. The community of Hoonah is approximately 45 miles to the north and
the city of Sitka is about 32 miles to the south. The area is bound by the
West Chichagof-Yakobi Wilderness (WC-Y) on the north and west, by Hoonah
Sound to the east and Peril Strait on the south. Access is by boat or
floatplane

There are roads in exclusion areas at Ushk Bay, Fick Cove and Patterson Bay
that provide foot or vehicle access to the associated river valleys There
is all-terrain vehicle (ATV) use on these roads as well as some off-road
use

(4) **Geography and Topography:** The large area displays a wide terrain
variation. The topography is typical of most of the larger island areas.
It is characterized by flat river valleys, surrounded by mountains.
Terrain relief ranges from sea level to more than 2,500 feet in elevation
at Pinnacle Peak. Although these mountains are not among the highest in
the area, they are steep and highly dissected by streams The lower
reaches of the rivers follow meandering courses in broad, flat floodplains,
while the headwaters are in steep, narrow valleys There are numerous
small lakes scattered about the area. Most of the smaller lakes lie above
the 1,000 foot elevation. There is a total of 380 acres of freshwater
lakes.

There are _____ miles of saltwater shoreline, _____ acres of beach
7,944 acres of small islands, 120 acres of snow and ice, 4,734 acres of
alpine tundra and 5,274 acres of rock.

(5) **Ecosystem:**

(a) **Classification:** The area is classified as being in the Northern
Outer Islands geographic province. This province is characterized by
rugged, highly dissected topography with exposed, extremely wet outer
coastal climate and extensive alpine environments, and productive
forests on over-steepened slopes and in river bottoms The Hoonah
Sound area is somewhat different than the norm and has some of the

alder, grasses, ferns, and currants

Muskegs, dominated by sphagnum mosses, sedges, and shrubs of the heath
family, are interspersed among low elevation timber stands where
drainage is restricted. Trees are sparse and consist mainly of
stunted hemlock, lodgepole pine, and Alaska-cedar. At elevations
above approximately 2,000 feet, the plant communities are
characterized by low shrubs, grasses, and sedges. Subalpine forests
and meadows occur at the interface between the forested communities
and the alpine tundra.

There are approximately 79,377 acres of forested lands, of which
39,646 acres are classified as commercial forest land (CFL). There
are 7,630 acres classified as riparian old growth and 29,639 acres as
nonriparian old growth. Approximately 4,734 acres are alpine tundra
vegetation, and 6,852 acres are classed as muskeg. Muskeg is
interspersed within other types in units too small to map. Therefore,
the acreage for muskeg may be substantially understated

(c) Soils: Glacial activity, combined with a basically sedimentary
bedrock, are primary factors in soil development in the evaluation
area. Other factors are high rainfall, cool summer temperatures and a
short growing season. Dense vegetative growth, combined with a slow
organic matter breakdown leaves a thick duff layer on most of the
subalpine soils

The roadless areas' soils are highly variable and range from exposed
bedrock and very shallow, poorly developed soils in the higher
elevations to deep fluvial and colluvial deposits in the flat river
bottoms. There are large areas of deep supersaturated or inundated
organic soils (muskeg) over much of the area. The steeper slopes are
generally well drained, shallow, moderately productive soils. The
valley bottoms are generally deep, well to poorly drained soils and
are highly productive. Many of the soils are highly leached because
of the rainfall.

(d) Fish Resource: There are four Pacific salmon (sockeye, coho,
pink and chum) valuable for commercial, subsistence and sport fishing
that spawn and rear in these waters. In addition, steelhead trout is
a favored and valuable sportfishing species. Other species include
Dolly Varden char, stickleback and smelt. Important saltwater
fisheries include crab, clams, sablefish and rockfishes

Fish resources have been rated as part of the Tongass Land Management Plan (1979) and by the Alaska Department of Fish and Game (ADF&G) in their Forest Habitat Integrity Program (1983). These ratings describe the value of VCU's for sport fish, commercial fish and estuaries. The following table lists seven VCUs rated high to very high for commercial and/or sport fisheries values and for highly valued estuaries.

		Sport	Commercial	Estuarine
Rapids Point	279C	-	X	X
Deep Bay	280C	X	X	X
Ushk Bay	281C	X	X	X
Fick Cove	282C	X	X	X
Patterson Bay	283C	X	X	X
South Arm	285C	X	X	X
Moser Island	286C	-	X	X

(e) **Wildlife Resource:** Wildlife is diversified in numbers and species. They include brown bear, Sitka black-tailed deer, pine marten, land otter, mink and beaver, as well as smaller mammals and several amphibians. There are few resident bird species, however, the area is used by many migratory species, including waterfowl. Eagles are common in the coastal zone. Sport and subsistence deer hunting is important in this area. This is a popular brown bear hunting area. In addition, there are pine marten and mink trapping and seal hunting.

Inventoried habitat for black-tailed deer, brown bear, pine marten and red squirrel totals 101,810 acres. Habitat for other management indicator species include mountain goat (40 acres).

(f) **Threatened and Endangered Species:** There are no known threatened or endangered species within the roadless area. The area may receive some migratory use by the peregrine falcon. The bald eagle, a protected species, uses the area for nesting and rearing.

(6) **Current Use and Management:** Land Use Designations (LUD) were allocated in the Tongass Land Management Plan (1979). There are three VCU's (17,753 acres) allocated to LUD 3, which allows for management of the land for a variety of uses, with emphasis on managing the uses and activities in a compatible and complementary manner to provide for the greatest combination of benefits. These areas have a high use or high amenity value in conjunction with a high commodity value. Four VCU's (84,057 acres) are allocated to LUD 4, which provides for intensive resource management and development, consistent with provisions to protect physical and biological productivity.

There are no management activities beyond some fish habitat improvement within the roadless evaluation area. There are inclusions of timber harvest and road construction in Patterson and Ushk Bays and Fick Cove, they are excluded from the roadless area. The entire evaluation area is within Management Area 5 of the Alaska Pulp Corporation Long-term Timber Sale Contract area, however, no activities outside of those mentioned have occurred or are currently planned. There are no special use permits for upland structures. Outfitter/guides use the evaluation area. There are no authorized structures, however, there are three or more unauthorized (trespass) cabins.

activities

The visual character type is the Admiralty-Chichagof Landforms are
generally rounded, but to range to steep, rugged mountains on the west of
the Hoonah Sound Roadless Area These mountains are snowcapped most of the
year. Rocky shorelines, interspersed with gravel beaches are found along
Hoonah Sound and Peril Straits. Streams are often short and swift, flowing
directly to saltwater. Bays and estuaries are common and show a wide range
of visual characteristics. Lower slopes are densely vegetated and are
interspersed with muskeg and small lakes. Upper slopes appear bare from a
distance, but often contain muskeg, alpine tundra vegetation and scattered
tree cover.

The evaluation area is inventoried as 13 percent Variety Class A
(Distinctive), 55 percent Variety Class B (Common) and 32 percent Variety
Class C (Minimal) The majority of the area (88 percent) is inventoried as
an Existing Visual Condition (EVC) I, which appears untouched by human
activity. The balance of the area (12 percent) is inventoried as an EVC
IV, or areas in which changes in the landscape are easily noticed by the
average visitor, and may attract some attention.

(8) **Surroundings (External Influences):** There are two small privately
owned tracts within, but excluded from, the roadless area These are
located at Deep Bay and Poison Cove Peril Strait is the Alaska Marine
Highway route connecting Sitka with the rest of Southeast Alaska There
are approximately ten weekly ferry passages during the summer months In
addition, there is some cruiseship and tourboat use The Strait is the
major connecting corridor between the west side of Baranof and Chichagof
Islands and the inland waterways Therefore, it is commonly used by sport
and commercial fishing boats, as well as barge traffic. Hoonah Sound gets
heavy pleasure and commercial fishing craft use Because the roadless area
is bound by water on the east and south and the WC-Y Wilderness to the
north and west, there is little activity in the adjoining surroundings that
would adversely affect the wilderness character of the area.

(9) **Attractions and Features of Special Interest:** Although the wildlife
and natural beauty of the area are attractions, there is little to
distinguish this from many other areas. Basic attractions are the
opportunity to "get away from it all" (solitude), sportfishing and hunting.
There are no Forest Service recreation facilities, such as cabins, nor are
there any developed/maintained trails. A public use recreation cabin is
planned for construction on Moser Island in 1990 A special interest may
be the diverse cultural resource sites in the general area, however there
are no interpretative or information programs at present There are 25
inventoried recreation places which total 22,855 acres

b. Capability of Management as Wilderness or in an Unroaded Condition

(1) Manageability and Management Area Boundaries: Manageability as
wilderness is high The boundaries are defined by the coastline or are not
critical because of the adjoining Wilderness Effects of adjoining
activities are minimal because these activities are transitory in nature
(ie saltwater-based or wilderness-related) Past activities (see (0)) may
detract from relatively small portions of the roadless area, however they
may provide better access, via the existing road system, into the interior
of the area Were the Hoonah Sound evaluation area left in an unroaded
state, it would complement the West Chichagof - Yakobi Wilderness
Conversely, the presence of the WC-Y Wilderness enhances the wilderness
character of the Hoonah Sound Roadless Area.

(2) Natural Integrity: The evaluation area is unmodified except for minor
activities (including the trespass cabins) and for early cabin and camp
sites, including Native activity sites. The early sites are deteriorated
and grown over, making them apparent only with close examination The
existing cabins are unobtrusive and infrequent, and do not detract from the
natural integrity of the total area.

(3) Opportunity for Solitude: The opportunity for solitude is very high
Terrain is such that activities in coastal waters have little influence on
areas away from the coastline The very large area, coupled with lack of
activities and low visitation, contribute to the feeling of solitude High
altitude overflights by commercial airliners (approximately six per day)
and occasional small aircraft flights may provide some distraction

(4) Opportunity for Primitive Recreation: The area provides primarily
primitive recreational opportunities, as inventoried with the Recreation
Opportunity Spectrum (ROS) system

ROS Class	Acres
Primitive I (P1)	80,679
Primitive II (2)	10,003
Semi-Primitive Non-Motorized (SPNM)	8,511
Semi-Primitive Motorized (SPM)	2,517
No ROS	100

The area contains 25 recreation places, totalling 22,855

ROS CLASS	# OF REC. PLACES	TOTAL ACRES	CAPACITY BY RVD
P1	6	11,167	1,370
P2	9	4,454	5,121
SPNM	7	5,314	8,478
SPM	3	1,919	5,144

(5) Special Features (Ecologic, Geologic, Scientific, Cultural). There is a high probability for numerous cultural resource sites, however, little study has been done in the area There are 13 known or suspected (unconfirmed) sites, dating back to about 3,000 years before present Future surveys may find sites contemporary with older sites in the general area and may add substantially to knowledge of pre-European culture Most known sites are located in the coastal zone. Further field investigation may reveal an opportunity to add to the pool of scientific or ecological knowledge for other resources, however, current indications are that there is nothing unique about the area

c   Availability for Management as Wilderness or in an Unroaded Condition

(1) **Resource Potentials**

(a) **Recreation Potential:** The potential exists to enhance primitive and/or semi-primitive recreation opportunities These include construction of trails and of recreation cabins, particularly along the coast in the several protected bays Potential also exists to provide interpretative information for cultural resource sites along the coast. The Tongass Land Management Plan, as amended in 1985-86 (TLMP), identified recreation facilities development for a day-use shelter construction in one VCU.

(b) **Fish Resource:** TLMP identified no projects for in-stream habitat or non-stream habitat improvement projects Watershed rehabilitation projects in the logged areas outside the evaluation are will benefit downstream fisheries by reduction of sediment and cooling of upstream waters.

(c) **Wildlife Resource:** The Tongass Land Management Plan, as amended, has no identified habitat improvement projects for the evaluation area.

(d) **Timber Resource:** There are 26,763 acres inventoried as tentatively suitable for harvest. This includes 5,893 acres of riparian old growth and 19,273 acres of nonriparian old growth The potential for managing timber in this roadless area is high in those areas of operable timber stands. The large areas of non-commercial timber and marginal operability because of accessibility limit management potential. However, there are large areas of mature-overmature timber that are operable and accessible These stands would be viable for timber harvest. Most of these stands exhibit old-growth habitat characteristics.

(e) **Land Use Authorizations:** There have been no special use permits have been issued for specific use of the evaluation area However the area is used by several outfitter/guides Possible future permits would be for subsistence or recreational facilities or for outfitter/guide services Potential is low for a significant increase in most types of permits, other than for incidental use However many special use permit applications are anticipated in conjunction

with the new herring pond fishery to be permitted by the State of
Alaska   Permits will be for on-shore pond storage, shore ties and
tent camps   Permits are expected for Eammons Island and near Ushk
Bay

(f) Minerals: The development potential for locatable minerals is
moderate in VCU 281, but is estimated to be low or non-existent on the
rest of the area

(g) Areas of Scientific Interest: There are no inventoried potential
Research Natural Areas within the Hoonah Sound evaluation area.

(2) Management Considerations

(a) Fire: The area has no significant fire history.

(b) Insects and Disease: Endemic tree diseases common to Southeast
Alaska are present, there are no know epidemic disease occurrences

(c) Land Status: There are no patented private lands within the
roadless area. There are two parcels of private land within the
boundaries, but excluded from the roadless area. There are four
unconveyed Native allotments within the roadless area   There are no
other non-Federal lands or withdrawals.

d. Relationship to Communities and Other Roadless and Wilderness Areas

(1) Nearby Roadless and Wilderness Areas and Uses: The West Chichagof -
Yakobi Wilderness forms the north and west boundary of the Hoonah Sound
area. Adjacent roadless evaluation areas are the North Kruzof, #326
(located south across Peril Strait), North Baranof, #330 (east across Peril
Strait) and Chichagof, #311 (north across Hoonah Sound)

(2) Distance From Population Centers (Accessibility): Approximate
distances from population centers are as follows:

Community		Air Miles	Water Miles
Juneau	(Pop 23,729)	70	120
Hoonah	(Pop. 870)	45	95
Sitka	(Pop. 8,041)	30	45

The closest Alaska Marine Highway terminals are at Angoon, Tenakee Springs,
Hoonah and Sitka. The nearest commercial airline service is available in
Sitka.

(3) Interest by Proponents:

(a) Moratorium areas: The Hoonah Sound Roadless Area is a part of
the Chichagof moratorium area proposed for study as a wilderness area
as described in S 341 ("Wirth Bill"), and is proposed for wilderness
in HR 987 ("Mrazek Bill")

(b) Local users/residents: The nearest communities are Tenakee
Springs (population 95), about 20 airmiles to the north. Angoon
(population 639) 40 airmiles to the east and Sitka Hoonah Sound and
inland within one-half mile of the coastline, is the primary zone of
use in the general area Heaviest use is indicated to be from Angoon
and Sitka. Activities are subsistence hunting and fishing, sport
hunting and fishing (particularly for salmon) and commercial fishing.
These activities do not necessarily take place within the roadless
area

(c) Concerns of local residents: Concerns expressed by residents of
the general area (Tenakee Springs, Angoon, Sitka and Hoonah) relate
primarily to subsistence uses and commercial fishing as affected by
timber harvest or to timber harvest that may be eliminated by the
creation of a wilderness, therefore, affecting jobs

e. Environmental Consequences

ALTERNATIVE ANALYSIS TO BE DONE LATER

INDIVIDUAL ROADLESS AREA DESCRIPTION

NAME: South Kruzof (329)   ACRES (GROSS): 56,701   ACRES (NFS) 56,701

GEOZONES: C10
GEOGRAPHIC PROVINCE: Northern Outer Islands

1989 WILDERNESS ATTRIBUTE RATING: 19

a. Description

(1) Relationship to RARE II areas: The table below displays the VCU 1/
names, VCU numbers, original WARS 2/ rating, and comments This enables
the reader to compare the roadless areas evaluated in Appendix C with
previous analyses.

		1979	
VCU Name	VCU No	WARS Rating	Comments
Cuvacan Cove	307*	- -	Not rated in 1979
Mount Edgecumbe	308	24	
Krestof Sound	309*	20	

*--The roadless area includes only part of this VCU

(2) History: This large area has a long and varied history of use dating
from Tlingit use in prehistoric and historic times to the present use by a
variety of Alaska residents and visitors Use of the area has been
primarily for hunting, fishing, recreation, and temporary occupancy This
area saw considerable military activity during World War II An army camp
was established on Shoals Point at the southeast corner of Kruzof Island.
This camp included miles of road and many buildings. Although the roaded
area was excluded from the roadless area, much evidence of the related
activities remains within the roadless area. Remains of structures and
other human cultural activity in varying degrees of deterioration can still
be found

(3) Location and Access: The area is located on the southern half of
Kruzof Island. It is bounded on the west by the Pacific Ocean, and on the
south and east by Sitka Sound. The northern boundary of the area is formed
by the road system and timber activity in the area between Shelikof Bay and
Mud Bay The area also includes a number of small offshore islands and
rocks.

1/ A VCU (Value Comparison Unit) is one of 867 watersheds which make up the
forest and were differentiated for planning purposes in the Tongass Land
Management Plan.
2/ Wilderness Attribute Rating System (WARS) was the nationwide system used to
rate the wilderness attributes of roadless areas in the Roadless Area
Review and Evaluation (RARE II).

The primary form of access to the area is by saltwater along all three
coastlines   Access to the area is generally good, and is due to proximity
to Sitka. The western and southern coasts have poor boat anchorages and
frequent rough water   The eastern coast is much more sheltered   The Mount
Edgecumbe Trail is a National Forest System Trail   It is 6 " miles in
length, beginning at Freds Creek Cabin along the eastern coast and ending
at the summit of the Mount Edgecumbe crater

(4) Geography and Topography· The area is generally characterized by a
large gently sloping shield volcano dominated by the volcanic cone named
Mount Edgecumbe   This is the result of a northeast trending line of
volcanic vents across the island that erupted to produce the Mount
Edgecumbe volcanic field covering about 100 square miles. Although the
3,200 foot Mount Edgecumbe and the 2,400 foot collapsed caldera, Crater
Ridge, dominate the Island, smaller cinder cones are scattered throughout
the area.

The Mount Edgecumbe volcanic field is a geologically recent feature with a
major ash eruption about 9,000 years ago, and the volcano only inactive
the last 200 years. The coastline is relatively smooth. It is not deeply
scalloped or indented as is typical of the glacially carved areas elsewhere
in the region. Semi-submerged rocks, reefs, and rock bluffs dominate the
coast, and the shoreline is characterized by forested lowlands with a
relatively gentle slope. Streams are generally short and flow directly to
saltwater.

There are _____ miles of shoreline along saltwater   There are 1,583 acres
of alpine tundra, 80 acres of ice and snow, and 80 acres of rock   There
are 20 acres of small islands located along the coastline and 20 acres of
freshwater lakes in the area   The only large lake in the area is Surprise
Lake

(5) Ecosystem:

     (a) Classification: The area is classified as being in the Northern
     Outer Islands Geographic Province. This province is generally
     characterized by rugged highly dissected topography, exposed extremely
     wet outer coastal environment, and extensive alpine environments with
     productive forested areas highly fragmented and usually concentrated
     on oversteepened slopes and on valley bottoms

     (b) Vegetation: The vegetation of this roadless area consists
     primarily of typical spruce-hemlock forests. Western hemlock-Sitka
     spruce dominate the overstory, while the understory is composed of
     shrubs such as red huckleberry, rusty menziesia, and devil's club.
     The forest floor is covered with a mat of mosses, liverworts, and
     plants such as deerheart, bunchberry dogwood, single delight, and
     skunk cabbage. Streamside riparian vegetation is characterized by
     salmonberry, devil's club, alder, grasses, ferns, and currants

Muskegs are abundant within this area, however due to their small size and association with forested sites, accurate acreage estimates are difficult These areas, dominated by sphagnum mosses, sedges, and shrubs of the heath family, are interspersed among low elevation timber stands where drainage is restricted Trees within the muskegs are sparse and consist mainly of stunted hemlock, lodgepole pine and Alaska-cedar

At elevations generally above 2,000 feet the plant communities are characterized by low shrubs grasses, and sedges Subalpine forests and meadows occur at the interface between the forested communities and the alpine tundra.

There are approximately 42,504 acres of forested land of which 17,829 acres are commercial forest land. Of the commercial forest land, 15,024 acres are non-riparian old growth and 2,765 acres are riparian old growth.

(c) Soils: Shallow mineral soils with good drainage can be found on steeper slopes due to rapid loss of material by erosion and efficient rainwater runoff. Deep, well-drained soils commonly occur below the shallow soils on the gentler slopes where transported soil materials have collected Poorly drained soils are found associated with low relief and impermeable subsurface layers In locations with poor drainage, deep organic soils (muskegs) tend to form In riparian areas, soil zones tend to contain sand and gravels as a result of flood deposition.

(d) Fish Resource: Fish resources have been rated as part of the Tongass Land Management Plan (1979) and by the Alaska Department of Fish and Game in their Forest Habitat Integrity Program (1983) These ratings describe the value of VCU's for sport fish, commercial fish, and estuaries

There is one VCU which is rated as having high value for sport fish Krestof Sound (309) There are two VCU's rated as highly valued for commercial fish, Mount Edgecumbe (308), and Krestof Sound (309) One VCU rated for highly valued estuaries is Krestof Sound (309)

(e) Wildlife Resource: There are many varied wildlife resources in this roadless area. Birds and waterfowl rearing and nesting areas are abundant in this area Generally, the area provides good habitat for Sitka black-tailed deer and brown bear Bald eagle habitat, nesting and roosting trees, encompasses this roadless area along the shorelines.

(f) Threatened and Endangered Species: The area contains no known resident threatened or endangered species This area has been identified as having habitats for two migrating endangered species The Peale's peregrine falcon passes through the forests during the spring and fall migration flights and the humpback whale inhabits nearby waters.

(6) Current Use and Management: The entire roadless area was allocated to
Land Use Designation (LLD) 3 in the Tongass National Land Management Plan.
Units allocated to LUD 3 are to be managed for a variety of uses   The
emphasis is on managing for both amenity and commodity oriented uses in a
compatible manner to provide the greatest combination of benefits   These
areas usually have high amenity values in conjunction with high commodity
values   Allowances in calculated potential timber yield have been made to
meet multiple use coordination objectives

Recreational use of the area is primarily for hunting and fishing, and
enjoying the scenery. This use is scattered across the area and with the
usual concentrations near lakes, streams, and shorelines

(7) Appearance (Apparent Naturalness): A vast majority of the area is
considered unmodified except for those areas primarily located near the
shoreline with evidence of current or historic use. Evidence of historic
use includes the World War II Army camp, old cabins, and other historic
occupancies   Current use includes recreational use of the trail and
recreation cabins, various short-term occupancies, and other evidence of
the use of the area and the surrounding waters. All of this evidence is
readily apparent to visitors that visit the specific sites

The visual character type of this roadless area is classified as
Admiralty-Chichagof. Landforms in this roadless area are generally
rounded. Rocky islands, reef, and rock bluffs are found frequently on the
outer coast. Rocky shorelines interspersed with small gravel beaches are
found throughout the character type   Streams are generally short and swift
on the west side of the roadless area. The streams are clear and many
offer considerable visual variety, e.g , pools, rapids, cascades, riffles
falls, and meandering forms   Saltwater bays and estuaries are numerous and
exhibit much variety, from small sheltered coves to large exposed forms
Often dramatic high energy seas occur on the outer coast.

The South Kruzof Roadless Area at the southern end of Kruzof Island is a
poor example of this visual character class as it is the only area within
the class that is of volcanic origin. It only has some of the features
described and the features are limited or poorly represented

None of this roadless area was inventoried in 1984 as being Visual Variety
Class B (Common). Approximately 29 percent was inventoried as Variety
Class C (Minimal Variety), and the remaining 71 percent of the acreage was
inventoried Variety Class A (Distinctive).

The majority (97 percent) of this roadless area was inventoried in 1984 as
having an Existing Visual Condition (EVC) I; these areas appear to be
untouched by human activity   Approximately 3 percent is in EVC V where
changes in the landscape are obvious to the average person. The changes
appear to be major disturbances

(8) Surroundings (External Influences): The area is bordered by salt
water on three sides. As a result, external influences on those sides are
limited to the sights and sounds of motorized boats   The northern boundary
adjoins an area of timber activity and its associated road system   This
development has had moderate impact on the northern part of the roadless
area.

(9) Attractions and Features of Special Interest: The major attractions and features of special interest in the South Kruzof Roadless Area are the volcanic landforms, and an area under the unique hydrological influence of volcanic ash soils The largest volcanic landform is Mount Edgecumbe, with Crater Ridge and Shell Mountain complimenting the view Mount Edgecumbe erupted between 6,000 and 9,000 years ago and deposited volcanic ash as far east as Sitkoh Bay on Chichagof Island , The volcanic activity on Kruzof is of particular interest as it is related to plate movements and the complex process of terrain accretion.

The natural features of the area, the scenery and the opportunity to see wildlife are all considered attractions High quality fishing opportunities in the streams and lakes also provide attractions The area contains six inventoried recreation places totaling 5,101 acres There is one National Forest System Trail in this roadless area, and two public recreation cabins

b. Capability of Management as Wilderness or in an Unroaded Condition

(1) Manageability and Management Area Boundaries: The South Kruzof Roadless Area is generally well defined by topographic features The boundaries determined by Shelikof Bay, the Pacific Ocean, Sitka Sound, Hayward Strait, and Krestof Sound are easily described and recognized Only the northern boundary, which is result of a road system and timber activity, is poorly defined It follows the edge of the development across terrain that is relatively gentle, without distinguishing topographic features

The feasibility of management of this area as Wilderness or in an unroaded condition is good as there are no significant motorized access or other current nonconforming uses

(2) Natural Integrity: The area is unmodified except for the evidence of current and historic use of the area. This includes the Freds Creek and Brents Beach Recreation Cabins, the Mount Edgecumbe Trail, and World War II developments along the southeastern coast. This evidence although locally significant, has a very low overall effect on the natural integrity of the area. Both the relative size of the developments and their location along the shoreline contribute to that low impact. The long-term ecological processes are intact and operating with the effect of human influences on natural processes unmeasurable

(3) Opportunity for Solitude: There is a moderate opportunity for solitude within the area. The limited amount of topographic screening and only moderate vegetative screening reduce opportunities for solitude The sight or sound of airplanes overhead and boats along the coastlines can occasionally intrude on a visitor's solitude. The area is on the primary flight path for jets arriving or departing Sitka's airport Although recreation use is concentrated near the two recreation cabins, it cannot be considered heavy Recreational use of the remainder of the area is relatively limited and dispersed, so that encounters with other visitors are unlikely There is some motorized recreational use occurring on the road system and in some unroaded areas along the northern boundary of the area that can be heard within the roadless area

(4) **Opportunity for Primitive Recreation:** The area provides a moderate opportunity for primitive recreation as a result of its size, vegetative screening, and physical challenges This area has a highly unique topography composed of a series of volcanic landforms surrounded by a gently sloping landscape terminating at the sea The unique landforms combine with the diverse vegetation to offer a setting capable of providing primitive recreation opportunities There are small ponds, streams, bays and a varied coastline that contribute to these opportunities The limited development of recreational facilities further enhances the the opportunity for primitive recreation.

The area provides primarily a Primitive recreation opportunity as inventoried with the Recreation Opportunity Spectrum (ROS) system. The acreage of each ROS class within the Roadless Area are listed below

ROS Class	Acres
Primitive I (P1)	24,614
Primitive II (P2)	2,466
Roaded Natural (RN)	2,759
Roaded Modified (RM)	160
Semi-Primitive Non-Motorized (SPNM)	25,745
Semi-Primitive Motorized (SPM)	1,278

The area contains six recreation places.

ROS CLASS	# OF REC. PLACES	TOTAL ACRES	CAPACITY BY RVD
P1	1	581	307
RN	3	2,740	9,127
RM	1	160	156
SPNM	1	1,620	1,593

There is one National Forest System Trail in the area, the Mt Edgecumbe Trail, and two Recreation Cabins.

(5) **Special Features (Ecologic, Geologic, Scientific, Cultural):** The most significant features of the area are volcanic landforms and the ecological effects of the volcanic activities

c. **Availability for Management as Wilderness or in an Unroaded Condition**

  (1) **Resource Potentials**

  (a) **Recreation Potential:** The Tongass Land Management Plan, Amended Winter 1985-86 did not identify any new opportunities for recreation in this roadless area. No potential trail locations or developed recreation sites have been identified at this time

  The unique volcanic features and vegetation, and the attractive scenery of this area provide opportunities for increasing dispersed recreation Additional trails and cabins or shelters are possible

(b) Fish Resource: The Tongass Land Management Plan, Amended Winter 1985-86 did not identify any opportunities for enhancement of the fish resource within the roadless area

(c) Wildlife Resource: The Tongass Land Management Plan, Amended Winter 1985-86 did not identify any opportunities for enhancement of the wildlife resource within the roadless area

(d) Timber Resource: The current Tongass Land Management Plan Amended Winter 1985-86 did not identify any new opportunities for management of the timber resource within the roadless area There are 7,568 acres inventoried as tentatively suitable for harvest This includes 1,202 acres of riparian old growth, and 6,326 acres of non-riparian old growth.

(e) Land Use Authorizations: There are no significant land use authorizations within the roadless area.

(f) Minerals: The roadless area does not have a high mineral development potential and there are no known claims

(g) Areas of Scientific Interest: The most significant features of scientific interest within the area are volcanic landforms and the ecological effects of the volcanic activities A portion of this area has been identified as having Research Natural Area (RNA) potential. This area has been identified in order to include examples of several major volcanic landforms and a small watershed under the unique hydrological influence of volcanic ash soils The area has been the subject of intensive study both from the standpoint of the structural development of the soils and ecosystem succession, and for geologic studies

Crater Ridge is a caldera (collapsed volcanic summit) on a subsidiary volcanic cone three kilometers northeast of Mount Edgecumbe Crater Ridge is a composite dome (made up of lava flows alternating with ash) and stands about 500 meters in elevation Freds Creek drains the east slope of the crater summit. This watershed from summit to tidewater will allow studies of the influence of recent (approximately 10,000 years ago) volcanic ash on stream flow and water chemistry

Important forest types in the area include western hemlock and riparian Sitka spruce, both are growing on special soils which may produce variants of the "typical" forest type. Small areas of western hemlock-Alaskan yellow-cedar and muskeg occur in the area Several plant species have been identified in this area that are uncommon or at edge of their range

(2) Management Considerations

(a) Timber: The potential for managing timber in this roadless area is dependent on the development of high market values and harvest methods which will allow extraction without need for extensive roading

(b) Fire: The area has no significant fire history.

(c) Insects and Disease: Endemic tree diseases common to Southeast Alaska are present in the area, however, there are no known epidemic disease occurrences

(d) Land Status: NOT YET AVAILABLE

d   Relationship to Communities and Other Roadless and Wilderness Areas

(1) Nearby Roadless and Wilderness Areas and Uses: The nearest Wilderness is the West Chichagof-Yakobi Wilderness that lies north of Salisbury Sound. Two other nearby Wildernesses are the Admiralty National Monument Wilderness, which lies east of Chatham Strait, and the South Baranof Wilderness south of Sitka.

Nearby roadless areas include North Kruzof and Middle Kruzof, both on Kruzof Island, and Sitka Sound, which includes the islands and Whitestone Peninsula in Sitka Sound.

(2) **Distance From Population Centers (Accessibility):** Approximate distances from population centers are as follows:

Community		Air Miles	Water Miles
Juneau	(Pop. 23,729)	100	160
Sitka	(Pop. 8,041)	10	10
Angoon	(Pop. 639)	50	80

The nearest stop on the Alaska Marine Highway is Sitka

(3) Interest by Proponents:

(a) **Moratorium areas:** The area has not been identified as a "moratorium" area or proposed as Wilderness in legislative initiatives to date

(b) **Local users/residents:** Most use of the area is associated with recreational boating, hunting and fishing, and viewing the wildlife and the scenery of the area

e. Environmental Consequences

ALTERNATIVE ANALYSIS TO BE DONE LATER

INDIVIDUAL ROADLESS AREA DESCRIPTION

NAME: North Baranof (330)   ACRES (GROSS): 343,617   ACRES (NFS)· 341,417

GEOZONES   C09 and C10
GEOGRAPHIC PROVINCE: Northern Outer Islands

1989 WILDERNESS ATTRIBUTE RATING.   25

a. Description

(I) Relationship to RARE II areas: The table below displays the VCU 1/
names, VCU numbers, original WARS 2/ rating, and comments This enables
the reader to compare the roadless areas evaluated in Appendix C with
previous analyses

VCU Name	VCU No	1979 WARS Rating	Comments
Fish Bay	287	19	
Range Creek	288	19	
Nixon Shoal	289	19	
Cozian Reef	290	19	
Peschani Point	291	--	Not rated in 1979
Rodman Bay	292		Not rated in 1979
Appleton Cove	293	--	Not rated in 1979
Saook Bay	·294	21	
Lake Eva	295	23	
Portage Arm	296	20	
Catherine Island	297	21	
Middle Arm	298	23	
Nakwasina Passage	300*	--.	Not rated in 1979
Neva Strait	302*	18	
Glacial River	314	24	
Kelp Bay	315	0	
Kasnyku Bay	316	23	
Takatz Bay	317	26	
Warm Springs Bay	326	22	
Cascade Bay	327	28	
Nelson Bay	328	26	

*--The roadless area includes only part of this VCU

1/ A VCU (Value Comparison Unit) is one of 867 watersheds which make up the
   forest and were differentiated for planning purposes in the Tongass Land
   Management Plan.
2/ Wilderness Attribute Rating System (WARS) was the nationwide system used to
   rate the wilderness attributes of roadless areas in the Roadless Area
   Review and Evaluation (RARE II).

(2) History: This large area has a long and varied history of use dating
from Tlingit use in prehistoric and historic times to the present use by a
variety of Alaska residents and visitors   Historic use of the area
includes sawmills, salmon and herring salteries, fisheries enhancement
facilities, and a variety of other occupancies and settlements   Remains of
structures and other human cultural activity in varying degrees of
deterioration can still be found.

(3) Location and Access: The area is located on the northern end and
northeastern side of Baranof Island   It is bounded on the north by Peril
Strait, on the east by Chatham Strait, and on the south by the South
Baranof Wilderness   The northwestern boundary of the area is formed by
Kakul Narrows and Neva Strait and the western boundary adjoins the Sitka
Urban Roadless Area (#331). The area also includes Catherine Island on the
northeast corner of Baranof Island and a number of offshore islands and
rocks.

The North Baranof Roadless Area, the Sitka Urban Roadless Area (#331) and
the Redoubt Roadless Area (#333) are all three subunits of a contiguous
roadless land mass that stretches from the South Baranof Wilderness to the
northern tip of Baranof Island.

There are two primary forms of access to the area. The first is by
floatplane, with Sitka the most frequent origin. The second access is by
saltwater along all coastlines. Due to the numerous bays and fiords that
provide sheltered anchorage for boats, and the proximity to Sitka, access
to the area is generally good.

There are three National Forest System Trails within the area, the
Lake Eva-Hanus Bay Trail, the Sadie Lake Trail, and the Warm Springs Bay
Trail. The Lake Eva-Hanus Bay Trail is 2 9 miles in length, beginning at
Hanus Bay and ending at the southwest end of Lake Eva   The Sadie Lake
Trail is 0.8 miles in length, beginning near the mouth of Baranof Lake and
ending at the south end of Sadie Lake. The Warm Springs Bay Trail is 0 5
miles in length, beginning at the Baranof Warm Springs and ending at the
east end of Baranof Lake.

(4) Geography and Topography: The area is generally characterized as an
irregular, rugged chain of mountains 2,000 to 5,300 feet in elevation
having a steep eastern slope and a more gentle slope in the northern half
of the area. The eastern coast is deeply indented with fiords while the
northern shore is characterized by numerous large bays. Numerous rocky
crests and sharp ridges are found at higher elevations. Snow can be seen
all year round on higher summits with a few cirque glaciers and small
permanent icefields in the southern part of the area.

Streams are generally short and flow directly to saltwater with the longest
about 10 miles long. Cascades are common and lakes are plentiful,
especially in the southern portion of the area. The largest lake is
Baranof Lake just west of the community of Baranof Warm Springs   It
stretches approximately three miles and lies at an elevation of 145 feet

There are _____ miles of shoreline along saltwater   Approximately 20
percent of the area consists of alpine tundra, ice, snow, and rock   This
includes 20,762 acres of alpine tundra, 13,577 acres of ice and snow   and
64,262 acres of rock   There are 1,080 acres of small islands located along
the coastline, and 4,561 acres of freshwater lakes in the area   Large
lakes in the area include Hidden Falls, Carbon and Baranof Lakes, and Lake
Eva   •

(5) Ecosystem:

(a) Classification: The area is classified as being in the Northern
Outer Islands Geographic Province   This province is generally
characterized by rugged highly dissected topography, exposed extremely
wet outer coastal environment, and extensive alpine environments with
productive forested areas highly fragmented and usually concentrated
on oversteepened slopes and on valley bottoms.

(b) Vegetation: The vegetation of this roadless area consists
primarily of typical spruce-hemlock forests. Western hemlock-Sitka
spruce dominate the overstory while the understory is composed of
shrubs such as red huckleberry, rusty menziesia, and devil's club.
The forest floor is covered with a mat of mosses, liverworts, and
plants such as deerheart, bunchberry dogwood, single delight, and
skunk cabbage   Streamside riparian vegetation is characterized by
salmonberry, devil's club, alder, grasses, ferns, and currants

Muskegs are abundant within this area, however due to their small size
and association with forested sites, accurate acreage estimates are
difficult   These areas, dominated by sphagnum mosses, sedges and
shrubs of the heath family, are interspersed among low elevation
timber stands where drainage is restricted   Trees within the muskegs
are sparse and consist mainly of stunted hemlock, lodgepole pine and
Alaska-cedar.

Tideflats are found at the heads of many of the bays and estuaries and
are usually associated with stream estuaries   The tideflats support
sea milkwort, glasswort, and algae   Beach meadows occur between the
shore and the forest. Lower beach meadows are composed of beach
ryegrass, reed bent grass, hairgrass, fescue grass, beach lovage,
goose tongue, and sedges   Upper beach meadow plants include yarrow,
bedstraw, starwort, ferns, western columbine, and cow parsnip   Oregon
crabapple, alder, devil's club, and blueberry occur along the border
of the beach meadow and the forest.

At elevations generally above 2,000 feet, the plant communities are
characterized by low shrubs, grasses, and sedges   Subalpine forests
and meadows occur at the interface between the forested communities
and the alpine tundra

There are approximately 227,611 acres of forested land of which
125,731 acres are commercial forest land   Of the commercial forest
land, 99,637 acres are non-riparian old growth and 10,087 acres are
riparian old growth

(c) **Soils:** Shallow mineral soils with good drainage can be found on steeper slopes due to rapid loss of material by erosion and efficient rainwater runoff Deep, well drained soils commonly occur below the shallow soils on the gentler slopes where transported soil materials have collected Poorly drained soils are found associated with low relief and impermeable subsurface layers In locations with poor drainage, deep organic soils (muskegs) tend to form In riparian areas, soil zones tend to contain sand and gravels as a result of flood deposition

(d) **Fish Resource·** Fish resources have been rated as part of the Tongass Land Management Plan (1979) and by the Alaska Department of Fish and Game in their Forest Habitat Integrity Program (1983) These ratings describe the value of VCU's for sport fish, commercial fish, and estuaries.

The three VCU's which are rated as high value for sport fish are 295, 300 and 326. VCU's rated as highly valued for commercial fish are 287, 292, 294, 300, and 314 There are seven VCU's rated as having highly valued estuaries These VCU's include 288, 293, 295, 296, 297, 302, and 315.

(e) **Wildlife Resource:** There are many varied wildlife resources in this roadless area. Birds and waterfowl rearing and nesting areas are abundant in this area. Generally, the area provides good habitat for Sitka black-tailed deer and brown bear Bald Eagle habitat, nesting and roosting trees, encompasses this roadless area along the shorelines.

(f) **Threatened and Endangered Species:** The area contains no known resident threatened or endangered species This area has been identified as having habitats for two migrating endangered species The Peale's peregrine falcon passes through the forests during the spring and fall migration flights and the humpback whale inhabits nearby waters.

(6) **Current Use and Management:** Six of the 21 VCU's in this area were allocated to Land Use Designation (LUD) 2 in the Tongass Land Management Plan. They include.

295	Lake Eva	326	Warm Springs Bay
316	Kasnyku Bay	327	Cascade Bay
317	Takatz Bay	328	Nelson Bay

VCU's allocated to LUD 2 are to be managed in a roadless state to retain their wildland character. This designation would permit wildlife and fish habitat improvement and primitive recreational facility development

Eight of the 21 VCU's in this area were allocated to Land Use Designation (LUD) 3 in the Tongass Land Management Plan This includes the following VCU's (the roadless area includes only part of the VCU's identified with an asterisk)

287	Fish Bay	296	Portage Arm
288	Range Creek	297	Catherine Island
289	Nixon Shoal	300*	Nakwasina Passage
290	Gorian Reef	302*	Neva Strait

Units allocated to LUD 3 are to be managed for a variety of uses   The emphasis is on managing for both amenity and commodity oriented uses in a compatible manner to provide the greatest combination of benefits   These areas usually have high amenity values in conjunction with high commodity values   Allowances in calculated potential timber yield have been made to meet multiple use coordination objectives

Seven of the 21 VCU's in this area were allocated to Land Use Designation (LUD) 4 in the Tongass Land Management Plan. This includes the following VCU's

291	Peschani Point	298	Middle Arm
292	Rodman Bay	314	Glacial River
293	Appleton Cove	315	Kelp Bay
294	Saook Bay		

VCU's allocated to LUD 4 provide opportunities for intensive development of resources. Emphasis is primarily on commodity, or market resources and their use while providing for amenity values   When conflicts over competing resource uses arise, conflicts would most often be resolved in favor of commodity values   Allowances in calculated potential timber yield have been made to provide for protection of physical and biological productivity

There are a number of authorized special uses existing within the area. The following are the major uses at this time   Northern Southeast Regional Aquaculture Association (NSRAA) has a special use permit for use of facilities at Takatz Bay for securing net pens for the rearing of salmon. The Alaska Department of Fish and Game (ADF&G) has a special use permit for use of facilities located at the head of Kasnyku Bay for the Hidden Falls Fish Hatchery   These facilities include hatchery buildings, residential buildings, water, hydroelectric, and waste disposal systems, roads trails boardwalks, and docks   The permit covers over 13 acres

There is also a Forest Service Radio Repeater located on Mount Furuhelm in the southern portion of the area.

Recreational use of the area is primarily for hunting and fishing, and enjoying the scenery   This use is scattered across the area and with the usual concentrations near lakes, streams, and shorelines

Four parcels of land within or adjacent to the roadless area are under other ownership. These include land around Takatz Lake selected by the State of Alaska, the proposed state selection of land at Baranof Warm Springs, and two small parcels in Rodman Bay and along Rodman Creek.

(7) Appearance (Apparent Naturalness)   A vast majority of the area is considered unmodified except for those areas primarily located near the shoreline with evidence of current or historic use   Evidence of historic use includes old salmon and herring salteries, old cabins, and other historic occupancies   Current use includes fish enhancement activities and facilities, fish hatchery facilities, various short-term occupancies, and other evidence of the use of the area and the surrounding waters   All of this evidence is readily apparent to visitors that visit the specific sites.

The visual character type of this roadless area is classified as Baranof Highland   Terrain in this roadless area consists of an irregular rugged asymmetrical chain of landforms 3,000-5,300 feet in elevation having a steep eastern slope and a more gentle western slope deeply indented with fjords. Generally, landforms are visually massive, bulky and stark throughout the character type. Shoreline forms are very rugged with steep-sided fjord country on both east and west coasts.

Rugged headwalls, cliffs and escarpments are common on the west side of the Baranof Highland character type, as a result of exposure to the sea wind and waves. Rock faces are sometimes visible on steep-sided fjords near saltwater throughout the roadless area   Numerous rocky crests, sharp ridges, horns, arétes and cirques are found at higher elevations   Snow can be seen all year found on the higher summits with cirque glaciers and small permanent ice fields, especially in the southern portion of the area

The North Baranof Roadless Area on the northern and eastern shore of Baranof Island presents an typical representation of the Baranof Highland visual character type. This area displays a coastline deeply and repeatedly scalloped by fjords and bays   A combination of historic glaciation and erosion from the high level of precipitation have further accentuated the carving of the topography   The glaciers, cirques, ice and snow fields in the souther half of the area are characteristic of this type.

Approximately 51 percent of this roadless area was inventoried in 1984 as being Visual Variety Class B (Common), and approximately 29 percent as Variety Class C (Minimal Variety)   The remaining 20 percent of the acreage was inventoried Variety Class A (Distinctive)

The majority (81 percent) of this roadless area was inventoried in 1984 as having an Existing Visual Condition (EVC) I, these areas appear to be untouched by human activity. Approximately 1 percent of the acreage is in EVC IV, which are areas in which changes in the landscape are easily noticed by the average person and may attract some attention   There appears to be disturbances but they resemble natural patterns   There is also 18 percent in EVC V where changes in the landscape are obvious to the average person. The changes appear to be major disturbances

(8) Surroundings (External Influences): The area is bordered by saltwater along a large percentage of its boundary   As a result, external influences on those sides are limited to the sights and sounds of motorized boats. The southern boundary adjoins the South Baranof Wilderness, and most of the western boundary adjoins the Sitka Urban Roadless Area   The adjoining

lands in both of these cases are in a natural condition In eighteen
locations around the edge of this roadless area, timber activities and
their associated road system development have taken place   These
activities have had a substantial influence on the roadless area

(9) Attractions and Features of Special Interest: Three features of
special interest in the North Baranof Roadless Area are Kelp Bay, Baranof
Warm Springs and the Baranof Island glaciers   Kelp Bay is a large
sheltered Bay with three arms and a number of subbasins   Baranof Warm
Springs consists of a small group of lakes, a hot springs, and warm springs
Bay Finally there are a string of glaciers, ice, and snow fields in the
mountain ranges of the roadless area   These glaciers are the southern most
island glaciers in North America

The natural features of the area, the scenery, and the opportunity to see
wildlife are all considered attractions. High quality fishing
opportunities in the streams and lakes also provide attractions   The area
contains 53 inventoried recreation places which contains 81,027 acres
Three National Forest System Trails are located within the area, as well as
two Recreation Cabins

b. Capability of Management as Wilderness or in an Unroaded Condition

(1) Manageability and Management Area Boundaries: The North Baranof
Roadless Area is generally well defined by topographic features   The only
exception is the many areas where the boundary is defined by previous
timber activities and the associated road system   The boundaries
determined by Neva Strait, Kakul Narrows, Peril Strait, Chatham Strait and
by the South Baranof Wilderness are easily described and recognized   Even
the western boundary adjoining the Sitka Urban Roadless Area (=331) follows
well-defined topographic divides In addition to the poor boundaries that
are a result of road systems and timber activity, there four land parcels
of other ownership within or adjacent to the roadless area which could
create management problems   These include land around Takatz Lake selected
by the State of Alaska, and the proposed state selection of land at Baranof
Warm Springs, and two small parcels in Rodman Bay and along Rodman Creek.

The feasibility of management of this area as Wilderness or in an unroaded
condition is good, as there are no significant motorized access or other
current nonconforming uses within the boundaries of the area

(2) Natural Integrity: The area is unmodified except for the evidence of
current and historic use of the area. This evidence, although locally
significant, has a very low overall effect on the natural integrity of the
area. Both the relative size of the developments and their location along
the shoreline contribute to that low impact. The long-term ecological
processes are intact and operating with the effect of human influences on
natural processes unmeasurable

(3) Opportunity for Solitude: There is a very high opportunity for
solitude within the area. Both the size of the area and the screening
offered by the topography increase the opportunity for solitude
Recreational use of the area is relatively limited and dispersed, so that
encounters with other visitors are unlikely Balancing those factors are
the effects of the numerous areas of previous timber activity and

associated road systems   The sight or sound of airplanes overhead and
boats along the coastlines can occasionally intrude on a visitor's
solitude   Along Peril Strait and Neva Strait, ferries of the Alaska Marine
Highway system can be observed or heard.

(4) Opportunity for Primitive Recreation: The area provides a very high
opportunity for primitive recreation as a result of its size, topographic
screening, diversity of recreation opportunities, and physical challenges
This area has a highly irregular topography and diverse vegetation that
combine to offer a setting capable of providing a variety of primitive
recreation opportunities   There are lakes, ponds, streams bays rugged
mountains, and a varied coastline that contribute to these opportunities.
The absence of developed recreational facilities further enhances the
opportunity for primitive recreation

The area provides primarily a Primitive recreation opportunity as
inventoried with the Recreation Opportunity Spectrum (ROS) system   The
acreage of each ROS class within the Roadless Area are listed below

ROS Class	Acres
Primitive I (P1)	161,899
Primitive II (P2)	10,802
Rural (R)	40
Roaded Natural (RN)	1,319
Roaded Modified (RM)	23,034
Semi-Primitive Non-Motorized (SPNM)	37,892
Semi-Primitive Motorized (SPM)	87,463
No ROS	860

The area contains 53 recreation places

ROS CLASS	# OF REC. PLACES	TOTAL ACRES	CAPACITY BY RVD
P 1			
P 2			
Rural			
R-NAT			
R-MOD			
SPNM			
SPM			

There are three National Forest System Trails within the area, the Lake Eva
- Hanus Bay Trail, the Sadie Lake Trail, and the Warm Springs Bay Trail
There are two Recreation Cabins within the Roadless Area, Lake Eva and
Baranof Lake.

(5) Special Features (Ecologic, Geologic, Scientific, Cultural): There
are no known features of ecologic, geologic, scientific, or cultural
significance.

. Availability for Management as Wilderness or in an Unroaded Condition

(1) Resource Potentials

(a) **Recreation Potential.** The current Tongass Land Management Plan.
Amended Winter 1985-86 identified opportunities for increasing
recreation potential   These opportunities included constructing a
Cross Baranof Trail from Baranof Warm Springs to Sitka, reclassif
the administrative cabins south of Kelp Bay as Recreation Cabins.
extending the Lake Eva Trail to the Adirondack Shelter at the inlet to
Lake Eva, constructing a Fish Bay Trail to the Fish Bay Hot Springs
and constructing a recreation facility at the Fish Bay Hot Springs.

The varied terrain, diverse vegetation, and attractive scenery of this
area provide unlimited recreation potentials for dispersed
recreation. Additional trails and cabins or shelters are possible.

(b) **Fish Resource:** The current Tongass Land Management Plan, Amended
Winter 1985-86 did not identify any opportunities for fish resource
enhancement within the roadless area.

(c) **Wildlife Resource:** The current Tongass Land Management Plan
Amended Winter 1985-86 identified opportunities for wildlife habitat
improvement in various areas within the roadless area through
management of second growth forest and thinning

(d) **Timber Resource:** The current Tongass Land Management Plan.
Amended Winter 1985-86 did not identify any opportunities for
management of the timber resource in this roadless area   There are
32,063 acres inventoried as tentatively suitable for harvest   This
includes 8,246 acres of riparian old growth, and 62,192 acres of
non-riparian old growth.

(e) **Land Use Authorizations:** The major land use authorizations are
the Northern Southeast Regional Aquaculture Association (NSRAA)'s
special use permit for use of facilities at Takatz Bay for securing
net pens for the rearing of salmon and the Alaska Department of Fish
and Game (ADF&G)'s special use permit for use of facilities located at
the head of Kasnyku Bay for the Hidden Falls Fish Hatchery   These
facilities include hatchery buildings, residential buildings, water.
hydroelectric, and waste disposal systems, roads, trails, boardwalks
and docks. The permit covers over 18 acres.

(f) **Minerals:** The area does not have a high mineral development
potential and there are not any known mining claims.

(g) **Areas of Scientific Interest:** One feature of scientific interest
is the area around Lake Eva, which has been identified as having
potential for Research Natural Area (RNA) status   The Lake Eva area
was identified because it represents a highly productive sockeye
fishery with an active history of research   Forest types present are
typical spruce and hemlock, which have the potential to serve as
baseline monitoring sites for nearby areas that have had historic
timber management   Lake Eva is a low elevation valley morainal lake

(2) Management Considerations

   (a) Timber: The potential for managing timber in this roadless area
   is dependent on the development of high market values and harvest
   methods which will allow extraction without need for extensive
   roading

   (b) Fire: The area has no significant fire history

   (c) Insects and Disease: Endemic tree diseases common to Southeast
   Alaska are present in the area, however, there are no know epidemic
   disease occurrences.

   (d) Land Status: NOT YET AVAILABLE

d. Relationship to Communities and Other Roadless and Wilderness Areas.

(1) Nearby Roadless and Wilderness Areas and Uses: There are three
Wilderness nearby: the West Chichagof-Yakobi Wilderness that lies north of
Salisbury Sound, the Admiralty National Monument Wilderness, which lies
east of Chatham Strait, and the South Baranof Wilderness south of Sitka and
adjoining this roadless area.

The North Baranof Roadless Area, in addition to being contiguous to the
South Baranof Wilderness, is also a part of a larger unroaded area which
stretches from the north tip of Baranof Island to the South Baranof
Wilderness, and from Baranof Warm Springs to Sitka and to Biorka Island
The three roadless areas are North Baranof (#330), Sitka Urban (=331), and
Redoubt (#333)

(2) Distance From Population Centers (Accessibility): Approximate
distances from population centers are as follows

Community		Air Miles	Water Miles
Juneau	(Pop. 23,729)	70	100
Sitka	(Pop 8,041)	10	10
Angoon	(Pop. 639)	20	20

The nearest stop on the Alaska Marine Highway is Sitka.

(3) Interest by Proponents:

   (a) Moratorium areas: The area has not been identified as a
   "moritorium area or proposed as Wilderness in legislative initiatives
   to date.

   (b) Local users/residents: Most use of the area is associated with
   recreational boating, hunting and fishing, and viewing wildlife and
   scenery of the area.

e. Environmental Consequences

   ALTERNATIVE ANALYSIS TO BE DONE LATER

INDIVIDUAL ROADLESS AREA DESCRIPTION

NAME. Sitka Urban (331)   ACRES (GROSS): 138,146   ACRES (NFS)· 120,520

GEOZONE: C10
GEOGRAPHIC PROVINCE: Northern Outer Islands

1989 WILDERNESS ATTRIBUTE RATING: 19

a. Description

(1) Relationship to RARE II areas: The table below displays the VCU 1/
names, VCU numbers, original WARS 2/ rating, and comments This enables
the reader to compare the roadless areas evaluated in Appendix C with
previous analyses.

VCU Name	VCU No	1979 WARS Rating	Comments
Annahootz Mountain	299	21	
Nakwasina Sound	301	--	Not rated in 1979
Gavanski Island	310*	16	
Sitka	311	--	Not rated in 1979
Katlian Bay	312	--	Not rated in 1979
Katlian River	313	21	
Blue Lake	318	21	
Green Lake	324	17	
Bear Cove	325	19	

*--The roadless area includes only part of this VCU.

(2) History: This large area has a long and varied history of use dating
from Tlingit use in prehistoric and historic times to the present use by a
variety of Alaska residents and visitors. Sitka was established between
2,000 and 9,000 years ago as a major Tlingit Indian village The Russians
settled in Sitka in 1799, made it the headquarters of the Russian American
Company, and later the capital of Russian America. After sale of Alaska to
the United States, Sitka served as the territorial capital until 1900 when
the capital was transferred to Juneau. Although the city of Sitka lies
outside the Roadless Area, its inhabitants have used the surrounding
roadless lands intensively.

Use of the area since 1900 has been primarily for hunting, fishing,
woodcutting, recreation, and occasional temporary occupancies Remains of
structures and other human cultural activity in varying degrees of
deterioration can still be found.

1/ A VCU (Value Comparison Unit) is one of 867 watersheds which make up the
Forest and were differentiated for planning purposes in the Tongass Land
Management Plan. .
2/ Wilderness Attribute Rating System (WARS) was the nationwide system used to
rate the wilderness attributes of roadless areas in the Roadless Area
Review and Evaluation (RARE II).

(3) Location and Access: The area is located on the western side of
Baranof Island just north of the center of the island It is generally
bounded on the west by Nakwasina Sound and Sitka Sound, with a major
portion of that boundary composed of private lands in the Sitka developed
area. The southern boundary adjoins the Redoubt Roadless Area (=333) and
the South Baranof Wilderness The north and eastern boundary of the area
is formed by the North Baranof Roadless Area (=330).

The Sitka Urban Roadless Area, the North Baranof Roadless Area (=330), and
the Redoubt Roadless Area (=333) are all three subunits of a contiguous
roadless land mass that stretches from the South Baranof Wilderness to the
northern tip of Baranof Island

There are two primary forms of access to the area. The first is on foot
from the Sitka road system along the western boundary of the area. The
second access is by saltwater along the western and southwestern
coastlines. Access to the area is generally very good due to its proximity
to Sitka and its road system, and the accessibility of Nakwasina, Katlian
and Silver Bays

There are four National Forest System Trails that provide access to the
area from the Sitka road system: Beaver Lake Trail, Gavan Hill Trail.
Harbor Mountain Ridge Trail, and Indian River Trail. In addition, there is
the Blue Lake River Trail which is 2.5 miles in length. It begins at the
east end of Blue Lake and ends at the south end of Glacier Lake

(4) Geography and Topography: The area is generally characterized as an
irregular, rugged chain of mountains 2,000 to 5,300 feet in elevation,
having a steep slope and deeply indented with bays and U-shaped valleys.
Numerous rocky crests and sharp ridges are found at higher elevations.
Snow can be seen all year round on higher summits with a few cirque
glaciers and small permanent ice fields along the eastern boundary of the
area.

Streams are generally short and flow directly to saltwater with the longest
about 10 miles long. Cascades are common and small mountain lakes are
plentiful.

There are _____ miles of shoreline along saltwater. Approximately 33
percent of the area consists of alpine tundra, ice, snow, and rock This
includes 22,273 acres of alpine tundra, 2,820 acres of ice and snow, and
39,381 acres of rock. There are 1,941 acres of freshwater lakes in the
area. Large lakes in the area include Blue and Glacier Lakes

(5) Ecosystem:

    (a) Classification: The area is classified as being in the Northern
    Outer Islands Geographic Province. This province is generally
    characterized by rugged highly dissected topography, exposed extremely
    wet outer coastal environment, and extensive alpine environments with
    productive forested areas highly fragmented and usually concentrated
    on oversteepened slopes and on valley bottoms

(b) Vegetation: The vegetation of this roadless area consists
primarily of typical spruce-hemlock forests   Western hemlock-Sitka
spruce dominate the overstory while the understory is composed of
shrubs such as red huckleberry, rusty menziesia, and devil's club.
The forest floor is covered with a mat of mosses liverworts, and
plants such as deerheart, bunchberry dogwood, single delight and
skunk cabbage   Streamside riparian vegetation is characterized by
salmonberry, devil's club, alder, grasses, ferns and currants

Muskegs are abundant within this area, however due to their small size
and association with forested sites, accurate acreage estimates are
difficult   These areas, dominated by sphagnum mosses, sedges and
shrubs of the heath family, are interspersed among low elevation
timber stands where drainage is restricted. Trees within the muskegs
are sparse and consist mainly of stunted hemlock, lodgepole pine, and
Alaska-cedar.

At elevations generally above 2,000 feet, the plant communities are
characterized by low shrubs, grasses, and sedges   Subalpine forests
and meadows occur at the interface between the forested communities
and the alpine tundra.

There are approximately 50,038 acres of forested land of which 27 038
acres are commercial forest land. Of the commercial forest land,
17,625 acres are non-riparian old growth and 2,761 acres are riparian
old growth.

(c) Soils: Shallow mineral soils with good drainage can be found on
steeper slopes due to rapid loss of material by erosion and efficient
rainwater runoff   Deep, well drained soils commonly occur below the
shallow soils on the gentler slopes where transported soil materials
have collected. Poorly drained soils are found associated with low
relief and impermeable subsurface layers   In locations with poor
drainage, deep organic soils (muskegs) tend to form   In riparian
areas, soil zones tend to contain sand and gravels as a result of
flood deposition.

(d) Fish Resource: Fish resources have been rated as part of the
Tongass Land Management Plan (1979) and by the Alaska Department of
Fish and Game in their Forest Habitat Integrity Program (1983) These
ratings describe the value of VCU's for sport fish, commercial fish
and estuaries.

There are three VCU's which are rated as high value for sport fish
These are Annahootz Mountain (299), Katlian Bay (312), and Blue Lake
(318). The four VCU's rated as highly valued for commercial fish are
Annahootz Mountain (299), Katlian Bay (312), Katlian River (313) and
Green Lake (324). There were no VCU's rated as having highly valued
estuaries

(e) **Wildlife Resource:** There are many varied wildlife resources in this roadless area. Birds and waterfowl rearing and nesting areas are abundant in this area · Generally, the area provides good habitat for Sitka black-tailed deer and brown bear Bald eagle habitat, nesting and roosting trees, encompasses this roadless area along the shorelines

(f) **Threatened and Endangered Species:** The area contains no known resident threatened or endangered species This area has been identified as having habitats for two migrating endangered species The Peale's peregrine falcon passes through the forests during the spring and fall migration flights and the humpback whale inhabits nearby waters.

(6) **Current Use and Management:** There are nine VCU's in the Sitka Urban Roadless Analysis Area. One VCU was allocated to Land Use Designation (LUD) 2 in the Tongass Land Management Plan; that VCU was Bear Cove #325 Areas allocated to LUD 2 are to be managed in a roadless state to retain their wildland character. This designation would permit wildlife and fish habitat improvement and primitive recreational facility development

Six of the VCU's in this area were allocated to Land Use Designation (LUD) 3 in the Tongass Land Management Plan. These are 310, 310, 311, 313, 318 and 324

Areas allocated to LUD 3 are to be managed for a variety of uses The emphasis is on managing for both amenity and commodity oriented uses in a compatible manner to provide the greatest combination of benefits These areas usually have high amenity values in conjunction with high commodity values Allowances in calculated potential timber yield have been made to meet multiple use coordination objectives

Two of the nine VCU's in this area were allocated to Land Use Designation (LUD) 4 in the Tongass Land Management Plan. This includes Annahootz Mountain (#299) and Katlian Bay (#312)

Areas allocated to LUD 4 provide opportunities for intensive development of resources Emphasis is primarily on commodity, or market resources and their use with provisions for amenity uses. When conflicts over competing resource uses arise, conflicts would most often be resolved in favor of commodity values Allowances in calculated potential timber yield have been made to provide for protection of physical and biological productivity.

Recreational use of the area is primarily for hunting, fishing, and enjoying the scenery. This use is scattered across the area and with the usual concentrations near lakes, streams, and shorelines.

(7) **Appearance (Apparent Naturalness):** A vast majority of the area is considered unmodified except for those areas primarily located near the streams, trails, and shorelines with evidence of current or historic use

The visual character type of this roadless area is classified as Baranof
Highland Terrain in this type consists of an irregular, rugged
asymmetrical chain of landforms 3,000-5,300 feet in elevation having a
steep eastern slope and a more gentle western slope deeply indented with
fjords Generally, landforms are visually massive, bulky and stark
throughout the character type Shoreline forms are very rugged with
steep-sided fjord country on both east and west coasts

Rugged headwalls, cliffs and escarpments are common on the west side of the
Baranof Highland character type, as a result of exposure to the sea
and waves Numerous rocky crests, sharp ridges horns, aretes and cirques
are found at higher elevations Snow can be seen all year round on the
higher summits with cirque glaciers and small permanent ice fields,
especially in the eastern portion of the area.

The Sitka Urban Roadless Area in the northcentral portion of Baranof Island
well represents the Baranof Highland visual character type This area
displays a mountain range deeply and repeatedly scalloped by bays and
U-shaped valleys A combination of historic glaciation and erosion from
the high level of precipitation have further accentuated the carving of the
topography. The mountains of this roadless area form the scenic backdrop
to the city of Sitka, and are a feature that attracts both residents and
tourists alike to this community

Approximately 49 percent of this roadless area was inventoried in 1984 as
being Visual Variety Class B (Common), and approximately 14 percent as
Variety Class C (Minimal Variety) The remaining 37 percent of the acreage
was inventoried Variety Class A (Distinctive)

The majority (79 percent) of this roadless area was inventoried in 1984 as
having Existing Visual Condition (EVC) I, these areas appear to be
untouched by human activity Approximately 14 percent was inventoried in
EVC IV, which are areas in which changes in the landscape are easily
noticed by the average person and may attract some attention There
appears to be disturbances but they resemble natural patterns There is
percent of the area in EVC V where changes in the landscape are obvious to
the average person. The changes appear to be major disturbances

(8) Surroundings (External Influences): The area is bordered on the north
and east by the North Baranof Roadless Area (#330), and on the south by the
South Baranof Wilderness and the Redoubt Roadless Area (#333) As a
result, there are no significant external influences on those sides of the
roadless area. The western boundary, however, adjoins the development
related to the community of Sitka, and areas of timber activity and
associated road systems The external influences from these developments
air traffic in the vicinity, and from a population center that utilizes the
area extensively, combine to substantially effect this roadless area

(9) Attractions and Features of Special Interest: There is one feature of major importance to this roadless area, that feature is the mountains east of Sitka. Those mountains form a scenic backdrop that enhances the beauty of Sitka to both the visitors and the residents Those same mountains also provide a watershed for the community that provides both water and power Finally, those mountains provide a location for the population of the community to recreate

The natural features of the area, the scenery, and the opportunity to see wildlife are all considered attractions High quality fishing opportunities in the streams and lakes also provide attractions The area contains 27 inventoried recreation places which contains -8 100 acres.   No National Forest System Trail is located in this roadless area but no public recreation cabins.

b. **Capability of Management as Wilderness or in an Unroaded Condition**

(1) **Manageability and Management Area Boundaries:** The Sitka Urban Roadless Area is only partially well defined by topographic features The northern, eastern, and southern boundaries are determined major watershed divides The western boundary is a ragged line that follows the boundary of private land and other land ownership, and which also is the result of a road system and timber activity. This is an extremely poor and difficult boundary to manage.

The feasibility of management of this area as Wilderness or in an unroaded condition is poor although there is no significant motorized access or other current nonconforming uses This is due to the heavy influence of the adjacent population center, road system, and timber activity, and the land ownership patterns.

(2) **Natural Integrity:** The area is unmodified except for the evidence of current and historic use of the area This evidence although locally significant, has a very low overall effect on the natural integrity of the area. Both the relative size of the developments and their location contribute to that low impact. The long-term ecological processes are intact and operating with the effect of human influences on natural processes unmeasurable.

(3) **Opportunity for Solitude:** There is a high opportunity for solitude within the area. Both the size of the area and the screening offered by the topography increase the opportunity for solitude Overall recreational use of the area is relatively limited and dispersed, so that encounters with other visitors are unlikely. However, recreational use along the trails at times may be moderate and concentrated, so that encounters with other visitors are likely. Because of its large size, there are many opportunities for solitude, however a visitor may have to work harder to find them. The sight or sound of airplanes overhead, boats along the coastlines, motor vehicles on adjacent roads or trails, and sights and sounds of the community of Sitka can occasionally intrude on a visitor's solitude

(4) **Opportunity for Primitive Recreation:** The area provides a high opportunity for primitive recreation as a result of its size, topographic screening, and physical challenges This area has a highly irregular topography and diverse vegetation that combine to offer a setting capable of providing a variety of primitive recreation opportunities There are lakes, ponds, streams, bays, rugged mountains, and a varied coastline that contribute to these opportunities The absence of developed recreational facilities further enhances the opportunity for primitive recreation.

The area provides primarily a Primitive recreation opportunity as inventoried with the Recreation Opportunity Spectrum (ROS) system The acreage of each ROS class within the Roadless Area are listed below

ROS Class	Acres
Primitive I (P1)	30,372
Primitive II (P2)	6,186
Rural (R)	40
Urban (U)	140
Roaded Natural (RN)	10,581
Roaded Modified (RM)	4,223
Semi-Primitive Non-Motorized (SPNM)	76,996
Semi-Primitive Motorized (SPM)	4,200
No ROS	860

The area contains 27 recreation places.

ROS CLASS	# OF REC. PLACES	TOTAL ACRES	CAPACITY BY RVD
P1	1	1,220	14
P2	2	1,304	277
RN	6	5,359	169,591
RM	3	4,182	3,391
SPNM	11	29,890	10,977
SPM	4	1,941	8,299

There are four National Forest System Trails within the roadless area which have trailheads on the Sitka road system: Beaver Lake Trail, Gavan Hill Trail, Harbor Mountain Ridge Trail, and Indian River Trail In addition there is the Blue Lake River Trail which begins at the east end of Blue Lake There are no recreation cabins

(5) **Special Features (Ecologic, Geologic, Scientific, Cultural):** There are no known features of ecologic, geologic, scientific, or cultural significance

c. Availability for Management as Wilderness or in an Unroaded Condition

(1) Resource Potentials

(a) **Recreation Potential:** The current Tongass Land Management Plan Amended Winter 1985-86 identified opportunities for expansion of the Starrigaven Campground adjacent to this roadless area and construction of the Indian River-Harbor Mountain Trail It also identified

opportunities to reconstruct the Beaver Lake Trail, the Blue Lake
Trail, the Lucky Chance Trail, and the Redoubt Lake Trail

The varied terrain, diverse vegetation, and attractive scenery of this
area provide unlimited recreation potentials for dispersed
recreation   Additional trails and cabins or shelters are possible
both accessible from the Sitka road system or within easy access by
boat from Sitka   With the large numbers of visitors to Sitka, use of
trails within walking distance of town or the campgrounds would be
substantial

(b) Fish Resource: The Tongass Land Management Plan, Amended Winter
1985-86 identified opportunities for fish stocking in Indian River

(c) Wildlife Resource: The Tongass Land Management Plan, Amended
Winter 1985-86 identified opportunities for wildlife habitat
improvement in the area between Katlian Bay and Nakwasina Sound, and
in the Katlian River Drainage through thinning of second growth
forest.

(d) Timber Resource: The Tongass Land Management Plan, Amended
Winter 1985-86 did not identify any opportunities for management of
the timber resource in this roadless area. There are 14,803 acres
inventoried as tentatively suitable for harvest   This includes 2,041
acres of riparian old growth, and 8,802 acres of non-riparian old
growth.

(e) Land Use Authorizations: No significant land use authorizations
exist within the roadless area.

(f) Minerals: The southwestern portion of the area contains a zone
of high mineral development potential with veins of valuable metallic
or nonmetallic minerals   The central portion of the area contains a
large zone of magmatic oxide or sulfide deposit. There are not any
known current claims

(g) Areas of Scientific Interest: There are no known areas of
scientific interest in this roadless area.

(2) Management Considerations

(a) Timber: The potential for managing timber in this roadless area
is dependent on the development of high market values and harvest
methods which will allow extraction without need for extensive
roading.

(b) Fire: The area has no significant fire history

(c) Insects and Disease: Endemic tree diseases common to Southeast
Alaska are present in the area, however, there are no know epidemic
disease occurrences

(d) Land Status: NOT YET AVAILABLE

d   Relationship to Communities and Other Roadless and Wilderness Areas

(1) Nearby Roadless and Wilderness Areas and Uses: The nearest Wilderness
is the South Baranof Wilderness which adjoins the southern tip of the
roadless area   Two other nearby Wildernesses are the Admiralty National
Monument Wilderness, which lies east of Chatham Strait, and the West
Chichagof-Yakobi Wilderness that lies north of Salisbury Sound

The Sitka Urban Roadless Area, in addition to being contiguous to the South
Baranof Wilderness, is also a part of a larger unroaded area which
stretches from the north tip of Baranof Island to the South Baranof
Wilderness, and from Baranof Warm Springs to Sitka and to Biorka Island.
The three roadless areas are North Baranof (#330), Sitka Urban (#331), and
Redoubt (#333).

(2) Distance From Population Centers (Accessibility): Approximate
distances from population centers are as follows·

Community		Air Miles	Water Miles
Juneau	(Pop. 23,729)	90	160
Sitka	(Pop. 8,041)	0	0
Angoon	(Pop 639)	40	90

The nearest stop on the Alaska Marine Highway is Sitka

(3) Interest by Proponents:

(a) Moratorium areas: The area has not been identified as a
"moratorium" area or proposed as Wilderness inlegislative initiatives
to date.

(b) Local users/residents: Most use of the area is associated with
recreational boating, hunting and fishing, and viewing wildlife and
scenery of the area

e. Environmental Consequences

ALTERNATIVE ANALYSIS TO BE DONE LATER

INDIVIDUAL ROADLESS AREA DESCRIPTION

NAME: Sitka Sound (332)   ACRES (GROSS): 20,934   ACRES (NFS): 19,475

GEOZONES: C10
GEOGRAPHIC PROVINCE. Northern Outer Islands

1989 WILDERNESS ATTRIBUTE RATING: 18

a. Description

(1) Relationship to RARE II areas: The table below displays the VCU 1/ names, VCU numbers, original WARS 2/ rating, and comments This enables the reader to compare the roadless areas evaluated in Appendix C with previous analyses

VCU Name	VCU No	1979 WARS Rating	Comments
Nakwasina Passage	300*	--	Not rated in 1979
Neva Strait	302*	18	
Krestof Sound	309*	20	
Gavanski Island	310*	16	

*--The roadless area includes only part of this VCU

(2) History: This large area has a long and varied history of use dating from Tlingit use in prehistoric and historic times to the present use by a variety of Alaska residents and visitors Use of the area has been primarily for hunting, fishing, recreation, and temporary occupancy Remains of structures and other human cultural activity in varying degrees of deterioration can still be found

(3) Location and Access: The area is generally located between Sitka Sound and Salisbury Sound, and between Kruzof Island and Baranof Island It is composed of Krestof Island, Halleck Island, the Siginaka Islands, the Magoun Islands and a number of small offshore islands and rocks In addition, this area includes a peninsula of Baranof Island separated from the remainder of Baranof Island by a road system and timber activity This peninsula lies adjacent to Neva Strait between St John Baptist Bay and Nakwasina Passage. For the lack of a better name, this peninsula will be referred to in this report as Whitestone Peninsula, named after Whitestone Cove at the southern end of the peninsula

The primary form of access to the area is by saltwater along all of the coastlines. Access to the area is good, mostly due to the proximity to Sitka. In addition, the numerous bays and channels provide both travel corridors and sheltered anchorage for boats.

1/ A VCU (Value Comparison Unit) is one of 867 watersheds which make up the forest and were differentiated for planning purposes in the Tongass Land Management Plan.
2/ Wilderness Attribute Rating System (WARS) was the nationwide system used to rate the wilderness attributes of roadless areas in the Roadless Area Review and Evaluation (RARE II).

(4) Geography and Topography· The area is generally characterized by three distinct features   Whitestone Peninsula, two moderate size islands Halleck and Krestof, and numerous small islands, islands groups, and offshore rocks   Whitestone Peninsula is a roughly triangular shaped piece of land of gentle slope and a maximum elevation of just over 1,400 feet It contains no stream or lakes of significant size

Halleck and Krestof are irregular shaped islands, with a mix of gentle and steep sloped terrain. Krestof is further defined by Promisla and De Groff Bays The maximum elevation of Krestof is over 1,600 feet and is over 1,900 feet on Halleck There are no lakes or named streams on either island

The small islands in the Sitka Sound Roadless Area are mostly under 100 feet in elevation and are scattered throughout the area. They are all irregular in shape and size.

There are _____ miles of shoreline along saltwater. There is 300 acres of alpine tundra and 20 acres of rock. Small islands totaling 9,197 acres or small islands located along the coastline

(5) Ecosystem:

   (a) Classification: The area is classified as being in the Northern Outer Islands Geographic Province   This province is generally characterized by rugged highly dissected topography, exposed extremely wet outer coastal environment, and extensive alpine environments with productive forested areas highly fragmented and usually concentrated on oversteepened slopes and on valley bottoms

   (b) Vegetation: The vegetation of this roadless area consists primarily of typical spruce-hemlock forests   Western hemlock-Sitka spruce dominate the overstory while the understory is composed of shrubs such as red huckleberry, rusty menziesia, and devil's club The forest floor is covered with a mat of mosses, liverworts and plants such as deerheart, bunchberry dogwood, single delight, and skunk cabbage   Streamside riparian vegetation is characterized by salmonberry, devil's club, alder, grasses, ferns, and currants.

Muskegs are abundant within this area, however due to their small size and association with forested sites, accurate acreage estimates are difficult. These areas, dominated by sphagnum mosses, sedges, and shrubs of the heath family, are interspersed among low elevation timber stands where drainage is restricted. Trees within the muskegs are sparse and consist mainly of stunted hemlock, lodgepole pine and Alaska-cedar

There are approximately 20,055 acres of forested land of which 11,417 acres are commercial forest land. Of the commercial forest land 9,878 acres are non-riparian old growth and 740 acres are riparian old growth

(c) Soils: Shallow mineral soils with good drainage can be found on steeper slopes due to rapid loss of material by erosion and efficient rainwater runoff Deep, well drained soils commonly occur below the shallow soils on the gentler slopes where transported soil materials have collected Poorly drained soils are found associated with low relief and impermeable subsurface layers In locations with poor drainage, deep organic soils (muskegs) tend to form In riparian areas, soil zones tend to contain sand and gravels as a result of flood deposition

(d) Fish Resource: Fish resources have been rated as part of the Tongass Land Management Plan (1979) and by the Alaska Department of Fish and Game in their Forest Habitat Integrity Program (1983) These ratings describe the value of VCU's for sport fish, commercial fish, and estuaries.

There are two VCU's which are rated as high value for sport fish These are Nakwasina Passage (300) and Krestof Sound (309) VCU's rated as highly valued for commercial fish are Nakwasina Passage (300) and Krestof Sound (309) VCU's rated as highly valued estuaries include Neva Strait (302) and Krestof Sound (309)

(e) **Wildlife Resource:** There are many varied wildlife resources in this roadless area. Birds and waterfowl rearing and nesting areas are abundant in this area. Generally, the area provides good habitat for Sitka black-tailed deer and brown bear Bald eagle habitat, nesting and roosting trees, encompasses this roadless area along the shorelines

(f) **Threatened and Endangered Species:** The area contains no known resident threatened or endangered species This area has been identified as having habitats for two migrating endangered species. The Peale's peregrine falcon passes through the forests during the spring and fall migration flights and the humpback whale inhabits nearby waters.

(6) **Current Use and Management:** The entire roadless area was allocated to Land Use Designation (LUD) 3 in the Tongass Land Management Plan Areas allocated to LUD 3 are to be managed for a variety of uses The emphasis is on managing for both amenity and commodity oriented uses in a compatible manner to provide the greatest combination of benefits These areas usually have high amenity values in conjunction with high commodity values. Allowances in calculated potential timber yield have been made to meet multiple use coordination objectives.

Recreational use of the area is primarily for hunting and fishing, and enjoying the scenery. This use is scattered across the area and with the usual concentrations near lakes, streams, and shorelines

(7) **Appearance (Apparent Naturalness):** A vast majority of the area is considered unmodified except for those areas primarily located near the shoreline with evidence of current or historic use Evidence of historic use includes old cabins, and other historic occupancies Current use includes various short term occupancies, and other evidence of the use of

the area and the surrounding waters   All of this evidence is readily
apparent to visitors that visit the specific sites.

The visual character type of this roadless area is classified as Baranof
Highland   Terrain in this type consists of an irregular, rugged
asymmetrical chain of landforms 3,000-5,300 feet in elevation having a
steep eastern slope and a more gentle western slope deeply indented with
fjords   Generally, landforms are visually massive, bulky and stark
throughout the character type   Shoreline forms are very rugged with
steep-sided fjord country on both east and west coasts

Rugged headwalls, cliffs and escarpments are common on the west side of the
Baranof Highland character type, as a result of exposure to the sea wind
and waves.   Rock faces are sometimes visible on steep-sided fjords near
saltwater throughout the unit.   The Sitka Sound Roadless Area is a poor
example of this visual character class as it has few of the described
features, or the features are limited or poorly representative

Approximately 11 percent of this roadless area was inventoried in 1984 as
being Visual Variety Class B (Common), and approximately 81 percent as
Variety Class C (Minimal Variety).   The remaining 8 percent of the acreage
was inventoried Variety Class A (Distinctive).

The majority (63 percent) of this roadless area was inventoried in 1984 as
having an Existing Visual Condition (EVC) I, these areas appear to be
untouched by human activity.   Twenty-six percent of the acreage is in EVC
IV, which are areas in which changes in the landscape are easily noticed by
the average person and may attract some attention   There appears to be
disturbances but they resemble natural patterns   Eleven percent is in EVC
V where changes in the landscape are obvious to the average person   The
changes appear to be major disturbances

(8) **Surroundings (External Influences):** The area is composed of islands
in Sitka Sound and the Whitestone Peninsula (which is bordered by salt
water on three sides).   As a result, external influences on those sides are
limited to the sights and sounds of motorized boats.   The eastern boundary
of Whitestone Peninsula adjoins an area of timber activity and its
associated road system   This development has had only local impact on the
roadless area.

(9) **Attractions and Features of Special Interest:** The major attraction of
the Sitka Sound Roadless Area is the islands themselves   Sitka is known
for the numerous islands lying off shore in Sitka Sound   Given the fact
that the ferries of the Alaska Marine Highway System pass through Neva
Strait and Olga Strait in this roadless area on their way to and from
Sitka, the beauty of the islands and of the two Straits themselves are seen
by many visitors to Sitka.

The natural features of the area, the scenery, and the opportunity to see
wildlife are all considered attractions   High quality fishing
opportunities in the streams and lakes also provide attractions   The area
contains 14 inventoried recreation places which contains 18,815 acres
These is one National Forest System Trail in this roadless area   but no
public recreation cabins

b   Capability of Management as Wilderness or in an Unroaded Condition

(1) Manageability and Management Area Boundaries: The Sitka Sound
Roadless Area is generally well defined by topographic features   All
areas, but one, are islands that have their boundaries determined by their
shorelines   The one exception is the Whitestone Peninsula of Baranof
Island, which has one boundary determined by previous timber activities and
the associated road system.

The feasibility of management of this area as Wilderness or in an unroaded
condition is good as there is no significant motorized access or other
current nonconforming uses

(2) **Natural Integrity:** The area is unmodified except for the evidence of
current and historic use of the area. This evidence although locally
significant, has a very low overall effect on the natural integrity of the
area. Both the relative size of the developments and their location along
the shoreline contribute to that low impact. The long-term ecological
processes are intact and operating with the effect of human influences on
natural processes unmeasurable.

(3) **Opportunity for Solitude:** There is a moderate opportunity for
solitude within the area. Recreational use of the area is relatively
limited and dispersed, so that encounters with other visitors are
unlikely. The sight or sound of airplanes overhead and boats along the
coastlines can occasionally intrude on a visitor's solitude   Along Neva
Strait and Olga Strait, ferries of the Alaska Marine Highway system can be
observed or heard.

(4) **Opportunity for Primitive Recreation:** The area provides a moderate
opportunity for primitive recreation as a result of its dense vegetative
screening, and physical challenges. This area has a unique topography and
diverse vegetation that combine to offer a setting capable of providing a
variety of primitive recreation opportunities   There are ponds, streams
bays, mountains, and a varied coastline that contribute to these
opportunities. The absence of developed recreational facilities further
enhances the the opportunity for primitive recreation

The area provides primarily a Primitive recreation opportunity as
inventoried with the Recreation Opportunity Spectrum (ROS) system   The
acreage of each ROS class within the Roadless Area are listed below

ROS Class	Acres
Rural (R)	20
Roaded Natural (RN)	5,558
Roaded Modified (RM)	260
Semi-Primitive Non-Motorized (SPNM)	13,017
Semi-Primitive Motorized (SPM)	2,519

The area contains 14 recreation places

ROS CLASS	# OF REC. PLACES	TOTAL ACRES	CAPACITY BY RVD
RN	3	4,359	14,930
RM	1	120	130
SPNM		13,017	2,698
SPM		1,180	4,567

There are no National Forest System trails in the area, and no recreation cabins

(5) Special Features (Ecologic, Geologic, Scientific, Cultural)   There are no known features of ecologic, geologic, scientific, or cultural significance.

c. Availability for Management as Wilderness or in an Unroaded Condition

(1) Resource Potentials

(a) Recreation Potential: The Tongass Land Management Plan, Amended Winter 1985-86 did not identify opportunities for additional recreational facilities or activities. No potential trail locations or developed recreation sites have been identified at this time

The varied terrain, diverse vegetation, and attractive scenery of this area provide unlimited recreation potentials for dispersed recreation. Additional trails and cabins or shelters are possible.

(b) Fish Resource: The Tongass Land Management Plan, Amended Winter 1985-86 did not identify additional opportunities for fish resource enhancement.

(c) Wildlife Resource: The Tongass Land Management Plan, Amended Winter 1985-86 did not identify additional opportunities for wildlife habitat improvement in the roadless area.

(d) Timber Resource: The Tongass Land Management Plan, Amended Winter 1985-86 did not identify any opportunities for management of the timber resource in this roadless area. There are 8,498 acres inventoried as tentatively suitable for harvest This includes 520 acres of riparian old growth, and 7,318 acres of non-riparian old growth.

(e) Land Use Authorizations: No significant land use authorizations exist within the roadless area.

(f) Minerals: The area does not have a high mineral development potential and there are no known claims

(g) Areas of Scientific Interest: There are no known areas of scientific interest in the roadless area

(2) Management Considerations

   (a) Timber: The potential for managing timber in this roadless area
   is dependent on the development of high market values and harvest
   methods which will allow extraction without need for extensive
   roading

   (b) Fire: The area has no significant fire history.

   (c) Insects and Disease: Endemic tree diseases common to Southest
   Alaska are present in the area, however, there are no know epidemic
   disease occurrences

   (d) Land Status: NOT YET AVAILABLE

d. **Relationship to Communities and Other Roadless and Wilderness Areas**

   (1) **Nearby Roadless and Wilderness Areas and Uses:** The nearest Wilderness
   is the West Chichagof-Yakobi Wilderness that lies north of Salisbury Sound
   Two other nearby Wildernesses are the Admiralty National Monument
   Wilderness, which lies east of Chatham Strait, and the South Baranof
   Wilderness south of Sitka.

   Nearby roadless areas include North Kruzof, Middle Kruzof, and South
   Kruzof, all three on Kruzof Island, and North Baranof and Sitka Urban,
   which lies east of Neva Strait and Sitka Sound on Baranof Island

   (2) **Distance From Population Centers (Accessibility):** Approximate
   distances from population centers are as follows

Community		Air Miles	Water Miles
Juneau	(Pop. 25,800)	90	160
Sitka	(Pop. 8,400)	0	0
Angoon	(Pop. 600)	40	90

   The nearest stop on the Alaska Marine Highway is Sitka

   (3) **Interest by Proponents:**

   (a) **Moratorium areas:** The area has not been identified as a
   "moratorium" area or proposed as Wilderness in legislative initiatives
   to date.

   (b) **Local users/residents:** Most use of the area is associated with
   recreational boating, hunting and fishing, and viewing the wildlife
   and the scenery of the area. It is also a nice place to have a
   picnic.

e. **Environmental Consequences**

   ALTERNATIVE ANALYSIS TO BE DONE LATER

INDIVIDUAL ROADLESS AREA DESCRIPTION

NAME: Redoubt (333)   ACRES (GROSS): 79,471   ACRES (NFS): 75,732

GEOZONE: C10
GEOGRAPHIC PROVINCE: Northern Outer Islands

1989 WILDERNESS ATTRIBUTE RATING: 17

a. Description

(1) **Relationship to RARE II areas:** The table below displays the VCU 1/
names, VCU numbers, original WARS 2/ rating, and comments This enables
the reader to compare the roadless areas evaluated in Appendix C with
previous analyses.

VCU Name	VCU No.	1979 WARS Rating	Comments
Sugarloaf Mountain	319	--	Not rated in 1979
Aleutkina Bay	320	17	
Redoubt Bay	321	--	Not rated in 1979
Deep Inlet	322	19	
Salmon Lake	323	20	
Big Bay	349	23	
Redoubt Lake	350	23	
Biorka Island	351	25	

(2) **History:** This large area has a long and varied history of use dating
from Tlingit use in prehistoric and historic times to the present use by a
variety of Alaska residents and visitors Use of the area by Russian
settlers began before 1800, and the Russian settlement, Ozerskoi Redoubt
was well established at the head of Redoubt Bay by 1818. Ozerskoi Redoubt
was established to supply New Archangel (Sitka) with fish. The Russians
constructed fish weirs and traps at the head of the rapids to obtain salmon
returning to Lake Redutsky (Redoubt Lake). By 1842, the saltery had
increased its production and was able to supply fish to other Russian
American Company settlements as well. In addition to the saltery, by 1832
Ozerskoi Redoubt included two mills for grinding flour with storage
facilities, a tannery, and a stockade.

In addition to evidence of use by the Russian settlers, use for fisheries
production and research, and other occupancies have occurred throughout the
area. Remains of structures and other human cultural activity in varying
degrees of deterioration can still be found.

1/ A VCU (Value Comparison Unit) is one of 867 watersheds which make up the
   forest and were differentiated for planning purposes in the Tongass Land
   Management Plan.
2/ Wilderness Attribute Rating System (WARS) was the nationwide system used to
   rate the wilderness attributes of roadless areas in the Roadless Area
   Review and Evaluation (RARE II).

(3) Location and Access: The area is located on the western side of
Baranof Island approximately half way between the north and south ends of
the island   It is bounded on the west and northwest by the Pacific Ocean
and Sitka Sound and on the northeast by Silver Bay and the Vodopad River
watershed   In addition, the area adjoins on the southeast side, the South
Baranof Wilderness

In addition to evidence of use by the Russian settlers, use for fisheries
production and research, and other occupancies have occurred throughout the
area   Remains of structures and other human cultural activity in varying
degrees of deterioration can still be found

The Redoubt Roadless Evaluation Area, in addition to being contiguous to
the South Baranof Wilderness, is also a part of a larger contiguous
roadless land mass which stretches from the north tip of Baranof Island to
the South Baranof Wilderness, and from Baranof Warm Springs to Sitka and to
Biorka Island. The three roadless areas that compose this contiguous
roadless land mass are North Baranof (#330), Sitka Urban (#331), and
Redoubt (#333).

The evaluation area includes a main section on Baranof Island and a
secondary section composed of numerous offshore islands   These islands
range in size from bare rocks that hardly stick out of the ocean at high
tide to Biorka Island.

The primary form of access to the area is by saltwater, with most people
arriving by boat from Sitka. There is also some floatplane access,
especially to Redoubt Lake in the center of the area   Due mainly to its
proximity to Sitka, access to the area is generally good " There are a
number of bays that provide sheltered anchorage for boats and several lakes
accessible by floatplane.

There is only one National Forest System Trail within the area, the Salmon
Lake-Redoubt Lake Trail. It is 5.9 miles in length, beginning at the head
of Silver Bay, and ending at the Redoubt Lake Recreation Cabin at the
northeast end of Redoubt Lake. There are also a couple of non-system
trails branching off of the Salmon Lake-Redoubt Lake Trail which lead up
Salmon Creek. One of the non-system trails leads to the Lucky Chance
Mountain mining areas.

(4) Geography and Topography: The area is generally characterized by
fingers of irregular, rugged mountains 2,000 to 4,400 feet in elevation
having steep slopes and deeply indented by Redoubt Lake and Deep Inlet
Numerous rocky crests and sharp ridges are found at higher elevations
Snow can be seen all year round on higher summits with a few cirque
glaciers and small permanent ice fields in the eastern corner of the area.
The shoreline is characterized by forested lowlands with a relatively
gentle slope. Forested islands, rocky islands, and reefs dominate the
coast along northern and western sides of the area.

Streams are generally short and flow directly to saltwater   The one
exception is the stream that empties into Redoubt Lake   Cascades are
common and the area contains three named lakes (Irina, Redoubt, and
Salmon). The largest lake and most dominant feature of the area is Redoubt

Four of the eight VCU's in this area were allocated to Land Use Designation (LUD) 3 in the Tongass Land Management Plan. This includes the following VCU's Sugarloaf Mountain (#319), Aleutkina Bay (#320), Deep Inlet (#321), Salmon Lake (#323)

VCU's allocated to LUD 3 are to be managed for a variety of uses The emphasis is on managing for both amenity and commodity oriented uses in a compatible manner to provide the greatest combination of benefits These areas usually have high amenity values in conjunction with high commodity values Allowances in calculated potential timber yield have been made to meet multiple use coordination objectives

Only the Redoubt Bay (#321) VCU was allocated to Land Use Designation (LUD) 4 in the Tongass Land Management Plan. VCU's allocated to LUD 4 provide opportunities for intensive development of resources. Emphasis is primarily on commodity, or market resources and their use with provision for amenity values When conflicts over competing resource uses arise, conflicts would most often be resolved in favor of commodity values Allowances in calculated potential timber yield have been made to provide for protection of physical and biological productivity

There are a number of authorized special uses existing within the area One use is an interagency agreement with the Alaska Department of Fish and Game for fisheries management facilities at Salmon Lake and at Redoubt Lake A second use is a special use permit with the Northern Southeast Regional Aquaculture Association (NSRAA) for fish net pens in Deep Inlet

Recreational use of the area is primarily for hunting, fishing, and enjoying the scenery This use is scattered across the area and with the usual concentrations near lakes, streams, and shorelines

(7) Appearance (Apparent Naturalness): A vast majority of the area is considered unmodified except for those areas primarily located near the shoreline with evidence of current or historic use. Evidence of historic use includes old fish production facilities, mineral prospecting, settlements, woodcutting, old cabins, and other historic occupancies Current use includes fish enhancement activities and facilities, fisheries research activities and facilities, various short-term occupancies, and other evidence of the use of the area and the surrounding waters All of this evidence is readily apparent to visitors that visit the specific sites.

The visual character type of this roadless area is classified as Baranof Highland. Terrain in this type consists of an irregular, rugged asymmetrical chain of landforms 3,000-4,400 feet in elevation having a steep eastern slope and a more gentle western slope deeply indented with fjords. Generally, landforms are visually massive, bulky and stark throughout the character type Shoreline forms are very rugged with steep-sided fjord country on both east and west coasts

Rugged headwalls, cliffs and escarpments are common on the west side of the Baranof Highland character type, as a result of exposure to the sea wind and waves Rock faces are sometimes visible on steep-sided fjords near saltwater throughout the unit. Numerous rocky crests, sharp ridges horns

aretes and cirques are found at higher elevations   Snow can be seen al
year found on the higher summits with cirque glaciers and small permanent
icefields, especially in the western portion of the area

The Redoubt Roadless Area on the western coast of Baranof Island presents a
good representation of the Baranof Highland visual character type   This
area displays a coastline deeply indented by fjords, and bays, and
especially Redoubt Lake and Deep Inlet   It is further characterized by the
hundreds of extremely irregular and exposed islands and rocks off the
western coast of the area   These islands and rocks provide a opportunity
for very dynamic surf waterforms

Approximately 41 percent of this roadless area was inventoried in 1984 as
being Visual Variety Class B (Common), and approximately 29 percent as
Variety Class C (Minimal Variety). The remaining 30 percent of the acreage
was inventoried Variety Class A (Distinctive)

The majority (95 percent) of this roadless area was inventoried in 1984 as
having an Existing Visual Condition (EVC) I; these areas appear to be
untouched by human activity   There is also 5 percent in EVC V where
changes in the landscape are obvious to the average person   The changes
appear to be major disturbances.

(8) Surroundings (External Influences): The area is bordered by saltwater
on the western side. As a result, external influences from that side is
limited to the sights and sounds of motorized boats. The southern boundary
adjoins the South Baranof Wilderness which could be considered a positive
influence. The northeastern boundary is the adjoining Sitka Urban Roadless
Evaluation Area, and is influenced occasionally by air pollution emitting
from the pulp mill located in Silver Bay   There are two areas of timber
activity and associated road systems. These developments are located in
Kizhuchia Creek and Camp Coogan Bay and have had only local impact on the
roadless area   This is due to the effects of topographic screening by
mountains surrounding both developments.

(9) Attractions and Features of Special Interest: Perhaps the feature of
greatest special interest in the Redoubt Roadless Area is Redoubt Lake.
This ten mile long lake sits at an elevation of 13 feet above sea level.
Its outlet is at the head of Redoubt Bay, and has been in the past served
by a boat tram, that lifted and moved small boats from the bay to the
lake. This tram is currently inoperable, however, it is scheduled for
repair. The size and location of this lake make it a prime attraction for
the Roadless Area.

The natural features of the area, the scenery, and the opportunity to see
wildlife are all considered attractions. High quality fishing
opportunities in the streams and lakes also provide attractions   The area
contains 20 inventoried recreation places which contains 22,405 acres.
These is one National Forest System Trail in this roadless area, and one
public recreation cabin.

The varied terrain, diverse vegetation, and attractive scenery of this area provide unlimited recreation potentials for dispersed recreation   Additional trails and cabins or shelters are possible.

(b) Fish Resource. The Tongass Land Management Plan, Amended Winter 1985-86 identified opportunities for fertilization of Redoubt Lake to enhance fish production

(c) Wildlife Resource   The Tongass Land Management Plan, Amended Winter 1985-86 did not identify any opportunities for wildlife habitat improvement in the roadless area

(d) Timber Resource: The Tongass Land Management Plan, Amended Winter 1985-86 did not identify any opportunities for management of the timber resource in this roadless area. There are 25,153 acres inventoried as tentatively suitable for harvest. This includes 3,040 acres of riparian old growth, and 21,098 acres of non-riparian old growth.

(e) Land Use Authorizations: The major land use authorization within the Roadless Area is the interagency agreement with the Alaska Department of Fish and Game for fisheries management facilities at Salmon Lake and at Redoubt Lake.

(f) Minerals: The area generally has a low potential for development of locatable minerals   There is one known active claim in the area.

(g) Areas of Scientific Interest: There is one feature of major ecologic and scientific interest within the Redoubt Roadless Area. That feature is Redoubt Lake   An area around this lake has been inventoried as having some potential for Research Natural Area (RNA) status.

Redoubt Lake is one of the only large meromictic lakes in the Tongass National Forest. Meromictic lakes are characterized by a stable bottom layer that does not mix or "turn over" during the fall when cooling surface waters sink. The factor responsible for the meromictic character of Redoubt Lake is the presence of a marine saltwater layer at the bottom of the lake   The surface of Redoubt Lake is only slightly above sea level and the lake is separated from Redoubt Bay only by a bedrock sill at the outlet. High tidal or storm surges push saltwater over the sill. Saltwater is denser than the freshwater of the lake and settles to the bottom no matter what the temperature.

The saltwater/freshwater density-stratified water column represents a chemocline. Once in place, the salt layer is generally stable and will not allow mixing   Nutrients contained in dead organisms filtering to the bottom are trapped in bottom sediments and subtracted from the ecosystem   However, freshwater springs seeping through fractures in the bedrock may enter the bottom of the lake and gradually degrade the chemocline by dilution until it is renewed by saltwater intrusion   In some situations meromictic lake systems have been reported to act as effective concentrators of solar energy in the

unmixed bottom layer, producing unusually warm temperatures at the
bottom Redoubt Lake offers the opportunity to conduct studies of
these physical and ecological phenomena.

(2) Management Considerations

(a) Timber: The potential for managing timber in this roadless area
is dependent on the development of high market values and harvest
methods which will allow extraction without need for extensive
roading

(b) Fire: The area has no significant fire history

(c) Insects and Disease: Endemic tree diseases common to Southeast
Alaska are present in the area, however, there are no know epidemic
disease occurrences.

(d) Land Status: NOT YET AVAILABLE

d. Relationship to Communities and Other Roadless and Wilderness Areas

(1) Nearby Roadless and Wilderness Areas and Uses: The nearest Wilderness
is the South Baranof Wilderness which adjoins the southern boundary of the
roadless area. Two other nearby Wildernesses are the Admiralty National
Monument Wilderness, which lies east of Chatham Strait, and the West
Chichagof-Yakobi Wilderness that lies north of Salisbury Sound

The Redoubt Roadless Evaluation Area, in addition to being contiguous to
the South Baranof Wilderness, is also a part of a larger contiguous
roadless land mass which stretches from the north tip of Baranof Island to
the South Baranof Wilderness, and from Baranof Warm Springs to Sitka and to
Biorka Island. The three roadless areas that make up this larger area are
North Baranof (#330), Sitka Urban (#331), and Redoubt (#333)

(2) Distance From Population Centers (Accessibility): Approximate
distances from population centers are as follows:

Community		Air Miles	Water Miles
Juneau	(Pop. 23,729)	90	160
Sitka	(Pop. 8,041)	0	0
Angoon	(Pop. 639)	40	90

The nearest stop on the Alaska Marine Highway is Sitka.

(3) Interest by Proponents:

(a) Moratorium areas: The area has not been identified as a
"moratorium" area or porposed as Wilderness in legislative initiatives
to date.

(b) Local users/residents: Most use of the area is associated with
recreational boating, hunting and fishing, and viewing wildlife and
the scenery of the area

e. Environmental Consequences

ALTERNATIVE ANALYSIS TO BE DONE LATER

INDIVIDUAL ROADLESS AREA DESCRIPTION

NAME: Port Alexander (334)   ACRES (GROSS): 126,636   ACRES (NFS): 126,120

GEOZONE: C11
GEOGRAPHIC PROVINCE: Northern Outer Islands

1989 WILDERNESS ATTRIBUTE RATING: 22

a. Description

   (1) Relationship to RARE II areas: The table below displays the VCU 1/
   names, VCU numbers, original WARS 2/ rating, and comments. This enables
   the reader to compare the roadless areas evaluated in Appendix C with
   previous analyses

| | | 1979 | |
VCU Name	VCU No	WARS Rating	Comments
Deep Cove	334	25	
Deep Lake	335	25	
Port Herbert	336	25	
Port Walter	337	27	
Port Lucy	338	25	
Port Alexander	339	23	
Puffin Bay	340	23	
Branch Bay	341	26	
Redfish Bay	342	28	
Snipe Bay	343	25	

   (2) History: This large area has a long and varied history of use dating
   from Tlingit use in prehistoric and historic times to the present use by a
   variety of Alaska residents and visitors. Use of the area since 1900
   includes fish canneries, herring reduction plants, whaling stations, and
   settlements. Remains of structures and other human cultural activity in
   varying degrees of deterioration can still be found.

   (3) Location and Access: The area is located on the southern tip of
   Baranof Island. It is bounded on the west by the Pacific Ocean and on the
   east by Chatham Strait. The area is bounded on the north by the southern
   boundary of the South Baranof Wilderness

   There are three primary forms of access to the area The first is by
   floatplane, with Sitka the most frequent origin. The second access is by
   saltwater on both the west and east side. The third access is from Port

1/ A VCU (Value Comparison Unit) is one of 867 watersheds which make up the
   forest and were differentiated for planning purposes in the Tongass Land
   Management Plan.
2/ Wilderness Attribute Rating System (WARS) was the nation-wide system used
   to rate the wilderness attributes of roadless areas in the Roadless Area
   Review and Evaluation (RARE II).

Alexander within the area. Access to the area is generally good   This is
due to the numerous bays and fiords that provide sheltered anchorage for
boats and the numerous lakes accessible by floatplane   The distance from
population centers is the primary restriction on access.

There is only one National Forest System Trail within the area, the Sashin
Lake Trail. It is 1 7 miles in length, beginning at the head of Little
Port Walter, and ending at the northeast end of Sashin Lake   There is also
a short non-system trail branching off of the Sashin Lake Trail which leads
to the north to Round Lake

(4) Geography and Topography: The area is generally characterized as an
irregular, rugged chain of mountains 2,000 to 3,800 feet in elevation
having a steep slope and deeply indented with fiords. Numerous rocky
crests and sharp ridges are found at higher elevations. Snow can be seen
all year round on higher summits with a few cirque glaciers and small
permanent ice fields in the northern part of the area.

Streams are generally short and flow directly to saltwater   The one
exception is the stream that empties into Big Branch Bay. This stream runs
in a southerly direction for over 12 miles. Cascades are common and lakes
are plentiful. The largest lake is Deer Lake in the northeast end of the
area which stretches approximately four miles and lies at an elevation of
386 feet. The west coastline exhibits areas of very dynamic surf
waterforms.

There are _____ miles of shoreline along saltwater. Approximately 19
percent of the area consists of alpine tundra, ice, snow, and rock   This
includes 12,731 acres of alpine tundra, 580 acres of ice and snow, and
10,830 acres of rock. There are approximately 19 acres of small islands
located along the coastline, and 5,857 acres of freshwater lakes in the
area. Large lakes in the area include Deer Lake, Borodino Lake, Betty
Lake, Tumakof Lake, and Antipatr Lake.

(5) Ecosystem:

(a) Classification: The area is classified as being in the Northern
Outer Islands Geographic Province. This province is generally
characterized by rugged highly dissected topography, exposed extremely
wet outer coastal environment, and extensive alpine environments with
productive forested areas highly fragmented and usually concentrated
on oversteepened slopes and on valley bottoms.

This area has possibly the highest rainfall zone in North America
The official Weather Service station at Little Port Walter, on the
east side of the area, records a long-term average annual
precipitation of 224 inches. The 1987 annual total precipitation was
292 inches. Because of orographic uplift (winds forced to rise over
mountains), total precipitation in the upper elevations of the area
are probably significantly higher.

(b) Vegetation: The proximity of this area to the open North Pacific
Ocean and the unimpeded movement of storms into the area from the
southwest results in a low freezing level and high snowfall total   As
a result, treeline is at a low elevation and much of the vegetation of
the steep watershed basins are alpine tundra. Conifer cover density
varies widely even on low slopes near saltwater and is usually
interspersed with muskeg and other lower forms of vegetation. Larger
intertidal grass and associated meadows species are infrequent   The
effects of wind and salt spray affect the character and, to some
extent, the species on the west side of this roadless area.

The vegetation of this roadless area consists primarily of typical
spruce-hemlock forests. Western hemlock-Sitka spruce dominate the
overstory while the understory is composed of shrubs such as red
huckleberry, rusty menziesia, and devil's club. The forest floor is
covered with a mat of mosses, liverworts, and plants such as
deerheart, bunchberry dogwood, single delight, and skunk cabbage
Streamside riparian vegetation is characterized by salmonberry,
devil's club, alder, grasses, ferns, and currants

Muskegs are abundant within this area, however due to their small size
and association with forested sites, accurate acreage estimates are
difficult. These areas, dominated by sphagnum mosses, sedges, and
shrubs of the heath family, are interspersed among low elevation
timber stands where drainage is restricted. Trees within the muskegs
are sparse and consist mainly of stunted hemlock, lodgepole pine, and
Alaska-cedar.

At elevations generally above 2,000 feet, the plant communities are
characterized by low shrubs, grasses, and sedges. Subalpine forests
and meadows occur at the interface between the forested communities
and the alpine tundra.

There are approximately 67,969 acres of forested land of which 31,489
acres are commercial forest land. Of the commercial forest land,
28,114 acres are non-riparian old growth and 3,275 acres are riparian
old growth.

(c) Soils: Shallow mineral soils with good drainage can be found on
steeper slopes due to rapid loss of material by erosion and efficient
rainwater runoff. Deep, well drained soils commonly occur below the
shallow soils on the gentler slopes where transported soil materials
have collected. Poorly drained soils are found associated with low
relief and impermeable subsurface layers. In locations with poor
drainage, deep organic soils (muskegs) tend to form. In riparian
areas, soil zones tend to contain sand and gravels as a result of
flood deposition.

(d) Fish Resource: Fish resources have been rated as part of the
Tongass Land Management Plan (1979) and by the Alaska Department of
Fish and Game in their Forest Habitat Integrity Program (1983) These
ratings describe the value of VCU's for sport fish, commercial fish,
and estuaries.

There are two VCU's which are rated as high value for sport fish
These are Deep Lake (335) and Redfish Bay (342). VCU's rated as
highly valued for commercial fish are Port Walter (337), Branch Bay
(341), and Redfish Bay (342). VCU's rated as highly valued estuaries
include Port Herbert (336), and Port Alexander (339)

(e) **Wildlife Resource:** There are many varied wildlife resources in
this roadless area. Birds and waterfowl rearing and nesting areas are
abundant in this area. Generally, the area provides good habitat for
Sitka black-tailed deer and brown bear. Bald eagle habitat, nesting
and roosting trees, encompasses this roadless area along the
shorelines.

(f) **Threatened and Endangered Species:** The area contains no known
resident threatened or endangered species. This area has been
identified as having habitats for two migrating endangered species
The Peale's peregrine falcon passes through the forests during the
spring and fall migration flights and the humpback whale inhabits
nearby waters.

(6) **Current Use and Management:** All ten of the VCU's in this area
(126,120 acres) were allocated to Land Use Designation (LUD) 2 in the
Tongass Land Management Plan. Areas allocated to LUD 2 are to be managed
in a roadless state to retain their wildland character. This designation
would permit wildlife and fish habitat improvement and primitive
recreational facility development.

There are a number of authorized special uses existing within the area
The following are the major uses at this time.

National Marine Fisheries Service - Interagency Agreement for the
Little Port Walter Fisheries Research Field Laboratory including the
Research Station at Little Port Walter and the area within the Little
Port Walter-Sashin Lake drainage encompassing approximately 2,400
acres.

Northern Southeast Regional Aquaculture Association (NSRAA) - Special
Use Permit for use of facilities at Upper Deer Lake, Deer Lake, Mist
Cove, Fawn Creek, Upper Rostilaf Lake, Lower Rostilaf Lake, Rostilaf
Beach, Borodino Lake, Cliff Lake, Deep Cove, and Osprey Lake.

Armstrong-Keta Inc. - Special Use Permit for water transmission lines
from Jetty Lake to the north shore of Port Armstrong for fish hatchery
operation and power generation.

Port Alexander - Special Use Permit for a water supply system.

Recreational use of the area is primarily for hunting, fishing, and
enjoying the scenery. This use is scattered across the area and with the
usual concentrations near lakes, streams, and shorelines.

There are two parcels of private land within the boundary of this roadless
area. They occur at Port Alexander and at Port Armstrong

(7) **Appearance (Apparent Naturalness):** The Port Alexander Roadless Area is considered unmodified except for those areas primarily located near the shoreline with evidence of current or historic use. Evidence of historic use includes old fish canneries and herring reduction plants, water diversion structures and pipelines, mineral prospecting, old cabins, and other historic occupancies. Current use includes fish enhancement activities and facilities, fisheries research activities and facilities, various short-term occupancies, the community of Port Alexander, and other evidence of the use of the area and the surrounding waters. All of this evidence is readily apparent to visitors that visit the specific sites.

The visual character type of this roadless area is classified as Baranof Highland. Terrain in this type consists of an irregular, rugged asymmetrical chain of landforms 3,000-5,300 feet in elevation having a steep eastern slope and a more gentle western slope deeply indented with fjords. Generally, landforms are visually massive, bulky and stark throughout the character type. Shoreline forms are very rugged with steep-sided fjord country on both east and west coasts.

Rugged headwalls, cliffs and escarpments are common on the west side of the Baranof Highland character type, as a result of exposure to the sea wind and waves. Rock faces are sometimes visible on steep-sided fjords near saltwater throughout the unit. Numerous rocky crests, sharp ridges, horns, aretes and cirques are found at higher elevations. Snow can be seen all year round on the higher summits with cirque glaciers and small permanent icefields, especially in the northern portion of the area.

The Port Alexander Roadless Area at the southern end of Baranof Island presents an extreme representation of the Baranof Highland visual character type. This area displays a coastline deeply and repeatedly scalloped by fjords and bays, the result of the Baranof landmass dipping down beneath the ocean surface. A combination of historic glaciation and erosion from the high level of precipitation have further accentuated the carving of the topography. One example, is that the head of bay of Port Lucy on the east coast of the area, reaches to within one-half mile of the head of Puffin Bay on the west coast. This occurs in an area where Baranof Island is approximately ten miles across, measured from the mouth Port Lucy to the mouth of Puffin Bay.

Approximately 65 percent of this roadless area was inventoried in 1984 as being Visual Variety Class B (Common), and approximately 4 percent as Variety Class C (Minimal Variety). The remaining 31 percent of the acreage was inventoried Variety Class A (Distinctive). The majority (95 percent) of this roadless area was inventoried in 1984 as having an Existing Visual Condition (EVC) I; these areas appear to be untouched by human activity.

(8) **Surroundings (External Influences):** The area is bordered by saltwater on three sides. As a result, external influences on those sides are limited to the sights and sounds of motorized boats. The northern boundary adjoins the South Baranof Wilderness which could be considered as having a positive influence on this area. The settlements along the eastern coast of the area probably have the greatest influence on the Port Alexander Roadless Area. These include the town of Port Alexander and the Fisheries Research Station at Little Port Walter

(9) **Attractions and Features of Special Interest:** Features of special
interest in the Port Alexander Roadless Area include three features related
to water. The first is the high precipitation in the area and the
ecological effects of that precipitation. The second is the large number
of lakes in the area, some at very low elevations and some at higher
elevations. Lastly, the extremely carved coastline that has resulted a
large number of deep fjords and bays.

The natural features of the area, the scenery, and the opportunity to see
wildlife are all considered attractions High quality fishing
opportunities in the streams and lakes also provide attractions The area
contains 19 inventoried recreation places which contains 17,771 acres
There is one National Forest System Trail in this roadless area, but no
public recreation cabins.

b. **Capability of Management as Wilderness or in an Unroaded Condition**

(1) **Manageability and Management Area Boundaries:** The Port Alexander
Roadless Area is well defined by topographic features. The boundaries
determined by Chatham Strait and the Pacific Ocean are easily,described and
recognized. Even the northern boundary, which follows the boundary of the
South Baranof Wilderness, lies on top of major watershed divides The only
area where the boundary is not defined by topographic features is around
private lands at Port Armstrong and Port Alexander and around the lands
selected by the State of Alaska at Port Alexander.

The feasibility of management of this area as Wilderness or in an unroaded
condition is good as there are no significant motorized access or other
nonconforming uses. The possible exception to this would be the fish
enhancement and fisheries research activities on the eastern edge of the
area.

(2) **Natural Integrity:** The area is unmodified except for the evidence of
current and historic use of the area. This evidence although locally
significant, has a very low overall effect on the natural integrity of the
area. Both the relative size of the developments and their location along
the shoreline contribute to that low impact, The long-term ecological
processes are intact and operating with the effect of human influences on
natural processes unmeasurable.

(3) **Opportunity for Solitude:** There is a very high opportunity for
solitude within the area. Both the size of the area and the screening
offered by the topography increase the opportunity for solitude
Recreational use of the area is relatively limited and dispersed, so that
encounters with other visitors are unlikely. The sight or sound of
airplanes overhead and boats along the coastlines can occasionally intrude
on a visitor's solitude.

(4) **Opportunity for Primitive Recreation:** The area provides a high
opportunity for primitive recreation as a result of its size, topographic
screening, and physical challenges. This area has a highly irregular
topography and diverse vegetation that combine to offer a setting capable
of providing a variety of primitive recreation opportunities There are
lakes, ponds, streams, bays, rugged mountains, and a varied coastline that

contribute to these opportunities. The absence of developed recreational
facilities further enhances the opportunity for primitive recreation

The area provides primarily a Primitive recreation opportunity as
inventoried with the Recreation Opportunity Spectrum (ROS) system. The
acreage of each ROS class within the Roadless Area are listed below

ROS Class	Acres
Primitive I (P1)	86,494
Primitive II (P2)	26,903
Rural (R)	57
Semi-Primitive Non-Motorized (SPNM)	9,059
Semi-Primitive Motorized (SPM)	3,509

The area contains 19 recreation places.

ROS CLASS	# OF REC. PLACES	TOTAL ACRES	CAPACITY BY RVD
P2	14	10,760	7,284
SPNM	2	4,487	1,575
SPM	3	2,165	3,951

There is one National Forest System Trail within the area, the Sashin Lake
Trail, and no recreation cabins.

(5) **Special Features (Ecologic, Geologic, Scientific, Cultural):** One
feature of ecological and scientific significance is the exceptionally high
precipitation and the effect that has on the ecology of the area. This
Roadless Area is located in possibly the highest rainfall zone in North
America. The official Weather Service station at Little Port Walter,
within the area, records a long term average precipitation of 224 inches
The 1987 annual total was 292 inches. Because of orographic uplift (winds
forced to rise over mountains), total precipitation in the upper elevations
of the area is probably significantly higher.

There are no other known features of ecologic, geologic, scientific, or
cultural significance.

c. **Availability for Management as Wilderness or in an Unroaded Condition**

   (1) **Resource Potentials**

   (a) **Recreation Potential:** The Tongass Land Management Plan, Amended
   Winter 1985-86 did not identify any opportunities for enhancing
   recreation in this roadless area. No potential trail locations or
   developed recreation sites have been identified at this time.

   The varied terrain, diverse vegetation, and attractive scenery of this
   area provide unlimited recreation potentials for dispersed
   recreation. Additional trails and cabins or shelters are possible.

   (b) **Fish Resource:** The Tongass Land Management Plan, Amended Winter
   1985-86 identified opportunities for fish stocking throughout the
   roadless area, and for constructing a fish passage in Big Branch Bay

(c) **Wildlife Resource:** The Tongass Land Management Plan, Amended Winter 1985-86 did not identify any opportunities for wildlife habitat improvement in this roadless area

(d) **Timber Resource:** The Tongass Land Management Plan, Amended Winter 1985-86 did not identify any opportunities for management of the timber resource in this roadless area. There are 12,660 acres inventoried as tentatively suitable for harvest. This includes 1,782 acres of riparian old growth, and 10,858 acres of non-riparian old growth.

(e) **Land Use Authorizations:** Major land use authorizations include the following:

> National Marine Fisheries Service - Interagency Agreement for the Little Port Walter Fisheries Research Field Laboratory including the Research Station at Little Port Walter and the area within the Little Port Walter - Sashin Lake drainage encompassing approximately 2400 acres

> Northern Southeast Regional Aquaculture Association (NSRAA) - Special Use Permit for use of facilities at Upper Deer Lake, Deer Lake, Mist Cove, Fawn Creek, Upper Rostilaf Lake, Lower Rostilaf Lake, Rostilaf Beach, Borodino Lake, Cliff Lake, Deep Cove, and Osprey Lake.

> Armstrong-Keta Inc. - Special Use Permit for water transmission lines from Jetty Lake to the north shore of Port Armstrong for fish hatchery operation and power generation.

> Port Alexander - Special Use Permit for a water supply system

(f) **Minerals:** The area generally has no known minerals development potential or current mineral claims. The only exception is a historic claim on a Nickel-Copper deposit, located on the north side of Snipe Bay. Prospecting and examination has occurred on and off since it was first staked in 1922.

(g) **Areas of Scientific Interest:** One feature of ecological and scientific significance is the exceptionally high precipitation and the effect that has on the ecology of the area. The Lover's Creek area has been inventoried as a potential Research Natural Area (RNA). The area was identified in order to represent several phenomena associated with exceptionally high precipitation. This area is located in possibly the highest rainfall zone in North America. The official Weather Service station at Little Port Walter, a few kilometers east of the potential RNA, records a long term average precipitation of 224 inches. The 1987 annual total was 292 inches. Because of orographic uplift (winds forced to rise over mountains), total precipitation in the upper elevations of the area is probably significantly higher

This inventoried potential RNA contains productive fisheries, and
alpine, rock, and snow communities that occupy unusually low
elevations. the proximity of the area to the open North Pacific and
the unimpeded movement of storms into the area from the southwest
probably results in a low freezing level and high snowfall total   As
a result, treeline occupies a low elevation and much of the vegetation
of the steep watershed basin is alpine tundra   The inventoried area
is also of interest because of the presence of Sitka spruce-western
hemlock and yellow cedar forest types that have developed under high
rainfall conditions

(2) **Management Considerations**

(a) **Timber:** The potential for managing timber in this roadless area
is dependent on the development of high market values and harvest
methods which will allow extraction without need for extensive
roading.

(b) **Fire:** The area has no significant fire history.

(c) **Insects and Disease:** Endemic tree diseases common to Southeast
Alaska are present in the area, however, there are no know epidemic
disease occurrences.

(d) **Land Status:** NOT YET AVAILABLE

d. Relationship to Communities and Other Roadless and Wilderness Areas

(1) **Nearby Roadless and Wilderness Areas and Uses:** The nearest Wilderness
is the South Baranof Wilderness which adjoins the northern boundary of the
roadless area. Two other nearby Wildernesses are the Admiralty National
Monument Wilderness, which lies east of Chatham Strait, and the West
Chichagof-Yakobi Wilderness that lies north of Salisbury Sound

(2) **Distance From Population Centers (Accessibility):** Approximate
distances from population centers are as follows:

Community		Air Miles	Water Miles
Juneau	(Pop. 23,729)	130	150
Sitka	(Pop. 8,041)	50	50
Angoon	(Pop. 639)	70	70

The nearest stop on the Alaska Marine Highway is Sitka.

(3) **Interest by Proponents:**

(a) **Moratorium areas:** The area has not been identified as a
"moratorium" area or proposed as Wilderness in legislative initiatives
to date.

(b) **Local users/residents:** Most use of the area is associated with
recreational boating, hunting and fishing, and viewing wildlife and
the scenery of the area.

e. Environmental Consequences

ALTERNATIVE ANALYSIS TO BE DONE LATER

INDIVIDUAL ROADLESS AREA DESCRIPTION

NAME: Brabazon Addition (338) ACRES (GROSS): 500,374   ACRES (NFS): 500,374

GEOZONE: C22
GEOGRAPHIC PROVINCE: Coast Range

1989 WILDERNESS ATTRIBUTE RATING: 27

a. Description

   (1) **Relationship to RARE II areas:** The table below displays the VCU 1/
   names, VCU numbers, original WARS 2/ rating, and comments. This enables
   the reader to compare the roadless areas evaluated in Appendix C with
   previous analyses.

VCU Name	VCU No.	1979 WARS Rating	Comments
Nunatak Gl.	353C*	25	LUD 1 Non-wilderness - released from wilderness recommendation in TLMP. Bounds Russell Fiord Wilderness Area.
Hidden Gl.	354C*	25	LUD 1 Non-wilderness - released from wilderness recommendation in TLMP. Bounds Russell Fiord Wilderness Area.
Black Tit	355C*	25	LUD 1 Non-wilderness - not included in wilderness in ANILCA Bounds Russell Fiord Wilderness Area
Russell Fiord	356C*	24	LUD 1 Non-wilderness - not included in wilderness in ANILCA. Bounds Russell Fiord Wilderness Area
Moser Creek	374C*	25	LUD 1 Non-wilderness - not included in wilderness in ANILCA. Bounds Russell Fiord Wilderness Area
Unnamed	888C*	--	Area added to NFS by ANILCA. No LUD, no WARS rating. Bounds Russell Fiord Wilderness Area, Glacier Bay NP & US/Canadian Border
Unnamed	999C*	--	Area added to NFS by ANILCA No LUD, no WARS rating. Bounds Russell Fiord Wilderness Area & US/Canadian Border

*--The roadless area includes only part of this VCU.

1/ A VCU (Value Comparison Unit) is one of 867 watersheds which make up the
   forest and were differentiated for planning purposes in the Tongass Land
   Management Plan.
2/ Wilderness Attribute Rating System (WARS) was the nationwide system used to
   rate the wilderness attributes of roadless areas in the Roadless Area
   Review and Evaluation (RARE II).

(2) History: The glaciated state of the entire area indicates there is no human history, other than occasional use, associated with the Brabazon Addition Roadless Area. It is believed that there was some passage over the glaciers by native peoples in the past, however, there is no evidence to support this   European use was been limited to exploration   Man's movement into the Yakutat Forelands (to the south of the Brabazon Range) is believed to have started about 1000 years ago, with the people coming from the north   Tlingit occupation, from the south, began approximately 300 ago   European ventures into the area started in the late 18th century, with Russian and English traders   There was little contact between whites and Indians until about 1874   A continuing white presence in the Yakutat area has been maintained since   Current activities in the evaluation area are scientific or recreational in nature.

(3) Location and Access: The Brabazon Addition Roadless Evaluation Area is located on the mainland, northeast of Yakutat. The area adjoins the Russell Fiord Wilderness to the west, the Canadian border to the east and the Glacier Bay National Park to the southeast. The southern boundary is the Yakutat Forelands roadless area. The center of the roadless area is approximately 40 miles northeast of Yakutat. Access to the roadless area is by foot from the end of Forest Highway 10 or from Russell Fiord/ Nunatak Fiord. Air access by ski-equipped small plane is possible.

(4) Geography and Topography: The Brabazon Addition is characterized by steep, rugged mountains, interspersed with or surrounded by glaciers   The glaciers moderate the terrain by providing large, relatively flat areas The highest point is approximately 9,310 feet above sealevel, at Boundary Peak 176. The majority of the area above 3,000 feet, with some areas below 1,000 feet; these are not common. Most surface features are hidden by the permanent glaciers. Major glaciers within the area are the Chamberlain (on the south), Novatak, Yakutat (feeding Harlequin Lake), Hidden (to Russell Fiord), East and West Nunatak (to Nunatak Fiord) and Battle (extending into Canada). There are two lakes located on the southeastern fringe of the roadless area. The visual character is the Coast Range. There are ___ acres of freshwater lakes, _____ acres of ice and snow, _____ acres of alpine tundra and _____ acres of rock.

(5) Ecosystem:

   (a) Classification: The area is classified as being in the Coast Range geographic province. This province is characterized by rugged, highly dissected, heavily glaciated terrain, with extensive alpine and ice field environments. The Brabazon Addition is typical of the province.

   (b) Vegetation: Vegetation is sparse and consists of lichens, mosses and grasses. Tree or brush species are unusual and infrequent, and are concentrated around the fringes, especially to the southeast in the Alsek River drainage. There are 120 acres classified as noncommercial forest land.

(c) **Soils:** There is little soil development because of recent glaciation. The primary feature (other than ice) is sharply uplifted bedrock, with steep, deeply incised slopes. Terrain is mountainous above the ice plains. Glaciers occupy much of this area.

(d) **Fish Resource:** There are no identified important fisheries in the roadless area. There is some fishing activity in the two lakes adjacent to the southeastern boundary.

(e) **Wildlife Resource:** Little is known about the wildlife in the Brabazon Addition. The only known use by wildlife is by mountain goats, with some possible use by bears. It may be assumed that some small mammals, such as pika, are present.

(f) **Threatened and Endangered Species:** There are no identified Threatened or Endangered species known to use the roadless area

(6) **Current Use and Management:** Five of seven VCU's were initially identified as LUD 1, or Wilderness, for inclusion in the Russell Fiord Wilderness. These were deleted for various reasons. They are now identified as LUD 1, Nonwilderness and total 25,382 acres. The other two have no LUD designation, but considering terrain, resources, accessibility, management potential, et cetera, are not characteristic of lands allocated a LUD 3 or 4 designation. No Forest Service management activities have occurred or are planned. There is some fishing in two lakes and may be some hunting, hiking or other recreational activity in the area; however, actual use is unknown. There is no known subsistence use.

(7) **Appearance (Apparent Naturalness):** The Brabazon Addition is unmodified; the appearance is entirely wild and natural. The remoteness and ruggedness seem to discourage modifications. The visual character of the area is the Coast Range. The landforms are generally massive, dissected by steep-walled canyons and valleys. Much of the area is glacier covered, making the sharp relief even more evident. The Existing Visual Condition (EVC) for the entire area is I, or the appearance of being untouched by human activity. The entire Brabazon Addition evaluation area is inventoried as a Variety Class A (Distinctive).

(8) **Surroundings (External Influences):** The surrounding areas are all roadless and unmodified. The area to the west is a designated wilderness management area, the areas to the north and south are rugged mountains surrounded by or containing glaciers and ice fields, and the area to the southeast is a National Park. While the area to the south is not in a protected status, it is in the Yakutat Forelands Roadless Management Evaluation Area. Additionally, the nature of the adjoining terrain is such that development of any kind is unlikely to occur. There are commercial flights to the south; however, none occur over the roadless area. There are occasional small aircraft overflights, generally on the southern roadless area boundary.

(9) **Attractions and Features of Special Interest:** Attractions of the area include sightseeing (primarily from aircraft), ice climbing and possibly rock climbing. The rugged mountains, springing from massive ice fields provide a spectacular view. Occasional sport hunting, particularly for

mountain goat, may occur   Some fishing occurs in two lakes accessible from
the Alsek River. Primary attraction would probably of scientific interest,
concentrating on the glacial features. There are no inventoried
recreational sites or trails

b   Capability of Management as Wilderness or in an Unroaded Condition

(1) Manageability and Management Area Boundaries: The roadless area lies
in a northwest to southeast orientation and is irregularly shaped   Length
is approximately 47 miles with an approximate 20 mile width   The
manageability of the boundaries is good; with the exception of the southern
boundary, the Brabazon Addition is surrounded by areas where management is
highly unlikely to change and the boundaries are described by law   The
southern boundary is a "point-to-point" straight line, approximately 24
miles long, and is not tied to physical points.

(2) Natural Integrity: The area is unmodified. Natural integrity has not
been compromised.

(3) Opportunity for Solitude: The opportunity for solitude is very high
over the whole of the Brabazon Addition. The very large area, coupled with
a high degree of difficulty of access and very low visitor numbers aids in
providing this solitude. There will be some disruption by overhead flights
of small aircraft; however, this should be infrequent.

(4) Opportunity for Primitive Recreation: The area provides primarily
primitive recreational opportunity, as inventoried with the Recreation
Opportunity Spectrum (ROS) system.

ROS Class	Acres
Primitive I (P1)	221,080
Primitive II (P2)	240,787

The area contains no recreation places.

(5) Special Features (Ecologic, Geologic, Scientific, Cultural): The area
is typical of much of the mainland coastal mountains   These are rugged,
heavily glaciated mountains, with little vegetation. The area is of
scientific interest for the effects of glaciation. The Brabazon Addition
Roadless Area is not unique within the Coastal Mountain character type
The primary interest probably lies with the association with the potential
of the Russell Fiord being isolated from saltwater by Hubbard Glacier and
becoming Russell Lake. The glaciers in the Brabazon Range would be the
primary contributors of freshwater to the lake.

c.   Availability for Management as Wilderness or in an Unroaded Condition.

(1) Resource Potentials

(a) Recreation Potential: Remoteness and rugged terrain limit
recreational opportunities to the primitive. Potential exists for the
development of trails and the possible construction of recreation
cabins. These facilities probably would receive little use because of
accessibility and very low visitor use of the area.

(b) **Fish Resource:** No known potential exists for fisheries habitat improvement activities.

(c) **Wildlife Resource:** No known potential exists for wildlife habitat improvement activities.

(d) **Timber Resource:** There are no timber resources and no potential for development of such

(e) **Land Use Authorizations:** There are no known special use permits or authorized land uses in the Brabazon Addition

(f) **Minerals:** The opportunity for mineral development appears low There are no known deposits of minerals with in the area. No known mineral exploration has occurred.

(g) **Areas of Scientific Interest:** The evaluation unit does not contain any inventoried potential Research Natural Areas.

(2) **Management Considerations**

(a) **Wilderness:** Maintenance of the area in a roadless state would be beneficial to the Russell Fiord Wilderness and the Glacier Bay National Park. The remoteness and accessibility will limit visitation to the Brabazon Addition, while the character of the area compliments the Wilderness and the Park.

(b) **Fire:** The area has no fire history.

(c) **Insects and Disease:** There is no known insect or disease occurrences.

(d) **Land Status:** There are no non-National Forest System lands located within the roadless area, nor any encumbrances or restrictions.

d. **Relationship to Communities and Other Roadless and Wilderness Areas**

(1) **Nearby Roadless and Wilderness Areas and Uses:** The Russel Fiord Wilderness is located along the entire western boundary of the Brabazon Addition. The Yakutat Forelands evaluation area lies along the southern boundary. The Glacier National Park, basically managed as wilderness, is the eastern boundary. The area to the north, across the Canadian border, is essentially a wild, unmanaged area with no development. Because of the surrounding areas, the Brabazon Addition evaluation area is part of a contiguous unroaded land mass of several million acres. National Forest System lands alone total over one million acres.

(2) **Distance From Population Centers (Accessibility):** Approximate distances from population centers are as follows:

Community		Air Miles	Water Miles *
Juneau	(Pop. 23,729)	180	255
Sitka	(Pop. 8,041)	190	225
Cordova	(Pop. 1,900)	270	285
Anchorage	(Pop. 235,000)	390	715

* No direct water access The closest water access points are in Russell Fiord (two miles) and Nunatak Fiord (one and one-half miles)

Yakutat has twice-daily commercial air service, both north- and southbound. There is no ferry service. The nearest Alaska Marine Highway terminals are at Hoonah to the east and Cordova to the west

(3) **Interest by Proponents:**

(a) **Moratorium areas:** The Brabazon Addition is neither a moratorium area, nor a proposed Wilderness

(b) **Local users/residents:** The nearest community is Yakutat (population 588), located 38 miles to the southwest. There is little use by local residents. This is some use by sport hunting guides in service to their customers and some small aircraft overflights for sightseeing.

(c) **Concerns of local residents:** There is no expressed concern by local residents for management within the evaluation area.

e. Environmental Consequences

ALTERNATIVE ANALYSIS TO BE DONE LATER

INDIVIDUAL ROADLESS AREA DESCRIPTION

NAME: Yakutat Forelands (339) ACRES (GROSS): 336,012 ACRES (NFS): 305,871

GEOZONE: C22 and C24
GEOGRAPHIC PROVINCE: Yakutat Forelands, Coast Range

1989 WILDERNESS ATTRIBUTE RATING: 20

a. Description

(1) **Relationship to RARE II areas:** The table below displays the VCU 1/ names, VCU numbers, original WARS 2/ rating, and comments. This enables the reader to compare the roadless areas evaluated in Appendix C with previous analyses.

VCU Name	VCU No.	1979 WARS Rating	Comments
Situk Lake	366C*	22	Road w/i VCU; Road, logging, pvt . land on boundary. LUD 2
Yakutat	367C*	--	Bound by pvt. land, road; Not rated in RARE II. LUD 3
Cannon Beach	370C*	--	Bound by pvt. land, road; Not rated in RARE II. LUD 2
Blacksand Is.	371C	--	Not rated in RARE II LUD 2
Arknklin R.	372C	20	LUD 2
Dark Forest	373C*	18	Bound by road. LUD 4
Miller Creek	375C*	23	Bound by road. LUD 4
Pike Lakes	376C*	20	Bound by road LUD 4
Dangerous R.	377C*	21	Bound by road LUD 2
Harlequin Lk.	378C*	21	Bound by road. LUD 3
Italio R.	379C	23	LUD 3
Italio Beach	380C	24	LUD 2
Awke Beach	381C	24	LUD 2
Triangle Lk.	382C	25	LUD 3
Cliff Mtn.	383C	22	LUD 2
Italio Lake	384C*	26	LUD 2
Awke Lake	385C	26	LUD 2
Ustay Flats	386C	23	LUD 3
Ustay R.	387C	24	LUD 3
Cannery Ck.	388C	21	LUD 3
Tanis Mesa	389C	24	LUD 3
Rodman Pass	390C	24	LUD 2
Tanis Lake	391C	25	LUD 2

*--The roadless area includes only part of this VCU.

1/ A VCU (Value Comparison Unit) is one of 867 watersheds which make up the forest and were differentiated for planning purposes in the Tongass Land Management Plan.

2/ Wilderness Attribute Rating System (WARS) was the nationwide system used to rate the wilderness attributes of roadless areas in the Roadlesss Area Review and Evaluation (RARE II).

VCU Name	VCU No.	1979 WARS Rating	Comments
Upper Alsek R.	392C*	26	Bounds Glacier Bay NP LUD 2
Canyon Glacier	393C	24	Bounds Glacier Bay NP LUD 2
Brabazon Gate	394C	24	Bounds Glacier Bay NP LUD 2
Alsek Rapids	395C	0	Bounds Glacier Bay NP LUD 2

(2) **History:** There is evidence of human occupation in Southeast Alaska
from 10,000 to 11,000 years before present Man's movement into the
Yakutat Forelands is believed to have started about 1,000 years ago, with
the people coming from the north (probably Eyak from the Copper River)
Tlingit occupation from the south began approximately 300 years before the
present. European ventures into the area started in the late 18th century
with Russian and English traders.

A Russian farming settlement was established in the approximate location of
Yakutat in 1796. Hostilities between the Russians and the Native
population ended with the total elimination of the settlement in 1805
Little contact between whites and Indians occurred from 1805 to about
1874. Activities since 1874 have included mining, fish canneries, fur
farms (mink and fox), manufactured native goods and tourism. Salmon
processing became a major industry, with the first salmon cannery
constructed in 1902. Others, located along the Gulf coast, followed over
the next 20 or so years. In the early 20th century, a railroad was planned
from Yakutat to Dry Bay for the service of the various canneries; however,
construction eventually went only to Johnson Slough, with lines serving the
Situk and Lost Rivers.

There was a large military presence, with attending activities, during
World War II. More recent activities within or adjacent to the roadless
area have included commercial logging operations, commercial fishing and
outfitter/guide services for sports fishing and hunting.

(3) **Location and Access:** The Yakutat Forelands Roadless Area is located
on the mainland, east and southeast of Yakutat. The area adjoins National
Forest System, State and private lands to the west and the Glacier Bay
National Park to the east. Forest Highway 10, the Russell Fjord
Wilderness and the Brabazon Range bound the Yakutat Forelands on the
north. The southern boundary is the Gulf of Alaska, from Dry Bay to
Johnson Slough. The center of the roadless area is approximately 30 miles
east of Yakutat.

There is small boat access, with numerous anchorages along most of the Gulf
Coast. Floatplane landing is possible in most of the bays, as well in
several lakes in the eastern half of the roadless area. There are seven
identified land-based aircraft landing areas. In addition, aircraft land
on the sandy beach fringes. Forest Highway 10 goes from Yakutat to the
Dangerous River, providing vehicle access to the upper reaches of several
rivers, as well as direct access to approximately 40 percent of the
northern boundary. All-terrain vehicles (ATV) are used along most of the
beaches, to access many of the river bottoms and from the road system to
access the uplands.

(4) **Geography and Topography:** The Yakutat Forelands is relatively flat over about 80 percent of the roadless area, with elevations ranging from sealevel to approximately 200 feet. The lowland terrain is characteristic of formerly glaciated topography, i.e , glacial outwash plains with lateral and terminal moraines, separated by low, flat areas with numerous streams and rivers as well as large marshes and muskegs. The rivers and streams are low gradient and follow wandering and braided channels, with wide floodplains.

Relief is such that a major runoff episode may completely change the location of streamcourses and may combine two or more totally divergent streams into one system. Were the Hubbard Glacier, located to the northwest, to close off Russell Fiørd, the resulting lake could reach overflow in a short period of time. The Situk River would be the overflow channel, drastically changing the landscape in this area. The eastern half also contains many lakes, varying in size to over 540 acres (Tanis Lake)

The northeast quadrant contains the southern slopes of the Brabazon Range, with elevations ranging from 200 feet to approximately 4,980 feet This mountainous area is steep and highly dissected with numerous streamcourses Several glaciers are present, and include the Rodman, Fassett, Canyon and Martin Glaciers.

The Gulf beach area is subject to drastic change due to open-water wave activity and ocean storms. The coastal area contains an extended stretch of sand dunes, formed by the wind. This dunes area is one of two found in Alaska.

There are _____ miles of shoreline on saltwater and _____ acres of beach Freshwater lakes total 2,930 acres. There are 1,516 acres of small islands, 344 acres of alpine tundra, 21,880 acres of ice and snow and 20,187 acres of rock.

(5) **Ecosystem:**

(a) **Classification:** The area is classified as being in the Yakutat Forelands geographic province. The province includes Glacier Bay north to Yakutat Bay and is characterized by recently uplifted beaches and fluvial processes related to icefields, valley glaciers and a cold wet climate. The climate is typical of the coastal maritime zone Total annual precipitation at Yakutat is 135 inches, with a 33-year snowfall average of 219 inches.

(b) **Vegetation:** Much of the vegetation in the lowlands are marsh and muskeg species or willows, cottonwoods and alders on the drier sites The wetland species are primarily sphagnum moss, sedges and heathers The drier sites contain low-growing species such as devils-club, salmonberry, blueberry, copper bush, hellesbore, ferns, skunk cabbage and huckleberry, over a carpet of mosses and liverworts.

Timbered areas contain primarily a dense overstory of Sitka spruce
and/or western hemlock over the "drained-site" species   Timber
stands, rated moderate to high (3 to 5 on a scale of 5) for management
activities, are concentrated in VCU's 379C, 382C, 386C, 387C, 388C and
389C. Even in heavily timbered areas, the tree species are found on
the drier sites on the ridges, separated by marsh or muskeg,
containing meandering streams

The sand dune area along the beach has a plant association, unique to
Southeast Alaska   Uncommon plants found here include species of the
Atriplex, Lupimachia and Saussurea genera

Outside of the VCU's above, the majority of the timber is not
considered operable, or does not constitute a significant component
There has been, and currently is, logging in the western and
northwestern portion of the lowlands, adjacent to the roadless area
boundaries.

There are approximately 152,510 acres of forested lands, of which
103,262 acres are classified as commercial forest land (CFL). There
are 6,215 acres classified as riparian old growth and 23,358 acres as
nonriparian old growth. Approximately 344 acres are alpine tundra
vegetation, and 64,806 acres are classed as muskeg   Muskeg is
interspersed within other types in units too small to map   Therefore
the acreage for muskeg may be substantially understated

.(c) Soils: The majority of the soils for the Yakutat Forelands
lowlands are youthful soils of glacio-fluvial and fluvial origin
Terrain is generally gently sloping. Base material is highly variable
and consists of igneous, metamorphic and sedimentary rocks   The
mountainous northeastern portion of the area consists of steep,
deeply incised slopes of exposed bedrock. Glaciers still occupy much
of this area.

Other features, such as mature soils (unglaciated remnants), steep
slopes and dunes occur, but to a limited extent. Recent glaciation
and ongoing uplift has, and does, affect soil development
Groundwater over most of the area is at or near the surface   Large
portions of the roadless area are poorly drained organic soils

(d) Fish Resource: Annual production for the evaluation area is
estimated at more than 250,000 salmon. Five species of Pacific
salmon, valuable for commercial, subsistence and sport use, spawn and
rear in the area. There are steelhead and cutthroat trout,
stickleback, Dolly Varden char, and smelt in many of the lowland
rivers and streams. Virtually all of the mountain streams are glacial
and support little or no resident fish populations

Commercial fisheries along the coast and in the bays take sea urchins,
salmon, shrimp, sablefish and crabs. Subsistence users take these,
plus herring, hooligan, clams and seaweed   In addition to the salmon
species, sportsfishers take steelhead and cutthroat trout

Fisheries habitat improvement projects have occurred in several
areas. Most notable are the efforts put coho habitat in the many
small rock pits along Forest Highway 10.

Fish resources have been rated as part of the Tongass Land Management
Plan (1979) and by the Alaska Department of Fish and Game (ADF&G) in
their Forest Habitat Integrity Program (1983) These ratings describe
the value of VCU's for sport fish, commercial fish and estuaries The
following table lists 26 VCU's rated high to very high for commercial
or sport fisheries values.

		Sport	Comm.			Sport	Comm
Situk Lake	366C	X	X	Triangle Lk.	382C	X	X
Yakutat	367C	X	X	Italio Lake	384C	X	X
Cannon Beach	370C	X	X	Awke Lake	385C	X	X
Blacksand Is.	371C	X	X	Ustay Flats	386C	X	X
Arknklin R.	372C	X	X	Ustay R.	387C	X	X
Dark Forest	373C	X	X	Cannery Ck.	388C	-	X
Miller Cr.	375C	X	X	Tanis Mesa	389C	X	X
Pike Lakes	376C	X	X	Rodman Pass	390C	-	X
Dangerous R.	377C	X	X	Tanis Lake	391C	-	X
Harlequin Lk.	378C	X	X	Upper Alsek R.	392C	X	X
Italio R.	379C	X	X	Canyon Glacier	393C	X	X
Italio Beach	380C	X	X	Brabazon Gate	394C	X	X
Awke Beach	381C	X	X	Alsek Rapids	395C	X	X

There are eight VCU's containing highly valued estuaries These are:

Situk Lake	366C	Dangerous R.	377C
Yakutat	367C	Italio Beach	380C
Cannon Beach	370C	Awke Beach	381C
Blacksand Is.	371C	Alsek Rapids	395C

(e) **Wildlife Resource:** The Yakutat Forelands support a rich wildlife
population, both in numbers and species diversity. Larger mammal
species include both brown and black bears (including the glacier
bear, a blueish color phase of the black bear), moose, wolverines and
wolves. There is a remnant Sitka black-tailed deer population, left
from transplant efforts in the 1940's. The smaller animals include
several furbearers (mink, marten, beaver) and rodents, such as mice,
snowshoe hare and pika, as well as several amphibian species There
are few resident bird species; however, the area is heavily used by
migratory species, both for nesting and resting and includes waterfowl
and raptors. Humpback and gray whales, seals, sealions, orcas,
dolphins and porpoises can be viewed from the beach areas.

There are 314,148 acres of habitat for both black and brown bears
Habitat for other management indicator species include mountain goat
(75,842 acres), red squirrel (314,148 acres) and 312,893 acres of pine
marten.

(f) Threatened and Endangered Species: There are no known Threatened
or Endangered plant or animal species resident to the Yakutat
Forelands. The peregrine falcon appears as a migratory user   The
bald eagle, a protected species, is found all along the coastal zone
and the larger rivers   There are several special interest plant
species within the roadless area

(6) Current Use and Management: There are 60 acres allocated as Land Use
Designation (LUD) 1 - Nonwilderness in the Tongass Land Management Plan
(1978). They were originally proposed as part of the Russell Fjord
Wilderness, but were not included in the final designation   There are 16
VCU's (171,419 acres) allocated to LUD 2, which provides for management of
the area in an unroaded state to retain the wildland character.

There are eight VCU's (134,740 acres) are designated as LUD 3, which allows
for management of the land for a variety of uses, with emphasis on managing
the uses and activities in a compatible and complementary manner to provide
for the greatest combination of benefits. These areas have a high use or
high amenity value in conjunction with a high commodity value. Three VCU's
(3,442 acres) are allocated to LUD 4, which provides for intensive resource
management and development, consistent with provisions to protect physical
and biological productivity.

Other than fisheries habitat enhancement and recreational cabins (some with
aircraft landing strips), few Forest Service management activities have
occurred. Habitat improvement activities for moose and fisheries are
planned for the 1989 field season. "There are four trails in the evaluation
area.

Other uses include sport fishing and hunting, subsistence fishing, hunting
and trapping, and commercial fishing. Outfitting and guide service is a
major business in the Yakutat area. Although oil and gas exploration has
been done in the recent past, such activities are not occurring at
present. There are many cabins and camps under special use permit - most
are concentrated along the coast - and are associated with fish camp and
outfitter/guide camps. There is some woodgathering, primarily along the
north and west boundaries and around cabin/camp areas   Logging and road
construction activities have taken place on the western and northwestern
boundaries.

(7) Appearance (Apparent Naturalness): The Yakutat Forelands generally
appear unmodified. Exceptions within the area are evidence of World War II
activities, former oil and gas exploration sites, abandoned fish canneries
and the various cabins/camps. The inland sites generally are not
obtrusive, except at short range or from the air. The coastal sites are
far more visible. Areas used in the past are reclaimed for the most part,
with differences in vegetation the primary indicators of use. Most of the
activity was, and is, concentrated along the coast, within one-half mile of
the beachfront.

There is widespread evidence of vehicular use, including all terrain
vehicle (ATV) trails and undesignated roads. Widespread ATV use is evident
along the beaches, river bottoms, muskegs, and upland trails The heaviest
cabin/fish camp concentrations are at Situk (the mouth of the Situk River),

on Blacksand Spit and on Blacksand Island   Many of the cabins have
impromptu small aircraft landing areas on the beach fringe   The airstrips
associated with the Forest Service cabins are highly visible from the air
These strips are maintained with heavy-duty mowing equipment

Harvest activity is visible along the northwestern and western boundaries
However, because of terrain, the logging is not visible from a distance and
does not affect the vast majority of the roadless area

The visual character type for about 80 percent of the evaluation area is
the Cordova-Yakutat, consisting of a coastal plain marked by longitudinal
beach and dune ridges, crossed by outwash plains and moraines, and backed
by marine ridges to several hundred feet in height   The Brabazon Range
provides a backdrop from outside the unit. The area is characterized by a
great variety of water forms, including glacial streams, meandering lowland
streams and small lakes. The ocean surf is a key water form. The balance
of the evaluation area lies in the Coast Range visual character type. The
land forms are massive and highly dissected. There is a great diversity in
geological features including cliffs, escarpments and jagged peaks.

There is little timber over 50 percent or more of the area; most of the
vegetation consists of groundcover or low-growing shrubs and short trees
The areas covered by timber contain stands with size classes from
seedling/saplings to large mature/overmature trees. The heavily timbered
areas are primarily in the eastern half. The view distance over much of
the area is relatively short because of terrain and vegetation. The view
to the south and west from the mountains shows most of the Yakutat
Forelands, and presents an unrestricted view of the coastal area

The evaluation area is inventoried as 32 percent Variety Class A
(Distinctive), 40 percent Variety Class B (Common) and 28 percent Variety
Class C (Minimal). The majority of the area (96 percent) is inventoried as
an Existing Visual Condition (EVC) I, which appears untouched by human
activity. The balance of the area is generally inventoried as an EVC II,
or areas in which changes to the landscape are not noticed by the average
visitor. The exception are areas which total less than 0.01 percent (100
acres) and are in an EVC IV, or areas in which changes in the landscape are
easily noticed by the average visitor, and may attract some attention

(8) Surroundings (External Influences): The area to the northwest and
west of the Yakutat Forelands has been highly modified by logging and
development. Forest Highway 10 runs along the northwestern boundary, with
the attendant vehicular traffic noise audible some distance into the
roadless area. The Yakutat airport is just outside the roadless area,
therefore, users in the western portion of the area may be subjected to
some aircraft noise. Most of the activities outside the roadless area are
not readily apparent to users because of the flat, rolling terrain   There
are commercial flights over the southern boundary, along the coast. There
is some water-borne activity in the coastal waters; however, there is no
disturbance from this traffic. There is one other roadless evaluation area
and the Russell Fiord Wilderness adjacent to the Yakutat Forelands
roadless area on the north, with Glacier Bay National Park to the east

(9) **Attractions and Features of Special Interest:** Attractions of the area include wildlife viewing, sports hunting and fishing, and camping in association with other activities. The numerous small lakes and streams provide a variety of fishing sites. There is driftboat fishing traffic on the Situk River, from the put-in site at Forest Highway 10 to the landing at the mouth of the river. There are small boat anchorages at various places along the coast. The very long stretches of sandy beach provide a opportunity for beachcombing, surfing, picnicking, and "dune running" with all-terrain vehicles. Sea mammal observation is a common activity

The area contains 26 inventoried recreation sites which contains 166,875 acres. There are four maintained trails within the roadless area. These are the Situk River #649, Lower Dangerous River #653, Middle Dangerous River #654, and Harlequin Lake #655. These trails total 10.7 miles. There are 10 Forest Service recreational cabin sites, with airstrips associated with six of the locations.

b. **Capability of Management as Wilderness or in an Unroaded Condition**

(1) **Manageability and Management Area Boundaries:** The roadless area is a long and relatively narrow, with a length of about 53 miles and a width varying from approximately seven to more than 15 miles. Most of the Yakutat Forelands is defined by a physical boundary, ie. the coastline, Dry Bay and the Alsek River, mountain ridgelines or Forest Highway 10 However, approximately 24 miles of the northeast boundary is a "point-to-point" straight line, and is not tied to readily identified physical points. In addition, the western boundary abuts private lands, roads or development. The presence of roads and/or private lands to the west may reduce the manageability of the area.

(2) **Natural Integrity:** The area is basically unmodified. There are modifications in the form of cabins and camps; however, other than the concentrations of fish camps at Situk and on Blacksand Spit and Island, most are widely scattered and are fairly unobtrusive. There are brushed-out landing strips associated with several of the Forest Service recreation cabins. There has been past modification of the area as evidenced by the abandoned fur farms, canneries and oil/gas exploration sites.

(3) **Opportunity for Solitude:** The opportunity for solitude is high over most of the Yakutat Forelands. The very large area, coupled with a high degree of difficulty of access and low visitor numbers aids in providing this solitude. Exceptions are locations along the western edge of the roadless area, and along Forest Highway 10. These are the locations people tend to concentrate. There will be some disruption by overhead flights of small aircraft, combined with some powerboat use along several of the rivers and the coast. The Situk River is heavily used by driftboaters, as well as having frequent use by permitted powerboats.

(4) **Opportunity for Primitive Recreation:** The area provides for the full spectrum of recreation opportunities. It is evident that both off-road and highway vehicles use the area. The following areas are as inventoried with the Recreation Opportunity Spectrum System.

ROS Class	Acres
Primitive I (P1)	78,200
Primitive II (P2)	104,437
Rural (R)	1,522
Roaded Natural (RN)	6,022
Roaded Modified (RM)	20
Semi-Primitive Non-Motorized (SPNM)	57,046
Semi-Primitive Motorized (SPM)	65,573
No ROS	1,788

The area contains 26 recreation places, totalling 166,875 acres.

ROS CLASS	# OF REC. PLACES	TOTAL ACRES	CAPACITY BY RVD
P1	_____	_____	_____
P2	_____	_____	_____
R	_____	_____	_____
RN	_____	_____	_____
RM	_____	_____	_____
SPNM	_____	_____	_____
SPM	_____	_____	_____

There are ten cabin sites (including two double cabins) located throughout the evaluation area. They receive some summer use (primarily fishers), but principle use is during the moose and bear hunting seasons.

(5) **Special Features (Ecologic, Geologic, Scientific, Cultural):** The area ranges from a constantly changing, uplifting coastal area to a remnant area untouched by the last glacial period to a young, developing ecosystem on immature or undeveloped soils. Of special ecological interest is the extensive sand dunes area along the coast. As one of only two such sites in Alaska, this feature is unique, even when compared to the rest of the Pacific Northwest. Their fairly recent development (estimated at less than 2,000 years), combined with unusual or uncommon plant associations, is of special interest.

Active glaciers in the northeast mountains are also of interest to visitors. The presence of species such as eagles, brown bears, black bears (including the glacier bear color phase), moose and mountain goats provide for wildlife observation. The many miles of sandy beach along the coast line provide for beachcombing opportunities. Cultural resource sites may provide special interest because of pre-contact mixing of peoples from the north and south, as well as relatively late prolonged direct contact with Europeans.

c. **Availability for Management as Wilderness or in an Unroaded Condition.**

(1) **Resource Potentials**

(a) **Recreation Potential:** Recreation potential includes the opportunity for trail corridors along several of the rivers and accessing several lakes Trailheads would have to be accessed from the coast, from aircraft landing strips or from the road system to the

west and northwest. Sport fishing and hunting are popular in the
area; moose hunting and steelhead fishing are major activities The
limited terrain features in the lowlands probably would not generate
much interest unto themselves. The Tongass Land Management Plan, as
amended in 1985-86 (TLMP), identified recreation facilities
development for shelters and trail construction in two VCU's

(b) **Fish Resource:** Fisheries management potential includes the
opportunity for the development of ground water spawning and rearing
channels, stock development for underutilized areas, large organic
debris placement for cover and habitat for rearing fish, lake
enrichment,and hatchery development. Much of the current management
emphasis centers around mitigation associated with the possible
overflow of Lake Russell. There are numerous fisheries research
projects in progress on the Situk River. The objectives of this
research are to recommend enhancement and mitigation projects on the
Yakutat Forelands. Projects identified in TLMP include stream habitat
improvement project in one VCU and non-stream habitat projects in 13
VCU's. Additionally, trail and public access projects can be
implemented to disperse sport fishing pressure.

(c) **Wildlife Resource:** Wildlife management potential includes
vegetation manipulation to enhance moose habitat, nest islands and
wetland enhancement to promote enhanced production, improved wildlife
viewing and interpretative areas and cooperative projects with the
State of Alaska. The Tongass Land Management Plan, as amended,
identified habitat improvement projects for moose in ten VCU's, for
trumpeter swans in eight VCU's, for waterfowl in seven VCU's and for
shorebirds in four VCU's.

(d) **Timber Resource:** There are 59,716 acres inventoried as
tentatively suitable for harvest. This includes 5,290 acres of
riparian old growth and 15,577 acres of non-riparian old growth The
potential for timber management is low, even with high quality, very
high volume stands. The cost of development and harvest, coupled with
a low value and no market make the timber essentially inoperable
Relaxation of export regulations and an upturn in the market may make
the timber profitable for a purchaser; however, this is unexpected in
the foreseeable future.

(e) **Land Use Authorizations:** There are approximately 130 special use
permits for uses such as fish camps, outfitter/guides, subsistence and
trapping camps and recreation cabins. The potential for increase of
number of permits is high. The increase will be in applications for
fish camps, outfitter/guide activities and facilities associated with
subsistence and outfitter/guide activities.

(f) **Minerals:** The opportunity for mineral development appears low
There are no known deposits of minerals important for development
Oil and gas exploration has occurred - the potential for development
appears to be high. The U.S.D.I., Geological Survey has identified
the Yakutat Forelands as a "Most Favorable Petroleum Reserve Area".
However, development activities have not been initiated

(g) **Areas of Scientific Interest:** There are five inventoried potential Research Natural Areas. These are Awke Beach, Awke-Ustay Lakes, Upper Situk, Italio River and Tidal Meadows

(2) **Management Considerations**

(a) **Fire:** The area has no significant fire history

(b) **Insects and Disease:** There are no epidemic insect or disease conditions. However, storm blowdown plays a historically important part in the ecology of the timbered areas. Blowdown is rapidly followed by a buildup of the striped ambrosia beetle. These attacks lead to rapid deterioration of the downed timber. In addition, the old growth timber stands are highly subject to mortality because of rots and windthrow.

(c) **Land Status:** There is one private parcel (Chief Situk Grave area) located within the roadless unit. There are no other non-National Forest System lands. A strip along the Situk River has tentatively been selected by Sealaska, the regional Native Corporation. While the transfer to other ownership has not occurred, the land is encumbered or land use restricted until such time as the selection is final or has been dropped. There are two unconveyed Native Allotments within the roadless area.

d. **Relationship to Communities and Other Roadless and Wilderness Areas**

(1) **Nearby Roadless and Wilderness Areas and Uses:** The Yakutat Forelands roadless evaluation area is located to the south of the Russell Fiord Wilderness. Roadless evaluation areas in the immediate area are the Brabazon Addition, #338 (adjoining to the north) and the Upper Situk, #341 (adjoining to the northwest).

(2) **Distance From Population Centers (Accessibility):** Approximate distances from population centers are as follows:

Community			Air Miles	Water Miles
Juneau	(Pop.	23,729)	180	240
Sitka	(Pop.	8,041)	190	210
Cordova	(Pop.	1,900)	250	270
Anchorage	(Pop.	235,000)	390	700

Yakutat has twice-daily commercial air service, both north- and southbound. There is no ferry service. The nearest Alaska Marine Highway terminals are at Hoonah to the east and Cordova to the west.

(3) **Interest by Proponents:**

(a) **Moratorium areas:** The Yakutat Forelands Moratorium area, as identified in Senate Bill 346 ("Wirth Bill") and as proposed for wilderness in House Resolution 987 ("Mrazek Bill"), represents approximately one-half of the evaluation area. It is located between

the Dangerous and Alsek Rivers and between the coast and the Brabazon
Range Addition boundary

(b) **Local users/residents:** The nearest community is Yakutat
(population 588), about 30 miles from the roadless area center and to
the west. Basically all use of the area comes from local residents,
except for sports hunting and fishing by fly-in nonresidents   Primary
activities are subsistence hunting and fishing   Set-net commercial
fisheries is a major use of the many river mouths and bays   Fish
camps for commercial fishers are common .

(c) **Concerns of local residents:** The general feelings of the local
residents seem to favor a primitive/semi-primitive designation without
the area becoming a Wilderness Management Area. The reasons revolve
around restrictions associated with the wilderness designation and the
lack of future management options were the area to be allocated to
wilderness.

e. Environmental Consequences

    ALTERNATIVE ANALYSIS TO BE DONE LATER

INDIVIDUAL ROADLESS AREA DESCRIPTION

NAME: Upper Situk (341)   ACRES (GROSS): 62,140   ACRES (NFS): 61,722

GEOZONE: C24
GEOGRAPHIC PROVINCE: Yakutat Forelands

1989 WILDERNESS ATTRIBUTE RATING: 22 .

a. Description

(1) **Relationship to RARE II areas:** The table below displays the VCU 1/
names, VCU numbers, original WARS 2/ rating, and comments. This enables
the reader to compare the roadless areas evaluated in Appendix C with
previous analyses.

VCU Name	VCU No.	1979 WARS Rating	Comments
Black Tit	355C*	25	LUD 1 Nonwilderness VCU primarily in Wilderness Area
Chicago Hbr.	361C*	22	LUD 1 Nonwilderness. VCU part. in Wilderness. Former Native selection
Dank Forest	362C*	21	LUD 1 Nonwilderness. VCU part in Wilderness. Former Native selection
Unnamed	363C*	--	LUD 3. Former Native selection
Old Situk	364C*	21	LUD 4
Lower Russell Fiord	365C*	24	LUD 1 Nonwilderness. VCU primarily in Wilderness area
Situk River	366C*	22	LUD 2. Native selection-tentatively selected, not yet conveyed
Dark Forest	373C*	18	LUD 4
Moser Creek	374C*	23	LUD 1 Nonwilderness VCU primarily in Wilderness Area
Miller Creek	375C*	23	LUD 4
Pike Lakes	376C*	20	LUD 4
Dangerous Rvr	377C*	21	LUD 2
Harlequin Lk	378C*	21	LUD 1 Nonwilderness VCU primarily in Wilderness Area.

*--The roadless area includes only part of this VCU.

(2) **History:** There is evidence of human occupation in Southeast Alaska
from 10,000 to 11,000 years before present. Man's movement into the
Yakutat Forelands is much more recent and is believed to have started about
1000 years ago, with the people coming from the north. Tlingit occupation
from the south began approximately 300 years ago.

1/ A VCU (Value Comparison Unit) is one of 867 watersheds which make up the
forest and were differentiated for planning purposes in the Tongass Land
Management Plan.
2/ Wilderness Attribute Rating System (WARS) was the nation-wide system used
to rate the wilderness attributes of roadless areas in the Roadless Area
Review and Evaluation (RARE II).

European ventures into the area started in the late 18th century, with Russian and English traders. A Russian farming settlement was established in the approximate location of Yakutat in 1796 Hostilities between the Russians and the Native population ended with the total elimination of the settlement in 1805 and resulted in little contact between whites and Indians until about 1874. Activities within or adjacent to the evaluation area since 1874 have included mining, fish canneries, fur farms, manufactured native goods and tourism. Tourism was first developed in the · 1880s to view Mount Saint Elias and the various glaciers. Salmon processing became a major industry, with the first cannery constructed in 1902. Others followed over the next 20 or so years

There was a large military presence, with attending activities, during World War II. More recent activities, within or adjacent to the roadless area, have included commercial logging operations, commercial fishing and outfitter/guide services for sports fishing and hunting

(3) Location and Access: The Upper Situk Roadless Evaluation Area is located on the mainland, east of Yakutat. The area adjoins National Forest System, State and private lands to the southwest, Forest Highway 10 and National Forest Systems lands to the south and the Russell Fiord Wilderness Area to the north. The western boundary is Yakutat Bay, from Eleanor Cove to Humpback Cove. The center of the roadless area is approximately 16 miles east of Yakutat.

There is small boat access, with several anchorages along the coastline of Yakutat Bay. Floatplane landing is possible along the Bay, as well in several lakes in the western portion of the roadless area. Forest Highway 10 goes from Yakutat to the Dangerous River, providing vehicle access to the upper reaches of several rivers, as well as direct access to all of the southern boundary of the Upper Situk. Connecting road systems, serving timber harvest units, provide access to areas immediately adjacent to the roadless area.

(4) Geography and Topography: The Upper Situk is relatively flat over about all of the roadless area, with elevations generally ranging from sealevel to approximately 200 feet. One point reaches about the 1,000 foot elevation. The terrain is characteristic of formerly glaciated topography, i.e., glacial outwash plains with lateral and terminal moraines, separated by low, flat areas with numerous streams and rivers as well as large marshes and muskegs. There are some areas, such as around Pike Lakes, that were unglaciated in the last glacial period; these remnant areas show the characteristics of an old-aged landform with highly developed soil profiles. The rivers and streams are low gradient and follow wandering channels, with wide floodplains.

Relief is such that a major runoff episode may completely change the location of streamcourses and may combine two or more totally divergent streams into one system. Were the Hubbard Glacier, located to the northwest, to close off Russell Fiord, the resulting lake could reach overflow in a short period of time. The headwaters of the Situk River would be the overflow channel, drastically changing the landscape in this area.

The far western portion also contains many lakes, varying in size to over 950 acres (Lake Redfield). There are many other scattered lakes, including the Pike Lakes in the headwaters of the Arhnklin River. The Yakutat Bay beach area is subject to change due to open-water wave activity and ocean storms.

There are _____ miles of shoreline on saltwater and _____ acres of beach Freshwater lakes total 897 acres There are 40 acres of small islands There is no alpine tundra, snow and ice or rock.

(5) Ecosystem:

(a) Classification: The area is classified as being in the Yakutat Forelands geographic province. This province includes from Glacier Bay north to Yakutat Bay and is characterized by recently uplifted beaches and fluvial processes related to icefields, valley glaciers and a cold wet climate. The climate is typical of the coastal maritime zone. Total annual precipitation at Yakutat is 135 inches, with a 33-year snowfall average of 219 inches.

(b) Vegetation: Much of the vegetation, even in the timbered areas, are marsh and muskeg species or willows, cottonwoods and alders on the drier sites. The wetland species are primarily sphgnaum moss, sedges and heathers. The drier, non-timber sites contain low-growing species such as devil's club, salmonberry, blueberry, copper bush, hellebore, ferns, skunk cabbage and huckleberry, over a carpet of mosses and liverworts.

Timbered areas (85 percent of the total unit) contain primarily Sitka spruce and/or western hemlock over the "drained-site" species Timber stands, rated moderate to high (3 to 5 on a, scale of 5) for harvest activities, are found over large areas. Even in heavily timbered areas, the tree species are found on the drier sites on the ridges, separated by marsh or muskeg containing meandering streams Outside of these heavy-timber areas, the majority of the timber is not considered operable, or does not constitute a significant component

Lodgepole pine is found in the Pike Lakes area and is probably at the western edge of its range. Other unique Pike Lakes area plant species are Oregon crabapple, deer cabbage, Labrador tea and mountain hemlock

There are approximately 12,940 acres of forested lands, of which 10,581 acres are classified as commercial forest land (CFL). There are 379 acres classified as riparian old growth and 5,723 acres as nonriparian old growth. Approximately 959 acres are classed as muskeg. Muskeg is interspersed within other types in units too small to map. Therefore, the acreage for muskeg may be substantially understated.

(c) Soils: The majority of the soils for the Upper Situk lowlands are youthful soils of glacio-fluvial and fluvial origin. The base material is variable and consists of igneous, metamorphic and sedimentary rocks. Terrain is generally gently sloping Other features, such as mature soils (unglaciated remnants) occur, but only

to a limited extent   Recent glaciation, and on-going uplift has, and
does, affect soil development. Groundwater over most of the area is
at or near the surface. Large portions of the roadless area are
poorly drained organic soils

(d) Fish Resource: There are the headwaters of two major stream
systems (the Situk and Arhnklin Rivers) in the area which are
identified by the Alaska Department of Fish and Game as important for
producing salmon. There is no estimate for fish production just for
the headwater areas, but total annual production for the two streams
is estimated at more than 80,000 salmon. Five species of Pacific
salmon, valuable for commercial, subsistence and sport use, spawn and
rear in the area. Steelhead and cutthroat trout, stickleback, Dolly
Varden char, and smelt are found in the many lowland rivers and
streams. A unique species, the northern pike, is located in Pike
Lakes; this is the only known population outside of the interior   It
is unknown how they came to be located here. There is some commercial
"set net" fishing along the coast. Sport fishing use is moderate to
light. Commercial fishers and subsistence users utilize fish camps
located along the Bay.

Fish resources have been rated as part of the Tongass Land Management
Plan (1979) and by the Alaska Department of Fish and Game (ADF&C) in
their Forest Habitat Integrity Program (1983). These ratings describe
the value of VCU's for sport fish, commercial fish and estuaries   The
following table lists nine VCU's rated high to very high for
commercial or sport fisheries values.

		Sport	Comm.			Sport	Comm
Dank Forest	362C	X	X	Situk River	366C	X	X
Unnamed	363C	X	X	Dark Forest	373C	X	X
Old Situk	364C	X	X	Moser Creek	374C	X	X
Lower Russell	365C	X	X	Miller Creek	375C	X	X
Fiord				Pike Lakes	376C	X	X

There are three VCU's containing highly valued estuaries· Chicago
Harbor (361C), Situk River (366C) and Lower Russell Fiord (365C)

(e) Wildlife Resource: The Yakutat Forelands area (which includes
the Upper Situk roadless area) support a rich wildlife population,
both in numbers and species diversity. Larger mammal species include
both brown and black bears, moose, wolverines and wolves   There is a
remnant Sitka black-tailed deer population, left from transplant
efforts in the 1940's. The smaller animals include several furbearers
(mink, marten, beaver) and rodents, such as mice and snowshoe hare, as
well as several amphibian species.

There are few resident bird species; however, the area is heavily used
by migratory species, both for nesting and resting and includes
waterfowl, such as the trumpeter swan, and raptors, such as the bald
eagle and peregrine falcon. While not within the boundaries of the
roadless area, humpback and gray whales, seals, sealions, orcas,
dolphins and porpoises can sometimes be seen from the beach areas

Inventoried habitat for black bear, brown bear, pine marten, and red
squirrel total 15,035 acres   Habitat for other management indicator
species include mountain goat (3,781 acres).

(f) **Threatened and Endangered Species:** There are no known Threatened
or Endangered plant or animal species resident to the Upper Situk
area. The peregrine falcon appears as a migratory user. The bald
eagle, a protected species, is found all along the coastal zone and
the larger rivers. There are several special interest plant species
within the roadless area

(6) **Current Use and Management:** There are six VCU's (1,836 acres)
allocated as Land Use Designation (LUD) 1 - Nonwilderness in the Tongass
Land Management Plan (1979). They were originally proposed as part of the
Russell Fiord Wilderness, but were not included in the final designation
There is two VCU's (359 acres) allocated to LUD 2 which provides for
management of the area in an unroaded state to retain the wildland
character.

There is one VCU (1,455 acres) designated as LUD 3, which allows for
management of the land for a variety of uses, with emphasis on managing the
uses and activities in a compatible and complementary manner to provide for
the greatest combination of benefits. This area have a high use or high
amenity value in conjunction with a high commodity value. Four VCU's
(6,224 acres) are allocated to LUD 4, which provides for intensive resource
management and development, consistent with provisions to protect physical
and biological productivity.

Other than fisheries habitat enhancement, few Forest Service management
activities have occurred within the roadless area. Habitat improvement
projects for moose and fisheries are planned for the 1989 field season
There is one maintained trail.

Additional uses include sport fishing and hunting, subsistence fishing,
hunting and trapping, and commercial fishing. Outfitting and guide service
is a major business in the Yakutat area. Although oil and gas exploration
has been done in the recent past, such activities are not occurring at
present. There are several cabins and camps under special use permit
associated with fish, outfitter/guide or subsistence camps   There is some
woodgathering primarily along the southern boundary around the harvest
areas and around cabin/camp areas. Logging and road construction
activities have occurred on the western and southern boundaries.

(7) **Appearance (Apparent Naturalness):**   The Upper Situk area itself
generally appears unmodified. Exceptions within the area are evidence of
former oil and gas exploration sites and the various cabins/camps. The
inland sites generally are not obtrusive, except at short range. The
coastal sites are more visible. Sites used in the past are mostly
reclaimed by vegetation. Most of the activity was, and is, located along
the coast.

Rock pits, used during road construction, are located in several sites
along Forest Highway 10, and are often served by short access roads These
are included in the evaluation area, but can be easily excluded Several
have been modified for fisheries habitat

All-terrain vehicle (ATV) use is highly evident along the beaches, river
bottoms, muskegs and upland trails. This activity does affect the apparent
naturalness from close range, the overall impact will rate moderate

Harvest activity is visible along the southwestern and southern boundaries
especially in the intrusion areas. However, because of terrain, the
logging is not visible from a distance and does not affect the vast
majority of the roadless area. There is little timber over approximately
15 percent of the area; most of the vegetation consists of groundcover or
low-growing shrubs and short trees. The areas covered by timber (85
percent) contain stands with size classes from seedling/saplings to large
mature/overmature trees. The heavily timbered areas are primarily in the
middle one-half of the evaluation area.

The visual character type for the evaluation area is the Cordova-Yakutat,
consisting of a coastal plain marked by longitudinal beach and dune ridges,
crossed by outwash plains and moraines, and backed by marine ridges to
several hundred feet in height. The area is characterized by a great
variety of water forms, including glacial streams, meandering lowland
streams and small lakes The ocean surf is a key water form The area
just to the north of the evaluation area lies in the Coast Range visual
character type, forming a strongly contrasting land form. The view
distance over much of the area is relatively short because of the flat,
rolling terrain combined with dense vegetation

The evaluation area is inventoried as 37 percent Variety Class A
(Distinctive), 16 percent Variety Class B (Common) and 47 percent Variety
Class C (Minimal). The majority of the area (97 percent) is inventoried as
an Existing Visual Condition (EVC) I, which appears untouched by human
activity. The balance of the area is generally inventoried as an EVC II (2
percent), or areas in which changes to the landscape are not noticed by the
average visitor and an EVC IV (1 percent), or areas in which changes in the
landscape are easily noticed by the average visitor, and may attract some
attention.

(8) Surroundings (External Influences): The area to the southwest and
south of the Upper Situk area has been highly modified by logging and
development. There has been, and currently is, logging in the western and
southern portion of the lowlands, adjacent to the roadless area
boundaries. Intrusions into the roadless area (but excluded from it) are
timber harvest areas, primarily associated with a blowdown episode in
1981. Forest Highway 10 runs along the entire southern boundary

The Yakutat airport is not far removed from the roadless area; therefore
users in the western portion of the area may be subjected to some noise
from the airport. There are commercial flights over the coast, to the
south. Most of the activities outside the roadless area are not visually
apparent to users because of the terrain/vegetation features; however,
traffic noise on Forest Highway 10 is audible for some distance into the

roadless area   There is some water-borne activity in the coastal waters,
however, there is no disturbance from these activities.

The Russell Fiord Wilderness Area is located adjacent to the Upper Situk
Roadless Area on the north, and the Yakutat Forelands (#339) Roadless
Evaluation Area is located to the south of Forest Highway 10.

(9) **Attractions and Features of Special Interest:** Attractions of the area
include wildlife viewing, sports hunting and fishing, and camping in
association with other activities. The numerous small lakes and streams
provide a variety of fishing sites   There are small boat anchorages at
various places along the coast

The area contains four inventoried recreation places which contain 6,140
acres. There is one trail, located along the Situk River, north from
Forest Highway 10.

b. **Capability of Management as Wilderness or in an Unroaded Condition**

(1) **Manageability and Management Area Boundaries:** The roadless area is a
long, very narrow strip, approximately 25 miles long and averaging less
than two miles in width (range is from a few hundred feet to more than five
miles). Only the southern and western boundaries are defined by a physical
boundary, i.e., Forest Highway 10 and Yakutat Bay. The intrusions of
timber harvest areas are defined by the treatment unit boundaries. The
entire northern boundary is the Russell Fiord Wilderness boundary, which is
legally described, but not tied to readily identified physical points   The
southwestern boundary abuts private lands, roads or development   The
presence of roads and/or private lands to the west may reduce the
manageability of the area. While the wilderness character of the
evaluation area may be questioned, if it were left in an unroaded
management condition (primitive unroaded, wilderness management, et
cetera), it would compliment the Russell Fiord Wilderness Area

(2) **Natural Integrity:** The area is basically unmodified. There is
modification in the form of cabins and camps; they are widely scattered and
are fairly unobtrusive. The western portion of the area has received heavy
off-road vehicle use, particularly in the muskegs. They are visually
apparent from the air, but are much less so from ground level   The entire
southern boundary has been highly modified by logging and road
construction. Past modification within the area has included fur farms and
and oil/gas exploration sites. These are evident to most on-site
observers.

(3) **Opportunity for Solitude:** The opportunity for solitude is high over
much of the Upper Situk, because of the proximity of the Russell Fiord
Wilderness. The area is relatively easy to access, has a moderate degree
of visitor use and is relatively close to various activities, including
timber harvest on private and National Forest lands and traffic on Forest
Highway 10. These are the locations people tend to concentrate   There
will be some disruption by overhead flights of small aircraft, combined
with some powerboat use along the coast. However, Lake Redfield, Pike
Lakes and other locations distant from the concentrated use areas are
relatively isolated and give an opportunity for solitude

(4) **Opportunity for Primitive Recreation:** The area provides primarily semi-primitive motorized and semi-primitive non-motorized opportunities It is evident that both offroad and highway vehicles use the area The following are as inventoried with the Recreation Opportunity Spectrum (ROS) system

ROS Class	Acres
Primitive I (P1)	100
Primitive II (P2)	20
Roaded Natural (RN)	620
Roaded Modified (RM)	80
Semi-Primitive Non-Motorized (SPNM)	8,138
Semi-Primitive Motorized (SPM)	5,559
No ROS	518

The area contains four recreation places, totalling 6,140 acres

ROS CLASS	# OF REC. PLACES	TOTAL ACRES	CAPACITY BY RVD
RN	1	540	1,680
RM	1	80	13,918
SPM	2	5,520	18,459

(5) **Special Features (Ecologic, Geologic, Scientific, Cultural):** The Pike Lakes area is of ecological and geological interest because of the unique plant associations, fish species and residual soils/geologic features The area ranges from a constantly changing, uplifting coastal area to a remnant area untouched by the last glacial period to a young, developing ecosystem on immature or undeveloped soils. The presence of wildlife species such as eagles, brown bears, black bears (including the glacier bear color phase), moose and the many different migratory bird species provide for wildlife observation. The coastline provides for beachcombing opportunities

c. **Availability for Management as Wilderness or in an Unroaded Condition**

(1) **Resource Potentials**

(a) **Recreation Potential:** Recreation potential includes the opportunity for trail corridors along several of the rivers and accessing several lakes. Trailheads could easily be accessed from the coast or from the road system to the south. Sport fishing and hunting are popular in the area; moose hunting and steelhead fishing are major activities. The limited terrain features in the lowlands probably would not generate much interest unto themselves.

There are no identified recreation facilities development planned in the Tongass Land Management Plan, as amended in 1985-86 (TLMP)

(b) **Fish Resource:** Fish management activities probably would increase production of salmonids within the evaluation area, however there are no estimates for increases. Past management activities have been aimed at downstream habitat improvement Much of the current management emphasis centers around mitigation associated with the

possible overflow of Lake Russell. There are numerous fisheries
research projects in progress on the Situk River. The objectives of
this research are to recommend enhancement and mitigation projects on
the Yakutat Forelands. Projects identified in TLMP include stream
habitat improvement project in one VCU and non-stream habitat projects
in five VCU's.

(c) **Wildlife Resource:** There is potential for improvement of moose
habitat with increases in numbers and survival There are no habitat
improvement activities currently underway; research plots are planned
for adjoining areas in the future. The Tongass Land Management Plan,
as amended, identified habitat improvement projects for moose in one
VCU.

(d) **Timber Resource:** There are 8,561 acres inventoried as
tentatively suitable for harvest. This includes 339 acres of riparian
old growth and 5,264 acres of nonriparian old growth. The potential
for timber management in the Upper Situk Roadless Area is high for
those areas containing operable timber stands. Present market
situations make the timber inoperable, because of export
restrictions. However, were the market to strengthen, the situation
could change. The existing road system combined with the flat terrain
makes access relatively simple. While marsh and muskeg areas restrict
road construction, it is not prohibitive. Most of the operable timber
stands are located in VCU's 364C, 366C, 373C and 375C. These stands
are generally mature/overmature and a high volume per acre.

(e) **Land Use Authorizations:** There are ten special use permits for
fish and subsistence camps and outfitter/guide activities. The
potential for increase in permit applications is moderate The
proximity to Yakutat and good access via the existing road system
makes the area popular for hunting. The probable increase in
applications would be in requests for facilities associated with
subsistence and outfitter/guide activities.

(f) **Minerals:** The opportunity for mineral development appears low
There are no known deposits of minerals suitable for development. Oil
and gas exploration has occurred - the potential for development
appears to be high. The entire Forelands have been identified by the
U.S.D.I., Geologic Survey as a "Most Favorable Petroleum Reserve
Area". However, development activities have not been initiated

(g) **Areas of Scientific Interest:** There are two inventoried
potential Research Natural Area, located at Pike Lakes and Mountain
Lake.

(2) **Management Considerations**

(a) **Fire:** The area has no significant fire history.

(b) Insects and Disease: There are no epidemic insect or disease conditions. However, storm blowdown is historically significant Blowdown is followed by widespread, very rapid buildup by the striped ambrosia beetle These attacks cause rapid deterioration (value loss) in the downed timber In addition, the-old growth stands are highly susceptible to mortality from rots and windthrow

(c) Land Status: There are no non-National Forest System lands located with in the roadless area. Lands along the Situk River have tentatively selected by Sealaska, the regional Native Corporation, however, the transfer of property rights has not occurred. Until such time as the transfer has taken place or has be dropped, land is restricted.

d. Relationship to Communities and Other Roadless and Wilderness Areas

(1) Nearby Roadless and Wilderness Areas and Uses: The Russell Fiord Wilderness forms the northern boundary of the Upper Situk area. The Yakutat Forelands (#339) Roadless Evaluation Area lies to the south, across Forest Highway 10. The Brabazon Addition (#338), another roadless evaluation area, is located five miles to the east and north, east of the Wilderness.

(2) Distance From Population Centers (Accessibility): Approximate distances from population centers are as follows.

Community		Air Miles	Water Miles
Juneau	(Pop. 23,729)	180	290
Sitka	(Pop. 8,041)	190	260
Cordova	(Pop 1,900)	230	250
Anchorage	(Pop. 235,000)	390	680

Yakutat has twice-daily commercial air service, both north- and southbound. There is no ferry service; the closest Alaska Marine Highway terminals at Hoonah to the east and Cordova to the west.

(3) Interest by Proponents:

(a) Moratorium areas: The Upper Situk Evaluation Area is not within any moratorium area, nor is it proposed for wilderness management

(b) Local users/residents: The nearest community is Yakutat (population 588), about 16 miles to the southwest. Basically all use of the area comes from local residents, except for some sports hunting and fishing by fly-in nonresidents. Primary activities are subsistence hunting and fishing.

(c) Concerns of local residents: The general feelings of the local residents seem to favor a primitive/semi-primitive designation for the area, without it becoming a Wilderness Management Area. The reasons revolve around restrictions associated with the wilderness designation and the lack of future management options, were the area to be allocated to wilderness.

e. Environmental Consequences

   ALTERNATIVE ANALYSIS TO BE DONE LATER

INDIVIDUAL ROADLESS AREA DESCRIPTION

NAME: Dall (501)   ACRES (GROSS): 137,329   ACRES (NFS): 108,260

GEOZONE: K09
GEOGRAPHIC PROVINCE: Southern Outer Islands

1989 WILDERNESS ATTRIBUTE RATING: 22

a. Description

(1) Relationship to RARE II areas: The table below displays the VCU 1/ names, VCU numbers, acres, original WARS 2/ rating, and comments This enables the reader to compare the roadless areas evaluated in Appendix C with previous analyses.

VCU Name	VCU No.	1979 WARS Rating	Comments
Meares	637	22	
Tlevak	638	22	
Bobs Bay	639	22	
Divers Bay	640	22	
Foul Bay	641	21	
Manhatten	642	23	
Sakle	643	22	
	644		Not rated
Cold Harbor	645	23	
Devil Lake	646	23	
Welcome	647	22	
Waterfall Bay	648	22	
	649		Not rated
Rose Inlet	650	22	
Gold Harbor	651	22	
Gooseneck	653	22	
Grace Harbor	654	22	
Ritter Point	655	22·	
	656		Not rated
	659		Not rated
Pond Bay	660	22	
Security Cove	661	22	
Kolgani	662	22	
Datzkoo	663	23	
Liscome Bay	664	20	
Wolk	665	22	
Mcleod Bay	666	22	
Cape Muzon	667	21	
Kolangles	668	22	
Stripe Mountain	866	23	

1/ A VCU (Value Comparison Unit) is one of 867 watersheds which make up the forest and were differentiated for planning purposes in the Tongass Land Management Plan.

2/ Wilderness Attribute Rating System (WARS) was the nationwide system used to rate the wilderness attributes of roadless areas in the Roadless Area Review and Evaluation (RARE II).

(2) **History:** Dall Island has a significant history in the Native
culture   Native cultures are known to have occupied sites on Dall Island
for two to three thousand years   Because of this history, large blocks
have been selected by the Native Corporations as part of their land
entitlement, and several traditional use sites have been selected

In recent history, the bays and harbors on the sheltered east side of the
island have served the commercial fishing industry as fish buying stations,
canneries, salteries, and anchorages.

There is one recreation use cabin located on the southern part of the
island.

(3) **Location and Access:** Dall Island is the largest island off the west
coast of the Prince of Wales Island. The northern tip of the island is
about 20 miles southwest of Craig. The island is about 50 miles long from
northern to southern tip. Access is by boat and floatplane

(4) **Geography and Topography:** The area is characterized by rugged
mountains, an irregular coast with many bays and inlets, numerous short
drainages, and a few freshwater lakes. The maximum elevation is 3,200 feet
with a significant amount of alpine vegetation above 2,000 feet. There are
232 miles of shoreline on saltwater. The Dall Island Roadless Area also
includes a number of small islands located off its coast and within its
bays and inlets.

.(5) **Ecosystem:**

   (a) **Classification:** This area is classified as being in the Southern
   Outer Island Geographic Province. The Southern Island Geographic
   Province is generally characterized as having rolling subdued to
   localized rugged topography.

   (b) **Vegetation:** Vegetation is typical Southeast Alaska coastal
   temperate rain forest. The forest is primarily western hemlock and
   Sitka spruce with a large cedar component. There are 1,737 acres of
   muskeg and 2,715 acres of alpine vegetation.

   There are approximately 94,551 acres of forested land of which 64,055
   acres are commercial forest land. Of the commercial forest land,
   53,225 acres are non-riparian old growth and 3,953 acres are riparian
   old growth.

   (c) **Soils:** These highly organic, low clay content soils are
   generally formed over bedrock. Soil depths are up to 40 inches

   (d) **Fish Resource:** Fish resources have been rated as part of the
   Tongass Land Management Plan (1979) and by the Alaska Department of
   Fish and Game in its Forest Habitat Integrity Program (1983)   These
   ratings describe the value of VCU's for sport fish, commercial fish
   and estuaries

Of the 30 VCU's comprising this roadless area 20 are rated as high value for sport fish. VCU's 643, 645, 655, 659, 661, 666, and 668 are rated high for estuary value.

(e) **Wildlife Resource:** Dall Island has large populations of Sitka black-tailed deer and black bear, otter, beaver, and other small land mammals. Sea birds and mammals are prevalent on the outside coast, islands, and rocks. An occasional puffin can be seen.

(f) **Threatened and Endangered Species:** None.

(6) **Current Use and Management:** About 95,913 acres were allocated to Land Use Designation 4 (LUD 4)in the Tongass Land Management Plan The LUD 4 area is to be managed for its commodity and market values. Small areas on the southern tip of Dall Island was allocated to LUD 2 (9,406 acres) and LUD 3 (2,883 acres). The LUD 2 area is to be managed in the roadless condition, and the LUD 3 area for mix of amenity and commodity values

There has been little active management of the land area. One recreation use cabin is located on the southern part of Dall Island. A few local residents travel to the east side of the island and hike overland to the beaches on the outer coast.

Subsistence use takes place on Dall Island.

(7) **Appearance (Apparent Naturalness):** The Dall Island Roadless Area is part of the Coastal Hills character type which is characterized by rolling to moderately steep terrain, with predominantly rounded summits, and elevations up to 4,000 feet. Dall Island is, for the most part, very representative of this character type, except for the extremely rugged coastline and terrain along portions of the outer coast

About 35 percent of this area is inventoried as Variety Class A (a high degree of landscape diversity relative to its character type) These Variety Class A landscapes are generally on the outer coast and include primarily the rugged headlands and rockforms found all along this coast

All of the National Forest lands in this area are rated as Type I Existing Visual Condition where the landscape has remained unaltered by human activity, though the Native lands adjacent to this roadless area (generally on the eastern half of Dall Island) have begun to be intensively roaded and logged.

(8) **Surroundings (External Influences):** Some portions of the roadless area provide views of intensively managed timber stands or Native lands on the east side of Dall Island.

(9) **Attractions and Features of Special Interest:** The natural features of the area, the scenery, the saltwater bays and inlets, and the opportunity to see wildlife and to study the processes which formed this country may all be attractions. The spectacular cliffs with sea caves and the beaches on the outer coast are of special interest. The area contains 13 inventoried recreation places totaling 38,800 acres

b. Capability of Management as Wilderness or in an Unroaded Condition

   (1) **Manageability and Management Area Boundaries:** The area is well
   defined by saltwater and adjacent Native owned lands are surveyed. There
   appears to be nothing that would prevent management of this area in the
   roadless condition The large amount of private land on the east side of
   Dall Island could reduce the wilderness experience level for small parts of
   the area.

   (2) **Natural Integrity:** The natural integrity of this area is rather good
   except for the large blocks of Native-owned land on the east boundary tend
   to fractionalize the east side of this roadless area.

   (3) **Opportunity for Solitude:** There is excellent opportunity for solitude
   within this roadless area with the possible exception of that area adjacent
   to the Native lands. In much of the roadless area people are unlikely to
   encounter others for the duration of their visit. The outer coast provides
   the opportunity for exceptional solitude on an ocean beach environment.

   (4) Opportunity for Primitive Recreation:

ROS class	Acres
Primitive I (P1)	76,763
Primitive II (P2)	24,630
Semi-Primitive Non-Motorized (SPNM)	4,850
Roaded Modified (RM)	778

ROS CLASS	# OF REC. PLACES	TOTAL ACRES	CAPACITY BY RVDS
P1	6	23,433	6,630
P2	6	15,108	9,100
RM	1	259	740

   (5) **Special Features (Ecologic, Geologic, Scientific, Cultural):** The
   high-energy outer coastline is a special feature. Along this coast there
   are several sea caves with evidence of ancient Native occupancy or use
   Also of interest are the rugged headlands and cliffs that face the ocean,
   particularly along the southern coast of this island.

c. Availability for Management as Wilderness or in an Unroaded Condition

   (1) Resource Potentials

      (a) **Recreation Potential:** This area has excellent potential for
      development of interesting cross-island trails. The only realistic
      way for most visitors to get to and use the outer coast beaches is to
      hike cross-country from east side bays and anchorages. Currently,
      there are no established trails to serve this purpose. There are
      excellent sites for Forest Service Public Use Cabins in the major bays
      on the outside coast. With careful planning, there may be
      opportunities to interpret cultural resources on Dall Island

(b) **Fish Resource:** The recently completed fish habitat inventory of Dall Island indicates that there is excellent opportunity to improve the quality and availability of salmon spawning habitat on a number of streams; although, no projects are planned at this time

(c) **Wildlife Resource:** There are no indications that habitat is deficient for any of the species living within this roadless area   No wildlife habitat improvement or population enhancement projects are planned.

(d) **Timber Resource**   There are 51,578 acres inventoried as tentatively suitable for harvest. This includes 3,953 acres of riparian old growth and 46,486 acres of non-riparian old growth

(e) **Land Use Authorizations:** There is one special use permit for a short powerline on the northeast corner of Dall Island.

(f) **Minerals:** There is some potential for mineral activity   There are several located mining claims on the south and southcentral part of Dall Island   None of these claims are currently in a development or production mode.

(g) **Areas of Scientific Interest:** None.

(2) **Management Considerations**

(a) Dall Island's west coast is exposed to the open ocean   This high-energy coast is not suitable for boat or floatplane access Natives have acquired almost all land surrounding good anchorages along the east coast   Ownership patterns and very rough topography complicate potential access for timber cutting, recreation facility construction, and other management activities.

(b) **Fire:** The area has no significant fire history

(c) **Insects and Disease:** Endemic tree diseases common to Southeast Alaska are present.

(d) **Land Status:** All of this roadless area is National Forest System land. There are no Native or State land selections pending within the area.

d. **Relationship To Communities and Other Roadless and Wilderness Areas**

(1) **Nearby Roadless and Wilderness Areas and Uses:** This roadless area is separated from nearby roadless areas by saltwater.

(2) **Distance From Population Centers (accessibility):** Approximate distances from population centers are as follows:

Community		Air Miles	Water Miles
Juneau	(Pop. 23,729)	.190	220
Ketchikan	(Pop. 12,705)	45	90
Craig	(Pop. 915)	18	30
Hydaburg	(Pop. 385)	15	20

Hollis, located on Prince of Wales Island, is the nearest stop on the
Alaska Marine Highway.

(3) Interest by Proponents:

(a) **Moratorium Areas:** The area has not been identified as a
"moratorium" area or proposed as Wilderness in legislative initiatives
to date.

(b) **Local Users/residents:** The area receives local use for
subsistence activities. Local residents travel to Dall Island and
hike overland to the west coast beaches for recreation purposes

e. Environmental Consequences

INDIVIDUAL ROADLESS AREA DESCRIPTION

NAME: Suemez (502)   ACRES (GROSS): 37,164   ACRES (NFS): 36,327 .

GEOZONE: K09
GEOGRAPHIC PROVINCE: Southern Outer Islands

1989 WILDERNESS ATTRIBUTE RATING: 18

a. Description

(1) **Relationship to RARE II areas:** The table below displays the VCU 1/
names, VCU numbers, acres, original WARS 2/ rating, and comments This
enables the reader to compare the roadless areas evaluated in Appendix C
with previous analyses.

VCU Name	VCU No.	1979 WARS Rating	Comments
Cabras	633	23	
Santa Cruz	634	23	
Port Rufugio	635	24	
Arena Cove	636	22	
Meares	637	22	

(2) **History:** Suemez Islands' history evolves around use by Native
cultures, early 1900 commercial fisheries and, in recent years, timber
harvest. The State has selected one parcel of land in the Port Delores
area.

Forest Service activity on the island has been confined to timber
management.

(3) **Location and Access:** Suemez Island is located off the west coast of
the Prince of Wales Island and about 15 miles southwest of Craig Access
is by boat and floatplane.

(4) **Geography and Topography:** The island is characterized by rugged
mountains around the coast and moderate to flat topography in its center
The highest elevation is 2,100 feet The 59 miles of saltwater shoreline
is very irregular, rugged, and includes several large bays

1/ A VCU (Value Comparison Unit) is one of 867 watersheds which make up the
forest and were differentiated for planning purposes in the Tongass Land
Management Plan.
2/ Wilderness Attribute Rating System (WARS) was the nationwide system used to
rate the wilderness attributes of roadless areas in the Roadless Area
Review and Evaluation (RARE II).

(5) Ecosystem:

(a) Classification: The area is in the Southern Outer Islands
geographic province   This province is characterized by rolling
subdued and localized rugged topography

(b) Vegetation: Vegetation is typical Southeast Alaska coastal
temperate rain forest. The forest is primarily western hemlock and
Sitka spruce with large components of cedar.

There are approximately 35,323 acres of forested land of which 22,105
acres are commercial forest land. Of the commercial forest land,
17,224 acres are non-riparian old growth and 3,879 are riparian old
growth.

(c) Soils: These highly organic, low clay content soils are
generally formed over bedrock and are typically about 40 inches deep

(d) Fish Resource: Fish resources have been rated as part of the
Tongass Land Management Plan (1979) and by the Alaska Department of
Fish and Game in its Forest Habitat Integrity Program (1983)   These
ratings describe the value of sport fish, commercial fish, and
estuaries.

VCU 635 rated as high value for commercial fish.

(e) Wildlife Resource: This area has populations of Sitka
black-tailed deer and black bear. There are small populations of
small mammals and land birds. Along the coast there are large numbers
of sea birds and a few sea mammals. The high cliffs may provide nest
sites for falcons.

(f) Threatened and Endangered Species: None.

(6) Current Use and Management: The Tongass Land Management Plan
allocated this area to Land Use Designation (LUD) 4. The LUD 4 areas are
to be managed for their commodity and market values. However, the Suemez
Island Management Plan does recognize and protect, to a great degree, the
recreation and scenic values of the Arena Cove and Cape Felix areas

The east-central part of the island has been harvested as part of an
independent timber sale. Currently, two independent timber sales are being
prepared for the east-central part of the island.

Some dispersed recreation occurs on the island, primarily deer and bear
hunting. There are no developed recreation facilities on the island and
none are planned at this time, though there has been much discussion of a
trail linking Port Refugio to the Arena Cove area.

Some subsistence use is occurring on Suemez Island.

(7) **Appearance (Apparent Naturalness):** This area is part of the Coastal Hills character type which is characterized by moderately steep landforms, predominantly rounded summits, elevations to 4,500 feet, and flat-floored, U-shaped valleys. Numerous island groups are common in this character type. This island, with its elevations over 2,000 feet, is very representative of this character type

Eighteen percent of this roadless area is inventoried as a Variety Class A (possessing landscape diversity unique for the character type) The outstanding scenic features are primarily along the southern coast of the island from Arena Cove to the Cape Felix area This coast exhibits a wide variety of unique scenic features, including long, broad sand beaches, diverse rocky beaches and coves, volcanic rock forms, and unique intertidal rock forms and other beach features. The rest of the area is inventoried as a Variety Class B (possessing landscape features common to the character type)

Almost the entire area is in a Type I Existing Visual Condition (where the natural landscape has remained unaltered by human activity) A small portion of the Port Refuge area is in a Type IV visual condition (where recent timber harvest has resulted in changes to the natural landscape that are easily noticeable to observers but tend to blend in with natural landscape features).

(8) **Surroundings (External Influences):** The timber harvest in the Port Rufugio area reduces the natural appearance of a small part of the island. Future logging will amplify this effect. It is probable that a small community or recreation residences will be developed on the State land located in Port Delores.

Waterfall, a world class fishing resort, is located across Ulloa Channel east of Port Rufugio

(9) **Attractions and Features of Special Interest:** The natural features of the area, the scenery, the saltwater bays and inlets, and the opportunity to see wildlife and to study the processes which formed this country may all be attractions. The spectacular cliffs with sea caves and volcanic formations on the south and west coast are of special interest, as are the long and wide sand beaches rimming Arena Cove The area contains six inventoried recreation places containing 7,068 acres.

b. **Capability of Management as Wilderness or in an Unroaded Condition**

(1) **Manageability and Management Area Boundaries:** The Pacific Ocean or large, open saltwater channels make up the southern, western and northern boundaries of this area, making these boundaries easy to manage. The eastern boundary of the roadless area is an irregularly shaped roaded and logged area. This boundary will be more difficult to manage because it crosses relatively flat terrain with no identifiable ridge lines or other natural boundary features.

(2) **Natural Integrity:** The natural integrity is limited because the existing timber harvest area extends into the center of the island causing the roadless area to be somewhat disjointed

(3) Opportunity for Solitude: When there is no logging occurring on the island, the opportunity for solitude within this roadless area is very good. Almost all of the hunting on the island occurs in the logged area Persons camped within the roadless area are unlikely to encounter other individuals during their stay.

(4) Opportunity for Primitive Recreation: Due to the coastal recreation attractions and the remoteness of the Island's outer coast, there are outstanding opportunities for primitive recreation.

ROS Class	Acres
Primitive I (PI)	9,305
Semi-Primitive Non-Motorized (SPNM)	17,043
Semi-Primitive Motorized (SPM)	2,138
Roaded Modified (RM)	7,568

The area contains six inventoried recreation places.

ROS CLASS	# OF REC. PLACES	TOTAL ACRES	CAPACITY BY RVD'S
PI	1	2,798	2,340
SPNM	2	1,907	1,950
SPM	1	658	4,826
RM	2	1,705	3,120

(5) Special Features (Ecologic, Geologic, Scientific, Cultural): The high coastal cliffs, including unique volcanic rock formations on the south and west sides, are of special interest. These cliffs have a number of sea caves that add to the interest.

c. Availability for Management as Wilderness or in an Unroaded Condition

(1) Resource Potentials

(a) Recreation Potential: Excellent potential exists for development of trails from the road system in Port Refugio to the Arena Cove beaches and the Cape Felix area. There are also identified recreation cabin or shelter sites in the Arena Cove area. Most of the present recreation use in the vicinity of this island is confined to offshore salmon fishing and crabbing in the bays.

(b) Fish Resource: The recently completed fish habitat inventory indicates some potential for habitat improvement for salmon.

(c) Wildlife Resource: The area is very good habitat for deer and bear. There are no plans for specific habitat improvement projects for these or other species of wildlife.

(d) Timber Resource: There are 20,663 acres inventoried as tentatively suitable for harvest. This includes 15,901 acres of non-riparian old growth and 3,953 acres of riparian old growth

(e) Land Use Authorizations: None.

    (f) **Minerals:** Mineral development potential is very low

    (g) **Areas of Scientific Interest:** None

(2) **Management Considerations**

    (a) The management emphasis for this area has been for timber management, except that the recreation, scenic and geologic values of the Arena Cove-Cape Felix area have been recognized by protecting the semi-primitive to primitive recreation experience in those areas Timber sales are being planned for the rest of the island

    (b) **Fire:** The area has no significant fire history

    (c) **Insects and Disease:** Endemic tree diseases common to Southeast Alaska are present.

    (d) **Land Status:** The State has made one small land selection in the Port Delores area. There are no private inholdings

d. **Relationship To Communities and Other Roadless and Wilderness Areas**

(1) **Nearby Roadless and Wilderness Areas and Uses:** This roadless area is separated from Dall Island and Outer Islands Roadless Areas by saltwater

(2) **Distance From Population Centers (accessibility):** Approximate distances from population centers are as follows.

Community		Air Miles	Water Miles
Juneau	(Pop. 23,729)	190	220
Ketchikan	(Pop. 12,705)	35	90
Craig	(Pop. 915)	15	18
Klawock	(Pop. 777)	20	24

Hollis, located on Prince of Wales Island, is the nearest stop on the Alaska Marine Highway.

(3) **Interest by Proponents:**

    (a) **Moratorium Areas:** The area has not been identified as a "moratorium" area or proposed as Wilderness in legislative initiatives to date.

    (b) **Local Users/residents:** The area receives some local use for subsistence and recreation activity.

e. **Environmental Consequences**

INDIVIDUAL ROADLESS AREA DESCRIPTION

NAME: Outer Islands (503)   ACRES (GROSS): 103,121   ACRES (NFS): 102,881

GEOZONE: K10
GEOGRAPHIC PROVINCE: Southern Outer Islands

1989 WILDERNESS ATTRIBUTE RATING: 24

a. Description

   (1) **Relationship to RARE II areas:** The table below displays the VCU 1/
   names, VCU numbers, acres, original WARS 2/ rating, and comments   This
   enables the reader to compare the roadless areas evaluated in Appendix C
   with previous analyses.

| | | 1979 | |
VCU Name	VCU No.	WARS Rating	Comments
Noyes	567	22	
Lulu	568	25	
Baker	569	25	
Palisade	626	23	
Point Pololano	627	22	
Point Amargura	628	23	
	629		Not Rated

   (2) **History:** The Outer Island group consists of six major of islands
   Lulu, Noyes, Baker, San Fernando, St Ignace, San Juan Bautista, and
   numerous smaller islands off the west coast of Prince of Wales Island   The
   area derives its Spanish place names from Spanish explorations which
   reached this area in the early 19th century, although no permanent
   settlements were established. The six major islands range in size from
   5,800 to 33,000 acres. The area has a significant history relating to the
   early day commercial fishing industry. These islands are located next to
   the major offshore salmon fishing grounds in Southeast Alaska. Noyes
   Island was a site for fish canneries and salteries. All islands served as
   shelters and anchorages for the offshore fishing fleet. Currently, these
   bays and anchorages are used by the floating fish-buying barges and the
   fishing fleet.

   These islands have a significant place in the history of the Alaskan Native
   culture. The Outer Islands are known traditional-use sites for the ancient
   and historic Native cultures. Accordingly, the Natives have selected
   traditional-use sites on the northern and southern ends of Noyes Island,
   and on San Juan Bautista Island.

1/ A VCU (Value Comparison Unit) is one of 867 watersheds which make up the
    forest and were differentiated for planning purposes in the Tongass Land
    Management Plan.
2/ Wilderness Attribute Rating System (WARS) was the nationwide system used to
    rate the wilderness attributes of roadless areas in the Roadless Area
    Review and Evaluation (RARE II).

(3) **Location and Access:** The Outer Island group is located five to ten miles west of Craig. Access is by boat and floatplane

(4) **Geography and Topography:** Noyes, Baker, and San Juan Bautista Islands are very rugged with elevations to 2,000 feet. This ruggedness extends from the water's edge to the mountaintops. San Fernando and Lulu Islands are characterized by moderate to flat terrain. There are 503 miles of shoreline on saltwater, 884 acres of alpine, and 341 acres of rock

The coastline of these islands varies, and ranges from highly irregular for Baker and Noyes Islands to smooth for San Juan Bautista and Lulu Islands The west coast of Noyes Island is noted for its high-energy coastline and its towering cliffs and headlands.

(5) **Ecosystem:**

(a) **Classification:** The islands are located in the Southern Outer Island Geographic Province. The major islands have gentle rolling topography with localized areas of rugged terrain.

(b) **Vegetation:** This area is typical Southeast Alaska coastal temperate rain forest. The forest is primarily western hemlock and Sitka spruce with a large cedar component. There are 722 acres of muskeg.

There are approximately 99,396 acres of forested land, of which 55,221 acres are commercial forest land. Of the commercial forest land, 49,390 acres are non-riparian old growth and 5,038 are riparian old growth.

(c) **Soils:** Soils are highly organic with a low clay content and are generally formed over bedrock. They are typically about 40 inches deep.

(d) **Fish Resource:** Fish resources have been rated as part of the Tongass Land Management Plan (1979) and the Alaska Department of Fish and Game in its Forest Habitat Integrity Program (1983) These ratings describe the value of these VCU's for sport fish, commercial fish, and estuaries

VCU 626 rated as high value for estuary habitat. No VCU's were rated highly either for commerical or sport fish.

(e) **Wildlife Resource:** All of the islands have populations of Sitka black-tailed deer, black bear, otter, beaver and other small land mammals. Sea birds and mammals are prevalent on the outside coast, islands and rocks. Puffins frequent the west coast and offshore rocks of Noyes Island.

(f) **Threatened and Endangered Species:** None

(6) **Current Use and Management:** All these islands were allocated to Land Use Designation (LUD) 4 in the Tongass Land Management Plan The LUD 4 area is to be managed for its commodity and market values

Preplanning has occurred for timber sales on Noyes Island but, for a
variety of reasons, these plans have never been executed. There is one
recreation use cabin located on San Fernando Island.

The commercial fishing fleet is the largest user of the island group
Boats and the floating fish-buying stations anchor in the major bays and
anchorages.

The inside waters around this island group are excellent for sport salmon
and halibut fishing. This attracts both tourists and local residents to
the island area. These people occasionally go ashore on the islands for
shore-based recreation such as beachcombing. Some deer and bear hunting
also takes place on the islands.

(7) **Appearance (Apparent Naturalness):** The Noyes and Baker Islands
portion of this roadless area is part of the Coastal Hills character type
which is characterized by moderately steep landforms, predominantly rounded
summits, elevations ranging up to 3,000 to 4,500 feet, and flat-floored
U-shaped valleys. Numerous island groups are also common. These two
islands are very representative of this character type with their steep
slopes and many short U-shaped valleys. The other islands are part of the
Kupreanof Lowlands character type which is characterized by lower and more
rolling relief with elevations seldom greater than 1,500 feet. Lulu and
San Fernando Islands possess terrain that is generally flatter than the
character type's norm.

About 11 percent of this area is inventoried as Variety Class A (possessing
landscape diversity that is unique for the character type) These landscapes
are primarily the outer coastal areas of Noyes and Baker Islands which
include rugged, rocky shorelines with many dramatic, steep-walled
headlands. About 32 percent of the area is rated as Variety Class C
(possessing a very low degree of landscape diversity relative to the
character type). These areas include the very flat terrain and relatively
featureless shorelines of Lulu and San Fernando Islands. The rest of this
roadless area is rated as Variety Class B (possessing landscape
characteristics common for the character type).

All the National Forest lands in this roadless area are in a Type I
Existing Visual Condition where the natural landscape has remained
unaltered by human activity, although some Native land on the east side of
Noyes has been logged.

(8) **Surroundings (External Influences):** The Native land on Noyes Island
is the only real external influence on this roadless area.

(9) **Attractions and Features of Special Interest:** The natural features of
the area, the scenery, the saltwater bays and inlets, and the opportunity
to see wildlife and to study the processes which formed this country may
all be attractions. The spectacular cliffs with sea caves and the beaches
on the outer coast are of special interest. An historic Native townsite on
Baker Island is being considered for development as an interpretive site
The proposed roadless area includes 14 inventoried recreation places
totaling 27,648 acres.

Capability of Management as Wilderness or in an Unroaded Condition

(1) **Manageability and Management Area Boundaries:** This island group can easily be managed in roadless condition. The private land boundaries on Noyes Island do not present a management problem

(2) **Natural Integrity:** This island group possesses outstanding natural integrity These islands appear to belong together as one geographic group in a marine setting. The small block of Native land located on Noyes Island does not seriously affect the apparent natural integrity of this or the other islands in the group.

(3) **Opportunity for Solitude:** With the possible exception of the area adjacent to Native lands, there is an excellent opportunity for solitude within this roadless area. In much of the area, a person is unlikely to encounter another during the duration of a visit. The outer coasts of Noyes and Baker Islands provide the opportunity for exceptional solitude on an ocean beach environment.

(4) **Opportunity for Primitive Recreation:** Due to their remoteness, there are outstanding opportunities for primitive recreation experiences, particularly on Noyes and Baker Islands with their various distinct and isolated bays, and the recreation and scenic attractions of the outer coastal areas.

ROS Class	Acres
Primitive I (P1)	46,512
Primitive II (P2)	34,794
Semi-Primitive Non-Motorized (SPNM)	9,696
Semi-Primitive Motorized (SPM)	12,059

The area contains 14 inventoried recreation places.

ROS CLASS	# OF REC. PLACES	TOTAL ACRES	CAPACITY BY RVD'S
P1	5	15,594	9,100
P2	5	6,954	4,680
SPM	4	5,100	10,168

(5) **Special Features (Ecologic, Geologic, Scientific, Cultural):** The high-energy outer coastlines of Noyes and Baker Islands are special features.

c. **Availability for Management as Wilderness or in an Unroaded Condition**

(1) Resource Potentials

(a) **Recreation Potential:** There are excellent opportunities to develop canoe/kayak routes through the protected inside waters, interpretation of cultural resources, additional recreation use cabins, and hiking trails from the inner bays to the outer coast beaches. All of the islands are accessible by boat through protected inside waters from Craig, thus providing the opportunity to develop recreation facilities in a unique offshore marine environment

(b) **Fish Resource:** The recently completed fish habitat inventory of
these islands indicates some potential to improve the quality and
availability of salmon spawning habitat on a number of streams   Most
of this potential relates to constructing fish passes around natural
barriers thus providing fish access to high quality spawning habitat

(c) **Wildlife Resource:** There are no indications that habitat for any
of the species living within this roadless area is deficient. There
are no plans for wildlife habitat improvement or population
enhancement projects.

(d) **Timber Resource:** There are 46,488 acres inventoried as
tentatively suitable for harvest. This includes 41,535 acres of
non-riparian old growth and 4,374 of riparian old growth.

(e) **Land Use Authorizations:** None.

(f) **Minerals:** The mineral potential is low

(g) **Areas of Scientific Interest:** The caves on the outer islands may
be significant for cultural resource research.

(2) **Management Considerations**

(a) There is considerable public concern over future management of
the Outer Islands. The most prevalent view is that these islands
should be managed for their recreation potential and that logging
should be excluded. The Forest Service has received written and
verbal comment that the Outer Islands should be designated as a
National Recreation Area.

(b) **Fire:** The area has no significant fire history.

(c) **Insects and Disease:** Endemic tree diseases common to Southeast
Alaska are present.

(d) **Land Status:** The Natives have selected blocks of entitlement
land and traditional use sites on Noyes and San Juan Bautista Islands

d. **Relationship To Communities and Other Roadless and Wilderness Areas**

(1) **Nearby Roadless and Wilderness Areas and Uses:** This roadless area is
separated from other nearby roadless areas by saltwater.

(2) **Distance From Population Centers (accessibility):** Approximate
distances from population centers:

Community		Air Miles	Water Miles
Juneau	(Pop. 23,729)	190	220
Ketchikan	(Pop. 12,705)	45	90
Craig	(Pop. 915)	20	24

Hollis, located on Prince of Wales Island, is the closest stop on the Alaska Marine Highway

(3) **Interest by Proponents:**

(a) **Moratorium Areas:** The area has not been identified as a "moratorium" area or proposed as Wilderness in legislative initiatives to date

(b) **Local Users/residents:** The area receives local use for subsistence and dispersed recreation activities

e. **Environmental Consequences**

INDIVIDUAL ROADLESS AREA DESCRIPTION

NAME: Sukkwan (504)   ACRES (GROSS): 53,256   ACRES (NFS): 44,607

GEOZONE: K08
GEOGRAPHIC PROVINCE: Southern Outer Islands

1989 WILDERNESS ATTRIBUTE RATING: 23

⌐ Description

(1) **Relationship to RARE II areas:** The table below displays the VCU 1/
names, VCU numbers, acres, original WARS 2/ rating, and comments. This
enables the reader to compare the roadless areas evaluated in Appendix C
with previous analyses.

VCU Name	VCU No.	1979 WARS Rating	Comments
Soda Bay	632	24	
Jackson	670	23	
Dunbar	671	23	
Hydaberg	672	22	

(2) **History:** This roadless area consists of Sukkwan and Goat Islands, two
small areas on Prince of Wales Island, plus a series of small islands All
of this area is within the principal traditional-use area of the Haida
Natives. Because of this history, the Haida Native Corporation made
extensive land selections in this area including all of Goat Island and
portions of Sukkwan Island. Subsequently, Goat Island and adjacent small
islands were purchased by the Forest Service through the recent enactment
of the Haida Land Exchange. Because of the Native interest and occupancy
of this land area, there is very little non-Native history associated with
this area.

(3) **Location and Access:** This area is located approximately 30 miles
south of Craig and seven miles south of Hydaburg. Access is by floatplane
or boat.

(4) **Geography and Topography:** This is, for the most part, an island
roadless area with Sukkwan and Goat Islands, being the main islands. There
are many unnamed small islands and a very irregular coastline within this
area. Many of the islands have low elevations with flat to rolling
topography, although Sukkwan Island reaches an elevation of 2,100 feet
There are 125 miles of saltwater shoreline.

1/ A VCU (Value Comparison Unit) is one of 867 watersheds which make up the
forest and were differentiated for planning purposes in the Tongass Land
Management Plan.
2/ Wilderness Attribute Rating System (WARS) was the nationwide system used to
rate the wilderness attributes of roadless areas in the Roadless Area
Review and Evaluation (RARE II).

(5) Ecosystem:

(a) **Classification:** The area is classified as being in the Southern
Outer Islands province. This province is characterized by rolling
subdued and localized rugged terrain

(b) **Vegetation:** This area is typical Southeast Alaska coastal
temperate rain forest. The forest is primarily western hemlock and
Sitka spruce, with a large cedar component

There are approximately 37,835 acres of forested land of which 14,102
acres are commercial forest land. Of the commercial forest land
12,365 acres are non-riparian old growth and 1,498 are riparian old
growth.

(c) **Soils:** These highly organic, low clay content soils are
generally formed over bedrock, and are typically about 40 inches deep

(d) **Fish Resource:** Fish resources have been rated as part of the
Tongass Land Management Plan (1979) and by the Alaska Department of
Fish and Game in its Forest Habitat Integrity Program (1983) These
ratings describe the value of VCU's for sport fish, commercial fish,
and estuaries

VCU 672 was rated as high value for sport fish. No VCU's were rated
highly for commercial fish or estuaries

(e) **Wildlife Resource:** This area has high populations of Sitka
black-tailed deer, black bear, otter, marten, mink, loon, and common
waterfowl. Marine mammals are common on the small islands

(f) **Threatened and Endangered Species:** None.

(6) **Current Use and Management:** The area was allocated to Land Use
Designation (LUD) 4 in the Tongass Land Management Plan The LUD 4 area is
to be managed for its commodity and market values.

The Sukkwan Roadless Area has received very little resource management
attention. There are no project-level activities planned for the
foreseeable future. The area receives occasional recreation use A few
Hydaburg area residents may participate in some subsistence activities
here.

(7) **Appearance (Apparent Naturalness):** The area is part of the Coastal
Hills character type, which is characterized by moderately-steep landforms,
predominantly rounded summits, elevations up to 4,500 feet, and
flat-floored, U-shaped valleys. The Sukkwan area exhibits more moderate
topography than is common in the character type. It also possesses a wide
variety of island clusters and prominent bays, more than is common in this
character type.

The entire area is inventoried as Variety Class B (possessing landscape
diversity which is common in the character type) The notable scenic
features are the diverse clusters of islands and coves, particularly in the
Dunbar Inlet area.

The Existing Visual Condition for the entire area is Type I where the natural landscape has remained unaltered by human activity

(8) **Surroundings (External Influences):** The external influence is mostly associated with the large blocks of Native land in the area These lands are in the process of being logged

(9) **Attractions and Features of Special Interest:** The natural features of the area, the scenery (particularly the island clusters and the saltwater bays and inlets), and the opportunity to see wildlife and to study the processes which formed this country are all attractions The area contains four inventoried recreation places containing 10,288 acres

b. **Capability of Management as Wilderness or in an Unroaded Condition**

(1) **Manageability and Management Area Boundaries:** The boundaries of this roadless area consist primarily of survey lines for the private land, or large expanses of saltwater. The area can easily be managed in its current roadless condition.

(2) **Natural Integrity:** The area has excellent natural integrity

(3) **Opportunity for Solitude:** The opportunity for solitude within this roadless area is excellent. Persons entering this area are unlikely to encounter others during their entire stay.

(4) **Opportunity for Primitive Recreation:** The area has good opportunity for primitive recreation, particularly on the outside shores of Sukkwan Island in the Dunbar Inlet area.

ROS Class	Acres
Primitive I (P1)	13,484
Primitive II (P2)	10,867
Semi-Primitive Non-Motorized (SPNM)	10,268
Semi-Primitive Motorized(SPM)	10,008

The area contains four inventoried recreation places.

ROS CLASS	# OF REC. PLACES	TOTAL ACRES	CAPACITY BY RVD'S
P1	2	8,210	4,724
SPNM	2	2,078	2,812

(5) **Special Features (Ecologic, Geologic, Scientific, Cultural):** There are no known special features within this roadless area.

c. **Availability for Management as Wilderness or in an Unroaded Condition**

(1) **Resource Potentials**

(a) **Recreation Potential:** This general area is identified as the southern end of a potential kayak route along the west coast of Prince of Wales Island. There are several identified dispersed campsites or

potential recreation shelter sites in the bays and inlets or islands
on the west side of Sukkwan Island The area has a few good
anchorages for large boats   There is no identified recreation
potential in the interior of Sukkwan Island due to the lack of
recreation attractions such as lakes, major streams or scenic alpine
areas

(b) **Fish Resource:** The area does have a few productive streams for
salmon, but few with significant potential for habitat improvement

(c) **Wildlife Resource:** There are no plans or identified need to
improve wildlife habitat conditions.

(d) **Timber Resource:** There are 13,024 acres inventoried as
tentatively suitable for harvest. This includes 11,346 acres of
non-riparian old growth and 1,318 acres of riparian old growth.

(e) **Land Use Authorizations:** None.

(f) **Minerals:** Mineral development potential is very low

(g) **Areas of Scientific Interest:** None

(2) **Management Considerations**

(a) This island group has received very little management attention
because of its lack of good access and rather low potential for
resource management. Public use is minor with little potential for
development of public use facilities, except for the development of a
few primitive campsites or shelters.

(b) **Fire:** The area has no significant fire history

(c) **Insects and Disease:** Endemic tree diseases common to Southeast
Alaska are present.

(d) **Land Status:** Native and State land selections have influenced
the boundary of this roadless area. There are no private inholdings
within this roadless area.

d. **Relationship To Communities and Other Roadless and Wilderness Areas**

(1) **Nearby Roadless and Wilderness Areas and Uses:** The area is isolated
from other roadless areas by wide expanses of saltwater.

(2) **Distance From Population Centers (accessibility):** Approximate
distances from population centers are as follows:

Community		Air Miles	Water Miles
Juneau	(Pop. 23,729)	190	220
Ketchikan	(Pop 12,705)	35	90
Hydaburg	(Pop 385)	6	6

Hollis, located on Prince of Wales Island, is the nearest stop on the
Alaska Marine Highway.

(3) Interest by Proponents:

(a) Moratorium Areas: The area has not been identified as a
"moratorium" area or proposed as Wilderness in legislative initiatives
to date.

(b) Local Users/residents: The area receives minor local use for
subsistence and recreation activity. Both the Haida Natives and the
Haida Native Corporation have a strong interest in the future of this
area because of its historic occupancy by the Haida and because of
adjacent corporation land selections.

e. Environmental Consequences

INDIVIDUAL ROADLESS AREA DESCRIPTION

NAME: Soda Bay (505)   ACRES (GROSS): 94,463   ACRES (NFS): 76,596

GEOZONE: K08
GEOGRAPHIC PROVINCE: Southern Outer Islands

1989 WILDERNESS ATTRIBUTE RATING: 23

a. Description

    (1) **Relationship to RARE II areas:** The table below displays the VCU 1/
names, VCU numbers, acres, original WARS 2/ rating, and comments   This
enables the reader to compare the roadless areas evaluated in Appendix C
with previous analyses.

VCU Name	VCU No.	1979 WARS Rating	Comments
	622		Not Rated
St. Nicholas	623	22	
Flat Creek	624	22	
Trocadero	625	23	
Port Estrella	630	23	
Shelikof	631	23	
Soda Bay	632	24	

    (2) **History:** The Soda Bay area is known to have been an important site
for the indigenous Native culture   For this reason, the Haida Native
Corporation, under its land entitlement, has made large land selections in
the area. The coast area was used from the late 1800's through the early
1900's as a base for the commercial fishing industry

In recent times, the community of Craig and the Native community of
Hydaburg have been connected with a road that now serves as the east
boundary of this roadless area   The construction of the road has resulted
in the Trocadero Bay and the Soda Bay areas to be more widely used for
recreation and subsistence by local residents

    (3) **Location and Access:** The Soda Bay Roadless Area is located in the
central part of the Prince of Wales Island midway between the communities
of Craig and Hydaburg. Access is by the Prince of Wales road system and by
boat through Trocadero and Soda Bays.

1/ A VCU (Value Comparison Unit) is one of 867 watersheds which make up the
    forest and were differentiated for planning purposes in the Tongass Land
    Management Plan.
2/ Wilderness Attribute Rating System (WARS) was the nationwide system used to
    rate the wilderness attributes of roadless areas in the Roadless Area
    Review and Evaluation (RARE II).

    (4) **Geography and Topography:** The area is characterized by by low
elevation and gently rolling topography. The maximum elevation is about

2,500 feet. There are 96 miles of saltwater shoreline. Approximately
1,100 acres are alpine tundra

The coast is dominated by Trocadero and Soda Bays   This area includes in
Soda Bay and Trocadero Bay

(5) **Ecosystem:**

   (a) **Classification:** The area is in the Southern Outer Islands
   Geographic Province. This province is characterized by rolling,
   subdued and localized rugged topography.

   (b) **Vegetation:** Vegetation is typical Southeast Alaska coastal
   temperate rain forest. The forest is primarily western hemlock and
   Sitka spruce, with a large cedar component. There are 3,493 acres of
   the muskeg vegetative type.

   There are approximately 69,711 acres of forested land of which 31,413
   acres are commercial forest land. Of the commercial forest land,
   25,845 acres are non-riparian old growth and 4,291 acres are riparian
   old growth.

   (c) **Soils:** These highly, organic, low clay content soils are
   generally formed over bedrock and are typically about 40 inches deep

   (d) **Fish Resource:** Fish resources have been rated as part of the
   Tongass Land Management Plan (1979) and by the State Department of
   Fish and Game in its Forest Habitat Integrity Program (1983) These
   ratings describe the value of VCU's for sport fish, commercial fish.
   and estuaries.

   VCU's 622, 623, 624, and 625 are high value for commercial fish, VCU's
   622, 624, and 630 are high value for estuary habitat, and VCU 623 is
   high value for sport fish.

   (e) **Wildlife Resource:** This area has high populations of Sitka
   black-tailed deer, bear, otter, marten, mink, loon, and common
   waterfowl.

   (f) **Threatened and Endangered Species:** None.

(6) **Current Use and Management:** The Tongass Land Management Plan
allocated this area to Land Use Designation (LUD) 4. The LUD 4 area is to
be managed for its commodity and market values.

The area has high value timber. Currently, Shelikof Island, off the coast
of the roadless area, is being logged, and is visible from the roadless
area.

Dispersed recreation, mostly associated with fishing and hunting, is the
primary recreation use of the area. A trail and a viewing/interpretive
site are located at Soda Springs.

Plans are being prepared for fish habitat improvement projects on streams
within the area.

North Fork Lake is the water source for the community of Craig The city operates a dam and pipeline system at this lake under the authorization of a special use permit

(7) **Appearance (Apparent Naturalness)** · The Soda Bay Roadless Area is part of the Coastal Hills character type which is characterized by moderately steep landforms, predominantly rounded summits, elevations to 4,500 feet, and flat-floored, U-shaped valleys Numerous island groups are also common. This area exhibits landscapes 'that are somewhat less rugged than is common in the character type Elevations in the roadless area average between 1,500 and 2,000 feet Several island clusters are present

The entire area is inventoried as a Variety Class B (possessing landscape diversity that is common in the character type). There are no outstanding large scenic features in the area, though small-scale scenic features may exist.

Ninety-nine percent of this roadless area is in Type I Existing Visual Condition (EVC) where the natural landscape has remained unaltered by human activity. A small portion is in EVC Type IV or V visual condition, where past logging has moderately or heavily altered the landscape in small portions of Soda and Trocadero Bays.

(8) **Surroundings (External Influences):** The large blocks of Native land to the west, north, and southeast of this roadless area have been extensively logged. Timber harvest is occurring on nearby Shelikof Island and on Suemez Island located to the southwest of this roadless area.

Waterfall, a world class fishing resort, is located on private land on the west side of this area. The road connecting Craig with Hydaburg forms the east boundary of this roadless area.

(9) **Attractions and Features of Special Interest:** The natural features of the area, the scenery, the saltwater bays and inlets, and the opportunity to see wildlife and to study the processes which formed this country may all be attractions. The excellent saltwater salmon fishing is a major attraction in the vicinity of this roadless area The area contains 16 inventoried recreation places containing 23,520 acres.

b. **Capability of Management as Wilderness or in an Unroaded Condition**

(1) **Manageability and Management Area Boundaries:** The boundaries of this roadless area consist primarily of roads or land survey lines for the private land making it an easily identified roadless area With one exception, the area can easily be managed in its current roadless condition. That exception is in the North Fork Lake area, located in the northwest corner, where the community of Craig's domestic water source facilities are located

(2) **Natural Integrity:** With the exception of the North Fork Lake area, the interior of this roadless area is unaltered

(3) **Opportunity for Solitude:** The opportunity for solitude within this roadless area is fair. The sights and sounds of adjacent logging activity

may be evident from much of the interior of this roadless area   During
fishing and hunting season people are likely to be encountered in the
Trocadero and Soda Bay tidal flats.

(4) **Opportunity for Primitive Recreation:** Most of the recreation
potential centers around semi-primitive opportunities of the marine
attractions in Trocadero and Soda Bays   Though portions of these bays are
fairly remote, one is likely to encounter recreation boaters or other
marine traffic in much of this area.

ROS Class	Acres
Primitive I (P1)	22,792
Primitive II (P2)	10,193
Semi-Primitive Non-Motorized (SPNM)	27,861
Semi-Primitive Motorized (SPM)	11,117
Roaded Natural (RN)	799
Roaded Modified (RM)	1,917

The area contains 16 inventoried recreation places.

ROS CLASS	# OF REC. PLACES	TOTAL ACRES	CAPACITY BY RVD'S
P1	1	5,233	2,080
P2	2	3,032	1,613
SPNM	5	8,986	6,612
SPM	4	5,270	21,692
RN	1	160	662
RM	3	838	2,672

(5) **Special Features (Ecologic, Geologic, Scientific, Cultural):** The
limestone formations in the Soda Bay area are a special geologic feature
The Forest Service has constructed a trail and interpretive signs to draw
attention to this site.

c. **Availability for Management as Wilderness or in an Unroaded Condition**

(1) **Resource Potentials**

(a) **Recreation Potential:** This area offers excellent opportunities
to connect the Prince of Wales Island road system to saltwater at
Trocadero Bay with short trails. This would support excellent fishing
and waterfowl hunting during the appropriate seasons as well as
provide day hiking opportunities for local residents and tourists
Much of the remaining area is well suited for dispersed recreation in
a semi-primitive setting.

(b) **Fish Resource:** The recently completed fish habitat inventory
indicates excellent potential for salmon enhancement projects,
including construction of fish passes, on several of the streams
within the area.

(c) **Wildlife Resource:** The tidal flats in Trocadero Bay are
excellent waterfowl habitat   There may be an opportunity for some

kind of waterfowl habitat improvement on this and other tidal flats in
the area.

(d) **Timber Resource:** There are 29,318 acres inventoried as
tentatively suitable for harvest. This includes 23,671 acres of
non-riparian old growth and 3,971 of riparian old growth

(e) **Land Use Authorizations:** Craig's water supply facilities located
at North Fork Lake are under special use authorization

(f) **Minerals:** The potential for mineral development is very low

Areas of Scientific Interest: None.

(2) **Management Considerations**

(a) The management emphasis for this area has been in the area of
dispersed recreation and fish habitat improvement. Craig's water
supply system at North Fork Lake is a on-going permit administration
activity.

A significant factor in the long-term management of this area is that
its location along saltwater midway between Craig and Hydaburg
Trocadero and Soda Bays are of special interest to residents of these
communities because of their ease of land access for fishing and
hunting (sport and subsistence) and for general recreation purposes.

(b) **Fire:** The area has no significant fire history

(c) **Insects and Disease:** Endemic tree diseases common to Southeast
Alaska are present.

(d) **Land Status:** Native and State land selections have influenced
the boundary of this roadless area. No private inholdings occur in
this roadless area.

d. **Relationship To Communities and Other Roadless and Wilderness Areas**

(1) **Nearby Roadless and Wilderness Areas and Uses:** Nearby roadless areas
are Karta and Polk to the northeast, and Sukkwan to the southeast. All of
these are separated from the Soda Bay area by roads, logged areas, private
land, or saltwater.

(2) **Distance From Population Centers (accessibility):** Approximate
distances from population centers are as follows:

Community		Air Miles	Water Miles
Juneau	(Pop. 23,729)	190	220
Ketchikan	(Pop. 12,705)	35	90
Craig	(Pop. 915)	10	12
Hydaburg	(Pop. 385)	8	16

Hollis, located on Prince of Wales Island, is the nearest stop on the
Alaska Marine Highway.

(3) **Interest by Proponents:**

(a) **Moratorium Areas:** The area has not been identified as a "moratorium" area or proposed as Wilderness in legislative initiatives to date.

(b) **Local Users/residents:** The area receives significant local use for subsistence and recreation activity.   .

e   **Environmental Consequences**

INDIVIDUAL ROADLESS AREA DESCRIPTION

NAME: Eudora (507)   ACRES (GROSS): 254,428   ACRES (NFS): 233,933

GEOZONE: K07
GEOGRAPHIC PROVINCE: Southern Outer Islands

1989 WILDERNESS ATTRIBUTE RATING: 23

a. Description

(1) **Relationship to RARE II areas:** The table below displays the VCU 1/
names, VCU numbers, acres, original WARS 2/ rating, and comments   This
enables the reader to compare the roadless areas evaluated in Appendix C
with previous analyses.

VCU Name	VCU No.	1979 WARS Rating	Comments
	614		Not Rated
West Arm	674	25	
Dora Bay	677	25	
South Arm	678	23	
Lancaster	679	26	
Windy Point	680	23	
Dolomi	681	24	
North Moria	682	26	
Myrtle	683	24	
Dickman	684	25	
West Moria	691	22	
Bokan	692	23	
Egg	693	23	
Ingraham	694	24	
Hidden Bay	695	24	
Hessa Lake	698	21	
Kendrick	699	23	
Short Arm	700	22	
Mclean	701	24	
Stone Rock	702	22	
Cape Chacon	703	21	
Nichols Bay	704	25	

1/ A VCU (Value Comparison Unit) is one of 867 watersheds which make up the
forest and were differentiated for planning purposes in the Tongass Land
Management Plan.

2/ Wilderness Attribute Rating System (WARS) was the nationwide system used to
rate the wilderness attributes of roadless areas in the Roadless Area
Review and Evaluation (RARE II).

(2) **History:** The Eudora Roadless Area has always been considered a remote area on Prince of Wales Island. The many major sounds and bays provide bases for commercial fishing including anchorages, fish processing facilities, boat repair sites, and fish buying stations. There has been an interest in the mineral resources since the early 1900's resulting in several patented mining claims and numerous unpatented claims that are currently active Sulzer Portage, a small boat and foot portage used since the early 1900's, connects the east and west sides of the island through Cholmondeley Sound and Hetta Inlet

In recent years, the Natives have made land selections in the northern part of this roadless area, and the State has made a number of selections scattered over its entire length.

The east coast has a rich history of prehistoric and historic use by Native cultures. This area has been, and is today, significant for subsistence hunting and fishing.

(3) **Location and Access:** Located on southeast Prince of Wales Island, the only access to the Eudora Roadless Area is by boat or floatplane

(4) **Geography and Topography:** Eudora has a varied topography The Cholmondeley Sound area has rugged and steep mountains with elevations up to 3,000 feet. Headlands separating the major bays and sounds have similar topography. The interior of the area has somewhat flat to moderate relief. There are 353 miles of saltwater shoreline. Freshwater lakes total 6,388 acres. Rock covers 10,931 acres.

(5) **Ecosystem:**

(a) **Classification:** Geographically, Eudora is classified as part of the Southern Outer Islands Geographic Province. The region is characterized by rolling subdued and localized rugged topography

(b) **Vegetation:** Vegetation is this area is that typical of Southeast Alaska coastal temperate rain forests. The forest is primarily western hemlock and Sitka spruce with a large cedar component There are less than 500 acres of muskeg and approximately 660 acres of alpine.

There are approximately 206,668 acres of forest land of which 112,656 acres are commercial forest land. Of the commercial forest land, 96,700 acres are non-riparian old growth and 12,511 acres are riparian old growth.

(b) **Soils:** Soils are generally highly organic with low clay content. They are formed over bedrock and their typical depth is 40 inches.

(c) **Fish Resource:** Fish resources have been rated as part of the Tongass Land Management Plan (1979) and by the Alaska Department of Fish and Game in its Forest Habitat Integrity Program (1983) These ratings describe the value of VCU's for sport fish, commercial fish, and estuaries.

VCU's 674, 678, 679, 682, 684, and 692 are rated high value for commercial fish; VCU's 674, 682, 683, 684 and 703 are high value for sport fish; and VCU's 679, 695, and 699 are high value for estuary habitat.

(d) Wildlife Resource: This area has populations of Sitka black-tailed deer, black bear, otter, marten, mink, loon, and common waterfowl. The Big Creek drainage is considered an excellent example of old-growth wildlife.

(e) Threatened and Endangered Species: None

(6) Current Use and Management: The area was allocated to Land Use Designation (LUD) 1 (11,666 acres), LUD 2 (24,460 acres), LUD 3 (60,080 acres), and LUD 4 (135,585 acres) in the Tongass Land Management Plan. The LUD 1 area is to be managed in the roadless condition. The LUD 2 area is at the west end of Moria Sound. This area is to be managed in the roadless condition, although fish and wildlife habitat improvements are allowed. The LUD 3 areas are located on the southwest end of Moria Sound and, in the Cholmondeley Sound area (the land around Dora Bay). The uses and activities in these areas are to be managed in a compatible and complementary manner. LUD 4 includes most of the eastern side of this area, and is to be managed for its commodity and market values.

There is a wide variety of mining and recreation use that occurs within the area. Three recreation use cabins, mooring buoys, trails, and a recreation residence are located within the area. A number of mining claims and mining patents are located in the areas around Green Mountain, Bokan Mountain, Niblack Mountain, and all around Moria Sound.

This is a significant subsistence use area.

(7) Appearance (Apparent Naturalness): The Eudora Roadless Area is part of the Coastal Hills character type which consists of moderately-steep landforms, predominantly rounded summits, elevations up to 4,500 feet and flat-floored, U-shaped valleys. This large area exhibits almost the full range of landscape characteristics of this character type from the rugged, diverse terrain of the West Arm of Cholmondeley Sound and the Eudora Mountain to the rugged coastline along Clarence Strait to the many island groups throughout the area.

About 24 percent of this area is inventoried as Variety Class A (possessing a high degree of landscape diversity relative to the character type). High scenic quality landscapes include the areas south of the West Arm of Cholmondeley Sound around Dora Bay, the Eudora Mountain area, and the complex of diverse lake basins and intricate saltwater shoreline to the south and east of this peak. The rest of the roadless area is inventoried as Variety Class B (possessing landscape characteristics common to the character type).

Virtually all of this roadless area is in Existing Visual Condition Type I where the natural landscape has remained unaltered by human activity. A few small pockets of old logging activity scattered throughout the area are the only exceptions to this unaltered condition. However, the large areas of recent harvest and potential future harvest on the Native lands throughout the eastern half of Cholmondeley Sound have had a significant impact on the highly scenic areas of this waterbody

(8) **Surroundings (External Influences):** The western boundary of the Eudora Roadless Area coincides with the South Prince of Wales Wilderness The eastern boundary is saltwater An irregular northern boundary results from the extensive Native land selections in the area.

The most significant external factor is the recent logging activity on the Native lands and the projection that almost all of their remaining standing merchantable timber will be removed. The State has made small land selections scattered along the entire coast for the purpose of creating communities sometime in the future

(9) **Attractions and Features of Special Interest:** The natural features of the area, the scenery, the saltwater bays and inlets, and the opportunity to see wildlife and to study the processes which formed this country may all be attractions. The extensive canoeing and kayaking opportunities within the area are outstanding attractions. Fishing and solitude are also attractions. The area contains 29 inventoried recreation places totaling 71,498 acres.

b. **Capability of Management as Wilderness or in an Unroaded Condition**

(1) **Manageability and Management Area Boundaries:** There are a few places where the mineral patents may affect the ability to manage the immediate surrounding area in a roadless condition. Despite this, the area, as a whole, can be easily managed in the roadless condition. Almost all of the State and Native land selections have been excluded from the boundary of the roadless area.

(2) **Natural Integrity:** The Eudora Roadless Area is a logical land unit The Native and State land selections have affected the natural integrity of isolated, limited areas, but these have not severely reduced the overall integrity of the roadless area The mining patents are inclusions within the roadless area, but these small areas do not seriously break the natural integrity.

(3) **Opportunity for Solitude:** There is excellent opportunity for solitude within the area excluding the very northern fringe where the sights and sounds of logging and vehicle traffic may be evident. Floatplanes and boats are used to transport people to the numerous fishing lakes and three recreation cabins within the area.

(4) **Opportunity for Primitive Recreation:** There are outstanding opportunities for primitive recreation due to the high scenic quality, the vastness of the area, and the wide variety of recreation opportunities These include saltwater related activities in protected, remote, and very scenic bays; opportunities to recreate at inland lakes; and alpine hiking opportunities through extensive areas of relatively open country.

ROS Class	Acres
Primitive I (P1)	109,001
Primitive II (P2)	70,076
Semi-Primitive Non-Motorized (SPNM)	26,173
Roaded Modified (RM)	17,617
Rural (R)	100

The area contains 29 inventoried recreation places

ROS CLASS	# OF REC. PLACES	TOTAL ACRES	CAPACITY BY RVD'S
P1	9	30,991	9,208
P2	10	34,157	11,930
SPNM	5	4,907	7,423
RM	4	1,342	7,800
R	1	100	508

(5) Special Features (Ecologic, Geologic, Scientific, Cultural): There are no known special features within the area.

c. Availability for Management as Wilderness or in an Unroaded Condition

(1) Resource Potentials

(a) Recreation Potential: There is great opportunity to manage this area for primitive and semi-primitive recreation. There is some opportunity to increase developed recreation facilities with additional cabins and new trails. This area has good road access to its northern boundary, and good boat access from the Ketchikan area.

(b) Fish Resource: The recently completed fish habitat inventory indicates that there is potential for salmon enhancement projects. such as constructing fish passes on several of the streams within the area.

(c) Wildlife Resource: There are no long range plans to accomplish habitat improvement project work within this roadless area

(d) Timber Resource: There are 95,161 acres inventoried as tentatively suitable for harvest This includes 80,666 acres of non-riparian old growth and 10,790 acres of riparian old growth

(e) Land Use Authorizations: None.

(f) Minerals: Mineral development potential is high. The number of existing mineral patents, located claims, and the expressed interest in the mineralized geology of the area indicate that mineral exploration and development is likely Explorations in 1988-89 are reported to indicate the presence of a variety of rare earth elements such as yttrium.

(g) Areas of Scientific Interest: The Big Creek-Chomondeley Sound area has been identified as a potential Research Natural Area

(2) Management Considerations .

(a) This roadless area offers a variety of resource management opportunities. There are many excellent opportunities to develop the recreation potential Outstanding freshwater fishing and scenic areas can be supported with additional shelters (cabins), trails, and mooring facilities.

There is excellent potential to enhance the salmon spawning habitat on many streams within Eudora, mainly through the construction of fish passes.

Timber management potential is very high. Almost all of the suitable timberland has good saltwater access. Mineral development potential is high.

An important management consideration is that the Haida Native Corporation has the right for further land selections that need to be made by 1995. It is known that they have interest in selecting lands in the northern third of the roadless area.

(b) **Fire:** The area has no significant fire history.

(c) **Insects and Disease:** Endemic tree diseases common to Southeast Alaska are present.

(d) **Land Status:** There are a number of mining patents within the boundary of this area. These inclusions total approximately 300 acres. All of the Native and State selected lands have been excluded from the boundary of this area.

d. **Relationship To Communities and Other Roadless and Wilderness Areas**

(1) **Nearby Roadless and Wilderness Areas and Uses:** This roadless area is part of a larger contiguous unroaded land mass consisting of the South Prince of Wales Wilderness, and the Nutkwa and Polk Roadless Areas These areas total 533,474 acres.

(2) **Distance From Population Centers (accessibility):** Approximate distances from population centers are as follows:

Community		Air Miles	Water Miles
Juneau	(Pop. 23,729)	190	220
Ketchikan	(Pop. 12,705)	25	30
Hydaburg	(Pop. 385)	15	30

Hollis, located on Prince of Wales Island, is the nearest stop on the Alaska Marine Highway.

(3) Interest by Proponents:

       (a) **Moratorium Areas:** The area has not been identified as a "moratorium" area or proposed as Wilderness in legislative initiatives to date.

       (b) **Local Users/residents:** The area receives local use for subsistence and recreation activity.

  e   Environmental Consequences

INDIVIDUAL ROADLESS AREA DESCRIPTION

NAME: Christoval (508)   ACRES (GROSS): 7,750   ACRES (NFS): 7,750

GEOZONE: K11
GEOGRAPHIC PROVINCE: Southern Outer Islands

1989 WILDERNESS ATTRIBUTE RATING: 22

a. Description

   (1) **Relationship to RARE II areas:** The table below displays the VCU 1/
   names, VCU numbers, acres, original WARS 2/ rating, and comments   This
   enables the reader to compare the roadless areas evaluated in Appendix C
   with previous analyses.

VCU Name	VCU No.	1979 WARS Rating	Comments
	561	--	Not Rated
Cone Bay	562	22	
Derrumba	563	23	

   (2) **History:** The Christoval Roadless Area consists primarily of a single
   steep mountain (Bald Mountain) on the southern end of Heceta Island
   Because of its steepness, and lack of safe anchorages, the area was not
   subject to the same level of historic development as other portions of
   Heceta Island.

   (3) **Location and Access:** This roadless area is located on the southern
   tip of Heceta Island. Access is via the Heceta Island road system   Heceta
   Island, itself, can be reached by boat or floatplane, but the roadless area
   does not contain lakes or sheltered harbors for boat or plane access

   (4) **Geography and Topography:** The roadless area is extremely rugged
   Mountains rise steeply from sea level to elevations up to 2,400 feet
   There are 12 miles of coastline consisting of rocky shores and towering
   cliffs. Most of this roadless area is forested. A few very short
   drainages also exist.

   (5) **Ecosystem:**

      (a) **Classification:** This area is in the Southern Outer Islands
      Geographic Province. This province is characterized by rolling
      subdued topography interspersed with localized rugged mountains

1/ A VCU (Value Comparison Unit) is one of 867 watersheds which make up the
   forest and were differentiated for planning purposes in the Tongass Land
   Management Plan.
2/ Wilderness Attribute Rating System (WARS) was the nationwide system used to
   rate the wilderness attributes of roadless areas in the Roadless Area
   Review and Evaluation (RARE II).

(b) Vegetation: Vegetation is typical Southeast Alaska coastal temperate rain forest. The forest is primarily western hemlock and Sitka spruce with large components of cedar.

There are approximately 7,369 acres of forested land, of which, 5,943 acres are commercial forest land Of the commercial forest land, 4,899 acres are non-riparian old growth and 562 acres are riparian old growth.

(c) Soils: Soils are generally formed over bedrock and are typically about 40 inches deep   Some soils are derived from limestone and marble.

(d) Fish Resource: Fish resources have been rated as part of the Tongass Land Management Plan (1979) and by the Alaska Department of Fish and Game in its Habitat Integrity Program (1983)   These ratings describe the value of VCU's for sport fish, commercial fish, and estuaries.

VCU 561 is rated high for commercial fish. No VCU's were rated highly for sport fish or estuaries.

(e) Wildlife Resource: Sitka black-tailed deer, black bear, wolves, mink, and bald eagles are the best known species that inhabit the area. There is an abundance of sea birds along the coast.

(f) Threatened and Endangered Species: None.

(6) Current Use and Management: TLMP allocated this area to Land Use Designation 4 which emphasizes intensive resource use and development of resources with commodity and market values. Timber management has been the emphasized resource management activity on Heceta Island.

(7) Appearance (Apparent Naturalness): The Christoval Roadless Area is part of the Kupreanof Lowland character type, which is characterized by predominantly low, rolling relief with elevations seldom over 1,500 feet Numerous island groups and intricate waterways are also common in this character type.

Christoval possesses much more rugged relief than is commonly found in this character type. For this reason, about 85 percent of the area is rated Variety Class A (having a high degree of landscape diversity relative to its character type). The key scenic feature in this area is the prominent peak of Bald Mountain and its broad flanks. This feature provides a dramatic backdrop from the saltwater channels to the east as they weave through the small islands just north of the village of Craig. Also noteworthy are the scenic grass meadows located at the base of this peak

About 75 percent of this area is in Type I Existing Visual Condition (EVC) where the landscape is essentially unaltered by human activity The rest of the area is in a Type IV EVC where alterations to the landscape are obvious but tend to blend with natural landscape features

(8) Surroundings (External Influences): The extensive amount of logging on Heceta Island on the opposite side of the Bald Mountain ridge is a major

influence on this roadless area. However, since logging activity on the
Island is near completion, there should be less influence in the
foreseeable future.

(9) **Attractions and Features of Special Interest:** The natural features of
the area, the scenery, and the opportunity to see wildlife and to study the
processes which formed this country may all be attractions The area
contains three inventoried recreation places totaling 3,012 acres There
are no improved trails in the area.

b Capability of Management as Wilderness or in an Unroaded Condition

(1) **Manageability and Management Area Boundaries:** The boundaries are
easily identifiable. The area can easily be managed in its unroaded
condition or as wilderness.

(2) **Natural Integrity:** This roadless area has good natural integrity
The coastline boundary and the rugged, mountainous terrain binds the area
together into a logical land unit.

(3) **Opportunity for Solitude:** Because access is difficult, an excellent
opportunity for solitude exists within the Christoval Roadless Area. Near
the boundary of the area however, one can expect to hear the sounds of
logging and, from some vantage points, actually see logging activity

(4) **Opportunity for Primitive Recreation:**

This area provides primarily Semi-Primitive Motorized or Semi-Primitive
Non-Motorized recreation opportunities because of the proximity to past
logged and roaded areas, and the moderate amount of motorized boat traffic
that passes by part of the area.

ROS Class	Acres
Semi-Primitive Non-Motorized (SPNM)	3,815
Semi-Primitive Motorized (SPM)	2,409
Roaded Modified (RM)	1,526

The area contains three inventoried recreation places.

ROS CLASS	# OF REC. PLACES	TOTAL ACRES	CAPACITY BY RVD
SPM	2	562	4,295
SPNM	1	2,449	3,120

(5) **Special Features (Ecologic, Geologic, Scientific, Cultural):** There
are no known special features within the area.

c. Availability for Management as Wilderness or in an Unroaded Condition

(1) Resource Potentials

(a) **Recreation Potential:** The rugged terrain and limited protected
anchorages around this area will somewhat restrict access into it
However, there is potential for a trail system into the Bald Mountain

area from logging roads on the opposite side of the ridge   There is
also potential for trail access from a small cove to the meadow areas
at the base of the mountain

(b) **Fish Resource:** The recently completed fish habitat inventory
indicates that there is some potential for salmon enhancement
projects, such as constructing fish passes, on several of the areas'
streams. The very difficult access is a limiting factor for
capitalizing upon this potential

(c) **Wildlife Resource:** No need has been identified for wildlife
enhancement projects within this area

(d) **Timber Resource:** There are 5,803 acres inventoried as
tentatively suitable for harvest. This includes 562 acres of riparian
old growth, and 4,899 acres of non-riparian old growth.

(e) **Land Use Authorizations:** None.

(f) **Minerals:** The mineral potential is low

(g) **Areas of Scientific Interest:** None.

(2) **Management Considerations**

(a) The rugged terrain over much of the area limits the opportunity
for management of its resources, particularly the timber   Those areas
on which timber harvest is economically feasible are included in
logging plans for the next five-year period (Ketchikan Pulp Company
Long-term Sale).

(c) **Insects and Disease:** Endemic tree diseases common to Southeast
Alaska are present.

(d) **Land Status:** All of the area is National Forest System lands

d. **Relationship To Communities and Other Roadless and Wilderness Areas**

(1) **Nearby Roadless and Wilderness Areas and Uses:** This is an isolated
roadless area about 10 miles north of the Maurelle Islands Wilderness,
separated from other roadless areas by the Gulf of Esquibel

(2) **Distance From Population Centers (accessibility):** Approximate
distances from population centers are:

Community		Air Miles	Water Miles
Juneau	(Pop. 23,729)	170	210
Ketchikan	(Pop. 12,705)	45	200
Craig	(Pop. 915)	20	26
Klawock	(Pop. 777)	16	20

Hollis, located on Prince of Wales Island, is the nearest stop on the
Alaska Marine Highway.

(3) Interest by Proponents:

(a) **Moratorium Areas:** The area has not been identified as a
"moratorium" area or proposed as Wilderness in legislative initiatives
to date.

(b) **Local Users/residents:** The only use of the area by local
residents is occasional hunting and some hiking out to the Bald
Mountain Ridge

e. Environmental Consequences

INDIVIDUAL ROADLESS AREA DESCRIPTION

NAME: Kogish (509)   ACRES (GROSS): 85,872   ACRES (NFS): 74,910

GEOZONE: K06
GEOGRAPHIC PROVINCE: Southern Outer Islands

1989 WILDERNESS ATTRIBUTE RATING: 22

a   Description

(1) **Relationship to RARE II areas:** The table below displays the VCU 1/ names, VCU numbers, acres, original WARS 2/ rating, and comments This enables the reader to compare the roadless areas evaluated in Appendix C with previous analyses.

VCU Name	VCU No.	1979 WARS Rating	Comments
	588		Not Rated
	589		Not Rated
	590		Not Rated
Nossuk	591	24	
St. Phillips	592	24	
Sombrero	593	25	
Shinaku	594	24	
Steelhead	595	21	
	596		Not Rated

(2) **History:** There is very little evidence of prehistoric or historic use of this roadless area Presently, the area is included in the primary sale area for the Ketchikan Pulp Company (KPC) Long-term Timber Sale

(3) **Location and Access:** The Kogish Roadless Area is located on the west side of central Prince of Wales Island. The only access is by way of the Staney Creek road system.

(4) **Geography and Topography:** This area is characterized by gently rolling relief with locally rugged areas. Kogish Mountain, with an elevation of 3,000 feet, is the highest point in the roadless area Shinaku Creek, and much of its watershed, exhibits fairly gentle relief It is the major drainage in the roadless area. There are 45 miles of saltwater shoreline. About 1,300 acres are alpine tundra

1/ A VCU (Value Comparison Unit) is one of 867 watersheds which make up the forest and were differentiated for planning purposes in the Tongass Land Management Plan.

2/ Wilderness Attribute Rating System (WARS) was the nationwide system used to rate the wilderness attributes of roadless areas in the Roadless Area Review and Evaluation (RARE II).

(5) Ecosystem:

(a) **Classification:** The area is in the Southern Outer Islands Geographic Province. This province is characterized by rolling subdued and localized rugged topography.

(b) **Vegetation:** Vegetation is typical Southeast Alaska coastal temperate rain forest. The forest is primarily western hemlock and Sitka spruce with a large cedar component   Numerous interspersed areas of muskeg total 5,056 acres

There are approximately 67,527 of forested land, of which, 34,811 acres are commercial forest land   Of the commercial forest land, 29,978 acres are non-riparian old growth and 4,352 are riparian old growth.

(c) **Soils:** Soils are generally formed over bedrock and are typically about 40 inches deep. Some of the soils in the area are derived from limestone and marble.

(d) **Fish Resource:** Fish resources have been rated as part of the Tongass Land Management Plan (1979) and by the Alaska Department of Fish and Game in its Forest Habitat Integrity Program (1983)   These ratings describe the value of VCU's for sport fish, commercial fish, and estuaries.

All VCU's in this roadless area were rated as high value for commercial fish. VCU's 588, 590, 596, and 597 were rated as high value for sport fish, and VCU's 589 and 592 were rated as high value for estuary habitat.

(e) **Wildlife Resource:** Sitka black-tailed deer, black bear, wolves, mink, and bald eagles are the best known species that inhabit the area. There is good alpine habitat for ptarmigan.

(f) **Threatened and Endangered Species:** None.

(6) **Current Use and Management:** The Kogish Roadless Area was allocated to Land Use Designation 4 (LUD 4) in the Tongass Land Management Plan   LUD 4 emphasis is on intensive development of commodity resources.

This area is in the KPC Long-Term Timber Sale primary sale area. Extensive timber harvest has occurred and is occurring to the north and west   The size of this roadless area continues to be reduced by timber harvest

Due to very difficult access to the usable parts of this roadless area and the lack of major recreation attractions such as major stream or lake systems, recreation use is low.

(7) **Appearance (Apparent Naturalness):** This area is within the Kupreanof Lowlands character type, which is characterized by predominantly low, rolling relief, with elevations seldom greater than 1,500 feet   Numerous island groups and intricate waterways are also common in this character type. Much of this area is quite representative of the character type,

though a major portion displays landscape features that have even less
diversity and distinctiveness than is common in that character type

About 50 percent of the area is inventoried as Variety Class B (possessing
a degree of diversity common to the character type in which it is located)
Over 33 percent of the area is rated as Variety Class C (possessing minimal
landscape diversity), while 17 percent is rated a Variety Class A (having a
high degree of landscape diversity)   These more scenic (Variety Class A)
areas are concentrated around the relatively rugged and diverse terrain of
Kogish Mountain and Staney Cone   Other scenic features are the intricate
shorelines and island groups in Salt Lake Bay and Nossuk Bay

The Existing Visual Condition of almost 90 percent of the area is Type I
(where the landscape has remained unaltered by human activity)   The
northern and eastern edges have been heavily modified by timber harvest

(8) **Surroundings (External Influences):** The major external influences on
most sides of this roadless area are road construction and logging   Native
corporation lands to the east have been completely logged over   To the
north, logging is an annual occurrence with new harvest planned in this
area as part of the KPC Long-term Sale for the 1989-94 operating period

(9) **Attractions and Features of Special Interest:** The natural features of
the area, the scenery, the saltwater bays and inlets, and the opportunity
to see wildlife and to study the processes which formed this country may
all be attractions   The fishing and solitude along some of the streams in
the southwestern portion of the area are an attraction   The area contains
five inventoried recreation places totaling 2,165 acres. There are no
improved trails with the area.

b. Capability of Management as Wilderness or in an Unroaded Condition

(1) **Manageability and Management Area Boundaries:** The boundaries are
easily identified. The area can easily be managed in its unroaded
condition or as wilderness.

(2) **Natural Integrity:** Even though roading and logging have occurred on
all sides, natural integrity of the area is very good.

(3) **Opportunity for Solitude:** Because of its difficult access, there is
excellent opportunity for solitude within the area   Near the boundary of
the area one can expect to hear the sounds of logging and, from some
vantage points, actually see logging activity.

(4) **Opportunity for Primitive Recreation:** There are no outstanding
opportunities for primitive recreation. Most recreation attractions are
associated with the saltwater bays, anchorages, and channels on the west
side of this roadless area where the experience level is primarily
semi-primitive motorized.

ROS Class	Acres
Semi-Primitive Non-motorized (SPNM)	49,351
Semi-Primitive Motorized (SPM)	3,432
Roaded Natural (RN)	520
Roaded Modified (RM)	21,607

There are five inventoried recreation places.

ROS CLASS	# OF REC. PLACES	TOTAL ACRES	CAPACITY BY RVD'S
SPM	4	2,125	13,000
RN	1	40	200

(5) **Special Features (Ecologic, Geologic, Scientific, Cultural):** There are no known special features within the area.

c. **Availability for Management as Wilderness or in an Unroaded Condition**

   (1) **Resource Potentials**

   (a) **Recreation Potential:** The rugged terrain and very difficult access into this roadless area severely constrain its recreation potential. Recognizing the small boat and kayak routes that pass through this area, the western and southern boundaries which border saltwater have potential for shelter sites and additional boat anchorages.

   (b) **Fish Resource:** The recently completed fish habitat inventory indicates that there is some potential for salmon enhancement projects, such as constructing fish passes, on several of the streams. The very difficult access limits capitalizing on this potential.

   (c) **Wildlife Resource:** No need has been identified for wildlife enhancement projects within this area.

   (d) **Timber Resource:** There are 32,134 acres inventoried as tentatively suitable for harvest. This includes 27,551 acres of non-riparian old growth and 4,112 of riparian old growth.

   (e) **Land Use Authorizations:** None.

   (f) **Minerals:** Although no mineral exploration has taken place in this area, the geology of the area indicates some potential for discovery of valuable minerals.

   (g) **Areas of Scientific Interest:** None.

   (2) **Management Considerations**

   (a) The rugged terrain over much of the area limits the opportunity for management of its usable resources, particularly the timber Those areas where logging is economically feasible are included in logging plans for the next five-year period (KPC Long-term Sale)

(b) Insects and Disease: Endemic tree diseases common to Southeast Alaska are present.

(c) Land Status: All National Forest System land

d. Relationship To Communities and Other Roadless and Wilderness Areas

(1) Nearby Roadless and Wilderness Areas and Uses: This roadless area is separated from the Thorne River and Karta Roadless Areas by a narrow strip of roaded and logged land

(2) Distance From Population Centers (accessibility): Approximate distances from population centers are as follows:

Community		Air Miles	Water Miles
Juneau	(Pop. 23,729)	170	210
Ketchikan	(Pop 12,705)	45	180
Craig	(Pop. 915)	12	12

Hollis, located on Prince of Wales Island, is the nearest stop on the Alaska Marine Highway.

(3) Interest by Proponents:

(a) Moratorium Areas: The area has not been identified as a "moratorium" area or proposed as Wilderness in legislative initiatives to date.

(b) Local Users/residents: The only use of the area by local residents is for occasional hunting.

e. Environmental Consequences

INDIVIDUAL ROADLESS AREA DESCRIPTION

NAME: Karta (510)   ACRES (GROSS): 129,664   ACRES (NFS): 121,440

GEOZONE: KO8
GEOGRAPHIC PROVINCE: Southern Outer Islands

1989 WILDERNESS ATTRIBUTE RATING: 21

a. Description

(1) **Relationship to RARE II areas:** The table below displays the VCU 1/ names, VCU numbers, acres, original WARS 2/ rating, and comments This enables the reader to compare the roadless areas evaluated in Appendix C with previous analyses.

VCU Name	VCU No.	1979 WARS Rating	Comments
	576		Not Rated
	586		Not Rated
Steelhead	595	21	
Control	596	21	
Goose Creek	597	21	
	598		Not Rated
	599		Not Rated
	601		Not Rated
North Creek	605	21	
Anderson	606	22	
Salmon Lake	607	23	
McGilvery	608	21	
	609		Not Rated
	610		Not Rated
	611		Not Rated
	622		Not Rated
	623		Not Rated

(2) **History:** The Karta River drainage has a rich aboriginal and recent cultural history. There are known prehistoric village sites, rock art, and other physical indications of aboriginal occupancy of sites within the area. In more recent times, the Karta area has seen considerable mineral exploration and active mining. The Flagstaff Mine produced silver and gold during the 1920's. Trapping was a common activity from the late 1800's to the 1950's.

1/ A VCU (Value Comparison Unit) is one of 867 watersheds which make up the forest and were differentiated for planning purposes in the Tongass Land Management Plan.

2/ Wilderness Attribute Rating System (WARS) was the nationwide system used to rate and evaluate wilderness attributes of roadless areas in the Roadless Area Review and Evaluation (RARE II).

The Karta Roadless Area is within the primary sale area for the Ketchikan
Pulp Company Long-term Timber Sale. In February 1989, a moratorium was
placed on timber harvest planning pending legislative action and possible
consideration of designating the area as Wilderness

(3) **Location and Access:** The Karta Roadless Area is located in the center
of the east side of the Prince of Wales Island and at the west end of
Kasaan Bay   Access to the Karta River is by boat or floatplane   The
north, west, and south sides are accessible by road

(4) **Geography and Topography:** The Karta River is a major west to east
trending drainage through a system of moderately rugged to rugged
mountains. The northern third of the area is relatively flat   Salmon
Lake, Karta Lake, and the Karta River form the principal water system
within the area and account for about 3,159 acres. There are 2,800 acres
of alpine. Shoreline on saltwater totals 32 miles.

(5) **Ecosystem:**

    (a) **Classification:** The area is in the Southern Outer Island
Geographic Province. This province is generally characterized by
rolling subdued and localized rugged topography.

    (b) **Vegetation:** Vegetation is typical Southeast Alaska coastal
temperate rain forest. The forest is primarily western hemlock and
Sitka spruce with large components of cedar. There are about 500
acres of muskeg.

There are approximately 99,687 acres of forested land of which 56,399
are commercial forest land. Of the commercial forest land, 48,122
acres are non-riparian old growth and 6,218 are riparian old growth

    (c) **Soils:** Soils are generally highly organic with low clay content
and are formed over bedrock. Soil depth is typically about 40 inches

    (d) **Fish Resource:** Fish resources have been rated as part of the
Tongass Land Management Plan (1979) and by the Alaska Department of
Fish and Game in its Forest Habitat Integrity Program (1983)   These
ratings describe the value of VCU's for sport fish, commercial fish,
and estuaries.

All VCU's with the exception of 598, 599, 601, and 611 are rated as
high value for commercial and sport fish. VCU 622 is rated as high
value estuary habitat. The Karta River is recognized as one of the
outstanding sport fishing streams in Southeast Alaska.

    (e) **Wildlife Resource:** This area has high populations of Sitka
black-tailed deer, black bear, otter, marten, mink, loon, and common
waterfowl. Alpine areas are excellent ptarmigan habitat

    (f) **Threatened and Endangered Species:** None

(6) **Current Use and Management:** The Tongass Land Management Plan
allocated the area to Land Use Designation (LUD) 1, Released. Released
LUD 1's are to be managed in their roadless condition, although fish and
wildlife improvement projects can be planned and implemented

The Karta River is a high recreation and subsistence use area. There are
five recreation use cabins and eight miles of trail within the area

(7) **Appearance (Apparent Naturalness):** This roadless area is part of the
Coastal Hills character type which is characterized by moderately steep
landforms, predominantly rounded summits, elevations ranging up to 4,500
feet, and flat-floored U-shaped valleys   Numerous island groups are also
common in this character type   This area is, for the most part, quite
representative of the Coastal Hills character type except for the very
rugged and scenic terrain near the south and west boundaries that make up
part of the Klawock Mountains.

About 20 percent of the area is inventoried as Variety Class A (having a
level of landscape diversity and scenic quality that is distinctive
relative to the character type in which it is located). The remaining 80
percent is rated as Variety Class B. The outstanding scenic features that
make up these Class A landscapes include the very rugged rock forms of the
Klawock Mountains. Significant also are the prominent waterforms including
the variety of lakes and river and stream features of this area.

About 85 percent of the area has a Type I Existing Visual Condition where
the natural landscape has remained unaltered by human activity   The rest
of the area has been moderately to heavily modified due to the logging and
roading activity along the northern and southern boundaries.

(8) **Surroundings (External Influences):** Extensive Native-owned
timberlands to the west of this roadless area are currently being
harvested. The areas to the north and south have also been roaded and
logged during different periods in the past. Major mountain ridges
physically isolate a great portion of the logging activity from the
roadless area. To the east is Kasaan Bay which is the main water access
route to Prince of Wales Island. It is this easy access route to the Karta
River along with the excellent fishing that creates the very heavy public
use of the Karta River area.

(9) **Attractions and Features of Special Interest:** The natural features of
the area, the scenery, the opportunity to see wildlife, and to study the
processes which formed this country may all be attractions. The
outstanding fishing in the Karta River water system is a premier
attraction. The area contains 22 inventoried recreation places containing
24,527 acres.

b. **Capability of Management as Wilderness or in an Unroaded Condition**

(1) **Manageability and Management Area Boundaries:** The boundaries of this
area are easy to identify and do not present any difficulty for management
as a roadless area boundary   The increasing popularity and use of the area
could cause some future difficulty in managing it as a wilderness due to
the decreasing solitude.

(2) **Natural Integrity:** Because it includes almost all of the Karta River drainage area, and includes no recent human-made intrusions except for the trail and cabins, natural integrity of this roadless area is very good The evidence of early day mining is no longer a significant influence on the area's naturalness

(3) **Opportunity for Solitude:** Between late June and September there is limited opportunity to find true solitude within the Karta River drainage The cabins at Salmon and Karta Lakes are generally fully booked for this use period   This causes near daily floatplane traffic to transport visitors in and out of the area   In addition, the eight-mile long Karta Trail is the only foot route into this roadless area. All visitors who access this area by boat use this trail. There is more opportunity for solitude on the alpine ridges that rim the Karta River basin.

(4) **Opportunity for Primitive Recreation:** There is good opportunity for semi-primitive to primitive recreation in the Karta River drainage which is the core of this roadless area. Much of the rest of this area borders on extensive timber harvest on both Native and National Forest lands, and hence is in a Roaded Modified or Semi-Primitive Motorized ROS class

ROS Class	Acres
Primitive I (P1)	20,395
Primitive II (P2)	11,017
Semi-Primitive Non-Motorized (SPNM)	54,919
Semi-Primitive Motorized (SPM).	2,998
Roaded Natural (RN)	3,218
Roaded Modified (RM)	26,335
Rural (R)	840

The area contains 22 inventoried recreation places.

ROS CLASS	# OF REC. PLACES	TOTAL ACRES	CAPACITY BY RVD'S
P2	2	11,017	4,680
SPNM	4	6,115	8,970
SPM	3	2,679	7,020
RN	4	1,699	3,060
RM	8	2,177	3,740
R	1	840	200

(5) **Special Features (Ecologic, Geologic, Scientific, Cultural):** There are no known special features within the area.

c. **Availability for Management as Wilderness or in an Unroaded Condition**

(1) **Resource Potentials**

(a) **Recreation Potential:** The current emphasis is to manage the area at about the present use level. Within the Karta River drainage, the present use level has already exceeded the capacity of the area for a primitive experience and is pushing the limits to allow for a semi-primitive experience   To this end outfitting and guiding is being limited to a rather low number, and no plans are contemplated to

construct additional cabins in the area A potential exists to
construct entry trails into the low use northern and southern edges of
this roadless area. There are also opportunities for alpine trails
along the ridges within the Klawock Mountains and along the Harris
ridge taking off from the Hollis-Klawock Highway

(b) **Fish Resource:** This roadless area has outstanding fish habitat
In addition, inventories show numerous opportunities for fish habitat
improvement on several of the streams within the area. Habitat
improvements would, for the most part, involve constructing fish
passes around natural barriers so salmon can reach high quality
spawning habitat that is currently unavailable.

(c) **Wildlife Resource:** There are no long-range plans to accomplish
habitat improvement project work within this roadless area.

(d) **Timber Resource:** There are 51,601 acres inventoried as
tentatively suitable for harvest. This includes 43,724 acres of
non-riparian old growth and 5,318 acres of riparian old growth.

(e) **Land Use Authorizations:** None.

(f) **Minerals:** The mineral potential within the area is considered to
be high. It is not unrealistic with an improvement in mining
economics that the Flagstaff Mine would reopen or that other old
claims would become viable mines in the future

(g) **Areas of Scientific Interest:** None

(2) **Management** Considerations

(a) It is anticipated that future management for most of this
roadless area will continue to be similar to that provided by the
LUD 1 designation in the current Tongass Land Management Plan; that
is, managed in the roadless condition with emphasis on recreation,
fish, and wildlife resources. Mining is a potential resource use that
cannot be planned for at this time. However, it is predicted that at
some time in the future mining activity will occur.

(b) **Fire:** The area has no significant fire history

(c) **Insects and Disease:** Endemic tree diseases common to Southeast
Alaska are present.

(d) **Land Status:** All National Forest System land.

d. **Relationship To Communities and Other Roadless and Wilderness Areas**

(1) **Nearby Roadless and Wilderness Areas and Uses:** This roadless area is
separated from the the Thorne River, Kogish, and Polk Roadless Areas by
roads and timber harvest units.

(2) **Distance From Population Centers (accessibility):** Approximate distances from population centers are as follows

Community			Air Miles	Water Miles
Juneau	(Pop	23,729)	170	200
Ketchikan	(Pop	12,705)	25	30
Hollis	(Pop	82)	6	10

Hollis, located on the Prince of Wales Island, is the nearest stop on the Alaska Marine Highway

(3) **Interest by Proponents:**

(a) **Moratorium Areas:** The area has been identified as a "moratorium" area pending congressional action on current wilderness initiatives

(b) **Local Users/residents:** The area receives substantial local use for subsistence and recreation activity

e. **Environmental Consequences**

INDIVIDUAL ROADLESS AREA DESCRIPTION

NAME: Thorne River (511)   ACRES (GROSS): 112,460   ACRES (NFS): 112,460

GEOZONE: K06
GEOGRAPHIC PROVINCE: Southern Outer Islands

1989 WILDERNESS ATTRIBUTE RATING: 22

a   Description

(1) **Relationship to RARE II areas:** The table below displays the VCU 1/
names, VCU numbers, acres, original WARS 2/ rating, and comments. This
enables the reader to compare the roadless areas evaluated in Appendix C
with previous analyses.

VCU Name	VCU No.	1979 WARS Rating	Comments
	571		Not Rated
Hatchery	574	22	
Thorne Lake	575	23	
Unnamed	576	21	
Logjam	577	21	
Snakey Lakes	578	20	
	579		Not Rated
	580		Not Rated
	581		Not Rated
	583		Not Rated
	584		Not Rated
	585		Not Rated
	588		Not Rated
	590		Not Rated
	595		Not Rated
	596		Not Rated
Goose Creek	597	21	

(2) **History:** This large and varied roadless area has received very little
use over time   Aboriginal cultures probably used the lower reaches of the
Thorne River for subsistence use   In recent history, trapping has occurred
in the Thorne River drainage. In the last twenty years there has been
increasing interest in the freshwater fishing and canoeing throughout the
water system.

1/ A VCU (Value Comparison Unit) is one of 867 watersheds which make up the
forest and were differentiated for planning purposes in the Tongass Land
Management Plan.
2/ Wilderness Attribute Rating System (WARS) was the nationwide system used to
rate the wilderness attributes of roadless areas in the Roadless Area
Review and Evaluation (RARE II).

The Thorne River Roadless Area is within the primary sale area for the
Ketchikan Pulp Company (KPC) Long-term Timber Sale   The periphery of the
area has been extensively roaded and logged and current plans include sale
units and roads within the roadless area boundary

(3) **Location and Access:** This roadless area includes a large part of the
center of Prince of Wales Island and almost all of the Thorne River
drainage

The southern boundary is formed by State Highway 929 and Forest Road 30
connecting the communities of Thorne Bay and Craig   These roads and other
logging roads provide land access to all sides of the roadless area   The
primary access to the interior of the roadless area is by floatplane   An
increasing means of access to the interior of the area is by canoe, but
this is limited to very skilled boaters.

(4) **Geography and Topography:** There are two distinct topographic types
within this roadless area. The larger is the broad, flat area essentially
made up of the Thorne River drainage. The other is the mountainous and
very rugged terrain of the eastern half of the area. Elevations range from
sea level to over 3,000 feet. There are 1,560 acres of alpine and 1,840
acres of fresh water within this roadless area. There are two miles of
saltwater shoreline.

(5) **Ecosystem:**

> (a) **Classification:** The area is in the Southern Outer Islands
> Geographic Province   This province is characterized by rolling
> subdued and localized rugged terrain.

> (b) **Vegetation:** Vegetation in this area is typical Southeast Alaska
> coastal temperate rain forest   The forest is primarily western
> hemlock and Sitka spruce with a large cedar component   There are
> 2,939 acres of muskeg.

> There are approximately 103,160 acres of forested land of which 61,514
> acres are commercial forest land. Of the commercial forest land,
> 55,351 acres are non-riparian old growth and 5,682 acres are riparian
> old growth.

> (c) **Soils:** These highly organic and low clay content soils are
> generally formed over bedrock and are about 40 inches deep

> (d) **Fish Resource:** Fish resources have been rated as part of the
> Tongass Land Management Plan (1979) and by the Alaska Department of
> Fish and Game in its Forest Habitat Integrity Program (1983)   These
> ratings describe the value of VCU's for sport fish, commercial fish,
> and estuaries.

> VCU's 574, 575, 576, 577, 578, 579, 580, 581, 588, 590, 595, 596, and
> 597 are rated high value for sport fish.

> VCU's 571, 574, 575, 576, 578, 579, 580, 581, 583, 588, 590, 595, 596,
> and 597 are rated high value for commercial fish.

VCU's 584 and 585 are rated high value for estuary habitat

(e) **Wildlife Resource:** This area has high populations of Sitka black-tailed deer, black bear, otter, marten, mink, loon, and common waterfowl. Alpine areas are excellent ptarmigan habitat The Thorne River and lakes in the area are known resting places for migrating trumpeter swans.

(f) **Threatened and Endangered Species:** None

(6) **Current Use and Management:** The Tongass Land Management Plan allocated this area to Land Use Designation 3 (LUD 3) (44,791 acres) and to LUD 4 (67,650 acres). The LUD 3 area is to be managed for a variety of uses and activities in a compatible and complementary manner. In the LUD 4 portion, the emphasis is on intensive resource use and development of resources with commodity and market values.

One recreation use cabin is located at Honker Lake. The trail/canoe system within the area is frequently used. Outfitting and guiding are becoming significant activities on the Thorne River system.

(7) **Appearance (Apparent Naturalness):** The northern half of this roadless area is part of the Kupreanof Lowlands character type which is characterized by low, rolling relief with elevations seldom greater than 1,500 feet. The southern half is part of the Coastal Hills character type which generally possesses steeper slopes, and more massive landforms The area exhibits the landscape characteristics of both character types, though not in a manner that corresponds to the character type boundaries The western half along the Hatchery Creek and Thorne River is characterized by low, rolling relief, while the eastern half is made up of large blocky landforms with rounded to flat ridges

Almost the entire area (90 percent) is inventoried as Variety Class B (possessing a level of landscape diversity that is common to the character type). Only about eight percent of the area is rated as Variety Class A (possessing a high degree of landscape diversity for the character type) These more scenic Variety Class A areas are primarily around the Snakey Lakes, an intricate complex of narrow, winding freshwater bodies north of the main Thorne Lake drainage. Other notable scenic areas are various portions of the Thorne River and its many areas of grassy meadows and large stands of spruce.

About 83 percent of this roadless area is in a Type I Existing Visual Condition where the natural landscape has remained unaltered by human activity. Most of the rest of the area is in a moderately to heavily modified visual condition due to the extensive logging around its edge

(8) **Surroundings (External Influences):** The Thorne River Roadless Area is bounded on the north, west, south, and most of the east by extensive timber harvest areas. A small segment of the eastern boundary is saltwater The southern boundary is formed by a Forest Highway which is one of the principal roads on Prince of Wales Island.

(9) **Attractions and Features of Special Interest:** The natural features of the area, the scenery, the opportunity to see wildlife, and to study the processes which formed this country may all be attractions   The extensive opportunity to canoe within the area is an outstanding attraction   The fishing and solitude, particularly along various segments of the Thorne River, are a major attraction. The area contains 17 inventoried recreation places totaling 49,121 acres

b   Capability of Management as Wilderness or in an Unroaded Condition

(1) **Manageability and Management Area Boundaries:** The existing timber harvest areas, the Forest highway, the ridge lines, and the muskeg areas form very definable and manageable boundaries

(2) **Natural Integrity:** The area is unmodified except for one recreation use cabin and a small trail system.

(3) **Opportunity for Solitude:** Very good opportunities for solitude exist within the area, excluding the very fringe where the sights and sounds of logging and vehicle traffic may be evident. Floatplanes and boats are used to transport people to the numerous fishing lakes and the recreation cabin within the area. Persons using this roadless area during the summer may encounter other recreation or subsistence users.

(4) **Opportunity for Primitive Recreation:** Due to the many lake and stream oriented recreation attractions and the remoteness and solitude of the area, the interior of the Thorne River Roadless Area offers outstanding opportunities for primitive recreation.

ROS Class	Acres
Primitive I (P1)	31,209
Primitive II (P2)	4,161
Semi-Primitive (SPNM)	58,817
Roaded Natural (RN)	4,302
Roaded Modified (RM)	13,971

The area contains 17 inventoried recreation places.

ROS CLASS	# OF REC. PLACES	TOTAL ACRES	CAPACITY BY RVD'S
P1	4	15,164	4,940
P2	1	4,161	1,560
SPNM	7	25,353	9,431
RN	4	2,642	19,084
RM	1	1,801	2,925

(5) **Special Features (Ecologic, Geologic, Scientific, Cultural):** There are no known special features within the area.

c Availability for Management as Wilderness or in an Unroaded Condition

    (1) Resource Potentials

        (a) Recreation Potential: The current management emphasis for the
Thorne River, Honker Divide, and Snakey Lakes area is for primitive
recreation. Future planning is centered upon completing a system of
canoe routes and portages, and identifying good, well-spaced campsites
rather than constructing shelters

        In general, the Thorne River Roadless Area has considerable potential
for developed and dispersed   However, to use it safely, this area
requires considerable wilderness skills   Even with well-developed
canoe trails and portages, the area is unforgiving and the
inexperienced visitor could be at risk using it. For these reasons,
the recreation potential of the area may not be developed in the
foreseeable future.

        (b) Fish Resource: This roadless area has outstanding fish habitat
This, notwithstanding, inventories show that there are numerous
opportunities for fish habitat improvement on several of the streams
within the area. Almost all of this potential is in constructing fish
passes around or over natural barriers so salmon can reach high
quality spawning habitat that is currently unavailable

        (c) Wildlife Resource: There are no long-range plans to accomplish
wildlife habitat improvement project work within this roadless area

        (d) Timber Resource: There are 54,972 acres inventoried as
tentatively suitable for harvest. This includes 49,430 acres of
non-riparian old growth and 5,042 acres of riparian old growth

        (e) Land Use Authorizations: None.

        (f) Minerals: The potential for finding and developing locatable
minerals low.

        (g) Areas of Scientific Interest: None.

    (2) Management Considerations

        (a) Located within the KPC Long-term Timber Sale primary sale area.
this roadless area contains significant volumes of merchantable
timber. For the remainder of the life of the long-term sale contract.
it is likely that harvest entries will continue to be made into the
existing unroaded area.

        One of the definitive management objectives for the area is to
preserve the recreational and natural values in the Honker Divide
area. To this end, the Tongass Land Management Plan directs that no
timber harvest may occur within a quarter-mile wide strip on either
side of the Thorne River, and that only a limited harvest occur within
the next quarter-mile strip on either side of the river

        (b) Fire: The area has no significant fire history

(c) **Insects and Disease:** Endemic tree diseases common to Southeast Alaska are present.

(d) **Land Status:** All of the area is National Forest System land

d   **Relationship To Communities and Other Roadless and Wilderness Areas**

(1) **Nearby Roadless and Wilderness Areas and Uses:** This roadless area is separated from the the Karta, Kogish, Sweetwater, and Ratz Roadless Areas by roads and timber harvest units

(2) **Distance From Population Centers (accessibility):** Approximate distances from population centers are as follows:

Community		Air Miles	Water Miles
Juneau	(Pop. 23,729)	170	200
Ketchikan	(Pop. 12,705)	35	45

Hollis, located on Prince of Wales Island, is the nearest stop on the Alaska Marine Highway

(3) **Interest by Proponents:**

(a) **Moratorium Areas:** The area has not been identified as a "moratorium" area or proposed as Wilderness in legislative initiatives to date.

(b) **Local Users/residents:** The area receives significant local use for subsistence and recreation activities.

e.   **Environmental Consequences**

INDIVIDUAL ROADLESS AREA DESCRIPTION

NAME: Ratz (512)   ACRES (GROSS): 8,349   ACRES (NFS): 8,349

GEOZONE: K06
GEOGRAPHIC PROVINCE: Southern Outer Islands

1989 WILDERNESS ATTRIBUTE RATING: 20

a. Description

(1) **Relationship to RARE II areas:** The table below displays the VCU 1/
names, VCU numbers, acres, original WARS 2/ rating, and comments This
enables the reader to compare the roadless areas evaluated in Appendix C
with previous analyses.

VCU Name	VCU No.	1979 WARS Rating	Comments
Baird Point	582	20	
	583	.	Not Rated
	584		Not Rated

(2) **History:** This area does not have a history of contemporary use or
activity. There may have been some aboriginal use within the area but this
has not been confirmed through cultural resource investigations Some
early day hand logging occurred along the saltwater of Ratz Harbor   .

The Ratz Roadless Area is within the primary sale area for the Ketchikan
Pulp Company (KPC) Long-term Timber Sale.

(3) **Location and Access:** The Ratz Roadless Area is located on the east
side of Prince of Wales Island approximately 15 miles north of Thorne Bay.
The only access to this area is by boat or floatplane through Ratz Harbor

(4) **Geography and Topography:** The area is characterized by very rugged
terrain except for the uplands west of Ratz Harbor where the topography is
flat wetlands and muskeg. The highest elevation is 3,000 feet There are
five miles of shoreline on saltwater.

(5) **Ecosystem:**

(a) **Classification:** The area is in the Southern Outer Islands
Geographic Province. This province is characterized by rolling
subdued and localized rugged topography.

1/ A VCU (**Value Comparison Unit**) is one of 867 watersheds which make up the
forest and were differentiated for planning purposes in the Tongass Land
Management Plan.
2/ Wilderness Attribute Rating System (WARS) was the nationwide system used to
rate the wilderness attributes of roadless areas in the Roadless Area
Review and Evaluation (RARE II).

(b) **Vegetation:** Vegetation in this area is typical Southeast Alaska coastal temperate rain forest The forest is primarily western hemlock and Sitka spruce with a large cedar component

There are approximately 7,588 acres of forested land of which 4,606 acres are commercial forest land Of the commercial forest land, 4,125 acres are non-riparian old growth and 461 acres are riparian old growth.

(c) **Soils:** These highly organic, low clay content soils are generally formed over bedrock Soil are typically about 40 inches deep.

(d) **Fish Resource:** The fish resources have been rated as part of the Tongass Land Management Plan (1979) and by the Alaska Department of Fish and Game in its Forest Habitat Integrity Program (1983) These ratings describe the value of VCU's for sport fish, commercial fish. and estuaries.

VCU 581 is high value for commercial and sport fish, and VCU 582 is high value for commercial fish and estuary habitat.

(e) **Wildlife Resource:** This area has populations of Sitka black-tailed deer, black bear, and a scattering of other animals and birds common to Prince of Wales Island.

(f) **Threatened and Endangered Species:** None.

(6) **Current Use and Management:** The Tongass Land Management Plan allocated this area to Land Use Designations (LUD) 3 (4,024 acres) and LUD 4 (4,325 acres). The area around Ratz Harbor is in LUD 3 and is to be managed for a variety of uses and activities in a compatible and complementary manner. The emphasis in the LUD 4 areas is to manage for intensive resource use, and for the development of resources with commodity and market values.

The only direct resource management activity of this area has been related to timber management. The perimeter of the roadless area has been reduced over time by road construction and logging, and there are harvest units planned in the peripheral area during the 1989-94 KPC Long-term Timber Sale operating plan.

An electronics site, authorized by a special use permit, is located on Baird Peak.

(7) **Appearance (Apparent Naturalness):** This roadless area is part of the Coastal Hills character type which is characterized by moderately steep landforms, predominantly rounded summits, elevations up to 4,500 feet and flat-floored, U-shaped valleys Numerous island groups are also common in this character type. This relatively small roadless area primarily includes one steep hillside and a long, rounded alpine ridge rising up from Clarence Strait

The entire area is inventoried Variety Class B (possessing landscape diversity common to the character type) The major scenic features are the diverse alpine terrain features and small lakes near the summit of Baird Peak.

About 53 percent of the area is in a Type I Existing Visual Condition where the natural landscape has remained unaltered by human activity. Due to the extensive timber harvest around the periphery of this area, the rest is in a moderately- to heavily-altered visual condition. Almost 20 percent is in a Type VI visual condition where the alterations create glaring contrasts with the natural landscape

(8) **Surroundings (External Influences):** The Ratz Roadless Area is bounded entirely by roads and timber harvest units or saltwater.

(9) **Attractions and Features of Special Interest:** The natural features of the area, the scenery, and the opportunity to see wildlife and to study the processes which formed this country may all be attractions. The area contains four inventoried recreation places totaling 5,043 acres

b. **Capability of Management as Wilderness or in an Unroaded Condition**

(1) **Manageability and Management Area Boundaries:** The existing timber harvest areas and roads form an irregular but very definable boundary Because of this, and the geographically well-defined nature of this ridge. the area can readily be managed as a roadless area.

(2) **Natural Integrity:** The area has good natural integrity.

(3) **Opportunity for Solitude:** Except when logging activity is taking place in nearby areas, the opportunity for solitude within the area is good. Persons camping or hiking within the area are unlikely to encounter other persons.

(4) **Opportunity for Primitive Recreation:** Due to the limited size of the area, and the proximity of extensive logging activities that are presently taking place, the potential for primitive recreation experiences is limited.

ROS Class	Acres
Semi-Primitive Non-Motorized (SPNM)	3,922
Semi-Primitive Motorized (SPM)	2,625
Roaded Modified (RM)	1,802

The area contains four inventoried recreation places.

ROS CLASS	# OF REC. PLACES	TOTAL ACRES	CAPACITY BY RVD'S
SPNM	1	3,362	3,120
SPM	1	780	7,800
RM	2	901	6,350

(5) **Special Features (Ecologic, Geologic, Scientific, Cultural):** There are no known special features within the area

c   Availability for Management as Wilderness or in an Unroaded Condition

    (1)   Resource Potentials

        (a)   Recreation Potential: There is relatively low potential for
        recreation development in the area. There is an identified potential
        for alpine hiking trails extending from existing logging roads to the
        various small alpine lakes in the area

        (b)   Fish Resource: The recently completed fish habitat inventory
        indicates that the streams and lakes within this area are supporting
        fish populations at about the optimum level, and no specific projects
        are planned.

        (c)   Wildlife Resource: There are no short- or long-range plans to
        accomplish habitat improvement project work within the area

        (d)   Timber Resource: There are 4,146 acres inventoried as
        tentatively suitable for harvest. This includes 3,685 acres of
        non-riparian old growth and 381 acres of riparian old growth

        (e)   Land Use Authorizations: Alaska Telecom's electronics site on
        Baird Peak is authorized by special use permit.

        (f)   Minerals: The potential for mineral development is low

        (g)   Areas of Scientific Interest: None.

    (2)   Management Considerations

        (a)   The rugged terrain limits plans for resource management within
        this roadless area. The roadless area is important as unaltered
        wildlife habitat adjacent to extensive timber harvest areas

        (b)   Fire: The area has no significant fire history

        (c)   Insects and Disease: Endemic tree diseases common to Southeast
        Alaska are present

        (d)   Land Status: All of this area is National Forest System land

d. Relationship To Communities and Other Roadless and Wilderness Areas

    (1)   Nearby Roadless and Wilderness Areas and Uses: This roadless area is
    separated from the the Thorne River and Sweetwater Roadless Areas by roads
    and timber harvest areas.

    (2)   Distance From Population Centers (accessibility): Approximate
    distances from population centers are as follows·

Community		Air Miles	Water Miles
Juneau	(Pop 23,729)	170	200
Ketchikan	(Pop. 12,705)	45	70

Hollis, located on Prince of Wales Island, is the nearest stop on the
Alaska Marine Highway

(3) Interest by Proponents:

(a) **Moratorium Areas:** The area has not been identified as a
"moratorium" area or proposed as Wilderness in legislative initiatives
to date.   •

(b) **Local Users/residents:** The area receives light use by local
people for recreation and subsistence.

e. **Environmental Consequences**

INDIVIDUAL ROADLESS AREA DESCRIPTION

NAME: Sweetwater (513)   ACRES (GROSS): 11,104   ACRES (NFS): 11,104

GEOZONE: K06
GEOGRAPHIC PROVINCE: Southern Outer Islands

1989 WILDERNESS ATTRIBUTE RATING: 21

.1 Description

(1) Relationship to RARE II areas: The table below displays the VCU 1. names, VCU numbers, acres, original WARS 2/ rating, and comments This enables the reader to compare the roadless areas evaluated in Appendix C with previous analyses.

VCU Name	VCU No.	1979 WARS Rating	Comments
	572		Not Rated
	573		Not Rated
Hatchery	574	22	
	581		Not Rated

(2) History: This area has no history of contemporary use or activity Some aboriginal use may have occurred within the area, but this has not been confirmed through cultural resource investigations

The Sweetwater Roadless Area is within the primary sale area for the Ketchikan Pulp Company (KPC) Long-term Timber Sale

(3) Location and Access: The Sweetwater area is located on the east side of Prince of Wales Island approximately 15 miles north of Thorne Bay Access to the area is by a road system that encircles the entire roadless area.

(4) Geography and Topography: The Sweetwater Roadless Area is characterized by fairly rugged terrain with elevations up to 2,500 feet The area primarily includes the broad, unroaded ridge tops between the Sweetwater and Luck Lake basins and does not include any saltwater shoreline.

(5) Ecosystem:

(a) Classification: The area is classified as being in the Southern Outer Islands Geographic Province. The region is characterized by rolling subdued and localized rugged terrain.

1/ A VCU (Value Comparison Unit) is one of 867 watersheds which make up the forest and were differentiated for planning purposes in the Tongass Land Management Plan.
2/ Wilderness Attribute Rating System (WARS) was the nationwide system used to rate the wilderness attributes of roadless areas in the Roadless Area Review and Evaluation (RARE II).

(b) **Vegetation:** Vegetation is typical Southeast Alaska coastal temperate rain forest. The forest is primarily western hemlock and Sitka spruce with a large cedar component. There are numerous interspersed areas of muskeg.

There are approximately 10,684 acres of forested land of which 5,922 acres are commercial forest land. Of the commercial forest land, 5,032 acres are non-riparian old growth and 560 acres are riparian old growth.

(c) **Soils:** These highly organic, low clay content soils are generally formed over bedrock and range to a depth of 40 inches

(d) **Fish Resource:** Fish resources have been rated as part of the Tongass Land Management Plan (1979) and by the Alaska Department of Fish and Game in its Forest Habitat Integrity Program (1983). These ratings describe the value of VCU's for sport fish, commercial fish, and estuaries

VCU's 574 and 581 have high value for commercial fish, VCU's 573, 574, and 581 high value for sport fish, and VCU 572 high value for estuary habitat.

(e) **Wildlife Resource:** This area has populations of Sitka black-tailed deer, black bear, and a scattering of other wildlife species common to Prince of Wales Island.

(f) **Threatened and Endangered Species:** None.

(6) **Current Use and Management:** The Tongass Land Management Plan allocated this area to Land Use Designation 4 (LUD 4). Emphasis in LUD 4 areas is to manage for intensive resource use, and development of resources with commodity and market values.

The only direct resource management activity of this area has been related to timber management. The perimeter of the roadless area has been reduced over time by road construction and logging. The area is within the primary sale area for the KPC Long-term Timber Sale.

(7) **Appearance (Apparent Naturalness):** This area is part of the Kupreanof Lowlands character type which is characterized by predominantly low relief, with elevations seldom greater than 1,500 feet. Numerous island groups and intricate waterways are also common in this character type. This area is generally representative of this character type except for slightly higher elevations. There are no outstanding, unique landscape features in this small area.

The entire area is inventoried as Variety Class B (possessing levels of landscape diversity common to the character type).

Because of the prominence of heavy logging surrounding this area, only 35 percent of the area is in a Type I Existing Visual Condition where the natural landscape has remained unaltered by human activity The rest of the area is in moderately to heavily modified state, including about 17 percent in Type VI visual condition where the heavy alterations to the landscape are in glaring contrast to its natural characteristics

(8) Surroundings (External Influences): The Sweetwater Roadless Area is entirely bounded by roads and timber harvest units This is a significant external influence upon the area

(9) Attractions and Features of Special Interest: Because of the very average scenic quality and the presence of extensive timber harvest around this small area, there are no major scenic attractions. Trumpeter Lake, a small waterbody near the alpine zone of the broad ridge, is probably the most significant natural feature in the area. The area contains two inventoried recreation places totaling 4,501 acres, but use is light

b. Capability of Management as Wilderness or in an Unroaded Condition

(1) Manageability and Management Area Boundaries: The existing timber harvest areas and roads form an irregular but very definable boundary The area is readily manageable in a roadless condition since it is primarily made up of a series of alpine ridges that are fairly identifiable

(2) Natural Integrity: This roadless area is unaltered, though the periphery of the area has been heavily modified. Its boundaries provide a logical land unit for management purposes

(3) Opportunity for Solitude: Within the area, the opportunity for solitude is excellent. Persons camping or hiking within the area are unlikely to encounter other persons

(4) Opportunity for Primitive Recreation: The limited size of the area, the extensiveness of adjacent timber harvest, and the limited number of recreation attractions result in limited primitive recreation potential

ROS Class	Acres
Semi-Primitive Non-Motorized (SPNM)	6,162
Roaded Modified (RM)	4,942

The area contains two inventoried recreation places

ROS CLASS	# OF REC. PLACES	TOTAL ACRES	CAPACITY BY RVD'S
SPNM	1	4,221	1,932
RM	1	280	437

(5) Special Features (Ecologic, Geologic, Scientific, Cultural): There are no known special features within the area.

c. Availability for Management as Wilderness or in an Unroaded Condition

(1) Resource Potentials

(a) **Recreation Potential:** Due to the minimal recreation attractions, the recreation potential of this area is relatively low. Identified alpine hiking opportunities lead from the Trumpeter Lake area Good hunting opportunities possibly exist.

(b) **Fish Resource:** The recently completed fish habitat inventory indicates that there is potential for salmon enhancement projects, such as constructing fish passes on several of the streams within the area.

(c) **Wildlife Resource:** There are no short- or long-range plans to accomplish habitat improvement project work within the area.

(d) **Timber Resource:** There are 5,382 acres inventoried as tentatively suitable for harvest. This includes 4,802 acres of non-riparian old growth and 520 acres of riparian old growth

(e) **Land Use Authorizations:** None.

(f) **Minerals:** Mineral development potential is low.

(g) **Areas of Scientific Interest:** None.

(2) Management Considerations

(a) The rugged terrain and the general lack of commercial timber limits resource management potential within this roadless area The area is important as unaltered wildlife habitat adjacent to extensive timber harvest areas.

(b) **Fire:** The area has no significant fire history.

(c) **Insects and Disease:** Endemic tree diseases common to Southeast Alaska are present.

(d) **Land Status:** All of the area is National Forest System land.

d. Relationship To Communities and Other Roadless and Wilderness Areas

(1) **Nearby Roadless and Wilderness Areas and Uses:** This roadless area is separated from the the Sarkar, Thorne River, and Ratz Roadless Areas by roads and timber harvest areas.

(2) **Distance From Population Centers (accessibility):** Approximate distances from population centers are as follows:

Community		Air Miles	Water Miles
Juneau	(Pop. 23,729)	170	200
Ketchikan	(Pop. 12,705)	45	70

Hollis, located on Prince of Wales Island, is the nearest stop on the
Alaska Marine Highway

(3) Interest by Proponents:

(a) Moratorium Areas: The area has not been identified as a
"moratorium" area or proposed as Wilderness in legislative initiatives
to date

(b) Local Users/residents: The area is not known to be of
significant interest to local residents or users   The area is not
used for recreation other than for deer hunting.

e. Environmental Consequences

INDIVIDUAL ROADLESS AREA DESCRIPTION

NAME: Sarkar (514)   ACRES (GROSS): 73,725   ACRES (NFS): 73,565

GEOZONE: K06
GEOGRAPHIC PROVINCE: Southern Outer Islands

1989 WILDERNESS ATTRIBUTE RATING: 23

a. Description

    (1) **Relationship to RARE II areas:** The table below displays the VCU 1/
    names, VCU numbers, acres, original WARS 2/ rating, and comments. This
    enables the reader to compare the roadless areas evaluated in Appendix C
    with previous analyses.

VCU Name	VCU No.	1979 WARS Rating	Comments
	538		Not Rated
Sarheen	549	21	
	550		Not Rated
	551		Not Rated
Barnes Lake	552	24	
Mable Creek	553	24	
Sarkar	554	23	
	571		Not Rated
	573		Not Rated
Logjam	577	21	

    (2) **History:** This area, used by prehistoric and historic Native cultures,
    contains what may be one of the larger-known Native summer camps Two
    traditional-use Native sites have been conveyed to Native Corporations in
    accordance with ANILCA. In the early 1900's, salteries were located on the
    west coast of this roadless area.

    The Sarkar Lake chain has a long history of subsistence and recreation
    use. Very old corduroy trail segments are in evidence. This same area is
    known for past and present use as a canoe route.

    The Sarkar Roadless Area is within the primary sale area for the Ketchikan
    Pulp Company (KPC) Long-term Timber Sale.

1/ A VCU (**Value Comparison Unit**) is one of 867 watersheds which make up the
    forest and were differentiated for planning purposes in the Tongass Land
    Management Plan.
2/ Wilderness Attribute Rating System (WARS) was the nationwide system used to
    rate the wilderness attributes of roadless areas in the Roadless Area
    Review and Evaluation (RARE II).

(3) **Location and Access:** The area is located on the north end of Prince of Wales Island and is bounded on all sides by roaded timber harvest areas. The area is accessed by saltwater on the east and west coasts of the Prince of Wales Island, by the network of roads around the exterior, and by floatplane to the several lakes within the area

(4) **Geography and Topography:** The area is characterized by low elevation, subdued topography, and low-lying muskeg systems. The maximum elevation is 2,000 feet. There are 21 miles of saltwater shoreline and numerous freshwater lakes totaling 5,316 acres

(5) **Ecosystem:**

(a) **Classification:** The area is in the Southern Outer Islands Geographic Province. This province is characterized by rolling subdued and localized rugged topography.

(b) **Vegetation:** Vegetation is typical Southeast Alaska coastal temperate rain forest. The forest is primarily western hemlock and Sitka spruce with a large cedar component. There are numerous interspersed areas of muskeg vegetative totaling 1,941 acres

There are approximately 65,308 acres of forested land of which 37,494 acres is commercial forest land. Of the commercial forest land, 33,394 acres are non-riparian old growth and 3,860 riparian old growth.

(c) **Soils:** Soils are highly organic, of low clay content, and generally formed over bedrock. They are typically about 40 inches deep.

(d) **Fish Resource:** Fish resources have been rated as part of the Tongass Land Management Plan (1979) and by the State Department of Fish and Game in its Forest Habitat Integrity Program (1983). These ratings describe the value of VCU's for commercial fish, sport fish and estuaries.

VCU's 538, 552, 553, 554, 573, and 570 are high value for sport fish and VCU's 538, 554, and 571 are high value for commercial fish. No VCU's were highly rated as estuaries

(e) **Wildlife Resource:** This area has populations of Sitka black-tailed deer, black bear, otter, marten, mink, loon, and common waterfowl. Sarkar Lake is a wintering area for trumpeter swan.

(f) **Threatened and Endangered Species:** None.

(6) **Current Use and Management:** The Tongass Land Management Plan allocated this area to Land Use Designations (LUD's) 2, 3, and 4. The center of the Sarkar Roadless Area is the LUD 2 area (25,406 acres) which is to be managed in the roadless condition with the exception that wildlife and fish habitat improvement projects are permitted. The LUD 3 area (26,140 acres) is to be managed for a variety of uses and activities in a compatible and complementary manner. Management emphasis in the LUD 4 area

(21,959 acres) is on intensive resource use and development of resources with commodity and market values.

There are three recreation use cabins located at Barnes, Sweetwater, and Sarkar Lakes. With the development of a few portages, Sarkar Lake and its associated lakes provide outstanding canoeing opportunities The main lake adjacent to the road system is presently used extensively for canoeing Sarkar is a significant subsistence use area.

(7) **Appearance (Apparent Naturalness):** The entire roadless area is part of the Kupreanof Lowlands character type which is characterized by predominantly low, rolling relief, and elevations seldom greater than 1,500 feet. Numerous island groups and intricate waterways are also common in this character type. This roadless area exhibits very gently rolling to almost flat landscapes. Though the landforms of the area are relatively featureless, the Sarkar Lakes area possesses a highly intricate and diverse network of freshwater channels, ponds, larger lakes, and islands.

About 18 percent of this area is inventoried as Variety Class A (possessing a high degree of landscape diversity relative to the character type). These landscapes include primarily the Sarkar Lakes and Gold and Galigan Lagoon areas. About 58 percent is inventoried as Variety Class B (possessing landscape diversity common in the character type Due to the large areas of low, featureless terrain much of this area (24 percent) is rated a Variety Class C (possessing a low degree of landscape diversity)

About 83 percent of the area is in a Type I Existing Visual Condition where the natural landscape has remained unaltered by human activity The rest of the area (17 percent) exhibits all the other levels of landscape modification, from Type II to Type VI, due to the moderate to heavy logging activity around the edge of this roadless area.

(8) **Surroundings (External Influences):** The Sarkar Roadless Area is bounded on the north, west, south, and most of the east by extensive timber harvest areas. A small segment of the eastern boundary is saltwater The pending Native land selections at South Neck Lake and South Whale Pass have been excluded from this roadless area but do form part of its boundary

(9) **Attractions and Features of Special Interest:** The natural features of the area, the scenery, the saltwater bays and inlets, and the opportunity to see wildlife and to study the processes which formed this country may all be attractions. The extensive canoeing opportunity within the area is an outstanding attraction. The fishing and solitude of the area are attractions. The area contains 14 inventoried recreation places totaling 26,482 acres.

b. **Capability of Management as Wilderness or in an Unroaded Condition**

(1) **Manageability and Management Area Boundaries:** The existing timber harvest areas along with ridge lines and muskeg areas form very definable and manageable boundaries.

(2) **Natural Integrity:** The area is unmodified except for the three recreation use cabins and the trail system

(3) Opportunity for Solitude: There is very good opportunity for solitude
within the area excluding the very fringe where the sights and sounds of
logging and vehicle traffic may be evident Floatplanes and boats are used
to transport people to the numerous fishing lakes and three recreation
cabins within the area. Persons using the Sarkar Lake water system during
the summer may encounter other recreation or subsistence users

(4) Opportunity for Primitive Recreation: There are excellent primitive
recreation opportunities, particularly in the northern end of the Sarkar
Lakes chain due to the remoteness and solitude of the area and to its
outstanding canoeing, fishing and camping opportunities

ROS Class	Acres
Primitive II (P2)	11,553
Semi-Primitive Non-Motorized (SPNM)	41,950
Semi-Primitive Motorized (SPM)	8,443
Roaded Natural (RN)	982
Roaded Modified (RM)	9,817

The area contains 14 inventoried recreation places.

ROS CLASS	# OF REC. PLACES	TOTAL ACRES	CAPACITY BY RVD'S
P2	1	7,504	3,888
SPNM	3	9,677	4,668
SPM	5	4,497	5,919
RN	2	321	5,458
RM	3	4,482	12,413

(5) Special Features (Ecologic, Geologic, Scientific, Cultural): There
are no known special features within the area.

c. Availability for Management as Wilderness or in an Unroaded Condition

(1) Resource Potentials

(a) Recreation Potential: There is potential for trail construction
and the development of canoe portages in the Sarkar Lakes area, and
additional recreation cabins throughout this area.

(b) Fish Resource: The recently completed fish habitat inventory
indicates that there is potential for salmon enhancement projects,
such as constructing fish passes on several streams within the area

(c) Wildlife Resource: There are long-range plans to accomplish some
habitat improvement project work within the fringe of this roadless
area.

(d) Timber Resource: There are 33,335 acres inventoried as
tentatively suitable for harvest This includes 31,515 acres of
non-riparian old growth and 3,620 acres of riparian old growth

(e) Land Use Authorizations: None.

(f) **Minerals:** Currently, no mining or known prospecting is occurring within this roadless area.

(g) **Areas of Scientific Interest:** The Sarkar Lakes area is under consideration as a Research Natural Area.

(2) **Management Considerations**

(a) The area cannot be easily managed for timber production because of the large number of lakes, streams, and riparian areas, and because the timber is arranged in small dispersed stands throughout the area. The area is important for wildlife as a place of unaltered habitat within a much wider area of extensive timber harvest

The area has considerable potential for developed and dispersed recreation activity.

(b) **Fire:** The area has no significant fire history.

(c) **Insects and Disease:** Endemic tree diseases common to Southeast Alaska are present.

(d) **Land Status:** All of the area is National Forest System land with no pending Native or State land selections

d. **Relationship To Communities and Other Roadless and Wilderness Areas**

(1) **Nearby Roadless and Wilderness Areas and Uses:** This roadless area is separated from the the Salmon Bay, Kosciusko, Sweetwater, and Thorne River Roadless Areas by approximately 10 miles of roaded timber harvest areas

(2) **Distance From Population Centers (accessibility):** Approximate distances from population centers are as follows.

Community		Air Miles	Water Miles
Juneau	(Pop. 23,729)	170	200
Ketchikan	(Pop. 12,705)	75	90

Hollis, located on Prince of Wales Island, is the nearest stop on the Alaska Marine Highway.

(3) **Interest by Proponents:**

(a) **Moratorium Areas:** The area has been identified as a "moratorium" area in pending Tongass reform legislation.

(b) **Local Users/residents:** The area receives significant local use for subsistence and recreation activity.

e. **Environmental Consequences**

INDIVIDUAL ROADLESS AREA DESCRIPTION

NAME: Kosciusko (515)   ACRES (GROSS): 70,597   ACRES (NFS): 70,216

GEOZONE: K11
GEOGRAPHIC PROVINCE: Southern Outer Islands

1989 WILDERNESS ATTRIBUTE RATING: 23

a. Description

(1) **Relationship to RARE II areas:** The table below displays the VCU 1/
names, VCU numbers, acres, original WARS 2/ rating, and comments   This
enables the reader to compare the roadless areas evaluated in Appendix C
with previous analyses.

VCU Name	VCU No.	1979 WARS Rating	Comments
	531		Not Rated
	536		Not Rated
	537		Not Rated
Shipley	541	24	
	542		Not Rated
	543		Not Rated
	546		Not Rated
Davidson Inlet	547	23	
Holbrook Mt.	548	24	
Sarheen	549	21	
	555		Not Rated
	556		Not Rated

(2) **History:** The coastal area was used by prehistoric and historic Native
cultures. The west coast area is known to have been used by the Russians
for trading with the Natives. There is some evidence of early day hand
logging along several of the sheltered bays. In the early 1900's, some
marble mining occurred in the Dry Pass area. The entire Kosciusko Roadless
Area is included within the primary area for the Ketchikan Pulp Corporation
Long-term Timber Sale.

(3) **Location and Access:** The area is located on the northwest end of
Prince of Wales Island. It is bounded by roaded and harvested areas on the
north, east, and south. Access to this area is by road, by boat through
Shakan and Shipley bays, and by floatplane.

1/ A VCU (Value Comparison Unit) is one of 867 watersheds which make up the
forest and were differentiated for planning purposes in the Tongass Land
Management Plan.

2/ Wilderness Attribute Rating System (WARS) was the nationwide system used to
rate the wilderness attributes of roadless areas in the Roadless Area
Review and Evaluation (RARE II).

(4) Geography and Topography: This area is within the low mountain arc of
the Pacific Mountain system   The maximum elevation is 3,100 feet
Numerous small streams drain to saltwater and the several freshwater lakes
within this roadless area. Shipley is the largest freshwater lake. There
are 104 miles of shoreline on saltwater, 3,000 acres are alpine tundra, and
2,000 acres are muskeg

(5) Ecosystem:

    (a) Classification: The area is in the Southern Outer Islands
    Geographic Province. This province is characterized by rolling
    subdued and localized rugged topography

    (b) Vegetation: Vegetation is typical Southeast Alaska coastal
    temperate rain forest. The forest is primarily western hemlock and
    Sitka spruce with large components of cedar. There are numerous
    interspersed areas of muskeg vegetative.

    There are approximately 62,949 acres of forest land of which 40,708 is
    commercial forest land. Of the commercial forest land, 35,469 acres
    are non-riparian old growth and 3,714 acres are riparian old growth

    (c) Soils: Soils are generally formed over bedrock and are typically
    about 40 inches deep. Some of the soils in the area are derived from
    limestone and marble.

    (d) Fish Resource: Fish resources have been rated as part of the
    Tongass Land Management Plan (1979) and by the Alaska Department of
    Fish and Game in its Forest Habitat Integrity Program (1983) These
    ratings describe the value of VCU's for sport fish, commercial fish
    and estuaries.

    VCU's 541 and 543 rated as high value for sport fish, VCU's 543, 546,
    and 548 as high value for commercial fish, and VCU's 531, 536, and 536
    as high value for estuary habitat.

    (e) Wildlife Resource: Sitka black-tailed deer, black bear, wolves,
    mink, and bald eagles are the best known species that inhabit the
    area. There is good alpine habitat for ptarmigan.

    (f) Threatened and Endangered Species: None

(6) Current Use and Management: The Tongass Land Management Plan
allocated this area to Land Use Designation 4. The emphasis in this
designation is on intensive resource use and development of resources with
commodity and market values. Due to the high cost of getting to the area,
recreation use, including the use of the one recreation cabin, is low

(7) Appearance (Apparent Naturalness): This area is part of the Kupreanof
Lowlands character type which is characterized by predominantly low,
rolling relief, with elevations seldom greater than 1,500 feet. Numerous
island groups and intricate waterways are also common in this character
type. Much of this roadless area includes terrain that is much more rugged
and diverse than is common in the character type

Just over 37 percent of this area is inventoried as Variety Class A
(possessing high level of landscape diversity relative to the character
type). Outstanding scenic features include the landscape around Mount
Francis, the highly diverse terrain around the The Nipples and particularly
the Odd Rock Creek drainage with its scenic meadows and dramatic steep
slopes enclosing this meadow   The rest of the area is inventoried as
Variety Class B (possessing landscape characteristics common in the
character type.)

About 75 percent of the area has a Type I Existing Visual Condition where
the landscape has remained unaltered by human activity   Due to the
influence of a moderate to heavy degree of logging in adjacent areas, the
rest of this area has a Type III, IV or V Existing Visual Condition

(8) **Surroundings (External Influences):** The adjacent areas to the north,
east, and south have been extensively roaded and logged. The southwest
boundary is a roaded and logged area with saltwater forming the remaining
boundary. This roadless area is separated from the Calder Roadless Area by
Shakan Strait.

(9) **Attractions and Features of Special Interest:** The natural features of
the area, the scenery, the saltwater bays and inlets, and the opportunity
to see wildlife and to study the processes which formed this country may
all be attractions. The fishing and solitude of the area is an
attraction. The area contains 20 inventoried recreation places containing
31,957 acres. There are no improved trails within the area.

b. Capability of Management as Wilderness or in an Unroaded Condition

(1) **Manageability and Management Area Boundaries:** Most of the area is
well-defined by saltwater. The southwest boundary is the roaded and logged
area at the base of Mount Francis, which offers a very manageable
boundary. Feasibility of management in a roadless condition is high

(2) **Natural Integrity:** The area is unmodified except for the recreation
cabin on Shipley Bay.

(3) **Opportunity for Solitude:** There is a high opportunity for solitude
within the area excluding the very fringe where the sights and sounds of
logging and vehicle traffic may be evident. The rugged terrain with many
isolated lake or alpine basins enhances the opportunity for solitude.
Floatplanes and boats are used to transport people to the Shipley Bay
cabin. Present recreation use levels are low. A person camped within the
area is unlikely to see others.

(5) **Opportunity for Primitive Recreation:** Several portions of this area
provide excellent opportunities for primitive recreation due to their
remoteness and to their many scenic and recreation attractions, including
lakes, scenic alpine areas, and protected saltwater bays

ROS CLASS	ACRES
Primitive I (P1)	6,586
Primitive II (P2)	3,955
Semi-Primitive Non-Motorized (SPNM)	41,311
Semi-Primitive Motorized (SPM)	11,499
Roaded Natural (RN)	261
Roaded Modified (RM)	6,544

The area contains 20 inventoried recreation places

ROS CLASS	# OF REC.PLACES	TOTAL ACRES	CAPACITY BY RVD'S
P1	1	2,168	780
P2	1	3,955	1,170
SPNM	6	18,428	18,120
SPM	6	5,478	8,985
RN	1	261	1,755
RM	5	1,666	7,150

(6) **Special Features (Ecologic, Geologic, Scientific, Cultural):** There are no special features within the area.

c. **Availability for Management as Wilderness or in an Unroaded Condition**

(1) **Resource Potentials**

(a) **Recreation Potential:** Potential exists for trail construction, additional recreation cabins, and anchor buoys throughout this area. El Cap Pass and Dry Pass, bordering the eastern and northern borders of this area, are part of an identified kayak route along the west coast of Prince of Wales Island. A few potential three-sided shelter sites have been noted along this route within this roadless area.

(b) **Fish Resource:** The recently completed fish habitat inventory indicates that there is some potential for salmon enhancement projects, such as constructing fish passes, on several of the streams within the area.

(c) **Wildlife Resource:** There is no identified need for wildlife enhancement projects within this area.

(d) **Timber Resource:** There are 38,621 acres inventoried as tentatively suitable for harvest. This includes 33,583 acres of non-riparian old growth and 3,553 of riparian old growth.

(e) **Land Use Authorizations:** None

(f) **Minerals:** One inactive claim is located within the area. Potential exists for development of the limestone and marble resources.

(g) **Areas of Scientific Interest:** None

(2) Management Considerations

(a) The area can easily be managed for timber production since the existing peripheral area has an extensive logging road network and there is ample opportunity to construct facilities for transferring logs to saltwater

The area is important unaltered habitat for wildlife within a much wider area of extensive timber harvest

The area has significant potential for developed and dispersed recreation activity.

(b) Fire: The area has no significant fire history

(c) Insects and Disease: Endemic tree diseases common to Southeast Alaska are present.

(d) Land Status: The entire area is National Forest System land

d. Relationship To Communities and Other Roadless and Wilderness Areas

(1) Nearby Roadless and Wilderness Areas and Uses: This roadless area is separated from the Calder Roadless Area by Shakan Strait

(2) Distance From Population Centers (accessibility): Approximate distances from population centers are as follows:

Community		Air Miles	Water Miles
Juneau	(Pop. 23,729)	170	210
Ketchikan	(Pop. 12,705)	85	150

Hollis, located on the Prince of Wales Island, is the nearest stop on the Alaska Marine Highway.

(3) Interest by Proponents:

(a) Moratorium Areas: The central part of this roadless area is part of a "moratorium" area in pending Tongass legislation

(b) Local Users/residents: Use by local residents is primarily excursions into the many bays and inlets for general boating, fishing, and hunting. There is subsistence use of the area.

e. Environmental Consequences

INDIVIDUAL ROADLESS AREA DESCRIPTION

NAME: Calder (516)   ACRES (GROSS): 12,687   ACRES (NFS): 12,687

GEOZONE: K11
GEOGRAPHIC PROVINCE: Kupreanof Lowland

1989 WILDERNESS ATTRIBUTE RATING: 22

a. Description

(1) Relationship to RARE II areas: The table below displays the VCU 1/
names, VCU numbers, acres, original WARS 2/ rating, and comments This
enables the reader to compare the roadless areas evaluated in Appendix C
with previous analyses.

VCU Name	VCU No.	1979 WARS Rating	Comments
Mt. Calder	528	22	
	531		Not rated

(2) History: The coastal area was used by prehistoric and historic Native
cultures. This roadless area includes a number of major and minor islands
in Shakan Bay. This bay (and its islands) was a homesite for aboriginal
people, and was and still is used as a gathering area for the fishing
fleet. The entire Calder Roadless Area is included within the primary area
for the KPC Long-Term Timber Sale.

(3) Location and Access: The Calder Roadless Area is located on the
northwest end of Prince of Wales Island. It is bounded on the north and
east by roaded and harvested areas. These roaded areas separate the Calder
Roadless Area from the El Capitan Roadless Area. The Pacfic Ocean and
Shakan Bay form Calder's western and southern boundaries. Access is by the
Prince of Wales Island road system or by boat and floatplane.

(4) Geography and Topography: The area is characterized by the rugged
terrain of Calder Mountain on Prince of Wales Island, and lower relief on
the smaller islands just to the south. Mount Calder is the highest point
with an elevation of 3,400 feet. Numerous small streams drain to Shakan
Bay. There are 34 miles of saltwater shoreline. Hamilton, Divide, and
Middle are the major islands within Shakan Bay. There are numerous small
islands and rocks along the coast.

1/ A VCU (Value Comparison Unit) is one of 867 watersheds which make up the
forest and were differentiated for planning purposes in the Tongass Land
Management Plan.
2/ Wilderness Attribute Rating System (WARS) was the nationwide system used to
rate the wilderness attributes of roadless areas in the Roadless Area
Review and Evaluation (RARE II).

(5) Ecosystem:

(a) Classification: The area is in the Southern Outer Islands
Geographic Province   This province is characterized by rolling
subdued and localized rugged topography.

(b) Vegetation: Vegetation is typical Southeast Alaska coastal
temperate rain forest   The forest is primarily western hemlock and
Sitka spruce with large components of cedar   There are 60 acres
classified as muskeg and 321 acres of rock.

There are approximately 11,864 acres of forested land of which 9,997
acres are commercial forest land. Of the commercial forest land,
8,512 acres are non-riparian old growth and 823 acres are riparian old
growth.

(c) Soils Resource: These highly organic, low clay content soils are
generally formed over bedrock and are typically about 40 inches deep

(d) Fish Resource: Fish resources have been rated as part of the
Tongass Land Management Plan (1979) and by the Alaska Department of
Fish and Game in its Forest Habitat Integrity Plan (1983)   These
ratings describe the value of VCU's for sport fish, commercial fish,
and estuaries.

One VCU, Mount Calder (528), is rated high for commercial fish and
estuary values. None of this area is rated high for sport fish
values.

(e) Wildlife Resource: Sitka black-tailed deer, black bear, wolves,
mink, and bald eagles are the best known species that inhabit the
area.

(f) Threatened and Endangered Species: None

(6) Current Use and Management: The Tongass Land Management Plan
allocated this area to Land Use Designation 4. The emphasis is on
intensive resource use and development of the commodity and market
resources.

(7) Appearance and Apparent Naturalness): This roadless area is part of
the Kupreanof Lowland character type, which is characterized by
predominantly low rolling relief, with elevations seldom greater than 1,500
feet. Numerous island groups and intricate waterways are also common in
this character type. This roadless area is dominated by Mount Calder which
exhibits greater relief and more distinctive rockforms than is common for
the character type.

About seventy percent of this area is inventoried as Variety Class A (a
high degree of landscape diversity relative to its character type)   The
rest of the area is Variety Class B. As mentioned above, the major
distinctive landscape features in this area are the limestone rock forms
that make up Mount Calder

About 60 percent of the area is in Existing Visual Condition (EVC) I where
the landscape has remained unaltered by human activity. About 18 percent is
in EVC IV where landscape alterations are easily noticed but tend to blend
in with the natural features of the landscape About 16 percent is in
EVC V where alterations are obvious and appear to be major disturbances

(8) **Surroundings (External Influences):** The adjacent areas to the north
and east have been extensively roaded and logged, and impact the east side
of the Mount Calder ridge There is a State selected parcel in the
southeast portion of the area on the east shore of Shakan Bay

(9) **Attractions and Features of Special Interest:** In addition to the
scenic features, attractions include the overall island environment, the
opportunity to see wildlife and to study the geologic processes which
formed this country, and the fishing and solitude of the Shakan Bay area
The area contains eight inventoried recreation places totaling 8,372
acres. There are no improved trails within the area.

b. **Capability of Management as Wilderness or in an Unroaded Condition**

(1) **Manageability and Management Area Boundaries:** Roads, harvest areas,
and saltwater form definite boundaries of this roadless area. Due to the
topography, the sight and sound of motor vehicles and timber harvest
activities are not apparent from within most of the roadless area
Feasibility of management in a roadless condition is high.

(2) **Natural Integrity:** The extensive logging on the eastern and northern
edges of this area, some of which includes the lower slopes of Mount
Calder, significantly impacts the natural integrity of this area

(3) **Opportunity for Solitude:** Excluding the very fringe of the area where
sights and sounds of logging and vehicle traffic may be evident, there is a
high opportunity for solitude Shakan Bay receives considerable use by the
fishing fleet and by recreation boaters. Recreation use levels are low
within the land and island areas. A person camped within the area is
unlikely to see others.

(4) **Opportunity for Primitive Recreation:** The area provides primarily a
Semi-Primitive recreation opportunity.

ROS Class	Acres
Semi-Primitive Non-Motorized (SPNM)	5 942
Semi-Primitive Motorized (SPM)	3 975
Roaded Natural (RN)	582
Roaded Modified (RM)	2,187

The area contains eight inventoried recreation places.

ROS CLASS	# OF REC. PLACES	TOTAL ACRES	CAPACITY BY RVD'S
SPNM	4	4,517	3,120
SPM	2	8,372	4,680
RM	2	1,867	2,230

(5) Special Features (Ecologic, Geologic, Scientific, Cultural): The
numerous islands offshore and within Shakan Bay are special features of the
area   Mount Calder is a prominent peak   This roadless area also contains
a limestone formation that is of geologic interest and has potential for
having large caves

c. Availability for Management as Wilderness or in an Unroaded Condition

   (1) Resource Potentials

      (a) Recreation Potential: Potential exists for some construction of
      trails and saltwater support facilities such as anchor buoys and
      docks   An identified potential kayak route goes through the islands
      in the roadless area along the west coast of Prince of Wales Island
      Recreation cabins are also a potential for this area.

      (b) Fish Resource: The recently completed fish habitat inventory
      indicates that there is some potential for salmon enhancement projects
      such as constructing fish passes on several of the areas' streams

      (c) Wildlife Resource: There is no identified need for wildlife
      enhancement projects within this area.

      (d) Timber Resource: There are 9,575 acres inventoried as
      tentatively suitable for harvest. This includes 763 acres of riparian
      old growth, and 8,170 acres of non-riparian old growth.

      (e) Land Use Authorizations: None

      (f) Minerals: The area is not currently mined and no known
      prospecting is taking place within this roadless area   The southern
      part of this area contains marble deposits

      (g) Areas of Scientific Interest: None

   (2) Management Considerations

      (a) The area can easily be managed for timber production since the
      existing peripheral area has an extensive logging road network and the
      necessary sites for transferring logs to saltwater   The area is
      important for wildlife as a place of unaltered habitat within a much
      wider area of extensive timber harvest   Mineral potential may be
      important because of the known, but undeveloped, deposits of marble
      located in the southern part of this roadless area.

      The area has good potential for developed and dispersed recreation
      activities. There is also good potential to manage for low density
      semi-primitive recreation experiences.

      (b) Fire: The area has no significant fire history

      (c) Insects and Disease: Endemic tree diseases common to Southeast
      Alaska are present

      (d) Land Status: All of the area is National Forest System land

d. Relationship To Communities and Other Roadless and Wilderness Areas

(1) **Nearby Roadless and Wilderness Areas and Uses:** The Calder Roadless Area is separated from the larger El Capitan Roadless Area by a Forest development road and harvest units.

(2) **Distance From Population Centers (accessibility):** Approximate distances from population centers are as follows:

Community		Air Miles	Water Miles
Juneau	(Pop. 23,729)	180	240
Ketchikan	(Pop. 12,705)	80	150

Hollis, located on the Prince of Wales Island, is the nearest stop on the Alaska Marine Highway.

(3) **Interest by Proponents:**

(a) **Moratorium Areas:** The area has been identified as a "moratorium" area.

(b) **Local Users/residents:** Use by local residents is primarily excursions into Shakan Bay by boat for subsistence and recreation purposes.

e. Environmental Consequences

INDIVIDUAL ROADLESS AREA DESCRIPTION

NAME: El Capitan (517)   ACRES (GROSS): 43,644   ACRES (NFS): 43,604

GEOZONE: K06 and K11
GEOGRAPHIC PROVINCE: Southern Outer Islands

1989 WILDERNESS ATTRIBUTE RATING: 21

⌐ Description

(1) **Relationship to RARE II areas:** The table below displays the VCU 1/ names, VCU numbers, acres, original WARS 2/ rating, and comments This enables the reader to compare the roadless areas evaluated in Appendix C with previous analyses.

VCU Name	VCU No.	1979 WARS Rating	Comments
Mt. Calder	528	22	
Alder	529	20	
Buster	530	22	
	531		Not rated
	532		Not rated
Red Lake	533	22	
	534		Not rated
	536		Not rated
	537		Not rated

(2) **History:** The area was used by prehistoric and historic Native cultures. This roadless area is one of the "moratorium" areas deferring timber harvest pending legislative action concerning wilderness. The entire El Capitan Roadless Area is included within the primary sale area for the Ketchikan Pulp Company (KPC) Long-term Timber Sale

(3) **Location and Access:** Located on the north end of Prince of Wales Island, the El Capitan Roadless Area is bounded by roaded and harvested areas on the north, west, and south. A road forms the eastern boundary separating El Capitan from the Salmon Bay Roadless Area. The area is accessed by logging roads. Freshwater lakes in the area are accessed by floatplane.

1/ A VCU (Value Comparison Unit) is one of 867 watersheds which make up the forest and were differentiated for planning purposes in the Tongass Land Management Plan.
2/ Wilderness Attribute Rating System (WARS) was the nationwide system used to rate the wilderness attributes of roadless areas in the Roadless Area Review and Evaluation (RARE II).

(4) **Geography and Topography:** The area is characterized by low elevation but rugged terrain. The maximum elevation is 2,500 feet. Numerous small streams drain into Red Lake, the largest body of water within the area. There is no saltwater shoreline. There are approximately 1,000 acres of alpine tundra above treeline.

(5) **Ecosystem:**

(a) **Classification:** The area is in the Southern Outer Islands Geographic Province. This province is characterized by rolling subdued and localized rugged topography. The El Capitan area is within the large limestone formation that occurs on the north of the Prince of Wales Island.

(b) **Vegetation:** Vegetation is typical Southeast Alaska coastal temperate rain forest. The forest is primarily western hemlock and Sitka spruce with large components of cedar. There are 261 acres of muskeg. About 1,000 acres is alpine.

There are approximately 42,829 acres of forested land of which 26,764 acres are commercial forest land. Of the commercial forest land, 23,759 acres are non-riparian old growth and 2,784 acres are riparian old growth.

(c) **Soils:** These highly organic, low clay content soils are generally formed over bedrock and are typically about 40 inches deep.

(d) **Fish Resource:** Fish resources have been rated as part of the Tongass Land Management Plan (1979) and by the Alaska Department of Fish and Game in its Forest Habitat Integrity Program (1983). These ratings describe the value of VCU's for sport fish, commercial fish and estuaries.

VCU's 528 and 534 are high value for commercial fish. VCU's 532, 533, and 534 are high value for sport fish. All VCU's with the exception of VCU 533 are high value estuary habitat.

(e) **Wildlife Resource:** Sitka black-tailed deer, black bear, wolves, mink, and bald eagles are the best known species that inhabit the area.

(f) **Threatened and Endangered Species:** None

(6) **Current Use and Management:** The Tongass Land Management Plan allocated the area to Land Use Designation (LUD) 3 (12,095 acres) and LUD 4 (31,509 acres). The emphasis in LUD 3 areas is on managing a variety of uses and activities in a compatible and complementary manner to provide the greatest combination of benefits. For LUD 4 areas, the emphasis is on intensive use and development of commodity or market resources. One recreation cabin is located at the north end of Red Lake.

(7) **Appearance (Apparent Naturalness):** This area is within the Kupreanof Lowlands character type which is characterized by predominantly low, rolling relief, with elevations seldom greater than 1,500 feet Numerous island groups are also common in this character type This area generally possesses slightly greater landform relief than is found in the character type

Almost all of this area is inventoried as Variety Class B. The outstanding scenic features in this area are the rugged terrain and rock faces just to the east of Calder Mountain, and the rugged landscapes at the head of the Red Lake valley

Due to the extensive timber harvest and roading along the edge of this area, about 38 percent of this roadless area is inventoried as a Type IV, V or VI Existing Visual Condition where alterations to the natural landscape are easily noticed and, for the most part, quite dominant

(8) **Surroundings (External Influences):** The adjacent areas to the north, west, and south have been extensively roaded and logged. A road forms the eastern boundary of this roadless area. The area east of this road is the Salmon Bay Roadless Area.

(9) **Attractions and Features of Special Interest:** The natural features of the area, the scenery, and the opportunity to see wildlife and to study the processes which formed this country may all be attractions The fishing and solitude of the Red Lake area is an attraction. El Capitan contains five inventoried recreation places totaling 12,422 acres There are no improved trails within the area.

Caves have been located in the limestone formations on the west side of this roadless area. Preliminary indications are that these caves may be of national significance because of their depths and general underground expanse.

b. **Capability of Management as Wilderness or in an Unroaded Condition**

(1) **Manageability and Management Area Boundaries:** Roads and harvest areas form definite boundaries of this roadless area. The influences of logging (sight and noise) as well as general vehicle traffic quickly dissipate within a short distance into the roadless area Feasibility of management in a roadless condition is high

(2) **Natural Integrity:** The existence of extensive timber harvest along the edge of this area significantly reduces its natural integrity

(3) **Opportunity for Solitude:** Excluding the very fringe where the sights and sounds of logging and vehicle traffic may be evident, there is a high opportunity for solitude within the area. Floatplanes are used to transport people to the Red Lake cabin. Present recreation use levels are low. A person camped within the area is unlikely to see others

(4) **Opportunity for Primitive Recreation:** The area primarily provides a semi-primitive recreation opportunity. Most of these opportunities are located in the Red Lake area and the alpine country around this lake and Red Bay Mountain and El Capitan Peak.

ROS Class	Acres
Primitive I (P1)	3,172
Semi-Primitive Non-Motorized (SPNM)	26,510
Roaded Natural (RN)	3,669
Roaded Modified (RM)	10,253

The area contains five recreation places

ROS CLASS	# OF REC. PLACES	TOTAL ACRES	CAPACITY BY RVD'S
P1	1	1,365	390
SPNM	3	9,953	5,850
RM	1	1,104	500

(5) **Special Features (Ecologic, Geologic, Scientific, Cultural):** El Capitan Mountain is a limestone formation. This formation extends westward of the mountain. Caves have been located in this formation.

c. **Availability for Management as Wilderness or in an Unroaded Condition**

(1) **Resource Potentials**

(a) **Recreation Potential:** There is potential for trail construction and possibly another cabin at Red Lake. The caves that have been found may provide a unique opportunity to develop destination recreation facilities in association with interpretation and viewing of these caves.

(b) **Fish Resource:** The recently completed fish habitat inventory indicates that there is some potential for salmon enhancement projects such as constructing fish passes on several of the streams within the area.

(c) **Wildlife Resource:** There is no identified need for wildlife enhancement projects within this area.

(d) **Timber Resource:** There are 23,316 acres inventoried as tentatively suitable for harvest. This includes 20,732 acres of non-riparian old growth and 2,383 acres of riparian old growth

(e) **Land Use Authorizations:** None

(f) **Minerals:** There are marble formations in the southwest corner of the area. There is no current mining or known prospecting within this roadless area.

(g) **Areas of Scientific Interest:** None.

(2) **Management Considerations**

(a) The area can easily be managed for timber production since the existing peripheral area has an extensive logging road network and the necessary sites for transferring logs to saltwater.

The area is important for wildlife as a place of unaltered habitat within a much wider area of extensive timber harvest

Mineral management may be of potential importance because of the known, but undeveloped, deposits of marble

The area is considered to have some potential for developed recreation activity and it does have good potential to manage for low density primitive recreation experiences.

(b) **Fire:** The area has no significant fire history

(c) **Insects and Disease:** Endemic tree diseases common to Southeast Alaska are present.

(d) **Land Status:** Entire area is National Forest System land

d. **Relationship To Communities and Other Roadless and Wilderness Areas**

(1) **Nearby Roadless and Wilderness Areas and Uses:** The El Capitan Roadless Area is separated from the Salmon Bay Roadless Area by a Forest development road.

(2) **Distance From Population Centers (accessibility):** Approximate distances from population centers are as follows

Community		Air Miles	Water Miles
Juneau	(Pop. 23,729)	150	180
Ketchik	(Pop. 12,705)	100	120
Port Protection & Point Baker	(Pop 91)	12	24

Hollis, located on the Prince of Wales Island, is the nearest stop on the Alaska Marine Highway.

(3) **Interest by Proponents:**

(a) **Moratorium Areas:** The area has been identified as a "moratorium" area and has been identified as potential Wilderness in recent legislative initiatives.

(b) **Local Users/residents:** Use by local residents is primarily for excursions into Red Lake using the recreation cabin as a base for fishing in the lake. Local subsistence use takes place within this roadless area.

e. **Environmental Consequences**

INDIVIDUAL ROADLESS AREA DESCRIPTION

NAME: Salmon Bay (518)   ACRES (GROSS): 36,426   ACRES (NFS): 36,426

GEOZONE: K06
GEOGRAPHIC PROVINCE: Southern Outer Islands

1989 WILDERNESS ATTRIBUTE RATING: 21

a. Description

(1) Relationship to RARE II areas: The table below displays the VCU 1/
names, VCU numbers, acres, original WARS 2/ rating, and comments. This
enables the reader to compare the roadless areas evaluated in Appendix C
with previous analyses.

VCU Name	VCU No.	1979 WARS Rating	Comments
Red Lake	533	22	
Salmon Bay	534	23	
	532*		Not rated **
	535*		" "
	537*		"
	538*		
	539*		
	540*		

*--The roadless area includes only part of this VCU.
**-The majority of this VCU was roaded prior to 1979 and was not rated
   in RARE II.

(2) History: The coastal portion of the Salmon Bay Roadless Area was used
by prehistoric and historic Native cultures. The Salmon Bay area was the
site of fish canneries in the early 1900's. The northern part of the
roadless area has been prospected for rare earth minerals. All of the area
is included within the primary area for the Ketchikan Pulp Company (KPC)
Long-term Timber Sale.

(3) Location and Access: Located on the north end of Prince of Wales
Island, the Salmon Bay Roadless Area is bounded by roaded and harvested
areas on the north, east, and south. A road forms the west boundary
separating it from the El Capitan Roadless Area. The area is accessed from
saltwater at Salmon Bay. Logging roads and floatplanes access the
interior.

1/ A VCU (Value Comparison Unit) is one of 867 watersheds which make up the
    forest and were differentiated for planning purposes in the Tongass Land
    Management Plan.
2/ Wilderness Attribute Rating System (WARS) was the nationwide system used to
    rate the wilderness attributes of roadless areas in the Roadless Area
    Review and Evaluation (RARE II).

(4) Geography and Topography: The area is characterized by low elevation but rugged terrain   The maximum elevation is 2,000 feet. Numerous small streams drain to Salmon Bay Lake, the largest body of water in the area There are 15 miles of saltwater shoreline

(5) Ecosystem:

(a) Classification: This area is characterized by low elevation mountains with steep slopes and moderately incised valleys   There are no known unique or uncommon plant/soil associations or geologic formations within the area

(b) Vegetation: Vegetation is typical Southeast Alaska coastal temperate rain forest. The forest is primarily western hemlock and Sitka spruce with large components of cedar.

There are approximately 74,378 acres classified as old growth of which 5,788 acres are riparian old growth; 819 acres are classified as muskeg.

(c) Soils: These highly organic, low clay content soils are generally formed over bedrock and are typically about 40 inches deep

(d) Fish Resource: Fish habitat potential has been inventoried in all streams. This inventory shows numerous streams and segments thereof which are high quality spawning habitat for the several species of salmon. These streams and Salmon Bay Lake also contain rainbow trout.

(e) Wildlife Resource: Sitka black-tailed deer, black bear, wolves. mink, and bald eagles are the best known species that inhabit the area.

(f) Threatened and Endangered Species: None.

(6) Current Use and Management: The Tongass Land Management Plan allocated this area to Land Use Designation (LUD) 3. The emphasis is on managing a variety of uses and activities in a compatible and complementary manner to provide the greatest combination of benefits. There is one recreation cabin at the north end of Salmon Bay Lake. Subsistence use in the area is minor

(7) Appearance (Apparent Naturalness): This roadless area is part of the Kupreanof Lowlands character type which is characterized by predominantly low rolling relief, with elevations seldom greater than 1,500 feet Numerous island groups and intricate waterways are also common in this character type. This area with its low rolling relief around Salmon Bay Lake and its coastal features is very representative of this character type.

About 74 percent of this area is inventoried as a Variety Class B
(possessing landscape diversity common for the character type)   About 23
percent is rated as a Variety Class C (possessing a minimal degree of
landscape diversity relative to the character type). A small portion of
the area (about three percent) is rated as a Variety Class A (possessing a
high degree of landscape diversity)   These Class A landscapes include the
Salmon Bay area with its diverse island groups, grass flats, and intricate
shorelines and saltwater channels.

About 75 percent of the area is in Type I Existing Visual Condition where
the natural landscape has remained unaltered by the human activity   The
remainder of the area is in Types III, IV, V, or VI condition due to the
moderate to heavy impacts of logging around the edges of this unit

(8) **Surroundings (External Influences):** The adjacent areas to the north,
east, and south have been extensively roaded and logged. A road forms the
western boundary of this roadless area. West of this road lies the El
Capitan Roadless Area.

(9) **Attractions and Features of Special Interest:** The natural features of
the area, the scenery, and the opportunity to see wildlife and to study the
processes which formed this country may all be attractions. The
outstanding stream and lake fishing and solitude of the Salmon Bay Lake
area is an attraction. The area contains nine inventoried recreation
places totaling 13,304 acres. One improved trail exists in this area -
from near the cabin at the outlet to Salmon Bay Lake downstream toward the
bay.

b. **Capability of Management as Wilderness or in an Unroaded Condition**

(1) **Manageability and Management Area Boundaries:** Roads and harvest areas
form definite boundaries of this roadless area. The influences of logging
(sights and sounds) as well as general vehicle traffic quickly dissipate
within a short distance into the roadless area. Management of this area in
a roadless condition is highly feasible

(2) **Natural Integrity:** The area is unmodified except for the recreation
use cabin at Salmon Bay Lake.

(3) **Opportunity for Solitude:** There is presently a good opportunity for
solitude within the area. Logging is planned for some areas near Salmon
Bay Lake. While the area is being harvested, the road building and logging
activity will periodically be heard from the lake. Floatplanes are used to
transport people to the Salmon Bay Lake cabin. Present recreation use
levels are low. A person camped within the area is unlikely to see others

(4) **Opportunity for Primitive Recreation:** Though there are outstanding
recreation opportunities in the Salmon Bay and Salmon Bay Lake area, the
proximity of these attractions to on-going logging operations presently
does not permit a strictly primitive recreation experience.

ROS CLASS	ACRES
Primitive (P1)	2,905
Semi-Primitive Non-Motorized (SPNM)	23,917
Semi-Primitive Motorized (SPM)	1,463
Roaded Natural (RN)	1,904
Roaded Modified (RM)	6,177

The area contains nine inventoried recreation places

ROS CLASS	# OF REC. PLACES	TOTAL ACRES	CAPACITY BY RVD'S
SPNM	3	11,772	5,357
SPM	3	435	1,566
RN	1	100	3,545
RM	2	997	1,402

(6) **Special Features (Ecologic, Geologic, Scientific, Cultural):** There are no known special features within the area.

c. **Availability for Management as Wilderness or in an Unroaded Condition**

(1) **Resource Potentials**

(a) **Recreation Potential:** There is potential for additional trails connecting Salmon Bay Lake to saltwater and connecting the logging road system to the southern end of Salmon Bay Lake. There is potential for one additional recreation cabin at Salmon Bay Lake

(b) **Fish Resource:** The recently completed fish habitat inventory indicates that there is some potential for salmon enhancement projects, such as constructing fish passes, on several of the streams within the area.

(c) **Wildlife Resource:** There is no identified need for wildlife enhancement projects within this area.

(d) **Timber Resource:** There are 15,881 acres inventoried as tentatively suitable for harvest. This includes 13,470 acres of non-riparian old growth and 2,193 acres of riparian old growth

(e) **Land Use Authorizations:** None

(f) **Minerals:** There is no current mining or known prospecting within this roadless area. The northern part of this area is known to contain some rare earth minerals.

(g) **Areas of Scientific Interest:** None

(2) **Management Considerations**

(a) The area can easily be managed for timber production since the existing peripheral area has an extensive logging road network and the necessary sites for transferring logs to saltwater.

The area is important for unaltered wildlife habitat within a much wider area of extensive timber harvest.

Because of the known but undeveloped deposits of rare earth minerals located in the northern part of this roadless area, mineral management may be of potential importance

The area is not considered to have much developed recreation potential but it does have good potential to manage for low density primitive recreation experiences

(b) Fire: The area has no significant fire history

(c) **Insects and Disease:** Endemic tree diseases common to Southeast Alaska are present.

(d) **Land Status:** All of this area is National Forest System land

d. Relationship To Communities and Other Roadless and Wilderness Areas

(1) **Nearby Roadless and Wilderness Areas and Uses:** The Salmon Bay Roadless Area is separated from the larger El Capitan Roadless Area by a Forest development road.

(2) **Distance From Population Centers (accessibility):** Approximate distances from population centers are as follows

Community		Air Miles	Water Miles
Juneau	(Pop. 23,729)	170	No water access
Ketchikan	(Pop. 12,705)	70	No water access

Hollis, located on Prince of Wales Island, is the nearest stop on the Alaska Marine Highway.

(3) **Interest by Proponents:**

(a) **Moratorium Areas:** The area has not been identified as a "moratorium" area or proposed as Wilderness in legislative initiatives to date.

(b) **Local Users/residents:** Use by local residents is primarily excursions into Salmon Bay Lake using the recreation cabin as a base for fishing in the lake.

e. Environmental Consequences

INDIVIDUAL ROADLESS AREA DESCRIPTION

NAME: Polk (519)   ACRES (GROSS): 173,024   ACRES (NFS): 149,205

GEOZONE: K07 and K08
GEOGRAPHIC PROVINCE: Southern Outer Islands

1989 WILDERNESS ATTRIBUTE RATING: 18

a. Description

(1) Relationship to RARE II areas: The table below displays the VCU 1/ names, VCU numbers, acres, original WARS 2/ rating, and comments   This enables the reader to compare the roadless areas evaluated in Appendix C with previous analyses.

VCU Name	VCU No.	1979 WARS Rating	Comments
	611		Not Rated
	612		Not Rated
Old Frank	613	21 ·	
Saltry Cove	614	22	
Trollers Cove	615	24	
Clover Lake	616	23	
Clover Bay	617	22	
McKenzie	618	23	
Polk	619	23	
Dog Salmon	620	22	
	621		Not Rated
	622		Not Rated
Flat Creek	624	22	
	674		Not Rated
Sunny	675	24	
North Chomly	676	23	
	679		Not Rated
	680		Not Rated
	691		Not Rated

(2) History: The Polk area has historically been the entry to Prince of Wales Island. The community of Hollis is adjacent to the northeast corner of this roadless area. Hollis began as a mining community, but it soon became the boat entry terminal through Kasaan Bay. Currently, Hollis is the only Alaska Marine Highway stop on the Prince of Wales Island Mining, trading/supply, boat repair, and, more recently, timber and tourism have been the influences on the Polk area.

1/ A VCU (Value Comparison Unit) is one of 867 watersheds which make up the forest and were differentiated for planning purposes in the Tongass Land Management Plan.

2/ Wilderness Attribute Rating System (WARS) was the nationwide system used to rate the wilderness attributes of roadless areas in the Roadless Area Review and Evaluation (RARE).

The Polk Inlet and Twelve-Mile Arm areas were important locales of
traditional use by the Haida Natives and before them, prehistoric cultures.
The Haida Native Corporation made large land entitlement selections in the
Polk Roadless Area's area of influence, and further land selections are
anticipated in this area before 1995.

The east coast side of the Polk Roadless Area has a rich chronology of
prehistoric and historic use by Native groups.

(3) **Location and Access:** The Polk Roadless Area is located on the
east-central part of Prince of Wales Island. Access is by the Alaska
Marine Highway System through Hollis, by the extensive road system around
the roadless area, by boat through Kasaan Bay and Skowl Arm, and by
floatplane.

(4) **Geography and Topography:** The area is characterized by moderate to
rugged topography. Most of this roadless area consists of rolling terrain,
however there are a few high ridges with elevations to 3,000 feet. Alpine
acres total 1,840 and 4,427 acres are rock. Freshwater lakes total 3,909
acres. There are 118 miles of saltwater shoreline.

(5) **Ecosystem:**

> (a) **Classification:** The area is classified as being in the Southern
> Outer Islands Geographic Province. This province is characterized by
> rolling subdued and localized rugged topography.
>
> (b) **Vegetation:** This area is typical southeast Alaska coastal
> temperate rain forest. The forest is primarily western hemlock and
> Sitka spruce with large components of cedar. There are 360 acres of
> muskeg.
>
> There are approximately 136,305 acres of forested land of which 60,230
> acres are commercial forest land. Of the commercial forest land,
> 52,527 acres are non-riparian old growth and 5,547 acres are riparian
> old growth.
>
> (c) **Soils:** These highly organic, low clay content soils are
> generally formed over bedrock and are typically about 40 inches deep
>
> (d) **Fish Resource:** Fish resources have been rated as part of the
> Tongass Land Management Plan (1979) and by the Alaska Department of
> Fish and Game in its Forest Habitat Integrity Program (1983) These
> ratings describe the value of VCU's for sport fish, commercial fish,
> and estuaries.
>
> VCU's 613, 618, 620,621, 622, 624, 674, 675, and 679 are high value
> for commercial fish, and VCU's 622, 624, and 679 are high value for
> estuary habitat.
>
> (e) **Wildlife Resource:** This area has high populations of Sitka
> black-tailed deer, black bear, otter, marten, mink, loon, and common
> waterfowl.
>
> (f) **Threatened and Endangered Species:** None.

(6) **Current Use and Management:** The Tongass Land Management Plan allocated this area to Land Use Designation (LUD) 3 (10,917 acres) and LUD 4 (138,228 acres) The LUD 3 areas are located around Hollis, and were intended to provide a greater degree of protection of aesthetic values near the community LUD 4 areas are to be managed for commodity and market values.

The Polk Inlet area contains active timber sales. Plans are being prepared for new timber sales that will extend into the Polk Roadless Area from the existing roaded and logged areas Dispersed recreation is also an important use in this area. The convenient road and boat accesses have made such places as the Harris River, Indian Creek, Rock Creek, and other streams popular fishing and hunting places. One recreation use cabin is located at Trollers Cove and a permitted floating fishing lodge in Clover Bay.

Fish habitat improvement is an ongoing activity. A major fish pass is being constructed on Dog Salmon Creek through a cooperative effort by the Forest Service and the timber industry.

(7) **Appearance (Apparent Naturalness):** The area is part of the Coastal Hills character type which is characterized by moderately steep landforms. predominantly rounded summits, elevations to 4,500 feet, and flat-floored. U-shaped valleys. This area exhibits a wide variety of landscape features present in this character type including prominent peaks, rolling terrain diverse lake basins, and rugged shorelines.

About 19 percent of the area is inventoried as Variety Class A (possessing landscape diversity that is unique for the character type) These class \ landscapes include the head of Polk Inlet from the estuary up to the Barren Mountain-Rock Butte Ridge, and the landscapes along the east side of this area between Cholmondeley Sound and Skowl Arm. This latter area is unique in that it exhibits low elevations but very rugged and diverse terrain, including a variety of different lake basins surrounded by steep slopes and rock cliffs. The shoreline of Skowl Arm and Cholmondeley Sound is very irregular and possesses many scenic coves. The rest of this area is rated a Variety Class B (possessing landscape diversity that is common for the character type).

About 92 percent of this roadless area is in Type I Existing Visual Condition where the natural landscape has remained unaltered by human activity. Due to past harvest around part of its edges, the rest is in a moderately to heavily altered visual condition (Type III, IV or V)

(8) **Surroundings (External Influences):** This area is significantly influenced by activity and uses adjacent it. Logging is active on both the National Forest and Native lands. This area receives higher use by people than most other places on Prince of Wales Island because of its close proximity to Hollis and the Prince of Wales Island road system. Because of the excellent fishing and close proximity to Ketchikan, the saltwater inlets and bays receive many visitors.

(9) **Attractions and Features of Special Interest:** The natural features of the Polk Roadless Area, the scenery, the saltwater bays and inlets, and the opportunity to see wildlife and to study the processes which formed this country are all attractions The excellent saltwater salmon fishing is a major attraction to people in the vicinity of this roadless area. The area contains 25 inventoried recreation places totaling 76,205 acres

b **Capability of Management as Wilderness or in an Unroaded Condition**

(1) **Manageability and Management Area Boundaries:** The extensive amount of on-going logging and that planned for the future makes managing this area in a roadless condition difficult. The boundaries are controlled by the constantly changing pattern of harvest units and roads.

(2) **Natural Integrity:** Because of the irregular pattern of intrusion caused by past and present logging, and by Native and State land selections, the natural integrity of the area, as a whole, is not ideal.

(3) **Opportunity for Solitude:** The opportunity for solitude within this roadless area is generally good to excellent on the eastern half of the area. On the western half, because of the sights and sounds of nearby logging, the sounds of boat use in the bays, and the good chance of encountering other people on the fishing streams, the opportunity becomes marginal.

(4) **Opportunity for Primitive Recreation:** Due to the many saltwater and upland recreation opportunities, and the rugged, diverse terrain that breaks up the area into many isolated bays and upland lake basins, there are excellent opportunities for primitive recreation, particularly in the eastern half of this area.

ROS Class	Acres
Primitive I (P1)	48,816
Primitive II (P2)	21,294
Semi-Primitive Non-Motorized (SPNM)	53,642
Semi-Primitive Motorized (SPM)	4,981
Roaded Natural (RN)	419
Roaded Modified (RM)	19,510
Rural (R)	502

The area contains 25 inventoried recreation places.

ROS CLASS	# OF REC. PLACES	TOTAL ACRES	CAPACITY BY RVD'S
P1	4	36,293	5,855
P2	4	10,127	8,802
SPNM	6	25,184	20,123
SPM	1	140	780
RN	1	419	1,737
RM	8	3,679	14,322
R	1	361	1,832

(5) Special Features (Ecologic, Geologic, Scientific, Cultural): There is
an existing Research Natural Area in the Old Tom Creek drainage

c   Availability for Management as Wilderness or in an Unroaded Condition

(1) Resource Potentials

(a) Recreation Potential: There is great opportunity to manage this
area for developed and dispersed recreation in a semi-primitive to
primitive setting   Long-range plans call for a campground at the head
of the Twelve-Mile Arm   There is opportunity, and an identified need,
for trails in the west half of this area   The potential is very good
for land or water based fishing resorts   There is also good potential
for trail development from the many protected coves along the east
side to the various lake basins just east of the coastline

(b) Fish Resource: The recently completed fish habitat inventory
indicates that there is excellent potential for salmon enhancement
projects, such as constructing fish passes, on several of the streams
within the area.

(c) Wildlife Resource: There are no long range plans for wildlife
habitat improvement projects

(d) Timber Resource: There are 53,605 acres inventoried as
tentatively suitable for harvest   This includes 46,217 acres of
non-riparian old growth and 4,966 acres of riparian old growth

(e) Land Use Authorizations: Fishing lodge in Clover Bay.

(f) Minerals: Mineral development potential is very low

(g) Areas of Scientific Interest: None.

(2) Management Considerations

(a) The Polk Roadless Area is in the primary sale area of the
Ketchikan Pulp Company (KPC) Long-term Timber Sale. Timber harvest
has been occurring around its perimeter for many years causing this
roadless area to shrink. Good potential exists to manage much of the
west half of the area for its timber potential.

The area has excellent potential to enhance the salmon spawning
habitat, mainly through the construction of fish passes, on many
streams within this area.

The close proximity of this area to Hollis, the Prince of Wales Island
road system, and to Ketchikan, coupled with the area's variety of
recreation opportunities have caused recreation management to be
highlighted in the long-term planning for management of this area
There is considerable private sector interest in developing commercial
fishing resorts on the saltwater fringe.

(b) Fire: The area has no significant fire history

(c) Insects and Disease: Endemic tree diseases common to Southeast Alaska are present.

(d) Land Status: Native and State land selections have influenced the boundary of this roadless area. There are no private inholdings

d   Relationship To Communities and Other Roadless and Wilderness Areas

(1) Nearby Roadless and Wilderness Areas and Uses: The Polk Roadless Area is part of a latger contiguous land mass consisting of the South Prince of Wales Wilderness, and the Eudora and Nutkwa Roadless Areas These areas total 533,474 acres.

(2) Distance From Population Centers (accessibility): Approximate distances from population centers are as follows:

Community		Air Miles	Water Miles
Juneau	(Pop. 23,729)	190	220
Ketchikan	(Pop. 12,705)	25	30
Hollis	(Pop. 82)	15	30

Hollis, located on the Prince of Wales Island, is the nearest stop on the Alaska Marine Highway.

(3) Interest by Proponents:

· (a) Moratorium Areas: The area has not been identified as a "moratorium" area or proposed as Wilderness in legislative initiatives to date.

(b) Local Users/residents: The area receives local use for subsistence and recreation activity.

e. Environmental Consequences

INDIVIDUAL ROADLESS AREA DESCRIPTION

NAME: Kasaan (520)   ACRES (GROSS): 8,676   ACRES (NFS)· 8,536

GEOZONE: K06
GEOGRAPHIC PROVINCE: Southern Outer Islands

1989 WILDERNESS ATTRIBUTE RATING: 15

.1 Description

    (1) **Relationship to RARE II areas:** The table below displays the VCU 1/
    names, VCU numbers, acres, original WARS 2/ rating, and comments. This
    enables the reader to compare the roadless areas evaluated in Appendix C
    with previous analyses.

VCU Name	VCU No.	1979 WARS Rating	Comments
Street Island	602	22	
	603		Not Rated
Cliffs	604	21	

    (2) **History:** The Kasaan Roadless Area includes Grindall Island and the
    southern tip of the Kasaan Peninsula. The records show that this roadless
    area does not have much in the way of prehistoric or historic human
    activity. Most of the land area on the Kasaan Peninsula was selected as
    Native entitlement land. In addition, the State of Alaska has nominated
    Grindall Island and sites on the peninsula for selection by the State

    (3) **Location and Access:** This roadless area is located on the southern
    tip of Kasaan Peninsula. Access is by boat or floatplane.

    (4) **Geography and Topography:** The peninsula part of this roadless area is
    characterized by rugged mountains and coastline. Grindall Island is a
    low-lying island just south of the tip of the peninsula Its main feature
    is the rocky reefs around much of the island. There are 20 miles of
    saltwater shoreline.

    (5) **Ecosystem:**

        (a) **Classification:** The area is classified as being in the Southern
        Outer Islands Geographic Province. This province is characterized by
        rolling subdued and localized rugged topography.

1/ A VCU (Value Comparison Unit) is one of 867 watersheds which make up the
    forest and were differentiated for planning purposes in the Tongass Land
    Management Plan.
2/ Wilderness Attribute Rating System (WARS) was the nationwide system used to
    rate the wilderness attributes of roadless areas in the Roadless Area
    Review and Evaluation (RARE II).

(b) **Vegetation:** Vegetation is typical Southeast Alaska coastal temperate rain forest. The forest is primarily western hemlock and Sitka spruce with large components of cedar.

There are approximately 8,415 acres of forested land of which 3,709 acres are commercial forest land Of the commercial forest land, 2,947 acres are non-riparian old growth and 481 acres are riparian old growth.

(c) **Soils:** These highly organic, low clay content soils are generally formed over bedrock and are typically, about 40 inches deep.

(d) **Fish Resource:** Fish resources have been rated as part of the Tongass Land Management Plan (1979) and by the Alaska Department of Fish and Game in its Forest Habitat Integrity Program (1983) These ratings describe the value of VCU's for sport fish, commercial fish, and estuaries. None of the VCU's comprising this roadless area rated high value for these categories.

(e) **Wildlife Resource:** This area has high populations of Sitka black-tailed deer, bear, otter, marten, mink, loon, and common waterfowl. Alpine areas are excellent ptarmigan habitat.

(f) **Threatened and Endangered Species:** None.

(6) **Current Use and Management:** The Tongass Land Management Plan allocated this area to Land Use Designation 3 (LUD 3) which allows a wide range of managemnet activities including timber harvest.

This roadless area receives very little use The only active management concerns the one recreation use cabin located on Grindall Island

(7) **Appearance (Apparent Naturalness):** The Kasaan Roadless Area is part of the Coastal Hill character type which is characterized by moderately steep landforms, predominantly rounded summits, elevations to 4,500 feet, and flat-floored U-shaped valleys. A variety of island groups are also common. The areas' landscapes are very representative of this character type.

All of the area is inventoried as a Variety Class B (possessing landscape diversity and features that are common to the character type). The entire area is made up of a long, rounded ridge with very steep slopes close to 2,000 feet in elevation.

The Existing Visual Condition for the entire area is Type I where the natural landscape has remained unaltered by human activity.

(8) **Surroundings (External Influences):** The area is bounded on the north by Native corporation land. Clarence Strait and Kasaan Bay make up the rest of the roadless area boundary.

(9) **Attractions and Features of Special Interest:** The natural features of the area, the scenery, the opportunity to see wildlife, and to study the processes which formed this country may all be attractions The rocks off the south side of Grindall Island are sea lion rookeries The area contains one inventoried recreation place totaling 1,425 acres

b **Capability of Management as Wilderness or in an Unroaded Condition**

(1) **Manageability and Management Area Boundaries:** The boundaries of this area are easily identified and do not present any difficulty for management as a roadless area boundary.

(2) **Natural Integrity:** This roadless area currently has good natural integrity. However, once the State land selections are concluded, the area will be fragmented and the key feature of this roadless area, Grindall Island, will be in State ownership.

(3) **Opportunity for Solitude:** The area does not provide the opportunity for solitude because the entire area is in close proximity or overlooks the shipping and marine channels of Clarence Strait and Kasaan Bay The near constant noise of boats can be heard over most of the area.

(4) **Opportunity for Primitive Recreation:** The area provides primarily primitive recreation opportunities·

ROS Class	Acres
Primitive I (P1)	2,182
Primitive II (P2)	6,353

(5) **Special Features (Ecologic, Geologic, Scientific, Cultural):** Grindall Island and the offshore rocks are noted places to view sea lions

c. **Availability for Management as Wilderness or in an Unroaded Condition**

(1) **Resource Potentials**

(a) **Recreation Potential:** The recreation potential of this area is very low. The one recreation cabin on Grindall Island is about the extent of recreation development possible. Access to the area is difficult due to the rugged terrain and limited coastal access, therefore, the recreation potential of the area is limited The pending State land selections include all land areas suitable for some type of recreation purpose.

(b) **Fish Resource:** Due to the lack of freshwater streams, this area has very little value for fish resources.

(c) **Wildlife Resource:** There are no long range plans for habitat improvement project work within this roadless area.

(d) **Timber Resource** There are 3,227 acres inventoried as tentatively suitable for harvest. This includes 2,706 acres of non-riparian old growth and 261 acres of riparian old growth.

(e) **Land Use Authorizations:** None.

(f) **Minerals:** The mineral potential within the area is considered to be low

(g) **Areas of Scientific Interest:** None.

(2) **Management Considerations**

(a) This area is now an isolated piece of National Forest System land and will become more so when the State land selections become final This and the rugged topography restrict resource management. Grindall Island has been managed for recreation purposes and this would continue at the current level if it remained in the National Forest system.

(b) **Fire:** The area has no significant fire history.

(c) **Insects and Disease:** Endemic tree diseases common to Southeast Alaska are present.

(d) **Land Status:** Grindall Passage (400 acres) has been selected by the State.

d. **Relationship To Communities and Other Roadless and Wilderness Areas**

(1) **Nearby Roadless and Wilderness Areas and Uses:** There are no roadless areas adjacent to the Kasaan Roadless Area. The nearest roadless areas are the Thorne River and Karta River drainages about 10 miles to the west

(2) **Distance From Population Centers (accessibility):** Approximate distances from population centers are as follows:

Community		Air Miles	Water Miles
Juneau	(Pop. 23,729)	170	200
Ketchikan	(Pop. 12,705)	25	30

Hollis, located on Prince of Wales Island, is the nearest stop on the Alaska Marine Highway.

(3) **Interest by Proponents:**

(a) **Moratorium Areas:** The area has not been identified as a "moratorium" area pending congressional action on current wilderness initiatives.

(b) **Local Users/residents:** The Grindall Island recreation cabin is used by local people

e   **Environmental Consequences**

INDIVIDUAL ROADLESS AREA DESCRIPTION

NAME: Duke (521)   ACRES (GROSS): 46,845   ACRES (NFS): 46,785

GEOZONE: K02
GEOGRAPHIC PROVINCE: Southern Outer Islands

1989 WILDERNESS ATTRIBUTE RATING: 22

a. Description

(1) **Relationship to RARE II areas:** The table below displays the VCU 1/
names, VCU numbers, acres, original WARS 2/ rating, and comments. This
enables the reader to compare the roadless areas evaluated in Appendix C
with previous analyses.

VCU Name	VCU No.	1979 WARS Rating	Comments
Percy Island	766	21	
Duke	767	22	
Mary Island	768	22	

(2) **History:** This roadless area consists of Duke, Mary, and Percy
Islands. These islands were used by Alaska Natives in both ancient and
historic times. All through the commercial fishing era, the Judd Bay area
on Duke Island has been used as anchorage for the fishing fleet During
the 1940's, fox farming occurred on Duke Island. Duke, Mary, and Perry
Islands are exposed to the frequent severe weather out of Dixon entrance.

(3) **Location and Access:** The Duke Island Roadless Area consists of an
island group located about 10 miles southeast of Annette Island. The lack
of safe anchorages and freshwater lakes for floatplane landings essentially
makes this roadless area inaccessible to the general public.

(4) **Geography and Topography:** The area is characterized by low elevation
subdued topography and low-lying muskeg systems. The maximum elevation is
500 feet. There are 150 miles of shoreline on saltwater.

(5) **Ecosystem:**

(a) **Classification:** This area is in the Southern Outer Island
Geographic Province and is characterized by rolling subdued
topography.

1/ A VCU (Value Comparison Unit) is one of 867 watersheds which make up the
forest and were differentiated for planning purposes in the Tongass Land
Management Plan.
2/ Wilderness Attribute Rating System (WARS) was the nationwide system used to
rate the wilderness attributes of roadless areas in the Roadless Area
Review and Evaluation (RARE II).

(b) Vegetation: These islands are forested with poor quality hemlock, spruce and cedar. There are 1,966 acres of muskeg.

There are approximately 42,829 acres of forested land of which 8,121 acres are commercial forest land. Of the commercial forest land, 6,735 acres are non-riparian old growth and 604 acres are riparian old growth.

(c) Soils: These highly organic, low mineral content soils are generally formed over bedrock and are typically about 40 inches deep

(d) Fish Resource: Fish resources have been rated as part of the Tongass Land Management Plan (1979) and by the Alaska Department of Fish and Game in its Forest Habitat Integrity Program (1983). These ratings describe the value of VCU's for sport fish, commercial fish, and estuaries. While there are no freshwater or anadromous fish resources, two VCU's, 766 and 767, are rated high quality for estuary habitat.

(e) Wildlife Resource: Duke Island has a fox population, some Sitka black-tailed deer, and, along the shoreline, the common sea mammals of Southeast Alaska. These islands are frequented by large numbers of sea birds.

(f) Threatened and Endangered Species: None.

(6) Current Use and Management: The Tongass Land Management Plan allocated this area to Land Use Designation 2 (LUD 2). LUD 2 areas are to be managed in the roadless condition with the exception that wildlife and fish habitat improvement projects are permitted. The lack of access, manageable timber, and freshwater systems has allowed no management of these islands. A few skilled boaters do land on the islands to beachcomb on the several sand beaches

(7) Appearance (Apparent Naturalness): This area is part of the Coastal Hills character type which is characterized by moderately steep terrain, rounded summits and elevations up to 4,000 feet. Though this roadless area has very flat landform characteristics, all of this area is inventoried as Variety Class B due to the vegetative and waterform diversity, and the diversity of its coastal features such as the very irregular shoreline and clusters of smaller islands.

The Existing Visual Condition for the entire Roadless Area is Type I where the landscape has remained unaltered by human activity.

(8) Surroundings (External Influences): The Duke Island Roadless Area is isolated from other land areas by saltwater. Annette Island is about 10 miles to the northwest.

(9) Attractions and Features of Special Interest: The isolation and the rugged coastline interspersed with sandy beaches are the special features of this roadless area. The opportunity to view sea birds and mammals on or near the shore is of special interest.

b. Capability of Management as Wilderness or in an Unroaded Condition

(1) **Manageability and Management Area Boundaries:** The essentially unapproachable shoreline makes this roadless area easy to manage in an unroaded condition.

(2) **Natural Integrity:** The area is unmodified; this, along with its isolation, provides excellent natural integrity

(3) **Opportunity for Solitude:** There is outstanding opportunity for solitude Persons using any one of these islands are unlikely to encounter another person during their stay

(4) **Opportunity for Primitive Recreation:** There is good opportunity for primitive recreation, primarily along the coastal areas. There are no recreation attractions inland such as large lakes, streams or alpine features.

ROS Class	Acres
Primitive I (P1)	31,797
Primitive II (P2)	14,767

The area contains four recreation places totaling 8,392 acres They are primarily associated with anchorages in the area.

ROS CLASS	# OF REC. PLACES	TOTAL ACRES	CAPACITY BY RVD
P1	1	1,732	1,560
P2	3	6,660	3,120

(5) **Special Features (Ecologic, Geologic, Scientific, Cultural):** The rugged, rocky coastline facing the open sea is a special feature

c. Availability for Management as Wilderness or in an Unroaded Condition

(1) **Resource Potentials**

(a) **Recreation Potential:** The lack of access to any of the islands precludes recreation facility development The only real recreation potential is low density dispersed recreation associated with the sand beaches.

(b) **Fish Resource:** None.

(c) **Wildlife Resource:** There are no plans for wildlife habitat management on these islands and little potential to do so

(d) **Timber Resource:** There are 7,659 acres inventoried as tentatively suitable for harvest; including 583 acres of riparian old growth and 6,372 acres of non-riparian old growth

(e) **Land Use Authorizations:** None

(f) Minerals: None

(g) Areas of Scientific Interest: None.

(2) **Management Considerations**

(a) The lack of quality timber, absence of fresh water, and lack of safe access preclude any active management of the resources on these islands.

(b) Fire: The area has no significant fire history

(c) Insects and Disease: Endemic tree diseases common to Southeast Alaska are present.

(d) **Land Status:** 2,170 acres of land have been selected by the State at Judd Harbor.

d. **Relationship To Communities and Other Roadless and Wilderness Areas**

(1) **Nearby Roadless and Wilderness Areas and Uses:** This roadless area is approximately 10 miles west of Misty Fiords National Monument across Revillagigedo Channel.

(2) **Distance From Population Centers (accessibility):** Approximate distances from population centers are as follows:

Community		Air Miles	Water Miles
Juneau	(Pop. 23,729)	300	375
Ketchikan	(Pop. 12,705)	30	35

(3) **Interest by Proponents:**

(a) **Moratorium Areas:** The area has not been identified as a "moratorium" area or proposed as Wilderness in legislative initiatives to date.

(b) **Local Users/residents:** The area receives an occasional visit by boaters who have the ability to land.

e. **Environmental Consequences**

INDIVIDUAL ROADLESS AREA DESCRIPTION

NAME: Gravina (522)   ACRES (GROSS): 61,841   ACRES (NFS): 38,952

GEOZONE: K04
GEOGRAPHIC PROVINCE: Southern Outer Islands

1989 WILDERNESS ATTRIBUTE RATING: 22

a   Description

(1) **Relationship to RARE II areas:** The table below displays the VCU 1/
names, VCU numbers, acres, original WARS 2/ rating, and comments   This
enables the reader to compare the roadless areas evaluated in Appendix C
with previous analyses

VCU Name	VCU No.	1979 WARS Rating	Comments
	761		Not Rated
Dall Ridge	762	22	
	763		Not Rated
	764		Not Rated
Dall Head	765	22	

(2) **History:** This roadless area includes all National Forest land on
Gravina Island. Gravina Island was used by prehistoric and historic Native
cultures, and has also been an integral part of the development of
Ketchikan and southern Southeast Alaska   The north end of Gravina Island
was reserved for the development of the city of Ketchikan Since the early
days of the developing fishing industry, almost all of the northern,
eastern, and some of the western coastline of the island have been
influenced by settlers building home and cabin sites, storage shelters, and
anchorage facilities. To this day, remnants of these sites can be found.

Significant State and Native land selections have occurred on the northern
third of the island and adjacent to the major bays.

Gravina Island has a long history of subsistence and recreation use by
residents of Ketchikan.

(3) **Location and Access:** This roadless area is located on Gravina
Island. To access the area from Ketchikan, one must first cross
Revillagigedo Channel by the public airport ferry and then hike across the
State owned lands by foot. It may also be accessed by boat and floatplane

1/   A VCU (Value Comparison Unit) is one of 867 watersheds which make up the
     forest and were differentiated for planning purposes in the Tongass Land
     Management Plan.
2/   Wilderness Attribute Rating System (WARS) was the nationwide system used to
     rate the wilderness attributes of roadless areas in the Roadless Area
     Review and Evaluation (RARE II).

(4) Geography and Topography: The area is characterized by low elevation subdued topography, a rugged backbone ridge, and muskeg flats. The maximum elevation is 2,700 feet. There are 44 miles of shoreline on saltwater and approximately 600 acres of muskeg.

(5) Ecosystem:

(a) Classification: The area is within the Southern Outer Island Geographic Province. This province is generally characterized by rolling subdued and localized rugged topography

(b) Vegetation: This area is typical Southeast Alaska coastal temperate rain forest. The forest is primarily western hemlock and Sitka spruce with a large cedar component. Muskeg totals approximately 600 acres.

There are approximately 37,186 acres of forested land of which 19,417 acres are commercial forest land. Of the commercial forest land, 16,641 acres are non-riparian old growth and 1,506 acres are riparian old growth.

(c) Soils: Soils are highly organic with low clay content and are generally formed over bedrock. Soil depths range to 40 inches

(d) Fish Resource: Fish resources have been rated as part of the Tongass Land Management Plan (1979) and by the Alaska Department of Fish and Game in its Forest Habitat Integrity Program (1983) These ratings describe the value of VCU's for sport fish, commercial fish, and estuaries.

VCU 766 rated high value for commercial and sport fish, and VCU 765 high for estuary value.

(e) Wildlife Resource: This area has high populations of Sitka black-tailed deer, some black bear, and populations of small furbearers and other mammals.

(f) Threatened and Endangered Species: None.

(6) Current Use and Management: The area was allocated to Land Use Designation 3 (LUD 3) in the Tongass Land Management Plan. The LUD 3 area is to be managed for a variety of uses, including timber harvest, while protecting amenity values.

There is one recreation use cabin on the southwest coast, and an electronics site on High Mountain. Current management is to maintain the existing cabin and electronics site.

(7) Appearance (Apparent Naturalness): This area is part of the Coastal Hills character type which is characterized by moderately steep landforms. predominantly rounded summits, elevations up to 4,500 feet, and flat floored, U-shaped valleys The Gravina Roadless Area is, for the most part, very representative of this character type

The entire area is inventoried as Variety Class B (possessing characteristics that are common in the character type)   The more distinctive and rugged landforms are found in the Dall Head area of Gravina Island.

Almost all of this area is inventoried as Type I Existing Visual Condition where the landscape has remained unaltered by human activity   The only exception is a 38-year-old clearcut at the head of Vallenar Bay, and evidence of human habitation along some of the coastal areas

(8) **Surroundings (External Influences):** Gravina Island is heavily influenced by the growth in the greater Ketchikan area   The Ketchikan airport is on the northern end of the island. Flight patterns cause noise and visual influence within the roadless area. State and Native land selections extend into the roadless area causing an irregular boundary State lands are dedicated for community development and expansion, therefore, their impact upon the roadless area will increase over time. The eastern, southern, and western boundaries are large bodies of saltwater.

(9) **Attractions and Features of Special Interest:** The natural features of the area, the scenery, the saltwater bays and inlets, and the opportunity to see wildlife and to study the processes which formed this country may all be attractions. The area contains seven inventoried recreation places totaling 18,169 acres.

b. **Capability of Management as Wilderness or in an Unroaded Condition**

(1) **Manageability and Management Area Boundaries:** The irregular State and Native land boundaries would make it difficult to manage this area in a roadless condition. These boundaries do not take advantage of natural topographic features and, in most cases, are on relatively flat ground Marking these boundaries would be difficult because the vegetation grows quickly. Access to unroaded areas would be difficult to control

(2) **Natural Integrity:** The area is unmodified except for the trace remains of human activity which occurred during the early 1900's   Because the area is surrounded primarily by large saltwater channels, the natural integrity of the area is preserved.

(3) **Opportunity for Solitude:** The opportunity for solitude within the area is somewhat marginal. Along the coast, there is near constant sports and commercial fishing causing a constant drone of boat engines   Within the area, persons can see jets and floatplanes overhead and hear their engines, although a person entering the interior of this roadless area is not likely to meet other humans.

(4) **Opportunity for Primitive Recreation:** There is good opportunity for primitive recreation in the interior of the island and along the southwest coast. The latter area possesses good saltwater fishing and a Forest Service cabin. Some of these primitive opportunities may be impacted in the future by development on the extensive State and private lands in the area   The eastern side of the island near Ketchikan is heavily influenced by jet and other airline and boat traffic.

ROS Class	Acres
Primitive I (P1)	16,160
Primitive II (P2)	9,510
Semi-Primitive Motorized (SPM)	12,243
Rural (R)	1,039

There are seven inventoried recreation places.

ROS CLASS	# OF REC. PLACES	TOTAL ACRES	CAPACITY BY RVD'S
P1	1	6,117	1,170
P2	1	2,466	1,560
SPM	4	9,326	3,360
R	1	260	400

(5) **Special Features (Ecologic, Geologic, Scientific, Cultural):** There are no known special features within the area.

c. **Availability for Management as Wilderness or in an Unroaded Condition**

(1) **Resource Potentials**

(a) **Recreation Potential:** There is potential for trail development connecting the east side of Gravina along Tongass Narrows to Bostwick Lake and Inlet or to Blank Inlet. The State of Alaska would be involved in this development.

(b) **Fish Resource:** Due to the lack of streams with fish habitat potential, there is little opportunity for fish habitat improvement projects.

(c) **Wildlife Resource:** There are no plans for wildlife habitat improvement project in this roadless area.

(d) **Timber Resource:** There are 16,578 acres inventoried as tentatively suitable for harvest. This includes 14,307 acres of non-riparian old growth and 1,406 acres of riparian old growth

(e) **Land Use Authorizations:** A permitted electronics site is located on High Mountain.

(f) **Minerals:** The southern end of Gravina Island has a history of mineral exploration and gold mining. Prospecting is presently occurring. There is potential for future mine development.

(g) **Areas of Scientific Interest:** None.

(2) **Management Considerations**

(a) This area has limited potential for commodity and market resource management. Potential for amenity values in terms of developed recreation, fish, and wildlife resources is also limited Minerals may or may not be of management concern in the future

(b) Fire: The area has no significant fire history

(c) Insects and Disease: Endemic tree diseases common to Southeast Alaska are present

(d) Land Status: All National Forest Land.

d   Relationship To Communities and Other Roadless and Wilderness Areas

(1) Nearby Roadless and Wilderness Areas and Uses: This roadless area is not adjacent to any other roadless areas

(2) Distance From Population Centers (accessibility): Approximate distances from population centers are as follows·

Community		Air Miles	Water Miles
Ketchikan	(Pop. 12,700)	3	5
Juneau	(Pop. 23,729)	250	300

(3) Interest by Proponents:

(a) Moratorium Areas: The area has not been identified as a "moratorium" area or proposed as Wilderness in legislative initiatives to date.

(b) Local Users/residents: The area receives significant local use for general hunting and some recreation activity.

e   Environmental Consequences

INDIVIDUAL ROADLESS AREA DESCRIPTION

NAME: South Revilla (523)   ACRES (GROSS): 71,998   ACRES (NFS): 71,358

GEOZONE: K04
GEOGRAPHIC PROVINCE: Central Interior Islands

1989 WILDERNESS ATTRIBUTE RATING: 21

a. Description

      (1) Relationship to RARE II areas: The table below displays the VCU 1/
      names, VCU numbers, acres, original WARS 2/ rating, and comments. This
      enables the reader to compare the roadless areas evaluated in Appendix C
      with previous analyses.

VCU Name	VCU No.	1979 WARS Rating	Comments
	747		Not Rated
	748		Not Rated
	753		Not Rated
Fish Creek	754	23	
Gokachin	755	22	
	756		Not Rated
	757		Not Rated
	758		Not Rated
Moth Bay	759	22	
Luckyikan Lakes	760	21	
	769		Not Rated
	770		Not Rated

      (2) History: Prehistoric and historic Native cultures used this roadless
      area but their primary influence areas are now within the private, Native
      and State lands. In more recent history, homesteading occurred in Ice
      House Cove and one site is still used as a summer residence. The Thorne
      Arm area has been prospected for minerals resulting in the Sealevel Mine
      being patented. In the 1950's, timber harvest was initiated and is
      continuing to progress into unroaded areas. The Forest Service camp and
      Coast Guard Loran station at Shoal Cove are excluded from the boundary of
      the South Revilla Roadless Area.

1/ A VCU (Value Comparison Unit) is one of 867 watersheds which make up the
    forest and were differentiated for planning purposes in the Tongass Land
    Management Plan.
2/ Wilderness Attribute Rating System (WARS) was the nationwide system used to
    rate the wilderness attributes of roadless areas in the Roadless Area
    Review and Evaluation (RARE II).

(3) **Location and Access:** The South Revilla Roadless Area is located on the southwest quarter of Revillagigedo Island. Access is gained through the Ward Lake road system and by saltwater through George and Carroll Inlets

(4) **Geography and Topography:** The area is characterized by a combination of rugged and gentle terrain The steep mountain slopes generally rise up to about 2,500 feet with the uppermost elevation being above timberline Most of the gentle terrain is located at the head end of the Thorne Arm There are 97 miles of saltwater shoreline.

(5) **Ecosystem:**

(a) **Classification:** The South Revilla Roadless Area is classified as being in the Central Interior Islands Geographic Province. This province is characterized by subdued, rolling topography.

(b) **Vegetation:** This area is typical Southeast Alaska coastal temperate rain forest. The forest is primarily western hemlock and Sitka spruce with a large cedar component There are interspersed areas of the muskeg and alpine vegetative types.

There are approximately 67,159 acres of forested land of which 33,410 acres are commercial forest land. Of the commercial forest land, 28,932 acres are non-riparian old growth and 3,618 are riparian old growth.

(c) **Soils:** These highly organic, low clay content soils are generally formed over bedrock and are typically about 40 inches deep.

(d) **Fish Resource:** Fish resources have been rated as part of the Tongass Land Management Plan (1979) and by the Alaska Department of Fish and Game in its Forest Habitat Integrity Program (1983) These ratings describe the value of VCU's for sport fish, commercial fish. and estuaries.

VCU's 747, 748, 754, 755, 758 and 760 are rated high value for sport fish, VCU's 747, 748, 754, and 760 are rated high value for commercial fish, and VCU's 769 and 770 are rated high value for estuary habitat.

(e) **Wildlife Resource:** This area has populations of Sitka black-tailed deer, black bear, otter, marten, mink, loon, and common waterfowl. Trumpeter swan use the major saltwater inlets and freshwater lakes as resting areas during their migrations.

(f) **Threatened and Endangered Species:** None.

(6) **Current Use and Management:** The Tongass Land Management Plan allocated this area to Land Use Designations (LUD's) 1 (8,577 acres), 2 (21,064 acres) and 3 (4,198 acres) LUD 1 areas are to be managed in the roadless condition. LUD 2 areas are to be managed in the roadless condition although wildlife and fish habitat projects are permitted LUD 3 areas are to be managed for a variety of uses and activities in a compatible and complementary manner

There is one Forest Service cabin, a mooring buoy, and a hiking trail at
Fish Creek. A timber sale and log transfer site are planned for the Elf
Point area on the east side of the Thorne Arm.

(7) **Appearance (Apparent Naturalness):** This roadless area is part of the
Coastal Hills character type which consists of moderately steep landforms
predominantly rounded summits, elevations to 4,500 feet, and flat-floored,
U-shaped valleys   Numerous island groups are also common in this character
type   The landscapes of this area range from very flat to gently rolling
or moderately rugged   The highest elevations are just over 2,100 feet

About 88 percent of the area is inventoried as Variety Class B (possessing
landscape diversity that is common in the character type). The rest of the
area is rated as Variety Class C (possessing minimal landscape diversity
relative to the character type). Though much of this area has low to very
average scenic quality, there are some specific areas that are notable
These include the Fish Creek-Low Lake drainage at the head of Thorne Arm,
and the cluster of lakes near the summit of Black Mountain.

About 98 percent of the area is in a Type I Existing Visual Condition where
the natural landscape has remained unaltered by human activity. The rest
of the area exhibits minimally to moderately altered landscapes resulting
from past timber harvest along its edge, primarily at the head of Thorne
Arm.

(8) **Surroundings (External Influences):** The area between the north ends
of Carroll Inlet and the Thorne Arm has been heavily logged. The remaining
adjacent areas to this roadless area are either saltwater or part of Misty
Fiords National Monument

(9) **Attractions and Features of Special Interest:** The main attraction of
the South Revilla Roadless Area is fishing in the streams and lakes at the
upper end of the Thorne Arm. The area contains five inventoried recreation
places containing 7,396 acres.

b. **Capability of Management as Wilderness or in an Unroaded Condition**

(1) **Manageability and Management Area Boundaries:** The boundaries of the
South Revilla Area consist mostly of Misty Fiords National Monument and
saltwater, making a very manageable roadless area boundary   Ridge lines
along the northern boundary could be used to separate the roadless from the
roaded/logged area. The area itself is very manageable as a roadless area

(2) **Natural Integrity:** South Revilla is unmodified except for the cabin
and trail system in the Fish Creek area. Some evidence of old mining
activity exists, but is very difficult to detect without knowing its exact
location.

(3) **Opportunity for Solitude:** There is excellent opportunity for solitude
within most of this area   A person camping or hiking in the Fish Creek
area during the steelhead and salmon fishing seasons is likely to encounter
other individuals   There will be sights and sounds of aircraft almost
anywhere within the area

(4) **Opportunity for Primitive Recreation:** Good opportunities for primitive recreation exist along the east shore of Thorne Arm and along potential trail corridors such as Gokachin Creek which lead into Misty Fiords National Monument Many of the recreation opportunities are in the Fish Creek area, and in the saltwater channels and coves of Carroll Inlet and Thorne Arm which provide a semi-primitive setting

ROS CLASS	ACRES
Primtive I (P1)	19,971
Primitive II (P2)	16,150
Semi-Primitive Non-Motorized (SPNM)	13,490
Semi-Primitive Motorized (SPM)	9,813
Roaded Modified (RM)	11,914

The area contains five inventoried recreation places.

ROS CLASS	# OF REC. PLACES	TOTAL ACRES	CAPACITY BY RVD'S
P1	1	4,476	1,170
P2	1	961	780
SPM	1	620	2,340
RM	2	1,339	3,436

(5) **Special Features (Ecologic, Geologic, Scientific, Cultural):** There are no known special features within the area.

c. **Availability for Management as Wilderness or in an Unroaded Condition**

   (1) **Resource Potentials**

   (a) **Recreation Potential:** There is potential for additional recreation cabins and trails within the Thorne Arm part of this roadless area. One potential trail corridor would lead into the Gokachin Lakes area in Misty Fiords National Monument. This lake system has been recognized as an outstanding canoeing opportunity The potential for primitive dispersed recreation is good

   (b) **Fish Resource:** The major streams provide excellent fish habitat and are widely known for high quality steelhead and salmon fishing The major lakes within the Fish Creek drainage have very good stocks of rainbow trout.

   (c) **Wildlife Resource:** There are Sitka black-tailed deer, black bear, marten, mink, wolves, and a variety of birds. Some hunting and trapping occurs.

   (d) **Timber Resource:** There are 23,807 acres inventoried as tentatively suitable for harvest. This includes 20,109 acres of non-riparian old growth and 2,838 acres of riparian old growth

   (e) **Land Use Authorizations:** None

(f) **Minerals:** Although no active mining is occurring at this time, there is interest in the mineral potential of the Black Mountain and Moth Bay areas.

(g) **Areas of Scientific Interest:** None

(2) **Management Considerations**

(a) Timber sales are currently planned in the Elf Point area in Thorne Arm. Most of this roadless area, with the exception of the LUD 2 and Fish Creek drainage areas, is being considered for future timber entry.

Some potential exists for additional recreation use cabins and trails within the area.

(b) **Fire:** The area has no significant fire history.

(c) **Insects and Disease:** Endemic tree diseases common to Southeast Alaska are present.

(d) **Land Status:** The one parcel of private land within the roadless area boundary is located about two miles north of Moth Bay The roadless boundary excludes the Sealevel Mine patent.

d. **Relationship To Communities and Other Roadless and Wilderness Areas**

(1) **Nearby Roadless and Wilderness Areas and Uses:** The east boundary coincides with the boundary of Misty Fiords National Monument The Revilla Roadless Area is to the north

(2) **Distance From Population Centers (accessibility):** Approximate distances from population centers are as follows:

Community		Air Miles	Water Miles
Juneau	(Pop. 23,729)	270	330
Ketchikan	(Pop. 12,700)	20	30

(3) **Interest by Proponents:**

(a) **Moratorium Areas:** The area has not been identified as a "moratorium" area or proposed as Wilderness in legislative initiatives to date.

(b) **Local Users/residents:** Sockeye salmon are harvested in the Thorne Arm area by local residents authorized for subsistence use Some trapping occurs within this roadless area. Sportfishing in the streams and lakes of the area is done primarily by local residents

e. **Environmental Consequences**

INDIVIDUAL ROADLESS AREA DESCRIPTION

NAME: Revilla (524)   ACRES (GROSS): 161,263   ACRES (NFS): 138,393

GEOZONE: K04
GEOGRAPHIC PROVINCE: Central Interior Islands

1989 WILDERNESS ATTRIBUTE RATING: 21

a   Description

(1) **Relationship to RARE II areas:** The table below displays the VCU 1/
names, VCU numbers, acres, original WARS 2/ rating, and comments. This
enables the reader to compare the roadless areas evaluated in Appendix C
with previous analyses.

VCU Name	VCU No.	1979 WARS Rating	Comments
Moser Bay	743	22	
Swan	745	22	
	746		Not Rated
Salt Lagoon	747	23	
	748		Not Rated
	749		Not Rated
	750		Not Rated
Ketchikan Lakes	751	23	
Whitmen Lakes	752	21	
	753		Not Rated
	754		Not Rated
	756		Not Rated
	776		Not Rated
Clover Pass	864	17	

(2) **History:** This area has a rich history in the development of southern
Southeast Alaska. The city of Ketchikan and its surroundings form the
southern boundary of this roadless area. Consequently, the southern part
of the Revilla Roadless Area has been influenced in the past, and continues
to be influenced, by human activity. The Ward Creek drainage was developed
by the combination of early 1900's mining, Civilian Conservation Corps
public works projects during the 1930's, and hydropower development in the
Swan Lake area. In recent times, the State and Native corporations have
made extensive land selections in the headwaters of Ward Creek, along
George and Carroll Inlets, and along the south boundary of this roadless
area. The State selections are for the express purpose of future community
development.

1/ A VCU (**Value Comparison Unit**) is one of 867 watersheds which make up the
    forest and were differentiated for planning purposes in the Tongass Land
    Management Plan.
2/ Wilderness Attribute Rating System (WARS) was the nationwide system used to
    rate the wilderness attributes of roadless areas in the Roadless Area
    Review and Evaluation (RARE II).

Prehistoric and historic Native cultures used the roadless area, but the areas they primarily influenced are now within private, Native and State lands.

(3) **Location and Access:** The area is located on the southwest quarter of Revillagigedo Island. Access is gained through the Ward Lake road system and by saltwater through George and Carroll Inlets.

(4) **Geography and Topography:** The area is characterized by rugged terrain. Mountain slopes are steep, causing deeply incised drainages. Elevations rise to over 3,000 feet. There are about 9,600 acres of alpine and 2,200 acres of rock terrain. There are 30 miles of saltwater shoreline. The numerous lakes account for about 4,300 acres.

(5) **Ecosystem:**

    (a) **Classification:** The area is classified as being in the Central Interior Islands Geographic Province. This province is characterized by rolling topography with localized rugged terrain and extensive muskeg areas.

    (b) **Vegetation:** This area is typical Southeast Alaska coastal temperate rain forest. The forest is primarily western hemlock and Sitka spruce with a large cedar component.

    There are approximately 117,245 acres of forested land of which 66,172 acres are commercial forest land. Of the commercial forest land, 59,095 acres are non-riparian old growth and 5,378 acres are riparian old growth.

    (c) **Soils:** These highly organic, low clay content soils are generally formed over bedrock and are typically about 40 inches deep

    (d) **Fish Resource:** Fish resources have been rated as part of the Tongass Land Management Plan (1979) and by the Alaska Department of Fish and Game in its Forest Habitat Integrity Program (1983). These ratings describe the value of VCU's for sport fish, commercial fish, and estuaries.

    VCU's 747, 748, 750, 751, 754, and 776 are high value for commercial fish. VCU's 745, 747, 748, 751, 752, 753, and 754 are high value for sport fish.

    (e) **Wildlife Resource:** This area has populations of Sitka black-tailed deer, black bear, otter, marten, mink, loon, and common waterfowl. Trumpeter swan use the major saltwater inlets and freshwater lakes as resting areas during their migrations.

    (f) **Threatened and Endangered Species:** The area contains no known threatened or endangered species, and has not been identified as an area of potential scientific value.

(6) **Current Use and Management:** The Tongass Land Management Plan allocated this area to Land Use Designation 3 (LUD 3). The LUD 3 area is to be managed for a variety of uses and activities in a compatible and complementary manner.

There are two Forest Service campgrounds, several picnic areas, and a day use trail at Ward Lake. The area has a number of trails, the most prominent being the Deer Mountain Trail which is designated as a National Recreation Trail. There are several outfitters and guides who operate within this roadless area The Ward Lake drainage receives heavy winter recreation activity.

This roadless area is the source of Ketchikan's domestic water supply Part of Ketchikan's hydropower comes from the Swan Lake power generation facility.

Future timber harvest is planned within this roadless area in the upper parts of George and Carroll Inlets.

(7) **Appearance (Apparent Naturalness):** This roadless area is part of the Coastal Hills character type which is characterized by moderately steep landforms, predominantly rounded summits, elevations up to 4,500 feet, and flat-floored, U-shaped valleys. A variety of island groups are also common. This area possesses some of the most rugged and diverse terrain in the character type.

About 17 percent of the roadless area is inventoried as Variety Class A (possessing a level of landscape diversity that is unique for the character type). These Class A landscapes are primarily centered around the rugged terrain behind Ketchikan from Deer Mountain north to the White River drainage and George Inlet. This area exhibits diverse alpine terrain, vegetative patterns, rock formations, and many lake basins and waterfalls The rest of the area is rated as Variety Class B (possessing landscape diversity common for the character type).

About 92 percent of this area is in a Type I Existing Visual Condition where the natural landscape has remained unaltered by human activity The rest of the area is in a moderately- to heavily-altered visual condition due to the impacts of a small level of timber harvest in the Ward Lake area and the Swan Lake transmission line.

(8) **Surroundings (External Influences):** The entire southern boundary of this roadless area is influenced by the development associated with Ketchikan. State and Native selections north of Ketchikan and in George and Carroll Inlets form much of the boundary of this roadless area. The Native lands are rapidly being roaded and logged.

(9) **Attractions and Features of Special Interest:** The main attraction of this area is its close proximity and accessibility to Ketchikan. It is the only National Forest land area that is accessible by road from Ketchikan The trail system is of interest because people can hike from Ketchikan to the alpine zone or take short day hikes at their leisure The area contains 27 inventoried recreation places totaling 40,618 acres.

b   Capability of Management as Wilderness or in an Unroaded Condition

    (1) **Manageability and Management Area Boundaries:** Private land along the
    southern and eastern sides of this roadless area results in irregular
    shaped boundaries. The boundary will therefore be difficult to define and
    manage. Parts of this roadless area are used by off-road vehicles during
    the winter for recreation and trapping. Prohibiting these uses would be
    very controversial.

    (2) **Natural Integrity:** The area is modified by the Swan Lake powerline
    and the trail system. The area's close proximity to Ketchikan, its history
    of mineral exploration, and its high recreation use in the southern part
    all contribute to evidence of human activity.

    (3) **Opportunity for Solitude:** There is opportunity for solitude within
    certain parts of the area. All along the roadless area's southern edge,
    the noise of the Ketchikan area can be heard. There are extensive
    overflights by fixed-wing aircraft and helicopters flying out of Ketchikan

    (4) **Opportunity for Primitive Recreation:** Due to the extensive human use
    of much of the area, the external influences of Native logging, the Swan
    Lake powerline, and other activities, the opportunities for primitive
    recreation are limited. There are many recreation attractions in this area
    but most are in a semi-primitive setting.

ROS Class	Acres
Primitive I (P1)	24,147
Primitive II (P2)	4,839
Semi-Primitive Non-Motorized (SPNM)	64,645
Semi-Primitive Motorized (SPM)	5,561
Roaded Natural (RN)	11,794
Roaded Modified (RM)	25,648
Rural (R)	879

The area contains 27 inventoried recreation places.

ROS CLASS	# OF REC. PLACES	TOTAL ACRES	CAPACITY BY RVD'S
P1	2	9,473	3,498
P2	3	4,839	2,343
SPNM	9	19,168	29,685
SPM	3	801	2,034
RN	6	4,578	88,675
RM	4	1,759	4,125

    (5) **Special Features (Ecologic, Geologic, Scientific, Cultural):** There
    are no known special features within the area.

c. **Availability for Management as Wilderness or in an Unroaded Condition**

    (1) **Resource Potentials**

        (a) **Recreation Potential:** This roadless area has high potential for
        development of roaded recreation. This is a priority objective for

the people in the Ketchikan area, since all direct road access to the
National Forest on Revillagigedo Island must be through the Revilla
unroaded area. Potential exists for trail construction and additional
recreation cabins throughout this area.

(b) Fish Resource: There is some potential for fish habitat
improvement on streams within the area. However, the best
opportunities are now within State and Native selected lands   There
is a desire by the Alaska Department of Fish and Game to improve
access to and the quality of freshwater fishing in this roadless area

(c) Wildlife Resource: There are no long-range plans for habitat
improvement projects within this roadless area. There is some hunting
and trapping within the area but, in general, the terrain is too rough
for quality sports hunting.

(d) Timber Resource: There are 50,638 acres inventoried as
tentatively suitable for harvest. This includes 44,501 acres of
non-riparian old growth and 4,778 acres of riparian old growth

(e) Land Use Authorizations: There is a special use permit for the
Swan Lake hydropower generating plant and powerline.   .

(f) Minerals: There are mining claims located on Mahoney Mountain

(g) Areas of Scientific Interest: None.

(2) Management Considerations

(a) The Revilla Roadless Area is the key to providing roaded
recreation opportunities for the residents of Revillagigedo Island
Any extension of the already limited road opportunities in the
Ketchikan Area must occur into and through the Revilla Roadless Area
There is a plan for extending the Ward Lake road into the upper end of
George and Carroll Inlets. A long-range plan proposes connection of
Ketchikan to the mainland with a road proceeding northward to the
Bradfield Canal. This route must go through the Revilla Roadless
Area.

Considerable potential exists for development of roaded recreation
opportunities, including campgrounds and additional trails, within
this area.

(b) Fire: The area has no significant fire history.

(c) Insects and Disease: Endemic tree diseases common to Southeast
Alaska are present.

(d) Land Status: No private land exists within the identified
roadless area boundary. The very irregular boundary, however,
resulted from State and Native corporation land selections

d   Relationship To Communities and Other Roadless and Wilderness Areas

(1) **Nearby Roadless and Wilderness Areas and Uses:** This roadless area is part of a larger contiguous unroaded land mass consisting of Misty Fiords National Monument, the South Revilla Roadless Area, and the North Revilla Roadless Area.

(2) **Distance From Population Centers (accessibility):** Approximate distances from population centers are as follows:

Community		Air Miles	Water Miles
Juneau	(Pop. 23,729)	250	300
Ketchikan	(Pop. 12,705)	Adjacent	

(3) **Interest by Proponents:**

(a) **Moratorium Areas:** The area has not been identified as a "moratorium" area or proposed as Wilderness in legislative initiatives to date.

(b) **Local Users/residents:** The area receives significant local use for subsistence and recreation activity.

e. **Environmental Consequences**

INDIVIDUAL ROADLESS AREA DESCRIPTION

NAME: Behm Islands (525)   ACRES (GROSS): 5,526   ACRES (NFS): 2,042

GEOZONE: K04
GEOGRAPHIC PROVINCE: Central Interior Islands

1989 WILDERNESS ATTRIBUTE RATING: 19

a. Description

(1) **Relationship to RARE II areas:** The table below displays the VCU 1/
names, VCU numbers, acres, original WARS 2/ rating, and comments   This
enables the reader to compare the roadless areas evaluated in Appendix C
with previous analyses.

VCU Name	VCU No.	1979 WARS Rating	Comments
	741		Not Rated
Clover Pass	864	17	

(2) **History:** The Behm Islands Roadless Area includes a chain of islands
extending from Point Higgins to Naha Bay. These islands form the sheltered
water known as Clover Pass and have been used for fox farms, navigational
aid sites, and for a recreation residence which is located on Benton
Island. In 1988, the Navy proposed to use Back Island as the shore
facility for their new acoustic test range located in Behm Canal   The
Forest Service has issued the Navy a Special Use Permit for the Back Island
site and construction has begun.

Prehistoric and historic Native cultures used this roadless area

(3) **Location and Access:** The area is located offshore of the southwest
corner of Revillagigedo Island. Access is by boat from the several marinas
in the area. ·

(4) **Geography and Topography:** The area is characterized by several low
relief islands and rocky shorelines with interspersed sand beaches.
There are 19 miles of saltwater shoreline and no freshwater streams on
these islands. All the islands are forested. There are no areas of ice,
snow, rock, or muskeg.

1/ A VCU (Value Comparison Unit) is one of 867 watersheds which make up the
forest and were differentiated for planning purposes in the Tongass Land
Management Plan.
2/ Wilderness Attribute Rating System (WARS) was the nationwide system used to
rate the wilderness attributes of roadless areas in the Roadless Area
Review and Evaluation (RARE II).

(5) **Ecosystem:**

(a) **Classification:** The area is in the Central Interior Islands Geographic Province. This province is characterized by rolling subdued and localized rugged topography.

(b) **Vegetation:** Vegetation is typical Southeast Alaska coastal temperate rain forest. The forest is primarily western hemlock and Sitka spruce with large components of cedar. There are numerous interspersed areas of the muskeg and alpine vegetative types

There are approximately 1,921 acres of forested land of which 1,581 acres are commercial forest land. Of the commercial forest land, 1,481 acres are non-riparian old growth and 60 acres are riparian old growth.

(c) **Soils:** These highly organic, low clay content soils are generally formed over bedrock and are typically about 40 inches deep

(d) **Fish Resource:** Fish resources have been rated as part of the Tongass Land Management Plan (1979) and by the Alaska Department of Fish and Game in its Forest Habitat Integrity Program (1983). Neither of these ratings indicate that there is high quality fish habitat within this roadless area.

(e) **Wildlife Resource:** There are few land mammals on these islands Marine mammals are occasionally seen on or near rocks along the shoreline.

(f) **Threatened and Endangered Species:** None.

(6) **Current Use and Management:** The Tongass Land Management Plan allocated this area to Land Use Designation 2 (LUD 2). The area is to be managed in a roadless condition except that wildlife and fish habitat improvements are permitted.

There is one recreation residence authorized by a special use permit on Betton Island. There are U.S. Coast Guard navigation aids installed on several of the islands. The Navy has recently been authorized to construct support buildings and a dock on Back Island for their acoustical test facility.

(7) **Appearance (Apparent Naturalness):** This roadless area is part of the Coastal Hills character type, which is characterized by moderately steep landforms, with generally rounded summits usually less than 4,000 feet, and also by island groups of different sizes and forms. This roadless area is typical of these island groups and is adjacent to other Coastal Hill landforms on Revilla Island.

All of this area is inventoried as Variety Class B (common or average scenic diversity relative to the character type of which it is a part) Though there are no highly distinctive scenic features, the combination of waterways, islands of different sizes, and the backdrop of more massive landforms around this popular fishing and boating area make this a very attractive landscape.

The Existing Visual Condition of this area is all Type I (the landscape is essentially unmodified by human). A few small structures scattered throughout this area are the only alterations to the natural landscape

(8) **Surroundings (External Influences):** The Islands are located one to two miles from the recreation, resort, and residential area on Revillagigedo Island The Clover Pass area has been designated a Scenic Recreation Area by the Ketchikan Borough. Several homes, marinas, and resort developments can be seen on the shore of Revilla Island from many portions of this area Logging on Native-owned land on the slopes east of Clover Pass have recently become partially visible from portions of the waterways and islands.

(9) **Attractions and Features of Special Interest:** There are no features or attractions on the islands that are of special interest. However, the Clover Pass area receives heavy fishing pressure and people fishing do land on the sandy beaches to rest, relax, and beachcomb. The area contains four inventoried recreation places or portions of recreation places totaling 1,761 acres.

b. **Capability of Management as Wilderness or in an Unroaded Condition**

(1) **Manageability and Management Area Boundaries:** Since the area is made up of small islands which have limited potential for timber harvest or other resource management activities, it could easily be managed in a roadless condition.

(2) **Natural Integrity:** The area is physically unaltered. The recreation summer home on Betton Island has little influence on the apparent natural integrity of the area. The Navy's acoustical test site on Back Island may break the apparent natural integrity of this island.

(3) **Opportunity for Solitude:** There is practically no opportunity for solitude within this roadless area. All of the island area is within sight and sound of saltwater. During the summer-long principal fishing season, both sport and commercial, there are the constant sights and sounds of powerboats. The frequent landings by boaters further decreases the opportunity for solitude.

(4) **Opportunity for Primitive Recreation:** The area provides primarily Roaded Natural and Semi-Primitive recreation opportunities:

ROS Class	Acres
Roaded Natural (RN)	560
Semi-Primitive-Motorized (SPM)	1,481

The area contains four inventoried recreation places.

ROS CLASS	# OF REC. PLACES	TOTAL ACRES	CAPACITY BY RVD
SPM	3	1,461	5,460
RN	1	300	2,000

(5) **Special Features (Ecologic, Geologic, Scientific, Cultural):** There are no known special features within the area.

c   Availability for Management as Wilderness or in an Unroaded Condition

(1) **Resource Potentials**

(a) **Recreation Potential:** This roadless area has minor potential for recreation development and use. There is some opportunity to provide unimproved or semi-improved rest/campsites for people kayaking in the area. The area will continue to receive the dispersed recreation use associated with the beaches.

(b) **Fish Resource:** None.

(c) **Wildlife Resource:** Sea mammals and birds will continue to use the shoreline environment. There is no plan to do any active habitat improvement work on any of the islands.

(d) **Timber Resource:** There are 1,361 acres inventoried as tentatively suitable for harvest. This includes 60 acres of riparian old-growth, and 1,281 acres of non-riparian old-growth.

(e) **Land Use Authorizations:** There is a permitted recreation summer home and an electronics site on Betton Island. The Navy is authorized to construct buildings and boat dock on Back Island. In addition, there are several sites reserved by the Coast Guard for placing navigation aids.

(f) **Minerals:** None.

(g) **Areas of Scientific Interest:** None.

(2) **Management Considerations**

(a) The Behm Canal Island group provides a scenic experience and backdrop for the significant amount of charter and independent fishing that occurs in the Clover Pass area. Recreation use is projected to remain incidental to the fishing activity unless some development to support kayaking activity takes place.

(b) **Fire:** The area has no significant fire history.

(c) **Insects and Disease:** Endemic tree diseases common to Southeast Alaska are present.

(d) **Land Status:** There is one parcel of private land on Grant Island.

d. Relationship To Communities and Other Roadless and Wilderness Areas

(1) **Nearby Roadless and Wilderness Areas and Uses:** This roadless area is isolated from the Revilla Roadless Area by Clover Pass and a strip of State and Borough land on Revillagigedo Island.

(2) **Distance From Population Centers (accessibility):** Approximate distances from population centers are as follows:

Community	Air Miles	Water Miles
Ketchikan (Pop 12,705)	15	18

(3)   **Interest by Proponents:**

(a) **Moratorium Areas:** The area has not been identified as a "moratorium" area or proposed as Wilderness in legislative initiatives to date.

(b) **Local Users/residents:** The area receives insignificant use by the local users/residents.

Environmental Consequences

INDIVIDUAL ROADLESS AREA DESCRIPTION

NAME: North Revilla (526)   ACRES (GROSS): 164,810   ACRES (NFS): 163,771

GEOZONE: K04
GEOGRAPHIC PROVINCE: Central Interior Islands

1989 WILDERNESS ATTRIBUTE RATING: 22

a. Description

(1) **Relationship to RARE II areas:** The table below displays the VCU 1/ names, VCU numbers, acres, original WARS 2/ rating, and comments. This enables the reader to compare the roadless areas evaluated in Appendix C with previous analyses.

VCU Name	VCU No.	1979 WARS Rating	Comments
Bell	731	22	
	732		Not Rated
	733		Not Rated
Orchard	734	24	
Klu	737	21	
	738		Not Rated
Traitors	739	23	
Francis Cove	740	23	
Loring	741	22	
	742		Not Rated
Naha	744	22	
	747		Not Rated
	749		Not Rated
	780		Not Rated
	781		Not Rated

(2) **History:** This area has a rich history in the development of southern Southeast Alaska. The commercial fishing industry established itself at Loring located in Naha Bay. This site has been continually occupied since the early 1900's. The Naha drainage was open to homesteading and the Orten Ranch owes its origin to this. A fish hatchery was constructed at Heckman Lake in the early 1900's.

1/ A VCU (Value Comparison Unit) is one of 867 watersheds which make up the forest and were differentiated for planning purposes in the Tongass Land Management Plan.
2/ Wilderness Attribute Rating System (WARS) was the nationwide system used to rate the wilderness attributes of roadless areas in the Roadless Area Review and Evaluation (RARE II).

Prehistoric and historic Native cultures used this roadless area Their activities mostly centered in the Naha Bay area and probably extended into the interior in the Naha drainage. The Naha River has been an important subsistence use area through recent history.

(3) **Location and Access:** The area is located on the west coast of Revillagigedo Island. Access is gained by way of Behm Canal through Naha Bay, Traitors Cove, Neets Bay, and Gedney Pass.

(4) **Geography and Topography:** The area is characterized by rugged terrain. Mountain slopes are steep, causing deeply incised drainages The North Revilla area is dominated by an extensive lake chain associated with the Naha River and its tributaries. Elevation ranges from sea level to 3,000 feet. There are 7,800 acres of alpine, 3,600 acres of rock, and 30 miles of shoreline on saltwater. Freshwater lakes cover 3,400 acres.

(5) **Ecosystem:**

(a) **Classification:** The area is in the Central Interior Islands Geographic Province. This province is characterized by generally subdued topography with localized intrusions of very rugged mountains

(b) **Vegetation:** Vegetation is typical Southeast Alaska coastal temperate rain forest. The forest is primarily western hemlock and Sitka spruce with large components of cedar. There are about 400 acres of muskeg.

There are approximately 142,305 acres of forest land of which 79,494 acres are commercial forest land. Of the commercial forest land, 70,010 acres are non-riparian old growth and 7,444 acres are riparian old growth.

(c) **Soils:** These highly organic, low clay content soils are generally formed over bedrock and are typically about 40 inches deep

(d) **Fish Resource:** Fish resources have been rated as part of the Tongass Land Management Plan (1979) and by the Alaska Department of Fish and Game in its Forest Habitat Integrity Program (1983). These ratings describe the value of VCU's for sport fish, commercial fish, and estuaries.

VCU's 731, 734, 737, 739, 742, 744, and 747 are rated as high value for sport fish.

VCU's 738, 739, 742, 744, 747 and 781 are rated as high value for commercial fish.

VCU 738 is rated as high value for estuary habitat.

(e) **Wildlife Resource:** This area has populations of Sitka black-tailed deer, bear, otter, marten, mink, loon, and common waterfowl. Trumpeter swans use the major saltwater inlets and freshwater lakes as resting areas during their migrations

(f) **Threatened and Endangered Species:** None.

(6) **Current Use and Management:** The Tongass Land Management Plan allocated this area to Land Use Designations (LUD's) 2, 3, and 4. The LUD 2 area (63,118 acres) takes in all of the Naha River drainage. This area is to be managed in its roadless condition except that wildlife habitat improvement and fish habitat improvement are allowed. This area is one of the "moratorium" areas. The LUD 3 portion (13,860 acres) takes in the northern part of this roadless area around Orchard Lake, and the headwaters of Traitors River The management emphasis is for a combination of compatible and complementary uses The LUD 4 (86,393) portion includes the head of Neets Creek, and the Carroll Creek and Orchard Creek areas These areas are managed emphasizing timber and other commodity uses

The Naha River drainage is managed for recreation use. It includes a boat dock, a small boat tram, the Naha Trail (which is designated as a National Recreation Trail), and six recreation use cabins. There is one recreation use cabin at the east end of Orchard Lake.

Timber harvest activity has occurred in the Gedney Pass, Neets Creek, and Traitors River areas during the 1970's. It is this activity that now forms the northwest boundary of this roadless area. There are no plans for timber harvest within this roadless area within the next five years.

There is a long range plan to connect the city of Ketchikan with Wrangell by highway. This route would pass through the east side of this roadless area.

(7) **Appearance (Apparent Naturalness):** The North Revilla Roadless Area is part of the Coastal Hills character type which is characterized by moderately steep landforms, predominantly rounded summits, elevations up to 4,500 feet and flat-floored, U-shaped valleys. Much of this areas' landscape is quite typical of this character type. The more rugged, diverse terrain is at the northern end in the Orchard and upper Carroll Creek valleys. The Naha River drainage at the southern end exhibits more subdued landscapes.

About 14 percent of the area is inventoried as a Variety Class A (possessing landscape diversity that is unique for the character type) The rest is rated a Variety Class B (possessing characteristics common in the character type). The class A landscapes are found in the Orchard Creek drainage. The main valley possesses steep, rock-faced walls, with distinct vegetative diversity, while the main channel of this creek also contains many diverse landscape features.

About 84 percent of the area is in a Type I Existing Visual Condition (EVC) where the natural landscape has remained unaltered by human activity The rest of the area is in an EVC Type III, IV, or V, where the landscape has been moderately to heavily altered by past logging activity. These latter areas primarily around the headwaters of Neets Creek and Traitors River

(8) **Surroundings (External Influences):** The southern boundary of this roadless area coincides with the boundary of the Revilla Roadless Area The east boundary is Misty Fiords National Monument. The north boundary is Behm Canal and the northwest boundary is the harvest areas in the Gedney Pass and Traitors Cove areas.

(9) **Attractions and Features of Special Interest:** The main attraction of this area is the excellent steelhead fishing and beauty of the Naha River. The recreation use cabins are very popular. The close proximity of the Naha River system to Ketchikan makes this a very popular day-use area for people living in Ketchikan. The North Revilla Roadless Area contains 21 inventoried recreation places containing 52,539 acres.

b. **Capability of Management as Wilderness or in an Unroaded Condition**

(1) **Manageability and Management Area Boundaries:** The area can easily be managed in its roadless condition, and as a roadless area, its boundaries will not be difficult to control. Orton Ranch (six acres), the Heckmen Lake fish hatchery (four acres), and the Loring townsite (200 acres) are private inholdings, but do not significantly impact the manageability of this area as roadless.

The long-range plan to connect Ketchikan with Wrangell by highway would reduce the size of this roadless area; probably the eastern one-third of the area would be affected by this proposal.

(2) **Natural Integrity:** The area consists of a number of east-west drainages that originate from the ridge line forming the western boundary of Misty Fiords National Monument. The other boundaries are either saltwater or major ridge lines that also bring a sense that all of the drainages making up this roadless area are tied together in a single land unit.

(3) **Opportunity for Solitude:** There is opportunity for solitude within certain parts of the area. A person is likely to encounter several other people when within the Naha River drainage. The youth groups staying at the Orten Ranch often recreate in this roadless area. The six recreation use cabins in the Naha River drainage are very popular. Frequent floatplane landings bring people to and from these cabins. The other drainages within this roadless area offer complete solitude with little chance of seeing other individuals.

(4) **Opportunity for Primitive Recreation:** There are outstanding opportunities for primitive or near-primitive recreation experiences due to the many recreation and scenic attractions and the remoteness of these attractions. Most of the area offers these primitive opportunities except portions of the Naha River area where periodic contacts with other parties or individuals may detract somewhat from this primitive experience.

ROS Class	Acres
Primitive I (P1)	70,752
Primitive II (P2)	23,291
Semi-Primitive Non-Motorized (SPNM)	43,657
Semi-Primitive Motorized (SPM)	3,060
Roaded Modified (RM)	22,151
Roaded Natural (RN)	680
Rural (R)	160

The area contains 21 inventoried recreation places.

ROS CLASS	# OF REC. PLACES	TOTAL ACRES	CAPACITY BY RVD'S
P1	3	25,126	2,358
P2	5	19,560	12,157
SPNM	2	4,671	2,340
SPM	1	1,440	3,120
RM	9	1,582	3,369
R	1	160	2,340

(5) Special Features (Ecologic, Geologic, Scientific, Cultural): There are no known special features within the area.

c. **Availability for Management as Wilderness or in an Unroaded Condition**

(1) **Resource Potentials**

(a) **Recreation Potential:** This roadless area will continue to receive significant recreation use. It has potential, and a probable need, for additional trails. While there is potential for additional recreation use cabins it may not be desirable to add more in order to preserve the present recreation experience within the area.

(b) **Fish Resource:** There is some potential for fish habitat improvement on streams within the area.

(c) **Wildlife Resource:** There are no long-range plans to accomplish habitat improvement project work within this roadless area. There is some hunting and trapping within the area but, in general, the terrain is too rough for quality sports hunting.

(d) **Timber Resource:** There are 61,763 acres inventoried as tentatively suitable for harvest. This includes 53,480 acres of non-riparian old growth and 6,244 acres of riparian old growth

(e) **Land Use Authorizations:** There are no special use authorizations within the roadless area boundary. A potential road corridor connecting Ketchikan with the Canadian highway system, by way of the Bradfield River, passes through the eastern part of this roadless area.

(f) **Minerals:** There are no mining claims located within this roadless area and the potential for mineral development is considered to be low.

(g) **Areas of Scientific Interest:** None.

(2) **Management Considerations**

(a) The long-term management intent for the North Revilla Roadless Area is to manage the Naha River drainage in its roadless condition with considerable emphasis on supporting the dispersed and developed (cabin) recreation use of this area. The northern part of this roadless area has some timber management capability, although there are no plans at this time to extend timber harvesting into the unroaded areas.

An important management consideration is the potential route for a road link to Canada from Ketchikan. While no specific route has been identified, any future road link must be through the North Revilla Roadless Area and the Revilla Roadless Area (524)

(b) Fire: The area has no significant fire history

(c) Insects and Disease: Endemic tree diseases common to Southeast Alaska are present.

(d) Land Status: There is a total of about 200 acres of private inholdings. These are the Loring townsite, Orten Ranch, and the Heckmen Lake fish hatchery.

d. Relationship To Communities and Other Roadless and Wilderness Areas

(1) Nearby Roadless and Wilderness Areas and Uses: This roadless area is one part of a much larger contiguous unroaded land mass. These other areas are:

Misty Fiords National Monument (Revillagigedo Is)	250,000 acres
Revilla Roadless Area (524)	138,393 acres
South Revilla Roadless Area (523)	69,998 acres

(2) Distance From Population Centers (accessibility): Approximate distances from population centers are as follows:

Community		Air Miles	Water Miles
Juneau	(Pop. 23,729)	200	280
Ketchikan	(Pop. 12,705)	10	25

(3) Interest by Proponents:

(a) Moratorium Areas: The Naha River drainage has been identified as a "moratorium" area and proposed as Wilderness in legislative initiatives.

(b) Local Users/residents: The area receives significant local use for subsistence and recreation activity.

e. Environmental Consequences

INDIVIDUAL ROADLESS AREA DESCRIPTION

NAME: Neets (527)   ACRES (GROSS): 6,315   ACRES (NFS): 6,315

GEOZONE: K04
GEOGRAPHIC PROVINCE: Central Interior Islands

1989 WILDERNESS ATTRIBUTE RATING: 22

a. Description

(1) **Relationship to RARE II areas:** The table below displays the VCU 1/
names, VCU numbers, acres, original WARS 2/ rating, and comments. This
enables the reader to compare the roadless areas evaluated in Appendix C
with previous analyses.

VCU Name	VCU No.	1979 WARS Rating	Comments
Hassler	735	22	
	736		Not Rated

(2) **History:** This roadless area is an isolated unroaded and unlogged area
surrounded by extensive timber harvest. There has been no evidence of
prehistoric or historic human use of this area.

(3) **Location and Access:** The area is located on the land area separating
Neets Bay from Gedney Pass. Access is by boat or floatplane to Neets Bay
or Gedney Pass and then hiking the road system to the area boundary

(4) **Geography and Topography:** The area is characterized by moderate to
rugged terrain. The highest elevation is about 3,000 feet. This roadless
area has no saltwater shoreline.

(5) **Ecosystem:**

(a) **Classification:** The area is in the Central Interior Islands
Geographic Province. This province is characterized by subdued
rolling topography and extensive muskeg areas.

(b) **Vegetation:** Vegetation is typical Southeast Alaska coastal
subalpine and alpine components of the temperate rain forest. The
forest is primarily western hemlock and Sitka spruce with large
components of cedar.

1/ A VCU (Value Comparison Unit) is one of 867 watersheds which make up the
forest and were differentiated for planning purposes in the Tongass Land
Management Plan.
2/ Wilderness Attribute Rating System (WARS) was the nationwide system used to
rate the wilderness attributes of roadless areas in the Roadless Area
Review and Evaluation.

There are approximately 5,914 acres of forest land of which 3,649
acres are commercial forest land. Of the commercial forest land 3,047
acres are non-riparian old growth and 521 acres are riparian old
growth.

(b) **Soils:** These highly organic, low clay content soils are
generally formed over bedrock and typically about 40 inches deep

(c) **Fish Resource:** Fish resources have been rated as part of the
Tongass Land Management Plan (1979) and by the Alaska Department of
Fish and Game in its Forest Habitat Integrity Program (1983). These
ratings describe the value of VCU's for sport fish, commercial fish,
and estuaries. VCU 735 rated as high value for estuary habitat

(d) **Wildlife Resource:** Sitka black-tailed deer, black bear,
ptarmigan and other species of small mammals and birds are found in
the area.

(e) **Threatened and Endangered Species:** None.

(6) **Current Use and Management:** The Tongass Land Management Plan
allocated the area to Land Use Designations (LUD's) 3 and 4. The LUD 3
area (1,484 acres) is to be managed for a variety of complementary resource
uses, and the emphasis for the LUD 4 area (4,832 acres) is primarily for
commodity or market resources.

(7) **Appearance (Apparent Naturalness):** This area is part of the Coastal
Hills character type which is characterized by moderately steep landforms,
predominantly rounded summits, elevations ranging up to 4,500 feet, and
flat-floored, U-shaped valleys. A variety of island groups are also
common.

The entire area is inventoried as a Variety Class B landscape (possessing
landscape characteristics that are common for the character type). There
are no outstanding scenic features in this area. It consists only of a
moderately steep, uniform, timbered slope and ridge top.

Only 19 percent of this area is in Type I Existing Visual Condition (EVC)
Due to the extensive logging surrounding this roadless area, almost the
entire remaining area is in EVC Type IV or V, where the landscape has been
moderately to heavily modified.

(8) **Surroundings (External Influences):** This area is surrounded by timber
harvest areas. Logging did not extend into this roadless area because of
its low quality timber.

(9) **Attractions and Features of Special Interest:** There are no known
features or attractions on the area that are of special interest. The area
contains one inventoried recreation place totalling 60 acres.

b. Capability of Management as Wilderness or in an Unroaded Condition

    (1) **Manageability and Management Area Boundaries:** Due to its small size,
lack of natural boundaries, and the influence of surrounding timber
harvest, future management as roadless area or Wilderness would be
difficult.

    (2) **Natural Integrity:** The area is physically unaltered, but the
proximity and visibility of extensive logging negatively affects the
natural integrity of the area.

    (3) **Opportunity for Solitude:** Extensive logging and roading are occurring
near the area; there is some opportunity for solitude except when logging
is taking place.

    (4) **Opportunity for Primitive Recreation:** Due to the small size of the
area, the proximity of past and future logging, and the lack of scenic and
recreation attractions, this area does not have much opportunity for
primitive recreation.

ROS Class	Acres
Semi-Primitive Non-Motorized (SPNM)	4,110
Semi-Primitive Motorized (SPM)	40
Roaded Modified (RM)	2,105

The area contains one inventoried recreation place

ROS CLASS	# OF REC. PLACES	TOTAL ACRES	CAPACITY BY RVD'S
RM	1	60	425

    (5) **Special Features** (Ecologic, Geologic, Scientific, Cultural): There
are no known special features within the area.

c. **Availability for Management as Wilderness or in an Unroaded Condition**

    (1) **Resource Potentials**

        (a) **Recreation Potential:** No potential exists for the development of
recreation facilities. Future use is likely to be primarily for
occasional deer hunting.

        (b) **Fish Resource:** None.

        (c) **Wildlife Resource:** There is no potential need to manage the
habitat conditions within this area; the area provides Sitka
black-tailed deer habitat of moderate quality.

        (d) **Timber Resource:** There are 2,667 acres inventoried as
tentatively suitable for harvest. This includes 2,185 acres of
non-riparian old growth and 401 acres of riparian old growth

        (e) **Land Use Authorizations:** None

(f) **Minerals:** None.

(g) **Areas of Scientific Interest:** None.

(2) **Management Considerations**

(a) This area does not have the resource conditions or use potential to warrant the development of specific management plans

(b) **Fire:** The area has no significant fire history.

(c) **Insects and Disease:** Endemic tree diseases common to Southeast Alaska are present.

(d) **Land Status:** All National Forest System land.

d. **Relationship To Communities and Other Roadless and Wilderness Areas**

(1) **Nearby Roadless and Wilderness Areas and Uses:** This roadless area is isolated from the North Revilla Roadless Area by roaded/timber harvest area.

(2) **Distance From Population Centers (accessibility):** Approximate distances from population centers are as follows:

Community	Air Miles	Water Miles
Juneau (Pop. 23,729)	200	280
Ketchikan (Pop. 12,705)	60	75

(3) **Interest by Proponents:**

(a) **Moratorium Areas:** The area has not been identified as a "moratorium" area or proposed as Wilderness in legislative initiatives to date.

(b) **Local Users/residents:** The area receives insignificant use by the local users/residents.

e. **Environmental Consequences**

INDIVIDUAL ROADLESS AREA DESCRIPTION

NAME: Cleveland (528)   ACRES (GROSS): 201,985   ACRES (NFS): 193,473

GEOZONE: K05
GEOGRAPHIC PROVINCE: Central Interior Islands

1989 WILDERNESS ATTRIBUTE RATING: 23

a. Description

   (1) **Relationship to RARE II areas:** The table below displays the VCU 1/
   names, VCU numbers, acres, original WARS 2/ rating, and comments. This
   enables the reader to compare the roadless areas evaluated in Appendix C
   with previous analyses.

VCU Name	VCU No.	1979 WARS Rating	Comments
Meyers Chuck	708	22	
Union Bay	709	25	
Cannery Creek	710	22	
Niblack	711	23	
Rainbow	712	23	
Caamano	713	22	
Bond	714	21	
Smugglers	715	23	
Helm Bay	716	24	
Granite Creek	717	23	
Vixen Lake	718	23	
Port Stewart	719	24	
Vixen Inlet	720	25	
Emerald	721	22	
Spacious	722	24	
Heckman	723	22	

   (2) **History:** The early settler history centers on the fishing industry.
   The community of Meyers Chuck was founded as a base for the fishing fleet
   and a cannery. Other cannery sites were located on the east side of the
   Cleveland Peninsula. A fox farm was located on Square Island within
   Spacious Bay. During the same period there was exploration for valuable
   minerals resulting in several patented claims.

   There is one Native land selection on the southwest coast and the State
   selected land in the Spacious Bay area.

1/ A VCU (**Value Comparison Unit**) is one of 867 watersheds which make up the
    forest and were differentiated for planning purposes in the Tongass Land
    Management Plan.
2/ Wilderness Attribute Rating System (WARS) was the nationwide system used to
    rate the wilderness attributes of roadless areas in the Roadless Area
    Review and Evaluation (RARE II).

(3) **Location and Access:** The area is located on the southern end of Cleveland Peninsula. Access is by boat or floatplane through the major bays. This part of the peninsula is the major land mass between Revillagigedo Island and Prince of Wales Island.

(4) **Geography and Topography:** This roadless area is located on the mainland, and is characterized by a combination of gently rolling topography to moderately rugged mountains. Elevations range from sea level to just over 3,000 feet. Many of the drainages are broad, flat areas There are a number of streams and lakes within the area.

There are 157 miles of shoreline on saltwater Approximately 600 acres are alpine tundra and 4,383 acres are classified as muskeg.

(5) **Ecosystem:**

(a) **Classification:** The area is in the Central Interior Islands Geographic Province. This province is generally characterized by rolling topography and extensive muskeg areas.

(b) **Vegetation:** This area is typical Southeast Alaska coastal temperate rain forest. The forest is primarily western hemlock and Sitka spruce with a large cedar component. There are numerous interspersed areas of the muskeg and alpine vegetative types

There are approximately 182,913 acres of forested land of which 101,438 acres are commercial forest land. Of the commercial forest land, 85,537 acres are non-riparian old growth and 13,522 are riparian old growth.

(c) **Soils:** These highly organic, low clay content soils are generally formed over bedrock and are typically about 40 inches deep

(d) **Fish Resource:** Fish resources have been rated as part of the Tongass Land Management Plan (1979) and by the Alaska Department of Fish and Game in its Forest Habitat Integrity Program (1983). These ratings describe the value of VCU's for sport fish, commercial fish, and estuaries.

VCU's 716, 718, 720, and 722 are rated as high value for commercial fish. VCU's 708, 715, 716, 717, and 720 are rated as high value estuary habitat.

(e) **Wildlife Resource:** This area has a high population of Sitka black-tailed deer, black bear, otter, marten, mink, loons, and common waterfowl. There is also a small population of brown bear which is estimated to be less than 10 individuals. Trumpeter swan use the major saltwater inlets and freshwater lakes as resting areas during their migrations.

(f) **Threatened and Endangered Species:** None

(6) **Current Use and Management:** The Tongass Land Management Plan allocated this area to Land Use Designations (LUD's) 3 and 4. The LUD 3 includes the Helm Bay area and 50,927 acres of the southern portion of this roadless area. The management emphasis in this portion is to manage for a mix of commodity and amenity values. The LUD 4 area includes 142,206 acres in the northern two-thirds of the roadless area. The management emphasis for LUD 4 is to manage for commodity and market resource values.

Most of the Cleveland Roadless Area is included within the contingency area for the Ketchikan Pulp Company (KPC) Long-term Timber Sale. Currently, there is an environmental impact statement in preparation for the KPC Long-term Timber Sale to analyze the effects of implementing a variety of management activities, including timber harvest. The current management emphasis is on the recreation use and fish habitat potential of the area. Three recreation use cabins, a special use right-of-way for a waterline and a powerline, an electronics site, and Coast Guard permits for aids to navigation are administered in this area.

(7) **Appearance (Apparent Naturalness):** This area is part of the Coastal Hills character type, which is characterized by moderately steep landforms, predominantly rounded summits, elevations up to 4,500 feet, and flat-floored, U-shaped valleys. This roadless area is very representative of this character type, particularly because of the rolling, but steep terrain and wide valleys. A few areas possess more distinctive, rugged terrain.

Most of this area is rated a Variety Class B (possessing a degree of landscape diversity that is common to the character type). About six percent of the area is rated as Variety Class A. These more scenic landscapes are found in the rugged terrain around Rainbow Lake, and in the area around Mount Burnett and Vixen Harbor.

The entire Cleveland Roadless Area, except for the village of Meyers Chuck, is rated a Type I Existing Visual Condition, where the landscape has remained essentially unaltered by human activity. The only development in the area is a few scattered small structures that exist for various uses

(8) **Surroundings (External Influences):** There are few external influences in this roadless area. The most significant influence is a Ketchikan Pulp Company-owned parcel of land in the center of the roadless area, which KPC plans to log. Logging will require a road across the Forest to saltwater There is also the Native-selected land on the southwest coast that will likely be logged in the future. The settlement of Meyers Chuck is now on State-owned land. Residents and visitors of Meyers Chuck venture into the roadless area.

(9) **Attractions and Features of Special Interest:** The main attraction to the area is the outstanding saltwater fishing in the major bays. Other areas of special interest are the large tidal flats at the ends of the bays, and the upland lakes between Helm Bay and Clarence Strait. The area contains 28 inventoried recreation places totaling 102,333 acres

b   Capability of Management as Wilderness or in an Unroaded Condition

(1) **Manageability and Management Area Boundaries:** The area and its
boundaries can easily be managed for roadless objectives.

(2) **Natural Integrity:** The area is unmodified and is not fragmented by
land ownership or land use patterns. Because it is surrounded by large
saltwater passages or other large roadless areas, it has a high degree of
natural integrity

(3) **Opportunity for Solitude:** There is excellent opportunity for solitude
in all parts of the area. Except for the Helm Bay area, a person is not
likely to encounter other people when boating, hiking or camping within
this roadless area.

(4) **Opportunity for Primitive Recreation:** Except around the southwestern
end of the peninsula and the shores around Helm Bay, this area offers many
primitive recreation opportunities.

ROS Class	Acres
Primitive I (P1)	97,883
Primitive II (P2)	41,571
Semi-Primitive Non-Motorized (SPNM)	80
Semi-Primitive Motorized (SPM)	15,969
Roaded Natural (RN)	2,744
Rural (R)	760

The area contains 28 inventoried recreation places.

ROS CLASS	# OF REC. PLACES	TOTAL ACRES	CAPACITY BY RVD
P1	10	62,319	15,080
P2	8	21,701	12,090
SPM	6	14,650	18,460
RN	1	2,744	1,560
R	2	761	6,240

(5) **Special Features (Ecologic, Geologic, Scientific, Cultural):** There
are no known unique or special features within this roadless area

c. **Availability for Management as Wilderness or in an Unroaded Condition**

(1) **Resource Potentials**

(a) **Recreation Potential:** The long-term recreation potential of the
area centers on continued management of the cabin system and
additional trails for dispersed recreation activity.

(b) **Fish Resource:** There is considerable potential for fish habitat
improvement and fish pass construction on the several streams in the
area, however, no projects are programmed at this time.

(c) **Wildlife Resource:** Although some hunting and trapping do occur within the area, there are no long-range plans for habitat improvement projects.

(d) **Timber Resource:** There are 83,219 acres inventoried as tentatively suitable for harvest. This includes 12,641 acres of riparian old growth, and 68,837 acres of non-riparian old growth.

(e) **Land Use Authorizations:** There are rights-of-way for a waterline and a powerline, a permitted residence on Square Island, an electronics site, and several Coast Guard reservations for navigation aids.

(f) **Minerals:** There are several located and patented claims within this roadless area and moderate potential for mineral development.

(g) **Areas of Scientific Interest:** None.

(2) **Management Considerations**

(a) The entire area has been managed in a roadless condition. Currently, an environmental impact statement is being prepared analyzing the effects of several management alternatives for the LUD 4 lands within this roadless area. Alternatives include road construction and timber harvest.

Active management to date has centered upon recreation use, fish habitat improvement projects, and the administration of special uses and mineral related activities.

(b) **Fire:** The area has no significant fire history.

(c) **Insects and Disease:** Endemic tree diseases common to Southeast Alaska are present.

(d) **Land Status:** There are no Native land selections within the area boundary. The State has selected 3365 acres within Spacious Bay The Ketchikan Pulp Company own 160 acres located in the Granite Creek drainage.

d. **Relationship To Communities and Other Roadless and Wilderness Areas**

(1) **Nearby Roadless and Wilderness Areas and Uses:** The North Cleveland Roadless Area (529) adjoins this areas' northern boundary.

(2) **Distance From Population Centers (accessibility):** Approximate distances from population centers are as follows:

Community		Air Miles	Water Miles
Ketchikan	(Pop. 12,705)	25	30
Juneau	(Pop 23,729)	200	250

(3) Interest by Proponents:

(a) **Moratorium Areas:** This roadless area is not included within the identified moratorium areas or proposed in any Wilderness legislative initiative.

(b) **Local Users/residents:** The area receives significant local use for subsistence and recreation activity.

e. Environmental Consequences

INDIVIDUAL ROADLESS AREA DESCRIPTION

NAME: North Cleveland (529)   ACRES (GROSS): 114,178   ACRES (NFS): 114,158

GEOZONE: K12
GEOGRAPHIC PROVINCE: Central Interior Islands

1989 WILDERNESS ATTRIBUTE RATING: 23

a. Description

(1) **Relationship to RARE II areas:** The table below displays the VCU 1/ names, VCU numbers, acres, original WARS 2/ rating, and comments. This enables the reader to compare the roadless areas evaluated in Appendix C with previous analyses.

VCU Name	VCU No.	1979 WARS Rating	Comments
Yes Bay	724	25	
Snipe	725	23	
Bailey	726	23	
Reflection	727	23	
Short Bay	728	23	
Anchor	729	22	
Bell	731	22	
Hassler	735	22	

(2) **History:** The interior of this area has seen little influence of human activity. Some coastal locations were occupied by prehistoric and historic Native cultures. Several of the bays and islands have been used by early commercial fishing interests and, in recent times, commercial recreation (lodges on Bell Island and in Yes Bay) and individual recreation users These land uses are closely tied to the excellent salmon fishing in the adjacent saltwater and streams.

(3) **Location and Access:** The area is located north of Revillagigedo Island. It includes land area on Cleveland Peninsula, an extension of the mainland, and the islands in Behm Canal.

1/ A VCU (**Value Comparison Unit**) is one of 867 watersheds which make up the forest and were differentiated for planning purposes in the Tongass Land Management Plan.
2/ Wilderness Attribute Rating System (WARS) was the nationwide system used to rate the wilderness attributes of roadless areas in the Roadless Area Review and Evaluation (RARE II).

(4) Geography and Topography: The area is characterized by very rugged terrain. The steep mountain slopes cause deeply incised drainages. There are large lakes at the headwaters of the larger streams, and numerous smaller lakes in most drainages. There are a few small glaciers. Elevations range from sea level to 4,000 feet. The major islands in Behm Canal are less rugged than the mainland, but are characterized by steep slopes starting at saltwater and ranging to 3,000 feet.

There are 93 miles of shoreline on saltwater, 5,200 acres of alpine tundra, and 6,800 acres of rock.

(5) Ecosystem:

   (a) Classification: The area is in the Central Interior Islands Geographic Province. This province is characterized by subdued rolling topography.

   (b) Vegetation: Vegetation is typical Southeast Alaska coastal temperate rain forest. The forest is primarily western hemlock and Sitka spruce with large components of cedar. There are numerous interspersed areas of the muskeg and alpine vegetative types.

   There are approximately 91,799 acres of forested land of which 50,720 acres are commercial forest land. Of the commercial forest land, 46,114 acres are non-riparian old growth and 4,103 acres riparian old growth. There are 300 acres of muskeg.

   (b) Soil: Soils are highly organic, have low clay content, are generally formed over bedrock, and are typically about 40 inches deep

   (c) Fish Resource: Fish resources have been rated as part of the Tongass Land Management Plan (1979) and by the Alaska Department of Fish and Game in its Forest Habitat Integrity Program (1983). These ratings describe the value of VCU's for sport fish, commercial fish, and estuaries.

   VCU's rated as high value for sport fish are 724, 726, 727, 728, and 731.

   VCU's 724, 727, and 728 are rated as high value for commercial fish

   VCU 735 is rated as high value estuary habitat.

   (d) Wildlife Resource: This area has habitat for deer, bear, otter, marten, mink, loon, and common waterfowl. Trumpeter swan use the major saltwater inlets and freshwater lakes as resting areas during their migrations.

   (e) Threatened and Endangered Species: None.

(6) Current Use and Management: The Tongass Land Management Plan allocates the area to Land Use Designations (LUD's) 2 and 3. The LUD 2 area (107,081 acres) takes in all of the mainland portion. This area is to be managed in its roadless condition with wildlife and fish habitat improvements allowed. The LUD 3 area (6,295 acres) contains the island

part of this roadless area. The management emphasis is to manage for a
combination of compatible and complementary uses.

Most of the current use is recreation along the coast and bay areas   There
are five recreation use cabins within the area and trails to lakes in the
Yes Bay and Short Bay areas. Private lodges at Yes Bay and on Bell Island,
cater to sport fishing but clients also use the hiking trails.

The current management emphasis of the North Cleveland Roadless Area is on
the recreation use and fish habitat potential.

(7) **Appearance (Apparent Naturalness)**: Most of this roadless area is part
of the Coast Range character type which is characterized by large massive
landforms that commonly rise to elevations of about 7,000 feet, steep
slopes or rock cliffs that plunge to saltwater, and deep, narrow saltwater
fiords that protrude into this land mass. Mountain ridges are generally
rounded with scattered jagged peaks rising above the surrounding rounded
ridge tops. This area does not have the massive landforms with the high
elevations that are found through much of the Coast Range character type,
however, it possesses a high degree of diversity due to the variety of lake
basins of all sizes, stream features, rock features and vegetative
patterns.

About 41 percent of the area is inventoried as a Variety Class A
(possessing landscape diversity that is unique for the character type)
The rest is rated as a Variety Class B (possessing landscape
characteristics that are common for the character type).

About 99 percent of the this roadless area is in a Type I Existing Visual
Condition (where the natural landscape has remained unaltered by human
activity). Only Hassler Island has been modified by development
activities. This is primarily from KPC Long-term Sale harvest completed in
the last 10-15 years.

(8) **Surroundings (External Influences)**: The east boundary coincides with
that of Misty Fiords National Monument. This roadless area is part of a
much larger contiguous unroaded land mass consisting of Misty Fiords
National Monument-Wilderness and the Cleveland Roadless Area.

The private lands at Yes Bay and Bell Island do not exert a strong
influence upon this roadless area.

(9) **Attractions and Features of Special Interest**: The main attraction of
this area is its remoteness and outstanding scenery. Excellent freshwater
fishing also attracts people to the area. The area contains 15 inventoried
recreation places totaling 45,184 acres. The hot springs at Lake Shelokum
are of special interest.

b. **Capability of Management as Wilderness or in an Unroaded Condition**

(1) **Manageability and Management Area Boundaries**: The area and its
boundaries can easily be managed for roadless objectives.

(2) **Natural Integrity:** The area has outstanding natural integrity   The boundaries all conform with natural terrain features. The physical features all tie together into one homogeneous unit   Large roadless areas are adjacent to most boundaries.

(3) **Opportunity for Solitude:** All parts of the area exhibit an excellent opportunity for solitude. A person is not likely to encounter other people when camping in and using this roadless area except possibly on the Lake McDonald, Shelokum Lake, or Reflection Lake trails.

(4) **Opportunity for Primitive Recreation:** Due to the vastness of the area, the high scenic quality, the abundance of saltwater and upland lake recreation attractions, and many trail opportunities, this area has outstanding opportunity for primitive recreation.

ROS Class	Acres
Primitive I (P1)	53,469
Primitive II (P2)	55,160
Semi-Primitive Motorized (SPM)	3,044
Roaded Modified (RM)	642
Rural (R)	682

The area contains 15 inventoried recreation places.

ROS CLASS	# OF REC. PLACES	TOTAL ACRES	CAPACITY BY RVD'S
P1	1	4,883	1,560
P2	12	36,575	20,554
SPM	1	3,044	9,120
R	1	682	7,571

(5) **Special Features (Ecologic, Geologic, Scientific, Cultural):** The hot springs at Lake Shelokum and the small glaciers are special features of the area.

c. **Availability for Management as Wilderness or in an Unroaded Condition**

(1) **Resource Potentials**

(a) **Recreation Potential:** The long-term recreation potential of the area centers on continued management of the cabin system, additional trails for dispersed recreation activity, and the possible development of the Lake Shelokum Hot Springs. There is some potential for additional mooring buoys in the popular bays. The bay areas have potential for fishing lodges.

(b) **Fish Resource:** There is considerable potential for fish habitat improvement and fish pass construction on several streams.

(c) **Wildlife Resource:** No long-range habitat improvement projects are planned within this roadless area. Some hunting and trapping occur in the area but, in general, the terrain is too rough for quality sports hunting.

(d) **Timber Resource:** There are 43,469 acres inventoried as tentatively suitable for harvest. This includes 39,223-acres of non-riparian old growth and 3,605 of riparian old growth.

(e) **Land Use Authorizations:** There is an electronics site at Syble Point and several lighthouse or navigational aid reserves. There are numerous proposals for recreation special uses on Bell Island

(f) **Minerals:** No mining claims are located within this roadless area and there is low potential for mineral development.

(g) **Areas of Scientific Interest:** Bailey Bay Hot Springs has been identified as a potential Research Natural Area.

(2) **Management Considerations**

(a) All of the area has been managed in a roadless condition, this is expected to be the continued emphasis. Although the LUD 3 area is within the KPC Long-term Sale Area, the 1989-1994 Operating Plan does not include timber harvest in the North Cleveland Roadless Area.

A potential road corridor which could link Ketchikan with the Canadian Highway system by way of the Bradfield River passes through the roadless area.

(b) **Wildlife:** There are no plans for fish or wildlife habitat improvement projects within the area.

(c) **Fire:** The area has no significant fire history.

(d) **Insects and Disease:** Endemic tree diseases common to Southeast Alaska are present.

(e) **Land Status:** There are two small parcels of private land located in Yes Bay and on Bell Island.

d. **Relationship To Communities and Other Roadless and Wilderness Areas**

(1) **Nearby Roadless and Wilderness Areas and Uses:** This roadless area is part of a larger contiguous unroaded land mass consisting of Misty Fiords National Monument, Cleveland Roadless Area and
---------- NOTE: Stikines to be added---------------------

(2) **Distance From Population Centers (accessibility):** Approximate distances from population centers are as follows:

Community		Air Miles	Water Miles
Ketchikan	(Pop. 12,705)	10	25
Juneau	(Pop. 23,729	200	300

(3) **Interest by Proponents:**

(a) **Moratorium Areas:** This roadless area is not included within the identified "moratorium" areas or proposed in any Wilderness legislative initiative.

(b) **Local Users/residents:** The area receives significant local use for subsistence and recreation activity.

e   Environmental Consequences

INDIVIDUAL ROADLESS AREA DESCRIPTION

NAME: HYDER (530)   ACRES (GROSS): 129,585   ACRES (NFS): 128,585

GEOZONE: K01
GEOGRAPHIC PROVINCE: Coast Range

1989 WILDERNESS ATTRIBUTE RATING: 23

a. Description

(1) **Relationship to RARE II areas:** The table below displays the VCU 1/ names, VCU numbers, acres, original WARS 2/ rating, and comments. This enables the reader to compare the roadless areas evaluated in Appendix C with previous analyses.

VCU Name	VCU No.	1979 WARS Rating	Comments
Texas Creek	804	22	
Thumb	805	22	
Hyder	806	24	
Soule	807	24	

(2) **History:** The area has a rich history of mining activity. It is for this reason that this roadless area was not made a part of Misty Fiords National Monument.

(3) **Location and Access:** The area lies east of Misty Fiords National Monument and west of the Canadian border and Hyder, Alaska. Access is by foot or helicopter. Due the lack of lakes large enough to accommodate them, floatplanes cannot land in the area.

(4) **Geography and Topography:** The area is extremely rugged and rises from saltwater to elevations over 7,000 feet. Glaciers cover large parts of the the area. Several medium-sized rivers flow through the area or originate within it. There are approximately 8,000 acres of alpine, 28,000 acres of snow and ice, and 37,000 acres of rock. There are 15 miles of shoreline on saltwater.

1/ A VCU (Value Comparison Unit) is one of 867 watersheds which make up the forest and were differentiated for planning purposes in the Tongass Land Management Plan.

2/ Wilderness Attribute Rating System (WARS) was the nation-wide system used to rate the wilderness attributes of roadless areas in the Roadless Area Review and Evaluation (RARE II).

(5) **Ecosystem:**

(a) **Classification:** The area is in the Coast Range geographic province. This province is generally characterized as a core of massive angular mountains capped with ice fields at high elevations along the Canadian Border, with somewhat lower mountains, deeply incised valleys and glacier-fed streams closer to the coast This roadless area is primarily characterized by the former

(b) **Vegetation:** Alpine vegetation dominates elevations above 2.500 feet. Below that elevation the steep mountainsides are heavily marked with snow and landslide paths which are typically covered with grass alder, and brush. Cottonwood trees may be occasionally found along valley bottoms and floodplains.

There are 33,867 acres of forested land of which 16,523 acres are commercial forest land. Of the commercial forest land, 13,743 acres are non-riparian old growth and 2,100 are riparian old growth.

(c) **Soils:** The soils are moderately-deep loam with inclusions of glacial till and moraine deposits.

(d) **Fish Resource:** Fish resources have been rated as part of the Tongass Land Management Plan (1979) and by the Alaska Department of Fish and Game in its Forest Habitat Integrity Program (1983). These ratings describe the value of VCU's for sport fish, commercial fish, and estuaries.

VCU's 804 and 805 are rated high value for commercial and sport fish and VCU's 806 and 807 high for estuary habitat.

(e) **Wildlife Resource:** A small population of mountain goat range over the area, as do black and brown bear and a small population of moose.

(f) **Threatened and Endangered Species:** None.

(6) **Current Use and Management:** Two drainages (67,710 acres) in the area were allocated to Land Use Designation (LUD) 2 in the Tongass Land Management Plan. This designation generally excludes timber harvest and roads. They are managed for roadless recreation. The other two drainages were allocated to LUD 3 (33,247 acres) and LUD 4 (27,608 acres) which allows road construction and timber harvest.

(7) **Appearance (Apparent Naturalness):** The Hyder Roadless Area is part of the Coast Range character type, which is characterized by large, massive landforms with upland elevations averaging 5,000 to 7,000 feet dissected by steep-walled U-shaped valleys. Though ridges are generally rounded, sharp. jagged peaks occasionally rise up to 9,000 feet. On the west side of this character type, narrow saltwater fiords often bounded by steep rock faces protrude into the terrain. Glaciers and ice fields are prominent in the interior of this character type. This roadless area is generally representative of the interior portions of this character type

The entire area is inventoried as a Variety Class B (possessing
characteristics that are common to the character type).

The entire area is inventoried as a Type I Existing Visual Condition
Except for scattered evidence of past mining activity, the landscape has
remained unaltered by human activity.

(8) **Surroundings (External Influences):** This area is contiguous to Misty
Fiords National Monument. Helicopters associated with mining operations in
Canada fly over and near the area. Aircraft flying to and from Hyder fly
over and near the area, and may cause temporary distractions to visitors
Otherwise, this area is surrounded by extremely remote areas

(9) **Attractions and Features of Special Interest:** The natural features of
the area, the scenery, and the opportunity to see wildlife and to study the
processes which formed this landscape are all attractions. The opportunity
to view glaciers, and the vast expanse of the Salmon River Valley are
special features of the area. There are seven inventoried recreation
places in this roadless area totaling 46,172 acres.

b. **Capability of Management as Wilderness or in an Unroaded Condition**

(1) **Manageability and Management Area Boundaries:** The Hyder Roadless Area
is generally well defined by topographic features. Feasibility of managing
the area in its roadless condition is excellent.

(2) **Natural Integrity:** The area is virtually unmodified, and surrounded
by vast areas of designated Wilderness and other undeveloped lands in
Canada.

(3) **Opportunity for Solitude:** Within the area, the opportunity for
solitude is high. Aircraft traveling to and from Hyder and mining
operations in Canada at times may pass over the roadless area and be
observed by people in it. Present recreation levels are low. Generally, a
person camped or traveling inland is unlikely to see others.

(4) **Opportunity for Primitive Recreation:** A vast majority of the area is
inventoried as Primitive I. There are two potential recreation cabins (old
mining cabins) in the area. The character of the landforms generally
allows the visitor to feel remote from sights and sounds of human
activity. The area is accessible by long hikes over difficult terrain or
by helicopter, though clearing an old, overgrown mining road might provide
easier access to a small part of the area. The rough terrain offers a high
degree of physical challenge. The presence of both black and brown bears
also presents a degree of challenge and a need for woods skills and
experience.

ROS Class	Acres
Primitive I (P1)	89,636
Primitive II (P2)	20,245
Semi-Primitive Non-Motorized (SPNM)	8,022
Roaded Natural (RN)	10,582

There area contains seven inventoried recreation places.

ROS CLASS	# OF REC. PLACES	TOTAL ACRES	CAPACITY BY RVD'S
P1	1	60	0
P2	2	14,644	3,120
SPNM	2	6,062	6,240
RN	2	10,582	8,200

Many of these recreation places are associated with old mining roads or trails that offer opportunities for improved recreation trails

(5) **Special Features (Ecologic, Geologic, Scientific, Cultural):** Opportunities to observe and study fish and wildlife and the various forces which formed these mountains are several of the attractions of this area Several alpine glaciers can be viewed in this area.

c. **Availability for Management as Wilderness or in an Unroaded Condition**

   (1) **Resource Potentials**

      (a) **Recreation Potential:** The potential exists for additional outfitter and guide permits, for development of additional cabins and shelters, and for the reopening of historic mining trails.

      (b) **Fish Resource:** The streams within the roadless area are heavily influenced by glacier melt runoff, preventing any opportunity for fish habitat improvements on those streams.

      (c) **Wildlife Resource:** No wildlife habitat improvements are planned as there is no apparent need.

      (d) **Timber Resource:** Approximately 11,882 acres have been inventoried as tentatively suitable for harvest. This includes 9,802 acres non-riparian old growth and 1,740 acres of riparian old growth

      (e) **Land Use Authorizations:** None.

      (f) **Minerals:** The level of mining activity in the area has elevated, due partially to mines reopening on the Canadian side of the border near the area.

      (g) **Areas of Scientific Interest:** None.

   (2) **Management Considerations**

      (a) Due to steep terrain and low timber volume, the potential for managing timber in this roadless area is low. Maintenance of the area in a roadless condition enhances opportunity to manage the adjacent Misty Fiords National Monument Wilderness and provide enhanced opportunities for solitude and primitive recreation for those capable of accessing it. It also maintains opportunities for wildlife, such as wolves, bears, and moose, to move freely through the area.

      (b) **Fire:** The area has no significant fire history.

(c) **Insects and Disease:** Endemic tree diseases common to Southeast Alaska are present; there are no known epidemic disease occurrences

(d) **Land Status:** The State has selected 160 acres of land at Fish Creek.

d. **Relationship To Communities and Other Roadless and Wilderness Areas**

(1) **Nearby Roadless and Wilderness Areas and Uses:** The area is adjacent to Misty Fiords National Monument Wilderness.

(2) **Distance From Population Centers (accessibility):** .

Community		Air miles	Water miles
Hyder	(Pop 80)	1	1
Ketchikan	(Pop 12,705)	90	160
Juneau	(Pop 23,729)	400	500

Stewart, British Columbia (Hyder, Alaska) is the nearest stop on the Alaska Marine Highway.

(3) **Interest by Proponents:**

(a) **Moratorium Areas:** The area has not been identified as a "Moratorium" area or proposed as Wilderness in legislative initiatives to date.

(b) **Local Users/residents:** Most of the area is used by local residents for trapping and recreation.

e. **Environmental Consequences:**

INDIVIDUAL ROADLESS AREA DESCRIPTION

NAME: Nutkwa (531)   ACRES (GROSS): 64,296   ACRES (NFS): 59,318

GEOZONE: K08
GEOGRAPHIC PROVINCE: Southern Outer Islands

1989 WILDERNESS ATTRIBUTE RATING: 25

a. Description

(1) **Relationship to RARE II areas:** The table below displays the VCU 1/·
names, VCU numbers, acres, original WARS 2/ rating, and comments. This
enables the reader to compare the roadless areas evaluated in Appendix C
with previous analyses.

VCU Name	VCU No.	1979 WARS Rating	Comments
	672		Not Rated
Hetta	673	26	
	674		Not Rated
Nutkwa	685	25	
Nutkwa Creek	686	24	
Hassiah	688	25	
Kassa	689	25	

(2) **History:** The Nutkwa Roadless Area has always been considered a remote
area on Prince of Wales Island. The major sounds and bays provide bases
for commercial fishing including anchorages, fish processing facilities,
and fish buying stations. Since the early 1900's, there has been an
interest in the mineral resources. As a result, there are several patented
mining claims, and numerous unpatented claims that are currently active

The Nutkwa area is one of the Haida Natives' traditional use areas. Prior
to use by the Haida culture, there is evidence that ·there was considerable
prehistoric use of coast sites. In recent years, the Natives have made
land selections in the northern part of this roadless area and the State
has made a number of selections scattered over the entire area.

(3) **Location and Access:** This roadless area is located on the southwest
corner of Prince of Wales Island. The only access is by boat or
floatplane.

1/ A VCU (Value Comparison Unit) is one of 867 watersheds which make up the
forest and were differentiated for planning purposes in the Tongass Land
Management Plan.
2/ Wilderness Attribute Rating System (WARS) was the nationwide system used to
rate the wilderness attributes of roadless areas in the Roadless Area
Review and Evaluation (RARE II).

(4) **Geography and Topography:** The area is characterized by moderately rugged topography. The mountain ridges are separated by rather broad drainages. The maximum elevation is about 2,500 feet. There are 1,060 acres of alpine, 2,441 acres of rock, and 67 miles of shoreline on saltwater. There are a number of large and small freshwater lakes that total 1,700 surface acres.

(5) **Ecosystem:**

   (a) **Classification:** The area is in the Southern Outer Island Geographic Province. This province is generally characterized by subdued rolling and localized rugged topography.

   (b) **Vegetation:** Vegetation is typical Southeast Alaska coastal temperate rain forest. The forest is primarily western hemlock and Sitka spruce with large components of cedar. There are about 60 acres of muskeg.

   There are approximately 51,297 acres of forest land of which 33,749 acres are commercial forest land. Of the commercial forest land, 30,209 acres are non-riparian old growth and 3,040 acres are riparian old growth.

   (c) **Soils:** These highly organic, low clay content soils are generally formed over bedrock and are about 40 inches deep.

   (d) **Fish Resource:** Fish resources have been rated as part of the Tongass Land Management Plan (1979) and by the Alaska Department of Fish and Game in its Forest Habitat Integrity Program (1983). These ratings describe the value of VCU's for sport fish, commercial fish, and estuaries.

   VCU's 672, 673, and 686 rated as high value for sport fish, VCU's 673, 674, 685, and 686 high for commercial fish, and VCU's 685 and 686 high for estuary habitat.

   (e) **Wildlife Resource:** This area has populations of Sitka black-tailed deer, black bear, otter, marten, mink, loon, and common waterfowl. The Big Creek drainage is considered an excellent example of wildlife habitat in the old-growth forest condition.

   (f) **Threatened and Endangered Species:** None.

(6) **Current Use and Management:** The Tongass Land Management Plan allocated the area to Land Use Designations (LUD's) 3 and 4. The LUD 3 areas (9,904 acres) are located on the southern tip and along the northern edge of this roadless area. The uses and activities in these areas are to be managed in a compatible and complementary manner. The LUD 4 area (49,414 acres) is to be managed for its commodity and market values.

The area's remoteness causes it to receive very little use. There is one recreation use cabin located in the northwest corner. Several mineral claims are located in the northwest corner.

(7) **Appearance (Apparent Naturalness):** The entire area is part of the Coastal Hills character type which is characterized by moderately steep landforms, elevations reaching 4,500 feet, and flat-floored, U-shaped valleys. Numerous island groups are also common. This roadless area is very representative of the character type, exhibiting all the above features except for the absence of any significant island clusters.

About 29 percent of the area is rated as Variety Class A (possessing landscape diversity that is unique for the character type) These outstanding landscapes are primarily the rugged, high elevations between the head of Nutkwa Lagoon and the West Arm of Cholmondeley Sound, and the alpine area around Josephine Lake near Copper Mountain. These landscapes exhibit a diversity of rugged alpine terrain, several different lake basins, and diverse vegetative patterns. The rest of the roadless area is rated as a Variety Class B (possessing landscape features that are common for the character type).

The entire area is in Type I Existing Visual Condition where the natural landscape has remained unaltered by human activity.

(8) **Surroundings (External Influences):** This roadless area is bounded on the east by the South Prince of Wales Wilderness and on the northeast by the Eudora Roadless Area. The upper west boundary is Native-selected land The remaining boundary is saltwater The Native land is currently being logged with little, if any, effect upon this roadless area

(9) **Attractions and Features of Special Interest:** The natural features of the area, the scenery, the saltwater bays and inlets, and the opportunity to see wildlife and to study the processes which formed this country may all be attractions. The extensive canoeing opportunity within the area is an outstanding attraction, as are the alpine lakes around the Lake Josephine recreation cabin. The fishing and solitude of the area are also attractions. The area contains seven inventoried recreation places containing 20,695 acres.

b. Capability of Management as Wilderness or in an Unroaded Condition

(1) **Manageability and Management Area Boundaries:** There are a few places where the mineral patents may affect the ability to manage the area around them in a roadless condition. Despite this, the area as a whole can be managed in the roadless condition with ease.

(2) **Natural Integrity:** The mineral patents in the northwest corner of this roadless area create the only break in its natural and logical integrity.

(3) **Opportunity for Solitude:** Excluding the very northern fringe where sights and sounds of logging and vehicle traffic may be evident, the area has excellent opportunity for solitude. The remoteness and difficult access make it unlikely that there will be much human activity in the area in the foreseeable future.

(4) Opportunity for Primitive Recreation: There are outstanding opportunities for primitive recreation in many parts of this area due to the scenic, fishing and canoeing attractions in the Nutkwa Lagoon area, and the scenic, hiking and camping attractions in the Lake Josephine area.

ROS Class	Acres
Primitive I (P1)	35,266
Primitive II (P2)	23,292
Semi-Primitive Non-Motorized (SPNM)	180

The area contains seven inventoried recreation places.

ROS CLASS	# OF REC. PLACES	TOTAL ACRES	CAPACITY BY RVD'S
P1	2	15,343	4,570
P2	5	9,593	3,752

(5) Special Features (Ecologic, Geologic, Scientific, Cultural): There are no known special features within the area.

c. Availability for Management as Wilderness or in an Unroaded Condition

(1) Resource Potentials

(a) Recreation Potential: There is good opportunity for primitive and semi-primitive recreation within this roadless area. Because of its remoteness and difficult access, it is unlikely that there will a need to develop facilities or trails in the rugged alpine areas However, there is the potential for campsites or recreation shelters in Nutkwa Lagoon area.

(b) Fish Resource: The recently completed fish habitat inventory indicates that there is potential for salmon enhancement projects, such as constructing fish passes, on several of the streams within the area.

(c) Wildlife Resource: There are no long-range plans for habitat improvement project work within this roadless area.

(d) Timber Resource: There are 29,311 acres inventoried as tentatively suitable for harvest. This includes 25,831 acres non-riparian old growth and 2,720 acres of riparian old growth.

(e) Land Use Authorizations: None.

(f) Minerals: There is potential for further mineral development in the northern part of the roadless area.

(g) Areas of Scientific Interest: None.

. (2) **Management Considerations**

(a) This roadless area is so remote and difficult to access that it receives very little management emphasis other than administration of the recreation use cabin and the mining claims in the area.

It is known that the Haida Native Corporation is interested in including much of the Nutkwa area into the next round of their entitlement land selections that must be completed by 1995.

The area has excellent potential to enhance the salmon spawning habitat on many streams within this area, mainly through the construction of fish passes.

The area has very good timber management potential. Almost all of the suitable timber land has good access to saltwater. Mineral development potential is moderate.

(b) **Fire:** The area has no significant fire history.

(c) **Insects and Disease:** Endemic tree diseases common to Southeast Alaska are present.

(d) **Land Status:** The northwest corner of this roadless area has three blocks of patented mining claims totaling about 300 acres.

d. **Relationship To Communities and Other Roadless and Wilderness Areas**

(1) **Nearby Roadless and Wilderness Areas and Uses:** This area is part of a larger contiguous unroaded land mass made up of the South Prince of Wales Wilderness, the Eudora and Polk Roadless Areas. This combined area totals 533,474 acres.

(2) **Distance From Population Centers (accessibility):** Approximate distances from population centers are as follows:

Community		Air Miles	Water Miles
Juneau	(Pop. 23,729)	190	310
Ketchikan	(Pop. 12,705)	45	75
Hydaburg	(Pop. 385)	15	24

Hollis, located on the Prince of Wales Island, is the nearest stop on the Alaska Marine Highway.

(3) **Interest by Proponents:**

(a) **Moratorium Areas:** This area has been identified as one of the "moratorium" areas in pending Tongass National Forest reform legislation.

(b) **Local Users/residents:** The area receives significant local use for subsistence and recreation activity.

e. **Environmental Consequences**

INDIVIDUAL ROADLESS AREA DESCRIPTION

NAME: Fake Pass (532)   ACRES (GROSS): 798   ACRES (NFS): 798

GEOZONE: K11
GEOGRAPHIC PROVINCE: Southern Outer Islands

1989 WILDERNESS ATTRIBUTE RATING: 19

a. Description

   (1) **Relationship to RARE II areas:** The table below displays the VCU 1/
   names, VCU numbers, acres, original WARS 2/ rating, and comments. This
   enables the reader to compare the roadless areas evaluated in Appendix C
   with previous analyses.

VCU Name	VCU No.	1979 WARS Rating	Comments
	545		Not Rated

   (2) **History:** This roadless area consists of a group of small islands,
   including Whale Head Island, located in Davidson Inlet. There is no
   prehistoric, historic or contemporary history related to this group of
   islands.

   (3) **Location and Access:** This roadless area is located off the southern
   coast of Kosciusko Island in Davidson Inlet. These islands are
   inaccessible to most except for very skilled boat handlers. Adjacent areas
   on the Kosciusko Peninsula have been harvested.

   (4) **Geography and Topography:** All of the islands in this roadless area
   are low-lying, rocky, and windswept. Whale Head Island is the largest in
   this group and its elevation rises to about 100 feet. There are 10 miles
   of shoreline on saltwater.

   (5) **Ecosystem:**

      (a) **Vegetation:** The larger islands of this group have limited tree
      growth, and the smaller islands are essentially devoid of trees and
      other kinds of vegetation.

1/ A VCU (Value Comparison Unit) is one of 867 watersheds which make up the
   forest and were differentiated for planning purposes in the Tongass Land
   Management Plan.
2/ Wilderness Attribute Rating System (WARS) was the nationwide system used to
   rate the wilderness attributes of roadless areas in the Roadless Area
   Review and Evaluation (RARE II).

There are about 718 acres of forested land, all of which are tentatively suitable forest land. Of this tentatively suitable forest land, 598 acres are non-riparian old growth and 40 acres riparian old growth.

(b) Soils: These island are essentially rock with some niches of soil located in crevices.

(c) Fish Resource: No freshwater fish habitat occurs on any of the islands

(d) Wildlife Resource: These islands provide habitat for sea birds and mammals. Bald eagles are often seen here

(e) **Threatened and Endangered Species:** None.

(6) **Current Use and Management:** These islands are not used now nor have they been used in the past. There is no active management objective for them.

(7) **Appearance (Apparent Naturalness):** The entire roadless·area is part of the Kupreanof Lowlands character type which is characterized by low, rolling relief, with elevations seldom greater than 1,500 feet. Numerous island groups and intricate waterways are also common in this character type. This area consists of a cluster of many islands of different sizes, and is thus quite characteristic of the character type.

The entire roadless area is inventoried as a Variety Class B (possessing landscape diversity common in the character type).

The entire area is also in a Type I Existing Visual Condition where the natural landscape has remained unaltered by human activity

(8) **Surroundings (External Influences):** These islands are not influenced by any external activity, land designation, land use or ownership.

(9) **Attractions and Features of Special Interest:** The natural features of the area, the scenery, and the opportunity to see wildlife and to study the processes which formed this country may all be attractions. The area contains two somewhat exposed anchorages. There is no freshwater.

b. **Capability of Management as Wilderness or in an Unroaded Condition**

(1) **Manageability and Management Area Boundaries:** Since this roadless area is a group of isolated islands with little activity, it would be fairly easy to manage in a roadless condition.

(2) **Natural Integrity:** This roadless area has excellent natural integrity, due in part to difficulty of access and lack of historic development.

(3) **Opportunity for Solitude:** There is excellent opportunity for solitude within of the area because of its difficult access.

(4) **Opportunity for Primitive Recreation:** Due to the limited recreation attractions, the difficult access to these islands due to the many rocks, and the proximity of small rural communities, there is not a high potential for primitive recreation.

ROS Class	Acres
Semi-Primitive Motorized (SPM)	717
Rural (R)	80

The area contains two inventoried recreation places

ROS CLASS	# OF REC. PLACES	TOTAL ACRES	CAPACITY BY RVD'S
SPM	2	717	3900

(5) **Special Features (Ecologic, Geologic, Scientific, Cultural):** There are no known special features within the area.

c. **Availability for Management as Wilderness or in an Unroaded Condition**

(1) **Resource Potentials**

(a) **Recreation Potential:** Due to the difficult access and lack of recreation opportunities, this roadless area does not have any potential for recreation development or enhancement. There are a couple of identified anchorages in the area which attract some use to the waters around these islands when the weather is satisfactory

(b) **Fish Resource:** None.

(c) **Wildlife Resource:** There is no identified need for wildlife enhancement projects within this area.

(d) **Timber Resource:** There are 718 acres of tentatively suitable timberland.

(e) **Land Use Authorizations:** None.

(f) **Minerals:** The mineral potential is low.

(g) **Areas of Scientific Interest:** None.

(2) **Management Considerations**

(a) The islands making up the Fake Pass Roadless Area do not have the basic resources to require active resource management plans or projects. The difficult access prevents general public use for recreation purposes.

(b) **Insects and Disease:** Endemic tree diseases common to Southeast Alaska are present.

(c) **Land Status:** The entire area is National Forest System lands

d. Relationship To Communities and Other Roadless and Wilderness Areas

(1) **Nearby Roadless and Wilderness Areas and Uses:** The Kosciusko Roadless Area is about 15 miles to the northeast. The Warren Islands' Wilderness is about 15 miles to the west.

(2) **Distance From Population Centers (accessibility):** Approximate distances from population centers are as follows:

Community		Air Miles	Water Miles
Juneau	(Pop. 23,729)	170	210
Ketchikan	(Pop 12,705)	70	200

Hollis, located on Prince of Wales Island, is the nearest stop on the Alaska Marine Highway.

(3) **Interest by Proponents:**

(a) **Moratorium Areas:** The area has not been identified as a "moratorium" area or proposed as Wilderness in legislative initiatives to date.

(b) **Local User/residents:** Rarely does a local area resident venture out to the islands making up this roadless area nor is there any kind of subsistence use.

e. Environmental Consequences

INDIVIDUAL ROADLESS AREA DESCRIPTION

NAME: Quartz (577)   ACRES (GROSS): 149,747   ACRES (NFS): 149,107

GEOZONE: K13
GEOGRAPHIC PROVINCE: Coast Range

1989 WILDERNESS ATTRIBUTE RATING: 23

a. Description

(1) **Relationship to RARE II areas:** The table below displays the VCU 1/
names, VCU numbers, original WARS 2/ rating, and comments. This enables
the reader to compare the roadless areas evaluated in Appendix C with
previous analyses.

| | | 1979 | |
VCU Name	VCU No.	WARS Rating	Comments
Blossom River	815	26	
Wilson Lake	817	25	
Lower Wilson	818	22	
Wilson Arm	819	22	
Bart Creek	823	24	
Smeaton	825	22	
Bakewell	826	25	
	840		Not Rated
Lower Keta	841	24	
Upper Keta	842	24	

(2) **History:** This area is a part of Misty Fiords National Monument.
ANILCA did not include this roadless area as wilderness because of the
pending plans to develop the Quartz Hill molybdenum mine.

(3) **Location and Access:** The area lies in the middle of the mainland
portion of Misty Fiords National Monument about 50 miles east of
Ketchikan. Access is by boat and foot or by helicopter. Due to the lack
of large enough lakes, floatplanes cannot land in the area.

(4) **Geography and Topography:** The area is extremely rugged and rises from
saltwater to elevations over 5,000 feet. There are 7,827 acres of exposed
rock, 1,060 acres of alpine tundra, and 1,700 acres of freshwater lakes
There are 38 miles of saltwater shoreline.

1/ A VCU (Value Comparison Unit) is one of 867 watersheds which make up the
forest and were differentiated for planning purposes in the Tongass Land
Management Plan.
2/ Wilderness Attribute Rating System (WARS) was the system used to rate the
wilderness attributes of roadless areas in the Roadless Area Review and
Evaluation (RARE II).

(5) **Ecosystem:**

(a) **Classification:** The area is classified as being in the Coast Range Geographic Province. This province is generally characterized by a core of massive, angular mountains capped with ice fields at high elevations along the Canadian Border, with somewhat lower mountains, deeply-incised valleys and glacier-fed streams closer to the coast The roadless area is more characteristic of the higher elevation areas, though no ice fields are present. There are no known areas of unique or uncommon plant/soils associations or geologic formations in the area.

(b) **Vegetation:** Alpine vegetation dominates above 2,500 feet elevation. Below that elevation the steep mountainsides are heavily marked with snowslide and landslide paths which are typically covered with grass, alder, and brush. Occasionally, cottonwood trees may be found along the valley bottoms and floodplains.

There are approximately 87,577 acres of forested land of which 48,863 acres are commercial forest land. Of the commercial forest land, 47,061 acres are non-riparian old growth and 1,361 acres of riparian old growth.

(c) **Soils:** The soils are moderately-deep loam with inclusions of glacial till and moraine deposits.

(d) **Fish Resource:** Fish resources have been rated as part of the Tongass Land Management Plan (1979) and by the Alaska Department of Fish and Game in its Forest Habitat Integrity Program (1983) These ratings describe the value of VCU's for sport fish, commercial fish, and estuaries.

VCU's 815, 817, 818, 826, 841, and 842 are high value for commercial and sport fish.

VCU 823 is rated high value for estuary habitat.

(e) **Wildlife Resource:** A small population of mountain goat ranges over the area, as do black and brown bear, and a small population of moose.

(f) **Threatened and Endangered Species:** None.

(6) **Current Use and Management:** The Tongass Land Management Plan allocated this area to Land Use Designation (LUD) 1. LUD 1 areas are to be managed in the roadless condition. The current management emphasis within this roadless area has been the administration of the permit involving access and pre-development exploration of the Quartz Hill molybdenum mine

(7) **Appearance (Apparent Naturalness):** This roadless area is part of the Coast Range character type which consists of large, massive landforms commonly rising to elevations of 7,000 feet, steep slopes or rock cliffs that plunge to saltwater, and deep, narrow saltwater fiords that protrude into this land mass. Mountain ridges are generally rounded with occasional jagged peaks rising above the surrounding smoother ridge tops This area

is fairly representative of this character type except for slightly lower elevations.

All of this roadless area is inventoried as a Variety Class B (possessing a level of landscape diversity that is common for the character type). Though this area does not possess the dramatic scenic features found in other portions of this character type, there are notable scenic landscapes at the head of Bakewell Arm, at the head of Wilson Arm around the Wilson and Blossom River estuaries, and along certain portions of Boca de Quadra

About 96 percent of this roadless area is in a Type I Existing Visual Condition where the natural landscape has remained unaltered by human activity. The only man-altered landscapes are the area of the U S. Borax mine site at Quartz Hill, and the mine access road corridor that runs along the Blossom River and the northeast shore of Wilson Arm.

(8) **Surroundings (External Influences):** This area is contiguous to Misty Fiords National Monument. The most significant influence is the noise and sight of large number of aircraft on flightseeing trips during the summer cruiseship season, and the helicopters that are making trips to Quartz Hill.

(9) **Attractions and Features of Special Interest:** The natural features of the area, the scenery, and the opportunity to see wildlife and to study the processes which formed this landscape may all be attractions.

b. **Capability of Management as Wilderness or in an Unroaded Condition**

(1) **Manageability and Management Area Boundaries:** The area is generally well defined by topographic features. Feasibility of management in a roadless condition is high with the possible exception of the area adjacent to the Quartz Hill Mine.

(2) **Natural Integrity:** The area is virtually unmodified with the exception of the Quartz Hill Mine and its access road.

(3) **Opportunity for Solitude:** There is a high opportunity for solitude within the area. Aircraft on flightseeing trips can be heard and seen during the summer season. Present recreation levels are low. Generally, a person camped or traveling inland is unlikely to see others.

(4) **Opportunity for Primitive Recreation:** Due to the remoteness of the area, the minimal sights and sounds of human activity, the great physical challenge presented by the rugged terrain and dense vegetation, and the presence of black and brown bear, there are good opportunities for primitive recreation. Because it is located inland, this area does not possess the variety of recreation attractions that are found in neighboring portions of the Monument, though the Wilson and Keta River corridors may have potential for hiking trails and offer good fishing and hunting opportunities.

ROS Class	Acres
Primitive I (P1)	102,146
Primitive II (P2)	23,280
Semi-Primitive Non-Motorized (SPNM)	17,575
Roaded Natural (RN)	4,844
Roaded Modified (RM)	1,261

The area contains three inventoried recreation places.

ROS CLASS	# OF REC. PLACES	TOTAL ACRES	CAPACITY BY RVD'S
P2	3	2,361	959

(5) **Special Features (Ecologic, Geologic, Scientific, Cultural):** There are opportunities to observe and study fish and wildlife and the various forces which formed these mountains.

c. **Availability for Management as Wilderness or in an Unroaded Condition**

(1) **Resource Potentials**

(a) **Recreation Potential:** The area is best suited for dispersed recreation activities.

(b) **Fish Resource:** The streams within the roadless area are important streams for salmon production. There may be some opportunity for fish habitat improvement projects within this roadless area.

(c) **Wildlife Resource:** There are no plans for wildlife habitat improvements within the area and there is no apparent need to conduct any habitat improvement projects.

(d) **Timber Resource:** None of the area has been inventoried as tentatively suitable for harvest.

(e) **Land Use Authorizations:** A special use permit has been issued to the Quartz Hill Mine for the construction and operation of a road and shore-related dock facilities.

(f) **Minerals:** There has been much mineral exploration activity associated with the Quartz Hill molybdenum deposit. It is still unclear, though, when actual mine development will take place

(g) **Areas of Scientific Interest:** When mining activity occurs, there will be much monitoring and research into the impacts of additional road building and mine excavation on fisheries habitat, and the effects of dumping mine tailings into saltwater.

(2) **Management Considerations**

(a) Timber management within this area is not a consideration because of the current LUD I designation. Maintenance of the area in a

roadless condition enhances opportunity to manage the adjacent Misty
Fiords National Monument Wilderness, and provide enhanced
opportunities for solitude and primitive recreation for those capable
of accessing it. It also maintains opportunities for wildlife, such
as wolves, bears, and moose, to move freely through the area.

(b) **Fire:** The area has no significant fire history.

(c) **Insects and Disease:** Endemic tree diseases common to Southeast
Alaska are present; there are no known epidemic disease occurrences

(d) **Land Status:** The Quartz Hill patents include 647 acres

d. **Relationship To Communities and Other Roadless and Wilderness Areas**

(1) **Nearby Roadless and Wilderness Areas and Uses:** The area is part of a
larger contiguous land mass consisting of Misty Fiords National Monument

(2) **Distance From Population Centers (accessibility):**

Community	Air miles	Water miles
Juneau (Pop. 23,729)	300	380
Ketchikan (Pop 12,005)	50	70

Ketchikan is the nearest stop on the Alaska Marine Highway.

(3) **Interest by Proponents:**

(a) **Moratorium Areas:** The area has not been identified as a
"moratorium" area or proposed as Wilderness in legislative initiatives
to date.

(b) **Local Users/residents:** Most of the area is used by local
residents for recreation.

e. **Environmental Consequences:**